# Real Estate Appraisal From <u>A</u> to <u>Z</u>

*Just a few of the many excellent book reviews our products hav*
*Top 50 book reviewers for Amazon.com have given this book the high*

 **A thorough exposition of how to appraise real estate.**
*Amazon Top 50 Book Reviewer: Harold McFarland from Florida*

*Real Estate Appraisal from A to Z -* **delivers up exactly what it promises - a thorough, understandable course on appraising.** The author discusses appraisals as a business and how to get into the appraisal business, but it is much more that just that. If you are looking at purchasing property for investing. If you are looking at purchasing a new home, wanting to know the value of vacant property, etc. **this is an excellent book. It covers all the bases when valuing a property.** Some of the subjects discussed include community factors, market influences, potential hidden problems and how to find them, building inspection, the cost approach to valuation, the income approach to valuation, and writing a proposal. **Given the thorough coverage and easy to understand writing style, this book is a highly recommended purchase for anyone** who might be interested in appraisals or investing in real estate.

 **Appraisal Know-How.**
*Reviewer: Author/Reviewer Denise Clark -* Denise's Pieces Book Reviews Site

*Real Estate Appraisal from A to Z -* Real estate appraisers are in demand these days, and get paid hundreds of dollars for their services. The best thing about becoming an appraiser is that you don't need a Master's Degree or any special schooling to become one. What you do need, however, is knowledge. In his **extensively researched and illustrated** Real Estate Appraising from A to Z, author Cozzi sets out to give anyone interested in moving into this quickly growing field the tools he or she will need, not only to do the job, but to do it right. Mr. Cozzi starts with the very basics. For instance, the purpose, benefits and explanation of what an appraiser is, what he does and how to become a certified appraiser. From there, he guides the reader step by step through what appraisers look for when inspecting homes, both their exteriors and interiors. He explains how to determine home values of not only single-dwelling homes, but condominiums as well. But Mr. Cozzi doesn't stop there. In basic, easily understood terms, he explains such topics as depreciation, the different types of home mortgages and appraisal accounts such as original home loan and refinance loan appraisals and foreclosure appraisals. Real Estate Appraising from A to Z is just what the title implies. **Mr. Cozzi's ability to instruct without 'talking down' to his audience is a plus and a rare treat -** even for those who know absolutely nothing about the 'home' business. Homeowners would do well to have a copy of this book on hand before obtaining an appraisal, and use Cozzi's inspection guidelines within the actual appraising section of the book to obtain the most favorable value for their homes. **Mr. Cozzi's easy to read, friendly writing style offers expert and timely advice and instruction** for both homeowners and aspiring appraisers. If you want to work for yourself, earn extra money, or increase the value of your home, **this edition is a definite must.**

 **Highly Recommended book for real estate appraisers. I simply love it!**
*Reviewer: Jennie S. Bev, Managing Editor of BookReviewClub.com*

*Real Estate Appraisal from A to Z -* Guy Cozzi is your guy, if you're serious about becoming a real estate appraiser. **I cannot recommend this book more. I simply love it.** This book teaches more than the techniques of appraising a property. More importantly, it teaches how to price, promote and insider tips and tricks, such as what to do in circumstances in which your work ethics are being tested and handling complaints. **The forms are also extremely useful** for those who have just started in this lucrative business. The author's humorous approach is also reflected in this book. He is not only a **good teacher**, but also possesses a very good funny bone. **He enlightens his readers about the hidden problems of a property without making them sleepy.** His technical chapters flow effortlessly and are sprinkled with jokes. **If you need to purchase only one book about the real estate appraising business, be it this one.**

 **He's an expert. You and I can learn from Guy Cozzi.**
*Reviewer: Barbara Bamberger Scott* - Curled Up With a Good Book - Book Reviews

***Real Estate Appraisal from A to Z -*** Guy Cozzi writes books about houses like yours and mine. His job, besides teaching people how to appraise houses, is appraising them himself. **He's an expert. You and I can learn from Guy Cozzi,** even if our goal is not to appraise houses, but just to understand the machine we live in. Cozzi's books are illustrated with black and white photos that look like they were smuggled out of the former Soviet Union by house appraisal spies at the height of the Cold War (detailed photos with arrows identifying problem conditions). I was sadly reminded of my guest room as I surveyed a photo of an overloaded electrical outlet bursting with wires that looked like spaghetti. But I took some comfort from the tree trunk for the basement foundation photo -- at least my main beams are not supported by a tree trunk, but by, as Cozzi obviously recommends, a "solid, metal support post." Cozzi suggests jumping vigorously to make sure floors are sound and spot-checking appliances by turning them briefly on. **This is simple, practical advice. No flowery prose. Just the facts.** Cozzi explains: "Every single thing I mention in this book is from actual experiences that I have personally encountered or that I have friends in this business encounter them." **Sincere. Pointed.** You won't be reading Cozzi for entertainment. But **you'll get "every single thing" you need to know about appraising, inspecting and improving your home.** Including the pitfall of over-improving. **Cozzi knows his stuff regarding finances, too.** An appraiser never advises a homeowner or buyer about bank loans. **But should you and I need financial advice, it's here in stark black and white.** Be warned - if you get paranoid just thinking about radon gas, asbestos, improperly covered wells and creosote damage, Cozzi will not comfort you. **He's been in the trenches of home inspection and appraisal** and it's not funny. It's a world where grown men fall through ceilings, and an honest comment about wood eating worms can earn you a call from somebody's lawyer. If you are, in fact, thinking of taking up a career or sideline job as a real estate appraiser, **I assure you Cozzi is right there with you every step of the way from basement crawlspace to attic and "asbestos heaven."** He'll help you design business cards, supply you with sample forms, run through the cost and income approaches to estimating values, depreciation, et al. Nemmar Real Estate Training and Cozzi keep making money with their series on home inspection and appraisal, **and if I were seriously thinking of buying or selling, especially an older house, I'd pick up one or more of their books for the straight poop. If you're a buyer, it will show you how to think like a seller, and vice versa.** And there's nothing wrong with that.

 **Appraiser's Dream Book for beginners or experts!**
*Reviewer: C. Robbinson from New York*

***Real Estate Appraisal from A to Z -*** We have one of the busiest appraisal and home inspection companies in our area. We exclusively work for mortgage lenders and banks who are very picky about getting high quality reports and evaluations. We have been using this "A to Z" appraisal book and the "A to Z" inspection book for years as **MANDATORY** reading for all of our appraisers and home inspectors when we hire and train them. It's the simplest to understand and the most thorough covering all necessary topics that we have found on the market. **This book will tell you the realities of evaluating real estate** without giving you a bunch of fluff - that's why we like it so much. Our appraisers and inspectors **get years of expertise and knowledge in one book** without having to make the mistakes they would to learn from their own experiences. It saves us a lot of time in getting our employees up to speed doing professional reports and evaluations for our clients. We can't afford to send our clients poor quality reports since there's a lot of competition in our business. This book keeps us at the top of our game and keeps our clients happy.

***Real Estate Press*** - "…the Real Estate from A to Z books and videos are the best we've ever seen."

***New Home Construction Journal*** – "…the best selling reference books available for home builders and buyers and cover every topic from A to Z."

***Seminar Progress Report*** - "…top-notch real estate investors, inspectors and appraisers agree the Real Estate from A to Z series is a great value."

***Real Estate Investors Journal*** - "…Real Estate from A to Z series is by far the most in-depth resource for every investor, beginner to expert."

## More excellent reviews and customer testimonials about our products and services

5 out of 5: "excellent book/excellent service"
Date: 11/9/2004 Rated by Buyer: davidleasparky

5 out of 5: "Excellent resource. Transaction successful"
Date: 10/17/2004 Rated by Buyer: gleach7

5 out of 5: "Quick Ship-Excellent book."
Date: 10/12/2004 Rated by Buyer: deje89

5 out of 5: "Highly recommended - superb service, fast shipment, great book! AAAAA+++!"
Date: 9/25/2004 Rated by Buyer: gemflint

5 out of 5: "fast service, great book"
Date: 9/13/2004 Rated by Buyer: mvolz92069

5 out of 5: "quick shipping honest seller great book"
Date: 9/12/2004 Rated by Buyer: patrinif

5 out of 5: "Great product, quick shipping"
Date: 08/17/2004 Rated by Buyer: bob2k

5 out of 5: "Fast shipping, great book. Thanks!"
Date: 04/24/2004 Rated by Buyer: atarikee

5 out of 5: "Great Communication! Great Book!!!"
Date: 04/11/2004 Rated by Buyer: robert a.

5 out of 5: "Very pleased! Thanks!"
Date: 02/05/2004 Rated by Buyer: hughesassociates2003

5 out of 5: "The book is the most informative I have read yet ! "
Date: 01/31/2004 Rated by Buyer: dirty123

5 out of 5: "Excellent real estate books!! They will save me thousands of dollars on my home purchase from the information I will learn in these books. "
Date: 12/27/2003 Rated by Buyer: happygoal

5 out of 5: "Fantastic product!! Great service and great products. You can't ask for more than that. Best product in it's category by far."
Date: 12/21/2003 Rated by Buyer: alberttrees

5 out of 5: "A++ Perfect transaction! I am a repeat customer since the book is the best real estate book I have ever read and I have seen a lot of books on real estate before!"
Date: 12/14/2003 Rated by Buyer: paul887

5 out of 5: "EXTREMELY happy with their book. Best books on real estate I've ever read."
Date: 12/06/2003 Rated by Buyer: aroundtee

5 out of 5: "Excellent transaction! Fast delivery and Excellent books!"
Date: 12/02/2003 Rated by Buyer: slaidl

Definitely worthwhile. Great seller!!! Buy confidently.
Buyer  subroc730 ( 58)  Oct-02-04 21:17 6304816459

Great product!!. Buy with complete confidence!!!.
Buyer  subroc730 ( 58)  Oct-02-04 21:15 6309285748

Great Book Would Buy Again AAAAA +++++
Buyer  frank-rubi ( 491)  Sep-27-04 10:29 6927595558

Great book! Thanks for the fast shipping!
Buyer  flohanajo ( 11)  Sep-23-04 11:43 6910449803

What a GREAT BOOK! Super-fast shipping and an excellent product! Recommended!
Buyer  shanekw ( 72)  Sep-16-04 10:55 6924938115

Thanks great item
Buyer  hellboy714 ( 22)  Sep-13-04 21:27 6321532616

Fast shipping great item thanks AAAA
Buyer  hellboy714 ( 22)  Sep-13-04 21:27 6321532663

Excellent transaction. product very informative. Thank you
Buyer  trader1128 ( 24)  Sep-07-04 15:16 6908719323

Great product! Very highly recommended! Thanks!
Buyer  mysbyu ( 40)  Aug-28-04 09:01 6314216042

Great book, fast delivery, was a good deal
Buyer  meliheim ( 205)  Aug-15-04 17:02 6914801318

A+ ALL THE WAY
Buyer  stitz14 ( 12)  Aug-09-04 08:45 6311529865

Quick transaction. No problems. Book is very informative.
Buyer  mariadaniellek ( 1 )  Aug-02-04 14:27 6914805667

Fast shipping and the book was better than I expected... thanks!
Buyer  arizona0926 ( 7 )  Jul-30-04 09:40 6912766573

GREAT
Buyer  alexand7 ( 81)  Jul-29-04 20:21 6908518676

Great A+++++
Buyer  raftermanfl ( 105)  Jul-24-04 19:55 6912772562

Great book! Thanks for the easy transaction.
Buyer  mighty_sultan ( 27)  Jul-21-04 19:21 6908518676

A++++ Thanks
Buyer  4everknight ( 109)  Jul-20-04 19:02 4182828782

Excellent service, great purchase. This seller rates an outstanding. A+A+A+A+
Buyer  gringo-rican ( 34)  Jul-19-04 16:02 6912771572

5 out of 5: "Excellent service, great product. Thanks"
Date: 08/17/2003 Rated by Buyer: sayu8

5 out of 5: "Excellent book and quick delivery!!"
Date: 07/21/2003 Rated by Buyer: hagomes

5 out of 5: "Great service, quick delivery, excellent book"
Date: 04/24/2003 Rated by Buyer: d9910

5 out of 5: "Arrived in good condition. Great book."
Date: 03/20/2003 Rated by Buyer: oldiesdude2

Material very well done. very informative
Buyer   yx981 ( 92)  Nov-24-04 11:22 6338256963

Great quality A+++++ great seller
Buyer   jotalong1000 ( 29)  Nov-19-04 17:11 6335074277

Quick delivery - excellent book on appraisals
Buyer   ziongroup ( 67)  Nov-15-04 21:38 2495215347

Excellent book highly recommended read
Buyer   juhlz ( 44)  Nov-08-04 09:13 6927595519

Great Book Thanks!!!!!
Buyer   ajok88 ( 109)  Nov-08-04 06:58 6922358202

A+A+A+ good transaction
Buyer   conestoga22 ( 152)  Nov-03-04 12:45 6919576348

Excellent Transaction Great Book
Buyer   hwkzrok ( 1 )  Oct-20-04 14:47 6922358298

AAAAAA++++++
Buyer   patric55 ( 842)  Oct-20-04 07:00 6929649552

Great book. Shipped promptly. Great Seller
Buyer   tjs_914 ( 19)  May-21-04 15:38 4205627517

Great seller. Great product. Immediate delivery. Thank you.
Buyer   leontennis ( 442)  May-19-04 17:21 4183684560

Great Book Thanks
Buyer   tachmedic ( 93)  May-17-04 20:05 4209383266

Great product, great response, many thanks
Buyer   edjafe ( 54)  Oct-15-04 15:19 6929649552

Fast delivery Great book Thanks!!
Buyer   mechanician477 ( 5 )  Oct-13-04 16:11 6908719323

Great product. Would love to start a business with seller!
Buyer   coreyratz ( 180)  Oct-11-04 21:35 6929649479

Excellent!
Buyer   jr333 ( 2992)  Oct-08-04 16:15 6316419120

Great Book, good doing business with you have a great day
Buyer   inspectorlake ( 126)  Jul-12-04 18:02 6908518676

GREAT book with helpful info!...Would deal w/again!...A+++
Seller!...Thank you!
Buyer   randj48 ( 84)  Jul-08-04 15:42 4205633335

Thank You A++++++++
Buyer   jims_son ( 144)  Jul-06-04 12:59 6908518749

Super DVD lots of info
Buyer   inspectorkid ( 115)  Jun-30-04 10:48 4183683333

A++++, Thank You!!!!
Buyer   mcclanesolo ( 1244)  Jun-24-04 22:47 4191424761

Great DVD! Fast shipper and good service... Thanks
Buyer   fc1sar ( 13)  Jun-21-04 13:30 4191422938

Fast Shipping, Quality Product, Awesome deal, A ++++
Buyer   info-ware ( 110)  Jun-09-04 18:51 4193612604

Great item, fast shipping, Highly recommend
Buyer   89_mustang ( 141)  Jun-08-04 09:13 4212285263

Very pleased with the book; its content and examples/case
studies. Excellent!
Buyer   tightwadtj ( 36)  Jun-07-04 11:40 6900685641

Great transaction! Thanks! I love the book! A+++++
Buyer   cwhitby91 ( 40)  May-15-04 14:18 4209383074

Great dvd's.......Thanks again and great doing business with you
Buyer   seahawks1 ( 507)  May-03-04 16:58 4183347687

Fast delivery-great value- thanks
Buyer   jotalong1000 ( 29)  Apr-25-04 17:53 4201591917

A++++++
Buyer   florino1964 ( 113)  Apr-22-04 20:05 3598166015

Great book. Fast service. Wonderful communication. What
more can you ask for?
Buyer   maggk ( 66)  Apr-17-04 09:34 4201591762

Great Seller! Great Product! Fast Shipping!
Buyer   hooverhouse ( 1658)  Apr-11-04 15:55 3596771099

Super smooth transaction! Excellent merchandise! A+++++
Buyer   pbbuysandsells ( 503)  Mar-26-04 15:31 3593483616

Great Product!!! Fast Delivery!!! A++++++
Buyer   imtabitha ( 23)  Mar-23-04 22:40 3593483397

Graph Pages

# What's In This For You?

Real Estate Appraisers earn **$375** or more for each appraisal. Many appraisers are so busy that they do two appraisals per day!

You don't need to have any background in real estate to become a highly paid real estate appraiser. All you need is to obtain the right knowledge and business plan, *(which we'll give you)*. Male or female, and your current age doesn't matter either, since there is *no* manual labor or hard work involved.

Here's just a few of the
benefits you get from this book:

**Earn Money** in one of the fastest growing businesses in the country.

**Be Your Own Boss** and work part-time or full-time. <u>You</u> set your own hours.

**Save Money** when you buy, sell, or renovate your own home.

**Eliminate Safety Hazards** to make your home safe for you and your family.

**Real Estate Related** knowledge to help people with the *biggest* investment they will ever make - their own home.

# What's The Income Potential?

Are you wondering about the income and growth potential of the real estate appraisal business?  Then look below because a picture is worth a thousand words.  Appraisers earn **high** incomes every year while working right out of their home.  The real estate appraisal industry has been growing by leaps and bounds every year.  And remember, this growth has gone on even during some of the worst economic recessions in history!  This book shows you the reasons why your real estate appraisal business can grow even during a recession.

### Growth Of Real Estate Appraisal Industry

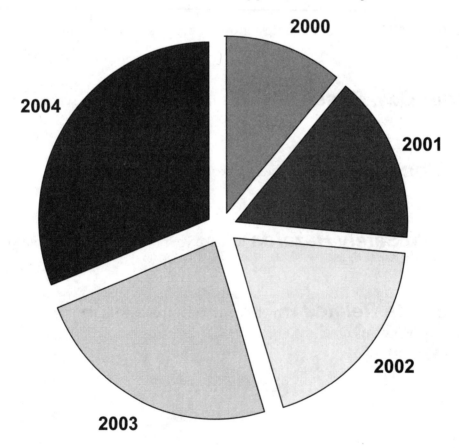

# What Houses Need Appraisals?

Are you wondering about the need for appraisals? Then look below because this data has been taken from evaluating thousands of homes. The graph shows the probability of finding aspects that negatively affect the market value of any house, *(including yours!)* This book shows you the reasons why <u>all</u> homes need to be appraised. **Do you really know the true market value of your house?**

### Average Changes To Market Value

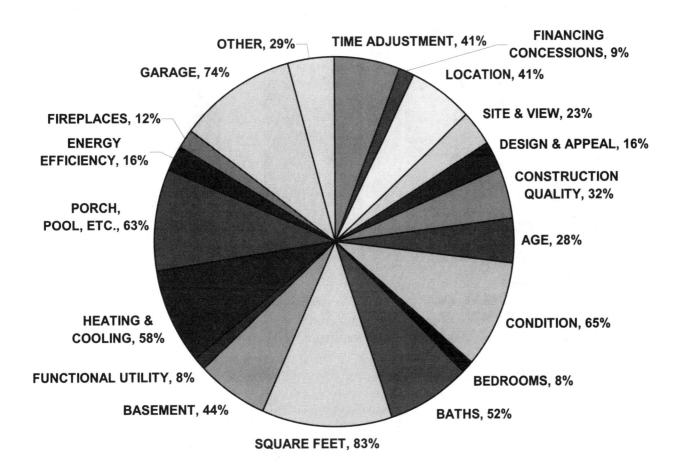

- OTHER, 29%
- TIME ADJUSTMENT, 41%
- FINANCING CONCESSIONS, 9%
- GARAGE, 74%
- LOCATION, 41%
- FIREPLACES, 12%
- SITE & VIEW, 23%
- ENERGY EFFICIENCY, 16%
- DESIGN & APPEAL, 16%
- CONSTRUCTION QUALITY, 32%
- PORCH, POOL, ETC., 63%
- AGE, 28%
- CONDITION, 65%
- HEATING & COOLING, 58%
- BEDROOMS, 8%
- FUNCTIONAL UTILITY, 8%
- BATHS, 52%
- BASEMENT, 44%
- SQUARE FEET, 83%

# What's A Buyer's Savings?

So you don't want a career change?  That's fine, but would you be interested in saving thousands of dollars when you buy your own home?  Then look below.

This graph shows some potential market value adjustments found when buying your home.  By identifying any negative aspects *before* you buy, you'll be able to negotiate a lower purchase price.

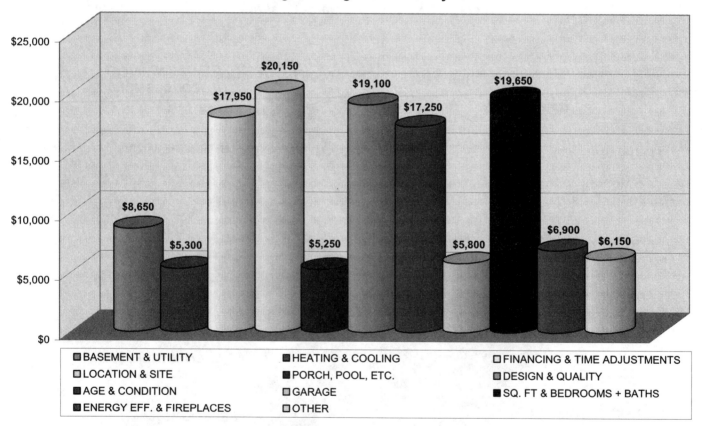

**Average $ Savings For Home Buyers**

Legend:
- BASEMENT & UTILITY
- LOCATION & SITE
- AGE & CONDITION
- ENERGY EFF. & FIREPLACES
- HEATING & COOLING
- PORCH, POOL, ETC.
- GARAGE
- OTHER
- FINANCING & TIME ADJUSTMENTS
- DESIGN & QUALITY
- SQ. FT & BEDROOMS + BATHS

Values: $8,650 · $5,300 · $17,950 · $20,150 · $5,250 · $19,100 · $17,250 · $5,800 · $19,650 · $6,900 · $6,150

# Don't Let Your Dream House...

# What's A Seller's Savings?

You're not buying a house at this time? Okay, but would you be interested in saving thousands of dollars when you renovate or sell your own home? Then look down. This graph shows your potential profit when selling your home. By properly evaluating these typical market value adjustments ahead of time, you can earn at least an additional $1.60 for each $1.00 you invested in your home. This $1.60 figure is based on an annual appreciation rate of only 10% over five years.

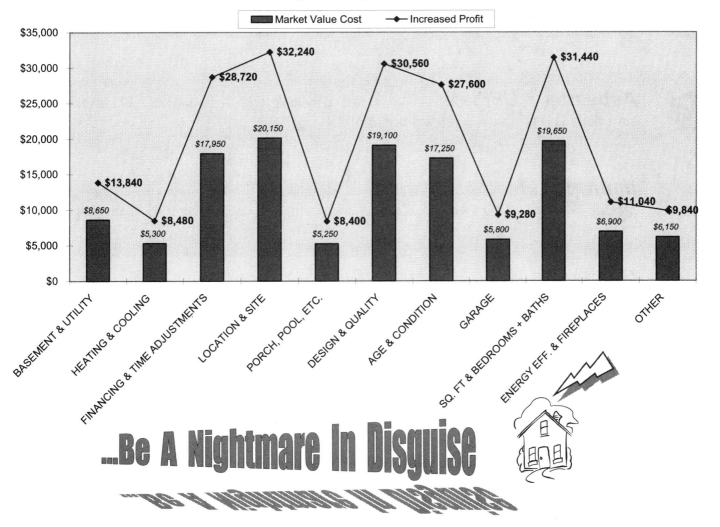

### Average $ Savings For Home Sellers

**Market Value Cost** — **Increased Profit**

| Category | Market Value Cost | Increased Profit |
|---|---|---|
| BASEMENT & UTILITY | $8,650 | $13,840 |
| HEATING & COOLING | $5,300 | $8,480 |
| FINANCING & TIME ADJUSTMENTS | $17,950 | $28,720 |
| LOCATION & SITE | $20,150 | $32,240 |
| PORCH, POOL, ETC. | $5,250 | $8,400 |
| DESIGN & QUALITY | $19,100 | $30,560 |
| AGE & CONDITION | $17,250 | $27,600 |
| GARAGE | $5,800 | $9,280 |
| SQ. FT & BEDROOMS + BATHS | $19,650 | $31,440 |
| ENERGY EFF. & FIREPLACES | $6,900 | $11,040 |
| OTHER | $6,150 | $9,840 |

## ...Be A Nightmare In Disguise

# What Safety Hazards?

So you think there are no safety hazards around your home?
Well, think again.

 **Lead In Water & Paint -** Do you know how to check for lead in your home?  Lead poisoning is the *number one* childhood disease in America!

 **Radon Gas -** Is it in your house?  The EPA, *(Environmental Protection Agency)*, has determined that radon is the *number two* leading cause of lung cancer behind cigarette smoking!

 **Asbestos & UFFI -** Do you know what they look like?  Asbestos and UFFI insulations have caused countless cancer related deaths.

 **Improper Electrical Wiring -** Do you know if your outlets meet the *National Electric Code* standards?  Improper electrical wiring can be found in over 90% of all homes!

 **Gas Leaks -** Do you know how to properly evaluate your gas meter and supply lines?  Natural gas is colorless and odorless before it gets to the utility company.  An undetected gas leak can explode and blow up an entire building!

We're not trying to scare you, we're trying to educate you.
We just want to open your eyes to the reality of some of the
safety hazards that can be found in *any* home.

# Customer Comments & Recommendations

From the Author

Thank you very much for purchasing my book. I invite you to view our web site at **www.nemmar.com** to see the other real estate products we offer that will save you thousands of dollars when you buy, sell, or renovate a home. You can sign up online to receive our **free** real estate newsletter with articles and updates that will definitely help you profit in real estate. Please email me and let me know what you think of my book after you have time to review it. Customer feedback and recommendations are greatly appreciated and help me to improve all of our products.
             Thank you,

             Guy Cozzi
             Nemmar Real Estate Training
*"Everything You Need To Know About Real Estate*
       *From **A**sbestos to **Z**oning"* ™


Nemmar Real Estate Training is ranked as the most exclusive real estate appraiser, home inspector and real estate investor training service since 1988. Our real estate books and DVDs are rated **number one** in their real estate categories nationwide! Our products have taught thousands of home buyers, sellers, and real estate professionals worldwide. You too can learn everything you need to know about Real Estate - from **A**sbestos to **Z**oning. With this knowledge you will save thousands of dollars when you buy, sell, or renovate your home. You will also learn how to eliminate safety hazards and properly maintain a home. Statistics show an average savings of at least **$4,700.00** per home for customers who have read our books.

Our home inspection, appraisal, and home improvement books have been called the "Bible" of the real estate industry. Written by Guy Cozzi who has decades of experience as a licensed appraiser, home inspector, consultant, and real estate investor. This top selling author has been quoted as a real estate expert by the *New York Times* and many other publications. He has been a guest speaker on real estate investment TV shows and has taught thousands of people how to inspect, appraise and invest in real estate and provides advice to many banks and mortgage lenders.

The real facts other books don't tell you! *You'll learn everything that your Realtor doesn't want you to know.* Realtors "sugar coat" the problem conditions in a house in order to close the deal and get paid their sales commission. This is unquestionably the only book of its kind that teaches you how to prevent those pitfalls. You get information that the professionals use to make you an educated consumer enabling you to negotiate a much better price on the purchase, renovation, or sale of your home.

*Do you really know the true market value of your house?* Don't let your **dream house** be a **nightmare** in disguise! Our *Real Estate From A to Z* books and DVDs will assist you with the biggest investment of your life - your own home! These products were originally designed to train top-notch, professional home inspectors, appraisers, investors, builders, contractors and Realtors and are now available at a price affordable to everyone.
             **All homes need to be inspected, appraised and updated for safety hazards,**
                         **routine maintenance, and energy efficiency.**

# Table of Contents

# Introduction To The Appraisal Business

## Introduction

This book is going to cover every aspect of the real estate appraisal business. I'm not going to paint some fairy tale, rosy picture or give you any fluff. I'm going to tell it like it is without holding anything back. **This book was originally designed to train top-notch, professional real estate appraisers. However, the book is extremely helpful to *anyone* involved in real estate.** This includes a home buyer, homeowner, home seller, Realtor, home inspector, etc. See section Benefits Of Knowledge Of Appraisals page 20 to see the reasons why **anyone** can benefit by knowing this material. A lot of the information in this educational material goes well beyond what's covered in other books. That's why I say it's "the *real facts* other books don't tell you!"

You may have purchased some of my other books and DVDs. If you have, then you will find that some of the information contained in this book is similar. This is because there are many important aspects that pertain to both the real estate appraisal and the home inspection businesses, as well as, real estate investing. I hope you don't feel that some of the information is redundant. It will only benefit you to read it several times to make sure you know the information well enough so it doesn't cost you time and money later. If you haven't purchased some of our other products, then do it now! I'm serious about that because our products are worth much more than the price we sell them for. Our customers email us all the time to tell us that.

There will be information in this book that you'll find very surprising and enlightening as to the inner workings of the real estate business. I certainly found it surprising when I got involved in real estate. The only problem was I had to find out the hard way. I'm going to tell you about it so you don't have to make the same mistakes that I made. They say a *Wise Man* learns by his mistakes, but a *Genius* learns by the mistakes of others. So I'll do the best I can to make you a genius!

I had a strong motivating factor for writing this book in the first place. I wrote it because I think there's a very important need for good, honest and thorough real estate appraisers. I sincerely want people to be more informed about the realities involved with the biggest investment decision they make - the purchase and sale of their own home. There is also a need to improve the integrity and professionalism of the real estate business overall. By being in the real estate

business, I've seen firsthand that there are many aspects about it that need to be improved upon. These improvements would be for the benefit of everyone involved, not just appraisers. I hope this book will help increase the integrity and professionalism of the real estate business. If it does, then I will feel that this information provides a much needed service and well worth my efforts.

> *I had a strong motivating factor for writing this book in the first place. I wrote it because I think there's a very important need for good, honest and thorough appraisers.*
> *I sincerely want people to be more informed about the realities involved with the biggest investment decision they make - the purchase and sale of their home.*

To get the most benefit, you have to read this book from cover-to-cover. So don't get lazy and cut corners; read everything! You have to read the book enough times until you've memorized enough of the information so you know what you're doing. You can't just read it once and expect to know enough to do a proper and thorough real estate appraisal. You can't "wing it" on an appraisal job because sometimes you'll get a client who asks a lot of questions. If you're fumbling for answers then you'll lose credibility and the client's respect.

This doesn't mean that you have to know the answer to every question the client asks. However, you need to be able to answer the vast majority of their questions. There are times that I tell clients *"I don't know"* when asked about a particular item. Because I know the answers to the vast majority of their questions, I have the client's respect for being knowledgeable. They realize that I can't be a walking encyclopedia. I just tell them that I will research their question and get back to them with the answer.

Don't expect to make big money overnight in this business, it's not a get rich quick scheme. It takes time to build up a referral business that brings in a lot of money. But don't worry. If you learn this material well enough and keep feeding your mind with new literature and training courses, you can make big money. Your referrals will begin to come automatically, without even advertising. The whole key to making a lot of money on a steady basis is to have satisfied clients. This is the same concept in every profession and not just the real estate appraisal business. Satisfied clients will refer their friends and business associates to you for appraisals. You'll become one of the best and busiest appraisers in your area if your knowledgeable and honest.

You will eventually get to the point when you're doing a lot of real estate appraisals. When you get to this point, don't book more than two appraisals in one day. If you try to do too many appraisals, you'll be rushing to get to the next appointment or you'll be tired before the end of the day. This can cause you to miss something that could create problems later with an angry phone call from your client.

Throughout this book you will see pull quotes and icon keys that will highlight important items. The icon keys are used to highlight important safety issues and "war stories". A *war story* refers to an actual appraisal or home inspection experience that myself or someone I know has had in the real estate business. I thought you might find these stories interesting and helpful since they can help you to understand the importance of the topics discussed in this book. Sometimes when people read about safety hazards, maintenance issues, market value factors, building department permits, etc., they don't take it very seriously – unless they've actually experienced their own war story concerning that topic! When people read about actual instances of these occurrences they tend to remember the advice easier, as opposed to taking it for granted. This will assist you in learning by actual experiences of other people and not make the same mistakes they did. That will save you time, money, aggravation, and stress. Sometimes it will even save your own LIFE! I hope you find the pull quotes and icon keys to be helpful while reading this book.

 = **Important Safety Issue**

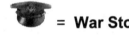 = **War Story**

In this book, when I use the term "Third Parties" I'm talking about people involved in the transaction, not including you or your client. This could be any number of people. The list includes but isn't limited to: the seller, the Realtor or broker, the appraiser, the home inspector, the mortgage lender, the title company, the attorney, the builder or repair contractor, the mailman, the Tooth Fairy, Santa Claus, the Easter Bunny, the seller's dog or cat, and anyone else who may have an interest in the deal. Also, when I use descriptive adjectives and refer to *immoral, greedy, dishonest, ignorant, incompetent, etc.* Third Parties, it does *NOT* refer to *all* third party people, just those that match the particular adjective used. I also want to make it clear that throughout this book both males and females are being referred to whenever the pronouns *he* or *she* are used. Both males and females are also referred to when I give examples of war stories that I've encountered in the real estate business. When the pronouns "he" or "she" are used, they are interchangeable.

Please send me an email and let me know what you think of this book and any recommendations you might have for improvements or new products. I accept positive and negative comments since both help me to improve the next version of the book. I am always looking to improve my products and services and I greatly appreciate customer feedback and suggestions. Also, you can sign up through our www.nemmar.com Nemmar Real Estate Training web site to receive our **free** real estate newsletter with articles and product updates that will definitely help you profit in real estate investing.

## What This Book Will NOT Teach You

I apologize if my grammar is not perfect in some sentences of this book. However, my objective is to teach real estate in an easy-to-understand way without being too formal, technical, *or boring!* My goal is to teach you as much as possible about the topics covered in this book. All of my books and DVDs are self-edited and self-published and I do the best I can with the time I have available.

This book will teach you a lot about topics related to the Real Estate Appraisal business. However, what this book will _not_ do is teach you EVERYTHING about **every single aspect** of the Real Estate Appraisal business. Why? Well, the reason is that no book ever written on any topic can teach you *everything* in one book. It's just not possible due to the cost and size limitations for printing a book. Every book can teach you **some**thing, but no book will teach you **every**thing. Seems obvious right? So are you wondering why I'm mentioning this at all since it's so obvious? The reason I mention it is that each year I receive thousands of emails from customers telling me they are very happy with my books and DVDs and feel my products are a great value for the price. Those emails I appreciate very much. Unfortunately, a few times per year I'll receive an email from a reader complaining that my $20 book or DVD did not teach them everything about **every single aspect** of the Real Estate Appraisal business!! It's pretty hard to imagine that there actually are some people who think that for $20 a book or DVD should give them the equivalent of decades of experience combined with a Masters Degree on the book subject. If it were that easy, then there would be no need for universities, training schools, or continuing education. All people would have to do is pay $20 for a book or DVD and have a world of information at their fingertips - *kind of like having **all** of the content from **every** web site on that topic available in **one** book*. Technology and information in all professions is constantly changing and improving. Even if it were possible to write and publish a book that covered *everything* about a topic, that book would not be up-to-date six months after it was printed due to the new technology and information that came out since the book publication date.

For the microscopic percentage of readers who expect to get the "world in the palm of their hands" for $20, let me explain how authors and publishers create and price their products - both large publishing houses and self-published authors. When any author or any company publishes a book or DVD they have to decide two things:
1) Who their target audience/customers are.
2) What the final retail price will be for the product.

Based upon these two criteria, the author and publisher will then determine how much money and time they will spend to create the book or DVD. For example, there are real estate training books and DVD packages that cost as much as $5,000.00. There are also many real estate schools that charge thousands of dollars for their training. A real estate Masters Degree program costs tens of thousands of dollars at universities. These authors, publishers and schools do not sell their training, books, or DVDs for $20 since they wouldn't be in business long if they did. The difference in the content of those products and my products is that their very expensive products are targeted for someone who is **already an EXPERT in that profession** and who is looking for continuing education credits and training materials that are **designed for professionals with many years of experience.** The reason why their training materials are so expensive is based upon their audience/customers who have to pay high prices to get more extensive and technical training materials. This enables the customer to receive the continuing education credits required by professional organizations they belong to. A general reader or a non-expert in that profession would be overwhelmed with the in-depth topics and technical details in a book or DVD *designed for someone who is already an expert in that field.* A book that an expert reads is too complex and technical for a beginner or intermediate level reader to comprehend. It's the same in all professions, not just in real estate.

Making all of my customers happy is my number one priority. If you are unhappy for any reason with your purchase then please email me so I can try to resolve the problem. With that said, I want to thank you for buying my book or DVD and I am confident that you will learn a lot and be a happy customer. *And yes, I very much appreciate my customer's sending me their comments, both positive and negative, since it helps me to improve my products and services.*

# *About The Author*

I'll briefly walk you through my background so you'll see how I ended up in the real estate appraisal business. My father died of cancer when I was 15, and as a result, I had to pay my own way through high school and college. I've worked many different types of service industry jobs to help pay my bills. I worked with a tree service company, a moving company, a house painting company, as a security guard, a day camp counselor, a golf caddie, in a restaurant as a dishwasher, a busboy, a waiter and a bartender, and the list goes on and on.

I studied Art History in college. When I graduated college I was working as a waiter at a local restaurant. You can see from my education and training that I had **no** experience in real estate and I knew virtually **nothing** about it. I didn't even know what a mortgage was! I knew a mortgage had something to do with real estate, but I didn't know exactly what it had to do with it. One day I saw an Infomercial TV show advertising products dealing with real estate investing. The show peaked my curiosity because it talked about buying real estate with "no money down." I ended up buying the products and I went through the material about 10 times. I memorized just about everything in that material. That's what got me started thinking about getting involved in real estate. The main problem was that I had almost no money in the bank! However, I was young and very ambitious and that can do a lot to help you get started. *(By the way, I wouldn't recommend buying the "no money down" books and products sold on TV infomercials. Statistics show that **less than 1%** of the people actually earn money who buy wealth making products, like the real estate "get rich quick" no-money down type of products. You have to be extremely ambitious, determined, plus be able to overcome major obstacles to use those products to get started in buying real estate. Moreover, many of the techniques they teach were much easier to use before the 1990's. Today they are just a pipe dream in the real world of real estate investing. The way they get customers is by preying on people's emotions. They pump you up with hyped-up customer testimonials and they make you think that with their material you'll be rich and financially independent in a few short years. It doesn't happen that way in the real world of real estate – unless you have a lot of money in the bank to start investing with).*

In the 1980's, while I was working as a waiter, my brother and I took out small personal loans to get down payment money to buy a rundown, old single-family house. This house was located in a low-income area of New York and it needed *a lot* of work. We gradually fixed this house up in our spare time, learning the ropes as we went along by trial and error. When we were finished, the house was appraised for twice what we paid for it. As a result, we refinanced the house. We used the money from this loan as a down payment to buy a two-family house that was in just as bad condition as the first house. We renovated the two-family house and then it was also appraised for twice what we paid for it. We refinanced this house and used the extra money to buy a six-family house. The six-family also needed a lot of work in repairs. So we did the same thing again, except this time when we were finished with the renovations, the house didn't appraise for twice what we paid for it. The six-family was appraised for <u>four times</u> what we paid for it!! *(We had bought the six-family at a bargain basement price.)*

We hired the best home inspector we could find to check these houses out before we purchased them. This inspector also inspected other houses we wanted to buy, however, things came up in the inspection that made us change our minds. We were beginning to learn the ropes about real estate and construction from buying, renovating and managing our own rental properties. This inspector coincidentally offered to train us to go into the home inspection business ourselves. The only catch was that we had to pay him $10,000 to do it! We saw that this inspector was earning over $135,000 per year while working right out of his home, and so we decided to take him up on his offer. I'm glad we did, because that $10,000 investment may have seemed like a lot of money back then, but it paid for itself many times over. I trained under this home inspector and did a lot of reading, research and memorization on my own. This learning process took a long time before I really felt that I knew what I was doing.

After getting into the home inspection business, I ran into a friend of mine from high school, named Mike, who was a local real estate appraiser. Mike had become a very qualified real estate appraiser. I was curious about how Mike trained to become an appraiser and what type of income someone could make in that profession. So I asked Mike some questions and found out that many appraisers earn over $140,000 per year while working out of their homes. He told me some of the aspects about the appraisal business but I just stored it all in the back of my mind and didn't think much about it.

Shortly after that, I received a phone call from another friend of mine from college, named Phil. Phil told me he was working for a bank in their foreclosure department. Phil said that he didn't hire home inspectors as much as he did appraisers for the properties the bank would foreclose on. After a bank forecloses on a property, they have an appraisal done to determine what the present market value is. A bank needs to estimate the market value to know what to try to sell the property for. Sometimes they need to have a home inspection done as well, but not as often. Anyway, this really got me thinking about learning how to do real estate appraisals. I was making a good income with my rental properties and home inspection business. However, I'm always looking for new opportunities that peak my interest. My friend Phil at the bank said that if I learned how to do appraisals well enough, he could give me plenty of work. This **really** set the wheels turning in my head.

I called back my other friend Mike, who was an appraiser, and asked if he could train me to do appraisals for a reasonable fee. Mike agreed to train me for one-half of the fee that I would charge the bank for each appraisal. This ended up amounting to over $8,500! I called Phil at the bank and told him I could do appraisals for him. I said that I will be getting trained by a qualified appraiser who had been in the business for years. This appraiser would also review all of my appraisals before they were mailed to the bank. Phil then

agreed to give me some appraisal work since I would have all of my appraisals reviewed by a qualified appraiser during my training.

It took about six months of working with Mike and writing up and reviewing many appraisals before I really felt that I knew what I was doing. I then went on to take the State Appraisal classes to get even more knowledge and expertise in real estate appraising. To continue building up my credentials and experience, I passed the State Appraisal examination to become a State Certified Real Estate Appraiser. With all of this training combined with my experience in the business, I have a big edge on many of the appraisers. This is because I have an extensive and diverse background in many different aspects of real estate.

In this book and educational series I'm going to tell you about all of the information and training I learned from a top-notch home inspector, a highly qualified appraiser, and the classes I have taken. Plus I'll tell you about all of the information I've learned from my own experience in real estate and in the inspection and appraisal businesses. The only part of that training I'm going to leave out is the $20,000 in up front fees and class tuition that I had to pay when I first started!! *I hope you don't mind me leaving that part out.*

## Purpose Of A Real Estate Appraisal

A real estate appraisal is needed to determine the estimated *market value* of a house, condominium, commercial property, vacant land, etc. It is used to assist someone in making a decision. They may be considering purchasing, selling, insuring, or lending money on a house, condo, commercial property, or vacant lot. Appraisals are also used for tax purposes to estimate how much money a property owner has to pay in taxes.

Here's a summary of some of the services a professional real estate appraiser can provide depending upon their qualifications:

◊ Residential and Commercial valuation estimates
◊ Estate planning and estate settlements
◊ Tax assessment review and advice
◊ Advice in eminent domain and condemnation property transactions
◊ Dispute resolution - including divorce, estate settlements, property partition suits, foreclosures, and zoning issues
◊ Feasibility studies
◊ Expert witness testimony
◊ Market rent and trend studies
◊ Cost/benefit or investment analysis, for example, what will be the financial return of remodeling a house, condo, or commercial property

◊   Land utilization studies
◊   Supply and demand studies

Banks and mortgage lenders need appraisals to assist them in figuring out how much money to lend someone for a mortgage loan application. There are many different aspects of a loan application that the banker has to consider, but mortgage lenders *always* require an appraisal since the real estate will be the collateral for the mortgage loan.

⚠ People get very emotional and excited about purchasing a house. When they're in this highly emotional and excited state, they tend to just look at the cosmetic appeal of a house instead of the important factors. They forget that they're not buying a **_CAR_**, they're buying a **_HOUSE!!_** There's a big difference between the two. One is a normal expense everyone has to incur occasionally. The other is the biggest financial decision most people will ever make. By becoming too emotionally attached to a deal, people often pay above market value for a home. This can cost them tens of thousands of dollars in an overpriced purchase. Since a house is such a major financial decision, it's prudent for them not to take any chances. They should try to eliminate as much risk as possible. It's a great feeling to have a client thank you for helping them out with the biggest investment they'll ever make.

> *A house is usually the biggest investment most people will make, so it's prudent for them not to take any chances. They should try to eliminate as much risk as possible.*

A pre-purchase appraisal will inform people of the true market value of a house. This will enable them to make an educated and intelligent decision on whether or not to purchase the home. They will also know the approximate amount to pay for it.

_All_ houses and condos should have a home inspection performed by a well qualified and thorough home inspector, before signing any contracts. The appraisal is generally done after the contracts are signed and the bank financing application has been filled out. There will be repairs or upgrading needed in all homes, even brand new ones. Sometimes people think that because a house is new it doesn't need to be inspected. They don't realize that builders are businessmen trying to make a profit. Any builder who doesn't do quality construction can cut corners to save a few dollars to try to try to increase their profit. When a house is built *"up to code"* it doesn't ensure a perfect house. Local building codes are the minimum standards that a builder or contractor has to follow to obtain a building permit or a Certificate of Occupancy for the work done. There's nothing to stop a builder or a contractor from exceeding the building codes other than saving some money for themselves or their client.

Pre-sale appraisals are recommended. Before someone puts their house up for sale they should have it appraised to estimate the true market value. This will prevent any last minute holdups because of problems found during the bank's appraisal. Any last minute problems will delay the sale or kill the deal altogether.

Homeowners can hire an appraiser to do a feasibility study to assist them before starting home remodeling and renovation work. The appraiser conducting the study analyzes the condition of the property and the cost of the renovations. The appraiser will then prepare an estimate of what the property's value will be **after** the improvements are made *(the improved value will affect the ad valorem real estate tax)*. This information will enable the homeowner to not spend too much or too little money with the renovations. The appraiser can also investigate whether a property qualifies for historic preservation benefits from Federal and local governments.

Homeowners can hire an appraiser when they need to insure the value of their home. *(This is different than private mortgage insurance)*. The *insurable value* is the cost of replacing the property if it were destroyed or damaged. This value can used to underwrite fire and hazard insurance on real estate. Although most reputable insurance brokers can tell you if your fire and hazard coverage is sufficient, there are properties that may require a closer examination, such as, older buildings, custom built homes, or properties with unusual features, such as solar energy collectors. An appraiser can give an opinion of the insurable value of the home by using the *Cost Approach*.

Homeowners can hire an appraiser to dispute the amount of their property taxes. Many people don't realize that they can be over charged for their property tax assessments. Homeowners need to hire an appraiser if they believe their property taxes are too high. An appraiser can estimate the market value of their house and then the homeowner can try to have their property taxes reduced.

Homeowners can hire an appraiser if they need to cancel *Private Mortgage Insurance* (PMI). New homeowners are frequently required to obtain private mortgage insurance, but as a result of legislation passed by Congress in 1998, homeowners can cancel this coverage when their loan to value ratio reaches 80 percent. An appraiser can estimate the current value of the home which will assist the homeowner in deciding whether or not to ask the lender to drop the PMI.

Relocation firms always need real estate appraisals during the process of employees being transferred to a new location by their employers. Sometimes, the relocation firm or employer will purchase an employee's home if the employee is unable to sell the home during a specified time period. A relocation appraisal is an estimate of the anticipated sales price which a home will sell in the current market within a reasonable length of time. The "length of time" in the appraisal valuation depends on the conditions in the area where the home is located. The definition of **anticipated sales price** indicates *"a reasonable marketing period, not to exceed 120 days and commencing on the date of appraisal (inspection), is allowed for exposure on the open market."*

Appraisers are needed during property condemnation proceedings, also known as, *Eminent Domain.* Appraisers often are asked to estimate "just compensation" in situations where the Federal or State governments take ownership of private property for public use. This happens in situations such as, to build a road, public park, expand an airport, etc. The law requires that owners of the condemned property, (property taken by the government in this manner), must be paid a fair price.

Appraisers are also hired to give an opinion of value of property for gift or inheritance taxes, lease rental schedules, and other investment purposes.

An *"A to Z Appraiser"* provides a much needed and highly respected service. People are trusting you to help them with the biggest decision they'll ever make!

# Benefits Of Knowledge Of Appraisals

Being an *"A to Z Appraiser"* will enable you to be involved in a recession-proof business. Real Estate is still bought and sold during a recession in the economy. In addition to the typical home sales, there are foreclosure sales, relocations, and distressed sales. The only difference about a recession is that houses are sold for a lower price. Also, during a recession the mortgage loan interest rates tend to drop. As a result, many people refinance their existing mortgages to take advantage of the lower rates. All of these houses still need to be appraised, and as a result, your business can grow during a slow economy.

Unfortunately, there are people who lose their homes due to tragic circumstances in their lives. However, you're not taking advantage of anyone or being unethical by appraising properties that are the result of a distressed sale or a foreclosure. All of these properties have to be appraised. Therefore, someone is going to be hired to do the job. Everyone will be much better off if the client hires an *"A to Z Appraiser"* who does top quality work.

Being an *"A to Z Appraiser"* can make you a much better home buyer or real estate investor. Before you buy a house or a rental property you can check it from top to bottom to figure out what it's worth. You can save up to tens of thousands of dollars by determining what price to pay. Many home buyers simply pay close to the asking price that the seller lists the house for. They tend to assume that the "listing price" must be close to the market value of the property. Often this is not so. The seller can ask any price they want for their property. However, the true market value could be much less than their asking price. If you have the knowledge of how to perform good, thorough appraisals then you can negotiate some price reduction or concessions. You can intelligently inform a seller if the asking price is too high.

Being an *"A to Z Appraiser"* can make you a much better home seller. Before you sell your house you can find out what the present market value is ahead of time. An awful lot of real estate deals are killed before the real estate appraisal or home inspection is done. The buyer and seller may come to an agreement on price and terms pending the appraisal or inspection. If the appraiser is thorough, they may find that the sales price agreed upon is too high. This ends up throwing a monkey wrench into the works by lowering the sales price or killing the deal. You can also learn if the asking price for your house is too low! You don't want to sell your house for a lot less than what it's worth, do you?

Being an *"A to Z Appraiser"* can make you a much better homeowner. See the *Purpose Of A Real Estate Appraisal* section for how homeowners can benefit from this knowledge. You can make your house safe for you and your family. You'll be able to identify electrical hazards, radon, asbestos, carbon monoxide and gas leaks, etc. Prevent accidents *before* they happen! Also, you can eliminate building code violations or protect yourself from being cheated by contractors.

Being an *"A to Z Appraiser"* can make you a much better Realtor. If you're presently a Real Estate Agent or Broker, you already know how a low appraisal or problems found during the home inspection can kill a deal. You can greatly increase the percentages of the deals you close. You can show the seller what the current market value is at the time you take the listing for the house or condo. As a Realtor, you can inform the home seller yourself without waiting for the bank appraiser to do it later. *(A Realtor CMA is only a ballpark range of the market value estimate of a property done by someone that **does not** have any experience as a licensed appraiser).*

I'm sure all of you that are presently Realtors are aware of houses that just sit on the market for long periods of time without selling. The *major* reason a house or condo doesn't sell within a reasonable amount of time is due to the asking price of the seller. Even if a house is in a bad area and needs work, someone will buy it if the price is right!! As a Realtor, you can help to reduce your headaches and wasted time showing clients' an overpriced house with a seller that won't come down in price. You can get more listings due to your knowledge and expertise, which any home buyer or seller will respect. This will enable you to increase your business and income.

Being an *"A to Z Appraiser"* can make you a much better real estate consultant. If you do any consulting work, you can gain much more respect and business due to your expertise and knowledge.

Being an *"A to Z Appraiser"* can make you a much better home inspector. I do inspections as well as appraisals and I can see things that the vast majority of inspectors in the business don't even know about. My inspections are much more thorough and informative for the client. Therefore, I can charge a lot more for my work than other home inspectors can.

---

> *So you see, I've got this baby set on automatic pilot.*
> *There's something in this material for just about anyone*
> *to benefit from.*

---

So you see, I've got this baby set on automatic pilot. There's something in this material for just about anyone to benefit from. There's only one type of individual that I can think of that can't benefit from this material. That's someone who has no intention of going into the real estate business in any way, shape or form. They also would need to have no intention of ever owning their own house or condominium. If that description fits you, then this book is not for you.

# Description Of A Real Estate Appraisal

A real estate appraisal is a little different depending on your regional area and the type of appraisal that is being done. However, you'll be dealing with the same general appraisal process and business. There are many different types of appraisers, some of which include: commercial real estate appraisers, residential real estate appraisers, furniture appraisers, jewelry appraisers, art appraisers, automobile appraisers, and the list goes on. We're going to concentrate on **residential** real estate appraising in this book.

*How does an appraiser estimate value?* Appraisers are taught to estimate value by following three recognized approaches. After analyzing the results of the analysis conducted, an appraiser then develops a final estimate or opinion of value. The 3 approaches to estimate value are:

◊ **Direct Sales Comparison Approach** - Compares similar, recently sold properties to the subject property.
◊ **Cost Approach** - Estimates the cost to replace or reproduce the subject property being appraised.
◊ **Income Approach** - Estimates what a prudent investor would pay for the subject property based on the income the property produces.

A real estate appraisal is an **estimate** of market value based upon the **opinion** of the appraiser. You're not stating the *exact* price that the property is worth in your appraisal report. You only give an estimate of the market value. Two separate appraisers are considered accurate if their value estimates differ by a maximum of 10% for the same property. The reason for this is that generally no two people will pay the identical price for a property. One buyer might like the house a little bit more than another buyer and so he would pay more, and vice versa. Therefore, when you estimate market value, you're merely giving your opinion. Your opinion will be based upon all of your field work and data. The estimated value in your appraisal report is the price you feel that the <u>majority</u> of the *typical buyers* in the area would pay for the subject property.

**Definition of Market Value** - The definition of market value that applies to HUD/FHA is cited from the Uniform Standards of Professional Appraisal Practice. *(HUD is the U.S. Department of Housing and Urban Development. FHA is the Federal Housing Administration).* This is the definition of value which must be used for all appraisals performed for FHA-insured mortgages:

◊ *"The most probable price which a property should bring in a competitive and open market under all conditions requisite to a fair sale, the buyer and seller each acting prudently and knowledgeably, and assuming the price is not affected by undue stimulus."*

Implicit in this definition is the consummation of a sale as of a specified date and the passing of title from seller to buyer under conditions whereby:

1. The buyer and seller are typically motivated.
2. Both parties are well informed or well advised, and each is acting in what they consider their best interest.
3. A reasonable time is allowed for exposure in the open market.
4. Payment is made in terms of cash in United States Dollars or in terms of a financial arrangement comparable thereto.
5. The price represents the normal consideration for the property sold unaffected by special or creative financing or sales concessions.

An appraisal involves a visual, limited time, nondestructive inspection of the subject property that you're appraising. There's no dismantling or using tools to take things apart. However, you will need some tools to help you on the appraisal. I'll tell you what tools you need a little further on in this book.

You're a real estate appraiser, you're not a repairman. Tell the client to have something checked out by a licensed contractor if it's not operating properly, or if you have any doubts about its present condition. This means that you don't need to know how to fix everything in a house. All you need to do is to be able to identify a problem, or identify whether the operating systems are working properly. To make this point more clear, I'll use an analogy with your car. Normally, you know when your car isn't running properly or if there's a problem with it. However, you don't need to know how to fix the car. All you need to do is identify that something is wrong and that a repairman needs to check it out further. You just bring the car to an auto mechanic and let them tell you exactly what's wrong and what it will cost to repair the problem.

As a real estate appraiser, you're not required to be the **Wizard of Oz**. You're not required to have a *magic wand* that reveals every, single problem with the house and site. You're not required to have *X-ray vision* to see things behind walls, ceilings or other finished areas. You're not required to have a *crystal ball* to foresee **all** potential problems that will arise in the future with the subject property. *(However some people expect you to have all of these qualities).*

As an appraiser you check all visible, accessible areas and operating systems, such as, heating, air-conditioning, electrical, plumbing, the roof, etc. Everything should appear to be operating properly and in satisfactory condition at the time of the appraisal.

You'll find that real estate appraising is a very interesting career. There are many different aspects that go into an appraisal report. There are photographs, some field work, some analysis of different data sources, some math calculations, etc. It's a very satisfying feeling to know that you can do very thorough appraisals.

Often when people find out that you're an appraiser they'll ask you, *"What's my house worth?"* For some strange reason people think that appraisers have some magical power. They believe an appraiser can just look at a property and be able to tell you what it's worth. You will get asked that question, *(many times if you go into this business)*. If you do, just politely tell them that an appraisal is a lot of field work. It's similar to doing a written report for school. There are no shortcuts to doing a good appraisal.

## Being A Licensed or Certified Real Estate Appraiser

To do real estate appraisals for federally related transactions, there are Federal and State licenses and/or certification requirements in all states. The regulations generally require you to work under someone else's wing until you learn the basics of the business and get some training. They also require you to take some appraisal classes to teach you the ropes. You'll find the appraisal classes to be very interesting if you have knowledgeable instructors for the courses.

If you decide to work with someone else's appraisal company, you'll find this will help you a lot in the beginning stages. You won't be calling the shots for a while, but you also won't have the overhead or liability problems. You will benefit by working with an experienced appraiser until you learn the basics. This book is a very in-depth look at the different aspects of real estate appraising. I think that you'll find it to be very helpful and enlightening. However, it will benefit you to get some field training alongside an experienced appraiser. That's because there are some aspects that are easier to learn if they are shown in person. If you're shown certain aspects on an actual appraisal assignment, it will be easier to understand and apply them properly. Although, the better the appraisal training manual, then the better your head start will be at becoming a qualified appraiser. I hope you find this book to be a good head start to being an appraiser.

See FHA Appraisal Roster – Appraiser FAQ's section page 198 and SELECTION OF APPRAISER section page 226 for details on the minimum requirements appraisers must meet

to be placed on the FHA Appraisal Roster. An appraiser listed on the FHA Appraisal Roster/Register is eligible to perform appraisals for FHA-insured mortgage loans. The success of the FHA mortgage insurance program and HUD's ability to protect its financial interest begins with selecting qualified and knowledgeable appraisers.

Here are some **Frequently Asked Questions** about real estate appraiser licensing and certification from the Appraisal Foundation web site. (See section Appraisal Related Web Sites page 406):

◊   **When and why was The Appraisal Foundation established?** In 1986, the instability in the real estate and mortgage lending professions led nine leading professional appraisal organizations in North America to form the Ad Hoc Committee on *Uniform Standards of Professional Appraisal Practice* (USPAP). These groups agreed upon a generally accepted set of standards that were then adopted by the eight American appraisal organizations. With the adoption of the Standards, *The Appraisal Foundation* was established in 1987 to implement the Uniform Standards of Professional Appraisal Practice through an independent board, the *Appraisal Standards Board* (ASB). The *Appraiser Qualifications Board* (AQB) was later incorporated in the Foundation structure in order to facilitate the development of meaningful qualification criteria for appraisers.

◊   **What public charge does the Foundation have and how was it obtained?** In 1989 Congress passed the *Financial Institutions Reform, Recovery and Enforcement Act* of 1989 (FIRREA), more commonly known as the *Savings and Loan Bailout Bill*. Title XI of FIRREA set up a real estate appraiser regulatory system involving the Federal government, the States and The Appraisal Foundation. *The Appraisal Subcommittee* (ASC) of the *Federal Financial Institutions Examination Council* has the authority to ensure that the States and the Foundation meet the requirements that the States use certifying appraisers and the standards of professional practice to which appraisers are held by the States *(the Uniform Standards of Professional Appraisal Practice - USPAP)*. As a result of the legislation, the Foundation has the following responsibilities: all certified appraisers must meet the qualification criteria established by the Appraiser Qualifications Board (*AQB*); all State appraisal examinations must be reviewed and approved by the AQB; all appraisals for Federally related transactions must conform to Uniform Standards of Professional Appraisal Practice promulgated by the Appraisal Standards Board.

◊   **What is the purpose of The Appraisal Subcommittee (*ASC*)?** The Appraisal Subcommittee mission is to ensure that real estate appraisers, who perform appraisals in real estate transactions that could expose the United States government to financial loss, are sufficiently trained and tested to assure competency and independent judgment according to uniform high professional standards and ethics. The ASC is responsible for monitoring the individual States in the licensing and certification of real property appraisers. In addition, the ASC acts as an oversight mechanism of activities of The Appraisal Foundation relating to real property appraisal. For additional information on the ASC and its activities, please visit the ASC website at www.asc.gov.

◊   **What is the relationship between The Appraisal Foundation and the Appraisal Subcommittee (ASC)?** These two entities are often confused by the public. The Appraisal Subcommittee is the Federal agency charged with oversight of the State appraisal regulatory programs. In addition, the ASC is responsible for monitoring the activities of The Appraisal Foundation and the ASB and AQB as well as providing a Federal grant to assist in the operations of these Boards.

◊   **What is the relationship between The Appraisal Foundation, the Appraisal Standards Board (ASB), and the Appraiser Qualifications Board (AQB)?** The Appraisal Foundation serves as an umbrella organization for two independent Boards, the Appraisal Standards Board and the Appraiser Qualifications Board. While these boards are independent, the Board of Trustees of The Appraisal Foundation is responsible for funding the activities of the ASB and AQB as well as appointing members to the Boards and providing oversight of their activities.

◊   **How is The Appraisal Foundation funded?** The Appraisal Foundation is funded in part by a Federal grant, sales of publications and services and from Sponsoring Organizations.

◊   **Is The Appraisal Foundation part of the Federal government?** No, The Appraisal Foundation is a private non-profit educational organization.

The following FAQ's are from the Appraisal Foundation brochures titled *"How to Enter the Appraisal Profession"* and *"How to Enter the Real Property Appraisal Profession"*. See section Appraisal Related Web Sites page 406.

◊   **What is an appraiser?** An appraiser is one who develops and reports an opinion of value on a specific type of property. Appraisers may opt to specialize in various disciplines such as:

- ▫   Real Property appraisal, which is the valuation of real estate. Real Property appraisers can choose specialties to practice within such as residential, commercial and agricultural.

- ▫   Personal Property appraisal, which encompasses all types of personal property such as fine and decorative arts, antiques, gems and jewelry and machinery and equipment.

- ▫   Business Valuation which is the valuing of businesses including all tangible and intangible assets ranging from the value of the equipment to the value of the business name or logo.

- ▫   Mass Appraisal which encompasses techniques that are used when valuing multiple types of real property

or personal property using general recognized formulas.

While most appraisers choose to specialize in just one area of practice, many appraisers practice in more than one discipline.

◊   **What skills are required to become an appraiser?** All appraisers must have good analytical skills and work well with numbers. In addition, appraisers spend much time interacting with clients and writing reports, so good communications skills are a must.

◊   **Does the federal government regulate appraisers?** Currently, the government regulates only real property appraisers. The power of regulation currently rests with the individual states and territories that issue licenses and certificates to real property appraisers. In addition, each individual State Real Property Appraisal Board is responsible for disciplining appraisers. At this time, there are no immediate plans for the regulation of appraisers who specialize in other forms of property.

◊   **How do I become an appraiser?** The process of becoming an appraiser differs according to the various appraisal disciplines. Most appraisers are required to have a certain number of hours of education and experience. In addition, if an appraiser wishes to become state licensed or certified in real property or if an appraiser wishes to become "designated" by an appraisal organization, they must also pass a comprehensive examination. The Appraiser Qualifications Board (AQB) of The Appraisal Foundation recommends the following minimum criteria for state licensed/certified real property appraisers:

|  | Experience Required | Education Required | Exam Required |
|---|---|---|---|
| Licensed Residential | 2,000 hrs | 90 hrs | Yes |
| Certified Residential | 2,500 hrs | 120 hrs | Yes |
| Certified General | 3,000 hrs | 180 hrs | Yes |

Please note that the criteria above is a recommended minimum and that the states may decide to increase this criteria as they see fit. The AQB has also established voluntary minimum criteria for personal property appraisers, as follows:

|  | Experience Required | Education Required | Exam Required |
|---|---|---|---|
| Personal Property Appraiser Minimum Qualification Criteria | * 1,800-4,500 hrs | 120 hrs | Yes |

\* Experience hours range from 1,800 of personal property appraisal experience, of which 900 hours must be specialized, to 4,500 hours of market related personal property non-appraisal experience in areas of specialization.

◊ **Do I need a college degree to become an appraiser?** Appraisal education in the United States has typically been provided by professional organizations. Accordingly, at present time it is not necessary to have a college degree in order to become an appraiser. Many appraisers choose to receive training through traditional methods, such as through professional appraisal organizations. It should be noted that some of these associations require a college degree for their advanced designations. On an increasing basis, appraisers are supplementing their education through courses at the community college or university level.

◊ **What is an appraisal "designation"?** An appraisal designation is awarded by one of many professional trade organizations that represent appraisers. Designations are awarded after an appraiser has completed a specific course of appraiser training through an organization. Each organization offers multiple designations in differing fields or specialties.

◊ **How do I become a designated appraiser?** You will need to contact one of the many professional organizations representing appraisers regarding membership and the course of action for designation.

◊ **Why should I join a professional appraisal organization?** A professional appraisal organization provides appraisers with the opportunity to network with other professionals, to keep abreast of pertinent issues such as regulatory changes and to receive continuing education.

◊ **How to I obtain trainee experience?** Trainee experience can be gained by aligning yourself with a professional, established appraiser as an apprentice as a trainee. Many appraisers work as an apprentice while completing the required education. For real property appraisers, many states have formal trainee programs.

◊ **What is the demand for qualified appraisers?** There is a wide array of clients that use appraisals such as lenders, insurance companies, attorneys, governments, museums and tax assessors.

◊ **What is The Appraisal Foundation?** The Appraisal Foundation is a non-profit educational organization dedicated to the promulgation of professional appraisal standards and appraiser qualifications for all appraisal disciplines. The Foundation accomplishes this mission through the work of two independent Boards, the Appraiser Qualifications Board (AQB) and the Appraisal Standards Board (ASB).

◊ **Why should I be interested in the work of the Foundation?** The Foundation, through its Appraisal Standards Board, publishes the *Uniform Standards of Professional Appraisal Practice* (USPAP), which is the generally accepted set of performance standards for appraisers. It is these standards that are enforced by state governments and various professional appraisal organizations. In addition, the minimum qualifications for certain appraisal disciplines are established by the Appraiser Qualifications Board of the Foundation.

**Real Property Appraisal Profession Questions**

The following is intended to provide basic information to individuals who are considering entering the real property appraisal profession. For specific information about the requirements in your state, please contact your state appraiser board. See section State Real Estate Appraiser Boards page 408.

◊ **What is the demand for qualified real property appraisers?** There is a wide array of clients that use real estate appraisals. For instance, lenders use them for loan collateral purposes; lawyers use them in property disputes, such as divorces; insurance companies use them to assist in determining the value of the property to be insured; and property owners may use them when appealing tax assessments, estate purposes and estimating a property's value when buying or selling real estate.

◊ **Do I need to obtain a credential or license in order to appraise real property?** Federal law requires all individuals appraising properties in a federally related transaction (e.g. a Federally insured lender is involved in the transaction) to be either state licensed or certified. In addition, many states have enacted laws that require any real property appraisal to be performed by an individual who is state licensed or certified. Professional appraisal organizations offer designations that often exceed the minimum requirements of state licensure. Since licensing/certification is required to show minimum competency, designations offer appraisers a way to further demonstrate their knowledge and professionalism.

◊ **Who regulates real property appraisers?** Each state and territory has a real property appraiser regulatory program. In the vast majority of instances, a board composed of between five and nine individuals governs the program. In addition to issuing licenses and certificates, the board is also responsible for disciplining appraisers.

◊ **What are the minimum qualifications I need in order to become a state licensed or certified appraiser?** The qualifications are set by the Appraiser Qualifications Board of The Appraisal Foundation and cover education, experience, examination and continuing education. For example, to become a state licensed appraiser, you will need at least 90 hours of classroom instruction, 2000 hours of experience, pass the state appraiser examination and complete 14 hours of continuing education annually. The minimum qualifications for all three categories (State Licensed, State Certified Residential and State Certified General) are contained in a publication entitled *Real Property Appraiser Qualification Criteria and Interpretations*, which is available on a complimentary basis from the Foundation.

◊ **How can I find out about available educational offerings in appraising?** Professional appraisal organizations are one of the primary providers of appraisal education. A listing of those organizations and their contact information is available at the Appraisal Foundation web site. See section Appraisal Related Web Sites page 406.

◊   **How can I gain the necessary experience?** One of the best ways to gain experience is to serve in an apprentice or trainee capacity with a state licensed or certified appraiser. Many states offer a trainee classification that formalizes the relationship between the state licensed or certified appraiser and someone who is wishing to become one. Professional appraisal organizations may also be helpful in assisting with mentor programs.

◊   **What do I have to do to qualify to sit for the examination?** In order to qualify to take the state examination, you must have completed your qualifying education classroom hour requirement.

◊   **How long is the examination?** Depending on the classification you are seeking to obtain, the examination is between 100 and 125 questions and takes approximately one to three hours.

◊   **Do appraisers have to follow any set of performance standards or guidelines?** The *Uniform Standards of Professional Appraisal Practice* (USPAP), which is promulgated by the Appraisal Standards Board of The Appraisal Foundation, are the generally recognized performance standards for the appraisal profession. Violation of these standards can lead to disciplinary action by government regulators and appraisal organizations. A copy of USPAP can be obtained from The Appraisal Foundation web site store.

◊   **May I appraise any type of real property once I become state licensed?** Generally, real property appraisers can obtain one of three types of credentials issued by a state. Each credential allows an appraiser to perform assignments within the following parameters:

- **State Licensed Appraiser**: may appraise non-complex 1-4 residential properties up to $1 million and commercial properties up to $250,000.
- **State Certified Residential**: may appraise 1-4 family residential units without regard to transaction value or complexity.
- **State Certified General**: may appraise all types of real property.

Although a license/certification might be obtained, competency in a specific field of expertise is needed. Certain state appraiser regulatory boards may have laws that differ from these (AQB) qualification criteria. All appraisers should consult their state laws prior to accepting certain appraisal assignments. See section State Real Estate Appraiser Boards page 408.

◊   **Why should I consider belonging to one of the professional appraisal organizations?** Professional appraisal organizations offer quality educational offerings and can keep you abreast of technological changes impacting the profession. Many offer "designations" that are awarded when you have completed a certain level of education and experience. These designations allow appraisers to demonstrate a higher level of expertise and specialization. In addition, they can serve as your voice on state and federal government issues. Many appraisal organizations are structured on a "chapter" basis, which allows members to network with their colleagues in a local area.

◊   **What does the future hold for the Appraisal Profession?** Of course, predicting the future is risky business, but the outlook for the appraisal profession is generally positive. Like most professions, the appraisal business is rapidly changing due to technology and globalization of the American economy. It is clear that these changes will open many doors to valuation experts, particularly those with a computer or statistical background. Appraisers are important when the economy is growing and also when it is in recession. Overall there may be fewer appraisers in the future but those that find their niche will be prosperous.

◊   **How do I become a designated appraiser?** You will need to contact one of the many professional organizations representing appraisers regarding membership and the course of action for designation.

◊   **Who are the Appraisal Sponsors of The Appraisal Foundation?** The Appraisal Sponsoring Organizations meet certain criteria to be a Sponsor and also provide financial support and advice to the Foundation. All of our Appraisal Sponsors offer educational programs and represent the interest of appraisers.

## Starting Out And Setting Up A Business

Set up a corporation in the State that you will be doing business in. This isn't a big expense. Consult an attorney in your area to assist you. You can use your home as an office. This is the most common way to start out. There's very little overhead and you don't have to pay rent and utilities for office space. Set up a separate phone line and create a professional web site. You don't have to hire a secretary if you can't afford one, just use an answering machine. **You** set your own hours and you can work part-time or full-time, whichever you prefer.

Have business cards, stationery and brochures made up at a local printer and drop them off and introduce yourself at: the local real estate offices, law offices, banks, home inspection offices and any businesses involved in real estate. I did this for months in my beginning stages. Banks are by far your best source of appraisal business. They need to order appraisals constantly for their mortgage loans. If you get on a bank's approved appraiser list you should have more than enough business to keep you busy and keep your own savings account growing.

Relocation companies are a great source of appraisals. I had a friend who was doing over a million dollars a year in business with relocation companies for appraisals and inspections. Get the relocation directories for the phone numbers and addresses of the people to contact. When a company relocates one of their employees they generally have two appraisals and two home inspections done. The company hires one appraiser and inspector, and the employee of the company hires the other appraiser and home inspector. The purpose of this is that they get two different opinions as to the current market value and condition of the employee's house. They then agree to a sales price and the company will reimburse their employee by buying the house from them. This enables the employee to move to the new location and buy a home. Sometimes when the first two appraisals are very different in estimating market value, they hire a *third* appraiser to settle the matter!

Some insurance companies hire appraisers before they write certain homeowner's policies. Contact some insurance agents in your area and see if they need appraisers. Attorneys and Accountants often hire appraisers to help settle an estate. An estate is created when someone dies and the heirs have to file the tax returns and disburse or manage the personal property and assets of the deceased person. The IRS requires an appraisal to figure out what the *estate tax* will be. The family members and/or relatives are taxed on the inheritance of the personal property and assets of the deceased person.

Get email lists of real estate offices, law offices, relocation companies, etc. to email them a link to your web site. Local billboards and other ads can be inexpensive for the exposure you get.

Work with another appraisal company. This is a great way to start out because you get to learn the business from someone who has been doing appraisals for years. There are many benefits to doing this. You will be earning money while building up business contacts during your training. You get to learn the basics of the business and you don't have the liability and overhead costs.

## Real Estate Appraisal Education

It's very important to keep educating yourself to stay up to date and knowledgeable. Join appraisal organizations and meet other appraisers. Some appraisal organizations have *Errors and Omissions* insurance offered to their members. Errors and Omissions insurance is <u>not</u> to be used as a safety net. Don't think that you can do bad appraisals and not have to worry about paying any penalties from lawsuits because you have E and O insurance. The purpose of E and O insurance is only in the event that you accidentally miss something on an appraisal. It's also used in the event that you get an unreasonable client who sues you for no-good reason. It only takes a small number of bad and dishonest appraisers that get a few really big lawsuits against them to cancel the E and O insurance program for everyone. So don't ruin Errors and Omissions insurance for everyone else. Do good, thorough and honest appraisals.

> *Errors and Omissions insurance is <u>not</u> to be used as a safety net. Don't think that you can do bad appraisals not have to worry about paying any losses from lawsuits because you have E and O insurance.*

I'll give you a perfect example of what you don't want to do concerning E and O insurance. There was some **Bozo** in my area who jumped into the home inspection business without knowing anything about it. Anyway, this new home inspector must have figured that he could learn the business overnight. He was telling potential customers, while giving them price quotes over the phone, that they should hire him because he had insurance which guaranteed they wouldn't have to pay for any problems in the house that he missed. These customers would call me and ask me if my company carried E and O insurance. I said yes but then I asked them why. When they told me what this other inspector was telling people, I was amazed at the absurdity and ignorance of this new inspector.

Just because someone has Errors and Omissions insurance doesn't mean that their insurance company is going to send checks out to anyone who wants one! If an inspector or appraiser gets slapped with too many lawsuits, then his insurance carrier will drop him like a bad habit. If that happens, then who is going to compensate all of his other clients who had totally useless home inspections or appraisals from this clown for their time and aggravation? Also, who would want to buy a house and then find out later about some major problems that should have been identified during the home inspection or appraisal? If the problems are overwhelming, then you wouldn't want to buy the house anyway, regardless of whether an insurance company was willing to compensate you for some damages.

The best insurance policy and client referral potential is to do good, honest and thorough appraisals. Each of your appraisals should take about one to two days to complete. This includes the on-site inspection, taking your field notes and photographs, finding comparable sales, gathering the pertinent data, and then writing up the appraisal report. You can work on several appraisals in one day but the overall time you spend on each report should amount to about 1-2 days. I've heard of some appraisers doing **three to four appraisals in one day.** I could not believe it when I heard that. I couldn't even get one appraisal report completed in a thorough, professional manner in that amount of time! So don't be a *"Walk-Thru"* appraiser by taking people's money and running. Do yourself and your clients' a favor. Spend enough time to check everything out properly at the job site, in obtaining the comparable sales, in gathering the data, and in doing the written appraisal report.

Some appraisal organizations have annual national seminars. They also have classes and real estate appraisal exams that are very good for keeping you on your toes and up to date. There are monthly newsletters that keep you up to date. You can get education credits for taking real estate appraisal classes. You need education credits to renew your Federal and State licenses and certifications, as well as, for any appraisal designation that you have.

I highly recommend you take some of the appraisal courses needed to obtain a State appraisers license. They have a class called *The Standards Of Professional Practice* that they require State licensed appraisers to take. This class will really open your eyes to the ethical and honest conduct that's required and expected of anyone in the real estate profession. *(Unfortunately, some people who take the course are either asleep or daydreaming when they're in the classroom! This you'll see from the war stories I mention in this book).*

Join home inspector organizations and meet other inspectors. I became a member of the leading home inspection organization in the country, as well as a State Certified Appraiser. That's something you may want to consider. Being a member of a top home inspection association gives you much more credibility in a potential client's eyes. You will have the edge over the competition when a client is calling around for price quotes and comparing the appraisal company services in your area. There are very, very, few people that are good home inspectors and appraisers. I mean top-notch home inspectors and State Certified and/or Licensed appraisers and not some guy who says he does both but has no extensive training in either.

Read books and talk to local appraisers, builders, contractors and building department inspectors to keep informed and educate your mind. There are constantly new technologies being applied to housing construction that you need to keep on top of. You also have to keep informed about the trends in the local real estate market.

Take some knowledgeable local contractors and appraisers out to lunch occasionally. This will enable you to find out about the new trends and technologies being used in new housing construction and you can compare your appraisal war stories. You may even be able to deduct it as a business expense! You'll be *amazed* at what you can learn from a contractor who specializes in a particular field. There are times when I come across something new that I haven't seen before during an appraisal. When this happens, I'll call a contractor who installs or repairs that item. I'll also call another appraiser and ask questions about it. People love to share their expertise with someone who's interested and willing to listen.

Take continuing education classes at local colleges. You may want to take a local building inspectors licensing course or test. This isn't required but it will give you more credibility and education.

## *Tools That Are Helpful*

◊  Road maps of your area and a car compass to find the job site.
◊  A clipboard with a notepad and pens to take your field notes.
◊  Standard appraisal forms.
◊  Home Inspection checklists (you can order these through our www.nemmar.com web site).
◊  A measuring wheel or 50-100 foot long measuring tape that can be reeled in for easy use and storage.
◊  Reliable camera to take interior, exterior and other photographs of the subject property, comparable sales and the neighborhood.
◊  Tool box to carry any tools.
◊  Reliable, powerful flashlight is a necessity.
◊  Lighted magnifying glass to view any data plates that are hard to read.
◊  Large probe and an awl to check wood for rot and termite damage.
◊  Hard hat, knee pads and a jump suit to wear in narrow crawl spaces.
◊  A marble and a six inch and a four-foot level to check walls and floors for being level.
◊  Pliers to help in necessary situations, such as lifting the corner of a rug to see the floor underneath.
◊  Binoculars to view the roof, chimney, siding and other parts of the house that you can't see clear enough from the ground.
◊  Folding ladder to look at the roof from a closer view.

## Booking Real Estate Appraisal Jobs

To give a price quote you have to determine the amount of time and liability that's involved with the appraisal. There are appointment and price quote cards that are included in this book. These index cards will help you give price quotes and keep track of your appraisal appointments with clients.

Explain to the client what's involved in doing a thorough appraisal. If you do work for banks, then they will already know the basics of what an appraisal report looks like. Let them know you're a very good, thorough real estate appraiser. Tell them how you give your clients much more data and photographs in your reports as compared to what other appraisers provide. This will help them with their decision about the subject property.

Don't make them think that your estimate of market value will be accurate to the penny because no appraisal report can be that accurate. Just make them realize how thorough you are and the realities of what an appraisal report involves. If you do this, then everything is up front for your clients to understand. They'll realize that your appraisal isn't some kind of guarantee that will exactly tell them the market value of the subject property. Remember it's an *estimate* of market value.

Sometimes you'll book jobs to appraise vacant houses. Some houses are left vacant when being sold for a number of different reasons. The homeowner could have died and it's an estate sale; the owner may have been relocated by his company for a new job position; the owner may be away for a long vacation; it could be a bank foreclosure sale, etc. If the subject property is vacant, then there are important items to be aware of. Often, vacant houses will have the utilities turned off. You should notify the client of this when booking the job. I've arrived at houses many times to do a home inspection or appraisal and the utilities were turned off. This limits what you can evaluate. For example, without electricity you can't check the outlets, switches or operating systems; without gas or oil you can't test the boiler/furnace or water heater; without the water supply turned on you can't test the plumbing pressure and drainage. There's another aspect to be aware of with vacant houses. If the property is located in cold weather areas, then the heating system must be kept on all winter or else the water pipes must be winterized. This protects the pipes from water freezing, expanding and cracking the pipes.

## Beginning The Appraisal

I'll go through the appraisal process. You can modify it to meet your own needs or desires. You'll be nervous for the first ten or so appraisals. This is normal. Just remember that you need to learn this material well enough, and keep up to date with all the new real estate and construction trends. If you do then you will earn the respect of the client and all third parties to the transaction by being so knowledgeable.

On your way to the subject property you should drive around the area before you get there. This will enable you to get a feel for the neighborhood. Take a good look around the neighborhood to see what condition and style the houses are in. See if there are any recreational facilities, such as, parks and playgrounds nearby. Check for the distance to any local transportation, shopping and employment centers. What are the negative and positive aspects of living in this area? Etc. Take note of the condition of the exterior of the house or condo, the terrain, if there are any ponds or streams, etc. Mark down the time the on-site appraisal work begins and ends. Mark down the weather conditions. Any snow covered areas will not be visible for inspection. Rain may have signs, or lack of signs, of water in the lower level and any roof leaks.

Greet the owner and Realtor and just tell them you have to ask some questions about the house or condo to get some background. You need this info to help you with the report and the appraisal. There are some aspects of the house that you can't always detect or verify without some additional information from the seller or Realtor. Often you'll find that you can't get all the information you need from the questions you ask the owner or Realtor. Just get whatever information you can and keep a record of it. Make sure that you put their answers in the written report to CYA, which stands for Cover Your Assets *(or Cover Your Ass)*. This will help in the event that you find out later that someone misrepresented the house or condo. You'll be able to show proof about what was stated and represented to you and your client at the time of the appraisal. This is why you want to stress to the client to arrange the on-site work at a time when the owner of the house is home. It's important to tell your client this when you're booking the appraisal. This way they'll have time to notify the owner to arrange the appointment. You should also get a copy of any real estate listing sheets, surveys, etc. that the third parties might have. See if there's anything important in these documents to help you or your client.

You have to be very gentle when you ask the seller of the house the following questions. Sometimes they get very upset and worried about all these questions. Just tell them that it's nothing personal or that you don't trust them, you just need this information to assist you with the appraisal. There are many aspects about a house that only the owner may know about and that's what you're trying to find out. If they (the seller) were buying the house, they'd want you to find out the same information from the seller as well. **Just remember that you're a guest in someone else's house! So don't be rude or get into an argument with anyone at the inspection site.**

You have to always be very diplomatic and professional in this or any other business if you want to be successful.

⚠ When you ask these preinspection questions, **make sure that you ask the owner or Realtor about information from any PRIOR owners of the house.** Meaning that if the seller tells you, *"No, we have never made any changes to the foundation or septic system,"* then ask them if they know of any prior owners having made any changes, repairs, etc. The reason you need to specifically ask that is because if you don't, then often the third parties will never mention any details they know about it. The Realtor, seller or seller's attorney may have information about what repairs, updating, problems there are/were with the house when the prior owners lived there. For example, the seller may have found problems in the house or with town hall records concerning the subject property after they moved in that were created or occurred with the prior owners. Third parties will rarely volunteer that type of information when you inspect the home for an appraisal client. They may not be trying to hide the information from you and they may think it's not relevant anymore because the situation occurred with a prior owner in the past. However, you need to make the third parties and your client aware that "yes" it is very relevant that you know all the details possible for your appraisal and evaluation of the subject property.

Some of the questions to ask:

◊ Age of House/Condo
◊ How long they lived there
◊ Any damaged areas to the floors, walls, and/or ceilings that they know about. Are any damaged areas hidden by carpets, furniture, sheetrock, etc.
◊ Any insulation added or removed to the floors, walls, and/or ceilings. Any UFFI foam or asbestos insulation removed must have licensed EPA contractor certification.
◊ Any past or present problems with the water pressure and drainage.
◊ Any past or present problems with electrical overloads, outlets, switches, etc.
◊ Does the fireplace draft properly and how often do they use it *(if applicable)*.
◊ Any exterior siding added after the original construction. What's behind it.
◊ Roof age and any past or present leaks.
◊ Any decks or additions added. If yes, are all valid permits and Certificate of Occupancies, *(C of O)*, filed at town hall.
◊ Any structural renovations done. If yes, is there a C of O for the work done.
◊ Furnace/Boiler Age. Dates and how often serviced. Are all rooms heated. Any oil tanks, used or unused, and their location. The age of any oil tanks.
◊ Age of the air-conditioning compressor. If it's too cold to test, did it operate properly last season. Dates and how often the system was serviced.
◊ Have they ever treated for termites or wood destroying insects. Date treated. Any damage from wood destroying insects, *(WDI)*. Any guarantees or documentation for any treatments performed.
◊ Any sump pumps in the house. Any water problems.
◊ Is house/condo connected to Municipal water & sewer systems. This is very important to get from them since there is no way to determine this at the site without checking the town hall records.

◊ Septic System:
◊ Any survey or plot plan showing the system.
◊ Any renovations or additions to the house that need septic system approvals, such as bathrooms added.
◊ Construction and size of septic tank.
◊ Is the tank original or was it upgraded.
◊ Date the tank was last pumped out and the times prior to this cleaning.
◊ Name of the septic service company for more info.

◊ Well Water System:
◊ Any survey or plot plan showing the system.
◊ Depth of the well.
◊ Is the well water pressure and volume adequate for normal use.
◊ Date the well pump was last serviced or replaced.
◊ Date the well water storage tank was last serviced and the age of the tank.
◊ Name of the well service company for more info.

◊ Swimming Pool:
◊ Age of the pool, filter, heater and liner.
◊ Do they have a Certificate of Occupancy and all valid permits.
◊ Any known leaks in the pool walls.
◊ Has it been properly winterized *(if applicable)*.
◊ Name of the pool service company for more info.

◊ Are there any outstanding building, zoning or other violations or any missing permits and/or approvals.
◊ Can I test all operating systems in the house or are there any that are being repaired or aren't functioning properly. Operating Systems refers to items such as the heating, air-conditioning, plumbing, electrical, wells, septics, etc.

*When you ask these preinspection questions, make sure that you ask the owner or Realtor about information from any **PRIOR owners** of the house. Meaning that if the seller tells you, "No, we have never made any changes to the foundation or septic system," then ask them if they know of any prior owners having made any changes, repairs, etc.*

# The On-Site Appraisal Inspection

Some areas of the country, like Florida, don't have basements in the houses due to a high groundwater table that would cause flooding. These houses are built on a concrete slab and therefore there is no lower level. As you move from the lower level through the interior and up to the attic, move in a clockwise direction. This will help prevent you from bouncing around from room to room which may cause you to skip a room by accident.

Another *very important* item to carry is your camera. I take many photographs for each appraisal I do. If you do this then you'll have plenty of pictures to help you when you write up the report. Don't just take the minimum number of photographs that are required to do a form appraisal report. Make the extra effort and take photos of interior rooms, the lower level, the operating systems, the attic and the exterior of the house. You should also take photos of the neighborhood and anything else needed to help your client in reading the appraisal report. If you include these photos with your appraisal your clients will appreciate the fact that you provide them with more than the minimum requirements in your reports.

> *Another very important item to carry is your camera. I take many photographs for each appraisal I do.*
> *If you do this then you'll have plenty of pictures to help you when you write up the report.*

You have to remember to bring a 50-100 foot long measuring tape or an appraisal measuring wheel to take any pertinent dimensions. Some of the items that must be measured are: the outside dimensions of the house to estimate square footage, any decks, patios or pools, any garages, etc. You have to also bring a notepad so that you can write down the dimensions and a diagram of the exterior and the interior of the house. On the interior you'll be drawing a diagram with the layout of the floor plan to include in your written report. You don't have to measure the interior rooms, except for the basement. You measure the *outside* of a building to estimate the square footage. If you take measurements on the interior of the house you should add about six inches to the figures. This is done because generally you should measure from the outside of the finished walls.

I'll always start the on-site inspection in the lower level because this is usually where the operating systems are located. For an appraisal, I usually spend at least 20 minutes in the lower level of a house looking at the operating systems and for structural, water and termite problems. When doing home inspections, I spend a lot of time in the lower level of a house. Appraisers don't have to do an in-depth analysis of the condition of a house like a home inspector would. Take a good look around since the lower level is an area that can really show a lack of maintenance and problems that need to be repaired. We'll go into more detail on how to do the on-site inspection in the following pages. But for now I'll go through some of the basics.

Some signs of structural problems are large cracks in the foundation walls that are wider than 1/4 of an inch. **Large horizontal cracks are very serious and must be evaluated by a licensed contractor!!** Signs of water problems are indicated by *efflorescence* on the walls and floors. Efflorescence is the white mineral salts that are the residue left on masonry construction materials due to moisture. Another indication of water problems is rotted wood members on the floors and walls. Check the base of any stored items in the lower level and underneath the corners of any carpets or floor coverings. Signs of wood destroying insect damage are indicated by wood beams that appear hollow and decayed. Probe the wood structural beams where visible and accessible.

When you look at the operating systems, check for any signs of aging and a lack of proper maintenance. Obviously if the boiler, or any other operating system, looks like they're on their last leg then you have to take this into account when determining the overall condition of the house. Check for insulation in the ceiling and if there is any heat or air-conditioning provided to finished rooms in the lower level. Look at the main electrical panel and all sub panels to see if there is any rust on them. I'll go into more detail in the following pages to show you how to evaluate the condition of the house. If you learn this material well enough, you'll be *light years* ahead of the competition!!

If there are any finished rooms or structural changes noted, make sure you find out if all valid permits and approvals have been obtained for this work. If there are no permits then this could be a building code violation that has to be corrected.

Before leaving this area, don't forget to take your measurements and photographs of the basement and all operating systems. This way when you get back to your office, you can refer to them while writing up the appraisal report. Just use your eyes and common sense when you're doing your inspections and make notes on anything that affects the value of the subject property.

# The Operating Systems Inspection

---

**The Operating Systems, Lower Level, Interior and Exterior Inspection sections are _EXTREMELY_ condensed versions of those found in our home inspection book:**

**_Home Inspection Business From A to Z_**

---

*Real Estate Appraisers are **not** required to be home inspectors. However, I will include these sections anyway to give you some basic details about home inspections.*

## Heating Systems

The average homeowner often improperly uses the term *furnace* when discussing their *boiler*. This same confusion happens with *heat pumps*. The difference between a Furnace, Boiler and Heat Pump:

◊ A *furnace* has a burner that heats the air and then blows it out of vents, sometimes called registers. You won't find any radiators if a furnace heats the house. Both a furnace and a heat pump use vents to discharge warm air in the house.

◊ A *boiler* heats by boiling water and making steam in a steam system. In a hot water system, a boiler heats water without reaching the boiling temperature, and circulates it through the pipes. The heated water or steam is sent through radiators to heat the house.

◊ A *heat pump* is a central air-conditioning system that works in reverse in the winter time. No matter how cold it is outside, there's always some heat in the air. The Freon in the heat pump can absorb this heat. The air is then blown over the Freon coils and the house is heated with warm air through the vents.

The basic operation of a heating system is this:

1. The temperature in the house falls below the setting on the wall *thermostat*. The thermostat then engages the *burner* or *heating coils* to turn on.

2. The air or water is then heated in an area called a *heat exchanger*. Picture the heat exchanger as a box where the burner or heating coils are located and the air or water passes around this area and the heat dissipates.

3. From the heat exchanger the water or steam in a boiler system goes through pipes to the *radiators* to heat the house. In a forced hot air system, *(FH Air)*, the air is heated as it passes over the heat exchanger. The heated air then moves through the *plenum*, which is the area just above the heat exchanger, and it goes through the *vents* to heat the house.

4. When the temperature in the house gets high enough to satisfy the thermostat setting, the thermostat tells the heating system burner or coils to shut off.

### Advantages of different heating systems:

◊ *Forced Hot Air Systems:* FH Air systems have the benefit of being used for central air-conditioning with the same ducts. If the furnace fails in the winter, there are no heating pipes to freeze. However, the house water pipes will freeze unless they've been drained. You can remove dust from the air and humidify it with a FH Air system.

◊ *Steam Systems:* Steam systems don't have water in the pipes that can freeze or leak. It doesn't dry out the air in the house. It takes a little longer to heat the house since the water must reach boiling temperatures of 212 degrees Fahrenheit first to make steam.

◊ *Forced Hot Water Systems:* Forced hot water systems heat faster than steam systems. You don't need to monitor the water level since the system is always filled with water.

◊ *Heat Pump Systems:* Heat pumps are central air-conditioning systems that work in reverse. They can remove dust and humidify the air. Heat pumps can be used as an A/C system in the warmer months.

## Disadvantages of different heat systems:

◊ ⚠ **_Forced Hot Air Systems:_**    Forced hot air systems have one main drawback. That is, if the heat exchanger leaks, there will be **lethal** carbon monoxide and products of combustion coming out of the vents in the rooms.

◊ _Steam Systems:_   Steam systems do not always have an automatic water feed on the system. When this is the case, the homeowner will have to monitor the water level in the boiler to make sure it doesn't get too high or too low.

◊ _Forced Hot Water Systems:_    Forced hot water systems heating pipes can freeze if the heating system fails in the winter. Also, the pipes can leak over time due to rust and corrosion from constantly being filled with water.

◊ _Heat Pump Systems:_    Heat pumps usually need a backup electric coil heater to assist them in very cold weather. This is because they may not be able to heat the house adequately in very cold weather. Heat pumps are mostly found in warmer climate areas and condo units.

The three most common ways to fuel a heating system are:  Oil, Gas and Electric. Heating systems generally have a life expectancy of 20-25 years. Heat pump compressors last about 7-10 years. Often heating systems will last longer, especially the old cast iron boilers. However, it's like an old used car, you never know when it can die. There will be many times that you'll find a heating system that is operating past its normal life expectancy. Just tell the client to budget for a replacement in case the system dies in the near future.

Check for a service card showing the last date of maintenance service for the heating system. The ceiling over the heating system should have a covering of sheet metal or 5/8 inch fireproof sheetrock to help prevent the spread of fires in this area.

See if there's a data plate on the heating system stating how many BTU's it is. The total heating capacity of a furnace or boiler system is usually measured in BTU's *(British thermal units)* or tonnage. One BTU is the amount of heat that's required to raise the temperature of one pound of water by one degree Fahrenheit. One BTU is about the amount of heat given off by an old-fashioned wood match. An average single family house that's about 2,500 square feet in size should have at least a 125,000 BTU heating system to heat the house adequately. This number will fluctuate up and down based upon many factors. Some of the factors are: how many windows the house has, what type of insulation, if it's a condominium that has a heated condo attached to it on each side, the efficiency rating of that particular heating system, etc. The biggest factors generally are the square footage, the amount and types of windows and insulation in the house.

These calculations must be carefully figured out by the heating contractor before they install the system.

There will be times when you find a house with a heating system that's too small to adequately heat in cold weather. Also, if the house has a lower level then your client may want to finish the basement to make a playroom. Another possibility is that your client may be planning to put an addition on the house. Make sure you remind your client that if they plan to heat additional areas of the house, then they need to speak to a heating contractor. Have the heating contractor figure out if the existing heating system is large enough to heat the expanded areas.

You'll also find houses with air-conditioning compressors that are too small to cool the house adequately. These types of problems are caused by an inexperienced contractor who didn't know what he was doing. It could also be caused by a homeowner who wanted to save a few dollars by installing a smaller heating or air-conditioning system instead of a properly sized unit.

> *The flue pipe is used to safely discharge the carbon monoxide and other products of combustion.*
> *These gases must be safely discharged from the house.*
> *They're lethal gases!!!*

⚠ Check the flue pipe on gas and oil fired heating systems. The flue pipe is usually located at the rear of the unit. This pipe is used to safely discharge the carbon monoxide and other products of combustion. All gas and oil fired burners discharge these products of combustion. These gases must be safely discharged from the house. They're lethal gases!!! It's similar to having the exhaust fumes from your car discharge inside your house. It'll kill everyone in the house! The sections of the flue pipe must be screwed together for safety. They must have an upward pitch and should not be within four inches of any combustible material, such as wood, to prevent fires.

Check the oil tank if it's located in the interior of the house and is visible. I prefer interior oil tanks more than underground tanks due to the potential expense of a leak. There have been recent Environmental Protection Agency court rulings about leaking oil tanks that incur stiff fines for the owner of the leaking tanks. It's also expensive to dispose of oil tanks because they're considered a contaminated waste like asbestos and toxic chemicals. If there's an underground oil tank, recommend that a licensed environmental contractor perform tests to find out if there are any leaks. There are a number of different tests to detect a leaking oil tank. Each test has positive and negative aspects to it. A Petro Test by a reputable oil contractor be performed to find out if there are any leaks. A Petro-Test is a pressure test that an oil contractor performs. What they do is seal off the oil tank vents and feed lines and pump air into the tank. They then monitor the pressure in the tank to determine if it drops which would indicate a leak. Another test is a Water Test. If an oil tank leaks there's a good chance water will enter it. The oil contractor will check the tank to find out if there's any water in it.

Determine if any C of O's, (Certificate of Occupancy), permits or surveys are needed in the local municipality with underground oil tanks. Interior and underground oil tanks generally last about 25 to 30 years and longer if they're maintained. If there are a lot of evergreen trees around the area where an oil tank is buried it'll cut down the life expectancy of the tank. This is because these trees add a lot of acid into the soil that rots the tanks quicker.

Check all heating pipe joints for rust or leaking conditions that'll require repairs. You'll usually find some rust unless it's a new unit.

# Air-Conditioning Systems

Don't turn on any central or window or wall air-conditioning units when the outdoor air temperature is 65 degrees Fahrenheit or lower. The interior pressure that's required to properly operate an air-conditioning system is too low when the temperature is 65 degrees or lower. If the unit is turned on, there are a number of ways that you could damage the compressor or the other components and end up buying the owner a new air-conditioning system.

> *Don't turn on any central or window or wall A/C units when the outdoor air temperature is 65 degrees Fahrenheit or lower. If the unit is turned on, there are a number of ways that you could damage the compressor or other components.*

Don't listen to anyone that says you can test the system anyway when the temperature is too cold. Let them turn on the system so if it blows, then they have to pay for it. I've heard a few war stories about poorly trained home inspectors that turned on A/C systems in the winter time and ended up blowing the compressors. Don't let this happen to you.

Check the exterior compressor unit while the air-conditioning system is on. See if it's making any unusual noises or if it's very old and rusty. Check the data plate to try to figure out the age and size of the unit. The life expectancy of a compressor is about 10 years depending upon the amount of usage. The life expectancy also depends on the quality of the unit and the maintenance given to the system over the years.

# Domestic Water Heaters

Usually the water heaters are a separate unit but can be immersion coils inside boilers. Separate water heater units can be gas, oil or electrically heated. An immersion coil system has water pipes that carry cold water inside a coil located in the side of the boiler. The coils are actually *immersed* in the hot boiler water, hence you get the name *immersion coils*.

The standard size water heater for a single family house is 40 gallons. Sometimes you'll find an oversized water heater in the house. It's not as energy efficient because a lot of water will be heated and then it will just sit in the tank without being used.

Check for any rust or water leaking conditions on the unit. The water heater should be kept on the warm setting for maximum efficiency and life expectancy. The life expectancy of a water heater is 10-12 years. A high temperature setting will cause the unit to constantly be heating water higher than is necessary which can cause premature failure.

During your interior inspection, check the water at some of the faucets and tubs. You want to make sure that adequate hot water is available.

# Plumbing System

Look at all visible plumbing lines. There will be very little to view in a finished basement or behind walls and ceilings. Check for any corrosion, leaks or any buildup of mineral deposits. There are several types of plumbing line materials including Copper, Brass, Galvanized Iron, Lead, PVC, and Cast Iron.

Often you'll see water stains on some of the floor joists, which are the beams that support the floor above. You'll also see water stains on the sub flooring, which is the base for the floor above. Minor water stains are normal, especially underneath kitchens and baths. You need to be concerned about extensive water damage. If any doubts exist, check the floor above the damaged or stained areas. Try bouncing on the floor above during your interior inspection to see if there are any problems.

Check the water main line where it enters the house. The water main for a house connected to a city water system is usually located in the lower level at the base of the foundation wall facing the street. The water main for a house connected to an on-site well water system is usually located in the lower level at the base of any of the foundation walls. Ask the owner or Realtor if you can't find the main water line. Sometimes they're behind personal items or finished walls in the lower level.

⚠️ Find out what type of pipe material the main water line is made of. Usually it'll be copper for a house with city water and it may be plastic for a house with well water. *Lead* piping is very rarely found in my area. It's not used any longer because the lead content can seep into the water supply which is very hazardous. These pipes will **always** leak some amount of lead content into the house water supply. A lead main entry line will be silver in color and may have a small bubble-type bulge in the beginning of the line. This bulge is known as a "wiped" joint. If you see a lead main water line or any lead piping in the house, highly recommend that the client have a laboratory water analysis done for safety. Also, recommend that all lead piping be replaced with a new pipe for safety. The reason for this is that lead poisoning is the ***NUMBER ONE*** childhood disease in the USA. Lead is an element that doesn't break down when it gets in your system. The effects of lead poisoning in children are *irreversible!!* Lead poisoning can damage the kidneys, nervous system and blood, and can cause permanent brain damage. So don't take any chances with this stuff.

⚠️ In older houses there will be lead in some of the soldered pipe joints. Gradually, over time the amount of lead in the solder will be reduced from leaching into the drinking water. **Ice makers are prone to very high lead levels.** The water in a freezer ice maker can sit in the pipe for days. This allows enough time for the lead to leach into the water at high levels. A lead abatement contractor told me that he's tested houses where the children had extremely high levels of lead in their bodies. He said that after the test results came back, **almost all the lead in their bodies was coming from the ice cubes!**

I'm telling you ahead of time, that if you come across any lead piping in a house, some Realtors and other third parties will try to sugarcoat the problem. They're going to tell your client that *"they only need to install a water filter and it'll be fine."* Don't let your client be snowed with that line! Tell them to remove all lead piping and eliminate the problem for good.

⚠️ Check for an electrical grounding wire. This is a **very important** safety item!!! It should be located by the water meter or the entry of the water main line. The purpose of this is to ground the house electrical system for safety. Electrical systems can also be grounded to an exterior metal rod driven 8-10 feet into the ground. The grounding wire doesn't have to be insulated like most electrical wiring because there's normally no current passing through this wire. It may be enclosed in BX cable or a conduit, which is a metal covering for protection from damage.

⚠️ The grounding clamps should not be rusty or loose, but often they are. The grounding wire should be clamped on both sides of the water meter, if there is a water meter installed. If there is no water meter, then the grounding wire should be clamped on both sides of the water main shutoff valve. Often it will only be clamped to one side of the water meter or main shutoff valve. Tell the client that they need to have a *jumper cable* installed with clamps to span the water meter. This is an inexpensive item to install and it's a safety requirement of the National Electric Code. A jumper cable is merely an additional heavy gauge wire about three feet long that's attached on both sides of the water meter. A jumper cable normally doesn't need to be an insulated wire because no electrical current should be passing through this wire unless there is a problem condition.

During the interior inspection check the water pressure and drainage by briefly running the faucets and tubs. In the bathrooms run the sink faucet, the tub or shower faucet and flush the toilet simultaneously. Watch the faucets to see if the pressure drops significantly. A minor pressure drop is normal but a large pressure drop can indicate either poor water pressure or clogged supply lines. Poor water pressure in some supply lines may be due to the street water pressure being too low. However, it's most likely caused by some supply pipes inside the house that have clogged over the years. Tell the client to have a licensed plumber check it out to determine if there are many clogged lines or just a small section that needs replacing.

Don't forget to turn off any faucets that you're testing during the inspection. You don't want to flood the house. Water damage can be very messy and expensive to repair.

# Well Water Systems

The main components of a well water system consist of a well pump, the water lines, the pressure gauge and the water storage tank. Well pumps are usually located inside the well and aren't visible. The life expectancy of a well pump is about 7-10 years but can be longer if the pump isn't overworked or neglected. The life expectancy also depends upon the type and quality of the pump installed and the acidity of the well water. Generally you should use the 7-10 year range during an inspection.

Try to get as much information as you can about the well from the owner or Realtor. Use the preinspection questions that I mentioned earlier for a guideline but don't be afraid to ask any other questions for further information. Don't be surprised if they don't know very much about the well system. Unfortunately, this is often the case. Don't be surprised if the answers you get don't seem to be the truth from the results of the well test.

Look at the well water lines to determine their overall condition. Take a look at the well water storage tank, if it's visible. Check for any rust or aging signs. The water storage tank should be painted and insulated to prevent any condensation from building up on the outside. The condensation causes rust over time. There should always be a pressure relief valve for safety in case the pressure in the system gets too high. It's usually set at 75 psi, *(pounds per square inch),* depending upon the type and capacity of the storage tank. Make sure the tank has an air fill valve to adjust the air-to-water ratio inside the tank during the periodic maintenance done by a well contractor.

> *The minimum acceptable flow for a well system is five gallons per minute, (GPM). Some local area codes may require a higher GPM rating, so check with your local building department.*

The minimum acceptable flow for a well system is five gallons per minute, *(GPM).* Some local codes may require a higher GPM rating, so check with your local building department. What you need to be concerned about, is an abnormal drop in pressure. Just ask yourself and the client, if they're present: Are the pressure and volume of the water flow enough to take a shower with? If the answer is no, then tell the client to have the system checked out by a licensed well service contractor.

Check to find out if there's a water filter installed on the system. I even recommend that the client use water filters when their house is connected to the city water system. Water filters are *highly* recommended for health reasons, especially with all of the pollutants going into the water supply these days.

# Septic Systems

The main components of a septic system consist of the drainage lines, the holding tank and the leaching fields or seepage pits. The life expectancy of a septic system is about 30 years depending upon the type of construction and the maintenance given it. Try to get as much information as you can about the septic from the owner or Realtor. Use the preinspection questions that I mentioned earlier for a guideline but don't be afraid to ask any other questions for further information. Don't be surprised if they don't know very much about the septic system. Unfortunately, this is often the case.

I'll tell you another war story that oughta jar you a little bit. I did an inspection once and the client, the Realtor, the seller, and the real estate listing all stated that the house was connected to the municipal sewer system. I always tell my clients that they need to confirm this with the town hall records since there is no way for me, or any inspector, to see underground to verify that the house is connected to the city sewers. *(I'm not Superman with X-ray vision).* Later during the backyard inspection, the client mentioned to me that he was thinking about putting a swimming pool in the backyard after he bought the house. So, as always, I told the client to check town hall to make sure he could get the approvals to install a pool and get price estimates ***BEFORE*** closing on the house.

Well, about four months later, I got a letter from this client's attorney. The letter stated that the client went to town hall to find out about installing a pool in his backyard – ***AFTER*** he bought the house. He was awfully surprised to find out that the house had a septic system and was **not** connected to the city sewer system! As a result, the client not only couldn't put a swimming pool in his yard, but he had to deal with a septic system that hadn't been maintained for who knows how long!! If the seller of the house didn't even know he had a septic system, then obviously he didn't call any septic contractors to clean out the tank and inspect it internally every few years. So the probability of having to pay to replace a decayed and neglected septic system and leaching fields, just added insult to injury for my client! I told this client and his attorney that they were "barking up the wrong tree" if they were even thinking about complaining to me. The seller, the Realtor, and the real estate listing, and even my client, all gave me incorrect information when they told me the house was connected to the city sewer system. Moreover, the client chose on his own to **not** follow my advice to check town hall records **before** he closed on the house. I also had a copy of this client's written inspection report that I had sent him. I explained to the client's attorney to read specific pages in the report which clearly stated my advice to this client *before* he closed on the house. As a result, I never heard a word from that attorney or client again about this complaint or problem. They realized the client himself was to blame and they could only consider suing the seller and Realtor – but certainly not me.

> *The point I'm trying to make, is that there's no way to know for sure whether or not the house is connected to the municipal sewer system.*
> *So you want to mention to the client that the only way for him to determine this is to check with town hall.*

There's no way to tell for sure if a main drainage line leads to a septic system or a city sewer system because they're identical. The point I'm trying to make, is that there's no way to know for sure whether or not the house is connected to the municipal sewer system. So you want to mention to the client that the only way for him to determine this is to check with the local building or health departments at town hall. Now do you see what I mean about being thorough and Covering Your Assets. This is why you need to ask the owner the preinspection questions and be up front and honest with your client.

Septic systems <u>must</u> be pumped out clean and inspected internally every two to three years at least. It should be more frequent than every two years if there are many people in the house or they do a lot of entertaining. I know a septic cleaning contractor in my area who has one customer that gets their tank cleaned every 3-4 *months* because they have a very high water usage.

You will encounter some homeowners who think you don't have to pump septic tanks clean. They believe in the fairy tale myth that the bacterial action inside the septic tank decomposes all the solid waste away. There are some products sold that claim to help the decomposition in septic tanks. Some homeowners think you merely have to use these products instead of pumping the tank periodically. You must tell your client that this is totally incorrect and the client needs to have the tank pumped and internally inspected. When this occurs you'll often have a third party say, *"If it's not broken, don't fix it."* My response to that is, *"Should you wait until you're terminally ill before going to the doctor for a physical?"*

# Electrical System

The main components of the electrical system consist of: the service entrance lines, the electrical conduit lines, the electrical meter, the main electrical panel and any sub panels, fuses or circuit breakers, the interior electrical wiring and the electrical system grounding cable.

 **Remember that electricity can kill you!!** Before touching the main panel or any sub panels check them with a voltage tester to make sure that it's not electrified. Voltage testers can be purchased very inexpensively at a local hardware or electrical supply store. There was a story in a home inspection newsletter about one inspector who noticed that the insulation on the service entrance line had worn off at the top of the main panel. This caused the main panel to be electrified. Luckily he tested the panel before touching it.

Also, don't go near any exposed wiring or any electrical panels or wiring if there's water on the floor or near the wires. Water and electricity *don't* mix! You're not paid to get electrocuted; you're paid to appraise the house. State appraisal and home inspection standards state clearly that home inspectors and/or appraisers are not required to do anything that can be hazardous to themselves or to others. So be careful.

Check the main panel for any rust or corrosion. If there's excessive rust or corrosion, then recommend that a licensed electrician evaluate the system. After testing the electrical panel with a voltage tester check to make sure it's installed on the wall securely by *gently* trying to shake the panel. Be careful - you don't want to loosen the electrical panel nor any wiring, you just want to see if it's secured properly. See if there are any hazardous conditions around the panel. Some hazards to watch out for are: potential water, objects in the way, the panel being too high to reach safely, etc.

Check to see whether the system has fuses or circuit breakers. Newer houses have *circuit breakers* which are the plastic switches that can easily be turned on or off by the homeowner. Older houses have *fuses* which are the glass screw-in type. <u>Do not turn any circuit breakers off or on or replace any fuses!!</u> Sometimes a circuit will be off because the homeowner is making repairs or the circuit was overloaded. Just inform the client of this and tell them to check with the owner or a licensed electrician to figure out the cause. You aren't allowed to turn any circuits on or off or replace any fuses for safety reasons.

Check to see if there are any open circuit breaker or fuse slots in the main panel or any sub panels. Open slots need to be covered with *blanks* or spare circuit breakers or fuses. This will prevent anyone from sticking their fingers or any objects inside the main panel and getting electrocuted. *Sub panels* are small electrical panels that branch off from the main electrical panel. The purpose of sub panels is to prevent very long branch circuit runs in the house. Long branch wires can cause a *"drop"* in the electrical current.

In the main panel you'll see the main disconnect for the entire electrical system in the house. This is similar to the water and gas main shutoff valves. Sometimes the main disconnect is located outside the house, next to the electrical meter. Check the main disconnect for an amperage rating number. It should be written right on the circuit breaker or fuse. Fuse systems have either a *pullout* fuse box or a *cartridge* fuse for a main disconnect. A pullout fuse box is simply a cartridge fuse inside a small box that's pulled out to shut off all the electrical power to the house. A cartridge fuse is a fuse that looks like a miniature stick of dynamite that has metal blades at the top and bottom.

⚠ **Do not remove any electrical panel covers unless you are a licensed electrician!! Do not pull out the main disconnect box or touch the cartridge fuse if you can't see their rating number!!** Just tell the client that you can't determine the amperage on these disconnects due to the type of system that it is. Tell them to have a licensed electrician find out the amperage for them.

⚠ It's **extremely** important that the electrical system be grounded to a properly working grounding cable attached to the water main line or a grounding rod in the soil. Make sure the client understands the importance of maintaining a properly operating grounding system of the electrical service for safety. Review the plumbing section that details the attachment of the electrical ground cable near the water meter.

As you go through the interior and exterior of the house check for any loose wiring that needs to be secured or any electrical hazards. Make sure you warn the client and the homeowner of any hazards. Remember, electricity can kill people so be very thorough and careful during the inspection. Check for loose electrical switches and outlets that need to be secured. Also, check for any "do-it-yourself" work in the house. All electrical repairs **must** be performed by a licensed electrician. All valid permits and building department approvals must be obtained for any work done. As a safety precaution, check to make sure that the outlets and switches in the bathroom **are not** reachable from the tub or shower. Remember that water and electricity don't mix! Remind your client of this.

> *All two prong outlets should be upgraded to the modern three prong grounded outlets by a licensed electrician.*

Older houses will have the two pronged outlets as opposed to the modern three prong types. The third prong is used for the grounding prong in electrical cord plugs. The purpose of this grounding prong is that most appliances today have an internal ground. All two prong outlets should be upgraded to the modern three prong grounded outlets by a licensed electrician.

In newer construction or recently renovated houses you may find *Ground Fault Circuit Interrupters* in some outlets. They're also called GFCI's for short. GFCI outlets have two buttons in the middle that are marked *test* and *reset*. A Ground Fault Circuit Interrupter is an electronic device that will trip or turn off the circuit when it senses a potentially hazardous condition. It's very sensitive and operates very quickly. The National Electric Code recommends that **GFCI's** be installed anywhere near water for safety. Water prone areas include basements, garages, kitchens, bathrooms and all exterior outlets. You should recommend the installation of GFCI's to all of your clients for safety reasons. They're an inexpensive item to have installed and they significantly increase electrical safety in the home.

> *The National Electric Code recommends that GFCI's be installed anywhere near water for safety. Water prone areas include basements, garages, kitchens, bathrooms and all exterior outlets.*

⚠ If the client has children, recommend that they install child proof caps for the electrical outlets. These are small plastic plugs to cover any unused outlets so a child won't stick anything into them and get electrocuted. You should also recommend that they use child guards for all cabinets to prevent children from opening cabinets that have cleansers and sharp objects inside.

# The Lower Level Inspection

## Lower Level

Some houses are built on a concrete slab and therefore there's no lower level to inspect. When you're inspecting the lower level of a house move in a clockwise or counter clockwise direction so you make sure you don't miss anything. Some lower level areas will be finished with rugs on the floors and sheetrock on the walls and ceilings and you can't view behind these finished coverings. Finished lower level areas add more value in price to a home but they make inspections more difficult for home inspectors and appraisers. Some lower level areas will be inaccessible due to personal items of the seller put there for storage. Just tell the client that you don't have X-ray vision and you'll try to evaluate as much as possible. Any inaccessible areas can't be evaluated so just do the best you can.

Check the lower level steps and any entrances to make sure they're in good condition and safe. All stairs need to have handrails and evenly spaced steps for safety. This will help prevent any tripping hazards.

Check the construction materials used for the foundation walls. The foundation will be made of poured concrete in new construction. Concrete block foundation walls are also common to find. Brick and stone constructed walls are usually found in older houses. Due to the cost of construction today, you probably won't find brick or stone foundation walls in newer houses.

The floor of the lower level should have a concrete covering. The vast majority of the time it will have a concrete covering. If there is a dirt floor, you should recommend that a concrete covering be installed. This will help prevent water, termite and radon entry in the house. Covering a dirt floor with concrete can be expensive, so tell the client to obtain an estimate before closing on the house.

Check for any large cracks in the walls and floors. You'll always find some minor settlement cracks in the walls and floors. These minor cracks are caused by the settling of the house and the expansion and contraction of the construction materials. As long as the settlement cracks are less the 1/4 inch wide, then it's a normal condition. Just tell the client to have the cracks caulked and sealed to prevent water entry and to monitor these cracks for future or further movement.

⚠ All construction materials will expand and contract with the weather and temperature changes during the year.

This can also create these minor cracks that you'll find. However, the cracks that you're looking for are long horizontal cracks or cracks over 1/4 inch in width. These cracks are much more serious, and if you find any, tell the client to have a licensed contractor evaluate them and give estimates for any repairs needed. Cracks over 1/4 inch wide indicate excessive differential settlement of the house and aren't normal. You'll find large cracks from time to time, so just remember to be careful and not to rush the inspection where you'll overlook them.

⚠ Long horizontal cracks are another indication of potentially serious problems with the foundation. You won't find these cracks as often, but if you do you better recommend that a licensed contractor evaluate the foundation for the client. Long horizontal cracks can indicate that the foundation wall is being pushed inward by the soil. The wall **will** collapse if this movement continues. Obviously, you can't see any cracks behind finished areas or personal items in the lower level. That's why you have to notify the client of the limits of the inspection due to inaccessible areas.

See if there are any areas of the foundation that have been altered from the time of the original construction of the house. If you notice any alterations, then recommend that the client check with town hall to make sure all valid permits and approvals have been obtained for the work performed. The last thing you need is to have someone buy a house and find out that the do-it-yourself work done to the original foundation doesn't pass the local building codes and is unsafe.

Check the main girder beams, all support posts, the floor joists, and the sub flooring where visible and accessible. Probe all wood members for rot or wood destroying insect damage. Sometimes in some newer construction you'll find a steel "I" beam as the main girder of the house. This is superior construction because the steel "I" beams have tremendous structural support. Check any steel beams for rust that will require painting or repairs.

Probe some wood floor joists for rot or wood destroying insect damage. Often you'll find damage from rot due to water leaks over the years in a bathroom or kitchen above. Check for any sagging sections of the floor joists that will suggest unusual settlement and sloping floors in the rooms above.

# Crawl Spaces

Some houses will have crawl spaces which are small areas underneath the house that aren't high enough to stand up in. You should ask the owner if there are any crawl spaces before starting your inspection. Ask this because the entrances to crawl space areas can be hidden by personal items or wall finishings.

> **A crawl space is an area that demands attention.
> There's a higher risk of rot and termite infestation due to these areas being dark and damp.**

You should use a jumpsuit, kneepads, a hardhat, gloves, and a flashlight to enter any crawl space areas that aren't too narrow for you to safely enter. A crawl space is an area that **demands** attention. Crawl spaces need attention because there's a higher risk of rot and termite infestation due to these areas being dark and damp most of the time. So don't get lazy and just assume everything is OK in the crawl space. You may end up regretting it if the client might call you up six months later to complain about the termite damage they found in the crawl space. You'll have a hard time defending yourself if you didn't check this area if it was accessible at the time of your inspection.

Check for the condition of the foundation walls, support posts, main girder, floor joists and sub flooring in the crawl space. Look for the same problems that were discussed in the lower level section.

# Gas Service

If the house is connected to the local gas utility lines in the street, check the condition of the gas meter and gas lines. If the house isn't connected to any gas service lines, recommend to the client that they check with the local utility company. They'll need to find out what the costs are to hook up or if it's even possible to get gas service in the house. Some areas don't have natural gas service and the client might not know this. Don't just assume your client is aware of the lack of gas service lines in the street. You don't want him to be confronted with any surprises after he moves into the house.

⚠ The gas meter is usually located in the lower level or just outside the house next to the foundation. All gas service lines should be approved black iron gas piping. There should not be any copper or other types of metals being used for gas supply lines. If there are, then you should recommend that they have a licensed plumber make any necessary repairs to bring the gas lines up to the building codes.

> *If you smell or detect any gas leaks IMMEDIATELY tell the client, all third parties and the homeowner to contact the local utility company to make repairs.
> Leaking gas will explode!!!*

⚠ If the gas lines are rusty, recommend that they be painted. Make sure that there's a main shutoff valve near the gas meter for safety. You might want to purchase a hand held combustible gas detector to check the visible gas lines and the meter for any gas leaks. If you smell or detect any gas leaks **IMMEDIATELY** tell the client, all third parties and the homeowner to contact the local utility company to make repairs. Any leaking gas will explode!!! Don't take any chances.

Natural gas is colorless and odorless when it comes from the earth. The gas utility companies put the odor into the gas before it reaches your house. The reason they put the odor in the gas is so that it's easier to detect a gas leak. If you couldn't see nor smell a gas leak, then you wouldn't be aware of a problem until *after* an explosion occurred.

Some houses have *Propane Gas* or *Liquid Petroleum Gas* (LPG) service. This is similar to getting oil deliveries because the tanks are filled by a local LPG gas supplier. Check the condition of the LPG gas tanks for any rust or corrosion. Also, make sure that the tank is properly leveled on a sturdy foundation. Recommend that the client check with town hall to make sure all valid permits are on file for the LPG tanks on the site.

⚠ Also, remind the client not to bring any gas tanks into the house, such as barbecue tanks or automobile gas cans. Barbecue gas tanks are under extreme pressure, like scuba diving tanks. *If they ever exploded, they would cause extensive damage and probably kill someone!!*

# Auxiliary Systems

Check for the existence of any alarm systems, fire detection systems, intercoms, burglar alarms, central vacuum systems, lawn sprinklers, etc. Often the control panels for these devices are located in the lower level.

You're not required to evaluate these systems during an appraisal. Just tell the client to get any manuals from the owner and find out how to operate these systems. Tell the client to find out if any fire or alarm systems are hooked up to any monitoring services and/or the local police or fire departments. Also, have them check to see what the fees are for this service.

# *Water Penetration*

While you're in the lower level you want to check for any signs of water problems in the house. This is something you *don't* want to forget. It certainly isn't life threatening to the occupant of the house to overlook water problems during an inspection. However, you will get phone calls from angry clients who have discovered that they get water in the lower level of their new home. Fortunately, I never got any angry phone calls but I know some inspectors who have. People get very upset if they get water in their basement. So watch out for this problem.

> *You're looking for excessive or abnormal signs of water problems, not just normal humidity and condensation stains.*

If you're inspecting the house during the rainy season, then the groundwater table will be higher than normal. You should always tell your client to visit the house after it rains, before the closing. This way they will be able to see for themselves if there is a potential problem with water penetration. Signs of water penetration can be white mineral salts on the concrete walls and floors. This is called *efflorescence* and it's caused by water seeping through the concrete and then drying on the exterior portion. After the water dries, it leaves the white, mineral salt from the concrete as a residue. Most lower level areas will get some minor efflorescence on the lower portion of the walls and floors. This is from the normal humidity in the lower level because these rooms are located underground. Recommend that the client use a dehumidifier to help prevent moisture.

In the corners you may see indications of water stains. Often the cause of these stains is due to the lack of gutters and downspouts on the house. Another cause is that the downspouts are draining right next to the foundation walls on the exterior. All downspouts should be piped away from the house by at least five feet so the rainwater won't drain next to the foundation and enter the lower level. Sometimes the downspouts drain into underground drain lines. These lines can become clogged due to leaves or small animals becoming stuck in them. Underground drain lines need to be checked periodically for proper operation.

The grading of the soil next to the exterior of the house can also cause minor water stains on the lower level walls and floors. All soil next to the foundation should slope away from the side of the house to help prevent rainwater from entering the lower level. We'll talk more about gutters, downspouts, and soil grading on the site in the exterior section of the book.

Another way to check for water problems is to probe the wood members that are in contact with the floor, such as, workbench posts, storage items, wood shelves, etc. Check under the corner of any carpeting or floor coverings in the lower level. If there's a water problem, then these areas will have signs of it. You're looking for excessive or abnormal signs of water problems, not just normal humidity and condensation stains. Be wary of recently painted lower level walls and floors. Sometimes the homeowner will paint just before selling a house. This can hide any indications of water problems.

Check for the existence of any sump pumps. *Sump pumps* are pumps that help carry water away from the house. Sump pumps are located in small pits dug into the lower level floor and have a drainage pipe to carry water to a more desirable location. When sump pumps are installed, it usually indicates that the lower level has a water penetration problem. Sometimes, you'll find a sump pump in a lower level that doesn't have any water problems. One reason for this is that some builders and homeowners install these pumps as a precautionary measure, even if they haven't had water penetration.

Check with the local building department to find out if the subject property is located in a designated flood hazard zone. A *flood hazard zone* is a designated area by the government. These areas have a certain potential of becoming flooded from time to time. Flood maps are located in every town hall and are available to the public to view for free. If a house is located in a flood hazard zone, the homeowner should obtain flood hazard insurance on top of the regular homeowner and title insurance for safety.

# The Interior Home Inspection

## Kitchen

After finishing in the lower level you're ready to begin inspecting the livable areas of the house. I usually start with the kitchen and move from room to room but feel free to adapt the inspection procedure to any method you like. Check the kitchen walls and floors for any structural problems or settlement cracks. Check the condition of the kitchen floor covering. The majority of houses have vinyl linoleum or ceramic tile floor coverings. In some houses you'll find hardwood on the kitchen floors. Hardwood isn't used as a kitchen floor often because of the possibility of it getting wet and damaged in this area. Be careful when inspecting older houses that have 9 inch x 9 inch floor tiles made of a very hard material. These tiles are usually a Vinyl and Asbestos material so you want to notify your client about the possible asbestos problems with them.

Check the kitchen cabinets by opening and closing a few of them. Make sure the cabinets are securely fastened to the wall and floor. I know a home inspector who was inspecting one home and the entire kitchen cabinet came right off the wall when he was checking it.

See if there are enough electrical outlets for modern usage and that they have Ground Fault Circuit Interrupter protection. Run the kitchen faucet hot and cold lines to make sure there's adequate hot water and there are no leaks underneath the sink. If there's a spray attachment in the sink area, check that as well. Sometimes they won't be operating properly and need to be replaced.

Ask the client, the seller or Realtor if the appliances are being sold with the house. Most of the time they are. If they're sold with the house, then spot check the appliances by turning them on and off briefly. For refrigerators, just open the doors to make sure they're cold inside. Tell the client you're very limited in what you can evaluate as to the life expectancy of appliances. This way the client won't think you're guaranteeing that the appliances will work for many years to come.

Note the condition and age of the appliances and recommend that any older units be upgraded for energy efficiency and convenience.

## Bathrooms

Check the bathroom walls and floors for any structural problems or settlement cracks. Check the condition of the bathroom wall and floor coverings. Most houses have ceramic tile floor coverings and part of the walls may have tile coverings. In some houses you'll find carpeting on the bathroom floors. Carpeting isn't used very often because of the possibility of it getting wet. Lift up a corner of the carpet to see what's underneath. Sometimes there are cracked and damaged tiles or water stains.

Press on some tiles, especially in the bathtub and shower area to see if any are loose. Check to see if the tiles need to be caulked between the joints to help prevent water leaks behind the walls. Some shower and tub areas are made of a premolded plastic and fiberglass material. Check these for any cracks and proper caulking around the edges.

Check the condition of the bathroom sink area for any cracks or loose sections. Make sure the drain stop mechanism in the sink is working. Often they won't be. Test any bathroom ventilation fans for proper operation. See if there's at least one electrical outlet and that it has Ground Fault Circuit Interrupter protection. Sometimes in older houses there won't be any grounded outlets in the bathroom which is an inconvenience and safety hazard.

Check the water pressure and drainage. There are usually local guidelines about what the minimum allowable water pressure should be, but generally, most houses will always meet the minimum criteria. After running the water for a few minutes check to see if the sink and tub drain properly. Sometimes they'll drain very slowly and need to be unclogged.

# Floors and Stairs

As you go through the house check the floors for any sagging or uneven areas that'll indicate structural settlement. Jump on the floor in each room to make sure they're sound. Don't jump so hard that you knock things off the walls, just do it lightly. Also, remember to look above you before you jump to test the floors. One time I forget to do this and I hit my head on a light fixture above me. Also, remember to look above you before you jump to test the floors. One time I forget to do this and I hit my head on a light fixture above me.

If there are hardwood floors, see if you notice any damaged areas or bowed sections. If there are carpets, check for signs of aging and worn areas that'll show the need for replacement. Check under the corner of some carpeting, if you can, to find out what's underneath. It's usually hardwood or plywood underneath but check to make sure and notify the client of what you see. The reason for this is that some people think that there's always hardwood floors underneath the carpeting. After they move into the house they may want to remove the carpets and leave the hardwood floors visible. You don't want them to be surprised about finding plywood as opposed to nice hardwood floors under the carpets.

> Check underneath the corner of some carpeting, if you can, to find out what's underneath. It's usually hardwood or plywood underneath but check to make sure and notify the client of what you see.

You also have to be careful about carpets that hide damaged areas underneath. I did an inspection once, where the client bought the house from a dishonest seller. After the client moved in, they found damage under the carpeting. The seller intentionally hid the damage during the home inspection. The seller had placed a couch over one section and put a large pile of toys and boxes over another section. I told the client to do a "walk-thru" inspection before the closing. This would enable them to check for any damaged areas after all furniture and personal items were removed from the house. The client did a walk-thru but they still didn't see this damage until after they removed the carpeting from the floor.

You also have to be careful to see if there are any moisture problems underneath hardwood floors. Moisture from basements, crawl spaces, water leaks, etc. will cause a hardwood floor to buckle. The reason the floor buckles, is that the wood absorbs the moisture and when it dries out, the wood will expand. If there are no gaps between the wood boards to allow for this expansion, then the boards will buckle upwards.

Check all staircases for sturdiness and secure handrails. Always recommend that they install handrails on both sides of the staircases for safety. There should be a light fixture and a light switch at the top and bottom of all stairways for safety. If there's a window at the base of a staircase its sill should be at least 36 inches above the floor. This will help prevent someone from falling through the window in the event they fell down the stairs. If the sill is less than 36 inches high, a window guard should be installed as a precautionary measure.

# Walls and Ceilings

Check all of the walls and ceilings for any structural problems or settlement cracks. You'll usually find some minor settlement cracks but you're looking for any major problems that could be hazardous. In older houses the walls will be made of *lath and plaster* which is also called *stucco*. Lath and plaster consists of an underlying layer of metal wiring, or lath, which has a layer of concrete over it. Lath and plaster walls are very rigid and have good sound insulating and fireproofing qualities. However, since these walls are so rigid they can develop cracks from any minor settlement in the house or with the temperature changes. Also, the metal lath can rust out over time and sections of the plaster can fall off which can be hazardous.

In newer houses the walls will be made of *sheetrock* which is also called *drywall*. Sheetrock consists of a gypsum material on the interior, usually about 1/2 inch thick, with exterior layers of a lightweight cardboard paper. The gypsum is a clay and plaster mixture. Sheetrock panels are sold in four feet by eight feet sections and are installed on the walls and ceilings with nails or screws. Screws are preferred to nails because they hold longer. Nails can pop loose over time which you'll see sometimes during an inspection. The joint sections where the different panels meet are sealed with finishing tape and spackled over to provide a smooth transition. Sheetrock is relatively inexpensive and is easy to install. Fireproof sheetrock is 5/8 inch thick and has a better fire resistance than the 1/2 inch sheetrock. However, it's also heavier and more difficult to install than 1/2 inch sheetrock.

Check for any water stains on the walls or ceilings, or around any skylights. If you see water stains, it indicates that there's probably damage to the areas behind the walls and ceilings that isn't visible due to the finished covering. So be very careful about telling the client anything such as the water damage appears minor because the stain isn't very large. Water can do an *awful* lot of damage behind the finished coverings. So if you're not sure then just tell the client to have the stained area opened and evaluated further.

> All linseed oil based paint prior to 1978 had lead in it because the lead is a good "binder" for the paint.
> Therefore, if a house was built before 1978, then there will be lead in some of the paint.

See if the house needs to be painted. Sometimes the client will ask you if there's lead paint in the house. The only way to identify lead paint is to have a sample taken to a lab for analysis. All linseed oil based paint prior to 1978 had lead in it. The reason for this is lead has a good wear quality and it is a strong "binder" for the paint. Therefore, if a house was built before 1978, then there will be lead in some of the paint. Latex based paint has never had a lead content in it and all paints today are non-toxic. When lead paint wears off it creates a dust. This lead dust causes soil contamination and health problems to anyone who breathes or drinks the lead. If the interior of the house has been painted after 1978, then the paint with the lead content will be encapsulated underneath the newer layers of non-lead paint. The main hazard of having lead in paint is if the paint is peeling and children can eat small sections of it. Also, if lead paint is sanded, then the dust created will have lead in it that will be breathed-in by the occupants of the house. Each State E.P.A. office has brochures with information about the hazards of lead in paint.

If there's wallpaper in the house, make sure it's not peeling off the walls. Tell the client that if they plan to remove the wallpaper, it is a time-consuming job that can be expensive. They should get estimates if they are not going to remove it themselves. You have to be careful removing when wallpaper from sheetrock walls because you can pull the light cardboard paper off the walls with the wallpaper. Some ceilings have acoustic tile coverings. These are also called *drop ceilings*. Try to lift some of these tiles to view underneath. Often these ceilings are installed to cover defects underneath.

> *Check for the existence and operation of any smoke detectors. Smoke detectors are required on all levels of a house or condo. Heat detectors are recommended in the garage area.*

Check for the existence and operation of any smoke detectors. Smoke detectors are **required** on all levels of a house or condo. Heat detectors are recommended in the garage area. If the smoke detectors are battery operated, they should have a small test button. Recommend that the client replace all batteries after moving in. Some smoke detectors have a *hard wired* installation. This simply means that they're electrically operated and not battery operated. Hard wired systems can't be evaluated during an inspection. Tell the client to get all instructions from the homeowner.

## Windows and Doors

Spot check the windows and doors by opening and closing all doors and at least one window in each room. Sometimes they'll be difficult to open and close due to excess paint or settlement of the house. This is common, so just notify the client about it. Check for cracked or broken panes of glass. Make sure you move any drapes or blinds. Sometimes they're hiding broken windows.

> *In some areas double key locks are against the local fire codes because a key is needed to exit in case of an emergency. This can cause people to get trapped inside a house during a fire.*

Check for any *double key* door locks. These are the locks that require a key to exit and enter through the door. The purpose of these locks is so that if a burglar breaks a door window, they can't just turn a bolt and open the door. They'll need a key to open the lock. However, in some areas these locks are against the local fire codes because a key is needed to exit in case of an emergency. This can cause people to get trapped inside a house during a fire. Tell the client to check with the local fire and building department for their recommendation about door locks. Recommend that the client change all of the house locks after taking possession for security reasons.

## Fireplaces

Check all fireplaces for any structural or back-smoking problems. Make sure the mortar joints are in satisfactory condition. Back-smoking is the result of downdrafts in the chimney flue that causes the smoke to come back into the house. Signs of back-smoking are black deposits, called *creosote*, on the front of the fireplace and mantel.

Sometimes the fireplace will have a metal firebox, a metal heat-a-lator, or a wood burning stove in it. You're limited in what you can evaluate with these because there's usually no access to view up the chimney flue.

# Attic Inspection

Most houses will have an attic space that you <u>must</u> inspect if there's access to it due to the potential problems you can find. Just like crawl spaces, don't get lazy and just assume everything's OK in the attic area. Some houses won't have any accessible attic areas. In that situation just do the best you can.

Sometimes the attic area has been finished and there are *knee wall* openings to the attic. These are small openings in the wall areas of the upper level that allow you to view a small portion of the attic and use it for storage. The access panels to most attics are located in the ceiling of the upper level hallway. Sometimes the access panel will be located in a bedroom closet. Ask the owner about this and don't assume there's no access panel because you didn't see one. It could be hidden.

---

*I always recommend that a handrail be installed inside the attic area surrounding the access opening. This will help prevent anyone in the attic area from falling through the access opening.*

---

⚠ I always recommend that a handrail be installed inside the attic area surrounding the access opening. This will help prevent anyone walking in the attic area from falling through the access opening. I have no idea why, but I haven't seen any building codes that require this handrail in new construction. What will happen is somebody is going to fall through the access panel and get killed someday and then the local building codes will add this safety precaution. Don't wait for that to happen, recommend they install a handrail now!

Usually you'll find most attics will have some wood board covering over the floor joists so the attic can be used to store lightweight items. If you see any very heavy objects, tell the client it's not recommended due to the excessive weight on the ceiling below. You have to be careful when you're in the attic area and not walk between any of the floor joists. If you do, then your foot will go right through the ceiling below!

Check the condition of the roof ridge beam, roof rafters and the roof sheathing while in the attic area. Look for any water stains that are due to water leaks or abnormal humidity in the attic area. Often there are old water stains from prior roof leaks that have been repaired. Just see if they look moist or recent. Check for any bowing in the wood members of the attic.

# Attic Ventilation

It's very important that the attic area be properly ventilated to prevent excessive humidity or heat in this area. Even in cold winter months humidity can cause problems in attics. As a result, ventilation to the exterior is needed in the winter. In the summer months attics can reach 150 degrees Fahrenheit which adds a big heat load on the house.

Check for an adequate number of attic vents. Check the condition of the screens on these vents. They need to be kept clean. Screens help to keep birds and bees out of the attic. Any bathroom fans should discharge to the exterior. Sometimes you'll find them discharging in the attic. This isn't recommended because it promotes moisture problems.

# Attic Insulation

Check to see if there is insulation in the floor joists of the attic area. The roof rafters don't need to be insulated because once heat has escaped through the upper level ceiling it's lost anyway. There's no sense trying to trap this heat in the attic. If you do, you'll only be trapping unwanted moisture in the attic by installing insulation between the roof rafters.

The benefit of having attic flooring is that you can use this area for storage. However, flooring prevents you from seeing if there's insulation throughout the attic area. Sometimes there's only insulation in the visible floor areas that aren't covered. The owner may have installed this insulation without bothering to remove the attic flooring that was there to insulate the entire attic.

⚠ Check to see how thick the insulation is. The insulation should be at least six inches thick. If it isn't just recommend that the client install an additional layer of insulation for better energy efficiency. Ask the owner if he/she has installed or knows of any prior owner's having installed insulation in the house. You want to warn you client about any *"blown-in"* type of insulation. In the past some houses had UFFI insulation blown-into the walls and floors. UFFI stands for *Urea Formaldehyde Foam Insulation*. Another possible hazard is older *Rockwool* or *Vermiculite* insulations in the attic area. The Environmental Protection Agency, *(EPA)*, has issued warnings about this type of insulation. If there's UFFI or older Rockwool or Vermiculite in the house, recommend that an air sample be taken to see if there are any health concerns.

# The Exterior Home Inspection

## *Roof*

When you finish inspecting the interior, you can start on the exterior. We'll start with the roof, but as I've said before, feel free to adapt the inspection process to any way you feel comfortable with. There shouldn't be any tree branches overhanging the roof. Overhanging trees cause damage to the roof structure and shingles if branches fall. Shade created by the branches can cause mold and deteriorate the roof shingles. If you can, use a ladder to get a close look at the roof from the edge. While inside the house, you should view the roof close up from the interior windows if possible. Evaluating the roof framing from the attic area is a necessity. This will enable you to make better conclusions and evaluations when you get to the exterior. If you can't view the roof closely, you should use a pair of strong binoculars to help you.

Check for any bowing sections of the roof ridge beam, roof rafters or the roof sheathing which would suggest expensive repairs are needed. If there are any bowing sections then make sure you have take another look at these areas in the attic, if it's accessible. You should see plumbing vent stack pipes protruding through the roof by one foot. These are needed to keep the plumbing drainage lines at atmospheric pressure. Maintaining atmospheric pressure is required so the plumbing lines drain properly. If there are no plumbing vent stacks then you might hear gurgling noises from the interior sinks and drains.

Check the flashing for all roof projections and adjoining sections. *Flashing* refers to the material used around all joints to prevent water penetration into the house. Areas of the roof that need this type of water protection are: the base of chimneys and plumbing vent pipes, roof valleys, skylights, and the joint where dormers protrude through the roof. A *roof valley* refers to the area where two slopes of a roof meet to form a drainage channel. A *dormer* refers to a window or room that projects outward from the roof structure. Flashing should be made out of copper or aluminum. On higher priced homes you may find lead-lined copper flashing. Lead-lined copper has a longer lifespan and costs more.

If you find a lot of roofing tar "slopped" around the base of a chimney or over existing flashing, recommend it be repaired. Roofing tar is only a temporary fix for water leaks. It's like putting a band-aid over a cut that needs stitches. Some homeowners cut corners and have tar installed to avoid the higher cost of new flashing.

Remember that if it's raining, the roof will look newer than it actually is because of the water on it. There is one benefit to doing a home inspection on a rainy day. That is you'll have a better chance of finding any roof leaks or water problems in the lower level. If there's snow on the roof, just tell the client that you can only evaluate the visible portions.

If the house has a shingle roof it must have a high enough pitch to prevent water leaks under the shingles. A minimum pitch of 4 on 12 is recommended for shingle roofs. This means the roof pitch should rise by at least 4 inches for every 12 inches of roofing area. The slope of the roof that has a southerly or southwesterly exposure faces the sun more often. This can cause roof shingles to become brittle and show signs of aging faster. The slope of the roof that has a northerly or northeastern exposure is more likely to have mold and decay fungi on the shingles. This is caused by the lack of sunlight.

In northern climates you may find wires along the bottom edges of the roof. These wires are used to heat the show and ice so it melts off the roof without causing an ice dam. An *ice dam* refers to ice and snow that has frozen at the base of the roof above the gutters. Since the ice is trapped by the gutter, it gradually melts and the water goes underneath the roof shingles. This leads to water penetration problems in the house roof and soffit areas. Some homeowners don't like the idea of wires in their roof. If this is the case with your client, then flashing can be installed under the bottom few rows of shingles to help prevent water leaks from ice dams.

> *You have to be careful when evaluating roofs. This is another aspect of houses that can scare a buyer.*

You have to be careful when evaluating roofs. This is another aspect of houses that can really scare a buyer. Often buyers have a good reason to be scared about roof problems, but sometimes they overreact to an aging roof. In either case, you don't want to get any phone calls in the middle of the night from some guy who says his roof is leaking. Especially, if it's within twelve months after your inspection and you never warned him about it.

The life expectancy of all roofs depends upon many factors. Some factors are: the quality of the shingles, the quality of the installation of the shingles and the roofing materials, the climate and exposure to the elements, and the maintenance given to the shingles. The vast majority of houses have five types of roofing shingles:

◊ Asphalt
◊ Wood Shingles and Wood Shakes
◊ Slate
◊ Tile
◊ Flat Roofing

# Chimneys

Use your binoculars to view the chimney. Check to make sure that the chimney isn't leaning which suggests a serious condition and it may need to be rebuilt. Make sure the mortar joints are in good condition and don't need to be repointed. The phrase *re-pointing* refers to patching any decayed areas of the mortar joints. This is a required maintenance item that needs to be done periodically. You may see the terra-cotta tile flue linings at the top of the chimney. Make sure they aren't cracked or broken where repairs are needed.

Some chimneys are made of metal piping. Check these for any rust. Often on condominiums you'll find the metal chimneys are covered with a finished wood siding to match the exterior wall siding. You'll be limited in what you can see with this type of installation. Just do the best you can.

# Siding

The siding on a house is used to provide weather protection. The siding doesn't support the house structurally. A load bearing wall is what provides the structural support of the house. If you find a building constructed of brick, stone or masonry, then these materials aren't considered the siding since they are load bearing walls. Check these types of structures for problems with bulging or leaning walls and deteriorated mortar joints. The different types of sidings that you'll generally encounter are:

◊ Wood Boards *(often called Clapboard Siding)*
◊ Wood Shingles and Wood Shakes
◊ Plywood Panels
◊ Aluminum Siding
◊ Vinyl Siding
◊ Asbestos-Cement Shingles
◊ Asphalt Siding
◊ Stucco
◊ Veneer Walls

*All siding should be at least eight inches above the soil all around the structure.*
*This will help prevent termite and rot problems.*

All siding should be at least eight inches above the soil all around the structure. This will help prevent termite and rot

problems. You'll often find siding too close or touching the soil. The moisture in the soil will rot out the siding. Also, when the siding is in contact with the ground, wood destroying insects can get behind the siding very easily.

Check with the seller to see if they've replaced any siding or if there's an underlying layer of older siding on the house. You want to try to find out what's underneath the exterior layer. The exterior maintenance of condo units is usually paid for by a monthly charge assessed to all of the condo owners in the complex. Recommend that the client check with the Condo/Owner's Association to find out what the fees and responsibilities are for each owner in the complex. We will discuss this topic of condominium units further into the book.

# Fascia, Soffits and Eaves

The *Fascia, Soffits* and *Eaves* are the molding areas at the bottom of the roof and the top of the siding. It's the small area where the roof overhangs the sides of the house. Check to see if the wood is rotted or if it needs to be painted or stained. Often you'll find there's an aluminum siding covering over the fascia, soffits and eaves. If you see vents at the bottom of the roof overhang area it indicates that the house may have soffit vents. *Soffit vents* allow air to enter the bottom of the attic area and help remove heat and moisture from the house.

# Gutters, Downspouts and Leaders

*Gutters* are installed along the bottom edge of the roof to catch the rainwater running off the roof. *Downspouts* are installed near the ends of the gutters and are used to drain the water from the gutters so they don't overflow. *Leaders* are installed at the bottom of the downspouts to direct the rainwater away from the side of the structure.

The majority of gutters, downspouts and leaders are made of aluminum because it's lightweight, inexpensive and rust and rot resistant. Sometimes on older houses the gutters, downspouts and leaders will be made of copper. If copper gutters are painted, the only way to know if they're copper is to look for soldered joints. Wood gutters are not recommended since they have a short life expectancy due to rot.

There should be at least one downspout for every 30 feet of gutter to prevent any excessive weight from the rainwater from damaging the gutters. All downspouts should have leaders to pipe the rainwater at least five feet away from the foundation to help prevent any water problems in the lower level.

Some downspouts drain directly into the ground. These lead to dry-wells or underground drainage lines. They need to be checked periodically for clogging due to leaves and small animals getting stuck in them. In most areas, the local building codes prohibit sump pumps, gutters and downspouts from discharging water into the house plumbing drainage lines. This restriction is designed to prevent an excessive amount of water from entering the municipal sewer system.

# Windows, Screens and Storms

Check the condition of the exterior window frames for any rot or if they need to be painted or stained. Check the condition of any storms and screens. If there are no storm windows you should recommend that they be installed in northern climates where the temperature gets cold. More heat is lost in a house through the windows than through any other area. Storm or thermal windows can reduce the heat loss by as much as 50%.

# Entrances, Steps and Porches

Check all entrances, steps and porches for structural sturdiness and any tripping hazards. Make sure there are no cracks or uneven sections in any of the steps. The landing platform is the standing area in front of a door. Make sure there is a large enough space to safely open the exterior doors while someone is standing in front of them. You don't want anyone to be knocked down the steps when the door is opened. *(Unless of course it's an unwanted guest).*

> *There should be handrails for all stairs that are more than two steps in height.*

There should be handrails for **all** stairs that are more than two steps in height. Make sure the handrails aren't loose or decayed. Recommend that they be installed when not noted. All steps should have an even and uniform height so that there's no tripping hazards. If there are any wood stairs, the base of the wood should be resting on concrete pads above the soil. This will prevent rot and termite infestation.

If there's an enclosed porch, tell the client to check with town hall to see if all valid permits and approvals have been filed. Sometimes people enclose an open porch area without knowing building permits are needed.

# Walks

Check all walks for any tripping hazards. There shouldn't be any weeds growing between the walkway sections. If there are any uneven sections, recommend that they be repaired. Sometimes the sidewalk at the street will be uneven due to tree roots. Tell the client to check with the local building department to find out whose responsibility it is to repair the sidewalk. In most areas, the homeowner is responsible for repairing and shoveling the sidewalk in front of their house.

My brother and I received a building violation once for a sidewalk that was a tripping hazard. The sidewalk in front of one of our rental properties had some cracks due to the growth of roots from a large tree planted there. We had the sidewalk repaired by a contractor and then the violation was removed. Also, we received a summons for not shoveling the snow immediately after a snowfall in front of one of our rental properties. We paid someone to shovel the snow whenever it was necessary in front of the building. However, one time he didn't do it fast enough after the snowfall stopped. As a result, we were given a ticket for this.

Sometimes you'll appraise a house that's located on a private street. In this situation, both you and the client need to determine what rights and responsibilities they have as a homeowner on that road. Often homeowners who live on private streets have to pay for repaving and maintenance of the street. This will have an affect on the market value of the property and it must be evaluated.

# Patios and Terraces

As with walks, check all patios and terraces for any tripping hazards. There shouldn't be any weeds growing between the joints of the sections. Any uneven sections need to be repaired. If the patio touches the side of the foundation, then it must be well caulked and sloped away to prevent water from draining toward the house. In most areas building permits and approvals are needed to build patios. You have to check this at town hall.

# Decks

Decks *always* require building department approvals because of the safety concern if they're improperly built. Check for any rotted sections of wood that need to be replaced. Some decks will be too low to the ground to view the structural members. Just do the best you can. The deck perimeter railings should be sturdy. The balusters under the railing must be spaced so that a maximum gap of four inches exists between them. This is to help prevent small children or dogs from falling through.

> **Decks always require building department approvals because of the safety concern if they're improperly built.**

⚠ There should be lag bolts in the main beam, called the *header beam*, where the deck is attached to the side of the house. *Lag bolts* are a **far superior** way to support the deck as opposed to just using nails. Copper flashing should be installed between the header beam and the side of the house. This will prevent water from getting trapped and rotting the wood.

The floor joists of the deck should have steel support hangers. Steel support hangers give the floor joists more support then by just nailing them. All deck support posts and girders should have steel brackets at the top and the base for support. This will also keep the wood from being in contact with the soil. The base should be resting on a concrete support post.

# Walls and Fences

Retaining walls are used to support the soil in areas, such as driveways or yards, which are dug into the earth. Check to see if any retaining walls are leaning. Any leaning conditions indicate that repairs **must** be made to prevent the wall from moving any further or collapsing. Some different types of retaining walls are:

◊ Stone and Cement Walls
◊ Dry Stone Walls
◊ Gabion Walls
◊ Concrete Block Walls
◊ Wood Timber Walls

All fences need to be checked for sturdiness. Tell the client to check with town hall to determine if the fence is within the subject property line. Often the homeowner or a neighbor will have a fence, wall, driveway or shed installed and the contractor will just guess where the property line is. This can lead to an *encroachment* on someone else's property. This topic will be discussed further into the book.

# Drainage and Grading

The soil next to the foundation should slope away from the house to prevent any rainwater from building up next to the foundation. Usually the soil only needs to slope 1/2 inch for every foot away from the house to properly drain the water accumulations. All bushes, shrubs and trees should be pruned away from the side of the house. This will allow enough sunlight and air next to the foundation to help prevent rot and wood destroying insect problems.

If the house is at the base of a hill there should be a *catch basin* to prevent water problems. These are large concrete underground drains. Both you and the client must check with the local building department to figure out if the house is located in a designated flood hazard zone. If it is, then flood hazard insurance will be needed.

# Driveways

Check all asphalt and concrete driveways for cracked and uneven sections. Asphalt driveways need to be sealed with a driveway sealer every two or three years to prevent them from drying out and cracking. Repaving an asphalt driveway can be expensive. If the driveway needs to be repaved, tell the client to get an estimate.

Some driveways don't have a finished surface and are made of gravel and dirt. Often they have holes which are tripping hazards that need to be repaired. Unfinished driveways lead to people tracking dirt into the house. These driveways also cannot be shoveled for snow removal in northern areas.

# Garage

The different types of garages you'll encounter are Detached, Attached and Built-in or Tuck-under garages.

◊ *Detached* garages are separate structures from the main house.

◊ *Attached* garages are attached to the main house.

◊ *Built-in* or *Tuck-under* garages are set underneath the house and take up a section of the lower level.

⚠ A benefit of having an attached or built-in garage is that you can park the car and enter the house without worrying about the weather conditions. A detached garage is safer in the event that a car is left running by mistake, the exhaust fumes can't enter the house easily. A detached garage is also safer in the event of a fire, the flames and smoke can't spread to the house easily.

The inspection procedure for the garage is the same as with the exterior and interior aspects of the main house. Review those sections to find more comments and recommendations. Check the floor for any oil or gas drippings. Gas and oil must be cleaned to help prevent fires from starting. Garage walls and ceilings should be covered with fireproof sheetrock to help prevent the spread of any fires. Masonry walls and ceilings are an acceptable fireproof covering.

⚠ If the garage is attached or built-in there should be a fireproof entry door leading to the house. Also, this door should have a self-closing device to prevent it being left open. This will prevent car exhaust fumes or fires from spreading into the house easily.

# Other Exterior Structures

Check all garden and tool sheds on the property for rot and wood destroying insect infestation. Make sure they're sturdy and there are no hazards. If there are any other exterior structures on the property, evaluate them just as you would the house itself. If there is anything you're unsure about, then just tell the client to have the structure evaluated further by a licensed contractor.

# Swimming Pools

All swimming pools require local town approvals that need to be verified by you and your client. All swimming pools need to have fences surrounding them to prevent any unattended children from falling into the water and drowning. Also, special homeowners' insurance is needed with swimming pools. This is due to the increased liability of having a pool on the property.

> *All swimming pools require local town approvals. All pools need to have fences surrounding them to prevent any unattended children from falling into the water and drowning.*

Check the area around the pool for any tripping hazards. Check the pool walls for any leaks, cracks or bulging sections. If it's winter time and the outdoor air temperature gets below 32 degrees Fahrenheit, then the pool must be properly winterized. When water freezes it expands and this can crack the walls of a pool if proper winter maintenance has not been taken care of. If you have doubts about the pool, tell the client to call a swimming pool contractor for further evaluations.

# Wood Destroying Insects

There are many different types of wood destroying insects, including 70 species of termites throughout the world. The wood destroying insects that you need to be the most concerned with are:

◊    *Subterranean Termites*
◊    *Dry Wood Termites*
◊    *Damp Wood Termites*
◊    *Powder Post Beetles*
◊    *Carpenter Ants*
◊    *Carpenter Bees*

> *If there was any aspect of home inspections that you would need X-ray vision, then this one takes the prize. If Superman really existed, he'd make a fortune as a Termite inspector.*

This is another concern with buying a house that really scares people. So make sure you check thoroughly for wood destroying insects. If there was any aspect of performing home inspections that you would need X-ray vision, then this one takes the prize. If *Superman* really existed, he'd make a fortune as a Termite inspector. I've heard an awful lot of war stories about inspectors getting complaints from people because they didn't notice the termites that were behind the sheetrock walls. Some people honestly believe that you should have told them that there were termites in areas that you couldn't even see. I have know idea where they get their logic from. If there are indications out in the open and you miss the signs, that's one thing. But don't expect someone to identify a problem that they can't even see!!

Occasionally you will have to rely on Lady Luck to help you find wood destroying insect damage. One time I was inspecting a house that was built on a concrete slab foundation. This type of construction doesn't have a basement area. As a result, termites can travel through cracks in the concrete slab. The wood beams and moldings of the livable rooms become an easy meal for the termites. I was just about finished with my inspection and only had one more closet to check. When I opened the closet door, there was termite damage all through the molding. The damaged wood was recently painted over and the termite tunnels were difficult to see. Had I cut corners by not checking that one last closet, I wouldn't have found the damaged wood. There were several times when I was in the lower level and Lady Luck was on my side. While looking around I randomly probed some wood beams. The screwdriver passed right through the beams due to wood destroying insect damage. I was lucky to find these damaged areas since there were no visible indications on the exterior of the wood.

**Termites** eat the wood and turn it into food. They have one-celled organisms in their digestive tracts that convert the cellulose of wood back into sugar which they can digest. In forests termites are beneficial since they help to decompose fallen trees and stumps. They help return the wood substances to the soil to be used again by other trees. Termite damaged wood will have channels in it and there won't be any sawdust around.

With *Subterranean Termites* you'll find mud in their tunnels. These termites bring mud into the wood channels since they can only survive in a warm, dark and moist environment. Probe wood with an awl or screwdriver, especially rotted or wet beams in dark areas, to check for termite infestation. You may see signs of mud on the outside sections of the wood indicating termite damage. What these termites do is they'll eat up to the very edge of the wood they are inside and leave a thin layer of wood on the exterior. This thin layer will prevent light or air from getting inside the channels and drying out the wood.

*Dry Wood Termites* are found in coastal warmer climate areas of the country. They have a caste system in their colonies similar to that of the Subterranean Termites. The difference is that they live and feed on sound, dry seasoned wood and they don't need to be in contact with the soil or a moisture source. As a result you won't see any mud tubes with these insects.

*Damp Wood Termites* are similar to subterranean termites but seldom live in the soil. They nest in damp wood and are associated with wood decay and don't construct tubing.

*Powder Post Beetle* larvae eat the wood and lay their eggs in it. They cannot convert the cellulose in the wood to sugar. Therefore, these insects must get their nourishment from the starch and sugar that the tree has stored in the wood cells. To these insects, the cellulose in the wood has no food value and is thus ejected from their bodies as wood powder or *frass*. They derive nourishment from the starch and sugar in the wood. Powder Post Beetle damaged wood will crumble like sawdust when you probe it. A common indication of these insects is the existence of tiny holes in the wood.

*Carpenter Ants* and *Carpenter Bees* merely excavate the wood to make nests. The damage they cause will leave sawdust outside the wood channels.

> *Often when you find damaged wood due to wood destroying insects, a Realtor, seller or other third party person will ask, "Oh, is it active or inactive." I just tell them that there's no way to know.*

Often when you find damaged wood due to wood destroying insects, Realtors and other third party people will ask, *"Oh, is it active or inactive."* I just tell them that there's no way to know since it's rare to actually find the termites in the damaged wood. The termites could just have moved to a different section of the house. There's just no way to know for sure. So **don't** let any Realtors or third parties tell your client that they don't have to worry about termites because you couldn't see them actually eating the wood. Often dishonest Realtors and other third parties will do this to *"gloss over"* and underestimate the potential termite problem in the house.

The damage caused by termites is sometimes over exaggerated. There are very few houses on record that had to be knocked down due to serious structural problems due to termites. A full colony of termites can only eat about three feet of a wooden 2 x 4 beam in a year. For them to do serious structural damage they would have to go unnoticed in the house for an awfully long time. I find minor termite damage in one out of every four houses that I inspect. Of these houses, I've only seen two or three of them that had very bad termite damage. But even those two or three houses could be repaired just be replacing some floor joists and treating the house with insecticide.

> *They say there are two kinds of houses: Houses that have termites and Houses that will have termites. That's a fact. All houses will get termite damage of some sort eventually.*

They say there are two kinds of houses: **Houses that have termites and Houses that will have termites**. That's a fact and from my experiences I've found this to be accurate. All houses will get termite damage of some sort eventually. Sometimes builders will install a termite shield along the top of the foundation wall. *Termite shields* are similar to the cap plate used at the top of concrete block walls. A termite shield is a small metal guard. However, these shields <u>do not</u> prevent termites. The only benefit from them is that they might deter termites or make it a little more difficult for them to reach the wood.

There are certain houses that many Pest Control Operators, *(PCO)*, **will not** treat for wood destroying insects. Or else there will only be a few of them that will treat the houses with insecticide.

1   One case is houses with on-site well water systems. The PCO has to worry about contaminating the well water supply. If the well is less than 100 feet from the house, your chances of finding a PCO to treat will diminish even further.

2   Another case is houses that have brick foundation walls. The PCO has to worry about contaminating the house by seepage through the brick walls.

3   Another case is houses that have air ducts embedded in the lower level cement floor for the heating or air-conditioning systems. The PCO has to worry about contaminating the ducts.

4   Also, if the inspection is being conducted on a condominium, then the By-Laws or Prospectus of the Condo/Owner's Association may have limitations. There could be requirements that can restrict wood destroying insect treatments.

## Home Inspection Photo Pages

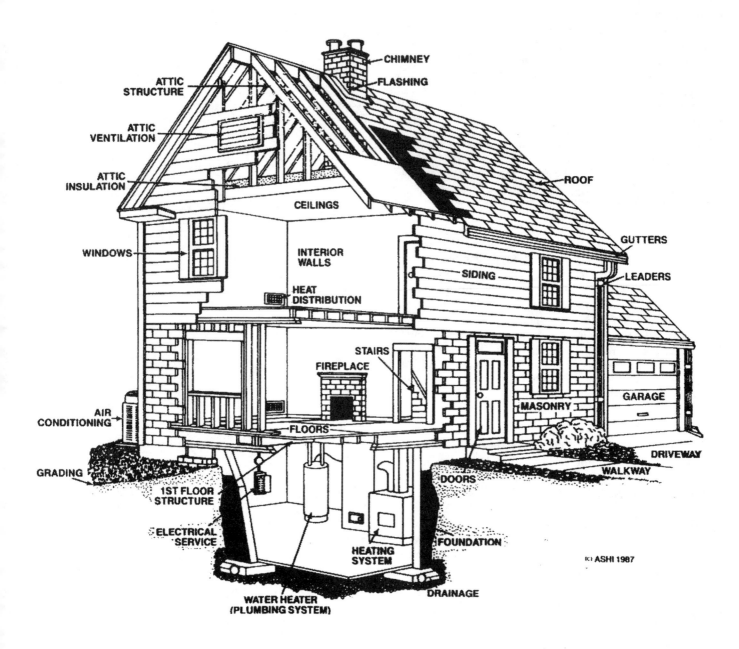

CHIMNEY

FLASHING

ATTIC STRUCTURE

ATTIC VENTILATION

ATTIC INSULATION

CEILINGS

ROOF

WINDOWS

INTERIOR WALLS

GUTTERS

SIDING

LEADERS

HEAT DISTRIBUTION

STAIRS

FIREPLACE

MASONRY

GARAGE

AIR CONDITIONING

FLOORS

DOORS

DRIVEWAY

GRADING

WALKWAY

1ST FLOOR STRUCTURE

ELECTRICAL SERVICE

HEATING SYSTEM

FOUNDATION

(c) ASHI 1987

WATER HEATER (PLUMBING SYSTEM)

DRAINAGE

P 2. *No, that's not a submarine periscope!* It's the oil supply pipe that is used to fill this underground oil tank. The longer, iron pipe by the house, is the tank vent pipe. This allows air to escape so the tank can be filled properly. Underground oil tanks are a major expense to clean up. EPA laws have become much more strict with oil and lead problems.

P 1. There is a small fuel level gauge on the top of this interior oil tank. This interior oil tank has some signs of oil stains on the top. This can happen when the tank is overfilled.

Notice the patch on the bottom of this tank. Due to humidity, the bottom of these tanks often rust out over time. The patch is a temporary repair and replacing the tank is recommended.

The oil supply line has a firematic shut-off valve for safety.

The copper oil supply line is embedded in the concrete floor to protect it against damage.

P 3. This is a properly installed water main line. The electrical grounding cable is clamped on both sides of the meter.
The bell shaped water pressure reducing valve indicates there is strong water pressure from the street main water line.
There are shut-off valves on each side of the meter for easy replacement of the meter. The lever shut-off valve *(upper right)* is more reliable than the knob type valve.
water meter

P 4. This is called a disaster!! This water main has so many problems that I don't know where to begin.
The water meter is very old, outdated, and probably gives inaccurate readings.
There is no electrical ground cable on the main!
The water shut-off valve is ancient and corroded.
The main water pipe is lead and must be replaced *(wiped joint noted by valve)!*
The water lines need to be properly secured to the wall. The wood board is not an acceptable support.

P 5. Electrical lines, conduits, and meters must be securely fastened to the side of the house. Tree branches need to be pruned away from the wires periodically. Three electrical lines at the service entrance head indicate 110/220 volts in this house. The "U" shape in the wires is called a drip loop. This is used to keep rainwater from entering the electrical conduit.

P 6. Caulking the joint on the top of the electrical meter and where the wires enter the house will prevent water penetration problems. Over time this exterior caulk will dry and crack and needs to be repaired.

The shingles on this house are made of asbestos/cement and are in excellent condition. EPA precautions must be taken when removing or tampering with any type of asbestos.

P 8. In the lower level of many homes, you'll find wiring installed through the floor joists. This is acceptable as long as it meets the NEC requirements. Also, the drill holes must be in the center of the wood and less than 1/4 of the height of the beam. This will preserve the structural integrity of the wood beam.

You can see Romex and Bx cables are installed through these floor joists.

P 7. Using adapters when there is a lack of electrical outlets is a safety hazard. Too many appliances plugged into an outlet can create a fire or shock. The NEC recommends one outlet for every six feet of horizontal wall space. This will help prevent the use of unsafe extension cord wiring and plug adapters.

To make matters even worse, this gas wall heater has a flexible supply line which is unsafe.

P 10. Here's a quiz: *How many problem conditions do you see in this photograph?*

1. There are remnants of asbestos that was unprofessionally removed from the old steam heating pipes.

2. The heating pipes and also between the floor joists should be insulated for energy efficiency.

3. The heating system flue stack has a downward pitch after the elbow which will slow the exhaust gases from exiting.

4. There is no pipe extending the water heater pressure relief valve to within eight inches above the floor.

5. On the lower, left of the tree trunk, the flexible pipe material is unsafe for the gas supply to the water heater.

6. This tree trunk could be put to better use somewhere else. In very old homes, you may find tree trunks being used to support the main girder beam. A solid, metal support post should be used instead.

P 9. A heating contractor took the easy route while installing this steam pipe. As a result, now there is a serious structural problem with the main girder beam. One-half of this beam was cut and removed which weakens the support. This pipe should have been routed around the girder. If that was not possible, then a hole, 1/4 of the height of the beam, could have been cut in the center of this girder.

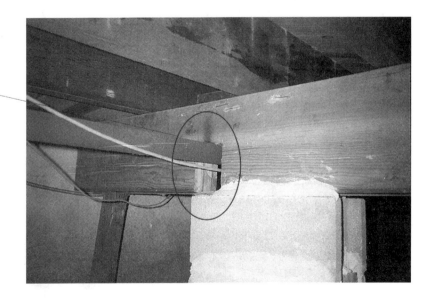

P 11. When inspecting the kitchen, spot check appliances by briefly turning them on. *Just remember to turn them off when you're done - except for the refrigerator!* The countertop and cabinets should be securely fastened. All outlets by the kitchen sink must have GFCI protection. Remodeled kitchens and bathrooms are like any other changes made to a house - building department permits and final approvals are neeed from town hall.

P 12. Bathroom tiles need to be evaluated for loose sections and open gaps. Loose areas can be detected by lightly banging on the tiles. The tiles in this bathroom are buckled and uneven. Prior water leaks behind the wall has caused this problem. To solve this problem, the tiles must be removed and the area behind must be repaired. Grout is used between ceramic tiles to prevent gaps that allow water penetration. Grout is a much harder material than caulk. Caulk is more flexible and used in areas where the joints will expand and contract more often.

P 13. This window is too close to the floor level and is a safety hazard. Not only can a child fall through, but if an adult tripped, there is no window sill to stop their fall. Child guards should be installed on this window. In many areas the height of the window sill and the use of child guards are regulated by the local building and fire codes. *Don't wait for accidents to happen - take precautions ahead of time.*

While you're inspecting the interior rooms, jump on the floors to make sure they're structurally sound.

Check underneath the corner of the wall-to-wall carpeting. The only way to know what type of flooring is underneath is to check it. Don't assume there are hardwood floors under carpets just because you see hardwood in other rooms in the house.

If there are any pets in the house, you should have the carpets removed or fumigated prior to moving-in. You don't want any fleas as house guests.

P 14. A vacuum seal is the air-tight space between the panes of glass in thermal windows and doors. Broken vacuum seals are indicated by dirt and condensation stains in between the two panes of glass, such as in this sliding glass door. Over time the moisture and dust stains will increase. Since this area can't be wiped clean, the window will become white and hazy. Repairing broken vacuum seals is expensive.

P 15. Wood burning stoves can save a lot of money on heating fuel bills. These stoves can heat a large area of a home. However, safety precautions must be taken. Since these stoves radiate heat from the iron casing, they must not be touched while in use. A guardrail will help prevent accidental burns. Also, the flue stack for these stoves must be properly installed. A fireproof lining is needed and the flue should not be near any combustible materials, such as wood. Wood burning stoves, like forced hot air heating systems, will dry out the air in the house. The metal pot on this stove is used to hold water. As the pot is heated, the water boils and turns to steam. This steam will add moisture back into the air so the occupants don't get sore throats or allergy problems from the dry air.

P 16. *Creosote* is a black soot found in chimneys. Creosote is caused by the smoke from burning wood. You may find excess creosote stains on the face of a chimney and mantle, such as this one. This indicates a back-smoking problem. Back-smoking is caused by a firebox area that is too narrow and/or a flue stack that does not extend high enough above the roof to prevent downdrafts.

P 17. *Here we have an accident waiting to happen!* Unfortunately, I have never seen any building codes that require railings around the attic access opening. Don't wait for someone to fall down this hole and break their neck *- install a guardrail NOW!* A handrail is also needed on the steps.

If plywood flooring is installed, the attic can provide storage space for lightweight items.

P 18. When inspecting the interior rooms make sure you look for signs of excessive structural settlement. Take a look at the floors where they meet the walls. You can see that this floor has separated from the baseboard molding due to abnormal settlement of the building over the years. It's a major expense to re-level and repair structural problems. Also, look at the window and door frames for signs of uneven and abnormal structural settlement.

P 20. Asphalt/fiberglass shingles come in different weights. A heavier shingle has a 30 year life expectancy. Light weight shingles last about 20 years. These shingles are in good condition and there are no signs of old age or curling shingles.

With cable TV, antennas should be removed from roofs and chimneys. Antennas move in the wind and create water leaks. A cap and screen keep animals and water out of the chimney.

The small pipe in the roof is the vent stack for the plumbing drainage lines.

P 19. A new roof will be needed on this house soon. These asphalt shingles are old and at the end of their life expectancy. When the shingles cup and curl and get frayed edges, it's a clear sign of old age. Get estimates prior to buying this house since a roof can be a major expense. If there are two layers of shingles on the roof, a third layer should not be installed on top. Three layers are too heavy for the roof. Remove the prior two layers of shingles and check the condition of the plywood sheathing before adding the new layer of roof shingles.

P 22. All vines, ivy, shrubbery and trees must be pruned away from the house. This ivy clearly needs to be trimmed.

A minimum of at least eight inches above the soil is needed at the base of all siding. This clearance allows air and sunlight to help prevent rot and wood destroying insect problems.

Downspouts must be cleaned periodically. Clogged downspouts and gutters will create water problems around the foundation.

P 21. *Here's an example of what can happen if you don't read my books!* The wood siding on this garage has rotted at the base. This decay was caused by the wood touching the soil. An eight inch clearance between the soil and the base of the siding would have prevented this problem.

P 23. This welcome mat is resting on top of a safety hazard. Instead of "Welcome" this door mat should read: *"Stand here at your own risk!"*

A landing platforms is the standing area in front of a door. Landing platforms need to be large enough so the door can open safely. This storm door would knock someone down the steps if it was opened hastily.

The riser height is the vertical distance between each step. All risers should be evenly spaced about eight inches in height. This will help prevent tripping hazards from uneven stair heights.

P 24. Do you know what's missing in this picture? *(No, it's not a matching gargoyle that's missing).* A handrail needs to be installed on these stairs. Whenever there are more than two steps in height, a handrail is needed for safety.

All stairways should have a light to prevent tripping hazards at night.

P 25. There are several problems with this exterior deck support post.

1) The metal bracket is not sturdy enough to support the post where it meets the deck girder beam. Proper metal brackets need to be installed.

2) The base of this post is resting on a 2 x 6" wood board. This board will eventually rot and the deck will settle unevenly. Metal brackets are also needed at the base to properly secure the deck post to the concrete foundation.

P 26. Clearly these deck support posts are unsafe! This is a high deck and if it collapses, *then someone is going to get hurt or killed!!* The posts have been installed improperly. The base of the wood is not resting evenly on the concrete foundation. The second post in the photo is off center on the concrete foundation. Metal brackets are needed to securely fasten deck supports to the concrete base.

P 28. Are you tempted to just dive into this pool?
Well, don't because it's only a photo and you'll hit your head on the table where you're reading this book! *(Unless my book already put you to sleep).*

Check for any bulging or cracked sections of in-ground pools. The area around the pool, called the apron, should be smooth without any tripping hazards. Fences are required around all pools to prevent unattended children from entering the water. Flotation devices should be within reach in case of an emergency.

P 27. Pools need to be winterized properly to prevent the walls from cracking due to freezing water during cold months.

P 30. Here we have the exposed termite damage in a lower level floor joist. This is a common area for damage since the wood is close to the soil. The termite channels can be seen when the wood is probed and opens up. The mud and termite tunnels are mostly hidden from the light under a thin, outer layer of the wood. This is because termites need a dark, warm and moist environment at all times.

P 29. On the exterior check the wood trim near the roofline. This area is prone to carpenter bee damage. The holes in this fascia board are an example of a carpenter bee nest. Carpenter bees and carpenter ants do not eat the wood for food, they merely excavate it to make a nest. Keeping a solid coat of stain or paint can reduce the chance of wood destroying insect damage.

# Appraising Real Estate

## Introduction To Appraising Real Estate

This is normally the first appraisal course that most people take if they are interested in becoming a licensed real estate appraiser. I will use my own notes from when I took the appraisal classes, along with my own comments and experience as a guideline for some of the following sections. The important items will be highlighted that I'm aware of from my experience as an appraiser and in the real estate business. I will try to keep these sections in a flowing format by including some additional comments and appraisal war stories. This will help explain anything that is new to you.

These courses have been renamed by State appraisal organizations to coincide with the Federal regulations of The Appraisal Foundation. Two of the class instructors that I had were some of the best teachers I've ever had. They were Anthony Fasanella and Dr. David Scribner. If you ever get a chance to take a class they're teaching, I suggest you do it (if they're not already retired). It'll be well worth your time and money. They are both true professionals with integrity and a sincere interest in improving the quality of real estate appraisers and the appraisal profession overall.

There are going to be appraisal math calculations in some of the following sections. If you're serious about real estate appraising then you're going to need to know this stuff. I hate math maybe as much as you do, so I'll keep it as simple as possible. I'm no rocket scientist myself, so if I can do the math then you certainly can too! I will round out the numbers when there are more than two decimal places. So please don't get angry if the answers you get on your calculator have more than two decimal points or if they don't appear to *exactly* match the numbers in the book.

---

*Some readers of this book, such as home buyers or sellers, may not be interested in becoming licensed real estate appraisers. They may only be interested in getting a general working knowledge of appraisal concepts. For those readers, I would recommend you don't get too caught up in trying to memorize the in-depth math and appraisal concepts discussed in some sections of this book. Choose the sections you feel are most useful to you for now, and then you can learn the more in-depth topics later if needed.*

---

Some readers of this book, such as home buyers or sellers, may not be interested in becoming licensed real estate appraisers. They may only be interested in getting a general working knowledge of appraisal concepts. For those readers, I would recommend you don't get too caught up in trying to memorize the in-depth math and appraisal concepts discussed in some sections of this book. Choose the sections you feel are most useful to you for now, and then you can learn the more in-depth topics later if needed.

I will repeat the definition of market value since it is such a **critically important and integral** part of every appraisal that you <u>cannot ever</u> forget when working on your reports! *(That's why I used both icon key symbols).*

**<u>Definition of Market Value</u>** - The definition of market value that applies to HUD/FHA is cited from the Uniform Standards of Professional Appraisal Practice. *(HUD is the U.S. Department of Housing and Urban Development. FHA is the Federal Housing Administration).* This is the definition of value which must be used for all appraisals performed for FHA-insured mortgages:

◊ *"The most probable price which a property should bring in a competitive and open market under all conditions requisite to a fair sale, the buyer and seller each acting prudently and knowledgeably, and assuming the price is not affected by undue stimulus."*

Implicit in this definition is the consummation of a sale as of a specified date and the passing of title from seller to buyer under conditions whereby:

1. The buyer and seller are typically motivated.
2. Both parties are well informed or well advised, and each is acting in what they consider their best interest.
3. A reasonable time is allowed for exposure in the open market.
4. Payment is made in terms of cash in United States Dollars or in terms of a financial arrangement comparable thereto.
5. The price represents the normal consideration for the property sold unaffected by special or creative financing or sales concessions.

You also need to review section HUD and FHA Guidelines page 220 and section Sample State Real Estate Appraiser Guidelines page 297 for more details and rules about appraisal standards and how to fill out the standard appraisal report forms.

# Real Estate Is Unique

There are at least four factors that make real estate unique and sophisticated as an investment:

1. It is *immobile* and therefore, external aspects around the building will affect the real estate. If an external aspect near the building turns away even **one** potential buyer, then it may reduce the market value of the subject property. For example, if a house is located on a very busy street, then that will generally have a negative impact on market value. The reason for this is that the typical buyer will want to live in a quiet, residential area. A commercial property will have more appeal on a busy street because a business would generally want the exposure to the public and the traffic.

Because of the immobility of real estate we have a distinct market for it and that market is imperfect. Meaning that since you can't just pick up and move a house, *(not easily of course)*, that house is subject to the current market and area that it exists in. When prices rise and fall in that local market, then generally all of the real estate is affected by this. This is why the market is said to be imperfect because it is constantly changing. When you appraise a property, you estimate the market value *"As Of"* a particular date. That same property will generally be worth a different price at any given time, such as, a year before today or a year after today.

2. Real estate tends to be bought by an investment team. The investment team consists of the *Equity* investor, which is the owner, and the *Debt* investor, which is the mortgage lender. Only the owner is listed on the deed for the property. The reason for this is that the lender or mortgage holder <u>does not</u> own the property. The lender has the owner sign a *note*. This note says that for a certain amount of interest and amortization period, the lender will let the owner borrow money to purchase or refinance the real estate. The lender also has the owner sign a *mortgage* which states that the real estate is the security for the loan. This way in the event that the borrower does not pay back the money as agreed to in the mortgage, then the lender can foreclose on the property. After foreclosing, the lender can sell the property to get their money back. The borrower generally cannot sell the property with a clear title until the loan is paid off.

3. Income property is only partially depreciable. Meaning that for tax depreciation purposes the land and the improvements are given two separate price values. *Improvement* means anything that is added to the land, such as the building. Land cannot be depreciated for tax purposes, only improvements can be depreciated. *Depreciation* simply means that you are allowed to take a small tax deduction over a specified number of years. The yearly tax deductions attempt to adjust for the depreciating value of the asset due to normal wear and tear. These deductions will allow you to spend the funds that you save from the tax deduction. You can use the funds to make repairs and maintain the building.

4. Real estate is ubiquitous. This means that real estate is always around, everywhere simultaneously. It's not like a rare mineral or hard to find commodity.

# The Bundle Of Rights

This section will cover some brief definitions concerning the rights of real estate. Land and anything attached to it is considered *Real Estate* because it is tangible and can be appraised for value. Real Estate refers to items that <u>cannot</u> be picked up and moved without dismantling anything. For example, when you appraise a home you don't evaluate the furniture which can be picked up and removed from the house. You evaluate the building itself which cannot be picked up and moved *(unless you hire a house moving company that actually uses huge cranes, jacks, and equipment to lift a house up off the foundation and move it to another location)*. *Real Estate* and *Realty* refer to the same thing. Personal items, such as the furniture, are called *Personalty*.

> *Real Estate refers to items that cannot be picked up and moved without dismantling anything.*
> *Personal items are called Personalty.*

*Real Property* refers to the rights of ownership of real estate which together are called the *Bundle of Rights*. When you sell real estate you're selling the <u>**rights**</u> of the real estate. The rights of real estate are:

1  The right to use. This refers to the owner's right to use his property as he wishes, as long as it isn't for an illegal purpose.
2  The right to exclude. This refers to the owner's right to rent out his property to whoever he wants to, as long as it isn't for an illegal purpose.
3  The right to dispose. This refers to the owner's right to sell his property when he wants.

There are *Sub-Surface*, *Surface* and *Air* Rights of real estate. This refers to the fact that the ownership of real estate is considered to start at the center core of the earth. This ownership extends up to the heavens like a big "V" encompassing the property. Therefore, when you purchase real estate you also will own the sub-surface, surface and air rights of that property, unless specified otherwise in the deed for the property.

*Fee Simple* and *Fee Simple Absolute* refer to having full ownership rights of a property. Let's say that someone has mineral rights (sub-surface) to your property. You or a prior owner may have purchased the property but later sold the mineral rights to someone else. For example, an oil speculator may have purchased the rights to any crude oil underneath your property. If that were the case then you would not have full Fee Simple ownership of the property. This must be taken into account when determining the market value of the real estate since it will affect the appraised value of the property.

> *The rights of real estate are severable and divisible.*
> *This means that the rights can be cut up and sold.*

The rights of real estate are severable and divisible. This means that the rights can be cut up and sold to other people. An example is a *life estate* which is the right granted to someone to use a property until they die. There was a house in my area that was sold by an old man to a builder. The agreement they had was that the builder would subdivide the vacant parts of the property and build three new homes to sell for a profit. The old man not only got his purchase price for the property, but he also was given the right to stay in the house until he died. At the time of the elderly man's death, the property would revert to the builder to sell the last house on the lot which he occupied. Both parties got what they wanted in the transaction.

A more common right granted with real estate is an *easement*. This is the right to provide access through your property for someone else to run utility lines, install driveways, build a walkway on your property, etc.

All ownership of real estate comes from the sovereign. The *sovereign* in the United States is the individual states and the Federal government.

# Public Limits On Real Estate

There are some **Public** limits on the **Private** ownership rights of real estate:

1.  *Condemnation*, also called *Eminent Domain* - This means that the State has the right to take your property from you for the benefit of the public. The State must compensate you by paying you the fair market value for the property that they condemn. For example, let's say the State determined that a new airport was needed. They may have decided that the best place to build the airport was in a location where there were existing houses. The State would first have to condemn all of the houses in that location. This could be done on the basis that a new airport being built, in that particular location, was for the good of the public overall. They would then have appraisals done on all of the real estate in that area to figure out what the fair market value was for each property. Then the State would pay the owners of all of the condemned real estate the fair market value to compensate them.

> *Condemnation, also called Eminent Domain - This means that the State has the right to take your property from you for the benefit of the public.*

Let's say an individual owner wanted to fight the State because they didn't want to sell. An owner might not want to move or may think that the condemnation sales price is too low. That owner would have to hire his own appraiser to find out if the State was paying him fair market value. If there was a large discrepancy between the two values, then the recourse would be to go to court to settle the matter.

I have a friend who is a home builder that was involved in a long, drawn out lawsuit against a town in my area over their condemnation values on his property. The town approved a large project for a company to build a shopping mall complex over an area of several city blocks. The town condemned all the houses and commercial buildings on the block and paid the owners the appraised value. My friend, along with another builder who owned property on the same block, fought the appraised values in court. It took about five years to settle the issue, but in the end they got millions of dollars for their properties. The other property owners didn't get nearly as much money because they didn't want to go to court, or they couldn't afford to fight a long, drawn out legal battle with the town.

2.  *Police Power* - This refers to the restrictions on real estate due to the zoning regulations, housing laws, building codes, etc.

I'll give you some appraisal trivia. *Zoning* laws started in 1916 when a building in New York City, located at 12 Broadway, was built so high that the adjacent property owners all complained to the city. The city then decided to impose restrictions on what property owners could do with their real estate. The purpose of zoning is to control the development of the land for the benefit of the general public. For example, if you live in a residential area you wouldn't want your neighbor building a warehouse. A warehouse next door would decrease your property value because buyers would pay less to live next to a warehouse.

It's the same thing with building codes. The State doesn't want people building unsafe housing, so they make sure that all construction is done to the minimum acceptable standards. Also, you wouldn't want your neighbor to be allowed to let his grass grow ten feet high would you? The building codes help protect the market value of your property. Building codes accomplish this by forcing a neighbor to maintain their property to conform with the other houses in the area.

Here's a funny war story. There was a homeowner who lived in an upper income area in Westchester County, New York that was furious with the local town because they had re-assessed the value of his house and raised his property taxes. This happened because the real estate market housing prices had increased dramatically in recent years. Apparently this homeowner didn't know how, or couldn't dispute his property taxes to get them lowered *(he should've read my book!)*. To "get even" with town hall, this angry homeowner protested the tax increase by hanging all of his laundry out in the front yard in full view from the sidewalk and street! Apparently he felt that if the neighbors all complained about his laundry being hung out in front of his house, then they would pressure the town to give in and lower this owner's taxes. Well, that's not what happened. The town not only didn't "give in" but they let this owner know that he was violating the building codes and creating problems for the property values of the neighborhood. So unless this guy took his laundry back inside the house and away from full view to the public, then he would have some building code violations and fines tacked onto his increased tax bills! As a result, this guy went back to doing his laundry inside the house with a washer and dryer, like everyone else in the area. *(This made his neighbors happy since they didn't have to look at his dirty underwear anymore! Just kidding.)*

3.  *Escheat* - This refers to a situation when someone dies without a Last Will and Testament drawn up or any heirs to inherit their assets. If this were the case, then all of the deceased person's assets would go to the sovereign, (State). A friend of mine, named Mike Roe, is a CPA accountant who used to deal with settling estates that were in an escheat situation in New York City. He said that there were people who had died that were worth millions of dollars but they had no heirs to inherit their assets. *(How about giving it to me?)* The city would take over the estate while they tried to locate an heir or relative of the deceased person. After a certain period of time, if there were any unclaimed assets then they would go to the State.

4.  *Taxation* - We all know what this is! This restricts the rights of real estate in the sense that the State can assess a tax for the ownership of the property. You can dispute your property taxes to get them lowered by hiring an appraiser to determine if the tax assessment is too high.

# Private Voluntary Limits On Real Estate

There are private **voluntary** limits that can be placed on the private ownership rights of real estate. This refers to restrictions that are voluntarily placed on the full rights of the real estate by the owner:

1.  *Deed Restrictions* - This refers to something in the deed restricting the use of the property. For example, someone may sell a house with the restriction that it can never have an addition installed or no tress can be intentionally cut down. Years ago some people put deed restrictions on their properties when they sold that today would be illegal. These restrictions stated that any future owners of the property could not sell or rent the house to a person of a particular nationality or race. That type of deed restriction is against the Federal discrimination laws and can't be enforced because it's no longer valid.

2.  *Easements* - This allows someone to have access to your property, such as, running utility lines or installing a driveway.

3.  *Leases* - This is simply granting the right to someone else to rent and use your property. Lease contracts can be written as simple or as detailed as both parties want. They outline specific rights and restrictions for the landlord and tenant.

4.  *Mortgages* - This refers to a lender who secures their loan with the real estate property. The property cannot be sold with a clear title without the lender being paid off or permitting the new owner to assume the existing terms of the loan.

# Private Involuntary Limits On Real Estate

There are private **involuntary** limits that can be placed on the private ownership rights of real estate. This refers to restrictions that are involuntarily placed on the full rights of the real estate by someone other than the owner. The involuntary limits are:

1.  *Liens* - This refers to a legal claim against a property to secure the payment of a debt. A lien is a record listed with the deed at town hall. A lien says that someone has an interest in the property so that it cannot be sold without the lien being paid off or resolved. It's similar to a mortgage, only it usually involves: money owed from a court judgment, a repairman that was not paid for work done at the property, unpaid tax bills, etc.

2.  *Encroachments* - This refers to something that is permanently located on someone else's property but it does not belong to the property owner of the real estate it is on. For example, let's say your neighbor has a driveway, fence, wall, or shed installed and the contractor accidentally places part of it on your property. Part of the driveway or fence is then said to be *encroaching* on your property.

> *If this encroachment goes unnoticed and unchallenged for many years, then that part of your property becomes the ownership of your neighbor.*

3.  *Adverse Possession* - This refers to a person obtaining ownership of some real estate that was originally owned by you. However, that person did not pay you for this property. For example, let's say your neighbor has a fence or a garage built and the contractor accidentally places part of it on your property. The part of the fence or garage that crosses over your property line is an encroachment. If this encroachment goes **unnoticed and unchallenged** for many years, then that part of your property becomes the ownership of your neighbor. This change in ownership happens **without any compensation or payment to you.**

4.  *Prescriptive Easement* - This refers to the fact that you must allow someone to have access to their property. For example, let's say someone purchased a lot behind your house. We'll assume that there was not an easement in your deed that granted them the right to walk through your yard, or build a driveway on your property, to get to their yard. You would *have to* allow them access to get to their property. You couldn't stop them by saying they're trespassing on your yard. They have the right to gain access to their property, with or without your consent.

# Basic Appraisal Concepts

The reason for an appraisal is to aid someone in making a decision. This could refer to: a mortgage lender, a potential home buyer or seller, an accountant who is trying to settle an estate, a homeowner disputing their property taxes, etc. An appraisal is an estimate of market value based upon the opinion of the appraiser.

> *An appraisal is a supportable and defensible estimate of value based upon the opinion of the appraiser. It's not a prediction which is what a crystal ball is for, and it's not a projection which is a mathematical forecast.*

The value of real estate is indeterminable due to the imperfect market. This means that real estate isn't like stocks and bonds where you can just look up its value in the newspaper. An appraisal is a supportable and defensible **estimate** of value based upon the **opinion** of the appraiser. It is a *forecast*. It's not a *prediction* (which is what a crystal ball is for), and it's not a *projection* which is a mathematical forecast. The difference between a forecast, a prediction and a projection:

◊  *Forecasting* is done with the best available information and facts that you have with reasonable conclusions to estimate the future.

◊  *Predictions* are less precise statements than forecasts. But a prediction has some basis (as opposed to something a fortune teller would tell you about the future).

◊  *Projections* are based on the past and don't allow for contingencies to estimate the future. It's similar to statistics that use projections of figures.

A forecast is an estimate. Appraisers forecast **not** predict because a forecast is based on whatever data is available and correct at the time of the report. Your appraised property value estimate is a forecast because it's value in future benefits. The value of a property is the present value of future benefits from the ownership of that real estate.

> *The appraiser measures the value; he doesn't determine the value. The market determines value.*

The appraiser **measures** the value of real estate; he doesn't **determine** the value. The **market** determines the value of real estate! This means that potential buyers decide the value based upon recent, similar sales of comparable properties in the area. All the appraiser is trying to do is *measure* what the potential buyers are willing to pay for the real estate. Value is always measured through the eyes and aspects of the buyers, and not the sellers. *People,* not a *property,* make value and determine the sale prices of real estate.

The **Use** of a property leads to its **Productivity**, which leads to it's **Value**. For example, if you have a two-family house, it will generally be worth more money than a one family house. The reason for this is that there is additional rental income from the second apartment. However, in some areas a single family house is worth more than a two-family house. That's because the single family fits-in with the other houses in the neighborhood, and there are no other two-family houses around. This is more common in a higher priced single-family area.

Another example is in the case of a legal rooming house with many small apartments. As a rooming house the structure brings in a substantial amount of income. However, if you converted that rooming house to a one family dwelling, then you eliminate all the extra rental income. By doing this, it will generally reduce the property's market value.

> **43,560 square feet equals one acre.**
> **There are 640 acres in one square mile.**

DON'T FORGET THESE FIGURES!!! Often you will need to know these figures to make calculations for an appraisal. You may come across the terminology of *"chains"* concerning an acre. Just remember that one chain is equal to 66 feet. An acre is equal to one chain times ten chains or:

66 feet x 660 feet = 43,560 square feet.

# Market Value - Subjective And Objective

To have value, a property must have all of the following items:

1   *U* = Utility
2   *S* = Scarcity
3   *E* = Effective Demand
4   *T* = Transferable

An easier way to remember it is by the abbreviations: *USE + T*. *Utility* refers to the property being useful to a buyer. *Scarcity* refers to the property being unique enough that there aren't many other properties for sale in the area for a lot less money. *Effective Demand* refers to their being enough interest from potential buyers for the property. *Transferable* refers to the ability to transfer the ownership of the property to a buyer. If you cannot transfer a clear title and deed to a buyer, then no one is going to want to purchase your property.

The value of something depends upon people's desires. This changes from time to time since the market is imperfect and always fluctuating. It's just like the value of money which constantly fluctuates with inflation and the economy. Value is perceived from the eyes of a typical buyer for the item or property you estimate the value of. You have to understand the market of the real estate you are appraising. You have to identify your market very carefully. Try to figure out what type of tastes and income level a person would need for this property to be appealing to them. Remember that you look at value and the market through the eyes of the typical buyer.

The market **price** of a property can be equal to the market **value** of that property. However, this is not always the case. I'll clarify this statement by starting with some basic appraisal definitions.

The appraisal textbook definition of Market Value:

◊   *"Market Value is the most probable price in terms of money which a property should bring in a competitive and open market under all conditions requisite to a fair sale, the buyer and seller each acting prudently and knowledgeable, and assuming the price is not affected by undue stimulus."*

The appraisal textbook definition of Market Price:

◊   *"Market Price is an amount actually paid for a property in a particular transaction; an historic fact; and it may be forecast as most probable selling price."*

**The market price is the actual sales price of a house. However, the sales price can be different from market value if the sale was not an "arms length" transaction.**

The market price is the actual sales price of a house. However, the sales prices can be different from market value because maybe the sale was not an *"arms length"* transaction. For an appraisal, you value property as though it were an all cash deal and with normal loan financing. I'll talk more about all of this later, but for now I'll just give you a little information. Most mortgages are conventional because they're not insured or guaranteed by the government. Any "seller financing" with flexible terms on the subject property may affect the **price** but it doesn't affect the **value** of the property. It's the value of the property that you appraise. For example, let's say that a buyer is a relative of the seller. That buyer may be given a very low interest rate, Purchase Money Mortgage loan by the seller. (See section Mortgages, Mortgages And More Mortgages page 170). This low interest loan can be used to pay for part, or all, of the sales price for the property. Then that will affect the **market price** (sales price) of the property. However, it doesn't affect the **market value** of the property. The reason for this is that the value doesn't change just because a particular buyer was given good terms for his purchase of the property. This is why you have to make an adjustment for favorable financing to the **sales comparables** that have non-conventional financing. By doing the adjustment, you'll make the comparables equal to an "arms length" transaction with conventional financing. *Do you understand?* If not, don't worry since this is covered in more detail later in the book. See section Narrowing Down The Search For Good Comps page 84.

You have to check to see what your State certification board gives as the definition of *market value*. Some States may have a slightly different definition to meet their particular needs. Also, there may be different definitions for *Condemnation Values,* etc. that you should check on. Call your State Certification Board for any information they can provide you with.

If something affects value then you *HAVE TO* include it in the market value estimate of your appraisal report. I once did a foreclosure appraisal on a horse stable that had a **negative** market value!! How about them apples! The appraiser who originally did the mortgage loan appraisal report stated that a horse stable was the Highest and Best Use for the property. This stable was located in an area of million dollar homes! This guy must have been drunk when he did that report. To top it off, some local contractors had dumped some waste and toxic materials on the vacant site and contaminated the soil. The bank that foreclosed on the property had price estimates of over $1.5 million dollars just to clean up the soil. This clean up fee didn't even include the costs to knock down the horse stable and subdivide the lot to build new houses.

**Market Value must be an objective value. Meaning, it must be an unbiased opinion of the value by the appraiser.**

*Market Value* must be an **objective** value. Meaning, it must be an unbiased opinion of the value by the appraiser. The appraiser should not include their personal opinions if they are different from the opinions and judgments of the typical buyer in that market. For example, let's say you're appraising an older Tudor style house in a low income section of town. We'll assume that you personally don't like older homes, Tudor style houses, and/or the low income section of town. If this were the case, then you do not estimate the market value to be unrealistically low just because **you** don't like the house or because **you** wouldn't want to buy it and/or live in that neighborhood. You only measure the potential value from the eyes and opinions of the typical purchaser that would consider buying that house. The reason for this is that just because you don't like that house and you wouldn't want to buy it, doesn't mean that no one else would buy it. There are many buyers that love older, Tudor style houses and maybe they can only afford to buy a house in a low income area. That's the estimated value you're determining because there are people who will pay a certain price for that house. Your job is to estimate what that price is.

*Value in Use* is a **subjective** value. Meaning, it is a biased opinion of the value by the buyer or the seller. One example is a person who doesn't want to sell their house or will only sell at a very high price. This may be because the property has more importance and value to him than it does to a typical purchaser. Possibly the house has been in his family for years and it has sentimental value, or any number of other reasons. This unrealistically high market value in that person's eyes is called Value in Use.

Another example of a subjective value is a person who is willing to buy a house at a much higher price than the typical buyer. This can occur because the property has more importance and value to him/her than it does to a typical purchaser. Possibly the house is located next door to their mother's house and he/she needs to live nearby to watch over her, or any number of other reasons.

One of my appraisal instructors told us a true story to explain the concept of Value in Use. There was an old woman who owned and lived in a small house in New York City that had been in her family for many years. A developer had purchased all of the buildings on a large section of the city block where this woman's house was located. The developer and investors needed to buy this last house from the woman in order to build a very large and expensive commercial building on the block. However, this woman would _NOT_ sell her house for any price! They offered her millions of dollars to buy her house - and this was **decades** before houses costing millions of dollars were common in or around New York City. They demolished all of the buildings and houses on the lot surrounding her home thinking that once she saw all the buildings gone, she might change her mind and sell before they started the new building construction. *Wrong!* This old lady wasn't going to budge from that house – no matter what. In the end, the developers and investors had to design and build the new building **around** her house to not encroach on her small property, which was located *right in the middle* of where the new building was supposed to be! This is an example of Value in Use *(an extreme example!)*, regardless of whether the woman accepted the buyout price offer or not.

The price offered by the potential buyers (the developers and investors) and not accepted by the potential seller (the old woman) cannot be used as an indication of property values in that area due to the extremely abnormal circumstances in this situation.

> *This is another reason why you want to get more than the minimum number of three sales comps for ALL of your appraisal reports.*

Let's say you were using a sales comparable that sold for an unusually high price due to the *Value in Use* of the buyer or seller. You must make an adjustment to the sales comp to reflect the personal opinions of the buyer or seller; if they paid a much higher price than the typical buyer would have in that market. Your adjustment amount should bring the total sales price of the comparable down to what it would have been if it were sold in an "arms length" transaction. This is another reason why you want to get more than the minimum number of three sales comps for **all** of your appraisal reports. When you're writing up the report, there will be times when you will find a problem with a comparable sale. Or you just get the feeling that a sales comp doesn't accurately reflect the local market and that something is wrong. If you have additional sales, then you can finish the report with the other sales comps that you have. Another option is that you can just apply less weight on that one comparable that's abnormal.

*Amenity* value is not really measurable in terms of money. This is similar to Value In Use, which was explained earlier. Amenity value is the value of something to a person due to their own tastes and desires. For example, someone may be willing to pay a very high price for a house that's located next to their mother-in-law's home. *(Well, maybe this example is a little far reaching, but it'll get my point across.)* This value of the property in their eyes is an amenity value because it doesn't reflect the opinion of the typical buyer. The amenity value to a particular person may not accurately reflect the value in the eyes of the typical buyer in the local market. Therefore, you can't really put a value on it because it's a subjective value and it's not tangible.

# The Principles Of Property Valuation

1. **Supply and Demand** - Physical, Economic, Government, and Social are the four forces that influence demand. The abbreviation makes it easier to remember as *PEGS*.

    *a*   P = Physical
    *b*   E = Economic
    *c*   G = Government
    *d*   S = Social

*Physical* refers to the actual physical property for sale and how appealing it is to potential buyers. The more appealing, the more potential buyers there are. *Economic* refers to the economic conditions in the area where the property is located. *Government* refers to the Federal, State and local government situation in that area. For example, perhaps the city politicians are planning to build an airport, or a huge garbage dump or waste disposal facility near the subject property. Obviously this will have a negative affect on the demand to buy that real estate. If the property is located in an excellent school district, this will increase demand from potential buyers. *Social* refers to the social conditions of the area around the subject property. For example, is the house located in a desirable community that typical buyers would want to live in?

*Effective Demand* is the desire for new housing *plus* the income potential to buy the new housing. For example, there are millions of people who would like to buy a large house overlooking the ocean. You could therefore conclude that the demand for large houses overlooking the ocean is extremely high. However, this doesn't mean that the market value of these houses suddenly shoots sky high because it is not an *effective* demand. Meaning that even though there are millions of people who have the desire to buy these houses, effective demand is measured **only** by the people who actually can afford these houses and who want to live in that particular area where the subject property is located.

The supply and demand are very important principles in estimating the market value of real estate. You relate it to the supply of houses for sale that the subject property is competing with. If there are many houses for sale in the area, then the market values will drop because there is too much supply. Supply is also called *standing stock* and is inelastic. This phrase "inelastic" is used because you can't build houses very quickly to meet a sudden increase in demand for them. Demand analysis can refer to whether people are moving into or out of the area. If an area has become undesirable, then the market values and sales prices of the homes will decrease due to a lack of buyers. Also, is it *Effective Demand* where the potential buyers have enough money and the desire to purchase the houses in the area.

2. **Highest and Best Use** - there are four forces that influence H&B Use, which in turn have an affect on the market value of real estate. These four are discussed in more detail in the Highest and Best Use section.

    a   Physically Permissible
    b   Legally Permissible
    c   Appropriately Supported *(access to it)*
    d   Economically Feasible

3. **Substitution** - the opportunity cost of making one investment decision over another has an affect on the market value of real estate. It's the choice someone has to make between different investment options. The *Principle of Substitution* is an alternative course of action open to a purchaser. The purchaser's alternative is to buy another property or investment with the same utility and depreciation as the subject property. This is the basis for the *Direct Sales* and *Cost Approaches* to estimate market value. It can also apply to the *Income Approach* to estimate market value. For example, let's say there's an area that has very similar designs of houses that are relatively all the same age. What if all of the houses in the area are on the market for sale at $200,000 and one house is on the market for $250,000. Then the chances of that seller getting the higher price of $250,000 is unrealistic. The reason for this is that the typical buyer would purchase a similar and competitive house in the area for the $200,000 sales price.

4. **Marginal Productivity** - the different contributions made to an investment by its aspects. In terms of real estate, adjustment amounts are made for the pluses and minuses of a property to account for the marginal productivity. For example, there may be something about the subject property that is more appealing to buyers than other properties for sale in the area, such as a swimming pool. The appraiser will need to make a plus adjustment in their report for this to increase the estimated market value of the house.

5. **Variable Proportions** - the increasing and decreasing rate of returns. This refers to the law of diminishing returns for any improvements made to a property. For example, let's say you have to spend $15,000 to make repairs to a house. Then how much will the value of the house increase when the work is finished? From an appraisal standpoint the normal rate of return for repairs should be at least one-to-one. This means that for each $1.00 you spend in repairs and improvements; you should increase the value of the property by at least $1.00. So using our example, if you spent the $15,000 then the market value of the property should increase by at least $15,000. If it doesn't, then your rate of return on your invested money will diminish or decrease. This will lower the estimated market value of the property.

6. **Change** - the real estate market is always fluctuating due to the physical, economic, government, and social conditions (*PEGS*). This change is reflected in the four stages which make up the lifecycle of a neighborhood.

    a   Growth
    b   Stability
    c   Decline
    d   Renewal

The *Principle of Change* is reflected in the lifecycle of a neighborhood. This means neighborhoods can change over time. The area may go through a period of *growth* during good economic times. Then the area will be *stable* for several or many years. Then the conditions could change and the area may start to *decline*. When the conditions change again, the area may begin a *renewal* process to complete the cycle.

The neighborhood where a property is located is **crucial** to the appraisal report. This is important because of the affect the external aspects have on the market value of a property. Every property takes on the characteristics of its neighborhood. As a result, if the neighborhood is in decline, then the property values will decline as well.

7.    **Anticipation** - the value of an investment at the end of a certain period of time is what an investor is interested in. This is also known as *appreciation* which is the gradual increase in market value of a house or asset. This is mainly more important for income producing properties. However, all homeowners want their properties to appreciate in value over time. The *Principle of Anticipation* is the basis for the Income Approach to estimate market value. It's the present value of future benefits for an investment. For example, if an investor is purchasing an income producing property, he's going to determine his purchase price based upon anticipated future profits in the deal.

# The Analysis Of A City

As was noted in the Principles of Property Valuation section for supply and demand: Physical, Economic, Government and Social (*PEGS*) are the four forces that will influence demand. Just as *PEGS* affects the value of a particular property, it also affects the value and appeal of a city or neighborhood.

*1*    P = Physical Boundaries
*2*    E = Economic Activity
*3*    G = Government
*4*    S = Sociological Characteristics

1.    **Physical Boundaries** - this refers to lakes, rivers, mountains, etc. that are some type of a divider between cities and/or neighborhoods. This <u>does not</u> mean that you just use the city boundaries listed on a map for an appraisal report. The boundaries that are on a map may be different from the actual physical boundaries of the area. Also, just because a street has heavy traffic, it doesn't make it a boundary for the neighborhood. When you do use a street as a boundary, you technically use the properties up to 1/2 of one side of the street, on either side, as the boundary for the neighborhood. Also, look at price ranges and incomes as possible boundaries to use for your appraisal reports.

2.    **Economic Activity** - this refers to the dominant economic activity of a city and/or neighborhood. Some examples of the different types found are: the nice areas of the city with the expensive homes and/or apartments, the expensive retail areas, the low income residential areas, the heavy industrial areas, transportation that's available in an area, such as, airports, bus terminals, railroad, etc.

*Linkages* refer to easy access to highways, job opportunities and employment centers, etc. of a neighborhood. Driving time is important for linkage with the supporting facilities for the subject property. *Supporting Facilities and Services* refers to hospitals, shopping centers, schools, recreational facilities, etc. to service the neighborhood. All of these will have an affect on the values of real estate in an area.

3.    **Government** - this refers to the jurisdiction and stability of the government, tax structure, building department regulations, zoning, etc. that is found in cities. Are the building department regulations and zoning very strict? This could limit a typical home buyer from building an addition to a house or garage, etc. All of which must be considered in estimating the market values of homes in that area for an appraisal.

4.    **Sociological Characteristics** - this refers to the quality of the schools and recreational facilities, diversity of the churches, culture, arts and theaters, etc. that are found in cities. The more diversity and appealing these are, then the higher the property values will be due to increased buyer demand.

# The Economic Base Of A City

You need to know the market and the economic conditions to be a good, thorough appraiser. To a certain degree you have to be an economist to really know what you're doing. The *Economic Base* of a community is the economic activity in that community which enables it to attract income from other areas outside its borders. It's not just referring to the job someone holds, but the type of industry their job comprises. For example, employment in areas of Texas is predominantly in the oil industry. Just like employment in Silicon Valley, California is predominantly in the computer related industries.

From an appraisal standpoint you're interested in the *Location Quotient*. The Location Quotient refers to the percentage of employment in a particular industry of an area as it compares to the national percentage in that industry for all areas. If the location quotient is greater than one, using the following math equations, then that industry is considered the **base industry** for the area. This means that in our examples above, Texas has a much higher Location Quotient percentage of employment in the oil industry, as compared to the national average of the oil industry employment for all areas of the country. Silicon Valley has a much higher Location Quotient percentage of employment in the computer industry, as compared to the national average of employment in the computer industry.

Remember that if the Location Quotient > 1 (greater than one) then it is a basic industry or service for that city. If the economic activity is being exported, then it's the Economic Base of a city.

Now let's see how all of this relates to an actual appraisal example. Let's say there was going to be an increase in the local population due to new jobs that opened in a particular industry. You have been hired by the company offering the new jobs to find out what amount of housing is needed for the new employees. Through you're research and knowledge of the local market; you have the following data to work with:

◊ LQ = Location Quotient
◊ LEi = Local Employment in an Industry
◊ LEt = Local Employment Total in all industries
◊ NEi = National Employment in an Industry
◊ NEt = National Employment Total in all industries
◊ LQ = (LEi/LEt)/(NEi/NEt)

◊ Et = Total Employment
◊ Eb = Base Employment
◊ Es = Service Employment
◊ Et = Eb - Es

◊ Ke = Employment Multiplier
◊ Ke = Et/Eb
◊ Pt = Total Population
◊ Kp = Population Multiplier

◊ Kp = Pt/Et

1 The total population, Pt, for the area is currently 60,000 people.

2 The increase in the population of the area created by the new job openings will be 857 people.

3 The current density of the population has been averaged out to determine there are 2.5 people for each apartment unit and 3.5 people for each single family house in the area.

4 The housing accommodations for the current population is averaged out to estimate that 40% of the people in the area live in apartments and 60% of the people live in single family houses.

To start we'll determine how many of the 857 people hired will live in apartments and how many will live in single family houses. To find this, simply use the percentages that currently exist in the area. We know that currently 40% of the people live in apartments and 60% of the people live in single family houses.

857 x 40% = 343 will live in apartments

857 x 60% = 514 will live in single family houses

Next, using these figures, we need to figure out how many apartments and how many single family houses are needed for the new employees. This is found by using the numbers that currently exist in the area. We know that currently there are 2.5 people for each apartment unit and 3.5 people for each single family house in the area. Simply divide the new employees for each type of dwelling unit by these amounts.

343/2.5 = 137 apartments will be needed

514/3.5 = 147 single family houses will be needed

137 + 147 = 284 total housing units will be needed

Add the total apartments needed to the total single family houses needed. The result is, that 284 units would be the increase in the total housing needed for the increased employment and population growth in the area, due to the new job openings.

# The "As Of" Date
# Of Valuation

An appraisal is a supportable and defensible estimate of value of a property "as of" a certain date. The *"As Of"* date sets up the conditions at the time of the value estimate, such as, physical conditions, economic conditions, etc. The date of sale is important due to the market condition "as of" the date of the sale.

The "As Of" date is **critical** in every appraisal report. It's critical because the house you're appraising is most likely worth a different price today than it was one year ago. The house will also be worth a different price one year after today. Changes in the market value are created by the fluctuating market. Therefore, you have to account for this fact. You decide what the typical buyer would pay in an "arms length" transaction, "as of" the date you are estimating the market value of the subject property. For example, let's say you're doing a house appraisal for an estate. Estate appraisals are always needed for tax purposes after someone dies. However, often the people overseeing the estate will order the appraisal many months or even years after the owner of the property has died. Let's say the person died four years ago. Then you would have to go back and find records of sales comparables from four years ago. You would also have to find the information needed for the Cost and Income Approaches at the time of the owner's death. If the person died 20 years ago, then you would have to go back 20 years to estimate the market value! The reason for this is due to the "As Of" date of your appraisal which in this example is 20 years ago.

One of my instructors for the appraisal courses told us that he has a friend who had to do an appraisal for a particular group of American Indians. They were trying to decide how much money the government owed these Indians, in today's dollar value, due to land that was taken from them many years ago. The "As Of" date of the appraisal wasn't just 20 years ago; it was 200 years ago!!! Imagine trying to find data from 200 years ago to do all three approaches to estimate market value of vacant land? To make it even more difficult, the appraiser had to figure out the value of the land in today's prices. Two hundred years ago many things were purchased with bartering instead of money. So instead of paying someone a $10 bill, you paid them with some food, or tools, or cattle, or anything else you could exchange with them. *(Do you think you would be able to do an appraisal assignment like that?)*

# The Highest And Best Use

You value property in relation to its *Highest and Best Use*. This may not always be its present use and the property's H&B Use can change over time. The H&B Use is based upon all factors, such as, the neighborhood data, market data, zoning, etc. **The Highest and Best Use of a property is the most profitable, likely use to which a property can be put.** Consider it as the use in which a property is put which will give the highest value to the site. Market Value is always estimated by the **Highest and Best Use** for the subject property and the **Date** of the appraisal. Highest and Best Use is one of the most **critical** factors in all appraisals. The "As Of" date of the appraisal is the other critical factor. **H&B Use and the "As Of" date, are the two factors that the entire appraisal is based upon.**

The type of improvement that someone puts on the site must yield the most value for it to be the H&B Use of that property. For example, if you build a single family house in an area mostly of four-family buildings, then the single family house is probably not the H&B Use of that site. The type of improvement must conform to the approved zoning for the site in order for it to be the H&B Use. Let's say you converted a single family home into a two-family house by separating the first and second floors to create two apartments. If the local zoning doesn't allow a two-family house on that site, then it cannot be the H&B Use of the property. Potential buyers will not want to purchase a property if it violates the zoning laws.

In the H&B Use, land is always *residual.* To estimate the land value by using a residual technique, you have to take sales comps and estimate the cost of only constructing the building. After that, you must take out for any depreciation that affected the sale. What you're left with is a *residual* value for the vacant land which is an estimate of the land value.

> *Highest and Best Use is one of the most CRITICAL factors in all appraisals. The "As Of" date of the appraisal is the other critical factor. H&B Use and the "As Of" date, are the two factors that the entire appraisal is based upon.*

To determine the highest and best use, you need to have *all* of the following factors:

1.   It must be a **legally permitted** use for the property. For example, let's say you're appraising a single family house. What if the zoning on the property states it can be used for a one-family or a two-family dwelling. If two-family houses are worth more money in that area, then you may determine that the highest and best use is a two-family. That is, if it is feasible for the house to be converted to a two-family. However, if the zoning is for a single family house only, then you cannot estimate the value based upon the possible conversion to a two-family house. That is, unless the conversion could be done without any extensive zoning changes.

2.    It must be a **physically possible** use for the property. For example, let's say you're appraising a two-family house that has a frame construction. *Frame* construction means that the walls of the house are made of wood materials and not masonry materials, like brick or stone. The zoning on the property may state that it can be used for a two-family *frame* dwelling or a four-family *masonry* dwelling. What if four-family houses are worth more money in that area. If this were the case, then you cannot decide that the highest and best use is a four-family. That is, unless you calculate into your analysis the cost of knocking down the existing *frame* house, and building a new four-family *masonry* structure.

3.    It must be an **appropriately supported** use for the property. For example, let's say you're appraising a vacant lot in a forest area. We'll assume that you want to determine if the H&B Use is a single family house as opposed to the current vacant lot. You would have to be able to get utility lines to the property and have some roadways providing access to it, in order to decide that the highest and best use is a single family house.

4.    It must be an **economically feasible** use of the property. For example, let's say you're appraising a one family house and you want to find out if the highest and best use is a three-family house. You would need to evaluate the following:

a    You must learn if a three-family house is marketable in the subject area. Marketability is determined by: the quality of the space *(demand for the real estate)*; the quantity of the space *(supply of other houses on the market for sale)*; the location of the real estate; and any special conditions that will enhance the marketability.

b    You must find out if a three-family house meets a typical investor's criteria. One requirement it would have to meet would be an adequate rent roll or appreciation to provide a good return on their money invested in the property.

# *Highest And Best Use Example*

Let's say, you're hired by an investor to find out the H&B Use of a property he's considering purchasing. The investor wants to know that if he buys this single family house, and then knocks down the house to build a four-family building; will a four-family be the H&B Use of the subject property?

From your field work and the data you have obtained, you make the following conclusions:

*Under The Current Use:*
◊    $40,000 = Site Value with the zoning for a single family house
◊    $150,000 = Building + Site Value

*Under The Proposed Use:*
◊    $10,000 = Demolition Cost of the single family house
◊    $180,000 = New Construction Cost of the four family house
◊    $75,000 = New Site Value with the zoning for a four family house
◊    $240,000 = New Construction Value of the four family house

The first step is to figure out the total loss in value for demolishing the existing improvements on the site. This is found by subtracting the current value of the building plus the site, from the current site value.

$$150,000 - \$40,000 = \$110,000$$

The next step, is to figure out what the costs will be for everything from the demolition of the single family house, to the construction of the four-family house. We find this by adding the current value of the site, plus the loss in value for demolishing the single family house, plus the cost of this demolition, plus the cost to construct the new four-family house.

$$40,000 + \$110,000 + \$10,000 + \$180,000 = \$340,000$$

Then we determine what the new value will be for the building plus the site with the four-family house on it. We find this by adding the new construction value plus the new site value with these improvements.

$$240,000 + \$75,000 = \$315,000$$

We then subtract the value of the current site plus the current building, from the value of the new site plus the new building. The purpose of this is to learn what the added value will be with the four-family house built.

$$315,000 - \$150,000 = \$165,000$$

The value added by this change in use is only $165,000. We have now found, that the cost to change the use of the site from a single family to a four-family is $340,000. The new total value of the site plus building will only be $315,000. This will give the investor a $25,000 loss if the change is made. Therefore, we can conclude that it's *not* the Highest and Best Use to change from the single family house to the four-family house. By making this change, it will cost the investor more money than he will gain in increased value when the conversion is all finished.

## Property Analysis

You must know the property you're appraising and the facts about it, the measurements, the negative and positive aspects, etc. It's important that you look at **all** areas of the house, top to bottom, and not the furniture. You look at the *building* when doing an appraisal, not the personal items like furniture. The exterior shell and roof, and the integrity of the interior must be maintained. These items have a lot to do with the remaining economic life of the building. The furniture and decorations may make the house more appealing on the inside, but they're not part of the real estate that you're appraising. Therefore, you have to picture the house for your value estimate as though the furniture and decorations weren't even there.

> It's important that you look at all areas of the house, top to bottom, and not the furniture. You look at the building when doing an appraisal.

Only include the aspects that affect the *value* in your report, not your own personal biases. The role of an appraiser is to reflect the *market* and not their own bias. When you walk around, notice what has to be repaired in and around the house. See how the rooms flow and the layout of the floor plan. Meaning that you should make sure you don't have to go through a bedroom to get to the only bathroom on a floor. This type of floor layout is similar to those found in the old railroad style apartments and will negatively affect the market value. See if the kitchen is located on the third floor, or if there are no bathrooms on the floor with the bedrooms. If this is the case, then it is a functional drawback because this is an abnormal room layout and will lower a potential buyer's purchase price.

Check the site to decide if it's too large or too small as compared to other houses in the area. Does the site have a very steep slope that makes most of the vacant land unusable? Is it located on a busy street that would decrease the market value? Is it located on a private street that has a positive or negative affect on value? Does the landscaping conform with the overall appearance of the other houses in the area? Etc. I think you get the picture here. Just open your eyes and use your common sense when you're doing appraisal reports.

One of the things that really helps me out on an appraisal is: *I try to look at the property the same way a typical purchaser for that house would look at it.* Try not to get too involved in the mathematical equations, the exact square footage, the adequacy and type of insulation in the house, if every faucet is working properly, etc. Not that these items shouldn't be accounted for; it's just that you don't want to forget to take a step back and look at the house as though you were a typical buyer. A typical buyer will look at the general appeal of the house and the area. They wouldn't go through the home with a microscope and nitpick with the seller about a stain in the carpet, or a peeling section of wallpaper, or other trivial items.

## Land And Site Valuation

In valuing vacant land, the best approach is generally the *Direct Sales Comparison Approach*. When you have improvements on the site, you have to consider what effect a building has on the land value. The improvements could have a positive or negative affect on the land value, as opposed to if the site were left vacant.

As always, the Highest and Best Use and the "As Of" Date of Valuation are critical factors for your appraisal. Subsoil conditions are also important. Such as, is the land part of a wetland or conservation area that can't be built upon? Or are there minerals in the soil that are worth money? Has the soil been contaminated with toxic substances or oil leaking from an underground tank? Or are there any other factors that affect the value? A site is valued from an appraisal standpoint as if it is vacant and available to be put to its Highest and Best Use. A *Site* is a buildable lot derived from taking vacant land and improving it so that it's ready to be built upon. For example, knocking down some trees, leveling the lot, running utility lines underground, etc. are all examples of improving vacant land. Location is important in H&B Use, and particularly important in land value.

> In valuing vacant land, the best approach is generally the direct sales comparison approach.

You value land on a physical basis or by its productivity. The productivity of the land refers to how many houses, apartments or the maximum building square footage amount that can be built upon it.

*Plottage* refers to two or more adjoining lots that when combined, they produce a higher utility and value. *Assemblage* refers to two or more lots that when they are combined, **do not** produce a higher utility and value. Meaning that just because you buy two lots that are next to each other, it doesn't necessarily mean that you increase their market value by combining them. Perhaps there are zoning restrictions or some other factor that wouldn't make it beneficial to be the sole owner of the two combined lots. You may get the same market value if the lots were owned by two different people.

There are many different ways of estimating land values. Some of these include:

1  *Front Foot Basis*
2  *Gross Area Basis*
3  *Price Per Acre Basis*

I'll give you some examples on how these work. We'll assume we have found a lot that sold for $56,000 and the dimensions are 40 feet wide by 128 feet long. *Front Foot*

*Basis* is calculated by the sales price of the lot divided by the total amount of frontage feet of the property. *Frontage Feet* simply refers to the length of the lot that is touching or facing the street. The larger the frontage feet the more property you have on the street. This is often more desirable than just having a narrow property by the street which widens as it goes inward more. This is especially true for commercial properties. Commercial businesses want as much exposure as possible to attract more customers off the street. Anyway, the estimated value of our example on a *Front Foot Basis* is:

$$\$56,000/40 = \$1,400 \text{ per } \textbf{frontage} \text{ foot}$$

*Gross Area Basis* is calculated by the sales price of the lot divided by the total square feet of the property. *Square Feet* simply refers to the length of the lot multiplied by the width of the lot. The estimated value of our example on a Gross Area Basis is:

$$40 \times 128 = 5,120 \text{ square feet}$$

$$\$56,000/5,120 = \$10.94 \text{ per } \textbf{square} \text{ foot}$$

*Price Per Acre Basis* is calculated by the sales price of the lot divided by the percentage of acres of the property. The first thing we need to do is to find out what the actual acreage is of the subject lot. To do this, we divide the square feet of the lot, by the number of square feet in an acre. You do remember that there are 43,560 square feet in an acre, don't you? *(I'll be disappointed if you forget that!)*

$$40 \times 128 = 5,120 \text{ square feet}$$

$$5,120/43,560 = .12 \quad \text{or} \quad 12\% \text{ of an acre}$$

We then take the sales price and divide it by the actual acreage. This will give us the estimated value of the property on a Price Per Acre Basis.

$$56,000/.12 = \$466,667 \text{ per } \textbf{acre}$$

# Direct Sales Comparison Approach

## The Direct Sales Comparison Approach

How does an appraiser estimate value? Appraisers are taught to estimate value by following three recognized approaches. After analyzing the results of the analysis conducted, an appraiser then develops a final estimate or opinion of value. The three approaches used to estimate market value of real estate are shown in the sample appraisals included in this book. Please review those appraisals as you read the sections outlining the following three approaches:

1. **The Direct Sales Comparison Approach** *(also called the Market Data Approach)* - Compares similar, recently sold properties to the subject property.

2. **The Cost Approach** - Estimates the cost to replace or reproduce the subject property being appraised.

3. **The Income Approach** - Estimates what a prudent investor would pay for the subject property based on the income the property produces.

You also need to review section HUD and FHA Guidelines page 220 and section Sample State Real Estate Appraiser Guidelines page 297 for more details and rules about appraisal standards and how to fill out the standard appraisal report forms.

> *The Direct Sales Comparison Approach is usually the most effective and accurate technique in appraising single family houses and condos.*

The *Direct Sales Comparison Approach (DSCA)* is based on the assumption that by using recent, closed sales in the local market, the appraiser can estimate market value of the subject property. "Closed sales" refers to properties that have sold and the deal was done (closed) on a date very close to the "as of" date for your appraisal. For example, let's say you were hired to appraise a condominium with an "as of" valuation date of two years ago for your report. You cannot choose condo sales comparables that sold two *months* ago because they won't accurately reflect the real estate market conditions two *years* ago. Using the DSCA, the appraiser evaluates and compares houses that have recently sold which

are located very close to, and are very similar to, the subject property to estimate market value of the subject property. This is usually the most effective and accurate technique in appraising single family houses and condominiums. The DSCA is the method that you will use most often for your final valuation analysis for single family and condo appraisals.

Basically, in order to estimate market value of the subject property using the DSCA, you analyze recent sales of **competitive** and **comparable** properties. You then make adjustments in your appraisal report to try to "equalize" the comparable sales as though they had the exact same characteristics as the subject property. Closed sales comparables for an appraisal report are chosen based upon many factors. Since no two properties are identical, cost adjustments must be made to **estimate what the sales comparable would have sold for if it was identical to the subject property.** You have to remember that with the DSCA technique you're always comparing the sales comps to the subject property, not vice versa. Don't get confused while writing up a report. For example, don't make a **plus** adjustment to a sales comp that has a two-car garage when the subject only has a one-car garage. In this example you would need to make a **minus** cost adjustment to the sales comparable since it has a two-car garage which adds more value than the one-car garage of the subject property in this example. Another example would be if the subject property had a swimming pool and the sales comp did not have a pool. In this example you would need to make a **plus** cost adjustment to the sales comparable since it does not have a pool which is less appealing to the typical buyer than a house with a swimming pool, like the subject property has in this example.

Let me give you one more example since this needs to be clearly understood. Sometimes people who are new to appraising get confused on this issue and they use the incorrect plus/minus signs in their written appraisal reports. Let's say the subject property had central air-conditioning installed and some of your sales comparables for this appraisal did not have central A/C. Would you give the sales comps without the A/C a plus or minus adjustment to account for this? In this example you would need to make a **plus** cost adjustment to the sales comparables since they do not have central air-conditioning which is less appealing to the typical buyer than a house with central A/C, like the subject property has in this example. I will describe the appraisal adjustment process and more details about this in the following sections.

Basically, in order to estimate market value of the subject property using the DSCA, you analyze recent sales of competitive and comparable properties.

The units of sales comparison to use when evaluating sales comparable properties include:

◊ *Physical* - compare acre to acre, square feet to square feet, etc.

◊ *Economic* - compare rental income to rental income, etc.

For the Direct Sales Comparison Approach you need to consult all data sources that accurately list recent sales in the area. An appraiser's own files should always be the primary source of data for an assignment. This means that you should have enough information, about the local market and recent sales, in your files to assist you on your appraisals. Obviously, the longer you're in business, the larger and more helpful your files will become in obtaining data. Some other helpful sources that you should use are: the local town hall, the real estate *Multiple Listing Service* (MLS), Internet services with real estate data, and any other sources that are available to you.

Just be careful when you're obtaining your data. If you find discrepancies between two different data sources, then you should always use the public record at town hall as the most reliable source. For example, let's say the local MLS has a sales comparable listed that sold for $135,000 four months ago. Well, since you're an **"A to Z Appraiser"** who does good, thorough appraisals, you will try to verify this information at the local town hall. You then find out that the public record for this sales comparable states that it sold for $127,000 five months ago. If this were the case then you should always use the public record as the final say in the matter.

I'm letting you know ahead of time that there will be many times that you'll find discrepancies in the data sources.

I'm letting you know ahead of time that there will be many times that you'll find discrepancies in the data sources. Some discrepancies will involve what the data source has listed, and what is actually at the site for the subject property and sales comps. For example, you'll often find a data source that says the property has a two-car garage. However, when you view the property personally, you find it only has a one-car garage. Or it says the house is in good condition and when you look at it, it's clearly a mess that needs work on the exterior. So you see, don't get lazy and cut corners or else you may end up in a very uncomfortable situation and you can't defend your actions.

If you read the MLS and other data sources, they clearly state that *"The information is believed accurate but not warranted."* This simply means that the data source company

is not guaranteeing that their information is 100% accurate. There will be many times when you'll find discrepancies in different data sources. You have to be very careful about using data sources that can be unreliable. Sometimes you have no choice, but that's why you always verify *all* information at the town hall. You should make copies of everything about the subject property, all sales comparables and any pertinent data that you can obtain. These copies should be kept with your own records in case you need them in the future to answer questions or refer back to an old appraisal report you did. This includes the deeds, tax information, zoning information, flood hazard zones, lot sizes, house square footage, age of the house, building department violations, etc.

You have to personally go out and look at all subject properties and all sales comparables if you're going to sign your name to the appraisal report.

*You have to personally go out and look at all subject properties and all sales comparables* if you're going to sign your name to the appraisal report. Don't just take it for granted that the site and building are OK and still standing. Remember that it's your neck on the line if you sign off on that appraisal. If you're the review appraiser, you don't have to go out and view the properties. However, you do have to at least see recent photographs taken for the appraisal report. You're probably wondering why I'm telling you that. Well, I'll give you a few war stories so you realize why.

One of my appraisal instructors told our class about a court case that he was working on. This case involved a lawsuit against an appraiser who never went out to view the comparable sales he used for a single family appraisal report. Apparently this appraiser had used sales comps that were abnormally low for his appraisal report. Upon reviewing this appraisal for the court case, the instructor found that the sales comps were **vacant land sales** and *not* single family house sales! **Even if the appraiser's data source incorrectly listed them as single family sales, the appraiser is still in trouble.** He's in trouble because he did not go out to verify this information with his own eyes. All he had to do, was drive to those addresses and he would have found that there were no houses at the site. Then he would have known that these sales were incorrectly listed in his data source. He must have gotten too lazy over the years and now he's going to pay for it.

Another one of my instructors told our class about an appraiser who never went out to view the subject property. When this appraiser turned in his report, the client called him to ask if he looked at the house on the "**as of**" date listed on his appraisal report. *(Remember, that the appraiser had to sign this report as being **truthful and accurate** to the best of his ability before sending it to the client.)* The appraiser was awfully surprised when the client informed him that **the house had burned down** the day **before** the "as of" date in which **he apparently inspected the subject property!!** This is another reason why the "as of" date is so crucial to an appraisal report. The day after that fire the subject property obviously was not worth as much as it was the day before. So learn a lesson from these two examples and make sure you personally view the subject property and all sales comps for all of your appraisal reports.

---

*This is another reason why the "as of" date is so crucial to an appraisal report. The day after that fire the subject property obviously was not worth as much as it was the day before.*

---

You can save a lot of time viewing and photographing the sales comps for an appraisal report by planning ahead. Map out your route to photograph and view the comparable sales for your reports before you leave your office. Purchase a good map of your area and photocopy the pages that have the subject property and the sales comparables on them. You can then use a highlighting marker to map out the best route to take. This will save you a lot of time and it will help prevent you from getting lost and driving around in circles. You can also use Internet map sources with driving directions to plan the routes. You should also purchase a good, reliable car compass. You'll be very surprised to find out how helpful an accurate compass is while you're driving around for your appraisal reports.

There will be times when you can't get inside the subject property or there will be inaccessible areas during some appraisals. For example, if you're doing a foreclosure appraisal for a bank, it's possible that the current tenant/occupant of the house will not allow you to come inside the home. Perhaps the basement or garage is sealed up and you don't have access. When you encounter a situation like this, just tell the client about it and make sure you mention this in your written report. If you have any doubts about the subject property or the sales comps, make sure you put that in the report as well. This way everything is up front and nobody can accuse you of being lazy or hiding something that you should have told them about.

---

*You should exceed the form requirements on all of your appraisals. This is how you do quality work that is far better than 90% of the appraisers in the business.*

---

Get extra sales comparables for all of your appraisals. Don't just stick to the minimum three sales to fill out the form reports. Don't just do the minimum requirements of the items listed on the standard appraisal forms. You should **exceed** the form requirements on all of your appraisals. This is how you do quality work that is far better than the vast majority of appraisers in the business. You should also include additional data in the addendum's, extra photos, etc.

There will be many times when you're writing up an appraisal report and you'll have a sales comparable that doesn't accurately reflect the local market. Possibly it has sold for an unusually high or low sales price. Maybe you will find some other problem with the comparable sale. You might just get the feeling that this sale doesn't accurately reflect the local market and that something is wrong. If you have additional

sales, then you can finish the report with the other sales comps that you have. You'll also have the option of just applying less weight in your evaluation to that particular sales comp. This is another reason why you want to get more than the minimum number of three sales comps for **all** of your reports.

# Narrowing Down The Search For Good Comps

There are many ways to narrow down your search for good sales comparables to use for an appraisal report. Some things to look for to narrow down your search for good comps are:

a   Sales that are an *"arms length"* transaction.

b   The most recent sales possible based upon the *"as of"* date of your appraisal report.

c   Sales that are located as close as possible to the subject property.

d   Sales that are as similar as possible to the subject property.

I'll elaborate on items A, B, C and D so they're easier to understand. (See Appraisal Form - URAR - FHLMC 70, FNMA 1004 section page 346 and the Sample Appraisal Reports section page 96).

**A:** Sales that are an "arms length" transaction refers to sales that have conventional financing terms for the purchase of the property. There also must be no known factors that abnormally affected the buyer's or seller's decisions in the deal. If the buyer obtained a mortgage loan at the market interest rate without any seller financing or lower than normal interest rates, then it can be assumed that the financing is *conventional*. Also, if there are no known factors that led to a *motivated* buyer or seller, then it can be considered an "arms length" transaction.

---

*Sales that are an "arms length" transaction refers to sales that have conventional financing terms for the purchase of the property.*

---

A motivated person could be someone who has to sell or buy the property for an important and urgent reason. For example, let's say the seller can't afford to make the mortgage payments anymore. We'll assume he cannot make the payments because his business is unfortunately going bankrupt. As a result, he will be motivated to sell the property for a lower price. The seller will be forced to sell the house before the bank can foreclose on his mortgage. Another possibility is that the seller is getting divorced and has to sell the house as part of the divorce settlement. In this case also, he will be motivated to sell the property for a lower price just to get rid of the house. Another example is if the buyer has to purchase a house next to a sick relative or family member. If he needs to be close enough to care for that person, then he'll be motivated to pay a higher price just because of the location of the house.

You adjust the sales comparables for *Sales and Financing Concessions* first and then time, locational, physical, etc. adjustments are made. The reason for this is that you first adjust the sales comps, if needed, to be "arms length" transactions on the date that they sold. The purpose of the adjustment process is to estimate what the sales comp would have sold for if it had possessed all the market recognized characteristics of the subject property. *Market recognized characteristics* refers to all items that affect the value of the property.

Financing adjustments in appraisal reports is normally required for *seller* financing on the comparable sales and not with *bank* financing. Seller financing is adjusted for if the financing was provided at a lower interest rate then the market lending rate, at the time of the sale of the **comparable**, not for the sale of the subject property. Meaning, that if the **subject property** is being sold with seller financing and good terms, then you *don't* adjust the sales comps downward if they were sold with conventional bank financing. The reason for this is that the flexible terms for the sale of the subject property will affect the market price (sales price). However, flexible terms do not affect the market value of the property. (See section Market Value - Subjective And Objective page 73). Any bank financing generally doesn't need to be adjusted for with the sales comparables. This is because bank loan financing is usually lent at the market interest rate at the time of the sale of that sales comparable property.

**B:** When you're looking for good sales comps, start checking the data sources for sales that have occurred within the last six months. You want to try to find the sales that have occurred within six months prior to the "as of" date of the appraisal. Hopefully you can find enough sales within the past six months for your report. The reason for this is that the more recent the sales are, then the more accurately they reflect the market conditions "as of" the date of your appraisal.

> *The reason for this is that the more recent the sales are, more accurately they reflect the market conditions "as of" the date of your appraisal report.*

It's not uncommon that you have to go back further than six months, so just do the best you can. If you can't find sufficient sales that have closed within the past six months, then go back up to one year. If you still can't find enough sales that have closed within the past year, then keep moving backwards until you find them. Just remember that you **have to make time adjustments** if necessary for the different market conditions at the time the sales comps closed. These time adjustments are made to reflect the market conditions at the time the comparables sold, as opposed to the "as of" date

for the appraisal of the subject property. Also, many lenders will not accept sales comps that are over one year old. That's why you have to make an extra effort to find sales that have sold within a six month period prior to the "as of" date. You don't want to finish a report and have a client bounce it back in your lap. They might do this if the sales are too old and they refuse to accept them as accurate comps.

Time adjustments in the appraisal report are also known as *Market-to-Market Comparisons*. The reason for this is that the time adjustments are used to factor in any changes in the local real estate market. Changes from the time that the sales comps sold, to the time of the "as of" date for the subject property valuation. The negative aspect of the Direct Sales Comparison Approach is that a closed sale is history and the market is constantly changing. This is why you need to use sales comparables that are no more than six months old. This way the comparables should accurately reflect the most recent market conditions "as of" the date of the appraisal.

Don't use the date the title of the property is recorded in the public record for the closing date of any sales comparables unless you have no other choice. The reason for this is that the title may not be recorded until long after the house was sold. One of my instructors gave our class an example of someone he met once that worked at a bank or a title company. This person had accidentally found a bunch of property titles in his desk drawer. The houses had sold a long time before that and this bank or title company employee had forgotten to record these property titles at town hall! If you used the title date for these properties as the actual closing date on your appraisal report, then you would be way off base. You'd be off because the market will be different from the actual date of the sale which was much earlier in time then the title recording date.

You can use the contract date for sales comparables because that is when the *meeting of the minds* between the buyer and the seller took place. Just make sure that if you do this, then you must use the contract date for all of your other sales comparables as well. Remember you have to compare the actual market conditions at the time of each sale. The contract date is normally at least several months before the actual closing date on the property. This is because there are mortgage applications that have to be approved, title searches and other legal work needs to be done, an appraisal must be ordered and then reviewed, etc.

**C:** Sales that are located as close as possible to the subject property is another factor to look for to narrow down your search for good comps. The closer a sale is to the subject property, the more it is similar to the subject, as far as how any external advantages or disadvantages affect it. Some items you have to consider when evaluating the subject and any sales comps are: the school district it's in; tax structure of the area; the town it's located in; proximity to highways, shopping, employment, and entertainment; the income level of the area; is it located on a private road; etc.

*The closer a sale is to the subject property, the more it is similar to the subject, as far as how any external advantages or disadvantages affect it.*

For example, if the subject property is located near an airport, there will probably be some negative affect on market value. Negative impact on value is caused by the noise from the airplanes flying over the houses in the area. If you pick a sales comparable from an area that isn't affected by the airport noise, then you <u>must</u> adjust for this factor. You have to adjust for the superior location because the airport didn't affect the sales price of the comp. Another example could be a different school district or the amount of taxes between the subject property and sales comparable. You have to try to compare apples-to-apples all the time. If the subject is located in an area that has a lower quality educational system, or lower taxes than a sales comparable, then you <u>must</u> adjust for these factors. An adjustment is needed because these factors would have affected the sales price of the comparable property if it was located in the same area as the subject property.

It's often said that in real estate the three most important factors are *Location, Location, Location.* The reason for this is that you can take two identical houses and place them in two different locations and have a big difference in their market values. For example, let's say you took an average house for your area and placed it onto a vacant lot that was overlooking the ocean. Does the market value suddenly increase? You bet it does! That's why location is so important in real estate.

<u>D:</u>  Sales that are as similar as possible to the subject property is something to look for to help you find good comps. The form appraisal reports list many different aspects you have to evaluate to determine how similar the comps are to the subject property. I'll go through the items listed on the back of the single family appraisal form and give you some descriptions to explain them in more detail. We have already discussed the first three items that are adjusted on the form: **A:** *Sales or Financing Concessions,* **B:** *Date of Sale/Time* and **C:** *Location.*

1.  **Site/View** - This refers to the topography and size of the site and the type of view there is from the site. Is the lot very hilly or is it relatively flat and does it have usable space? A very hilly lot will not be as usable to the homeowner as a flat lot. *(Unless they like to roll giant snowballs down the hill).* What size is the lot? If the lot sizes are different, then determine what adjustment is needed to compensate for this in the eyes of the typical buyer. If the lots are only slightly different in size, then an adjustment may not be needed. The reason for this is that the typical buyer may not lower or higher the purchase price due to a slight difference in two lots. What type of view does the property owner have? If one house overlooks a nice forest area and the other house overlooks a busy street, then an adjustment is needed.

2.  **Design and Appeal** - This refers to the style and appeal of the house. Is the house a Ranch style in an area of mostly Colonial style homes? The typical buyer will probably be looking for a house that conforms with the other homes in the area. What type of appeal does the house have? Is the overall design and appeal something that the typical buyer would find a nice home to live in or not?

3.  **Quality of Construction** - This refers to the type and quality of the construction of the house. Is the house built of brick construction in an area of mostly wood frame constructed homes? The typical buyer will probably be willing to pay more for a house made of brick or stone, as opposed to a wood frame structure. What is the quality of the construction? Is it something the typical buyer would find to be an overall well made home to live in or not?

4.  **Age** - This refers to the age of the house. Is there a significant difference between the age of the subject property and that of the comparable sales? The typical buyer will probably be willing to pay more for a house that is newer. If the ages are significantly different, then decide what adjustment is needed to compensate for this in the eyes of the typical buyer. If the ages are only slightly different, then an adjustment may not be needed. An adjustment may not be needed because the typical buyer may not lower or higher the purchase price due to a slight difference in age of the two houses. You can also account for a slight age difference by making an adjustment in the *Condition* section on the appraisal form, instead of adjusting for it in the *Age* section.

5.  **Condition** - This refers to the overall interior and exterior condition of the house. Is there a significant difference between the condition of the subject property and that of the comparable sales? The typical buyer will probably be willing to pay more for a house that is in "move-in" condition where no significant work is needed. If the conditions are significantly different, then determine what adjustment is needed to compensate for this in the eyes of the typical buyer. You won't have access to the interiors of the comparable sales because the owners of the sales comps don't have any interest in the appraisal of the subject property. They obviously don't want strangers knocking on their doors asking them to go inside, inspect their homes, take photos, measurements, etc. Just do the best you can with the data sources and information you have concerning the interior condition of the sales comps. You must at least view the sales comps on the outside from the street and take photos to evaluate the overall condition of the property.

6.  **Above Grade Room Count** - This refers to the room count of the house. The total number of rooms in a house refers to the rooms in the *livable* areas that are *above grade*. The total number of rooms <u>does not</u> include the bathrooms nor any rooms in the basement or attic. Bathrooms are counted and listed separately. Although the bedrooms are listed separately on the form, they are included in the total room count number. Is there a significant difference between the number of total rooms, bedrooms and bathrooms of the subject property, in relation to the comparable sales? The typical buyer will be willing to pay more for a house that has more total rooms, bedrooms and baths.

> *The total number of rooms in a house refers to the rooms in the livable areas that are "above grade."*

If the room numbers are significantly different, then decide what adjustment is needed to compensate for this in the eyes of the typical buyer. If the room counts are only slightly different, an adjustment may not be needed. The reason for this is the typical buyer may not lower or higher the purchase price due to a slight difference in the room count of two houses. You can also account for a slight room count difference by making an adjustment in the *Gross Living Area* section on the appraisal form, instead of in the *Above Grade Room Count* section. Generally the difference in the number of bathrooms is adjusted for in this section. The difference in the total room count and the number of bedrooms is adjusted for in the *Gross Living Area* section.

7. **Gross Living Area** - *(No, this doesn't refer to a dirty, disgusting living area!)* This refers to the total livable square feet of space inside the house. The gross living area, (GLA), in a house refers to the square footage in the *livable* areas that are *above grade,* which doesn't include the basement or attic areas. Is there a significant difference between the GLA of the subject property and that of the comparable sales? The typical buyer will probably be willing to pay more for a house that is larger. If the GLA's are significantly different, then determine what adjustment is needed to compensate for this in the eyes of the typical buyer. If the GLA's are only slightly different then an adjustment may not be needed. This is because the typical buyer may not lower or higher the purchase price due to a slight difference in size of two houses.

> *The gross living area, (GLA), in a house refers to the square footage in the livable areas that are "above grade," which doesn't include the basement or attic areas.*

You need to estimate what standard GLA multiplier would be good to use for the local market. You can obtain this information from other more experienced appraisers that do appraisals in the local market area of the subject property and sales comps. You then multiply this figure by the difference between the GLA for each sales comparable as opposed to the subject property. This simplifies the adjustment process for the Gross Living Area in your comps. For example, let's say Sale #1 was 235 square feet larger than the subject and Sale #4 was 140 square feet smaller than the subject. Let's say you estimated that the GLA multiplier is $35 per square foot for the local market. Then the adjustment for Sale #1 would be $35 x (-235) = -$8,225 and the adjustment for Sale #4 would be $35 x (+140) = +$4,900.

8. **Basement and Finished Rooms Below Grade** - This refers to whether there is a basement and/or finished lower level rooms in the house. These are areas that are *below grade.* This means that these rooms are 3/4 or more below the soil line on the exterior of the house. Is there a full or a partial basement? Is it completely finished, partly finished or unfinished? By saying "finished" it means that there are wall, ceiling and floor coverings in this room so that it can be used

as livable space. The typical buyer will probably be willing to pay more for a full basement because they can use that area for a playroom, laundry room, etc. Also, if the lower level is finished with carpeting, sheetrock, outlets, etc. it will increase the market value of the house.

9. **Functional Utility** - This refers to the overall flow of the interior rooms of the house or other functional items. Is there a significant problem with the functional layout of the subject property or with any of the comparable sales? The typical buyer will probably be willing to pay more for a house that has a typical room layout where no significant changes are needed. If there are functional problems with the house, then determine what adjustment is needed to compensate for this using an amount a typical buyer would account for.

For example, a house that has a kitchen on the third floor can be considered to have a functional problem. The house has a functional problem because this type of floor plan is very uncommon and can be inconvenient for the occupants. Other examples of functional problems that you might encounter are: having no bathrooms on a floor where the bedrooms are located, or a floor of the home that has only one bathroom that can only be reached by going through someone's bedroom.

10. **Heating/Cooling** - This refers to the type, age and condition of the heating and/or air-conditioning systems in the house. Is the house lacking a central air-conditioning system in an area where most homes have central A/C? The typical buyer will pay more for a house with central A/C and a newer heating system.

11. **Garage/Carport** - This refers to the type, size and condition of the garage or carport of the house. A *carport* is just a small roof covering over the driveway area; it's not enclosed on the sides. Is the house lacking an enclosed garage in an area where most homes have them? The typical buyer will probably pay more for a house with an enclosed garage than one with just a carport. Also, a two-car garage is more desirable than a one-car garage due to the extra car and/or storage capacity for the owner.

12. **Porches, Patio, Pools, etc.** - This refers to any porches, patios, swimming pools, decks, etc. on the property. Is the house lacking a pool or a deck in an area where most homes have them? The typical buyer will pay more for a house with a pool, porch or a nice deck, etc.

13. **Special Energy Efficient Items** - This refers to any extra insulation installed, thermal windows, etc in the house. Is the house lacking thermal windows in an area where most homes have these items? The typical buyer will pay more for an energy efficient house because it will save them money on utility bills. Newer houses have better insulation. Older houses sometimes have no insulation in exterior walls.

14. **Fireplace(s)** - This refers to the number of fireplaces. Is the house lacking a fireplace in an area where most homes have them? Is there only one fireplace instead of several? The typical buyer will probably pay more for a house with a fireplace.

**15. Other (e.g., remodeling, kitchen equip.)** - This refers to any other aspects about the house that have an affect on value that weren't covered in the other adjustment areas on the appraisal form. Is there a burglar/fire alarm system, a central vacuum system, etc.? Is the kitchen of the house modern or is it outdated? Are the fixtures and appliances modern or very old? The typical buyer will pay more for a house with a nice kitchen, bath, fixtures, etc. that have been upgraded and remodeled. Kitchens and bathrooms can have a BIG effect on many home buyers when they're looking at a house to buy.

---

*See APPENDIX D: COMPREHENSIVE VALUATION PACKAGE PROTOCOL section page 274 for more details and guidelines about how to evaluate and fill out the standard URAR appraisal form for FHA-insured mortgage loans.*

---

See APPENDIX D: COMPREHENSIVE VALUATION PACKAGE PROTOCOL section page 274 for more details and guidelines to evaluate and fill out each line on standard URAR appraisal forms for FHA-insured mortgage loans.

# The Adjustment Process

The adjustment process refers to the price changes you make to the comparable sales to equalize them to have the same characteristics as the subject property. For example, let's say the subject property has a full, finished basement and the sales comp has a partial, unfinished basement. The sales comp would have sold for a higher price if it had a full, finished basement like the subject property. Therefore, you have to adjust the actual sales price of the sales comparable **upward** to equalize it to the subject. It's the same thing if it were vice versa, with the sales comparable having the more appealing aspect than the subject property. Then the sales comp's actual selling price would be adjusted **downward** to equalize it to the subject. This is how you accurately estimate market value.

The adjustment process for the Direct Sales Comparison Approach can be done on a dollar basis or on a percentage basis. You can use a dollar amount to adjust the sales comparable for a particular item. You also can use a percentage amount of the sales price to adjust a sales comp. There is a sequence on the appraisal forms that follow the adjustment process. There are four aspects to adjust first:

*1   Real Property Rights Conveyed* - this refers to whether the rights sold with the real estate are fee simple, leasehold, etc.

*2   Financing Terms* - this refers to what type of financing terms were given with the sale, such as, a conventional loan, an FHA or VA loan, a purchase money mortgage, etc.

*3   Conditions of the Sale* - this refers to what type of terms were given with the sale other than financing, such as, was the deal an "arms length" transaction, was the house sold to a family member for an abnormally low price, was there a motivated seller or buyer involved in the deal, etc.

*4   Date of the Sale* - this refers to what the conditions of the real estate market were "as of" the date of the sale, any time adjustments needed for changes in the local market, etc.

**There are some very important points you need to be aware of when writing up your appraisal reports. Please read this *Adjustment Process* section carefully to make sure you understand it clearly.** *(That's why I used both icon symbols for this paragraph.)*

The first point is that you have to be very careful not to **double dip** your comparable sales adjustments. Meaning, you don't want to adjust for the same item in two different places on the appraisal form. If you do this, then you will be making an exaggerated cost adjustment. An exaggerated adjustment will throw off your final adjusted sales price for that comp. For example, often you'll need to make an adjustment due to the difference in the condition between the subject property and a sales comp. Sometimes the condition of the sales comparable is inferior to the condition of the subject property because the comp is an older house. If this were the case, then you could pick up the condition difference in the *Age* section adjustment, instead of in the *Condition* section, or vice versa. You don't want to make two adjustments for the same thing in this type of situation by making an adjustment in both sections of the form. If you did that, then you would be "double dipping" the adjustment.

The second point I want to make is that you ***don't*** have to stick to the standard appraisal form layout! You can add items, comments, sections, etc. to the form by using addendums and other explanatory comments. This will help you clarify something that affects the value that isn't found on the form. Too many appraisers restrict themselves by only sticking to the exact layout of the standard appraisal form. Remember that you should adapt the appraisal forms to meet the particular needs of the appraisal assignment that you're working on!

The next point that I want to make sure you understand is that **there are NO set percentages or mathematical formulas used to make adjustments in an appraisal report that apply to all situations!** I will repeat that since it's important and I want to make sure you are aware of this: *there are no set percentages or mathematical formulas used to make adjustments in an appraisal report that apply to all situations!* Sometimes people who are new to appraising don't realize this. Real estate appraising is **not** an exact science where you can apply a specific formula, percentage amount, or mathematical calculation that will work for all areas of the country in all situations.

The reason there are no standard adjustment amounts that are used nationwide is because **each local market in the country is <u>DIFFERENT</u>!! This applies to <u>*ALL*</u> aspects of an appraisal report!** You should find an experienced appraiser in your area to assist you with learning how to make the proper adjustments for your local market. This will help you get a feel for the adjustment process. Your local real estate market will have different adjustment amounts needed for the identical item on/in a property located in a different market. For example, the adjustment amount for a 500 square foot difference in size for a sales comparable located in New York City will be *very* different than a 500 square foot adjustment made to a property in Tulsa, Oklahoma.

> *The first point is you have to be very careful not to double dip your comparable sales adjustments.*
> *The second point I want to make is that you don't have to stick to the standard appraisal form layout!!*
> *The next point that I want to make sure you understand is that there are NO set percentages or mathematical formulas used to make adjustments in an appraisal report that apply to all situations!*

Let me explain this further for the readers who are not already experienced real estate appraisers. There are aspects of appraising that you will need to learn in-person from an appraiser in your local area.  That is because each local neighborhood in the country has its own particular aspects that need to be adjusted for to estimate the market value of the subject property. When I say "*neighborhood*", I am not talking about an entire town/city or even a large section of a town. I am referring to only a very precise section of a town/city where the houses have the **same** market conditions.  In many situations, this comprises a distance from the exact location of the subject property of only a few blocks for a metropolitan city or only about one mile for a suburban area. If you went a few miles away from the subject property, let alone going to another town or city, then the market conditions and market value adjustments will usually be very different for an appraisal report. This is why there are no set amounts, percentages, or math formulas used to estimate market value that apply to *every* neighborhood in the country.

Even if someone wrote a book covering specific percentage adjustments to apply in your exact local neighborhood, that book would be outdated as soon as the real estate market conditions change. Since real estate market conditions change constantly, then a book like that would only be helpful for a short time in *your specific neighborhood only.* This is why people have to train to become real estate appraisers. If a book could give you exact adjustment amounts, percentages, or math formulas to apply to all situations, then there would be no need to pay a real estate appraiser. All a bank or home buyer would need to do is plug some numbers into a software program and the software would automatically calculate the market value of the property. That's not *appraising*, that's *science fiction!*

A real estate appraiser is required to use their own training, judgment and experience in their local market when estimating the market value of a property. A computer or mathematical formula does not "think" like a person does, it does not use "judgment" in making decisions like a person does. The reason the Federal government and all States require you to get in-field appraisal training, pass exams to get an appraiser's license, and take continuing education classes, is because they know that a person who can think and reason, based upon their own experience, is required to accurately appraise real estate - not a computer or mathematical formula. Surprisingly, in 2003 some major mortgage lenders began using *electronic appraisals* which are touted as a fast-growing "alternative" to traditional, full-cost appraisals. See Electronic Appraisals section page 93 and You Get What You Pay For section page 388 for more information on why using electronic appraisals is a **huge mistake** for mortgage lenders. "Intelligent" decisions like that may come back to haunt these lenders later with foreclosure loans and enormous financial losses – as it did in the late 1980's.

Let me give you an example using an explanation I gave to a customer who had a very hard time realizing this. This customer was convinced that there **had to be** specific math formulas or percentages to appraise real estate. He said he knew a lot about building and he used an example of a lead water main pipe in a house. *(I gotta tell ya, this guy was a piece of work. He was convinced he was an expert in real estate - yet he had never done an appraisal or home inspection in his life!).* For example, let's say you were a very thorough **"A to Z Appraiser"** and you found a lead water main pipe in a house. You then decided that you wanted to adjust the market value for that in your written appraisal report. Here are a few aspects you would have to evaluate in your appraisal report for that property:

1) Do the sales comparables have lead pipes?  Did you go inside the sales comparables to determine if they have lead pipes? If you ask any appraiser in your area if they go inside the sales comparable homes they use in their reports then you will find the answer is "no". As an appraiser, you cannot go knocking on people's doors and bothering them to assist you with an appraisal report that has nothing to do with them. Since you cannot go into the home for a sales comp, then you have to make a judgment call on whether you think all or some of the sales comps have lead pipes in their homes. Once again, this cannot be done by a computer or mathematical calculation. It is a judgment call by a human being with many years of  appraisal experience that determines this. Is it possible that the local town hall has accurate records indicating whether or not there is a lead pipe in **all** of the sales comps? Yes, it's *possible*. However, is it *probable*? Maybe not, because even if you find something at town hall that states there is a lead water main pipe in some or all of the sales comparables, then my next question to you would be - how do you know that is accurate? For example, there are often errors and discrepancies in data sources. That's a fact of life. People are not perfect, they make mistakes. Often you will find real estate MLS listings, town hall records, etc., which state something that is incorrect. So if you did not go into the homes of the sales comps to see with your own two eyes that there is, or is not, a lead water main pipe, then you would have

to make a judgment call on how much to adjust the market value for this factor in the subject property appraisal report.

2) While we're still on the subject of the lead water main pipe: Let's say you encountered someone and they told you something like *"if you find a lead pipe in the subject property then you have to adjust the market value by .7%"*. This would be an incorrect assumption unless they specifically told you that the .7% was the market value adjustment used in that **exact** neighborhood under the **exact** real estate market conditions for the **"As Of" date of valuation** for the subject property appraisal report. Let me tell you why this is a fact and not an opinion. I don't know what town you live in or what the houses sell for. Nevertheless, I can give you an example for a local neighborhood where I have a lot of appraisal experience. To change a water main pipe that is lead to a copper pipe you have to contact the local water company, town hall, and a licensed plumber. They have to dig up the soil from the street water main line to your house foundation to remove the lead pipe and replace it with a new copper water main pipe. What does that cost in your neighborhood? Does it cost $3,500 - $6,000 depending upon the time involved, length and depth of the soil removal, and difficulty with the new water main pipe installation? If not then you have different prices for this type of work in your neighborhood then another neighborhood in the USA *(which is the same situation for all aspects of real estate appraising)*.

Then my next question: What is the market value of the subject property that has this lead pipe?  Is the market value range of houses in this exact neighborhood between $500,000 and $750,000? If not, then you appraise in a neighborhood that has very different market values than another neighborhood in the USA, where I have experience appraising. On top of that, you can drive about two miles and go from this market value range neighborhood, and arrive in a neighborhood in that same town (Bell Haven in Greenwich, Connecticut) where there are *extremely* high priced homes. Houses located in the Bell Haven neighborhood range from $5,000,000 to $10,000,000 and higher! And that is only a **few miles away** from the other neighborhood in Greenwich, Connecticut. Perhaps where you appraise the neighborhoods don't fluctuate in prices as dramatically. However, the prices definitely change in different neighborhoods, wherever you are located. Therefore, you can see that if someone applied a specific formula to use for every neighborhood in the country then they would be incorrect and their appraisals would not be worth the paper they were written on.

To explain further: For example, let's say you applied a specific formula of .7% in all of your appraisals to adjust for a lead water main pipe when you found one in a subject property. First, you need to determine accurately **if** some or all of the sales comps have lead pipes. Then when you make your cost adjustments, if you apply the .7% adjustment to a $500,000 subject property, then you will see that the adjustment would be $3,500 to replace the lead water main pipe. However, if the subject property had a market value of $750,000 and located in the **same** neighborhood, and you adjusted for a lead pipe using a specific formula of .7% then you would make an adjustment for $5,250 to replace the lead

water main pipe. Now you have the problem of determining *(if you want to use specific formulas and not your judgment and experience)* whether or not you incorrectly assumed that the water main replacement was not a more complicated job. For example, as I explained, if the two properties are not exact in their length from the street water main, the depth of the soil, and the difficulties in replacing the main pipe, then the prices to replace those lead pipes are different even though those two houses ($500,000 and $750,000) are located in the **same** neighborhood. For example, it's possible the water main replacement for the $500,000 house would cost $6,000 to replace and the pipe replacement for the $750,000 house would only cost $3,500 to replace. And these houses are located in the **same** neighborhood, let alone different cities across the USA. Moreover, if you went to the Bell Haven neighborhood, just two miles away, and applied the same .7% cost adjustment, then you can see how drastically incorrect you would be! For example, if you applied the .7% specific formula to a $6,500,000 home for replacing a water main pipe, then your adjustment amount would be **$45,500!!** Obviously it doesn't cost $45,500 to replace a water main pipe – not even in Bell Haven. Now that you can see that there are differences in even this one aspect of appraising real estate in just two neighborhoods, you can now see how impossible it is for any appraisal book or class to give you "specific formulas" that apply to **all** areas of the country for **all** situations.

You also have to remember to round out your adjustment amounts because appraising is not an exact science. For example, you shouldn't use adjustments like $8,739.24 in your report. You should just round out to the nearest $50 or $100 mark, or some other figure, that's used in the local area. So instead of using $8,739.24 in your report, you would use $8,750. Remember, an appraisal is an *estimate* of market value. Appraising is not an exact science and that's why you round out the adjustment figures.

Don't expect to find identical comparable sales on your appraisals. It just doesn't happen, or at least it's a *very* rare occurrence. This is why there are appraisers! If there were identical sales all the time, then the client wouldn't need to hire an appraiser, he could estimate the market value himself. You're the professional. You're the expert with the knowledge of how to compare different houses and make the proper adjustments to estimate market value. Just try to find the best comps you can. By doing this you won't have to exceed the adjustment guidelines to "make a sale work" as a comparable for the subject property. If you send a client an appraisal report with comps that have an abnormally high number of adjustments, then the client is going to wonder if you really took the time to do the field work. If this were the case, don't be surprised if the client sends the report back to you and asks you to find them better comps for the appraisal. There will be times when you can't find very good sales to use as comparables and you'll want to pull your hair out trying to find good comps. Just make that the exception and not the norm by taking the time to know the local market and get all the pertinent data.

Once I did a foreclosure appraisal for a bank on a funeral home. There certainly weren't many recent sales comps of funeral homes to use in the valuation report for the DSCA. If you ever get an appraisal assignment like that, then I'll warn you ahead of time - trying to find comparable sales for a funeral parlor can "kill" you! You may end up *needing* a funeral home for your memorial services after you go out of your mind trying to get good comps for that appraisal!! It was an interesting appraisal assignment since I was surprised to learn that a funeral home/parlor business can be lucrative and bring in a lot of money. *(I guess you could say that their customers are just "dying" to get there to do business with them. Just kidding!)*

---

*When you make adjustments to the comp sales, remember to look at the difference between the subject property and the sale through the eyes of the typical buyer!!*

---

When you make your adjustments to the comparable sales, just remember to look at the difference between the subject property and the sales comps **through the eyes of the typical buyer!!** I want to stress that point. Sometimes appraisers get carried away doing all of the field work, photographs, and math calculations, etc. By doing this, they forget to take a step back and look at the subject and the sales comps the way a typical buyer would. A *typical buyer* refers to someone who has enough income and would be looking to purchase a competitive or similar property in the area, under "arms length" transaction conditions. Just ask yourself before you make any adjustment: *"How would the typical buyer in this local market compensate his purchase price for the difference between these two competing and similar properties?"* Significant differences need to be adjusted for, but very minor items don't really have an affect on market value and don't need to be adjusted for. So be thorough, but don't get carried away and go overboard in your adjustments. If you go too far by making unnecessary or exaggerated adjustments, then you may end up opening a can of worms. This means that the client might bounce the appraisal back in your lap asking for it to be rewritten.

Use your common sense and think about your adjustments. For example, let's say the subject property had a septic system and a well water system. We'll assume that the sales comparables you're using, along with most of the houses in the area, are connected to the municipal water and sewer systems. Since they do not have their own septic and well water systems, you should make an adjustment for this. The logic behind this adjustment would be, that the typical buyer is willing to pay more for a house that is connected to the municipal water and sewer systems. An identical house in the area that has a septic and well system, would not be as appealing as having the home hooked up to the city water and sewer lines. The reason is, if a house is connected to the municipal water and sewer systems, then the homeowner will not have to worry about the costs of maintaining a well water and septic system.

---

*When making adjustments remember that you're comparing the sales to the subject property so don't forget to use the proper plus and minus signs!!!*

---

When making adjustments remember that you're comparing the sales comps to the subject property so **don't forget to use the proper plus and minus signs!!!** I want to stress that point as well. Sometimes appraisers get carried away with all of the field work, the photos, math calculations, etc. When appraisers do this, they forget to properly use the proper plus and minus signs in their adjustment figures for the comparable sales. You have to adjust the sales comparable as though it had the same exact characteristics as the subject property. For example, let's say you're appraising a house that does not have central air-conditioning and does have a two-car garage. One of the sales comparables you're evaluating **does** have central air-conditioning and only has a **one**-car garage. Well, when you make your adjustments next to the sales comp on the appropriate line, you have to remember that the adjustment for the central A/C will have a minus sign. Also, the adjustment for the one-car garage will have a plus sign. The reason for this is that the sales price of the comparable would have been lower if it didn't have central A/C and the sales price would have been higher if the comparable had a two-car garage.

You'll be doing a thorough interior and exterior inspection of the subject property; you'll have photographs; you'll be getting information about the house from the seller, Realtor, or another third party; and you'll also be checking things out at town hall. Therefore, you obviously will have more information and knowledge about the subject property than you will for the comparable sales. You're going to have to make some assumptions about the sales comps when you're evaluating them and making your adjustments. For example, you'll be viewing the operating systems and the interior of the subject property with your own eyes. As a result, you'll know exactly what to write in the report about the condition. Obviously you can't get access to the interior of the comparable sales. As a result, you have to go by whatever information you have on the sales comps and use your own judgment. Just do the best you can with the information you have and always use your common sense. If you have the opportunity to call one of the real estate agents or the owner involved in the sale of the comp, then great! Give them a call and ask them some questions. Just make notes of your conversation and the info you obtained and put it in the written appraisal report.

Please review the sample appraisals included in this book to view examples of the Direct Sales Comparison Approach adjustment process for an actual written appraisal report.

# Guidelines For The Adjustments

I'll go through the basic guidelines for making adjustments to the sales comps. These guidelines are used to assist the appraiser in evaluating comparable sales for an appraisal report.

10% is the maximum adjustment that should be made on the appraisal form for an <u>individual</u> item as compared to the selling price of the sales comparable. This is a **horizontal** adjustment on the form. The 10% does not account for the plus or minus signs in the dollar amount for an adjustment on the form. This means it is the absolute value of the number that is considered. The *absolute value* of a number disregards the plus or minus sign of that number, such as, +/- 10%.

15% is the maximum adjustment that should be made on the appraisal form for all <u>combined</u> items as compared to the selling price of the sales comparable. This is a **vertical** adjustment on the form. The 15% maximum adjustment for all of the combined items does account for the plus or minus signs in the total *dollar* amount. However, the 15% does not account for the plus or minus signs in the total *percentage* amount. This means it is the absolute value of that number.

25% is the maximum overall adjustment that should be made on the appraisal form for all <u>combined</u> items as compared to the selling price of the sales comparable. This is a **vertical** adjustment on the form. However, this differs from the 15% maximum adjustment for all of the combined items. It differs because this adjustment *does not* account for the plus or minus signs in the total dollar adjustment *dollar* amount, as well as in the total *percentage* amount. Meaning that you take the absolute value and disregard all of the plus and minus signs in your adjustment amounts and just add up the numerical amounts.

For example, let's say you had the following six adjustments for a sales comparable that had a recorded selling price of $170,000:

-11,500, +6,250, +3,000, +5,750, -2,750, -9,000

The largest horizontal adjustment would fall below the 10% maximum amount. Remember that this is an absolute value we're considering that does not account for any plus or minus signs:

$11,500/$170,000 = .07   or   7%

The combined vertical adjustment, accounting for the *individual* dollar amount plus or minus sign but disregarding the *total* dollar amount plus or minus sign, would fall below the 15% maximum amount:

-11,500 +6,250 +3,000 +5,750 -2,750 -9,000 = -$8,250

$8,250/$170,000 = .05   or   5%

The combined vertical adjustment, disregarding the *individual* and the *total* dollar amount plus or minus signs, would fall below the 25% maximum amount of the appraisal guidelines:

11,500 + 6,250 + 3,000 + 5,750 + 2,750 + 9,000 = $38,250

$38,250/$170,000 = .23   or   23%

Therefore, we can conclude that this sales comparable may be used on the appraisal form. The reason it can be used is that the adjustments that we deemed necessary for the sales comparison approach, all fall within the recommended percentage guidelines.

Let's take another example of a sales comparable that has adjustments that do not fall within the guidelines of the appraisal form. We'll use the same six adjustments as in our example above for our new sales comparable, but it has a selling price of only $95,000:

-11,500, +6,250, +3,000, +5,750, -2,750, -9,000

The largest horizontal adjustment would fall above the 10% maximum amount. Remember that this is an absolute value we're considering that does not account for any plus or minus signs:

$11,500/$95,000 = .12   or   12%

The combined vertical adjustment, accounting for the *individual* dollar amount plus or minus sign but disregarding the *total* dollar amount plus or minus sign, would fall below the 15% maximum amount:

-11,500 +6,250 +3,000 +5,750 -2,750 -9,000 = -$8,250

$8,250/$95,000 = .09   or   9%

The combined vertical adjustment, disregarding the *individual* and the *total* dollar amount plus or minus signs, would fall above the 25% maximum amount of the appraisal guidelines:

11,500 + 6,250 + 3,000 + 5,750 + 2,750 + 9,000 = $38,250

$38,250/$95,000 = .40   or   40%

Therefore, we can conclude that this sales comparable **should not** be used on the appraisal form. It should not be used because the adjustments that we deemed to be necessary for the sales comparison approach, do not all fall within the recommended percentage guidelines. The 15% maximum adjustment does fall within the guidelines, but the other two adjustments do not. The purpose for these guidelines is to try to help the appraiser to obtain only good comparable sales for the appraisal report. If you have a sales comparable that does not fall within the recommended guidelines, then it should immediately raise a red flag in your mind. The guidelines help you identify sales comparables that should not be used. Some sales should not be used because there may be factors involved in the deal that you can't determine in your adjustments and/or that you're not aware of.

For example, maybe the house was sold to a friend of the family. Another possibility could be that there was some type of tradeoff of services or personal items. A tradeoff of services or other items could lead to a reduction in the sales price between the buyer and seller, etc. Sales with terms and agreements such as these cannot necessarily be detected by the appraiser from the public record. Sometimes you'll find that you have a sales comparable that just doesn't seem right. After you make your adjustments and are reviewing the appraisal, you can see that something's wrong. You may conclude that there may be more to the deal than meets the eye. Therefore, you should not use that sales comparable in your appraisal report. If you don't have extra sales comparables, you will have to wait until you do some more field work to dig-up additional comps to finish writing the appraisal report.

Please review the sample appraisals included in this book to view examples of the Direct Sales Comparison Approach guidelines for the adjustment process for an actual written appraisal report.

# *Electronic Appraisals - Fact or Fiction?*

In 2003 some major mortgage lenders began using *electronic appraisals* which are touted as an "alternative" to traditional, full-cost appraisals. For some mortgages, like refinance loans, the lenders started using these "insured", exterior site-inspected electronic appraisals at deeply-discounted prices. The basic concept of electronic appraisal services is that they tap into large database sources that have comparable sales data throughout the entire country. They can search by criteria location, price, date of sale, etc. to find recent comparable sales that are located near the subject property. Some *(not all)* of these services and/or mortgage lenders follow up the electronic appraisal by sending a Realtor or appraiser to the property for an exterior assessment of the house and the surrounding neighborhood conditions. An exterior checklist must be filled out on-site answering questions about traffic, quality of the property maintenance, and any conditions that could decrease, or increase, the market value of the property.

Some lenders justify the use of these electronic appraisal services because it's much cheaper for them *(about 50% less than paying a trained, qualified appraiser),* and because the turn around time for the finished valuation on the property is a few days instead of a few weeks. Well, the major problem with using electronic appraisals, (as I've already mentioned - see section The Adjustment Process page 88), is that a computer can't **think** nor use **logic, reason,** nor **common sense** based on experience. Only a human being with a brain and many years of training can properly and accurately appraise real estate. Moreover, the Realtor or appraiser sent to

view the exterior of the subject property **does not** go into the interior of the house. They merely view the exterior and the neighborhood. *(Human appraisers are required to view the interior of the **subject property** but not the interior of **sales comps**).* As a result, the electronic appraisal report has no accurate data on the condition, appeal, functional utility, etc. of the **inside** of the subject home. The Realtor or appraiser also are not required to view the sales comps, neither interior nor exterior, that are used in the report. This further severely limits the validity of electronic appraisal service reports. And if that's not enough, these lenders may add insult to injury: If they send a Realtor involved in the deal to do this exterior assessment, then obviously you're going to have a serious conflict of interest! That Realtor will certainly want to make sure the deal goes through so they get their sales commission. The "intelligent" lenders using these low-budget appraisals are stepping over dollars to pick up pennies!! Using electronic appraisals is a **huge mistake** for mortgage lenders. Being **ONLY** concerned about the cost paid for the appraisal report may come back to haunt these lenders later with foreclosure loans and enormous financial losses – as it did in the late 1980's. (See section You Get What You Pay For page 388).

I checked the Internet web sites for some of these electronic appraisal services. This you'll find interesting about how on the one hand these services, and the lenders hiring them, **verbally** market electronic appraisals as being equal to the quality and accuracy of a live, trained, human appraiser. Yet, on the other hand, they use **written** caveats to *Cover Your (their) Assets* in case of lawsuits due to inaccurate property valuations. Here is the wording some of these sites use to describe their services to consumers and the public:

◊ *What are the benefits of your service?* Did you ever wonder what your home was worth or what homes have sold for in your neighborhood? It used to be that only large institutions had access to critical public record information that could be used to determine real estate values. They say knowledge is power, now electronic appraisals put information in your hands and provide a powerful automated valuation analysis. This is the same information used by banks, appraisers and realtors to make lending, valuation and other important decisions.

▫ My comment: Notice the last sentence, *"This is the SAME info used by... important decisions".* So basically what they're trying to convince you of is that electronic appraisal valuations are **EQUAL** to the quality of human created appraiser reports.

◊ *What is an appraisal?* An appraisal is an estimate of a properties fair market value prepared by a licensed professional who takes into consideration many items, including: recent sales of comparable properties, location, home size and a physical inspection. An appraisal may run anywhere from $250-$500.00 or higher and usually takes from 1-3 weeks to prepare. Appraisal standards are set by the Appraisal Institute and are required by lenders under various federal and state banking laws. Our reports are not an appraisal, but an excellent and inexpensive way to help determine value.

□ My comment: Notice the last sentence, *"Our reports are NOT an appraisal, but an excellent... way to help determine market value."* So let me get this straight now because I'm confused. Didn't they just tell me in the prior paragraph that their *"powerful automated valuation analysis"* info is the **SAME** as those used by appraisers, banks, lenders, etc.?

◊ **What is a comparative market analysis?** A comparative market analysis is an unscientific and informal estimate of the market value of a property prepared by a real estate broker/agent based on their knowledge of a particular market area and recent sales of similar properties in that market. Realtors often use this method when advising clients what the listing price of homes for sale should be.

□ My comment: Well, this I have to agree with since it's telling people that the CMA's performed by Realtors are **not** appraisals. *"A CMA is an UNSCIENTIFIC and INFORMAL estimate..."* They must be telling people this to promote the use of electronic appraisals instead of people relying on the Realtor's CMA. If you're in a situation where you can't hire a human appraiser, then I would choose an electronic appraisal instead of a CMA. At least the computer database that creates the electronic appraisal report doesn't **lie, mislead people, or compromise their morals to earn money** – *unlike some Realtors and other third parties.*

◊ **What is an automated valuation analysis?** An automated valuation is what you get when you buy a report from us. We prepare our automated home valuations through a continuously updated nationwide data store of billions of records, we gather specific data on the subject property and then estimate the value of that property in real time. Our valuations are based on comparable sales data, a price and time comparison and a complex valuation engine. Our reports are the most accurate in business, second only to a physical inspection and opinion by a qualified professional. An automated valuation is not an appraisal and no human interaction or inspection is involved in such an analysis; however banks and lenders routinely use such analysis to check the accuracy of appraisals in what is known as the appraisal review process. Further, appraisers and realtors use the same type of information when conducting valuations and market analysis.

□ My comment: OK, so now they've finally 'come out of the closet' and 'spilled the beans' in the fine print! Let's break it down line by line.

□ a) *"We prepare our... valuations through a continuously updated nationwide data store of BILLIONS of records, we gather SPECIFIC DATA on the SUBJECT PROPERTY..."* The 'billions of records' and 'specific data on the subject property' phrases certainly give the impression that these people know **every** important detail about the subject home. It's as though they're practically living there themselves or are relatives of the property owner!

□ b) *"Our reports are the MOST ACCURATE in business, SECOND only to a physical inspection and opinion by a QUALIFIED professional."* They write that their appraisal reports are the 'most accurate' **BUT** they are 'second' to a 'qualified professional'. Well, now wait a second because I'm getting confused again from the mixed messages they're sending. What happened to the 'billions of records' and 'specific data on the subject property' phrases? So now we've got the **real facts** that they put in the written caveats about their service to CYA. They're now admitting that an appraisal report done by a trained, human appraiser with two eyes and a brain is better and more accurate then their computer database with 'billions of records' and 'specific data'. I wonder what the chances are of their salesman verbally explaining this when they are marketing their electronic appraisal services to banks, lenders, consumers, and real estate professionals?

□ c) *"An automated valuation is NOT an appraisal and NO human interaction or INSPECTION is involved in such an analysis..."* There you have it. Straight from the horses mouth! 'An automated valuation IS NOT an appraisal...'. That is a very clear and direct statement in the caveats or fine print. Moreover, it's coming from a service company that some lenders and consumers use since they're led to believe electronic appraisals are as good as a human appraiser's report.

□ d) *"...however banks and lenders routinely use such analysis to check the accuracy of appraisals in what is known as the appraisal review process. Further, appraisers and realtors use the same type of information when conducting valuations and market analysis."* OK, this I will agree with. This is a valid purpose and logical reason to use electronic appraisals. '...routinely use such analysis to check the accuracy of appraisals in what is known as the appraisal review process.' An appraiser, lender, and real estate professional has a **fiduciary responsibility** to do the best job they can when obtaining information to present a report to a client. Using electronic appraisal data to **ASSIST** with an appraisal report, a mortgage loan, appraisal review process, etc. is perfectly fine, and makes a lot of good business sense. An appraiser has to rely on many different data sources to make sure their market value estimate is accurate and reliable. As an appraiser, the data available from an electronic appraisal service can certainly **assist** you with your report, but it cannot do the report for you; nor can it replace you!

◊ **How is the automated valuation analysis limited?** The automated valuation analysis is not an appraisal and no site inspection is completed as part of the process. Excess depreciation or wear and tear as well as property upgrades which are not contained in public record information will not necessarily be reflected in the automated model and the analysis is limited in discerning these types of conditions.

□ My comment: OK, here they're giving you the straight talk without the hype – in the written caveats. They again state that an electronic appraisal, '...*is NOT an appraisal and NO SITE INSPECTION is completed...'.* That's a key problem. It's **NOT** an appraisal and **NO** site inspection is completed. Even the electronic appraisal services that do send someone by for the exterior site inspection of the subject property, do NOT send their inspectors inside the subject home to evaluate the interior. Why is that a major problem with the accuracy of their appraisal reports? Well, I'll let the electronic appraisal service answer and tell you why: *'Excess depreciation or wear and tear as well as property upgrades... will not necessarily be reflected... and the analysis is limited in discerning these types of conditions.'*

◊ **How is our service different from an appraisal or comparative market analysis?** A licensed appraiser certifies to the estimate of value in an appraisal based on a physical inspection during an onsite visit. The automated valuation model is designed to duplicate and take into consideration the same functions as an appraisal but is limited in the things it can discern as noted above. A comparative market analysis is a "guesstimate" of value based on the particular level of expertise possessed by the realtor preparing the analysis and this may lack critical information not available to the realtor at the time. A comparative market analysis lacks the complex valuations analysis that you get when completing a valuation through electronic appraisal services.

▫ My comment: Here again, the problem is stated. a) An electronic appraisal report *'...is LIMITED in the things it can discern as noted above...'*. Yes, it is a limited tool that can **assist** in decision making and estimating market value. But it cannot **replace** a human appraisal report for accuracy.

▫ b) *'A comparative market analysis is a "guesstimate"... and this may lack CRITICAL information...'*. This I agree with. A Realtor CMA is only a ballpark range of the market value estimate of a property done by someone that **does not** have any experience as a licensed appraiser.

▫ c) *'A comparative market analysis lacks the complex valuations analysis that you get when completing a valuation through electronic appraisal services.'* Yes, I agree. An electronic appraisal may be better than a Realtor CMA. However, an electronic appraisal, and/or a CMA, are definitely **NOT** more accurate than an appraisal report done by a trained human appraiser!

OK, so let's recap here. As you can see they tell you **three** times in their written caveats that an electronic appraisal is **not** an appraisal!!! They didn't write it once or twice, but actually three times! Clearly, they're trying to CYA and notify people about that very important fact. So my next question that I would like to ask these electronic appraisal companies is: If it's not an **appraisal**, then why do you market it and call it an "Electronic **Appraisal**"? That is a misleading name because it gives people the impression that you're doing an **appraisal** report. The reason the *National Association of Realtors* doesn't call a CMA a *Comparative Market Appraisal* is because they are well aware that a CMA is not an **appraisal** and it would be misleading to the public if they used that term.

In 2004, there was a State that actually forced these electronic appraisal services to **change their names** and remove the term *"appraisal"* from their service name!! This was because the State appraisal laws do not allow the use of the term "appraisal" for any report or market value estimate **unless the work is done by a State certified/licensed appraiser.** A computer database cannot be a certified/licensed appraiser, but a human being can. As a result, the electronic appraisal services had to remove the word "appraisal" from their names when doing business in that State. It would be great if more States or the Federal government enforced the same laws for the use of the term "appraisal" so consumers would not be misled.

I'm not trying to discredit electronic appraisal services *(you probably find that hard to believe after reading this section).* Electronic appraisals can provide valid and useful services to the real estate profession. I'll repeat what I said earlier to stress the point I'm trying to make: If electronic appraisal information is used to **ASSIST** someone, then that is a valid purpose and logical reason to use electronic appraisal services. '...banks and lenders routinely use such analysis to check the accuracy of appraisals in what is known as the appraisal review process.' An appraiser, lender, and real estate professional has a **fiduciary responsibility** to do the best job they can when obtaining information to present a report to a client. Using electronic appraisal data to **assist** with an appraisal report, a mortgage loan, appraisal review process, etc. is perfectly fine, and makes a lot of good business sense. An appraiser has to rely on many different data sources to make sure their market value estimate is accurate and reliable. As an appraiser, the data available from an electronic appraisal service can certainly **assist** you with your report, but it cannot do the report for you; nor can it replace you!

## Sample Appraisal Reports

You can find a complete set of appraisal report forms and lots of advice on our web site www.nemmar.com.

Single Family Appraisal Report

Northeast Management, Maintenance and Realty, Inc.

# APPRAISAL OF

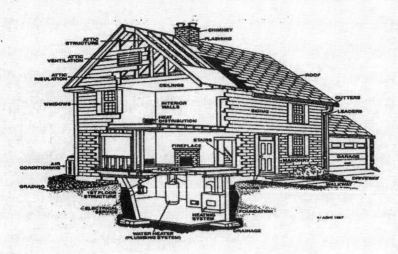

## A SINGLE FAMILY RESIDENCE

**LOCATION** : 42 Beekman Hill Drive
Stillwater, CT  09589

**CLIENT** : Mr. & Mrs. Tom Appleseed for a presale
estimate of market value before listing the home.

**AS OF DATE** : January 6, 1993

This is a sample single family appraisal report used for demonstration purposes only.  It is used to show the reader some of the aspects covered in a real estate appraisal report.  All names, dates, numbers, addresses, etc. are fictitious.  Any similarities to real life individuals or situations is purely coincidental.  This is not a complete appraisal report since the photographs, location map and other data is not included for the sake of brevity.  This report is reproduced with the permission of: *Fannie Mae, Freddie Mac, ASHI,* and *Day One.*  All brand and product names are trademarks of their respective holders.

Northeast Management, Maintenance and Realty, Inc.

Property Description & Analysis **UNIFORM RESIDENTIAL APPRAISAL REPORT**   File No. A9834D92

| | | |
|---|---|---|
| Property Address 42 Beekman Hill Drive | Census Tract | **LENDER DISCRETIONARY USE** |
| City Stillwater   County Rockland   State CT   Zip Code 09589 | | Sale Price $ |
| Legal Description District C, Lot 24, Map 286-247, Block 402 | | Date |
| Owner/Occupant Mr. & Mrs. Tom Appleseed   Map Reference Hagstrom | | Mortgage Amount $ |
| Sale Price $ N/A   Date of Sale 01/06/93 | **PROPERTY RIGHTS APPRAISED** | Mortgage Type |
| Loan charges/concessions to be paid by seller $ N/A   Presale | [X] Fee Simple | Discount Points and Other Concessions |
| R.E. Taxes $ +/- 5,860   Tax Year 1992   HOA $/Mo. N/A | [ ] Leasehold | Paid by Seller $ |
| Lender/Client Mr. & Mrs. Tom Appleseed for a presale | [ ] Condominium (HUD/VA) | |
| estimate of market value before listing the home. | [ ] De Minimis PUD | Source |

| | | | | | |
|---|---|---|---|---|---|
| LOCATION | [ ] Urban | [X] Suburban | [ ] Rural | **NEIGHBORHOOD ANALYSIS** | Good Avg. Fair Poor |
| BUILT UP | [X] Over 75% | [ ] 25-75% | [ ] Under 25% | Employment Stability | [ ] [X] [ ] [ ] |
| GROWTH RATE | [ ] Rapid | [X] Stable | [ ] Slow | Convenience to Employment | [ ] [X] [ ] [ ] |
| PROPERTY VALUES | [ ] Increasing | [X] Stable | [ ] Declining | Convenience to Shopping | [ ] [X] [ ] [ ] |
| DEMAND/SUPPLY | [ ] Shortage | [X] In Balance | [ ] Over Supply | Convenience to Schools | [ ] [X] [ ] [ ] |
| MARKETING TIME | [ ] Under 3 Mos. | [X] 3-6 Mos. | [X] Over 6 Mos. | Adequacy of Public Transportation | [ ] [X] [ ] [ ] |

| PRESENT LAND USE | % | LAND USE CHANGE | | PREDOMINANT | SINGLE FAMILY HOUSING | | NEIGHBORHOOD ANALYSIS | Good Avg Fair Poor |
|---|---|---|---|---|---|---|---|---|
| | | | | | PRICE | AGE | Recreation Facilities | [ ] [X] [ ] [ ] |
| Single Family | 80 | Not Likely | [X] | OCCUPANCY | $ (000) | (yrs) | Adequacy of Utilities | [ ] [X] [ ] [ ] |
| 2-4 Family | | Likely | [ ] | Owner [X] | 350 Low New | | Property Compatibility | [X] [ ] [ ] [ ] |
| Multi-family | | In process | [ ] | Tenant [ ] | 550 High 35 | | Protection from Detrimental Cond. | [ ] [X] [ ] [ ] |
| Commercial | | To: | | Vacant (0-5%) [X] | Predominant | | Police & Fire Protection | [ ] [X] [ ] [ ] |
| Industrial | | | | Vacant (over 5%) [ ] | 475 . 10 | | General Appearance of Properties | [X] [ ] [ ] [ ] |
| Vacant | 20 | | | | | | Appeal to Market | [ ] [X] [ ] [ ] |

Note: Race or the racial composition of the neighborhood are not considered reliable appraisal factors.
COMMENTS: The subject neighborhood is located by the Westchester County line about 3 miles north of the Merritt Parkway. The area consists of mostly Colonial & Contemporary style dwellings. The subject neighborhood maintenance level is judged to be good. Most of the homes are newer construction.

| | | | |
|---|---|---|---|
| Dimensions +/- 296.8 x 175-195 feet | | Topography | Gently Rolling |
| Site Area +/- 1.2 Acres   Corner Lot No | | Size | Typical For Area |
| Zoning Classification R A-1, 1 Acre Single Fam   Zoning Compliance Yes | | Shape | Irregular |
| HIGHEST & BEST USE: Present Use Yes   Other Use No | | Drainage | Fair, pond next to home |

| UTILITIES | Public | Other | SITE IMPROVEMENTS | Type | Public | Private | View | Average |
|---|---|---|---|---|---|---|---|---|
| Electricity | [X] | 200 Amp CB | Street | Asphalt Paved | [X] | [ ] | Landscaping | Good |
| Gas | [ ] | None | Curb/Gutter | Asphalt | [X] | [ ] | Driveway | Gravel/Fair |
| Water | [ ] | Privat Well | Sidewalk | None | [ ] | [ ] | Apparent Easements | Yes, for pond maint |
| Sanitary Sewer | [ ] | Septic Sys. | Street Lights | None | [ ] | [ ] | FEMA Flood Hazard Yes* [ ] No XX |
| Storm Sewer | [ ] | | Alley | None | [ ] | [ ] | FEMA* Map/Zone | 090015 0002 B, Zn C |

COMMENTS (Apparent adverse easements, encroachments, special assessments, slide areas, etc.): Flood Map dated 01/16/81. Site is a typical suburban lot for this neighborhood. No known encroachments. There is an easement listed on the deed for repairs and maintenance to the pond and retaining walls.

| GENERAL DESCRIPTION | | EXTERIOR DESCRIPTION | | FOUNDATION | | BASEMENT | | INSULATION | |
|---|---|---|---|---|---|---|---|---|---|
| Units | 1 | Foundation | Concrete Block | Slab | No | Area Sq.Ft. | 400 | Roof None | [ ] |
| Stories | 2.5 | Exterior Walls | Wood Clapboard | Crawl Space | Part | % Finished | 100 | Ceiling Good | [X] |
| Type (Det./Att.) | Detached | Roof Surface | Asphalt Shingl | Basement | Part | Ceiling Sheetrock | | Walls Good | [X] |
| Design (Style) | Contemporary | Gutters & Dwnspts. | Aluminum | Sump Pump | None Noted | Walls Sheetrock | | Floor Good | [X] |
| Existing | Yes | Windows Type | Alum/Thermal | Dampness | Not in home | Floor Carpeting | | None | |
| Proposed | No | Storm Sash | Thermal Units | Settlement | Normal | Outside Entry Yes, | | Adequacy Good | [X] |
| Under Construction | No | Screens | Yes | Infestation | None Noted | Permits and | | Energy Efficient Items: | |
| Age (Yrs.) | +/- 10 | Manufactured House | No | | | approvals are | | Thermal | |
| Effective Age (Yrs.) | 2 | | | | | needed for finish | | Windows | |

| ROOMS | Foyer | Living | Dining | Kitchen | Den | Family Rm. | Rec. Rm. | Bedroom | # Baths | Laundry | Other | Area Sq. Ft. |
|---|---|---|---|---|---|---|---|---|---|---|---|---|
| Basement | | | | | 1 | | | | | | | +/- 400 |
| Level 1 | 1 | 1 | 1 | 1 | | | | | .5 | | | 1,438 |
| Level 2 | | | | | | | | 2 | 1 | 1 | | 468 |
| 3rd | | | | | | | | 1 | 1 | | | 1,078 |

Finished area above grade contains: 8 Rooms; 3 Bedroom(s); 2.5 Bath(s); 2,984 Square Feet of Gross Living Area.

| SURFACES | Materials/Condition | HEATING | | KITCHEN EQUIP. | | ATTIC | | IMPROVEMENT ANALYSIS | Good Avg. Fair Poor |
|---|---|---|---|---|---|---|---|---|---|
| Floors | Carpet/Good | Type F Hot Air | Refrigerator [X] | None | [ ] | | | Quality of Construction | [X] [ ] [ ] [ ] |
| Walls | Drywall/Good | Fuel Oil | Range/Oven [X] | Stairs | [ ] | | | Condition of Improvements | [X] [ ] [ ] [ ] |
| Trim/Finish | Softwood/Good | Condition Good | Disposal [X] | Drop Stair | [X] | | | Room Sizes/Layout | [X] [ ] [ ] [ ] |
| Bath Floor | Marble/Good | Adequacy Good | Dishwasher [X] | Scuttle | [ ] | | | Closets and Storage | [X] [ ] [ ] [ ] |
| Bath Wainscot | Marble/Good | COOLING | Fan/Hood [ ] | Floor | [ ] | | | Energy Efficiency | [X] [ ] [ ] [ ] |
| Doors | Hollow Wood/Average | Central Yes | Compactor [ ] | Heated | [ ] | | | Plumbing-Adequacy & Condition | [X] [ ] [ ] [ ] |
| | | Other None | Washer/Dryer [X] | Finished | [ ] | | | Electrical-Adequacy & Condition | [X] [ ] [ ] [ ] |
| Fireplace(s) Brick / 1 | | Condition Good | Microwave [X] | Storage | [X] | | | Kitchen Cabinets-Adequacy & Cond. | [X] [ ] [ ] [ ] |
| | | Adequacy N/Test | Intercom [ ] | | | | | Compatibility to Neighborhood | [X] [ ] [ ] [ ] |
| CAR STORAGE: | Garage [X] | Attached [ ] | Adequate [X] | House Entry [X] | | | | Appeal & Marketability | [X] [ ] [ ] [ ] |
| No. Cars 2 | Carport [ ] | Detached [ ] | Inadequate [ ] | Outside Entry [X] | | | | Estimated Remaining Economic Life | 95 Yrs. |
| Condition Good | None [ ] | Built-In [X] | Electric Door [X] | Basement Entry [X] | | | | Estimated Remaining Physical Life | N/A Yrs. |

Additional features: Marble in baths and new fixtures installed, flagstone patio, new carpeting, finished lower level, driveway lighting, water softener, central vacuum, cedar closet, security system, sump pump alarm, jacuzzi with large master bathroom, 2 decks.

Depreciation (Physical, functional and external inadequacies, repairs needed, modernization, etc.): Physical: Subject is judged to be about 2% depreciated using the Age/Life Method. There are no significant functional or external inadequacies noted. Large living room windows need child guards for safety, upper deck has rotted boards, handrails needed for exterior walks, metal brackets needed for deck supports.

General market conditions and prevalence and impact in subject/market area regarding loan discounts, interest buydowns and concessions: Market Values have begun to stabiliz in some areas after a long period of decline. Buydowns and concessions are not common in pre-owned homes. Many lenders are being very conservative with their lending policies.

Freddie Mac Form 70  10/86  12 CPI                                                                Fannie Mae Form 1004  10/86

Valuation Section

## UNIFORM RESIDENTIAL APPRAISAL REPORT

File No. A9834D92

Purpose of Appraisal is to estimate Market Value as defined in Certification & Statement of Limiting Conditions.

| BUILDING SKETCH (SHOW GROSS LIVING AREA ABOVE GRADE) If for Freddie Mac/Fannie Mae, show only square foot calculations & cost approach comments. | ESTIMATED REPRODUCTION COST - NEW - OF IMPROVEMENTS: | | |
|---|---|---|---|

ESTIMATED REPRODUCTION COST - NEW - OF IMPROVEMENTS:

| | | | |
|---|---|---|---|
| Dwelling | 2,584 Sq. Ft. @ $ 90.00 | = $ | 232,560 |
| Bsmnt | 400 Sq. Ft. @ $ 70.00 | = | 28,000 |
| Extras | Jacuzzi, Marble baths | = | 15,000 |
| | Alarm Sys, Central Vac, etc | = | 12,500 |
| Special Energy Efficient Items | | | |
| Porches, Patios, etc. | 2 Decks | = | 10,000 |
| Garage/Carport | 530 Sq. Ft. @ $ 25.00 | = | 13,250 |
| Total Estimated Cost New | | = $ | 311,310 |

The site value represents 42% of the total value

| | Physical | Functional | External | | |
|---|---|---|---|---|---|
| Less 2% Depreciation | 6,300 | | | = $ | 6,300 |
| Depreciated Value of Improvements | | | | = $ | 305,010 |
| Site Imp. "as is" (driveway, landscaping, etc.) | | | | = $ | |
| ESTIMATED SITE VALUE | | | | = $ | 205,000 |
| (If leasehold, show only leasehold value.) | | | | | |
| INDICATED VALUE BY COST APPROACH | | | | = $ | 510,010 |

(Not Required by Freddie Mac and Fannie Mae)

Does property conform to applicable HUD/VA property standards? ☐ Yes ☐ No

If No, explain: _____

Construction Warranty ☐ Yes ☐ No _____

Name of Warranty Program _____

Warranty Coverage Expires _____

The undersigned has recited three recent sales of properties most similar and proximate to subject and has considered these in the market analysis. The description includes a dollar adjustment, reflecting market reaction to those items of significant variation between the subject and comparable properties. If a significant item in the comparable property is superior to, or more favorable than, the subject property, a minus (-) adjustment is made, thus reducing the indicated value of subject; if a significant item in the comparable property is inferior to, or less favorable than, the subject property, a plus (+) adjustment is made, thus increasing the indicated value of the subject.

| ITEM | SUBJECT | COMPARABLE NO. 1 | | COMPARABLE NO. 2 | | COMPARABLE NO. 3 | |
|---|---|---|---|---|---|---|---|
| Address | 42 Beekman Hill D Stillwater, CT | 280 Beekman Hill Dr. Stillwater, CT | | 98 Beekman Hill Dr. Stillwater, CT | | 30 Beekman Hill Dr. Stillwater, CT | |
| Proximity to Subject | | 1 block | | 1 block | | 250 feet | |
| Sales Price | $ N/A | $ 545,000 | | $ 475,000 | | $ 515,000 | |
| Price/Gross Liv. Area | $ 0.00 ☑ | $ 136.25 ☑ | | $ 143.94 ☑ | | $ 180.70 ☑ | |
| Data Source | Inspection | MLS / RE Broker | | MLS / RE Broker | | MLS / RE Broker | |
| VALUE ADJUSTMENTS | DESCRIPTION | DESCRIPTION | +(-)$ Adjustment | DESCRIPTION | +(-)$ Adjustment | DESCRIPTION | +(-)$ Adjustment |
| Sales or Financing Concessions | | None Known | | None Known | | None Known | |
| Date of Sale/Time | 01/06/93 | 07/24/92 | | 05/01/92 | | 04/30/92 | |
| Location | Average | Average | | Average | | Average | |
| Site/View | +/- 1.2/Aver | +/- 1.0 A/Av | | +/- 1.2 A/Av | | +/- 1.2 A/Av | |
| Design and Appeal | Contemp/Good | Contemp/Good | | Colonial/Avg | 10,000 | Contemp/Good | |
| Quality of Construction | Frame/Good | Frame/Good | | Frame/Good | | Frame/Good | |
| Age | 1983 | 1979 | | 1980 | | 1986 | |
| Condition | Good | Good | | Good | | Good | |
| Above Grade Room Count | Total 8 / Bdrms 3 / Baths 2.5 | Total 8 / Bdrms 4 / Baths 3 | -1,500 | Total 9 / Bdrms 3 / Baths 4 | -3,000 | Total 8 / Bdrms 3 / Baths 3.5 | -2,000 |
| Gross Living Area | 2,984 Sq. Ft. | 4,000 Sq. Ft. | -30,480 | 3,300 Sq. Ft. | -9,480 | 2,850 Sq. Ft. | 4,020 |
| Basement & Finished Rooms Below Grade | Part Finished | Part Finished | | Full Finished | | Full Unfinished | 3,000 |
| Functional Utility | Average | Share Drvway | 15,000 | Average | | Share Drvway | 8,000 |
| Heating/Cooling | FHA/Central | FHA/Central | | FHA/Central | | FHA/Central | |
| Garage/Carport | 2 Car Attach | 2 Car Attach | | 2 Car Attach | | 2 Car Attach | |
| Porches, Patio, Pools, etc. | 2 Deck, Alrm Marble, HTub | Patio, Deck Alarm System | 5,000 | Deck, Terrac Alarm System | 5,000 | Deck, Patio Alarm System | 5,000 |
| Special Energy Efficient Items | Good Efficiency | Good Efficiency | | Good Efficiency | | Good Efficiency | |
| Fireplace(s) | One | Two | -1,500 | One | | One | |
| Other (e.g. kitchen equip., remodeling) | Modern Kitchen | Modern Kitchen | | Modern Kitchen | | Modern Kitchen | |
| Net Adj. (total) | | ☐ + ☑ - $ | -13,480 | ☑ + ☐ - $ | 2,520 | ☑ + ☐ - $ | 18,020 |
| Indicated Value of Subject | | -2 %Net 10 %Gr $ | 531,520 | .53 %Net 6 %Gr $ | 477,520 | 3.5 %Net 4 %Gr $ | 533,020 |

Comments on Sales Comparison: See attached sheet.

| | |
|---|---|
| INDICATED VALUE BY SALES COMPARISON APPROACH | $ 485,000 |
| INDICATED VALUE BY INCOME APPROACH (If Applicable) Estimated Market Rent $ N/A /Mo. x Gross Rent Multiplier N/A = $ | 0 |

This appraisal is made ☑ "as is" ☐ subject to the repairs, alterations, inspections or conditions listed below ☐ completion per plans and specifications.

Comments and Conditions of Appraisal: The income approach is not applicable due to the lack of sales/rental data.

Final Reconciliation: The sales comparison analysis is the most reliable approach as it reflects the actions of buyers and sellers in the marketplace.

This appraisal is based upon the above requirements, the certification, contingent and limiting conditions, and Market Value definition that are stated in

☐ FmHA, HUD &/or VA instructions.

☑ Freddie Mac Form 439 (Rev.7/86) / Fannie Mae Form 1004B (Rev.7/86) filed with client _____ 19___ ☑ attached.

I (WE) ESTIMATE THE MARKET VALUE, AS DEFINED, OF THE SUBJECT PROPERTY AS OF January 6 19 93 to be $ 485,000

I (We) certify: that to the best of my (our) knowledge and belief the facts and data used herein are true and correct; that I (we) personally inspected the subject property, both inside and out, and have made an exterior inspection of all comparable sales cited in this report; and that I (we) have no undisclosed interest, present or prospective therein.

APPRAISER(S)  REVIEW APPRAISER

Signature _____  (If applicable) Signature _____ ☐ Did ☐ Did Not

Name Harry Simpson  Name _____ Inspect Property

Freddie Mac Form 70  10/86  12 CPI  LaserForm Software by DAY ONE, Inc. 1987  Fannie Mae Form 1004  10/86

File No. A9834D92

These recent sales of properties most similar and proximate to subject have been considered in the market analysis. The description includes a dollar adjustment, reflecting market reaction to those items of significant variation between the subject and comparable properties. If a significant item in the comparable property is superior to, or more favorable than, the subject property, a minus(-) adjustment is made, thus reducing the indicated value of subject; if a significant item in the comparable is inferior to, or less favorable than, the subject property, a plus(+) adjustment is made, thus increasing the indicated value of the subject.

| ITEM | SUBJECT | COMPARABLE NO. 4 | +(-)$ Adjustment | COMPARABLE NO. 5 | +(-)$ Adjustment | COMPARABLE NO. 6 | +(-)$ Adjustment |
|---|---|---|---|---|---|---|---|
| Address | 42 Beekman Hill D Stillwater, CT | 66 Beekman Hill Dr. Stillwater, CT | | 102 Spring Lane Stillwater, CT | | 723 Milton Avenue Stillwater, CT | |
| Proximity to Subject | | 250 feet | | 2 blocks | | 3 blocks | |
| Sale Price | $ N/A | $ 412,500 | | $ 421,000 | | $ 483,000 | |
| Price/Gross Liv. Area | $ 0.00 | $ 165.00 | | $ 120.29 | | $ 182.26 | |
| Data Source | Inspection | MLS / RE Broker | | MLS / RE Broker | | MLS / RE Broker | |
| VALUE ADJUSTMENTS | DESCRIPTION | DESCRIPTION | | DESCRIPTION | | DESCRIPTION | |
| Sales or Financing Concessions | | None Known | | None Known | | None Known | |
| Date of Sale / Time | 01/06/93 | 12/21/92 | | 12/18/92 | | 09/18/92 | |
| Location | Average | Average | | Average | | Average | |
| Site / View | +/- 1.2/Aver | +/- 1.1 A/Av | | +/- 1.2 A/Av | | +/- 1.0 A/Av | |
| Design and Appeal | Contemp/Good | Ranch/Avg | 10,000 | Colonial/Avg | 8,000 | Contemp/Good | |
| Quality of Construction | Frame/Good | Frame/Good | | Frame/Good | | Frame/Good | |
| Age | 1983 | 1968 | 25,000 | 1964 | 25,000 | +/- 1980 | |
| Condition | Good | Good | | Good | | Good | |
| Above Grade Room Count | Total 8 / Bdrms 3 / Baths 2.5 | Total 8 / Bdrms 3 / Baths 2.5 | | Total 8 / Bdrms 3 / Baths 3.5 | -2,000 | Total 7 / Bdrms 3 / Baths 2.5 | |
| Gross Living Area | 2,984 Sq.Ft. | 2,500 Sq.Ft. | 14,520 | 3,500 Sq.Ft. | -15,480 | 2,650 Sq.Ft. | 10,020 |
| Basement & Finished Rooms Below Grade | Part Finished | Full Finished | | Full Unfinished | 3,000 | Full Unfinished | 3,000 |
| Functional Utility | Average | Average | | Average | | Average | |
| Heating / Cooling | FHA/Central | HW/Central | | FHA/Central | | FHA/Central | |
| Garage / Carport | 2 Car Attach | 2 Car Attach | | 1 Car | 4,000 | 2 Car Attach | |
| Porches, Patio, Pools, etc. | 2 Deck, Alrm Marble, HTub | Porch, Patio Alarm System | 5,000 | Patio, Alarm System | 10,000 | Similar to subject prop | |
| Special Energy Efficient Items | Good Efficiency | Average Efficiency | 3,500 | Average Efficiency | 3,500 | Good Efficiency | |
| Fireplace(s) | One | One | | Two | -1,500 | One | |
| Other (e.g. kitchen equip., remodeling) | Modern Kitchen | Modern Kitchen | | Modern Kitchen | | Modern Kitchen | |
| Net Adj. (total) | | [X]+ []- | $ 58,020 | [X]+ []- | $ 34,520 | [X]+ []- | $ 13,020 |
| Indicated Value of Subject | | 14 %Net / 14 %Grs | $ 470,520 | 8.2 %Net / 17 %Grs | $ 455,520 | 2.7 %Net / 3 %Grs | $ 496,020 |

Comments on Market Data

Sales 2, 4 & 5 were judged to be slightly less appealing and adjusted accordingly. Age adjustments were deemed necessary for sales 4 & 5. The condition for these older houses was accounted for in the age adjustment.
Sales 1 & 3 were adjusted for having a common driveway with one and two neighbors. The gross living area adjustments are based upon about $30.00 per square foot.

In this appraisal assignment, the existence of potentially hazardous material used in the construction or maintenance of the building, such as the presence of Urea-formaldehyde foam insulation, asbestos, underground oil tanks and/or the existence of toxic waster or radon gas, which may or may not be present on the subject property, was not observed by the appraiser, nor do I have any knowledge of the existence of such materials on or in the property. The appraiser is not hired, required and/or qualified to detect such substances. The existence of Urea-formaldehyde insulation, asbestos, underground oil tanks, radon gas or other potentially hazardous waste mterial may have an effect on the value of the property. It is our opinion, that the client should retain an expert in this field if desired or any doubts exist.

## SUBJECT PHOTOGRAPH ADDENDUM

| | |
|---|---|
| Borrower Client | Mr. & Mrs. Tom Appleseed |
| Property Address | 42 Beekman Hill Drive |

| City | Stillwater | County | Rockland | State | CT | Zip Code | 09589 |
|---|---|---|---|---|---|---|---|

| | |
|---|---|
| Lender | Mr. & Mrs. Tom Appleseed for a presale |

**FRONT OF
SUBJECT PROPERTY**

**REAR OF
SUBJECT PROPERTY**

**STREET SCENE**

## COMPARABLES PHOTOGRAPH ADDENDUM

Borrower Client     Mr. & Mrs. Tom Appleseed

Property Address    42 Beekman Hill Drive

City     Stillwater          County  Rockland          State  CT     Zip Code  09589

Lender     Mr. & Mrs. Tom Appleseed for a presale

**COMPARABLE SALE # 1**

**280 Beekman Hill Dr.**
Date of Sale: 07/24/92
Sale Price  : 545,000
Sq. Ft.     : 4,000
$ / Sq. Ft. : 136.25

**COMPARABLE SALE # 2**

**98 Beekman Hill Dr.**
Date of Sale: 05/01/92
Sale Price  : 475,000
Sq. Ft.     : 3,300
$ / Sq. Ft. : 143.94

**COMPARABLE SALE # 3**

**30 Beekman Hill Dr.**
Date of Sale: 04/30/92
Sale Price  : 515,000
Sq. Ft.     : 2,850
$ / Sq. Ft. : 180.70

## COMPARABLES 4 5 6 PHOTOGRAPH ADDENDUM

| | |
|---|---|
| Borrower Client | Mr. & Mrs. Tom Appleseed |
| Property Address | 42 Beekman Hill Drive |
| City | Stillwater   County Rockland   State CT   Zip Code 09589 |
| Lender | Mr. & Mrs. Tom Appleseed for a presale |

**COMPARABLE SALE # 4**

**66 Beekman Hill Dr.**
Date of Sale: 12/21/92
Sale Price : 412,500
Sq. Ft. : 2,500
$ / Sq. Ft. : 165.00

**COMPARABLE SALE # 5**

**102 Spring Lane**
Date of Sale: 12/18/92
Sale Price : 421,000
Sq. Ft. : 3,500
$ / Sq. Ft. : 120.29

**COMPARABLE SALE # 6**

**723 Milton Avenue**
Date of Sale: 09/18/92
Sale Price : 483,000
Sq. Ft. : 2,650
$ / Sq. Ft. : 182.26

## Location Map

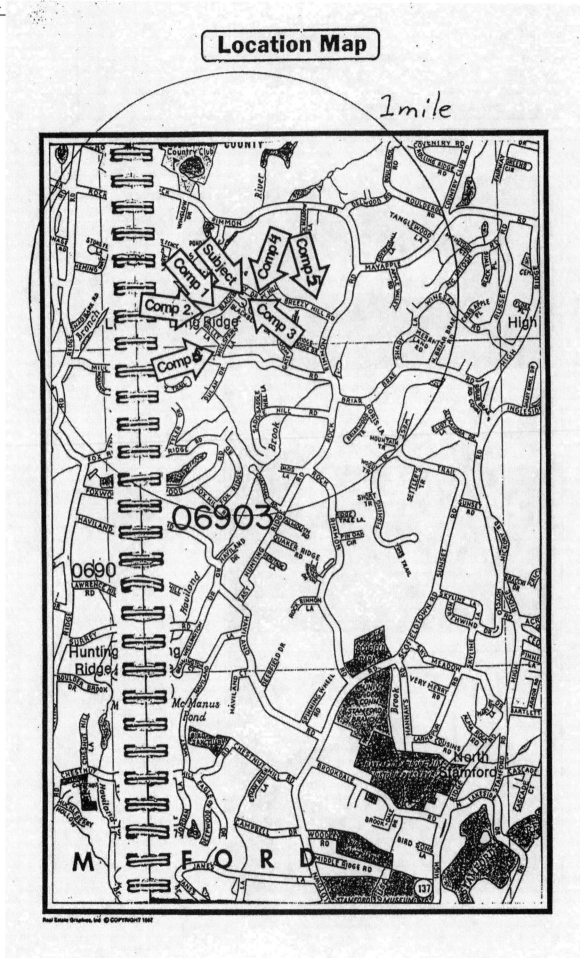

Borrower Name: **Mr. & Mrs. Tom Appleseed**         File No. **A9834D92**

**DEFINITION OF MARKET VALUE :**     The most probable price which a property should bring in a competitive and open market under all conditions requisite to a fair sale, the buyer and seller, each acting prudently, knowledgeably and assuming the price is not affected by undue stimulus. Implicit in this definition is the consummation of a sale as of a specified date and the passing of title from seller to buyer under conditions whereby: (1) buyer and seller are typically motivated; (2) both parties are well informed or well advised, and each acting in what he considers his own best interest; (3) a reasonable time is allowed for exposure in the open market; (4) payment is made in terms of U.S. dollars or in terms of financial arrangements comparable thereto; and (5) the price represents the normal consideration for the property sold unaffected by special or creative financing or sales concessions* granted by anyone associated with the sale.

*Adjustments to the comparables must be made for special or creative financing or sales concessions. No adjustments are necessary for those costs which are normally paid by sellers as a result of tradition or law in a market area; these costs are readily identifiable since the seller pays these costs in virtually all sales transactions. Special or creative financing adjustments can be made to the comparable property by comparisons to financing terms offered by a third party institutional lender that is not already involved in the property or transaction. Any adjustment should not be calculated on a mechanical dollar for dollar cost of the financing or concession, but the dollar amount of any adjustment should approximate the market's reaction to the financing or concessions based on the appraiser's judgment.

## CERTIFICATION AND STATEMENT OF LIMITING CONDITIONS

CERTIFICATION:     The Appraiser certifies and agrees that:

1. The Appraiser has no present or contemplated future interest in the property appraised; and neither the employment to make the appraisal, nor the compensation for it, is contingent upon the appraised value of the property.

2. The Appraiser has no personal interest in or bias with respect to the subject matter of the appraisal report or the participants to the sale. The "Estimate of Market Value" in the appraisal report is not based in whole or in part upon the race, color, or national origin of the prospective owners or occupants of the property appraised, or upon the race, color or national origin of the present owners or occupants of the properties in the vicinity of the property appraised.

3. The Appraiser has personally inspected the property, both inside and out, and has made an exterior inspection of all comparable sales listed in the report. To the best of the Appraiser's knowledge and belief, all statements and information in this report are true and correct, and the Appraiser has not knowingly withheld any significant information.

4. All contingent and limiting conditions are contained herein (imposed by the terms of the assignment or by the undersigned affecting the analyses, opinions, and conclusions contained in the report).

5. This appraisal report has been made in conformity with and is subject to the requirements of the Code of Professional Ethics and Standards of Professional Conduct of the appraisal organizations with which the Appraiser is affiliated.

6. All conclusions and opinions concerning the real estate that are set forth in the appraisal report were prepared by the Appraiser whose signature appears on the appraisal report, unless indicated as "Review Appraiser." No change of any item in the appraisal report shall be made by anyone other than the Appraiser, and the Appraiser shall have no responsibility for any such unauthorized change.

**CONTINGENT AND LIMITING CONDITIONS:**     The certification of the Appraiser appearing in the appraisal report is subject to the following conditions and to such other specific and limiting conditions as are set forth by the Appraiser in the report.

1. The Appraiser assumes no responsibility for matters of a legal nature affecting the property appraised or the title thereto, nor does the Appraiser render any opinion as to the title, which is assumed to be good and marketable. The property is appraised as though under responsible ownership.

2. Any sketch in the report may show approximate dimensions and is included to assist the reader in visualizing the property. The Appraiser has made no survey of the property.

3. The Appraiser is not required to give testimony or appear in court because of having made the appraisal with reference to the property in question, unless arrangements have been previously made therefor.

4. Any distribution of the valuation in the report between land and improvements applies only under the existing program of utilization. The separate valuation for land and building must not be used in conjunction with any other appraisal and are invalid if so used.

5. The Appraiser assumes that there are no hidden or unapparent conditions of the property, subsoil, or structures, which would render it more or less valuable. The Appraiser assumes no responsibility for such conditions, or for engineering which might be required to discover such factors.

6. Information, estimates, and opinions furnished to the Appraiser, and contained in the report, were obtained from sources considered reliable and believed to be true and correct. However, no responsibility for accuracy of such items furnished the Appraiser can be assumed by the Appraiser.

7. Disclosure of the contents of the appraisal report is governed by the Bylaws and Regulations of the professional appraisal organizations with which the Appraiser is affiliated.

8. Neither all, nor any part of the content of the report, or copy thereof (including conclusions as to the property value, the identity of the Appraiser, professional designations, reference to any professional appraisal organizations, or the firm with which the Appraiser is connected), shall be used for any purposes by anyone but the client specified in the report , the borrower if appraisal fee paid by same, the mortgagee or its successors and assigns, mortgage insurers, consultants, professional appraisal organizations, any state or federally approved financial institution, any department, agency, or instrumentality of the United States of any state or the District of Columbia, without the previous written consent of the Appraiser; nor shall it be conveyed by anyone to the public through advertising, public relations, news, sales, or other media, without the written consent and approval of the Appraiser.

9. On all appraisals, subject to satisfactory completion, repairs, or alterations, the appraisal report and value conclusion are contingent upon completion of the improvements in a workmanlike manner.

**ENVIRONMENTAL DISCLAIMER:** The value estimated in this report is based on the assumption that the property is not negatively affected by the existence of hazardous substances or detrimental environmental conditions. The Appraiser is not an expert in the identification of hazardous substances or detrimental environmental conditions. The Appraiser's routine inspection of and inquiries about the subject property did not develop any information that indicated any apparent significant hazardous substances or detrimental environmental conditions which would affect the property negatively unless otherwise stated in this report. It is possible that tests and inspections made by a qualified hazardous substance and environmental expert would reveal the existence of hazardous substances or detrimental environmental conditions on or around the property that would negatively affect its value. The Appraiser assumes no responsibility for the presence of radon gas, as the Appraiser has no expertise in this area.

Date **January 6, 1993**          Signature: _____

                                          **Harry Simpson**

# Sample
# Condo / Co-Op
# Appraisal Report

# APPRAISAL OF

# A CONDOMINIUM

**LOCATION** : 162 82nd Street
Union, NY 11203

**CLIENT** : Richmond Savings Bank
27 Main Street, Oakdale, NY

**AS OF DATE** : April 5, 1992

**APPRAISER** : Steve Smith

**Northeast Management, Maintenance and Realty, Inc.**
**APPRAISAL REPORT - INDIVIDUAL** ☐ CONDOMINIUM OR ☐ PUD UNIT          File No. A0238D92

| | |
|---|---|
| Borrower **Stephen Jones** | Census Tract **0036**  Map Reference **HAG22A16** |
| Unit No. **E-27**  Address **162 82nd Street** | Project Name/Phase No. **Ridge Hill** |
| City **Union**  County **Oakdale** | State **NY**  Zip Code **11203** |

Actual Real Estate Taxes $ **Incl in maint.** (yr.) Sale Price $ **58,000** Property Rights Appraised ☐ Fee ☒ Leasehold
Loan charges to be paid by seller $ **N/A** Other sales concessions **N/A**
Lender/Client **Richmond Savings Bank** Lender's Address **27 Main Street, Oakdale, NY**
Occupant **Occupied** Appraiser _____ Instructions to Appraiser **Estimate market value**
☐ FNMA 1073A required   ☐ FHLMC 465 Addendum A required   ☐ FHLMC 465 Addendum B required

### NEIGHBORHOOD

| | | | | NEIGHBORHOOD RATING | Good | Avg. | Fair | Poor |
|---|---|---|---|---|---|---|---|---|
| Location | ☒ Urban | ☐ Suburban | ☐ Rural | Adequacy of Shopping | ☐ | ☒ | ☐ | ☐ |
| Built up | ☒ Over 75% | ☐ 25% to 75% | ☐ Under 25% | Employment Opportunities | ☐ | ☒ | ☐ | ☐ |
| Growth Rate | ☒ Fully Developed | ☐ Rapid | ☐ Steady ☐ Slow | Recreational Facilities | ☒ | ☐ | ☐ | ☐ |
| Property Values | ☐ Increasing | ☒ Stable | ☒ Declining | Adequacy of Utilities | ☐ | ☒ | ☐ | ☐ |
| Demand/Supply | ☐ Shortage | ☒ In Balance | ☒ Oversupply | Property Compatibility | ☒ | ☐ | ☐ | ☐ |
| Marketing Time | ☐ Under 3 Mos. | ☒ 4-6 Mos. | ☒ Over 6 Mos. | Protection from Detrimental Conditions | ☒ | ☐ | ☐ | ☐ |

Present Land Use **25** % 1 Family **40** % 2-4 Family **15** % Apts **15** % Condo          Police and Fire Protection ☐ ☒ ☐ ☐
**5** % Commercial ___ % Industrial ___ % Vacant          General Appearance of Properties ☒ ☐ ☐ ☐
Change in Present Land Use ☒ Not Likely ☐ Likely ☐ Taking Place*          Appeal to Market ☒ ☐ ☐ ☐
*From ___ To ___

| | | | | | | Distance | Access or Convenience |
|---|---|---|---|---|---|---|---|
| Predominant Occupancy | ☒ Owner | ☐ Tenant | ___ % Vacant | | | | |
| Condominium: | Price Range $ **35,000** to $ **125,000** Predominant $ **60,000** | | | Public Transportation | | **1 blk** | ☐ ☒ ☐ ☐ |
| | Age **25** yrs. to **75** yrs. Predominant **50** yrs. | | | Employment Centers | | **NYC** | ☐ ☒ ☐ ☐ |
| Single Family: | Price Range $ **125,000** to $ **325,000** Predominant $ **200,000** | | | Neighborhood Shopping | | **3 blks** | ☐ ☒ ☐ ☐ |
| | Age **50** yrs. to **100** yrs. Predominant **65** yrs. | | | Grammar Schools | | **.25 mi** | ☐ ☒ ☐ ☐ |

Describe potential for additional Condo/PUD units in nearby area **Additional Co-Ops may**          Freeway Access **6 blks** ☐ ☒ ☐ ☐
**not be feasible at this time due to the poor Co-Operative market. The area appears to be fully**
Note: FHLMC/FNMA do not consider race or the racial composition of the neighborhood to be reliable appraisal factors. **developed.**
Describe those factors, favorable or unfavorable, affecting marketability (e.g. public parks, schools, noise, view, mkt. area, population size, financial ability). **The subject**
**neighborhood is located along the Narrows Lower Bay shoreline, one mile north of the Fort**
**Hamilton Army Base. Neighborhood maintenance level is judged to be good.**

### SITE

Lot Dimensions (if PUD) **N/A** = ___ Sq. Ft. ☐ Corner Lot   Project Density When Completed as Planned ___ Units/Acre
Zoning Classification **Residential** Present improvements ☒ do ☐ do not conform to zoning regulations
Highest and best use: ☒ Present use ☐ Other (specify) ___

| | Public | Other (Describe) | OFF-SITE IMPROVEMENTS | | Project Ingress/Egress (adequacy) **Average/Average** |
|---|---|---|---|---|---|
| Elec. | ☒ | **No Access** | Street Access: | ☒ Public ☐ Private | Topo **Rolling** |
| Gas | ☒ | | Surface **Asphalt paved** | | Size/Shape **Average For Area/Mostly Rectangular** |
| Water | ☒ | | Maintenance: | ☒ Public ☐ Private | View Amenity **Average – Residential** |
| San. Sewer | ☒ | | ☒ Storm Sewer ☒ Curb/Gutter | | Drainage/Flood Conditions **Minimal Flood Hazard** |
| | ☒ Underground Elec. & Tel. | | ☒ Sidewalk ☒ Street Lights | | Is the property in a HUD identified Special Flood Hazard Area? ☒ No ☐ Yes |

Comments (including any easements, encroachments or other adverse conditions) **Flood Map 360497-63. Site is lightly tree shaded and**
**well landscaped and maintained. No known adverse conditions.**

### PROJECT IMPROVEMENTS

| | | | PROJECT RATING | Good | Avg. | Fair | Poor |
|---|---|---|---|---|---|---|---|
| ☒ Existing Approx. Year Built 19 **56** Original Use **Rentals** | | | Location | ☐ | ☒ | ☐ | ☐ |
| ☐ Condo ☐ PUD | ☒ Converted (19 **83** ) | | General Appearance | ☐ | ☒ | ☐ | ☐ |
| TYPE ☐ Proposed | ☐ Under Construction | | Amenities and Recreational Facilities | ☐ | ☒ | ☐ | ☐ |
| ☐ Elevator | ☒ Walk-up No. of Stories **6** | | Density (units per acre) | ☐ | ☒ | ☐ | ☐ |
| PROJECT ☐ Row or Town House | ☒ Other (specify) **Mid Rise Building** | | Unit Mix | ☐ | ☒ | ☐ | ☐ |
| ☒ Primary Residence | ☐ Second Home or Recreational | | Quality of Constr. (mat'l & finish) | ☐ | ☒ | ☐ | ☐ |
| If Completed: No. Phases **1** No. Units **178** No. Sold **167** | | | Condition of Exterior | ☐ | ☒ | ☐ | ☐ |
| If Incompleted: Planned No. Phases **N/A** No. Units **N/A** No. Sold **N/A** | | | Condition of Interior | ☐ | ☒ | ☐ | ☐ |
| Units in Subject Phase: Total **178** Completed **178** Sold **167** Rented **11** | | | Appeal to Market | ☐ | ☒ | ☐ | ☐ |
| Approx. No. Units for Sale: Subject Project **N/A** Subject Phase **N/A** | | | | | | | |

Exterior Wall **Brick** Roof Covering **Built-Up Roof** Security Features **Deadbolts, intercom**
Elevator: No. **2** Adequacy & Condition **Average** Soundproofing: Vertical **Average** Horizontal **Average**
Parking: Total No. Spaces **Street** Ratio **N/A** Spaces/Unit Type **Street** No. Spaces of Guest Parking **Average**
Describe common elements or recreational facilities **Hall, laundry room**
Are any common elements, rec. facilities or parking leased to Owners Assoc.? **None known** If yes, attach addendum describing rental, terms and options.

### SUBJECT UNIT

☒ Existing ☐ Proposed ☐ Under Constr. Floor No. **5** Unit Livable Area **629** ☑ Basement **0** % Finished **N/A**
Parking for Unit: No. **0** Type **Street** ☐ Assigned ☐ Owned Convenience to Unit **Average**

| Room List | Foyer | Liv | Din | Kit | Bdrm | Bath | Fam | Rec | Lndry | Other | UNIT RATING | Good | Avg. | Fair | Poor |
|---|---|---|---|---|---|---|---|---|---|---|---|---|---|---|---|
| Basement | | | | | | | | | | | Condition of Improvement | ☐ | ☒ | ☐ | ☐ |
| 1st Level | | | | | | | | | | | Room Sizes and Layout | ☐ | ☒ | ☐ | ☐ |
| 2nd Level | | | | | | | | | | | Adequacy of Closets and Storage | ☐ | ☒ | ☐ | ☐ |
| 5th Level | x | 1 | | 1 | 1 | 1 | | | | | Kit. Equip., Cabinets & Workspace | ☐ | ☒ | ☐ | ☐ |

Floors: ☒ Hardwood ☐ Carpet over ___ ☐ ___          Plumbing - Adequacy and Condition ☐ ☒ ☐ ☐
Int. Walls ☐ Drywall ☒ Plaster ☐ ___          Electrical - Adequacy and Condition ☐ ☒ ☐ ☐
Trim/Finish: ☐ Good ☒ Average ☐ Fair ☐ Poor          Adequacy of Soundproofing ☐ ☒ ☐ ☐
Bath Floor: ☒ Ceramic ___ ☐ Wainscot ☒ Ceramic ☐          Adequacy of Insulation ☐ ☒ ☐ ☐
Windows (type): **Aluminum Double Hung** ☒ Storm Sash ☒ Screens ☒ Combo          Location within Project or View ☐ ☒ ☐ ☐
Kitchen Equip: ☒ Refrig. ☒ Range/Oven ☐ Fan/Hood ☐ Washer ☐ Dryer          Overall Livability ☐ ☒ ☐ ☐
☒ Intercom ☐ Disposal ☐ Dishwasher ☐ Microwave ☐ Compactor          Appeal and Marketability ☐ ☒ ☐ ☐
HEAT: Type **Steam** Fuel **Oil** Cond. **No Access**          Est. Effective Age ___ to **5** yrs.
AIR COND.: ☐ Central ☒ Other **Window** ☒ Adequate ☐ Inadequate          Est. Remaining Economic Life ___ to **55** yrs.
☐ Earth sheltered Housing Design ☐ Solar Design/Landscape ☐ Solar Space Heat/Air Cond. ☐ Solar Hot Water
☐ Flue Damper ☐ Elec./Mech. Gas Furn. Ignition ☐ Auto Setback Thermostat ☒ Dble/Triple Glazed Windows ☒ Caulk/Weatherstrip
INSULATION (state R-Factor if known) ☐ Walls **U/K** ☐ Ceiling **U/K** ☐ Floor **U/K** ☐ Roof/Attic **U/K** ☐ Water Heater **No Access**
If rehab proposed, do plans and specs provide for adequate energy conservation? ___ If no, attach description of modification needed.
ENERGY EFFICIENCY APPEARS: ☐ High ☒ Adequate ☐ Low          Energy Audit: ☐ Yes (attach, if available) ☒ No
COMMENTS (special features, functional or physical inadequacies, modernization or repair needed, etc.) **Subject unit is judged to be about 9%**
**physically depreciated. There appears to be no significant functional or external inadequacies.**

FHLMC Form 465 Rev. 9/80 12 CPI          ATTACH DESCRIPTIVE PHOTOGRAPHS OF SUBJECT PROPERTY AND STREET SCENE          FNMA Form 1073 Rev. 9/80

**BUDGET ANALYSIS**

Unit Charge $ 290 /Mo. x 12 = $ 3,480 /Yr. ($ 5.53 /Sq. Ft./year of livable area) Ground Rent (if any) $ N/A /yr.

Utilities included in unit charge: ☐ None ☒ Heat ☐ Air Cond. ☐ Electricity ☐ Gas ☒ Water ☒ Sewer

Note any fees, other than regular Condo/PUD charges, for use of facilities None known.

| | ☐ High | ☒ Adequate | ☐ Inadequate |
|---|---|---|---|
| To properly maintain the project and provide the services anticipated, the budget appears | | | |
| Compared to other competitive projects of similar quality and design subject unit charge appears: | ☐ High | ☒ Reasonable | ☐ Low |

Management Group: ☐ Owners Association ☐ Developer ☒ Management Agent (identify) J.C. Kemper 347-9248

Quality of Management and its enforcement of Rules and Regulations appears: ☐ Superior ☐ Good ☒ Adequate ☐ Inadequate

Special or unusual characteristics in the Condo/PUD Documents or otherwise known to the appraiser, that would affect marketability(if none, so state) Lisa in the sales office provided information. Could not get any further data from a Mr. Benson.

Comments None.

NOTE: FHLMC does not require the cost approach in the appraisal of condominium or PUD units.

**COST APPROACH**

Cost Approach (to be used only for detached, semi-detached, and town house units):

| | | |
|---|---|---|
| Reproduction Cost New _____ Sq. Ft. @ $ _____ per Sq. Ft. = | $ | 0 |
| Less Depreciation: Physical $ _____ Functional $ _____ Economic $ _____ | ( | 0 ) |
| Depreciated Value of Improvements: | | 0 |
| Add Land Value (if leasehold, show only leasehold value - attach calculations) | | |
| Pro-rata Share of Value of Amenities | $ | |
| Total Indicated Value: ☐ FEE SIMPLE ☐ LEASEHOLD | $ | 0 |

Comments regarding estimate of depreciation and value of land and amenity package The Cost Approach is not applicable to this report.

The appraiser, whenever possible, should analyze two comparable sales from within the subject project. However, when appraising a unit in a new or newly converted project, at least two comparables should be selected from outside the subject project. In the following analysis, the comparable should always be adjusted to the subject unit and not vice versa. If a significant feature of the comparable is superior to the subject unit, a minus (-) adjustment should be made to the comparable; if such a feature of the comparable is inferior to the subject, a plus (+) adjustment should be made to the comparable.

**MARKET DATA ANALYSIS**

LIST ONLY THOSE ITEMS THAT REQUIRE ADJUSTMENT

| ITEM | Subject Property | COMPARABLE NO. 1 | +(-)$ Adjustment | COMPARABLE NO. 2 | +(-)$ Adjustment | COMPARABLE NO. 3 | +(-)$ Adjustment |
|---|---|---|---|---|---|---|---|
| Address-Unit | 162 82nd Street Unit E-27 | 28 Tree Lane Unit 4B | | 971 Overton Street Unit 3N | | 7290 Ridge Drive Unit 5A | |
| Project Name | | | | | | | |
| Proximity to Subj. | | 22 Blocks | | 3 Blocks | | 5 Blocks | |
| Sales Price | $ 58,000 | $ 67,000 | | $ 54,000 | | $ 50,000 | |
| Price/Living Area | $ 92.21 ☐ | $ 100.90 ☐ | | $ 99.63 ☐ | | $ 72.99 | |
| Data Source | Inspection | SREA Data | | SREA Data | | SREA Data | |
| Date of Sale and | DESCRIPTION | DESCRIPTION | | DESCRIPTION | | DESCRIPTION | |
| Time Adjustment | 04/05/92 | 06/10/91 | -1,650 | 07/15/91 | -1,175 | 12/16/91 | -450 |
| Location | Average | Average | | Inferior | 2,500 | Average | |
| Site/View | 5thLevel/Avg | 4thLevel/Avg | 500 | 3rdLevel/Avg | 1,000 | 5thLevel/Avg | |
| Design and Appeal | MidRise/Avg | MidRise/Avg | | MidRise/Avg | | MidRise/Avg | |
| Quality of Constr. | Average | Average | | Average | | Average | |
| Age | 1956 | +/- 1954 | | +/- 1931 | | +/- 1950 | |
| Condition | Average | Average | | Average | | Average | |
| Living Area, Room Count & Total | Total 3 B-rms 1 Baths 1 | Total 3 B-rms 1 Baths 1 | | Total 3 B-rms 1 Baths 1 | | Total 3 B-rms 1 Baths 1 | |
| Gross Living Area | 629 Sq. Ft. | 664 Sq. Ft. | -1,050 | 542 Sq. Ft. | 2,610 | 685 Sq. Ft. | -1,680 |
| Basement & Bsmt. Finished Rooms | N/A | N/A | | N/A | | N/A | |
| Functional Utility | Average | Average | | Average | | Average | |
| Air Conditioning | Window Units | Central AC | -2,500 | WindowUnits | | Wall Units | |
| Storage | Average | Average | | Average | | Average | |
| Parking Facilities | Street | Street | | Street | | Street | |
| Common Elements and Recreation Facilities | Hall,Laundry Room | Hall, Laundry Room | | Hall, Laundry Room | | Hall, Laundry Room | |
| Mo. Assessment | +/- 290.00 | +/- 385.00 | 1,000 | +/- 524.00 | 4,250 | +/- 589.00 | 4,750 |
| Leasehold/Fee | Leasehold | Leasehold | | Leasehold | | Leasehold | |
| Special Energy Efficient Items | Average Efficiency | Average Efficiency | | Average Efficiency | | Average Efficiency | |
| Other (e.g. fire-places, kitchen equip., remodeling) | No Fireplace Std. Kitchen Appliances | No Fireplace Std. Kitchen Appliances | | No Fireplace Renovated Appliances | -2,000 | No Fireplace Std. Kitchen Appliances | |
| Sales or Financing Concessions | None Known | None Known | | None Known | | None Known | |
| Net Adj. (total) | | ☐ Plus ☒ Minus $ | -3,700 | ☒ Plus ☐ Minus $ | 7,185 | ☒ Plus ☐ Minus $ | 2,620 |
| Indicated value of Subject | | -6 %Net 10 %Gr $ | 63,300 | 13 %Net 25 %Gr $ | 61,185 | 5.2 %Net 14 %Gr $ | 52,620 |

Comments on Market Data Analysis SEE ATTACHED ADDENDUM

INDICATED VALUE BY MARKET DATA APPROACH $ 58,000

INDICATED VALUE BY INCOME APPROACH (If applicable) Economic Market Rent $ N/A /Mo. x Gross Rent Multiplier N/A = $ 0

This appraisal is made ☒ "as is" ☐ subject to repairs, alterations, or conditions listed below ☐ subject to completion per plans and specifications.

Comments and Conditions of Appraisal: The cost and income approaches are not applicable to this report.

Final Reconciliation: The market data analysis is the only reliable approach as it reflects the behavior of buyers and sellers in the marketplace. No repairs or modernization were deemed necessary at this time.

Construction Warranty ☐ Yes ☐ No Name of Warranty Program _____ Warranty Coverage Expires _____

This appraisal is based upon the above requirements, the certification, contingent and limiting conditions, and Market Value definition that are stated in

☒ FHLMC Form 439 (Rev. 7/86)/FNMA Form 1004B (Rev. 7/86) filed with client _____ .19 _____ ☒ attached.

I ESTIMATE THE MARKET VALUE, AS DEFINED, OF SUBJECT PROPERTY AS OF April 5 .1992 to be $ 58,000

Appraiser(s) Steve Smith Review Appraiser (if applicable) Harry Jones

Date Report Signed May 6 .1992 ☐ Did ☒ Did Not Physically Inspect Property

FHLMC Form 465 Rev. 9/80 LaserForm Software by DAY ONE, Inc. 1987 FNMA Form 1073 Rev. 9/80

# MARKET DATA ANALYSIS

File no. A0238D92

The appraiser, whenever possible, should analyze two comparable sales from within the subject project. However, when appraising a unit in a new or newly converted project, at least two comparable should be selected from outside the subject project. In the following analysis, the comparable should be adjusted to the subject unit and not vice versa. If a significant feature of the comparable is superior to the subject unit, a minus (-) adjustment should be made to the comparable; if such a feature of the comparable is inferior to the subject, a plus (+) adjustment should be made to the comparable.

## LIST ONLY THOSE ITEMS THAT REQUIRE ADJUSTMENT

| ITEM | Subject Property | COMPARABLE NO. 4 | +(-)$ Adjustment | COMPARABLE NO. 5 | +(-)$ Adjustment | COMPARABLE NO. 6 | +(-)$ Adjustment |
|---|---|---|---|---|---|---|---|
| Address-Unit | 162 82nd Street | 255 Baybowl Place Unit 4H | | 255 Baybowl Place Unit 8S | | | |
| Project Name | Unit E-27 | | | | | | |
| Proximity to Subj. | | 7 Blocks | | 7 Blocks | | | |
| Sale Price | $ 58,000 | $ 60,000 | | $ 63,000 | | $ | |
| Price/Living Area | $ 92.21 | $ 81.30 | | $ 90.00 | | $ | |
| Data Source | Inspection | SREA Data | | SREA Data | | | |
| Date of Sale and Time Adjustment | 04/05/92 | 07/26/91 | -1,250 | 07/27/91 | -1,325 | | |
| Location | Average | Inferior | 2,500 | Inferior | 2,500 | | |
| Site / View | 5thLevel/Avg | 3rdLevel/Avg | 1,000 | 4thLevel/Avg | 500 | | |
| Design and Appeal | MidRise/Avg | MidRise/Avg | | MidRise/Avg | | | |
| Quality of Construction | Average | Average | | Average | | | |
| Age | 1956 | +/- 1963 | | +/- 1963 | | | |
| Condition | Average | Average | | Average | | | |
| Living Area, Room Count & Total | Total 3  B-rms 1  Baths 1 | Total 3  B-rms 1  Baths 1 | | Total 3  B-rms 1  Baths 1 | | Total  B-rms  Baths | |
| Gross Living Area | 629 Sq.Ft. | 738 Sq.Ft. | -3,270 | 700 Sq.Ft. | -2,130 | Sq.Ft. | |
| Basement & Bsmt. Finished Rooms | N/A | N/A | | N/A | | | |
| Functional Utility | Average | Average | | Average | | | |
| Air Conditioning | Window Units | WindowUnits | | WindowUnits | | | |
| Storage | Average | Average | | Average | | | |
| Parking Facilities | Street | Street | | Street | | | |
| Common Elements and Recreation Facilities | Hall, Laundry Room | Hall, Laundry Room | | Hall, Laundry Room | | | |
| Mo. Assessment | +/- 290.00 | +/- 263.00 | | +/- 327.00 | | | |
| Leasehold/Fee | Leasehold | Leasehold | | Leasehold | | | |
| Special Energy Efficient Items | Average Efficiency | Average Efficiency | | Average Efficiency | | | |
| Other (e.g. fireplaces, kitchen equip., remodeling) | No Fireplace Std. Kitchen Appliances | No Fireplace Std. Kitchen Appliances | | No Fireplace Std. Kitchen Appliances | | | |
| Sales or Financing Concessions | None Known | None Known | | None Known | | | |
| Net Adj. (total) | | ☐ Plus ☒ Minus $ | -1,020 | ☐ Plus ☒ Minus $ | -455 | ☐ Plus ☐ Minus $ | 0 |
| Indicated Value of Subject | | -2 %Net  13.5%Gr  $ | 58,980 | -1 %Net  10 %Gr  $ | 62,545 | %Net  %Gr  $ | 0 |

Comments on Market Data  All sales were adjusted .25% per month due to the declining Co-Op market.
    Sales 2, 4, & 5 were judged to be inferior in location due to their being on busier streets and being closer to commercial activities.
    All sales, except 3, were adjusted for the view.
    The gross living area adjustments are based on $30.00 per square foot.
    Sales 1, 2 & 3 were adjusted for the monthly maintenance charge in relation to their square footage, as compared to the subject.

    No evaluations are made as to the existence or potential effects on market value for any environmental conditions or substances on or near the subject property. Any environmental concerns must be analyzed and reported by a professional in that field of expertise. The appraiser is not qualified and makes no evaluations or determinations of these matters in the estimated market value of the subject property or in evaluating the comparable sales.

## SUBJECT PHOTOGRAPH ADDENDUM

| | |
|---|---|
| Borrower Client | Stephen Jones |
| Property Address | 162 82nd Street |
| City | Union County Oakdale State NV Zip Code 11203 |
| Lender | Richmond Savings Bank |

**FRONT OF SUBJECT PROPERTY**

**REAR OF SUBJECT PROPERTY**

**STREET SCENE**

LaserForm Software by DAY ONE, Inc. 1990

## COMPARABLES PHOTOGRAPH ADDENDUM

Borrower Client   Stephen Jones

Property Address   162 82nd Street

City   Union          County   Oakdale          State   NY      Zip Code   11203

Lender   Richmond Savings Bank

**COMPARABLE SALE # 1**

**28 Tree Lane**
Date of Sale: 06/10/91
Sale Price  : 67,000
Sq. Ft.     : 664
$ / Sq. Ft. : 100.90

**COMPARABLE SALE # 2**

**971 Overton Street**
Date of Sale: 07/15/91
Sale Price  : 54,000
Sq. Ft.     : 542
$ / Sq. Ft. : 99.63

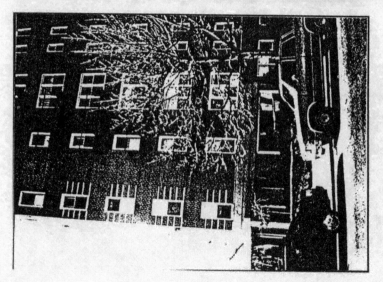

**COMPARABLE SALE # 3**

**7290 Ridge Drive**
Date of Sale: 12/16/91
Sale Price  : 50,000
Sq. Ft.     : 685
$ / Sq. Ft. : 72.99

Borrower Client  Stephen Jones

Property Address  162 82nd Street

City  Union  County  Oakdale  State  NY  Zip Code  11203

Lender  Richmond Savings Bank

**COMPARABLE SALE # 4**

**255 Baybowl Place**
Date of Sale: 07/26/91
Sale Price  : 60,000
Sq. Ft.    : 738
$ / Sq. Ft. : 81.30

**COMPARABLE SALE # 5**

**255 Baybowl Place**
Date of Sale: 07/27/91
Sale Price  : 63,000
Sq. Ft.    : 700
$ / Sq. Ft. : 90.00

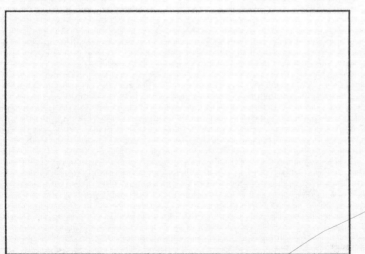

**COMPARABLE SALE # 6**

Date of Sale:
Sale Price  :
Sq. Ft.    :
$ / Sq. Ft. :

## Location·Map

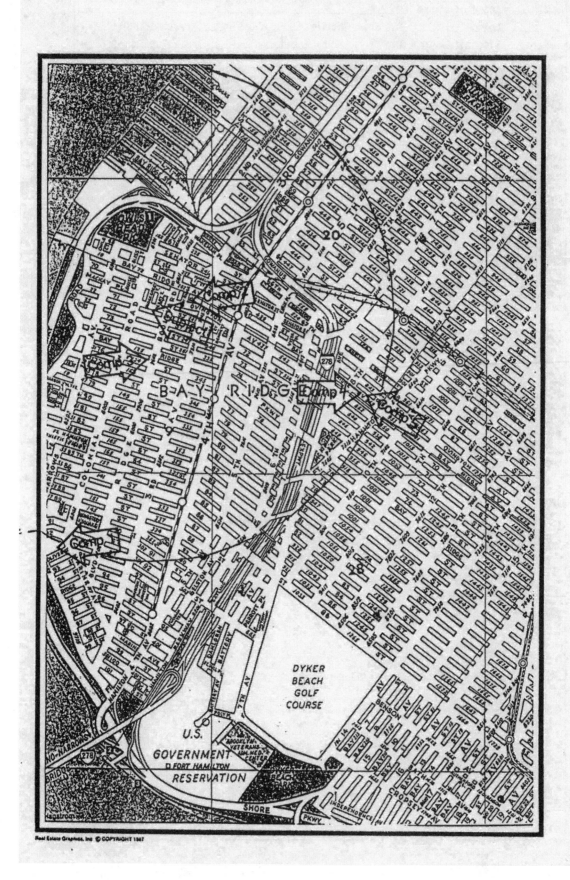

Borrower Name: **Stephen Jones**                           File No. **A0238D92**

**DEFINITION OF MARKET VALUE :**    The most probable price which a property should bring in a competitive and open market under all conditions requisite to a fair sale, the buyer and seller, each acting prudently, knowledgeably and assuming the price is not affected by undue stimulus. Implicit in this definition is the consummation of a sale as of a specified date and the passing of title from seller to buyer under conditions whereby: (1) buyer and seller are typically motivated; (2) both parties are well informed or well advised, and each acting in what he considers his own best interest; (3) a reasonable time is allowed for exposure in the open market; (4) payment is made in terms of cash in U.S. dollars or in terms of financial arrangements comparable thereto; and (5) the price represents the normal consideration for the property sold unaffected by special or creative financing or sales concessions* granted by anyone associated with the sale.

*Adjustments to the comparables must be made for special or creative financing or sales concessions. No adjustments are necessary for those costs which are normally paid by sellers as a result of tradition or law in a market area; these costs are readily identifiable since the seller pays these costs in virtually all sales transactions. Special or creative financing adjustments can be made to the comparable property by comparisons to financing terms offered by a third party institutional lender that is not already involved in the property or transaction. Any adjustment should not be calculated on a mechanical dollar for dollar cost of the financing or concession but the dollar amount of any adjustment should approximate the market's reaction to the financing or concessions based on the appraiser's judgment.

## CERTIFICATION AND STATEMENT OF LIMITING CONDITIONS

CERTIFICATION:      The Appraiser certifies and agrees that:

1. The Appraiser has no present or contemplated future interest in the property appraised; and neither the employment to make the appraisal, nor the compensation for it, is contingent upon the appraised value of the property.

2. The Appraiser has no personal interest in or bias with respect to the subject matter of the appraisal report or the participants to the sale. The "Estimate of Market Value" in the appraisal report is not based in whole or in part upon the race, color, or national origin of the prospective owners or occupants of the property appraised, or upon the race, color or national origin of the present owners or occupants of the properties in the vicinity of the property appraised.

3. The appraiser has personally inspected the property, both inside and out, and has made an exterior inspection of all comparable sales listed in the report. To the best of the Appraiser's knowledge and belief, all statements and information in this report are true and correct, and the Appraiser has not knowingly withheld any significant information.

4. All contingent and limiting conditions are contained herein (imposed by the terms of the assignment or by the under-signed affecting the analyses, opinions, and conclusions contained in the report).

5. This appraisal report has been made in conformity with and is subject to the to the requirements of the Code of Professional Ethics and Standards of Professional Conduct of the appraisal organizations with which the Appraiser is affiliated.

6. All conclusions and opinions concerning the real estate that are set forth in the appraisal report were prepared by the Appraiser whose signature appears on the appraisal report, unless indicated as "Review Appraiser." No change of any item in the appraisal report shall be made by anyone other than the Appraiser, and the Appraiser shall have no responsibility for any such unauthorized change.

## CONTINGENT AND LIMITING CONDITIONS:    The certification of the Appraiser appearing in the appraisal report is subject to the following conditions and to such other specific and limiting conditions as are set forth by the Appraiser in the report.

1. The Appraiser assumes no responsibility for matters of a legal nature affecting the property appraised or the title there-to, nor does the Appraiser render any opinion as to the title, which is assumed to be good and marketable. The property is appraised as though under responsible ownership.

2. Any sketch in the report may show approximate dimensions and is included to assist the reader in visualizing the property. The Appraiser has made no survey of the property.

3. The Appraiser is not required to give testimony or appear in court because of having made the appraisal with reference to the property in question, unless arrangements have been previously made therefor.

4. Any distribution of the valuation in the report between land and improvements applies only under the existing program or utilization. The separate valuations for land and building must not be used in conjunction with any other appraisal and are invalid if so used.

5. The Appraiser assumes that there are no hidden or unapparent conditions of the property, subsoil, or structures, which would render it more or less valuable. The Appraiser assumes no responsibility for such conditions, or for engineering which might be required to discover such factors.

6. Information, estimates, and opinions furnished to the Appraiser, and contained in the report, were obtained from sources considered reliable and believed to be true and correct. However, no responsibility for accuracy of such items furnished the Appraiser can be assumed by the Appraiser.

7. Disclosure of the contents of the appraisal report is governed by the Bylaws and Regulations of the professional appraisal organizations with which the Appraiser is affiliated.

8. Neither all, nor any part of the content of the report, or copy thereof (including conclusions as to the property value, the identity of the Appraiser, professional designations, reference to any professional appraisal organizations, or the firm with which the Appraiser is connected), shall be used for any purposes by anyone but the client specified in the report , the borrower if appraisal fee paid by same, the mortgagee or its successors and assigns, mortgage insurers, consultants, professional appraisal organizations, any state or federally approved financial institution, any department, agency, or instrumentality of the United States or any state or the District of Columbia, without the previous written consent of the Appraiser; nor shall it be conveyed by anyone to the public through advertising, public relations, news, sales, or other media, without the written consent and approval of the Appraiser.

9. On all appraisals, subject to satisfactory completion, repairs, or alterations, the appraisal report and value conclusion are contingent upon completion of the improvements in a workmanlike manner.

Date **April 5, 1992**    Signature _____
                                              **Steve Smith**

Freddie Mac                                                    Fannie Mae
Form 439 JUL 86                                               Form 1004B Jul 86

Multi-Family Appraisal Report

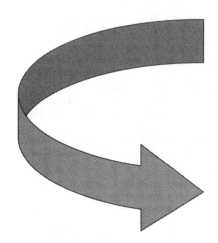

# APPRAISAL OF

## A SMALL RESIDENTIAL INCOME PROPERTY

**LOCATION**   :   8427 Lawrence Drive
                      Hicksville, NY  10288


**CLIENT**        :   Kings Savings and Loan


**AS OF DATE**   :   December 27, 1992

**PROPERTY DESCRIPTION & ANALYSIS**

## Northeast Management, Maintenance and Realty, Inc.
### SMALL RESIDENTIAL INCOME PROPERTY APPRAISAL REPORT
File no. A0451H92

### Subject

| | | |
|---|---|---|
| Property address 8427 Lawrence Drive | | Lender discretionary use |
| City Hicksville | County Kings | State NY | Zip Code 10288 | Sale price $ |
| Legal description Block 5441, Lot 6 | | Gross monthly rent $ |
| Owner/occupant Unknown/3 tenants | Tax Year 1992 R.E. taxes $ +/- 2,350 | Closing date |
| Sale price $ 220,000 Date of Sale 12/27/92 Census tract 158 Map Reference Hagstrom | | Mortgage amount $ |
| Property rights appraised [X] Fee Simple [ ] Leasehold [ ] Condominium or [ ] PUD HOA$ N/A /Mo. | | Mortgage type |
| Borrower N/A Project Name N/A | | Discount points and other concessions |
| Loan charges/concessions to be paid by seller $ N/A | | Paid by seller $ |
| Lender/client Kings Savings and Loan | | Source |
| Appraiser Harry Richmond | | |

### Neighborhood

| | | | | | Good | Avg. | Fair | Poor |
|---|---|---|---|---|---|---|---|---|
| Location [X] Urban [ ] Suburban [ ] Rural | Predominant Occupancy | Single family housing PRICE $(000) / AGE (yrs) | Neighborhood Analysis | | | | | |
| Built up [X] Over 75% [ ] 25-75% [ ] Under 25% | | 180 Low / 10 | Employment stability | | | X | | |
| Growth rate [ ] Rapid [ ] Stable [X] Slow | [X] Owner | 240 High / 75 | Convenience to employment | | | X | | |
| Property values [ ] Increasing [X] Stable [ ] Declining | [ ] Tenant | Predominant | Convenience to shopping | | X | | | |
| Demand/supply [ ] Shortage [X] In balance [ ] Over supply | [X] Vacant (0-5%) | 200 / 55 | Convenience to schools | | X | | | |
| Marketing time [ ] Under 3 mos. [X] 3 - 6 mos. [ ] Over 6 mos. | [ ] Vacant(over5%) | | Adequacy of public transportation | | X | X | | |
| Typical 2-4 family bldg. Type Detachd | Present land use % | 2-4 family housing PRICE $(000) / AGE (yrs) | Recreation facilities | | | X | | |
| No. stories 2 No. units 2 | One family 30 | Land use change | 200 Low / 12 | Adequacy of utilities | | | X | | |
| Age 55 yrs. Condition Average | 2-4 family 50 | [X] Not likely | 270 High / 75 | Property compatibility | | X | | | |
| Typical rents $ 550 to $ 875 | Multifamily | [ ] Likely | Predominant | Protection from detrimental cond. | | | X | | |
| [ ] Increasing [X] Stable [ ] Declining | Commercial 20 | [ ] In process | 240 / 55 | Police & fire protection | | | X | | |
| Est neighborhood apt vacancy 2 % | Industrial | To: | | General appearance of properties | | X | | | |
| [ ] Increasing [X] Stable [ ] Declining | Vacant | Rent controls [X] Yes [ ] No [ ] Likely | Appeal to market | | X | X | | |

Note: Race and the racial composition of the neighborhood are not considered reliable appraisal factors.

Description of neighborhood boundaries: North and East to I-295 Throggs Neck Expwy, West to East Tremont Avenue, South to Cross Bronx Expwy. See location map

Description of those factors, favorable or unfavorable, that affect marketability (including neighborhood stability, appeal, property conditions, vacancies, *rent control, etc.):
The subject neighborhood is located in the Schuylerville section of the east portion of the Bronx, 3 blocks from the Throggs Neck Expwy, the Cross Bronx Expwy, Intermediate School #192, the NY Public Library Throggs Neck branch, and a nursing home. The area is comprised of mostly attached and detached two family dwellings. There are commercial businesses on East Tremont Avenue. The vast majority of the houses are of the same style, Brick Row houses, and the same approximate age. The neighborhood maintenance level is judged to be average.

The following available listings represent the most current, similar, and proximate competitive properties to the subject property in the subject neighborhood. This analysis is intended to evaluate the inventory currently on the market competing with the subject property in the subject neighborhood and recent price and marketing time trends affecting the subject property. (Listings outside the subject neighborhood are not considered applicable).

| ITEM | SUBJECT | COMPARABLE LISTING NO. 1 | COMPARABLE LISTING NO. 2 | COMPARABLE LISTING NO. 3 |
|---|---|---|---|---|
| | 8427 Lawrence Dri | 2290 Prospect Ave. | 2986 Kenneth Ave. | 982 Marytill Drive |
| Address | Hicksville, NY | Hicksville, NY | Hicksville, NY | Hicksville, NY |
| Proximity to subject | | 2 blocks | 9 blocks | 5 blocks |
| Listing price $ | 245,000 | [X] Unf. [ ] Furn. $ 295,000 | [X] Unf. [ ] Furn. $ 275,000 | [X] Unf. [ ] Furn. $ 250,000 |
| Approximate GBA | +/- 2,330 | +/- 2300 | +/- 2300 | +/- 2300 |
| Data Source | Inspection | MLS / REDI Data | MLS / REDI Data | MLS / REDI Data |
| #Units/Tot. rms/BR/BA | 3 14 6 4 | 2 12 4 2 | 2 13 5 2 | 2 13 4 2 |
| Approximate year built | +/- 1971 | +/- 65 years | +/- 65 years | +/- 60 years |
| Approx. days on market | N/A | +/- 2 years | +/- 4 months | +/- 4 months |

Comparison of listings to subject property. All listings are located in similar neighborhoods to the subject neighborhood. All listings are reported to be similar in quality to the subject.

Reconciliation: Description and analysis of the general market conditions that affect 2-4 family properties in the subject neighborhood (including the above neighborhood indicators of growth rate, property values, demand/supply, and marketing time) and the prevalence and impact in the subject/market area regarding loan discounts, interest buydowns, and concessions; and identify trends in listing prices, average days on market and any change over past year, etc.: There does not appear to be an oversupply of multi-family dwellings in the area due to a number of recent sales. However, it is a buyer's market in some areas with real estate prices "bottoming out" after a long period of decline. Sales concessions have been offered recently by some developers of new homes to stimulate sales. These concessions usually consist of a partial or full payment of the closing costs by the developer. Fixed and adjustable rate mortgages are typical.

### Site

| | |
|---|---|
| Dimensions +/- 100 x 28 x 26 = 2,700 SF | Topography Gently Sloping |
| Site Area +/- .6 A Corner lot [X] No [ ] Yes | Size Typical For Area |
| Specific zoning classification and description Tax Class Residential Dwelling 2 fam | Shape Irregular |
| Zoning Compliance [X] Legal [ ] Legal nonconforming (Grandfather use) [ ] Illegal [ ] No zoning | Drainage Appears Adequate |
| Highest & best use as improved [X] Present Use [X] Other use(explain) First floor apartmnt was added by the owner and is an illegal dwelling. | View Average |
| | Landscaping Fair |

| Utilities | Public | | Off-site Improvements | Type | Public | Private | Driveway Concrete |
|---|---|---|---|---|---|---|---|
| Electricity | X | 3 meters | Street | Asphalt Paved | X | | Apparent easements Noted in deed and client was notified. Reel 155, Page 531. |
| Gas | X | 2 meters | Curb/gutter | Concrete | X | | |
| Water | X | | Sidewalk | Concrete | X | | FEMA Special flood hazard area [ ] Yes* [ ] No |
| Sanitary sewer | X | | Street lights | Yes | X | | *FEMA Zone/Map Date Map N/A at town hall |
| Storm sewer | X | | Alley | None | | | *FEMA Map No. |

Comments (apparent adverse easements, encroachments, special assessments, slide areas, illegal or legal nonconforming zoning, use, etc.): There is a third kitchen located in the finished area of the first level. This apartment is an illegal dwelling. This is a safety and health hazard that MUST be resolved prior to closing. NO evaluations are made of the restrictions in the deed for this appraisal report. The client was notified.

Freddie Mac Form 72 10/89  2-4 units 12CH          PAGE 1 OF 4          LaserForm software by DAY ONE, INC.          Fannie Mae Form 1025 2-4 units 10/89

**PROPERTY DESCRIPTION & ANALYSIS, continued**

## SMALL RESIDENTIAL INCOME PROPERTY APPRAISAL REPORT

### Description of improvements

| General description | | Exterior description | (Materials/condition) | Foundation | | Insulation | (R-value if known) |
|---|---|---|---|---|---|---|---|
| Units/bldgs. | 3/ 1 | Foundation | P Concrete/Average | Slab | Yes | ☐ Roof | Concealed |
| Stories | 2 | Exterior walls | Brick/Average | Crawl space | No | ☐ Ceiling | Concealed |
| Type (det./att..) | Semi-Attachd | Roof surface | Ashpalt Shing/Avg | Sump Pump | None Noted | ☐ Walls | Concealed |
| Design | Row House | Gutters & downspouts | Aluminum/Average | Dampness | None Noted | ☐ Floor | Concealed |
| Existing/proposed | Yes / No | Window type | Metal Slider/Avg | Settlement | Normal | ☐ None | |
| Under construction | No | Storm sash/Screens | Poor Condition | Infestation | None Noted | Adequacy | Average |
| Year Built | +/- 1971 | Manufactured housing | ☐ Yes ☒ No | Basement | 0 % of 1st floor area | Energy efficient items | Average |
| Effective age (yrs.) | 6 | (Complies with the HUD Manufactured Housing Construction and Safety Standards) | | Basement finish | N/A | Efficiency | |

| Units | Level(s) | Foyer | Living | Dining | Kitchen | Den | Family rm. | # Bedrooms | # Baths | Laundry | Other | Sq. ft./unit | Total ☐ |
|---|---|---|---|---|---|---|---|---|---|---|---|---|---|
| 1 N/ | 1 | 1 | 1 | | 1 | | | 1 | 1 | | | 570 | 570 |
| 1 | 2 | | 1 | 1 | 1 | | | 3 | 2 | | | 880 | 880 |
| 1 | 3 | | 1 | 1 | 1 | | | 3 | 2 | | | 880 | 880 |

Improvements contain: 14 Rooms; 7 Bedroom(s); 5 Bath(s); 2,330 Square feet of GROSS BUILDING AREA*

*GROSS BUILDING AREA(GBA) IS DEFINED AS THE TOTAL FINISHED AREA(INCLUDING COMMON AREAS) OF THE IMPROVEMENTS BASED UPON EXTERIOR MEASUREMENTS.

| SURFACES | (Materials/condition) | HEATING | | Kitchen equip. (#/unit-cond.) | Attic | | Improvement Analysis | Good | Avg. | Fair | Poor |
|---|---|---|---|---|---|---|---|---|---|---|---|
| Floors | Wood/Carpet/Avg | Type | FH Air | Refrigerator 3/Avg | ☒ None | | Quality of construction | | X | | |
| Walls | Drywall/Average | Fuel | Gas | Range/oven 3/Poor | | Stairs | Condition of improvements | | X | | |
| Trim/finish | Softwood/Average | Condition | Good | Disposal | | Drop stair | Room sizes/layout | | X | | |
| Bath floor | Ceramic/Average | Adequacy | Good | Dishwasher | | Scuttle | Closets and storage | | | X | |
| Bath wainscot | Ceramic/Average | COOLING | | Fan/hood | | Floor | Energy efficiency | | X | | |
| Doors | Hollow Wood/Fair | Central | None | Compactor | | Heated | Plumbing - adequacy & condition | | X | | |
| | | Other | None | Washer/dryer | | Finished | Electrical - adequacy & condition | | X | X | |
| | | Condition | N/A | Microwave | | Unfinished | Kitchen cabinets - adequacy & cond. | | X | | |
| Fireplace(s) None | # 0 | Adequacy | N/A | Intercom | | | Compatibility to neighborhood | X | X | | |
| Car storage: | ☒ Garage | ☒ Attached | | ☒ Adequate | | ☐ None | Appeal & marketability | X | X | | |
| No. cars | 1 | ☐ Carport | ☐ Detached | ☐ Inadequate | | ☐ Offstreet | Estimated remaining economic life | | 95 | | yrs. |

Comments on repairs needed, additional features, modernization, etc.: Client commissioned a home inspection along with the appraisal. Review the written home inspection report for details on the repairs and upgrading needed.

### Additional comments on neighborhood, site & description of improvements

Depreciation (physical, functional, and external inadequacies, etc): The subject is judged to be approximately 6% physically depreciated using the Age/Life Method. No functional or external inadequacies were noted.

Environmental conditions observed by or known to the appraiser: No environmental factors were noted or known to the appraiser. The value estimated in this report is based on the assumption that the property is not negatively affected by the existence of hazardous substances or detrimental environmental conditions. The appraiser is not an expert in the identification of hazardous substances or detrimental environmental conditions. The appraiser's routine inspection of and inquiries about the subject property did not develop any information that indicated any significant hazardous substances or detrimental conditions which would negatively affect property value.

### VALUATION ANALYSIS

Purpose of Appraisal is to estimate Market Value as defined in the Certification & Statement of Limiting Conditions

### Cost approach

Comments on cost approach, accrued depreciation, and estimated site value:

ESTIMATED REPRODUCTION COST-NEW-OF IMPROVEMENTS:

| | | | |
|---|---|---|---|
| 570 Sq. Ft. @ $ | 75.00 | = $ | 42,750 |
| 880 Sq. Ft. @ $ | 75.00 | = | 66,000 |
| 880 Sq. Ft. @ $ | 75.00 | = | 66,000 |
| Sq. Ft. @ $ | | = | |
| Extras (Garage = 250 SF) | | = | 12,000 |

The site value is about 40% of the total value.

| | | |
|---|---|---|
| Special Energy Efficient Items | = | |
| Porches, Patios, etc. | = | |
| Total Estimated Cost New | = $ | 186,750 |

| | Physical | Functional | External |
|---|---|---|---|
| Less Depreciation | 11,205 | | |

| | | |
|---|---|---|
| Depreciation 11,205 | = $ | 11,205 |
| Depreciated Value of Improvements | = $ | 175,545 |
| Site Imp. "as is" (driveway, landscaping, etc.) | = $ | |
| ESTIMATED SITE VALUE | = $ | 95,000 |
| (If leasehold, show only leasehold value.) | | |
| INDICATED VALUE BY COST APPROACH | = $ | 270,545 |

VALUATION
ANALYSIS, continued

## SMALL RESIDENTIAL INCOME PROPERTY APPRAISAL REPORT

### Sales comparison analysis

The undersigned has recited three recent sales of properties most similar and proximate to the subject property and has described and analyzed these in this analysis. If there is a significant variation between the subject and the comparable properties, the analysis includes a dollar adjustment reflecting the market reaction to the items or an explanation supported by the market data. If a significant item in the comparable property is superior to, or more favorable than, the subject property, a minus(-) adjustment is made, thus reducing the indicated value of the subject; if a significant item in the comparable is inferior to, or less favorable than, the subject property, a plus (+) adjustment is made, thus increasing the indicated value of the subject.
[ (1) Sales Price / Gross Monthly Rent) ]

| ITEM | SUBJECT | COMPARABLE SALE NO. 1 | +(-) $ Adjustment | COMPARABLE SALE NO. 2 | +(-) $ Adjustment | COMPARABLE SALE NO. 3 | +(-) $ Adjustment |
|---|---|---|---|---|---|---|---|
| Address | 8427 Lawrence Drive Hicksville, NY | 943 Porch Avenue Hicksville, NY | | 3387 Victory Lane Hicksville, NY | | 23 Lucastone Drive Hicksville, NY | |
| Proximity to subject | | 1 block | | 1.5 blocks | | 3 blocks | |
| Sales price | $ 220,000 | X Unf. Furn. $ 230,000 | | X Unf. Furn. $ 232,000 | | X Unf. Furn. $ 220,000 | |
| Sales price/GBA | $ 94.42 | $ 95.83 | | $ 116 | | $ 88 | |
| Gross monthly rent | $ 1,775 | $ 1,700 | | $ 1,750 | | $ 2,000 | |
| Gross mo. rent mult. (1) | 123.93 | 135.29 | | 132.57 | | 110 | |
| Sales price per unit | $ 110,000 | $ 115,000 | | $ 116,000 | | $ 110,000 | |
| Sales price per room | $ 18,333 | 19,170 | | 19,330 | | 15,710 | |
| Data Source | | MLS/REDI D/Town Hal | | MLS/REDI D/Town Hal | | MLS/REDI D/Town Hal | |
| ADJUSTMENTS | DESCRIPTION | DESCRIPTION | | DESCRIPTION | | DESCRIPTION | |
| Sales or financing concessions | | None Known | | None Known | | None Known | |
| Date or sale/time | 12/27/92 | 02/19/92 | | 10/19/92 | | 07/30/92 | |
| Location | Average | Average | | Average | | Average | |
| Site/View | +/- .6 A/Avera | +/- .10 A/A | -11,000 | +/- .05 A/A | | +/- .13 A/A | -12,000 |
| Design and appeal | 2 Fam/Semi-Att | 2 Fam/Detac | -10,000 | 2 Fam/Attac | 10,000 | 2 Fam/Detac | -10,000 |
| Quality of construction | Brick/Avg | Brick/Avg | | Brick/Avg | | Frame/F-Avg | 20,000 |
| Year built | +/- 1971 | +/- 1930 | 22,500 | +/- 1960 | 3,500 | +/- 1960 | 3,500 |
| Condition | Average | Average | | Average | | Average | |
| Gross Building Area | 2,330 Sq. ft. | 2,400 Sq. ft. | -1,750 | 2,000 Sq. ft. | 8,250 | 2,500 Sq. ft. | -4,250 |

| UNIT BREAKDOWN | No. of units | Tot | Room count Br. | Baths | No. Vac | | No. of units | Tot | Room count Br. | Baths | No. Vac | +(-) | No. of units | Tot | Room count Br. | Baths | No. Vac | +(-) | No. of units | Tot | Room count Br. | Baths | No. Vac | +(-) |
|---|---|---|---|---|---|---|---|---|---|---|---|---|---|---|---|---|---|---|---|---|---|---|---|---|
| | 1 | 6 | 3 | 2 | 0 | | 1 | 6 | 3 | 1 | 0 | 1,750 | 1 | 6 | 2 | 2 | 0 | | 1 | 7 | 3 | 2 | 0 | |
| | 1 | 6 | 3 | 2 | 1 | | 1 | 6 | 3 | 1 | 0 | 1,750 | 1 | 6 | 2 | 2 | 0 | | 1 | 7 | 3 | 2 | 0 | |

| | | | | | | | |
|---|---|---|---|---|---|---|---|
| Basement description | N/A | None | | None | | None | |
| Functional utility | Average | Average | | Average | | Average | |
| Heating/cooling | FH Water/None | Steam/None | | Hot W/None | | FH W/None | |
| Parking on/off site | 1 Car Garage | 1 Car Garag | | None | 4,000 | 1 Car Garag | |
| Project amenities and fee (If applicable) | Additional apartment | Additional apartment | | None | 6,000 | None | 6,000 |
| Other | N/A | N/A | | N/A | | N/A | |
| Net Adj. (total) | | X + - $ | 3,250 | X + - $ | 31,750 | X + - $ | 3,250 |
| Adj. sales price of comparables | | 1.4 Net% 21 Gross % $ | 233,250 | 14 Net % 14 Gross % $ | 263,750 | 1.5 Net % 25 Gross % $ | 223,250 |

Comments on sales comparison (including reconciliation of all indicators of value as to consistency and relative strength and evaluation of the typical investors'/purchasers' motivation in that market) No time adjustments were deemed necessary. Condition adjustments were accounted for in the age adjustments. The gross living area adjustments are based on about $25.00 per square foot. The appraiser is not taking into account any deed easements, restrictions, etc. The client was notified of this. Any problems in the deed WILL affect the market value of the property. Investigate this condition fully!

INDICATED VALUE BY SALES COMPARISON APPROACH $ 235,000

Prior sales of subject and comparables within one year of the date of this appraisal : None Known

### Income Approach

Total gross estimated rent $ 1,720 /month x gross rent multiplier 123.93 = $ 213,159.6 INDICATED VALUE BY INCOME APPROACH

Comments on income approach (including expense ratios, if available, and reconciliation of the GRM) The total gross monthly estimated rent was arrived at from the comparable rents listed above. However, the first level apartment rental of $600 per month was not calculated into the income approach because it is an illegal apartment.

### Reconciliation

INDICATED VALUE BY SALES COMPARISON APPROACH ............................................ $ 235,000
INDICATED VALUE BY INCOME APPROACH ...................................................... $ 213,159.6
INDICATED VALUE BY COST APPROACH ........................................................ $ 270,545

This appraisal is made X "as is"  subject to repairs, alterations, inspections or conditions listed below  subject to completion per plans and specifications.

Comments and conditions of appraisal: This appraisal is subject to a free and clear title report and a deed with no adverse easements, encroachments, violations, etc.

Final reconciliation: The sales comparison analysis is the most reliable indicator of value as it reflects the actions of typical buyers and sellers in the marketplace.

This appraisal is based upon the above conditions and the certification, contingent and limiting conditions, and Market Value definition that are stated in

Freddie Mac Form 439/Fannie Mae Form 1004B (Rev. 07/86 ) X attached or  filed with client _____ or  other attached.

I (WE) ESTIMATE THE MARKET VALUE, AS DEFINED, OF THE SUBJECT PROPERTY AS OF December 27, 1992 to be $ 235,000

I (We) certify that to the best of my (our) knowledge and belief the facts and data used herein are true and correct; that I (we) personally inspected the subject property, both inside and out, and have personally made an exterior inspection of all comparables cited in this report; and that I (we) have no undisclosed interest, present or prospective therein.

| APPRAISER(S) | REVIEW APPRAISER (if applicable) | |
|---|---|---|
| SIGNATURE | SIGNATURE |  Did  Did not |
| NAME Harry Richmond | NAME | inspect property |

## SMALL RESIDENTIAL INCOME PROPERTY APPRAISAL REPORT

VALUATION ANALYSIS, continued

### Comparable rental data

At least three rental comparables should be reported and analyzed in this section. The rental comparables should represent the most current rental information on properties as similar and proximate to the subject property as possible. (This comparison is based on current rental data, therefore, the rental comparables typically are not the same comparables used in the sales comparison analysis.) The appraisal report should assure the reader that the units and properties selected as comparables are comparable to the subject property (both the units and the overall property) and accurately represent the rental market for the subject property (unless otherwise stated within the report).

| ITEM | SUBJECT | COMPARABLE RENTAL NO. 1 | COMPARABLE RENTAL NO. 2 | COMPARABLE RENTAL NO. 3 |
|---|---|---|---|---|
| Address | 8427 Lawrence Drive Hicksville, NY | 3982 Uptown Road Hicksville, NY | 198 Downhill Ave. Hicksville, NY | 9037 Procall Lane Hicksville, NY |
| Proximity to subject | | 2 blocks | 9 blocks | 5 blocks |
| Lease Dates (if available) | N/A | N/A | N/A | N/A |
| Rent survey date | 12/92 | 09/92 | 08/92 | 08/92 |
| Data source | | MLS / REDI Data | MLS / REDI Data | MLS / REDI Data |
| Rent concessions | N/A | None Known | None Known | None Known |
| Description of property-units, design, appeal, age, vacancies, and conditions | No. Units 2 No. Vac. 0 Yr. Blt: +/- 1971 Location/Avg Quality/Avg Condition/Avg | #Units 2 No.Vac. 0 Yr.Blt:1927 Location/Average Quality/Average Condition/Average | #Units 2 No.Vac. 0 Yr.Blt:1927 Location/Average Quality/Average Condition/Average | #Units 2 No.Vac. 0 Yr.Blt:1933 Location/Average Quality/Average Condition/Average |

| Individual unit breakdown | Rm. Count Tot/Br/Bath | Size Sq. Ft. | | Rm. Count Tot/Br/Bath | Size Sq. Ft. | Total Monthly Rent | Rm. Count Tot/Br/Bath | Size Sq. Ft. | Total Monthly Rent | Rm. Count Tot/Br/Bath | Size Sq. Ft. | Total Monthly Rent |
|---|---|---|---|---|---|---|---|---|---|---|---|---|
| | 6 3 2 | 880 | | 4 1 1 | 700 | 550 | 5 2 1 | 900 | Owner | 5 2 1 | 900 | Owner |
| | 6 3 2 | 880 | | 6 3 1 | 1,000 | 725 | 6 3 1 | 1,000 | 775 | 4 2 1 | 850 | Family |

| Utilities, furniture and amenities included in rent | N/A | Heat & Hot W includ in the rent payment | Heat & Hot W includ in the rent payment | Heat & Hot W includ in the rent payment |
|---|---|---|---|---|
| Functional utility, basement, heating/cooling, project amenities, etc. | Functional/Avg Extra apartmnt FH Water/None | Functional/Avg Extra apartment Hot Water/None | Functional/Average Extra apartment Steam heat/None | Functional/Average Extra apartment Steam heat/None |

Reconciliation of rental data and support for estimated market rents for the individual subject units (including the adjustments used, the adequacy of comparables, rental concessions, etc.) All rentals are located in the subject neighborhood. Quality and condition of all of the rentals are reprted to be similar to the subject. All monthly rent figures are based on comparable market rent.

### Subject's rent schedule

The rent schedule reconciles the applicable indicated monthly market rents to the appropriate subject unit, and provides the estimated rents for the subject property. The appraiser must review the rent characteristics of the comparable sales to determine whether estimated rents should reflect actual or market rents. For example, if actual rents were available on the sales comparables and used to derive the gross rent multiplier (GRM), actual rents for the subject should be used. If market rents were used to construct the comparables' rents and derive the GRM, market rents should be used. The total gross estimated rent must represent rent characteristics consistent with the sales comparable data used to derive the GRM. The total gross estimated rent is not adjusted for vacancy.

| Unit | Lease Date Begin | End | No. Units Vacant | ACTUAL RENTS Per Unit Unfurnished | Furnished | Total Rents | ESTIMATED RENTS Per Unit Unfurnished | Furnished | Total Rents |
|---|---|---|---|---|---|---|---|---|---|
| N/A | No lease | | 0 | $ 600 | $ | $ 0 | $ | $ | $ 0 |
| 1 | No lease | | 0 | 875 | | 875 | | | 0 |
| 1 | No lease | | 0 | 900 | | 900 | | | 0 |
| | | | | | | 0 | | | |
| 2 | | | 0 | | | $ 1,775 | | | $ 0 |

Other monthly income (itemize) N/A $

Vacancy: Actual last yr U/K % Previous year U/K % Estimated: 3 % $ 640 Annually TOTAL GROSS ESTIMATED RENT $ 1,720

Utilities included in estimated rents: ☐ Electric ☒ Water ☒ Sewer ☒ Gas ☐ Oil ☒ Trash collection ☒ Hot Water and Heat

Comments on the rent schedule, actual rents, estimated rents (especially regarding differences between actual and estimated rents), utilities, etc.: The rent schedule is based on the appraiser's research and analysis of market rent in the subject area. Data sources include: REDI Data, Multiple Listing Service, and local real estate offices. Utilities included in the projections are considered typical. The total gross estimated rent is adjusted for vacancy.

**SUBJECT PHOTOGRAPH ADDENDUM**

| | |
|---|---|
| Borrower Client | N/A |
| Property Address | 8427 Lawrence Drive |
| City | Hicksville   County Kings   State NY   Zip Code 10288 |
| Lender | Kings Savings and Loan |

**FRONT OF
SUBJECT PROPERTY**

**REAR OF
SUBJECT PROPERTY**

**STREET SCENE**

Borrower Client   N/A
Property Address   8427 Lawrence Drive
City   Hicksville         County   Kings         State   NY         Zip Code   10288
Lender   Kings Savings and Loan

**COMPARABLE SALE # 1**

**943 Porch Avenue**
Date of Sale: 02/19/92
Sale Price  : 230,000
Sq. Ft.     : 2,400
$ / Sq. Ft. : 95.83

**COMPARABLE SALE # 2**

**3387 Victory Lane**
Date of Sale: 10/19/92
Sale Price  : 232,000
Sq. Ft.     : 2,000
$ / Sq. Ft. : 116

**COMPARABLE SALE # 3**

**23 Lucastone Drive**
Date of Sale: 07/30/92
Sale Price  : 220,000
Sq. Ft.     : 2,500
$ / Sq. Ft. : 88

# Location Map

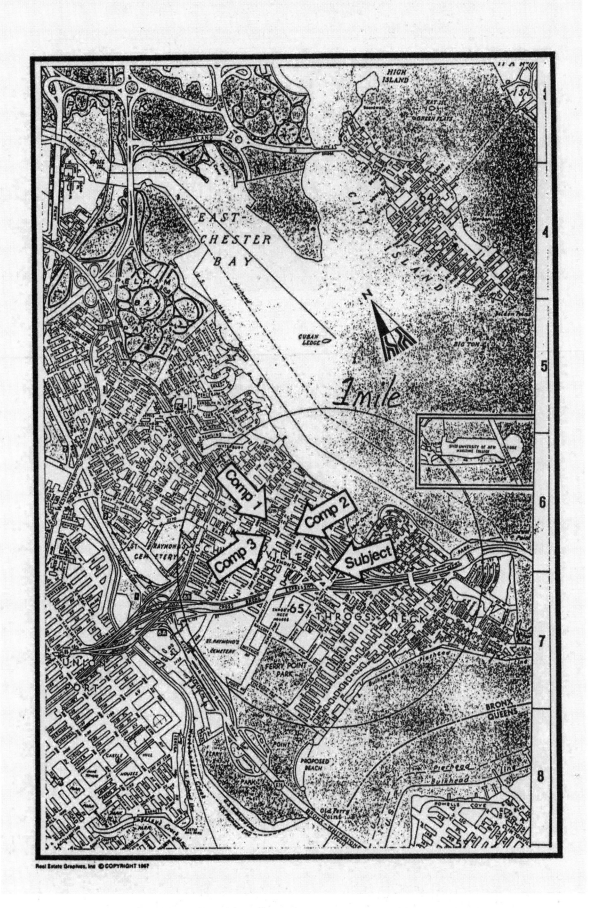

Borrower Name : N/A                    File No. A0451H92

## DEFINITION OF MARKET VALUE :

**DEFINITION OF MARKET VALUE :**   The most probable price which a property should bring in a competitive and open market under all conditions requisite to a fair sale, the buyer and seller, each acting prudently, knowledgeably and assuming the price is not affected by undue stimulus. Implicit in this definition is the consummation of a sale as of a specified date and the passing of title from seller to buyer under conditions whereby: (1) buyer and seller are typically motivated; (2) both parties are well informed or well advised, and each acting in what he considers his own best interest; (3) a reasonable time is allowed for exposure in the open market; (4) payment is made in terms of cash in U.S. dollars or in terms of financial arrangements comparable thereto; and (5) the price represents the normal consideration for the property sold unaffected by special or creative financing or sales concessions* granted by anyone associated with the sale.

*Adjustments to the comparables must be made for special or creative financing or sales concessions. No adjustments are necessary for those costs which are normally paid by sellers as a result of tradition or law in a market area; these costs are readily identifiable since the seller pays these costs in virtually all sales transactions. Special or creative financing adjustments can be made to the comparable property by comparisons to financing terms offered by a third party institutional lender that is not already involved in the property or transaction. Any adjustment should not be calculated on a mechanical dollar for dollar cost of the financing or concession but the dollar amount of any adjustment should approximate the market's reaction to the financing or concessions based on the appraiser's judgment.

## CERTIFICATION AND STATEMENT OF LIMITING CONDITIONS

**CERTIFICATION:**    The Appraiser certifies and agrees that:

1. The Appraiser has no present or contemplated future interest in the property appraised; and neither the employment to make the appraisal, nor the compensation for it, is contingent upon the appraised value of the property.

2. The Appraiser has no personal interest in or bias with respect to the subject matter of the appraisal report or the participants to the sale. The "Estimate of Market Value" in the appraisal report is not based in whole or in part upon the race, color, or national origin of the prospective owners for occupants of the property appraised, or upon the race, color or national origin of the present owners or occupants of the properties in the vicinity of the property appraised.

3. The appraiser has personally inspected the property, both inside and out, and has made an exterior inspection of all comparable sales listed in the report. To the best of the Appraiser's knowledge and belief, all statements and information in this report are true and correct, and the Appraiser has not knowingly withheld any significant information.

4. All contingent and limiting conditions are contained herein (imposed by the terms of the assignment or by the undersigned affecting the analyses, opinions, and conclusions contained in the report).

5. This appraisal report has been made in conformity with and is subject to the to the requirements of the Code of Professional Ethics and Standards of Professional Conduct of the appraisal organizations with which the Appraiser is affiliated.

6. All conclusions and opinions concerning the real estate that are set forth in the appraisal report were prepared by the Appraiser whose signature appears on the appraisal report, unless indicated as "Review Appraiser." No change of any item in the appraisal report shall be made by anyone other than the Appraiser, and the Appraiser shall have no responsibility for any such unauthorized change.

## CONTINGENT AND LIMITING CONDITIONS:

**CONTINGENT AND LIMITING CONDITIONS:**    The certification of the Appraiser appearing in the appraisal report is subject to the following conditions and to such other specific and limiting conditions as are set forth by the Appraiser in the report.

1. The Appraiser assumes no responsibility for matters of a legal nature affecting the property appraised or the title thereto, nor does the Appraiser render any opinion as to the title, which is assumed to be good and marketable. The property is appraised as though under responsible ownership.

2. Any sketch in the report may show approximate dimensions and is included to assist the reader in visualizing the property. The Appraiser has made no survey of the property.

3. The Appraiser is not required to give testimony or appear in court because of having made the appraisal with reference to the property in question, unless arrangements have been previously made therefor.

4. Any distribution of the valuation in the report between land and improvements applies only under the existing program or utilization. The separate valuations for land and building must not be used in conjunction with any other appraisal and are invalid if so used.

5. The Appraiser assumes that there are no hidden or unapparent conditions of the property, subsoil, or structures, which would render it more or less valuable. The Appraiser assumes no responsibility for such conditions, or for engineering which might be required to discover such factors.

6. Information, estimates, and opinions furnished to the Appraiser, and contained in the report, were obtained from sources considered reliable and believed to be true and correct. However, no responsibility for accuracy of such items furnished the Appraiser can be assumed by the Appraiser.

7. Disclosure of the contents of the appraisal report is governed by the Bylaws and Regulations of the professional appraisal organizations with which the Appraiser is affiliated.

8. Neither all, nor any part of the content of the report, or copy thereof (including conclusions as to the property value, the identity of the Appraiser, professional designations, reference to any professional appraisal organizations, or the firm with which the Appraiser is connected), shall be used for any purposes by anyone but the client specified in the report , the borrower if appraisal fee paid by same, the mortgagee or its successors and assigns, mortgage insurers, consultants, professional appraisal organizations, any state or federally approved financial institution, any department, agency, or instrumentality of the United States or any state or the District of Columbia, without the previous written consent of the Appraiser; nor shall it be conveyed by anyone to the public through advertising, public relations, news, sales, or other media, without the written consent and approval of the Appraiser.

9. On all appraisals, subject to satisfactory completion, repairs, or alterations, the appraisal report and value conclusion are contingent upon completion of the improvements in a workmanship like manner.

Date **December 27, 1992**   Signature _____

                                          Harry Richmond

Freddie Mac                                                      Fannie Mae
Form 439 JUL 86                                                  Form 1004B Jul 86

Additional Appraisal Photos

P 31. The style/design
of this house is:

**Split Level**

P 32. The style/design of
this house is:

**Ranch**

P 33. The style/design of
this house is:

**Colonial**

P 34.
The style/design of
this house is:

**English Tudor**

P 35.
The style/design of
this house is:

**Contemporary**

P 36.
The style/design of
this house is:

*BIG!!*

P 37. Above: This is what you'll see on most appraisal assignments - a home filled with furniture and personal items.

Below: *So why did I include two photos of an empty home?* Because this is how you have to picture the interior of a house, condo or building in your mind when doing your appraisals. Remember, you're appraising the **building** - not the appeal and value of the furniture and personal items!

P 38. A private tennis court can increase the market value and appeal of a house.

You have to take this into account when writing up your appraisal reports. Remember to make adjustments for this when evaluating the sales comparables in your appraisals.

P 39. This is a very appealing finished basement area. This adds usable space for the occupants of a home. Finished basements can increase the market value of a house or condo.

P 40. I encountered this on one of the foreclosure appraisals and inspections I did for a bank. The prior owner had spent his money on building an indoor basketball court, indoor swimming pool, sauna and Jacuzzi room, along with some other luxurious and expensive additions to the house and site. The problem was, that after he spent all this money he couldn't pay his mortgage payments and the bank had to foreclose on the property! I guess you could say that it wasn't "money well spent" *(or should I say it was "money spent down the well").*

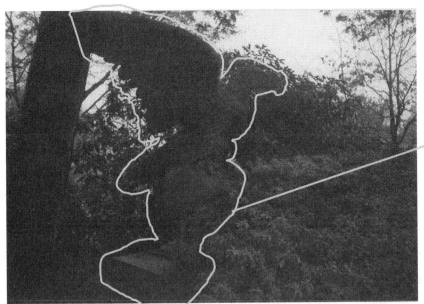

P 41. *Can you see what I outlined in this photo?* The picture is dark because it was overcast on the day of the appraisal so you might not be able to see the image clearly. It's a metal statue of a very large eagle standing on a globe with it's wings spread out wide (side view). The frontal view photo of this statue is below. This is one of the eagle statues from Grand Central Station in New York City. I don't know how the homeowner of the property got a hold of this statue, but I'm sure you won't find many of these during your appraisals! This thing was about 20 feet high.

P 42. *No, it's not a junkyard or auto salvage site.* It's actually the yard of a home I had to appraise and inspect for a client. I doubt you'll ever encounter a situation like this one. However, if you do just remember to make adjustments in your report based upon how all of this junk would affect the purchase price offered by potential buyers of this property. *(You better make it a BIG negative adjustment!)*

P 43.

**Jack and Jill went up the hill, to fetch a pail of water,**

But because the homeowner didn't properly seal up the well,

**Jack fell down and broke his crown, and Jill came tumbling after!**

So you see what happens when you don't take the advice in my *Home Inspection From A to Z* book? Jack and Jill ended up getting hurt because of the negligence of the property owner.
*(I wonder if Jack and Jill got an "ambulance chaser" attorney to file a lawsuit against the homeowner?)*

All unused wells must be properly sealed for safety. This well has a sealed cover over it.

Appraisal Stationery

# Sample Business Card, Brochures, Stationery, & Price Quote Card

## Sample Business Stationery

## Sample Business Card

### Sample Envelope

**Capitol R.E. Appraisers**

1234 Little Hill Road
Anytown, CT  12345-6789

John Doe  -  Real Estate Appraiser

PHONE  (123) 456-7890
FAX  (123) 456-7890
 info@capitol.com    www.capitol.com

**Capitol Real Estate Appraisers**
John Doe
1234 Little Hill Road
Anytown,  CT  12345-6789

## Capitol Real Estate Appraisers

John Doe
1234 Little Hill Road
Anytown,  CT  12345-6789

PHONE  (123) 456-7890     FAX  (123) 456-7890

Email:  info@capitol.com     Web:  www.capitol.com

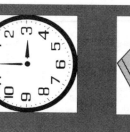

## 3 Days of Appraisal Analysis

## Narrative, In-Depth Reports

## Available 7 Days A Week

## Clients Encouraged To Attend The On-Site Evaluation

Your home is the most important investment of your life! Have a professional appraiser take the risk out of your decision.

# Call Capitol and hire the best appraiser!

Home and Condominium Appraisals

We do extensive research to provide our clients with an in-depth analysis of the subject property.

Serving all towns in the New England area.

## Capitol Real Estate Appraisers

1234 Little Hill Road
Anytown, CT 12345

Phone (123) 456-7890
Fax (123) 456-7890
Email: info@capitol.com
Web: www.capitol.com

Capitol Real Estate Appraisers
1234 Little Hill Road
Anytown, CT  12345-6789

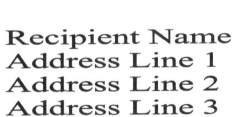

**Recipient Name**
**Address Line 1**
**Address Line 2**
**Address Line 3**

## Our Real Estate Appraisals Include:

◇ Subject Property Analysis for overall condition and appeal

◇ Appraisal Depreciation Aspects

◇ Land and Site Valuation

◇ Highest and Best Use Analysis

◇ Town Hall Records Search

◇ Neighborhood Evaluation

◇ Numerous Comparable Sales evaluated to estimate market value of the property

# Price Quote Card

Report Number

Date of Inspection/Appraisal

Bldg. Address                                    Zip

Day of Week & Time

Inspector/Appraiser          Present Owner          Phone

Client                                           Comments, Directions, etc.

Address

Zip

Home Phone

Work Phone

Attorney

Address

Zip

R.E. Agent

(c) 1992 Guy Cozzi

# Price Quote Card

Report Number

Date of Inspection/Appraisal

Bldg. Address                                    Zip

Day of Week & Time

Inspector/Appraiser          Present Owner          Phone

Client                                           Comments, Directions, etc.

Address

Zip

Home Phone

Work Phone

Attorney

Address

Zip

R.E. Agent

(c) 1992 Guy Cozzi

Inspection

Appraisal

| Date Price Quoted |
| How You Heard of Us |
| Type of Property        Condo        1 Family |
| Square Footage |
| Bedrooms / Bathrooms / Garage |
| Reported Age of Bldg. |
| Overall Condition    Very Good    Good    Average    Fair    Poor |
| Basement / Crawl Space |
| Air Conditioning |
| Septic System Test |
| Well System Test |
| Water Lab Test |
| Termite Inspection |
| Radon Test |
| Location Factor |
| Selling Price |

**TOTAL FEE $**

---

Inspection

Appraisal

| Date Price Quoted |
| How You Heard of Us |
| Type of Property        Condo        1 Family |
| Square Footage |
| Bedrooms / Bathrooms / Garage |
| Reported Age of Bldg. |
| Overall Condition    Very Good    Good    Average    Fair    Poor |
| Basement / Crawl Space |
| Air Conditioning |
| Septic System Test |
| Well System Test |
| Water Lab Test |
| Termite Inspection |
| Radon Test |
| Location Factor |
| Selling Price |

**TOTAL FEE $**

## More Nemmar Products

### Energy Saving Home Improvements From A to Z ™

*Don't let your dream house be a money pit in disguise!* Our **5-star rated** book that teaches you how to **save** thousands of dollars **and** help the environment by making minor improvements to your home. You'll learn how to **lower your utility bills by 50%,** live more comfortably, and help the environment. Includes many photographs with detailed descriptions.

### Home Inspection Business From A to Z ™

*The REAL FACTS the other books don't tell you!* Our **number one** selling home inspection book. This is **definitely** the best home inspection book on the market and has been called the "Bible" of the inspection industry. *Every* aspect of home inspections is covered with precise steps to follow. Includes many photographs with detailed descriptions.

### Real Estate Appraisal From A to Z ™

*The REAL FACTS the other books don't tell you!* Our **number one** selling appraisal book. This is **definitely** the best real estate appraisal book on the market. *Every* aspect of real estate appraising is covered with precise steps to follow. Includes sample professional appraisal reports and many photographs with detailed descriptions.

### Real Estate From A to Z ™

*Don't let your dream house be a nightmare in disguise!* You'll learn information the professionals use to inspect, appraise, invest, and renovate real estate. This book covers every aspect of Real Estate from A to Z and contains abbreviated versions of our three **5-star rated** books: *Home Inspection Business, Real Estate Appraisal, and Energy Saving Home Improvement From A to Z.*

### DVD's - Home Inspection From A to Z ™

Our **5 star rated** DVD's have two hours of video plus you get the 80 page *HIB* **DVD** *Companion Guidebook!*
**OPERATING SYSTEMS** DVD topics including: heating systems, air-conditioning, water heaters, plumbing, well water system, septic system, electrical system, gas service, and auxiliary systems. Health Concerns topics including: asbestos insulation, radon gas, and water testing.
**INTERIOR and EXTERIOR** DVD topics including: roof, chimneys, siding, eaves, gutters, drainage and grading, windows, walkways, entrances and porches, driveways, walls and fences, patios and terraces, decks, swimming pools, exterior structures, wood destroying insects, garage, kitchen, bathrooms, floors and stairs, walls and ceilings, windows and doors, fireplaces, attics, ventilation, insulation, basement/lower level, and water penetration.

### Home Buyer's Survival Kit ™

***Don't buy, sell, or renovate your home without this!*** Includes: Four of our **top selling** books – *Real Estate Home Inspection Checklist From A to Z, Energy Saving Home Improvements From A to Z, Home Inspection Business From A to Z,* and *Real Estate Appraisal From A to Z.* Plus, you get both of our *Home Inspection From A to Z – DVD's.* As an added bonus you also get the 80 page *HIB* **DVD** *Companion Guidebook.*

### Narrative Report Generator and On-Site Checklist

*The report generator and checklist the others don't have!* CD-Rom with the *best* Narrative Report Generator and On-Site Checklist on the market! These will enable you to *easily* do 30 page narrative, professional home inspection reports to send to your clients. These will assist you at the inspection site to be sure that you properly evaluate the subject property. Designed to walk you through the entire inspection process with very detailed instructions on how to properly evaluate the condition and status of **all** aspects of a home in a fool-proof, step-by-step system and create professional, narrative reports.

### Appraiser and Home Inspector "A to Z Coach" School Training ™

**Personal One-to-One Training** with an "A to Z Coach" where you are the only student! Your training is personalized to meet your specific requirements and needs. Your questions are answered to make sure you learn everything you need to know about real estate - from Asbestos to Zoning. No crowded classrooms filled with students - unlike other real estate training schools. You'll learn how to become a highly paid Real Estate Appraiser or Home Inspector from top experts with many years of experience in the business!

**Telephone and Email Training** with an "A to Z Coach" via telephone and email. Our training school meets and exceeds the standards of all the leading home inspection and appraisal organizations. Regardless of where you live, you can enroll as a student in Nemmar Real Estate Training's "A to Z Coach" School.

# Just some of our books, CD's, DVD's and much more!

# Email info@nemmar.com for prices.

# Visit us at www.nemmar.com

# The Cost Approach

## The Cost Approach

The *Cost Approach* uses the reproduction cost to estimate the market value of the subject property. The appraiser uses an estimate based on the cost to replace or reproduce the subject property being appraised. This approach takes into account the cost to build an identical house to the subject property. The cost of the identical house is determined at today's prices (if today is the "as of" date), minus the three forms of depreciation, *(physical, functional and external)*. I will describe the three forms of depreciation a little later. The result of the cost analysis at today's prices minus the depreciation will give you the depreciated value of the building. The site value with the site improvements is then added to the depreciated value of the building to get the final estimated market value of the subject property. Please review the sample appraisals in this book to view examples of the Cost Approach for an actual written appraisal report.

You also need to review section HUD and FHA Guidelines page 220 and section Sample State Real Estate Appraiser Guidelines page 297 for more details and rules about appraisal standards and how to fill out the standard appraisal report forms.

> *The Cost Approach is based on the assumption that a typically informed buyer would not pay more for the subject property then it would cost him to build a similar property.*

The Cost Approach is based on the assumption that a typically informed buyer would not pay more money for the subject property then it would cost him to build a similar property. The similar property being considered would have the same utility and depreciation as the subject property. Meaning, that if a house was selling for $215,000 and the typical buyer could have a similar house built for about $190,000, then the buyer would probably build a similar house. The buyer might want to build a similar house, rather than pay more money for the existing subject property. Now you have to remember that the cost of the similar house the buyer would be pricing to have built for himself must take into account all of the three forms of depreciation that the subject property currently has.

The Cost Approach uses the *Replacement Cost* and the *Reproduction Cost*. The Replacement Cost estimates the cost of replacing the **utility** of the subject property. This takes into account the three types of depreciation of the subject property: physical, functional and external. The Reproduction Cost is

the cost to **reproduce** the subject property by building it with all new construction, from the ground up. The construction will be in the identical style, square footage, room layouts, construction materials, etc. as the subject property. The Reproduction Cost is the dollar amount of reproducing the building with its current materials, (plaster, stone, sheetrock, wood frame, etc.). In this reproduction cost, it also includes all of the building's current depreciation, (physical, functional and external).

Basically, the Cost Approach takes the Reproduction Cost New of the building, minus the depreciated items, plus the site value. The result is used as an estimate of current market value. Four methods used with the Cost Approach:

1   *Quantity Survey Method - A method of cost estimation that replicates the contractor's original procedure in detail.* This is the most detailed way to estimate market value using the Cost Approach.

2   *Unit In Place Method - A method of cost estimation that includes materials and labor in the unit cost of component sections of the structure "in place."*

3   *Trade Breakdown* or *Segregated Cost Method - A method of cost estimation that breaks the major functional parts of the structure into an installed unit cost.* It's the breakdown to cost out the structure as though you were building it new.

4   *Comparable Unit Method - A method of cost estimation that lumps together all components of the structure and converts the lump sum amount to a unit basis (e.g., per square ft, per cubic foot).* This is the method that is most often used to fill out the form appraisal reports. Cost estimate books are used to assist the appraiser. Unfortunately, it's also the least accurate method to use for the Cost Approach to estimate market value.

> *The Cost Approach also DOES NOT have to be the highest estimate of value for all three approaches to value.*
>
> *Many appraisers will try to tell you that the Cost Approach has to be the highest estimated value in a report. Baloney!!*

The cost estimate that you arrive at in the Cost Approach does not have to equal the value of the property. This means that the estimate of value in the Direct Sales Comparison or Income Approaches, doesn't have to equal the value you estimate in the Cost Approach. The Cost Approach also

*DOES NOT* have to be the highest estimate of value for all three approaches to value, (Direct Sales, Income and Cost Approaches). I'll elaborate on that again so you don't forget it. Don't use the assumption that the Cost Approach should always be the highest value for the subject property. This is an old myth that some appraisers are led to believe is always true. Because of this myth, all of their appraisal reports intentionally show the Cost Approach as the highest estimate of value. You have to keep an open mind about this. Many appraisers, and some third parties, will try to tell you that the Cost Approach **has to be** the highest estimated value in a report. Baloney!! Anyone who tells you that doesn't know what they're talking about. See section The Cost Approach page 181 for an explanation of the logic and reason on this.

It's true that often the Cost Approach may be the highest estimate of value. However, let's say you're appraising a house and you do the cost analysis of the construction materials to duplicate the site and improvements. After you do this cost analysis, you find that it costs less money to build the subject property than it's estimated value using the Direct Sales Comparison Approach. The difference between the <u>cost</u> of the site and improvements and the <u>value</u> of the site and improvements, could be due to the builders profit! This has to be figured into the calculations of the cost to reproduce the property. The Cost Approach doesn't have to always be higher than the other approaches to value. The reason for this is: *Why would someone go through all the work, problems and risks of building a house just to have a small profit, or no profit at all?* The builder will certainly want to make a big profit on the deal for all of his/her time, effort and financial risk involved in building a house. If the <u>cost</u> of the site and improvements is greater than the <u>value</u> of the site and improvements, then the builder will lose money on the deal! How long could you stay in business if you lost money on every house you built? Not very long. If you want, you can include a figure in your cost analysis amounts to account for the builder's profit.

The Cost Approach is only really effective when used for relatively new buildings that are the Highest and Best Use of the site. This approach isn't very effective for older houses. It's not effective due to the margin for error with an older house in estimating the three types of depreciation. Also, with older houses there is a large margin for error in estimating the cost of using the same construction materials today. The Cost Approach is used more effectively when there are no good comparable properties available to assist the appraiser. A reason for a lack of sales could be due to unique or unusual improvements on the subject site.

> *The Cost Approach is only really effective when used for relatively new buildings that are the Highest and Best Use of the site. This approach isn't very effective for older houses.*

For buildings in crowded urban areas, like a big city, there are probably very few (if any) vacant land sales to analyze and so the Cost Approach isn't very effective. If you have no vacant land sales, then you have to estimate the land value by using a **residual** technique. This simply means that you have to take sales and estimate the cost of only constructing the building. After that, you must take out for any depreciation that affected the sale. What you're left with is a *residual* value for the vacant land which is an estimate of the land value. There are three types of residuals used for appraisal purposes:

1  **Land**
2  **Building**
3  **Property**

Land doesn't depreciate from wear and tear over the years. It can lose or gain value, but it doesn't depreciate from a tax deduction standpoint. You can use the residual values to help you in estimating the depreciation of a site or the improvements. For example, let's say you were doing the Cost Approach for a single family appraisal. We'll assume that you were trying to estimate the value of the lot for a sales comparable. However, you can't find any vacant land sales because the area is too built-up and/or there are no recent vacant lot sales to use as comparables. You could estimate the Reproduction Cost New of the building, and then subtract the depreciation amount. Then take this figure, plus the site improvements, and subtract it from the value of the property. You're left with an estimated value of the vacant lot.

You can also use the *Assessed Value Ratio* for the area to help you figure out the vacant land value. Do this if there are no vacant land sales in the subject neighborhood. See section Tax Assessments page 165 for more information about the Assessed Value Ratio. There are various other techniques you can use. However, they're much more involved and you would be better off learning them while taking the State appraisal courses. They're too involved to teach properly outside a classroom atmosphere.

# Basics Of Appraisal Depreciation

There are three types of depreciation that you have to consider for an appraisal report. These depreciation items are also evaluated for the Cost Approach. *(Obsolescence* is also used to describe *depreciation).* This section covers some definitions and explanations that you will need to know for the depreciation and Cost Approach examples later in this book:

1    **Physical Depreciation**
2    **Functional Depreciation**
3    **External Depreciation**

I'll explain the differences between *Curable* and *Incurable* items from an appraisal standpoint. Let's say you want to repair, change, update, and/or add something to a house. We'll assume that the repairs will have a neutral or positive impact on the market value of the house. Well, if this were the case, then from an appraisal standpoint you should make the repairs and/or additions to the house. To determine if something is a <u>curable</u> item, simply ask yourself whether it's worth it to repair the problem. If the repair costs <u>do not</u> equal or exceed the value that the repaired item will add to the property, then you should go ahead and repair the item and/or make the changes. In order to make it a **curable** problem, you should at least break even with the money you spend to repair the problem. The break-even point we're referring to, is in relation to what the increased value of the property will be when you're finished. For example, let's say the cost to remodel and update a bathroom in your house is $5,250. If you make these repairs then the market value of your house will increase by $7,750. You could then conclude that the repairs are *curable* since the increase in market value will be $2,500 **more** than the costs to do the work.

To determine if something is an <u>incurable</u> item, simply use the same logic. Ask yourself whether or not it's worth it to repair the problem. From an appraisal standpoint, if the repair costs <u>do</u> exceed the value that the repaired item will add to the property, then you should <u>not</u> repair the item and/or make the change. It's an **incurable** problem if you will not at least break even with the money you spend to repair the problem. The break-even point is in relation to what the increased value of the property will be when you're finished with the repairs. For example, let's say the cost to add a garage to your home is $10,500. If you build this addition then the market value of your house will increase by only $8,000. You could then conclude that the repairs are *incurable* since the increase in market value will be $2,500 **less** than the costs to do the work.

## Physical Depreciation:
1.    **Physical Curable** - refers to physical items that are worth paying the expense to repair the problem because of the neutral or positive impact on market value it will have for the subject property.

2.    **Physical Incurable** - refers to physical items that <u>are not</u> worth paying the expense to repair the problem because they will not have a positive market value impact for the subject property.

3.    **Physical Short-Lived Items** - refers to physical items and operating systems of a house that have normal depreciation and wear and tear on them over time. Such items can be the roof, heating system, air-conditioning system, appliances, etc.

4.    **Physical Long-Lived Items** - refers to the basic structure of the building, such as, the foundation, the walls, etc.

## Functional Depreciation:
1.    **Functional Curable** - refers to functional items that are worth paying the expense to repair and/or change the problem because of the neutral or positive impact on market value it will have for the property.

2.    **Functional Incurable** - refers to functional items that <u>are not</u> worth paying the expense to repair and/or change the problem because they will not have a positive impact on market value for the subject property.

## External Depreciation:
1.    **External Obsolescence** (Incurable) - refers to external items that negatively influence the market value of the subject property. External items are very rarely curable because resolving the problem is out of the hands of the owner of the subject property. Some examples of external depreciation items are: locational problems with the area; environmental problems; economic problems in the economy and the local market; etc.

Physical and Functional depreciation in the Cost Approach should be the same, or compatible, with the like adjustments that you make in the Direct Sales Comparison Approach. This means that, let's say you make an adjustment in the Direct Sales Comparison Approach for a physical or functional depreciation item. Then you should make an adjustment that's equal to or accurately reflects, the same depreciation adjustment for this item which you make in the Cost Approach. For example, let's say you determine that an adjustment of $3,250 is needed in the Cost Approach to account for a large wood deck on the house. If this were the case, then you would have to make the same or a compatible adjustment in the Direct Sales Comparison Approach to accurately reflect the wood deck. You can't make adjustments in each approach that contradict one another. Remember that you have to be consistent throughout the entire appraisal report!

An example of *Functional Obsolescence* is a property that has been over-improved *(obsolescence* is the same thing as saying depreciation). An *over-improvement* occurs when a homeowner makes an improvement or change to a property that costs more  money than the increased value it brings to the property (see the *functional incurable depreciation* definition).

An example of *External Obsolescence* is a property that is located next to a highway or on a very busy street. External Obsolescence items have to be allocated proportionately to the land and the building for depreciation purposes. For example, let's say a house is located on a busy street and this has a negative impact on market value. Well, even if the house was knocked down, the vacant lot would still be negatively affected by the busy street. That's why you have to figure out the dollar or percentage amount of the negative impact that is allocated separately to the land and to the building. External, location, and economic obsolescence are all synonyms and they're measured in the neighborhood for appraisal reports.

Economic Obsolescence *(External)* depreciation refers to: high interest rates, high labor costs, high taxes, drop in the employment in the base industry, etc. You can use economic obsolescence for an external depreciation adjustment in the Cost Approach if there's a poor real estate market in the area. You must apply the percentage to the building and the percentage to the site, as **separate** amounts for economic obsolescence.

*Accrued Depreciation* and *Diminished Utility* are interchangeable because they essentially are the same. The appraisal course definition for Accrued Depreciation *(diminished utility)* is:

*"Total depreciation from all sources, measured as the difference between reproduction cost new of the improvements and the present worth of those improvements as of the date of the appraisal."*

*Total* or *Remaining Economic Life* refers to how long the improvements (the house itself) will add value to the land. Meaning, that for how many more years do you feel that the property will be worth more with the existing house still standing. As opposed to, knocking down the house to build a new one or just knocking down the house and leaving the land vacant.

*Physical Age* refers to how old the improvements (the house) actually are. In simple terms, what is the actual age of the house listed at town hall in the public record. *(Don't just use the age the owner tells you or what is stated in the real estate listing. Often they're wrong, so use the age listed in the public record).*

*Effective Age* refers to how old the improvements (the house) appear to be. This means that if you didn't know what the actual age of the house was, then when would you estimate the house last had any major repairs and upgrading. Effective Age is often different from the actual age of the house. The cause of this difference is due to the normal maintenance and upgrading done over the years, or the lack of it not being done over the years. For example, let's say you're appraising a house that's 85 years old. Chances are very good that the house has gone through several major upgradings over the years by different owners to keep up with the changing times. The Effective Age you estimate would be the last time you felt that the house has had some significant repairs and upgrading done

to it. Pay particular attention to the kitchens, bathrooms, windows and doors. These areas really can show the age of a house that is outdated due to the lack of any significant upgrading over the years.

# Cost Approach Example #1

Let's use a depreciation example to walk you through the Cost Approach process. We'll assume the following figures were obtained during our appraisal field work and inspection of the subject property.

◊ Actual Age = 10 years
◊ Effective Age = 5 years
◊ Total Economic Life = 50 years
◊ Reproduction Cost New = $75,000

## Physical Curable:
◊ Painting needed = $750
◊ Gutters needed = $450
◊ $750 + $450 = $1,200 is the total Physical Curable depreciation

## Short Lived Items:

|  | Cost | Effect-ive Age | Useful Life | % of Deprec | $ of Deprec |
|---|---|---|---|---|---|
| Roof | $2,000 | 10 | 20 | 50 | $1,000 |
| Heat System | 1,500 | 10 | 25 | 40 | 600 |
| Carpets | 600 | 2 | 6 | 33 | 200 |
| Kitch. Appl. | 1,800 | 10 | 15 | 67 | 1,206 |

| Total Cost of Items: | **$5,900** | Actual Depre-ciation Cost: | **$3,006** |
|---|---|---|---|

There's a point to remember when estimating the Total Physical depreciation amount for the structure. That is, to use the **Actual Depreciation Cost,** and not the total cost new of the items, as your *Short Lived Items* depreciation amount. This means that the Short Lived Items are still in operating order but they have aged and won't last as long as a similar new item. For example, the roof is 10 years old but it has a life expectancy of 20 years. This gives the roof another 10 years before it will need to be replaced. If it costs $2,000 to install a new roof and it's 50% depreciated now, then the current depreciated dollar amount value of the roof is $1,000. It's similar to buying a used car. A used car may still be operating properly but you wouldn't buy it for the same price you could get a new one for, would you?

The percentage of depreciation for the value of the *Long Lived items* (the structure) is estimated by dividing the *Effective Age* by the *Total Economic Life* of the subject property. This is also referred to as the *Age/Life Method* for estimating the physical depreciation of a building. The Total Economic Life is also called the Remaining Economic Life. Therefore, in our example it would be:

Effective Age/Total Economic Life = % of Depreciation

$$5/50 = .10 \quad or \quad 10\%$$

We will use the 10% depreciation figure to estimate the depreciation dollar amount for the Long Lived Items. But first we must subtract the Physical and Short Lived Items from the Reproduction Cost New, before estimating the depreciation for the Long Lived Items. We do this by taking the depreciation cost of the Physical Curable depreciation items, and then adding this amount to the total cost _new_ of the Short Lived Items. We then subtract this amount from the Reproduction Cost New. In our example we end up with the following formula.

$$\$75,000 - (\$1,200 + \$5,900) = \$67,900$$

Therefore, $67,900 is the amount left to be depreciated by the percentage amount we derived earlier. This is needed to estimate the depreciation dollar amount for the Long Lived Items.

$$\$67,900 \times .10 = \$6,790$$

Therefore, we are left with the following dollar amounts of depreciation:

| | | |
|---|---|---|
| Physical | = | $1,200 |
| Short Lived Items | = | $3,006 |
| Long Lived Items | = | $6,790 |

We add these to get our Total Physical Depreciation for the building.

$$\$1,200 + \$3,006 + \$6,790 = \$10,996$$

You **have to** remember, that you must subtract the Physical Curable depreciation and the _total cost new_ of the Short Lived Items, from the Reproduction Cost New <u>before</u> estimating the depreciation for the Long Lived Items. The reason for this is that if you don't, you'll be "double dipping" when you estimate your depreciation amounts. Meaning that the depreciation amount that you subtract for the Long Lived Items, will be incorrectly increased by the inclusion of the depreciation amounts for the Physical Curable and Short Lived Items. You would then be taking out more depreciation then you should be. We'll use our example to show you the **incorrect** way of doing this so you can see what I mean by "double dipping."

$$\$75,000 \times .10 = \$7,500$$

The increase would be $7,500 - $6,790 = $710. This would incorrectly increase the amount of Total Physical Depreciation for the subject property by $710.

Now we'll take an example of _Functional Obsolescence_. Remember that _obsolescence_ is the same as saying depreciation. Let's say the vast majority of houses in the area that are similar to the subject property have central air-conditioning. Therefore, we can conclude that a typical buyer would expect the house to have central A/C. If the house did not have central A/C, then the buyer would pay a little bit lower purchase prices to compensate for the air-conditioning not being installed. This is considered a Functional Depreciated item, as opposed to a Physical Depreciated item. The reason for that is the central air-conditioning <u>is not</u> installed in the house, so there's no physical depreciation on it to account for.

We have to first estimate what the cost would be to install a central air-conditioning system "as of" the date of the appraisal. Let's say we asked a local A/C contractor, or checked the published cost manuals, and get an estimate. We'll assume that the estimate is $1,750 to correct the problem by installing the central air-conditioning. We then must estimate what it would have cost to install the central air-conditioning at the time the house was built. Our research tells us that during construction of the property it would have cost $1,500 to install central air-conditioning.

We can now conclude the _Accrued Functional Depreciation_ for the subject property. We do this by subtracting the two figures.

$$\$1,750 - \$1,500 = \$250$$

From our research we have found that a comparable house to the subject property would sell for an additional $2,800 if central air-conditioning was installed. We have already estimated that it would cost $1,750 to install. Therefore, the central air-conditioning is a _Functional Curable Item_ because the value added to the subject property by installing it, is equal to or greater than the cost of installing the A/C.

Now we'll take an example of _Locational Obsolescence_. This is also called External or Economic Obsolescence. Let's say, there's a gas station next to the subject property. From our knowledge of the area, we conclude that the typical buyer would pay less for the house to compensate for the location next to a gas station. The typical buyer would rather have a house with only other residential properties around it and not any commercial properties in view.

You **have to** apply any Locational Obsolescence values _separately_ to the building and the land of the subject property. This is because the land is not a depreciable item. However, site improvements do have depreciated values, such as, driveways, landscaping, etc. The land will be affected by a Locational Obsolescence and you have to take that into account in your site value estimate.

In order to estimate the total Locational Obsolescence depreciation amount, we need to make some evaluations. We must first decide what percentage of the value of the subject property is allocated to land, and what percentage is allocated to the building. This is called the *Land Value to Building Value Ratio*. This technique is also used for tax purposes. The technique is used to figure out the depreciation amount on your tax returns for real estate. Let's say our research of the area has shown that typically the estimate of value is 20% allocated to the land and 80% allocated to the building. Another way of saying this is that the *Land Value to Building Value Ratio* is 1:4. Meaning the ratio is one part land plus four parts building. This tells us that 1/5 (or 20%) of the value is allocated to the land.

From our research, we have found that a comparable house to the subject property would sell for an additional $4,200 if it was not located next to the gas station. We simply multiply this figure by the percentage of value allocated to the building, to get our Locational Obsolescence amount.

$$\$4,200 \times .80 = \$3,360$$

Now we will add up all of the three depreciation amounts we have estimated. We do this to obtain the depreciated value of the Reproduction Cost New of the subject property.

| | | |
|---|---|---|
| Total Physical Depreciation | = | $10,996 |
| Total Functional Depreciation | = | $250 |
| Total Locational Depreciation | = | $3,360 |

We add these to get our *Total Depreciation* for the building.

$$\$10,996 + \$250 + \$3,360 = \$14,606$$

Now we simply subtract the total depreciation amount from the Reproduction Cost New.

$$\$75,000 - \$14,606 = \$60,394$$

Therefore, the *depreciated value* of the Reproduction Cost New of the subject property is estimated to be **$60,394**.

# Cost Approach Example #2

I know how much you liked the first one, so let's try another depreciation example to walk you through the Cost Approach process again! Let's say, you've been hired to appraise a single family house that's 20 years old. It's similar to the other houses in the neighborhood and it has an effective age of 20 years.

◊ The estimated cost of the items which you decided need to be repaired is: Painting of the trim work $1,000, a broken door $200, and a hole in the kitchen wall $100.

◊ During your inspection and field work you noted some depreciated short-lived items and have made the following calculations:

### Short Lived Items:

| | Cost | Effect-ive Age | Useful Life | % of Deprec | $ of Deprec |
|---|---|---|---|---|---|
| Refrigerator | $800 | 5 | 20 | 25 | $200 |
| Furnace | 2,500 | 15 | 30 | 50 | 1,250 |
| Oven | 400 | 5 | 20 | 25 | 100 |
| Roof | 5,000 | 10 | 20 | 50 | 2,500 |

| | | |
|---|---|---|
| Total Cost of Items: | **$8,700** | Actual Depre-ciation Cost: **$4,050** |

◊ The estimated reproduction cost new of the structure is $100,000. The site improvements have a depreciated value of $5,000. After analyzing the market you estimate that the value of the vacant site is $20,000.

◊ After curing all forms of physical depreciation the remaining structure has an effective age of 15 years. An analysis of the market has shown that similar houses have an economic life of 50 years.

◊ The subject property has a one-car garage and most homes in the area have a two-car garage. The subject property is currently rented for $1,000 per month. (This is also known as the *contract rent*.) An analysis of the market shows that comparable homes which are rented with two car garages, bring in $1,075 per month in rental income. You have analyzed many recent sales, and a gross rent multiplier of 100 is determined to be a good estimate for the area. A local contractor has estimated that the cost of enlarging the garage now to have a two-car capacity would be $6,000. If the second car capacity was included during the original construction it would have cost $4,000.

◊ You have not found any external factors that negatively affect the market value of the subject property. Therefore, there is no external obsolescence depreciation amount.

### What is the estimated market value of the subject property using the Cost Approach to value?

Reproduction Cost New        =    $100,000

Physical Curable Deferred Maintenance:
| | | |
|---|---|---|
| Trim Painting | = | $1,000 |
| Broken Door | = | $ 200 |
| Kitchen Wall Hole | = | $ 100 |

Total Physical Curable    =    $1,300

Physical Incurable Short Lived Items:

| | Cost | Effect-ive Age | Useful Life | % of Deprec | $ of Deprec |
|---|---|---|---|---|---|
| Refrigerator | $800 | 5 | 20 | 25 | $200 |
| Furnace | 2,500 | 15 | 30 | 50 | 1,250 |
| Oven | 400 | 5 | 20 | 25 | 100 |
| Roof | 5,000 | 10 | 20 | 50 | 2,500 |

Total Cost of Items:  **$8,700**      Actual Depreciation Cost:  **$4,050**

Physical Incurable Long Lived Items:
| | | |
|---|---|---|
| Reproduction Cost New | = | $100,000 |
| Minus Physical Curable | = | $1,300 |
| Minus Cost New Physical Incurable Short Lived Items | = | - $10,000 |
| Cost of Bone Structure | = | $90,000 |

Percent of Depreciation    =    $\dfrac{\text{Effective Age (after curing)}}{\text{Economic Life}}$

$$30\% = 15/50$$
$$\$90,000 \text{ x } .30 = \$27,000$$

Summation of Physical Depreciation:
| | | |
|---|---|---|
| Physical Curable Deferred Maintenance | = | $ 1,300 |
| Physical Incurable Short Lived | = | $ 4,050 |
| Physical Incurable Long Lived | = | $27,000 |
| Total Physical Depreciation | = | $32,350 |

Functional Obsolescence:
For a one-car garage as opposed to a two-car garage.

Market Rent minus Contract Rent = Rent Differential
$$\$1,075 - \$1,000 = \$75$$

Loss in Value  =  Rent Differential x Gross Rent Multiplier
$$\$7,500 = \$75 \text{ x } 100$$

If the increase in value to the subject property for installing a two-car garage is equal to or greater than the Cost to Cure then it is a Curable item.
$$\$7,500 \geq \$6,000 \text{  Cost to Cure}$$

If the item is curable then the depreciated Functional Obsolescence value is:  Cost New minus Cost if it was included during the original construction = the depreciated value amount.

$$\$6,000 - \$4,000 = \$2,000$$

External Obsolescence:
There were no external obsolescence items noted that affected the subject property.

### Estimated Market Value Using The Cost Approach:

| | | |
|---|---|---|
| Reproduction Cost New | = | $100,000 |
| Physical Depreciation | = | $32,350 |
| Functional Obsolescence | = | $ 2,000 |
| External Obsolescence | = | $ 0 |
| Total Depreciation | = | - $34,350 |

$$\$100,000 - \$34,350 = \$62,650$$

| | | |
|---|---|---|
| Depreciated Reproduction Cost | = | $65,650 |
| Depreciated Site Improvements | = | $ 5,000 |
| Depreciated Improvements Value | = | $70,650 |
| Plus Land Value | = | $20,000 |

$$\$70,650 - \$20,000 = \$90,650$$

**Total Indicated Value By The Cost Approach =**

## $90,650

## Cost Approach Example #3 & 4

There are two additional examples of the Cost Approach method in the sample Singe Family appraisal report and the sample Multi-Family appraisal report included in this book. Please review those sample appraisals.

# The Income Approach

## The Income Approach

The following sections will cover the Income Approach and other income related methods used by real estate appraisers. Using the Income Approach, the appraiser estimates what a prudent investor would pay for the subject property based on the income the property produces. Today, any computer can do all the math calculations for you which greatly simplifies the process, unlike many years ago. However, as always, the appraiser __MUST__ use their own training, experience, and judgment when determining what numbers and amounts need to be plugged into the calculations. There is an additional example of the Income Approach method in the sample Multi-Family appraisal report included in this book. Please review that sample appraisal.

You also need to review section HUD and FHA Guidelines page 220 and section Sample State Real Estate Appraiser Guidelines page 297 for more details and rules about appraisal standards and how to fill out the standard appraisal report forms.

> *The Income Approach is more effective in appraising income producing properties in which the typical buyer would be an investor who will rent out the property.*

The *Income Approach* uses the potential income generated by the property to estimate the market value of the subject property. The Income Approach is based on the assumption that a typically informed buyer would estimate the value of a property based upon the anticipated future benefits of purchasing it. Future benefits could be in dollar amounts or in amenities of ownership. The Income Approach is more effective in appraising income producing properties in which the typical buyer would be an investor who will rent out the property. The anticipated future income is discounted to what the present value is worth today. For example, a dollar earned by someone today is worth more money than a dollar earned five years from now. The reason for this is inflation which is the cause of rising prices over the years. Also, if you have a dollar today you can invest it or put it in the bank to earn interest. Therefore, in five years you can end up with much more money than the original dollar you started with. Whether you're talking about one dollar or a million dollars, the concept is the same.

The Income Approach is not very effective for appraising a single family house or condominium. The reason for this is that single family homes and condos are generally not purchased based on the net rental income that they earn. Single family houses and condos tend to be purchased as a residence for the owner, as opposed to being purchased by an investor to rent out.

## Basic Algebra

Now here's the part that you've all been waiting for. Let's get into some math formulas and calculations! I tried to include the more serious math sections as far back in the book as I could to "break it to you gently". **When you read the *Cash Equivalency Example #3* you'll see how all the following math sections relate to an actual appraisal report.** So don't get bored and put this book on the shelf to collect dust. Instead of looking at the math with a negative attitude, try to be like Dorothy from the *Wizard of Oz* and keep repeating to yourself over and over: *"There's no place like math class. There's no place like math class. There's no place like math class."* If you do it with your eyes closed while you click your heels, then you might start to believe what you're saying! Just use your computer to handle most of the math calculations which takes the tedious work out of the process. I will round out the numbers when there are more than two decimal places. So please don't worry if you get answers with more than two decimal places and they don't appear to *exactly* match the numbers in the book.

> *When you read the Cash Equivalency Example #3 you'll see how all the following math sections relate to an actual appraisal report. Instead of looking at the math with a negative attitude, try to be like Dorothy from the Wizard of Oz and keep repeating to yourself over and over:*
> *"There's no place like math class..."*

We'll start off with some simple algebra. In algebra you always multiply and divide before you do any other calculations in a formula, unless there are parentheses around part of the formula. Anything inside the parenthesis is always calculated first. To solve the equation $5/7 + 6/11$ you have to first make the *denominator* (lower figure) equal for both sets of numbers. You do this by multiplying each number by the opposite number's denominator. For example, the *numerator* (top figure) and the denominator in $5/7$ would be multiplied by 11 to give you:

$$5/7 \times 11 = 55/77$$

The numerator and the denominator in 6/11 would then be multiplied by 7:

$$6/11 \times 7 = 42/77$$

This leaves us with:

$$55/77 + 42/77 = 97/77$$

The *reciprocal* of a number is that number turned upside down. For example:

The reciprocal of $X = 1/X$
The reciprocal of $4 = 1/4$
The reciprocal of $6/11 = 11/6$

The *complement* of a number is 1 minus that number. For example:

The complement of $X = 1 - X$
The complement of $4 = 1 - 4$
The complement of $75\% = 1 - .75$

Let's try to solve the equation:

$$(8X - 4) \, 2 = 3 \, (14 - 3X)$$

First we'll multiply the numbers that are located inside the parenthesis:

$$16X - 8 = 42 - 9X$$

Then we'll add 8 to each side of the equation to eliminate the non-X number on one side:

$$16X = 50 - 9X$$

Then we'll add 9X to each side of the equation to eliminate the X number on one side:

$$25X = 50$$

Then we'll divide each side of the equation by 25 to find the X value. This will give us our answer:

$$X = 2$$

## Leverage Example

There are three types of leverage:

1. *Negative Leverage* - This is also called unsuccessful leverage because the investor or lender ends up **losing** on their money invested in the deal.

2. *Neutral Leverage* - This is called neutral leverage because the investor or lender ends up **breaking even** on their money invested in the deal.

3. *Positive Leverage* - This is also called successful leverage because the investor or lender ends up making a **profit** on their money invested in the deal.

◊   Vo or Price = $100,000
◊   Ym = 10%
◊   Rate = Income/Value
◊   ADS = $100,000 x 10% which equals $10,000. *ADS* stands for the Annual Debt Service. Meaning that the total mortgage payments for the year on this loan will be $10,000.

Let's say you were buying an investment property for $100,000 and your mortgage interest rate was 10%. If your rate of return on this investment is greater than 10%, than you have positive leverage. You have positive leverage because the return on investment exceeds the interest rate you pay as the borrower of the money needed to purchase the property.

Let's say this property has a $15,000 total positive cash flow for the year. A *positive cash flow* simply means that the rental income from the apartments can pay all of the bills on the property each month, and there will still be extra money left over.

$$\$15,000/\$100,000 \; = \; .15$$
or
15% rate of return

The 15% rate of return on investment is greater than the 10% you're being charged by the bank for the mortgage funds. Therefore, you have positive leverage on this deal. That's the way to go!

# *Effective Interest Rate Example*

◊  Vm = The Value of the Mortgage
◊  Rm = The Rate of the Mortgage *(also called the mortgage constant)*
◊  Ym = Yield of the Mortgage *(also called the interest rate or the return on investment)*
◊  Vo = Value of the Property
◊  ADS = Annual Debt Service *(the amount of the total yearly payments on the mortgage)*
◊  n = Term of the loan *(the length of time that the mortgage is amortized)*
◊  b = balloon payment or loan balance due. A balloon refers to the remaining balance amount of a loan that comes due in one large sum at a specified time in the future.
◊  M = Loan-to-Value ratio *(amount of money lent divided by total value of property,* Vm/Vo*)*
◊  Ve = Value of the Equity *(the amount of equity in the property which is the total value of the property minus any existing mortgage loans)*
◊  Points = Points on a loan refers to the extra charge assessed by the lender to process the loan application and provide the funds. This is in addition to the interest payments made on the loan. One point is equal to 1% of the total amount of the loan given. For example, a $50,000 mortgage loan that has 3 points. The total amount the borrower has to pay for the points is $50,000 x 3% = $1,500
◊  Amortization = The monthly payment schedule to gradually pay off the loan balance of principal plus interest over a specified period of time.

Let's take an example so we can put all these abbreviations to work:

◊  Vm = $100,000
◊  Ym = 12%
◊  n = 20 years
◊  Points = 6
   Six points are equal to 6 x 1% = .06

$$.06 \text{ x } \$100,000 = \$6,000$$

$$\$100,000 - \$6,000 = \$94,000$$

This tells us that the borrower has to pay back $100,000 but he actually only receives $94,000 from the lender. The $6,000 is kept by the lender to pay for the points on the loan.

◊  ADS = Vm x Ym which in this equation would be $100,000 x 12% = $12,000

$$\$12,000/\$100,000 = .12 \text{ or } 12\%$$

$$\$12,000/\$94,000 = .1277 \text{ or } 12.77\%$$

Therefore, the *contract* interest rate for this loan is 12% but the *effective* interest rate for this loan is 12.77%. This simply means, that due to the additional cost for the loan points, the actual interest rate that the borrower is being charged for the money is 12.77% and not just 12%. This is why all loan agreements state the effective interest rate at the top of the loan document. By doing this, the borrower can see the full amount of interest, and the total of all of the payments, that they are being held responsible for.

*Nominal* interest rate is the <u>annual</u> rate charged for a loan and it's the same thing as the contract interest rate. It's just another phrase used to describe what the interest rate is that's stated in the loan contract.

The monthly *effective* interest rate charged for the loan is the effective rate divided by 12.

$$.1277/12 = .0106 \text{ or } 1\%$$

# *ITAO Example #1*

Let's try another example and we'll use the ITAO tables. ITAO stands for the *Installment To Amortize One* dollar. You can purchase ITAO tables at a bookstore that sells loan amortization tables. Today, you can do these calculations with any computer and some basic software. However, I will still go through the ITAO tables and calculation process since this was part of the State licensing appraisal courses when I took them.

If you look at the ITAO tables, you'll see two column headings listed for each different interest rate listed. The first column heading, *ITAO*, is used to figure out the monthly loan payment on a particular loan. The second column heading, *Rm*, is used to figure out 12 of the loan payments or 1 full year of the annual debt service, ADS, to amortize a particular loan. If you multiply the ITAO figure by 12 you'll get the Rm figure, and if you divide the Rm figure by 12 you'll get the ITAO figure. The row headings on the left side of the tables correspond to the remaining term of the loan.

Let's say the you wanted to determine the monthly payment for a $50,000 loan that had a term of 30 years and an interest rate of 10%. First you would go to the ITAO table with the 10.00% interest rate. Next you would go down the list until you reached the 30 year column heading, giving you an ITAO figure of 0.008776. You then multiply $50,000 x 0.008776 = $438.80 which is the monthly loan payment to amortize that loan over a 30 year period.

If you wanted to figure out the total loan payments for 1 year, or the ADS, you could multiply the $438.80 x 12 = $5,265.60. Or you could go down the Rm list until you get to the 30 year figure of 0.105312. Multiply the loan amount of $50,000 x 0.105312 = $5,265.60 which is the same yearly amount. Either way you arrive at the same answer.

◊   Vo or Price = $125,000
◊   Vm or Mortgage = $100,000
◊   Ym or Interest Rate = 10%
◊   n or Term = 30 year payment term *(amortization)* with a balloon payment for the remaining balance due in 10 years.
◊   b or balloon payment due date = 30 - 10 = 20 years will be left on the loan balance amount at the time the balloon payment will be due.
◊   Rate = Income/Value  *(Mortgage Rate = Mortgage Income/Mortgage Value)*
◊   Value = Income/Rate
◊   Income = Value x Rate
◊   CRRT = Contract rate for the remaining term of the loan
◊   ADS = Vm x CRRT x 12

◊   $100,000 x 0.008776 = $877.60 is the monthly loan payment as determined by the ITAO tables. The ADS is $877.60 x 12 = $10,531.20.

Now in this example the loan has a balloon payment due in 10 years. This means that the remaining 20 year balance of the loan is due after only 10 years of loan payments have been made. A balloon payment enables a borrower to have lower monthly payments before the balloon amount comes due. For example, let's say this loan was fully amortized over a 10 year period. This would mean that it would be totally paid off after 10 years including the loan principal and the loan interest amounts. If this were the case then we take the ITAO for 10 years and multiply it by the loan amount to get $100,000 x 0.013215 = $1,321.50. The loan payment to fully amortize this loan over 10 years instead of 30 years would be $1,321.50 instead of the $877.60.

So what we want to do now is figure out what the balloon payment amount will be for the loan in our example. We do this by dividing the original loan term ITAO for 30 years, by the ITAO for the balloon payment date of 20 years. *(There is another way of doing this: by dividing the monthly payment by the new ITAO, or by dividing the yearly ADS by the new Rm figure to get the same result. This will be covered in the next section.)*

$$0.008776/0.009650 = 0.90943$$

To figure out the balloon payment, just multiply this new number by the original loan amount.

$$0.90943 \text{ x } \$100,000 = \$90,943$$

Therefore, our balloon payment is $90,943. You might be wondering why the balloon payment is so close to the original $100,000 loan amount borrowed. The reason is that in the first 15 years of a 30 year loan, the vast majority of your monthly loan payments go toward paying off the interest amount. In the first half of the loan, the monthly payments barely pay off any of the loan principal amount. Each monthly loan payment gradually reduces your loan principal amount. When you get to the last 7 years of the loan, you begin to reduce more

principal with each payment, as opposed to reducing the interest payment.

Another way to figure out the balloon payment is to divide the Rm figure for 30 years by the Rm figure for 20 years.

$$0.105312/0.115800 = 0.90943$$

$$0.90943 \text{ x } \$100,000 = \$90,943$$

Either way you get the same result. Just remember that you have to use the same column heading for your calculations on this. Don't take the 30 year *ITAO* figure and divide it by the 20 year *Rm* figure or vice versa. If you do, your calculations will be **wrong!!** You have to compare apples to apples and not apples to oranges.

◊   DSCR = Debt Service Coverage Ratio. This is what a property will generate in net operating income and the amount of the debt service that the property income could pay. Net income refers to the amount of money left over after all of the bills *(operating expenses)* are paid. It's also called cash flow and it can be positive, neutral *(break even)* or negative. Banks like to see a positive cash flow when they're lending money on a rental property.
◊   GI = Gross Income. Gross income refers to the total amount of income received before the bills have been paid.
◊   OE = Operating Expenses
◊   NOI = Net Operating Income

For this example we'll assume:

◊   GI = $20,000
◊   OE = $5,960

$$GI - OE = NOI$$
$$or$$
$$\$20,000 - \$5,960 = \$14,040$$

Now let's take this a step further. Remember we found out that $100,000 x 0.008776 = $877.60 is the monthly loan payment as determined by the ITAO tables for our sample mortgage.
The ADS is $877.60 x 12 = $10,531.20.

$$DSCR = NOI/ADS$$

The property in our example has a NOI of $14,040 per year. We want to find the DSCR.

$$\$14,040/\$10,531.20 = 1.33$$

Our answer of 1.33 is a positive number. It's a number that the bankers would like to see if they were lending money on this property. Bankers like to see a positive cash flow balance to make their mortgage loan more secure.

Let's take it a step further and try to figure out the Loan-to-Value ratio.

$$M = Vm/Vo$$
or
$$\$100,000/\$125,000 = 0.8$$

Our answer of 0.8 is the same as an 80% loan-to-value ratio

In our example, we'll now try to determine the rate of the mortgage, Rm, *without* looking at the ITAO tables. Remember that Rate = Income/Value which is the same as Rm = ADS/Vm.

◊　ADS = $10,531.20
◊　Vm = $100,000

$$\$10,531.20/\$100,000 = 0.105312$$

If you check the ITAO tables for a 10% loan that has a 30 year amortization period, you will see it matches our answer.

## ITAO Example #2

Let's try to solve another ITAO problem:

◊　Vm or Mortgage = $80,000
◊　Ym or Interest Rate = 12%
◊　n or Term = 30 year payment term *(amortization)*
◊　b or balloon payment due date = 20 years
◊　CRRT = Contract rate for the remaining term of the loan
◊　ADS = Vm x CRRT x 12

To figure out the ADS, annual debt service, we find that the Rm in the ITAO tables for a 12% interest rate loan, with a 30 year amortization term, is 0.123432.

$$\$80,000 \times 0.123432 = \$9,874.56$$

Another way to find the ADS, is to take the figure under the ITAO column, which is the monthly loan payment figure, and multiply it by 12. The result will give you one full year's loan payment amount.

$$\$80,000 \times 0.010286 = \$822.88$$

$$\$822.88 \times 12 = \$9,874.56$$

Now we'll figure out the remaining loan balance when the balloon payment is due after 20 years of loan payments. We can do this two ways, using either the ITAO column figure or the Rm column figure. *(There is another way of doing this: by dividing the original ITAO figure by the new ITAO figure, or by dividing the yearly Rm figure by the new Rm figure to get the same result. This was covered in the prior section.)*

First we find that the ITAO figure for a 12% interest loan at the 10 year term is 0.014347. Since we are using the *monthly* ITAO then we must use the *monthly* loan payment to figure out the balloon payment.

$$\$822.88/0.014347 = \$57,355.54$$

Or we can find that the Rm figure for a 12% interest loan at the 10 year term is 0.172164. Since we are using the *yearly* Rm then we must use the *yearly* loan payment to determine the balloon payment.

$$\$9,874.56/0.172164 = \$57,355.54$$

Using both methods we come up with the same answer. The balloon payment due after 20 years of loan payments in our example will be $57,355.54.

## Cash Equivalency Example #1

*Cash equivalencies* will make the market price higher than the market value due to flexible terms given to the buyer by the seller. The market *price* (sales price) can be equal to the market *value* but this is not always the case. (See section Market Value - Subjective And Objective page 73). If necessary, you have to make the adjustment with the sales comparables for flexible terms given. This is done to bring the market value of the sales comparable down to what an all cash deal would have brought the seller. If the market interest rate at the time of the sale is the same as the interest rate paid by the buyer for a seller financed purchase money mortgage to buy the property, then no cash equivalency adjustment is needed. For example, let's say the market interest rate was 13% and the buyer paid only 10% for his/her interest on the mortgage. Then an adjustment for cash equivalency has to be made because the buyer might actually be paying about $110,000 for the property. However, due to the favorable financing, the adjusted sales price may be around $95,000 after you make the proper ITAO calculations.

You could even take this a step further, if you wanted to figure out the *Present Value* of flexible financing terms. You can buy Present Value tables that are used in a similar manner to the ITAO tables. Present Value calculations and adjustments are used to estimate what a future amount of money would be worth in today's market. For example, let's say you had a mortgage loan that was due in 25 years. You would use these tables to estimate what the mortgage loan balance would be worth to a lender *today.* The value of the loan to the lender today, would be compared to the lender waiting 25 years to fully amortize the loan and get all of their money from the borrower.

Now before you get angry at me for including all these math formulas, let me show you an actual *Cash Equivalency* example. By showing you an actual example, you can see how this relates to doing real estate appraisals. We'll use the same loan as we did in the prior example.

◊    Vm or Mortgage = $80,000
◊    Ym or Interest Rate = 12%
◊    n or Term = 30 year payment term *(amortization)*

We already found out the monthly mortgage payment is $822.88. Let's assume that after you have been making payments on this loan for 4 years, the loan interest rates the banks are charging go up from 12% to 15%. The 15% is now the *market* interest rate. We need to now determine what the *book value* of this loan is in today's market.

◊    Book Value = Monthly Loan Payment/ITAO at CRRT
◊    ITAO at CRRT = The Installment To Amortize One dollar at the *Contract* Rate for the Remaining Term of the loan.

You've been making payments on the loan for 4 full years. So we need to figure out the remaining term of this loan at that point in time.

$$30 - 4 = 26 \text{ years remaining}$$

If you check the tables, the ITAO for a loan term of 26 years at 12% interest is 0.010470. Now we'll find out the remaining loan balance with 26 years remaining on this loan. Remember we can do this two ways, using either the ITAO column figure or the Rm column figure. We'll use the ITAO column figure.

Since we are using the *monthly* ITAO, then we must use the *monthly* loan payment to determine the remaining loan balance at 26 years.

$$\$822.88/0.010470 = \$78,594.08$$

Now we'll figure out what this loan is worth at the *market* interest rate, which is 15% in our example. You have to compare apples to apples, so we use the same ITAO remaining loan term. The remaining loan term is 26 years in our example.

◊    ITAO at MRRT = The Installment To Amortize One dollar at the *Market* Rate for the Remaining Term of the loan.

If you check the tables, the ITAO for a loan term of 26 years at 15% interest is 0.012765. Now we'll figure out the remaining loan balance with 26 years remaining on this loan, at the *market* interest rate and the *contract* monthly loan payment. Remember we can do this two ways, using either the ITAO column figure or the Rm column figure. We'll use the ITAO figure.

Since we are using the *monthly* ITAO, then we must use the *monthly* loan payment to find out the remaining loan balance at 26 years.

$$\$822.88/0.012765 = \$64,463.77$$

We now have determined what our current loan balance is at the contract interest rate of 12%. We have also figured out what the loan balance would be with the contract monthly loan payment at the market interest rate of 15%. Now we will determine what our loan is worth to the lender **today**. We do this by dividing the market rate by the contract rate figure.

$$\$64,463.77/\$78,594.08 = 0.82$$

Our answer is 0.82 which is the same as 82%. This indicates that the existing loan at a 12% interest rate, is only worth 82% of what the exact same loan would be worth in today's market of 15% interest. That is a discount of 18% (100% - 82% = 18%). This simply means that if your banker lent the equivalent of your unpaid loan balance to someone in today's market, he would get an additional 18% profit over what he is getting from you for the same loan amount. So the $78,594.08 outstanding loan balance at the contract interest rate of 12% is only worth $64,463.77 in today's market at current market interest rates of 15%. This is why an adjustment is often needed to a sales comparable that has seller financing and flexible terms.

Using the above example, let's say a seller decided to finance part of the sales price of his house. The seller did this by giving the buyer a 12% purchase money mortgage. If the banks were lending money to everyone else at 15%, then that buyer would be getting the seller financed loan at an 18% discount! This means that an adjustment would have to be made to this sale if you were using it as a comparable for a house that you were appraising. The flexible terms with the low interest rate can cause a buyer to pay more than someone else would normally pay for that same house at that particular time.

## *Cash Equivalency Example #2*

We'll use our prior ITAO example for another problem. Let's say we wanted to find out what the separate loan principal and interest amounts were for the **first** monthly payment.

◊   Vm or Mortgage = $80,000
◊   Ym or Interest Rate = 12%
◊   n or Term = 30 year payment term *(amortization)*

Using the ITAO tables for the 30 year term we found the correct monthly loan payment amount:

$$\$80,000 \times 0.010286 = \$822.88$$

We need to figure what amount of the $822.88 first monthly payment is applied toward loan principal and what amount is toward loan interest. To do this we first need to find the monthly interest rate. The *nominal* interest rate is given to us as 12%. The monthly interest rate is simply the nominal rate divided by 12.

$$.12/12 = .01 \quad or \quad 1\% \text{ interest per month}$$

The total loan principal amount for the first monthly payment is given to us as $80,000. If the monthly interest rate is 1%, we then multiply this by the outstanding loan principal amount to determine what the interest payment is, for that particular monthly payment.

$$\$80,000 \times .01 = \$800.00$$

Now we have found the interest payment for the first month to be $800.00. All we need to do is subtract this amount from the total monthly loan payment to figure out the loan principal amount for that month.

$$\$822.88 - \$800.00 = \$22.88$$

The amortization of the loan principal or the *recapture of capital* for the first monthly loan payment is $22.88. This may seem surprisingly low, but I noted the reason for this earlier. The vast majority of the loan payments made in the early years are applied toward paying down the loan **interest** balance, instead of the loan **principal** balance.

We'll use this same example for another problem. Let's say we wanted to find what the remaining loan principal balance is after the first **year** of loan payments. As shown in prior examples, we can do this two ways, using either the ITAO column figure or the Rm column figure. First we find the ITAO figure for a 12% interest loan at the 29 year term is 0.010324. Since we are using the *monthly* ITAO, then we must use the *monthly* loan payment to find the remaining loan principal amount.

$$\$822.88/0.010324 = \$79,705.54$$

Or we can find that the Rm figure for a 12% interest loan at the 29 year term is 0.123888. Since we are using the *yearly* Rm, then we must use the *yearly* loan payment to determine the loan principal amount.

$$\$9,874.56/0.123888 = \$79,705.54$$

Using both methods, we come up with the same answer. The loan principal balance that is outstanding after 1 year of loan payments will be $79,705.54.

We can figure out the amount of loan principal paid during the first year of loan payments. To do this, we simply subtract the original loan principal amount from the remaining amount after 1 year of payments.

$$\$80,000 - \$79,705.54 = \$294.46$$

The amortization of the loan principal, or the *recapture of capital,* after the first year of loan payments is $294.46.

We'll use this same example to see how the loan amortizes over 5 year intervals. Let's say we wanted to determine what the remaining loan principal balance is after **10** years of loan payments. As shown in prior examples, we can do this two ways, using either the ITAO column figure or the Rm column figure.

First we find that the ITAO figure for a 12% interest loan at the 20 year term is 0.011011. Since we are using the *monthly* ITAO, then we must use the *monthly* loan payment to find out the remaining loan principal amount.

$$\$822.88/0.011011 = \$74,732.54$$

Or we can find that the Rm figure for a 12% interest loan at the 20 year term is 0.132132. Since we are using the *yearly* Rm, then we must use the *yearly* loan payment to determine the loan principal amount.

$$\$9,874.56/0.132132 = \$74,732.54$$

Using both methods, we come up with the same answer. The loan principal balance that is outstanding after 10 years of loan payments will be $74,732.54.

We can determine the amount of loan principal paid during the first 10 years of loan payments. Simply subtract the original loan principal amount from the remaining amount after 10 years of payments.

$$\$80,000 - \$74,732.54 = \$5,267.46$$

*(Yes, we're going to keep practicing it until you can do this in your sleep!)* Now we'll learn what the remaining loan principal balance is after **15** years of loan payments.

First we find that the ITAO figure for a 12% interest loan at the 15 year term is 0.012002.

$$\$822.88/0.012002 = \$68,561.91$$

Or we can find that the Rm figure for a 12% interest loan at the 15 year term is 0.144024.

$$\$9,874.56/0.144024 = \$68,561.91$$

Using both methods, we come up with the same answer. The loan principal balance that is outstanding after 15 years of loan payments will be $68,561.91.

Now we'll find out what the remaining loan principal balance is after **20** years of loan payments.

First we find that the ITAO figure for a 12% interest loan at the 10 year term is 0.014347.

$$\$822.88/0.014347 = \$57,355.54$$

Or we can find that the Rm figure for a 12% interest loan at the 10 year term is 0.172164.

$$\$9,874.56/0.172164 = \$57,355.54$$

Using both methods, we come up with the same answer. The loan principal balance that is outstanding after 20 years of loan payments will be $57,355.54.

*(OK, this is the last one - practice makes perfect!)* Now we'll learn what the remaining loan principal balance is after **25** years of loan payments.

First we find that the ITAO figure for a 12% interest loan at the 5 year term is 0.022244.

$$\$822.88/0.022244 = \$36,993.35$$

Or we can find that the Rm figure for a 12% interest loan at the 5 year term is 0.266928.

$$\$9,874.56/0.266928 = \$36,993.35$$

Using both methods, we come up with the same answer. The loan principal balance that is outstanding after 25 years of loan payments will be $36,993.35.

# Cash Equivalency Example #3

Now we'll use some of this information to put together another *Cash Equivalency* example to see how it would relate to an actual appraisal report. Let's say, you were appraising a house and you found a sales comparable that was sold with an assumable mortgage loan. An assumable mortgage means that a buyer can "assume" or take over the mortgage loan when buying the house instead of having to get a new loan to pay off the existing mortgage. Basically, the buyer just makes the remaining payments on the existing mortgage. This makes the sale of the house more flexible and easier to find potential buyers who may be willing to pay a higher price for the convenience of being able to assume the existing loan. The buyer will not have to go through the hassle and expense of getting a new mortgage and pay the points, bank fees, and maybe even a higher interest rate. Assumable loans were easy to get years ago but today they are hard to find.

Now back to our example: The recorded sales price of the house was $100,000. The mortgage loan that was assumed by the buyer was the same loan and terms that we've used in our examples; $80,000 loan at a 12% interest rate for a 30 year term. The seller of the house has been making loan payments for 10 years on this mortgage loan before the buyer assumes it. We already found out, (from our prior examples), that the monthly mortgage payment is $822.88. However, at the time of the sale when the buyer assumed this loan, the market interest rates were 16.5% for conventional financing mortgages.

We first need to determine what the remaining loan principal balance is at the time the new buyer assumes the mortgage. This loan in our example has a principal balance remaining after 10 years of making loan payments of:

$$\$822.88/0.011011 = \$74,732.54$$
$$\text{or}$$
$$\$9,874.56/0.132132 = \$74,732.54$$

Using both methods, we come up with the same answer. The loan principal balance that is outstanding after 10 years of loan payments will be $74,732.54.

Next we need to figure out what the down payment amount was that the buyer had to pay to purchase this house. We find this by simply subtracting the balance of the assumable loan from the total sales price.

$$\$100,000 - \$74,732.54 = \$25,267.46$$

The amount of the buyer's down payment is determined to be $25,267.46.

As I said, the seller has been making payments on this loan for 10 years. The loan interest rates that the banks are charging at the time of the sale, have gone up from 12% to 16.5%. The 16.5% is now the *market* interest rate. We need to now determine what the *book value* of this loan was at the time that the loan was assumed by the buyer.

◊    Book Value = Monthly Loan Payment/ITAO at CRRT
◊    ITAO at CRRT = The Installment To Amortize One dollar at the *Contract Rate for the Remaining Term* of the loan.

The seller has been making payments on the loan for 10 full years. So we need to find out the remaining term of this loan.

$$30 - 10 = 20 \text{ years remaining}$$

Now we'll figure out what this loan is worth at the *market* interest rate which is 16.5% in our example. You have to compare apples to apples, so we use the same ITAO remaining loan term, which is 20 years in our example.

◊    ITAO at MRRT = The Installment To Amortize One dollar at the *Market Rate for the Remaining Term* of the loan.

If you check the tables, the ITAO for a loan term of 20 years at 16.5% interest is 0.014289. Now we'll find what the remaining loan balance is with 20 years remaining on this loan, at the *market* interest rate and the contract monthly loan payment. Remember we can do this two ways, using either the ITAO column figure or the Rm column figure. We'll use the ITAO column figure. Since we are using the *monthly* ITAO, then we must use the *monthly* loan payment to find the remaining loan balance at 20 years.

$$\$822.88/0.014289 = \$57,588.35$$

We now have determined what the current loan balance is at the contract interest rate of 12%. We've also found what the loan balance would be with the contract monthly loan payment, at the market interest rate of 16.5%. Now we will figure out what the loan is worth to the lender today. We do this by dividing the market rate figure by the contract rate figure.

$$\$57,588.35/\$74,732.54 = 0.77$$

Our answer is 0.77 which is the same as 77%. This indicates that the existing loan, at a 12% interest rate, is only worth 77% of what the exact same loan would be worth in today's market of 16.5% interest. That's a discount of 23% (100% - 77% = 23%). This simply means, that if the seller's banker lent the equivalent of the unpaid loan balance to someone in today's market, **the bank would get an additional 23% profit** over what they are getting from the seller for the same loan amount! So the $74,732.54 outstanding loan balance at the contract interest rate of 12%, is only worth $57,588.35 in today's market at the current market interest rate of 16.5%.

Now since we are using this sale as a comparable for one of our appraisals, we **have to** make a cash equivalency adjustment to the sales price of the comp. We do this because the loan that was assumed by the buyer has a lower interest rate than a loan that a typical buyer would obtain, at the time that the sale of the comparable took place. An adjustment is needed because the recorded sales price does not reflect an "arms length" transaction. This is because the buyer had received a lower than normal interest rate loan to buy the house which probably caused them to pay a higher sales price due to the favorable terms.

We can figure out the adjustment to make by subtracting the *recorded* sales price of the comparable, from the *adjusted* sales price. The adjusted sales price takes into account the low interest rate loan. To do this, we first need to decide what the adjusted sales price is. This is calculated by adding the buyer's down payment to the *market* rate of the loan balance assumed.

$$\$57,588.35 + \$25,267.46 = \$82,855.81$$

The adjusted sales price of the comparable in our example is $82,855.81. Meaning that this is what the house actually sold for because of the low interest rate of the loan assumed by the buyer. The $100,000 recorded sales price of that sales comparable then is not an "arms length" transaction.

Now we need to determine the adjustment to make in the appraisal report. We do this by simply subtracting the adjusted sales price of the comparable from the recorded sales price. Remember that you have to round out your adjustment amounts because real estate appraising is not an exact science.

$$\$82,855.81 - \$100,000 = -\$17,144.19$$

The rounded adjustment in the appraisal report that we would make to the recorded sales price of the comparable in our example is -$17,150.

> *Now do you see why I had to teach you all of this math? I hope so. Believe me, I wouldn't have included all of these math examples in the book unless it was a necessary part of teaching the techniques and methods of real estate appraising. The math calculations can get boring but there will be times when you need to know this stuff for an appraisal report.*

Now do you see why I had to teach you all of this math? I hope so. Believe me, I wouldn't have included all of these math examples in the book unless it was a necessary part of teaching the techniques and methods of real estate appraising. The math calculations can get boring but there will be times when you need to know this stuff for an appraisal report.

# How To Make Big Money With The ITAO Tables

Now I'll really try to get you interested in all this math by showing you how you can use it to save yourself tens of thousands of dollars!! And I'll even give you a real life example. One of my instructors told our class this story while he was teaching the appraisal course. His friend had a 12% *contract* interest rate loan with a bank. The current *market* interest rates were 16.5% at the time his friend was selling his house. The remaining loan balance on the mortgage was $75,000 at the 12% interest rate. Using the ITAO tables, his friend showed the banker that the *book value* of the bank's loan was worth less than $65,000 with the market interest rates at 16.5%. He told the banker that if they would accept $65,000 as **full** payment for the loan, instead of the $75,000 that was the actual balance due, he would pay them off in a few months. He would pay off the loan early, rather than the bank having to wait many more years of just getting monthly loan payments. Believe it or not, the banker accepted the guy's offer and he put an additional $10,000 in his pocket when he sold his house!

> Now I'll really try to get you interested in all this math by showing you how you can use it to save yourself tens of thousands of dollars!!

This guy must have been an appraiser or an economist to figure this technique out. But either way, I think it's a brilliant idea to try to save a lot of money when you pay off any of your loans. However, it's like negotiating anything else, some lenders will say "yes" to the idea, and some lenders will say "no". If you have the courage to ask for a discount, you can only get two answers and one of them is great!

Obviously, my class instructor's friend didn't tell the banker that he was selling his house. I think he just said that he had gotten some extra money to pay them off with. If you're going to do this and you don't tell the lender that you're selling the house, then it becomes a business decision for the bank to make. The bank has to decide if it would be more profitable for them to take a discount on the loan and receive a lump sum now. This would enable them to lend that money out again at a higher interest rate. If they do this, then they won't have to wait for their monthly payments to fully amortize the loan. The banker may say "no" to the discount if he feels that you're going to sell the house anyway. In order to sell your house, and give the buyer a "clear" title, you'll have to pay off all of the existing mortgages and liens on the house. If the lender knows you're getting the money to pay off the loan from the sale proceeds, he also knows that you have no choice if he insists on getting the full loan balance from you. However, if the lender thinks that he's going to have to wait many more years of only receiving monthly loan payments to fully amortize his loan, then he has some incentive to give you the discount. Try it out on your own mortgage and see what your bank says. Hey, you never know, if they say yes you'll profit big time!

# Income Capitalization Example

When you buy a property, you buy either the amenities it offers or the income it offers. It's sometimes assumed that the income property market behaves rationally, whereas, the residential market doesn't. Meaning, that the income properties are purchased by investors who look at the deal as a business decision. Residential properties are generally purchased by people looking for the amenities in the deal and they can get too emotionally involved in the purchase to act rationally and may pay too much.

Here's some abbreviations you'll need for the following sections concerning the Income Approach:

◊ GI = Gross Income
◊ PGI = Potential Gross Income
◊ GI = PGI = Rent Roll
◊ V = Vacancy
◊ EGI = Effective Gross Income
◊ NOI = Net Operating Income
◊ OE = Operating Expenses
◊ (GI or PGI) - (V + Collection Losses) = Effective Gross Income
◊ Effective Gross Income - Operating Expenses = Net Operating Income
◊ Operating Expense Ratio = OE/EGI
◊ ADS = Annual Debt Service
◊ CTO = Cash Throw Off
◊ NOI - ADS = CTO

Capital costs, such as, depreciable items, do not appear in the equation. Capital costs or depreciable items refer to items whose cost to purchase and install cannot be totally deducted in the year the expense is incurred. The expense deduction for these items must be depreciated over a specified number of years according to the tax laws. Any payments to the debt or equity investors, (mortgage lender and owner), as well as income taxes paid do not appear in the equation.

Income property is always treated on an <u>annual</u> basis. This accounts for the winter and summer expenses in the calculations. Income property is always treated on a cash method of accounting and not an accrual method of accounting. A *cash method* of accounting simply means that any income is reported as "earned" when it's *actually* received. Any expenses are reported as "paid" when the money is *actually* spent to pay the bills. An *accrual method* of accounting simply means that any income is reported as "earned" at the time the work or service is performed. The income **is not** reported as earned at the time it's *actually* received. Any expenses are reported as "paid" at the time the bills are *supposed* to be paid and not when they're *actually* paid. According to a friend of mine who is a CPA, the accrual method of accounting is a "truer" method to use.

Let's try an income capitalization example:

The GI or PGI or Rent Roll includes 20 apartments at $200 per month rental income.

(20 x $200) x 12 = $48,000 rental income per year

The Vacancy and Collection Losses are estimated to be 5% per year.

$48,000 x .05 = $2,400 lost income per year

There is additional income that is estimated to be $100 for each occupied apartment unit. This additional income is from the coin operated laundry and soda machines plus rented garage spaces. However, there is a vacancy factor to account for in this calculation.

20 x .05 = 1 vacant unit per year

20 - 1 = 19 occupied units per year

19 x $100 = $1,900 additional income per year

Therefore, we add these calculations to determine the *Effective Gross Income* for the property.

$48,000 + $1,900 = $49,900

$49,900 - $2,400 = $47,500 in Effective Gross Income

Next we need to figure out the *Operating Expenses* for the building. This simply refers to the expenses to operate the building for one full year. *Fixed Expenses* refers to expenses that **don't** really fluctuate depending upon the occupancy of the building, such as, real estate taxes and insurance. *Variable Expenses* refers to expenses that **do** fluctuate depending upon the occupancy of the building, such as, management fees, electricity, heating fuel, etc.

*Fixed Expenses:*

| | | |
|---|---|---|
| Real Estate Taxes | | $6,600 |
| Insurance | | 600 |
| | Total | *$7,200* |

*Variable Expenses:*

| | | |
|---|---|---|
| Management Fees are 3% of EGI | | $1,425 |
| Electricity | | 250 |
| Water + Sewer Fees | | 190 |
| Heating Fuel | | 4,560 |
| Miscellaneous | | 240 |
| | Total | *$6,665* |

| | | |
|---|---|---|
| Repairs and Maintenance | | $8,635 |

**Total Operating Expenses  =**     *$22,500*

*Operating Expense Ratio* is then determined to be:

$22,500/$47,500 = 47%

To figure out the *Net Operating Income,* we subtract the total *Operating Expenses* from the *Effective Gross Income.* The *Debt Service* amount is not added to the expenses to figure out the Net Operating Income.

$47,500 - $22,500 = $25,000

Now we'll assume that this property has a $187,500 mortgage at 8% interest for a 20 year term. No payments have been made yet on the mortgage since it's a new loan. So we will find out the monthly payment from the ITAO tables for 8% interest.

$187,500 x 0.008364 = $1,568.25

Now we'll determine the ADS or *Annual Debt Service* from the monthly payment calculation.

12 x $1,568.25 = $18,819

To figure out the CTO or *Cash Throw Off,* (the positive cash flow on the property), we need to do the following calculations:

$25,000 - $18,819 = $6,181

---

*The **most important** criteria in analyzing an income producing property is where Capital Recapture, also called Recapture or Capital Recovery, will come from.*

---

**The most important criteria in analyzing an income producing property is where *Capital Recapture,* also called *Recapture* or *Capital Recovery,* will come from.** Recapture or Capital Recovery refer to someone receiving back the initial amount of money that they have invested in the deal. This is determined by the following equations:

◊     Ro = Capitalization Rate
◊     NOI = Net Operating Income
◊     Vo = Value of the Property
◊     Ro = NOI/Vo
◊     NOI/Ro = Vo

We can find the equity in this building using these equations with our example. We'll assume the subject property is worth $250,000 in the current market.

25,000/250,000 = .10
or
10% Capitalization Rate

Let's assume that we didn't know what the value of the property was. However, we did know that the investor in the deal was looking for a *Capitalization Rate* of at least 10%. The investor then asks you during your appraisal process, what the subject property would have to be worth in order for him to obtain his 10% Capitalization Rate. This is found by dividing the *Net Operating Income* by the *Capitalization Rate.*

$$\$25,000/.10 = \$250,000$$

The answer is that the subject property would have to be worth $250,000 in order for the investor to obtain his 10% Capitalization Rate.

The return **of the initial investment** made by an investor in a deal is called *Capital Recapture*. The return **on the initial investment** made by an investor in a deal is called *Interest Rate* or *Risk Rate*. If you wanted to use a straight line method (equal yearly amounts) to determine the Capital Recapture, then the following equation would apply:

◊   ARR = Annual Recapture Rate
◊   YUL = Years of Useful Life
◊   ARR = 100%/YUL
◊   YUL = 100%/ARR

Using the figures in our example, let's say the investor asks you to determine the number of *Years of Useful Life* of the investment for him to obtain his 10% Capitalization Rate. The following equation applies:

$$100\%/10\% = 10$$
or
10 Years of Useful Life

For an investor, the return amount **of** or **on** their initial investment that they will require before making the deal will depend upon the amount of risk they are assuming with the investment. The more risk, then the higher the returns need to be to make the deal worthwhile. A **low risk** investment will generally have a **low** Capitalization Rate and the price of the subject property will be **high**. A **high risk** investment will generally have a **high** Capitalization Rate and the price of the subject property will be **low**.

## Income Approach and Statistics Example

You will encounter situations where knowledge of statistics is needed for real estate appraising and the Income Approach. For example, you will need to analyze the sales comparables for the Income Approach on an appraisal assignment. Using statistics will enable you to determine if the sales comps you have are what is considered a "tight fit". When you have a "tight fit", then you can assume your data is an acceptable representation of the market. Meaning that the sales you're analyzing are probably good comps to use and accurately reflect the local market. A tight fit from an appraisal standpoint is generally one in which the Percentage Deviation is 10% or less.

When someone refers to *population* in statistics, it doesn't have to mean that they are talking about "people". It refers to whatever units of measurement or values you're analyzing. For example, it could refer to cars, houses, rents, dollar amounts, etc. In statistics an *absolute* number is the number without any negative or positive signs before it. If you're analyzing a set of numbers, your first step should always be to set them up in an ascending or descending order. This order is based on the values of the numbers. For example, let's say you're analyzing some recent comparable sales of houses for an appraisal assignment. You're analyzing the sales prices *(SP)* of the houses; their gross monthly rents *(GMR)* for unfurnished apartments; and their gross rent multipliers *(GRM)* in your area; to assist you on the appraisal. GRM (Gross Rent Multiplier) is equal to the SP (Sales Price) divided by the monthly rent of unfurnished units. The *Gross Rent Multiplier* is used for the Direct Sales Comparison Approach for small residential income properties. You use unfurnished apartment rental figures.

Your field work for this appraisal assignment has found the following information:

1   The **Sales Prices** of the houses are: $125,000, $92,000, $87,000, $116,000, $147,000, $138,000.

2   The **GMR** of the houses are: $370, $290, $285, $355, $405, $390.

3   The **GRM** of the houses are: 337.84, 317.24, 305.26, 326.76, 362.96, 353.85.

Your first step is to place this information in an order that makes it easier to analyze the data statistically.

| Sale No. | Sales Price | G.M.R. | G.R.M. |
|---|---|---|---|
| 1 | $147,000 | $405 | 362.96 |
| 2 | $138,000 | $390 | 353.85 |
| 3 | $125,000 | $370 | 337.84 |
| 4 | $116,000 | $355 | 326.76 |
| 5 | $92,000 | $290 | 317.24 |
| 6 | $87,000 | $285 | 305.26 |
| | $705,000 | $2,095 | 2,003.91 |

**Mean** - refers to the number that is the **average** of all of the values. We find the Mean by dividing the total *amount* of the values, by the total *number* of values we are analyzing. In our example the Mean for the Sales Prices, the GMR, and the GRM would be calculated with the following equations:

$$\$705,000/6 = \$117,500 \text{ is the}$$
Mean or average Sales Price

$$\$2,095/6 = \$349.17 \text{ is the}$$
Mean or average GMR

$$2,003.91/6 = 333.99 \text{ is the}$$
Mean or average GRM

**Median** - refers to the number that is the **midpoint** of all of the values. When you have an even number of figures, for example the six that we are using, you have to add the two middle figures and then divide them by two. Think of the Median as a *position* on the scale of values that you're dealing with. In our example the Median for the Sales Prices, the GMR, and GRM would be calculated with these equations:

($125,000 + $116,000)/2 = $120,500  is the
Median or midpoint Sales Price

($370 + $355)/2 = $362.50  is the
Median or midpoint GMR

(337.84 + 326.76)/2 = 332.3  is the
Median or midpoint GRM

**Mode** - refers to the number that is **repeated** most often in all of the values. For example, let's say sale #1 and sale #2 both sold for $138,000. Since the two sales prices are identical then the Mode would be $138,000 for the Sales Prices. It's the same thing for the GMR and the GRM, or any other values your analyzing. If you have values that have several different numbers that are identical, then the Mode would be the number that is found the most frequently. For example, let's say sale #1 and sale #2 both sold for $138,000 but sales #4, #5, and #6 all sold for $92,000. The Mode in this situation would be $92,000 because there are 3 values with that identical number. In our example there is no Mode because none of the values are repeated.

**Range** - refers to the number that is the **difference** of all of the values. You simply subtract the lowest value from the highest value to get the Range. In our example the Range for the Sales Prices, the GMR, and the GRM would be calculated with the following equations:

$147,000 - $87,000 = $60,000  is the
Range or difference of Sales Prices

$405 - $285 = $120  is the
Range or difference of GMR

362.96 - 305.26 = 57.7  is the
Range or difference of GRM

**Absolute Deviation** - refers to the number that is the difference from the **Mean** for each of the individual values. Remember that an absolute number disregards any plus or minus signs for the values. First we have to set up another table to be able to analyze the values clearly. Then you simply subtract each value from the Mean number, and then add those amounts together to get the Absolute Deviation. This would be calculated as follows:

| Sale No. | Sales Price | Mean | Absolute Deviation |
|---|---|---|---|
| 1 | $147,000 | $117,500 | $29,500 |
| 2 | $138,000 | $117,500 | $20,500 |
| 3 | $125,000 | $117,500 | $7,500 |
| 4 | $116,000 | $117,500 | $1,500 |
| 5 | $92,000 | $117,500 | $25,500 |
| 6 | $87,000 | $117,500 | $30,500 |
| | **$705,000** | | **$115,000** |

The total of the Absolute Deviation from the Mean of the Sales Prices is determined to be $115,000.

Now we'll find the Absolute Deviation from the Mean of the Gross Monthly Rent values:

| Sale No. | G.M.R. | Mean | Absolute Deviation |
|---|---|---|---|
| 1 | $405 | $349.17 | $55.83 |
| 2 | $390 | $349.17 | $40.83 |
| 3 | $370 | $349.17 | $20.83 |
| 4 | $355 | $349.17 | $5.83 |
| 5 | $290 | $349.17 | $59.17 |
| 6 | $285 | $349.17 | $64.17 |
| | **$2,095** | | **$246.66** |

The total of the Absolute Deviation from the Mean of the Gross Monthly Rent values in our example is determined to be $246.66.

Now we'll find the Absolute Deviation from the Mean of the Gross Rent Multiplier values:

| Sale No. | G.R.M. | Mean | Absolute Deviation |
|---|---|---|---|
| 1 | 362.96 | 333.99 | 28.97 |
| 2 | 353.85 | 333.99 | 19.86 |
| 3 | 337.84 | 333.99 | 3.85 |
| 4 | 326.76 | 333.99 | 7.23 |
| 5 | 317.24 | 333.99 | 16.75 |
| 6 | 305.26 | 333.99 | 28.73 |
| | **2,003.91** | | **105.39** |

The total of the Absolute Deviation from the Mean of the Gross Rent Multiplier values in our example is determined to be 105.39.

Now we'll find the *Arithmetic Deviation* for all three sets of values that we're analyzing:

**Arithmetic Deviation** - refers to the number that is the **average** of the **total** of the Absolute Deviation values. You simply divide the total Absolute Deviation value by the number of values to get the Arithmetic Deviation. In our example the Arithmetic Deviation for the Sales Prices, the GMR, and the GRM would be calculated with the following equations:

$$\$115,000/6 = \$19,166.67 \text{ is the}$$
Arithmetic Deviation for the Sales Prices

$$\$246.66/6 = \$41.11 \text{ is the}$$
Arithmetic Deviation for the GMR

$$105.39/6 = 17.57 \text{ is the}$$
Arithmetic Deviation for the GRM

Now we'll use all these calculations, to show you how statistics math equations can help you to do an actual appraisal report. As we said earlier, we'll assume that you're analyzing these recent sales prices *(SP)* of houses; their gross monthly rents *(GMR)* for unfurnished apartments; and their gross rent multipliers *(GRM)* in your area; to assist you on an appraisal assignment.

We've found the Arithmetic Deviation for all three sets of values. Now we will use this data to decide whether these sales are good comparables which accurately reflect the local market. We learn this by finding out the percentage difference of the Arithmetic Deviation from the Mean of each set of values. We calculate this percentage by dividing the Arithmetic Deviation by the Mean of each set of values. Therefore, in our example the percentage difference for the Sales Prices, the GMR, and the GRM would be calculated with the following equations:

$$\$19,166.67/\$117,500 = .16 \text{ or } 16\% \text{ is the}$$
Percentage Deviation of the Sales Prices

$$\$41.11/\$349.17 = .12 \text{ or } 12\% \text{ is the}$$
Percentage Deviation of the GMR

$$17.57/333.99 = .05 \text{ or } 5\% \text{ is the}$$
Percentage Deviation of the GRM

Now, I'll repeat what I said earlier in this section so you see why we had to go through all these statistics examples for an Income Approach appraisal. When you have what is considered a "tight fit" then you can assume that your data is an acceptable descriptive representation of the market. Meaning that the sales you're analyzing are probably good comparables to use and accurately reflect the local market. A tight fit from an appraisal standpoint is generally one in which the Percentage Deviation is 10% or less. Using the example sales, we have learned that the only "tight fit" for the three different sets of values we're analyzing is in the Gross Rent Multiplier amounts. The Gross Rent Multiplier amounts only deviate from the Mean by 5%. One way to estimate market value using the Income Approach is to multiply the Monthly Total Gross Estimated Rent *(GMR)* by the Gross Rent Multiplier amount *(GRM)*. An example is shown in the sample Multi-Family appraisal report in this book.

# Income Approach GRM Example

We'll use the same data and sales comparables from the prior example for another Income Approach appraisal. For this assignment you have to use the Gross Rent Multiplier *(GRM)* of the sales comparables to estimate the market value of the subject property. Let's say that you've analyzed the Sales Prices of the houses; their Gross Monthly Rents for unfurnished apartments; and their Gross Rent Multipliers. You use unfurnished apartment rental figures for this. The following equations are needed:

◊   SP = Sales Price
◊   GMR = Gross Monthly Rents
◊   GRM = Gross Rent Multiplier
◊   GRM = SP/GMR

Your field work for this appraisal assignment has found the following information:

1   The **Sales Prices** of the houses are: $125,000, $92,000, $87,000, $116,000, $147,000, $138,000.

2   The **GMR** of the houses are: $370, $290, $285, $355, $405, $390.

3   The **GRM** of the houses are: 337.84, 317.24, 305.26, 326.76, 362.96, 353.85.

4   The **GMR** of the **Subject Property** is: $380.

Your first step is to place this information in an order that makes it easier to analyze.

| Sale No. | Sales Price | G.M.R. | G.R.M. |
|---|---|---|---|
| 1 | $147,000 | $405 | 362.96 |
| 2 | $138,000 | $390 | 353.85 |
| 3 | $125,000 | $370 | 337.84 |
| 4 | $116,000 | $355 | 326.76 |
| 5 | $92,000 | $290 | 317.24 |
| 6 | $87,000 | $285 | 305.26 |
| **Subject** | $ ? | $380 | ? |

We need to determine the GRM for the subject property. We do this by taking the **average** of the GRM figures for the sales comparables.

$$362.96 + 353.85 + 337.84 + 326.76 + 317.24 + 305.26 = 2003.91$$

$$2003.91 / 6 = 333.99$$

334 is the rounded out GRM amount

Next we need to use this figure to estimate the market value of the subject property. We do this by multiplying the GRM amount by the GMR amount for the subject property.

334 x $380 = $126,920

**$127,000** is the rounded out
estimated market value of the subject property.

You would use these Income Approach figures to fill out the appraisal form for this report. You can estimate market value by multiplying the Monthly Total Gross Estimated Rent *(GMR)* by the Gross Rent Multiplier amount *(GRM)*. An example is shown in the sample Multi-Family appraisal report in this book.

## *Income Approach GIM Example*

We'll use the same data and sales comps from the prior example for another Income Approach appraisal on a different subject property. For this appraisal you have to use the Gross Income Multiplier *(GIM)* of the sales comparables to estimate the market value of the subject property. Let's say you've analyzed the Sales Prices of the houses; their Gross Annual Income *(GAI)* for unfurnished apartments; and their Gross Income Multipliers *(GIM)*. You will use unfurnished apartment rental figures. The following equations are needed:

◊   SP = Sales Price
◊   GAI = Gross Annual Income
◊   GIM = Gross Income Multiplier
◊   GIM = SP/GAI

Your field work for this appraisal assignment has found the following information:

1   The **Sales Prices** of the houses are: $125,000, $92,000, $87,000, $116,000, $147,000, $138,000.

2   The **GAI** of the houses are: $4,440, $3,480, $3,420, $4,260, $4,860, $4,680.

3   The **GIM** of the houses are: 28.15, 26.44, 25.44, 27.23, 30.25, 29.49.

4   The **GAI** of the **Subject Property** is: $4,200.

Your first step is to place this information in an order that makes it easier to analyze.

| Sale No. | Sales Price | G.A.I. | G.I.M. |
|----|----|----|----|
| 1 | $147,000 | $4,860 | 30.25 |
| 2 | $138,000 | $4,680 | 29.49 |
| 3 | $125,000 | $4,440 | 28.15 |
| 4 | $116,000 | $4,260 | 27.23 |
| 5 | $92,000 | $3,480 | 26.44 |
| 6 | $87,000 | $3,420 | 25.44 |
| **Subject** | **$ ?** | **$4,200** | **?** |

We need to determine the GIM for the subject property. We do this by taking the **average** of the GIM figures for the sales comparables.

28.15, 26.44, 25.44, 27.23, 30.25, 29.49 = 167

167 / 6 = 27.83

28 is the rounded out GIM amount

Next we need to use this figure to estimate the market value of the subject property. We do this by multiplying the GIM amount by the GAI amount for the subject property.

28 x $4,200 = $117,600

**$117,600** is the rounded out
estimated market value of the subject property.

## *HUD/FHA Gross Rent Multiplier Form*

HUD/FHA guidelines state that when using the URAR appraisal form for three and four unit properties, the appraiser is to complete the Gross Rent Multiplier calculations and analysis. If the FNMA 1025 - Small Residential Income Property Appraisal Report form is used then completion of the GRM section on the form is acceptable. See Appraisal Form - FHLMC 72, FNMA 1025 section page 347, Appraisal Form - HUD/FHA SA HOC GRM section page 351, and 4-7 INCOME APPROACH section page 250. The following is a sample of a filled out GRM form:

---------------------------------------------------------------------------------------------------------------------

SAMPLE    **GROSS RENT MULTIPLIER ANALYSIS**    SAMPLE
Information Required for 3 & 4 Unit Properties

FHA Case Number: __111-1234577_____    *(FHA does not require this information for 1 and 2 unit properties.)*

Property Address: ___1111 Subject Place, Housing Town, Washington 22222_____

| COMPARABLE PROPERTIES (Addresses) | Liv-ing Units | LIVING AREA AND ROOM COUNT PER LIVING UNIT | | | | ACTUAL GROSS MONTHLY RENT PER LIVING UNIT | | | | GROSS Monthly RENT | SALE PRICE | GRM |
|---|---|---|---|---|---|---|---|---|---|---|---|---|
| | | UNIT 1 | UNIT 2 | UNIT 3 | UNIT 4 | UNIT 1 | UNIT 2 | UNIT 3 | UNIT 4 | | | |
| **Subject:** 1111 Subject Pl. | 4 | 592 | 592 | 592 | 592 | $350. | $300. | $350. | $300. | $1300. | | |
| Housing Town, | | 4-2-1 | 4-2-1 | 4-2-1 | 4-2-1 | | | | | | | |
| **Comp #1:** 1113 Subject Pl. | 4 | 592 | 592 | 592 | 592 | $350. | $300. | $350. | $300. | $1300. | $142,000 | 109 |
| Housing Town, | | 4-2-1 | 4-2-1 | 4-2-1 | 4-2-1 | | | | | | | |
| **Comp #2:** 292 Any Street, | 4 | 600 | 600 | 600 | 600 | $350. | $350. | $350. | $300. | $1350. | $142,000 | 105 |
| Housing Town, | | 4-2-1 | 4-2-1 | 4-2-1 | 4-2-1 | | | | | | | |
| **Comp #3:** 97264 That Pl. | 4 | 740 | 700 | 740 | 700 | $300. | $250. | $300. | Vacant ($250.) | $1100. | $116,000 | 106 |
| Housing Town, | | 4-2-1 | 4-2-1 | 4-2-1 | 4-2-1 | | | | | | | |
| | | | | | | | | | | | | |
| | | | | | | | | | | | | |
| Fair Gross Monthly Rent (Economic) For Subject Property | | | | | | $350. | $300. | $350. | $300. | **$1300.** | | |

| Indicated Gross Rent Multiplier for Subject Property: | **106** |
|---|---|

**Remarks:**    Comp 1 & 2 = Same as subject property, best indicator of value.
Comp 3 = Inferior location, older unit, no CAC, no carports or garages, over 10% adjustment required.
Used best comps available - there is a lack of 4 unit sales in area.

### $1300 x 106 = $137,800 value by income approach.

| Signature: | License #: WA-CGI-12024231 | Date Signed: April 16, 1999 |
|---|---|---|

SA HOC GRM -01    SAMPLE

# Miscellaneous Appraisal Info

## Tax Assessments

Real estate tax assessments are based upon the *Assessed Value*, which may be based on the market value of a property depending upon the local municipalities rules. However, the assessment value should be based on the Highest and Best Use, even if it's not the present use of the subject property. A residential house can be taxed as a commercial property if it's located in an area of businesses. By being in a business location, this could make the H&B Use of the subject property a commercial use. An apartment building can be taxed as a condominium building because it's located in an area of condo buildings. You may come across the term *depth tables* which are used by tax assessors. They're not accurate enough to estimate market value for an appraiser to use them.

*How can you appeal your property tax assessment?* In most areas real estate taxes are based on an ad valorem ("according to value") assessment of your property's value. If you believe the assessed value is incorrect, then you may have the right to appeal the tax assessor's valuation. A qualified appraiser can give you an independent opinion of value to assist you with your appeal to the tax assessor.

> The building department is a separate entity from the tax department. As a result, the building department doesn't care how your property is taxed, they only care that it meets all of the local building code requirements.

I've seen many cases where single family, or small multi-family dwellings, have a higher tax rate than they should. This is because these buildings have illegal apartment units. For example, let's say you had a single family house and you made an apartment in the basement and rented it out. Even though the property doesn't have the legal zoning for two apartments, your property can still be taxed as a two-family building. A two-family tax base will generally be a higher tax rate than a single family. And to make matters even worse, the building department will give you a building code violation for having the illegal, second apartment! Just because you're taxed as a two-family, it doesn't mean that the apartment suddenly becomes a legal rental unit. You don't have the right to go ahead and rent this extra apartment out to someone. It's still an illegal apartment until you have a building inspector sign-off on it as a safe and acceptable living area that meets all of the local regulations. The building department is a separate entity from the tax department. As a result, the building department doesn't care how your property is taxed. They only

care that your property meets all the local building code requirements.

The *Effective Tax Rate* is the rate based upon the full amount of the estimated market value of the property. This rate is **not** based on the Assessed Value of the property. It's similar to the Effective Interest Rate example that we discussed. (See section Effective Interest Rate Example page 151). The Effective Tax Rate is the actual amount the owner is paying in taxes, in relation to the market value of his property. The assessed value of a property is usually less than the actual market value of the property. To calculate the effective tax, divide the taxes paid for the property by the market value of the property. For example, let's say a house is worth $185,000 and the current taxes on the property were $6,750 per year. The effective tax rate would be:

$$\$6,750 / \$185,000 = 0.04 \quad \text{or} \quad 4\%$$

The *actual* real estate taxes that a property owner pays are usually based on the *assessed value* of the house. Actual real estate taxes are <u>not</u> normally based on the actual *market value*. To calculate the actual tax rate, multiply the assessed value for the property, by the tax millage rate or "mill rate" for the property. For example, let's say a house is assessed for $147,000 and the current mill rate for the yearly tax on the property is $53 per $1,000 of assessed value. The actual tax rate per year would be:

$$\$147,000 / \$1,000 = 147$$

$$147 \times \$53 = \$7,791$$

The *Assessed Value Ratio* is the ratio between the assessed value amount of the subject property and the current market value amount. It's the *percentage* that the owner is paying in taxes, as compared to the market value of his property. To calculate the assessed value ratio, divide the assessed value of the property by the current market value of the property. In our example above the assessed value is $147,000 and the current market value for the property is $185,000. The assessed value ratio would be:

$$\$147,000 / \$185,000 = .79 \quad \text{or} \quad 79\%$$

166    www.nemmar.com                                      REA From A to Z

# Obtaining Information
# At Town Hall

You have to make a trip to town hall to check **all** of the records pertaining to the subject property. You also need to verify the pertinent information concerning the sales comparables that you'll be using for the appraisal report. There will be times when you'll find discrepancies between some data sources. A real estate listing, for example, may have different information from what is recorded at town hall for the subject property and sales comps. When you encounter a situation like this, you may not be able to accurately determine which data source is correct. When this happens, you should always use the public record at town hall as the final say in the matter. You'll be much better off "Covering Your Assets" with the info from the public record than you will from any other data source.

> You have to make a trip to town hall to check all of the records pertaining to the subject property.
> You also need to verify the pertinent information concerning the sales comparables you'll be using for the appraisal.

In most areas you can purchase copies of the flood maps, tax maps, zoning maps, and other information from the local municipality or you can obtain them via the Internet. If you purchase these maps you can do some of the appraisal field work at your office. This can save you time at town hall. You'll also be able to get some appraisal information before you go out to view the subject property.

Years ago the records were all kept on paper and in files so it was a lot more work to find what you needed. Now everything is in computer databases which greatly simplifies checking the records on a property. When you get to town hall you usually have to visit several different departments to obtain all of the information that you need. Ask the employees in each department to assist you. You can save **a lot** of time by having them help you out. They know exactly where the information will be and they can help you with any questions you might have about it. As long as you're polite and friendly, they're usually willing to assist you. Don't go in there with an attitude like you're something special because you pay taxes in that town and they have to cater to your needs. If you have a nasty attitude or if you talk down to them, then you're not going to get much help from them. *Sounds basic doesn't it?* Well, believe me, I've seen people go into town hall with an attitude toward the workers there like they were saying, *"gimme, gimme, gimme."* They have no consideration for the town employees. People with an attitude like that end up wasting a lot of time because they have to find everything out for themselves. I have found that if you're friendly to the town hall employees they can help you tremendously in finding information. This will save you time and money. However, there will be times when you'll encounter a town hall employee who has an attitude problem or is just plain lazy and/or nasty. Just do the best you can if you find yourself in a situation like that.

Not all local town halls are the same. Some have more information than others and some have a filing and recording system that makes it easier to find the information. Just do the best you can with what you have to work with in your area. Here's a list of some of the information you need to check at town hall. **Don't limit yourself to this list!** Always get as much data and information as you can for your appraisals. The more you get, the better your report will be.

1. Check the **field card or building papers** that describe the house and/or site. This should tell you the square footage of the house; type of construction materials used; the size of any decks, pools, garages; the age of the house; number of rooms; the site acreage etc. Determine if there is/was an underground septic system, well water system, and/or an underground oil tank on the site. Also, find out if all valid permits and approvals have been obtained for the installation and/or the discontinued use of these underground items. Any problem conditions will have a negative affect on the property market value.

> Check to make sure that all necessary building dept. permits have been filed and all building department approvals have been obtained.

2. Check to make sure that all necessary **building department permits** have been filed and that all **building department approvals** have been obtained. This is _required_ for any changes to the house and/or site from the time of the original construction or inspection by the local building department. Any decks, pools, garages, additions, updated kitchens and baths, etc. that have been added *must* have building department permits and approvals. Don't just take it for granted that they were filed. Check it out yourself to verify the information! Often the permits and approvals have not been obtained for work/repairs done. Any missing permits or approvals will have a negative affect on the market value of the property.

3. Check to see if there are any **building code violations** against the subject property. This is something that the client and the title company will need to know. A building code violation is generally a safety hazard item found at the subject property that was recorded at town hall by the building inspector. Violations can be for any number of items that do not meet the standards and regulations of the local town. A violation must be repaired and then reinspected by the town building department inspectors to be removed from the record against the house. Any code violations will have a negative affect on the property market value.

4. Check to make sure that there is an up-to-date **Certificate of Occupancy** (C of O) for the subject property. The C of O is a certificate issued by a local building department to a builder, renovator or homeowner indicating that the building is in proper condition to be occupied. A Certificate of Occupancy is required for the occupancy, use, or change of use of a property and usually certifies that the construction meets both the building code and the zoning

ordinance of the town/city. However, if the property has a C of O, it **doesn't guarantee** that there are no building or zoning violations and/or missing permits and approvals. The reason for this is that if the homeowner has repairs or changes made to the house and/or site, then the C of O will not reflect those changes _UNLESS_ the town hall has been notified of those repairs/changes. Therefore, the existing C of O at town hall will <u>not</u> be a valid one based upon the new repairs/changes made to the house or site. An invalid C of O will have a negative affect on the property market value.

5.   Check the **zoning** for the subject property. You have to make sure that there are no zoning violations against the property. You also need to see what the conversion potential is for the property to decide what the Highest and Best Use will be. For example, let's say the property has the zoning potential of being converted to a two-family house from the current single family house. Then you have to decide if a two-family house would be the H&B Use for the subject property, as opposed to a single family house. Any zoning violations will have a negative affect on the property market value.

6.   Check the **deed** for the subject property and all sales comps. This will list the legal description of the property, what the sales price was for the last sale, and sometimes the sales prices of prior sales of the property, when these sale(s) took place, if there are any easements on the property, etc. Any problems with the deed will have a negative affect on the property market value.

> Check to see what the current taxes are on the property. Also, see when the next assessment is due so that you can find out if the taxes are going to go up soon.

7.   Check to see what the **current taxes** are on the property. Also, see when the **next assessment** is due so that you can find out if the taxes are going to go up soon. For example, the property taxes might not be high now. However, what if there's going to be a new tax assessment in the area that will greatly increase the yearly tax bill. This is something that the client will need to know and it will also have an affect on market value. For example, in Greenwich, Connecticut in the 1990's the real estate taxes had not been reassessed for 10 years. When the city finally got around to reassessing the property taxes, they raised the taxes by as much as 60% for many homeowners! So many homeowners complained that the town had to roll-back part of that property tax increase. A very high tax rate will have a negative affect on the market values of real estate.

8.   Check the **flood hazard map** for the subject property. These are maps that the government publishes to figure out if a property is located in a designated flood hazard zone. A _flood hazard zone_ is an area that is determined to have some potential for flooding from time to time. The cause of the flooding could be a river, lake, stream, etc. that is close to the subject property. A high groundwater table in the area could also cause the flooding. If a property is located in a designated flood hazard zone, then special flood hazard insurance will be needed. If an area has occasional flood problems, then this will have a negative affect on property market values.

9.   Check the **survey** for the property. Surveys are very difficult to read so just do the best you can. Surveys are used to find the property line boundaries of real estate. The United States government survey applies in the whole country except the original 13 states: Texas, Tennessee, Kentucky and the New England area states. _Mete_ is the name referring to a distance on a survey. _Bound_ is the name referring to a direction on a survey. The direction can be a compass direction or the name of an adjacent property owner. If you ever see a surveyor at work you'll be amazed to find how precise their measurements are. I had a survey done on one of my rental properties before I sold it and the surveyor's were taking down measurements up to 1/1000 of an inch! I couldn't believe how precise they were about it. Any problems with the survey will have a negative affect on the property market value.

# Condominium and Co-Operative Units

Appraising Condos and Co-Ops is the same as appraising single family houses. There are a few additional factors that you have to consider on Condos and Co-Ops. All areas of the country have Condominium units. Co-Operatives are only found in some areas. Condominiums are usually owned with _Fee Simple_ ownership rights. The idea of a condominium complex is that it provides the condo buyer with a less expensive form of home ownership. A condo owner will not have to spend as much money as is needed to buy a single family house. Also, many people like having the exterior of their home and the grounds maintained by someone else for a monthly fee assessed to all the condo owners. Condos are attached units with common areas that all of the owners in the whole complex have the right to use. The common areas usually have a _Tenancy in Common_ ownership. This ownership is spread between all the individual unit owners in the complex. There are _monthly assessment fees_ that all of the individual unit owners have to pay to maintain the exterior of the complex and the common areas. The individual owners cannot paint, change or alter the exterior of their units in any way unless the Condo Board approves the changes.

> Condos are attached units with common areas that all of the owners in the whole complex have the right to use. The common areas usually have a Tenancy in Common ownership.

There is a Board of some elected Condo owners as well as a _Prospectus_ that outlines the rules and regulations of owning a condominium in the complex. The reason for this is to keep the exterior and common areas looking very uniform and well kept. You wouldn't want your neighbor to paint the outside of his Condo fluorescent pink would you? The regulations have guidelines on how the common areas can be used. Sometimes there are rules of whether the individual Condo units can be rented out to tenants or whether you can have pets. The whole intent of the rules and regulations in the Prospectus of each complex is to try to keep a uniform and pleasant environment. This is for the benefit of <u>all</u> the unit owners, as opposed to catering to each person's individual needs and tastes.

Co-Operatives are owned with *Leasehold* ownership rights. The idea of Co-Ops is that it provides the owner with an alternative to renting. It is a less expensive form of home ownership than having to spend more money to buy a single family house. Again, many people like the idea of having the exterior of their home and the grounds maintained by someone else for a monthly fee assessed to all the Co-Op owners. Co-Operatives are similar to Condos, however, Co-Ops are generally only found in converted apartment buildings in urban areas, like New York City. Often an apartment building will be converted to a Co-Op building just by selling off the individual apartments. The first step is that the current owner of the building, called the *Sponsor*, will set up a corporation with shares of stock. Rather than selling the buyer Fee Simple ownership, they purchase shares of stock from the corporation. The larger your apartment, or Co-Op unit, then the more shares of stock you obtain. The sales price is higher when you buy more shares of the stock. The owner of a Co-Operative unit in a building is legally a renter. By owning that particular share of the stock, which is *Personalty*, it gives him the right to rent a certain apartment from the corporation. The important document is the *Proprietary Lease*.

It's important that you understand that with a Co-Op you're legally still a renter. However, as a shareholder you have the right to live in one of the apartments. The reason behind the whole concept of Co-Operatives is that in a large, built-up urban city, like New York City, there aren't single family houses, like suburban or rural areas. The only option is to sell off individual units in an existing apartment building which gives people an opportunity to buy their home as opposed to renting an apartment.

> *The individual owners cannot paint, change or alter the exterior of their units in any way unless the Condo/Co-Op board approves the changes.*

As with Condos, Co-Ops have common areas that all of the owners in the whole building have the right to use. There are *monthly assessment fees* that all of the individual unit owners have to pay to maintain the exterior of the building and the common areas. The individual owners cannot paint, change or alter the exterior of their units in any way unless the Co-Op board approves the changes. Co-Ops have elected Board members but instead of a Prospectus they have *By-Laws*. The *By-Laws* outline the rules and regulations of owning a Co-Op unit, (shares of stock), in the building, (corporation). The reason for this is to keep the exterior and common areas looking very uniform and well kept. Co-Op By-Law regulations are usually **very** strict. Much more strict than many Condo rules. The By-Laws regulate how the

common areas can be used and whether the individual Co-Op units can be rented out to tenants, or whether you can have pets. As with Condos, the whole intent of the rules and regulations in the By-Laws is to try to keep a uniform and pleasant environment in the complex. This is for the benefit of <u>*all*</u> the unit owners as opposed to catering to each person's individual needs and tastes.

**With Co-Ops there is a Co-Op board that has to approve any potential tenants that you can rent your unit to, if the rules allow tenants. The board also has to approve any potential buyers that you have for your unit when you try to sell it. This is the strict part of the By-Laws that can really bother some people.** It's similar to having someone "approve" you to become a member of a private country club. One possible reason for this is that Co-Op corporations have an underlying mortgage for the purchase of the building. The *underlying mortgage* is the mortgage that is taken out by the corporation to originally purchase the entire building from the current owner, (sponsor). The unit owners purchase the building when the individual shares of stock are sold to them. Each buyer or stockholder has a monthly assessment charge to pay their portion of the underlying mortgage payment. It's similar to the monthly assessment for Condos. However, with Co-Ops you not only have the underlying mortgage but you also have the monthly assessment fee. The monthly assessment fee pays for the maintenance of the exterior of the building and the common areas.

> *Sometimes you'll find that a particular complex has unusually strict rules that can affect the market value of the individual units.*

Some things you have to watch out for when appraising Condos and Co-Ops are the rules and regulations of the Prospectus and By-Laws. Sometimes you'll find that a particular complex has **unusually strict rules** that can affect the market value of the individual units. Remember that if a typical buyer is turned away because of something about the subject property; then that is something that must be considered in the appraisal report. This is because that aspect may have a negative influence on market value.

I've done quite a few foreclosure appraisals on Co-Ops where the bank had taken the property back from the defaulting mortgagee. The bank would often find potential buyers at lower than normal sales prices just because they wanted to sell the Co-Op quickly. However, the sale wouldn't go through. The Co-Op Board members of the complex would come up with all sorts of bogus reasons why they wouldn't approve the sale to this potential buyer. One bank in particular had to actually get to the point of threatening some of the Co-Op Boards with a lawsuit. The bank did this because the Co-Op Boards kept denying approval for the sale to all interested buyers that the bank could find. The bank employees told me that the reason the Co-Op Boards did this is that the sales prices were lower than normal. The low sales prices were the result of the property being a foreclosure. These Co-Ops generally needed a lot of work on the interior of the unit. If the

Board approved a low-priced sale, then it would bring down the market value of **all the other units in the complex.** Market values would drop because that low sale could be used as a sales comparable for an appraisal that involved other units in the complex. This would hurt the market value of **all** of the units in the building.

---

*The reason for this is that banks do not want to be in the property management business.*
*They make their profits by lending money out, not by selling houses, Condos or Co-Ops.*

---

Some banks will often find potential buyers at lower than normal prices because the bank is not concerned with trying to wait to get top dollar for the unit. They merely want to sell the unit for a lower than normal price just to get rid of it quickly. The reason for this is that banks do not want to be in the property management business. They make their profits by lending money out, not by selling houses, Condos or Co-Ops. If they tried to get top dollar for a foreclosure property on their books, then they might have to wait a long time before a qualified buyer came along. The longer a bank keeps a property on their books, then the more money it costs the bank in monthly fees for the property management, maintenance, taxes, etc. These fees can become extremely costly, especially when the bank has already paid high legal fees to go through the entire foreclosure process.

Another aspect you need to consider with Co-Ops is the **underlying mortgage balance** and the **due date** of this mortgage. Many underlying mortgages have *balloon* payments. This refers to a set date in the future when the remaining balance of the loan becomes due and payable to the lender. When the mortgage comes due, then the Co-Op corporation has to secure new financing to pay off the balance. **If they cannot obtain financing then the whole building and corporation will go into foreclosure for the loan!** If the underlying mortgage is due in the near future, then a typical buyer will be hesitant about buying stock, (an apartment), in that building. This will have a negative affect on market value. The reason for this is that I've seen a number of cases where the underlying mortgage loan was in foreclosure proceedings started by the lender. **This means that if you were a stockholder, and you had been making all of your monthly mortgage and monthly assessment payments, you could still lose your equity position!!** Your equity would be lost because the lender was foreclosing on the underlying mortgage. That will definitely negatively affect the market value of all the Co-Ops in that building. A foreclosure proceeding on the underlying mortgage will make a typical buyer alter their purchase price *drastically* or they will probably back out of the deal altogether.

---

*Remember that the monthly assessment is not a mortgage payment that benefits the individual unit owners. It's merely used to pay for the maintenance of the exterior and common areas*

---

The monthly assessments have to be considered when you're appraising Condos and Co-Ops. Two units in two separate complexes can have the same asking price and be very similar in construction. However, if the monthly assessment fees are different, then the typical buyer will take this into account. Remember that the monthly assessment *is not* a mortgage payment that benefits the individual unit owners. It's merely used to pay for the maintenance of the exterior and the common areas. This monthly fee will increase with inflation as prices go up in the economy and the costs of maintaining and managing the complex increase. It's no different from paying a small rent payment each month. That payment does not increase the equity for the individual unit owner. You should find out what the rules in the complex are for increases in monthly assessment charges. *Can they double in a year?* If so, then it's going to have a negative affect on market value.

You have to check all Condo and Co-Op complexes for the number of individual units that have been sold and how many are rented or owned by the builder or sponsor of the complex. The reason for this is that when most or all of the units are sold, then the complex normally has a steady cash flow from the monthly assessments to pay all the common area charges. **But when the builder or sponsor owns most of the complex, then you have many vacancies and the cash flow may not be enough to pay the monthly bills. This can lead to the common areas being neglected and/or the underlying mortgage not being paid!** To offset a cash flow problem or large expenses, most complexes will have a "special assessment" fee. This is an increased monthly payment that all the current unit owners have to pay. This payment is in addition to the regular monthly payments and it's needed to compensate for the poor cash flow. This will have an affect on market value so make sure you do your homework and check these things out completely.

## Over Improvements

Be wary of houses that have *over improvements*. A homeowner creates an "over improvement" when they spend more money in repairs and/or upgrading than they gain in increased market value for the property. See section Basics Of Appraisal Depreciation page 144.

For example, I once did an appraisal on a house located in a neighborhood of homes that ranged from $475,000 to $700,000. The homeowner had purchased the house for about $525,000 and then a year later they spent another **$430,000** to do more improvements to the house. They didn't just remodel the kitchens and baths for $430,000. They added a new floor on the house, they built an addition on the side of the house, they remodeled the entire interior, etc. When the work was completed the house was beautiful. The only problem was that they spent about $250,000 too much!! That's what you call an *over improvement*.

Since this house was located in an area where all of the houses ranged in value from $475,000 to $700,000, then this homeowner could not expect to sell the house for more money than the area could demand. If a typical buyer wanted to spend $955,000 on a house, ($525,000 + $430,000), that potential buyer wouldn't purchase this property because the market values of the other houses in this neighborhood weren't even close to that price. The potential buyer would spend $955,000 in an area where the value of the other houses all fell within that range. Therefore, the additional work the homeowner in this example had done, was not well-spent money from an investment standpoint. Now that doesn't mean that the homeowner isn't happy with the work they did. There is an **amenity** value for the property owner by living in a remodeled house that they're in love with. However, this is a *subjective* opinion of that particular homeowner. If the typical buyer would not agree with that same reasoning, then the excess renovation funds were not well spent from an investment standpoint.

> *Some people don't realize that just because they spend $1.00 in repairs and/or upgrading to their house, it doesn't guarantee that they're going to increase the market value by at least $1.00.*

Some people don't realize that just because they spend $1.00 in repairs and/or upgrading to their house, it doesn't guarantee that they're going to increase the market value by at least $1.00. That's why homeowners need to properly evaluate any extensive work they're planning on doing *before* they spend the money to have it done. One of the best things for a homeowner to do is to hire a good appraiser to give them an *"As Repaired"* market value estimate. This is simply an estimate based upon certain conditions and/or repairs being completed. Sometimes, this type of appraisal is referred to as a *Feasibility Study*. An "as repaired" appraisal will be like telling the client, *"Well, if you make the renovations and build the addition according to the building plans your architect has shown me, then the estimate of market value for your house when it's all completed will be $_____."*

## Other Types Of Housing

A *Planned Unit Development*, (PUD), is <u>not</u> a form of ownership like a condominium or a co-operative unit. A PUD is just a land plan and it usually centers around manufactured housing, such as a trailer park. Manufactured Housing and Mobile Homes can be well made housing with today's technology. Many people think you only get junk when you buy a prefabricated house, but that's not true. The reason for this is that all of the essential construction parts of the house are built in large warehouses that are like an assembly line. Since the sections are put together in a controlled environment, they can be very well made because the weather doesn't affect the workers or the materials. The different parts are then shipped to the vacant site and put together to form a finished house.

*Row Houses* generally all look the same as units that are next to them. Row houses are mostly found in older cities. *Town Houses* generally look a little different from the units that are next to them.

## Mortgages, Mortgages And More Mortgages

Some states have *Deeds of Trust* as opposed to *Mortgages*. One difference between the two is that a Deed of Trust generally takes less time to foreclose on someone than a mortgage does. The mortgage or deed of trust is the collateral for the money lent. A *mortgagee* is the lender of a loan. A *mortgagor* is the borrower of a loan. A *Deed* is a document to transfer title of a property. Title passes on real estate when the buyer accepts the deed. The deed **does not** require the buyer's signature in order to pass title.

> *All mortgages and liens should be recorded at the local town hall to notify the public that someone has a lien or collateral against the property*

A **First Mortgage** refers to the mortgage that is paid off first in case of a foreclosure or sale of the property. All mortgages and liens should **always** be recorded at the local town hall to notify the public that someone has a lien or collateral against the property. This is done to make sure that nobody else records a new mortgage against the subject property before any existing mortgages are recorded. For example, let's say a bank lent you money to refinance your house. Well, if the bank's attorney or the title company forgot to record that mortgage at town hall, then you could take out another mortgage on your house and the second lender wouldn't even know the other mortgage existed! A second mortgage on a property is called a *Junior Mortgage* because it's recorded **after** the existing first mortgage.

**Mortgages take priority in the order in which they are recorded at the town hall.** For example, let's say there are five mortgages on a house and the house is sold. At the closing, the seller must pay off all of the mortgage holders to give the buyer a "clear" title. A clear title simply means that the new buyer will obtain the deed for the property without any encumbrances against it. The only encumbrances will be those that the new buyer incurs to purchase the property, such as his own bank financing mortgage. The mortgage holders that are paid off at the closing will sign a *Satisfaction of Mortgage*. This is a document stating the lenders have removed any claims or liens they have against the subject property.

If a house has five mortgages against it and the house is foreclosed on by one of those mortgage holders, then the person with the **first** mortgage is paid off **first**. Then the **second** mortgage holder is paid off **second**, the third mortgage holder is paid off next, etc. so on down the line. However, if there isn't enough money to pay off any or all of the mortgage holders, then they get stuck holding the bag and end up losing money. In some states an unpaid mortgage holder can then sue the property owner to be paid through the personal funds or assets of that person. Because of the order in which the mortgage holders are paid off, it's more desirable for a lender to have a first mortgage as opposed to a second or third mortgage. The lower on down the line you get, the less secure the mortgage loan becomes in case of a foreclosure sale. That's why many junior mortgages have higher interest rates and lower loan-to-value ratios. The lender is at a greater risk with their loan so they have a higher interest rate and a lower loan-to-value ratio to try to compensate for this additional risk.

The **Loan-To-Value Ratio** simply refers to the amount of money lent against the property as opposed to what is the actual market value of the property. For example, let's say a house is appraised at $275,000 and the lender is willing to give the borrower a 75% loan-to-value ratio loan for a first mortgage. That means that if the loan application is approved, then the lender will lend the borrower $275,000 x 75% = $206,250. Let's say that same lender is asked by the borrower to lend him money secured by a *second* mortgage on his house, instead of a first mortgage. In this case the lender may only have a 50% loan-to-value ratio for a second mortgage because it's a riskier loan to grant someone. That means that if the loan application is approved, then the lender will lend the borrower $275,000 x 50% = $137,500.

> *The fifth mortgage holder can still foreclose on the property even though everyone else is getting paid on time.*

**Any of the mortgage holders can foreclose on the property owner for not living up to the terms of the mortgage note agreement.** For example, let's say the owner

of the property makes all of his loan payments on time to the first four mortgage holders but doesn't pay the fifth mortgage holder. The fifth mortgage holder can still foreclose on the property even though everyone else is getting paid on time. However, the fifth mortgage holder will only get paid from the money that's left over from paying off the first four mortgages with the foreclosure sale proceeds. As a result, this lender's chances of getting all of their money back can be greatly reduced by a foreclosure sale on the property. This generally will give the lender some incentive to "work out" a new loan payment agreement with the borrower instead of rushing into a foreclosure proceeding.

Now I don't want to give you the wrong impression by making you think that there are a lot of houses out there that have four or five mortgages on them. The vast majority of houses have only one mortgage on them and sometimes you'll find a second mortgage as well.

> *From an appraisal standpoint you have to be careful when you find out that a comparable sale has had a purchase money mortgage involved in the financing.*

A **Purchase Money Mortgage** is given in lieu of receiving cash. It's often called *seller financing*. This is what happens when you buy a house and the seller takes part of the sales price amount in a mortgage. No cash changes hands for the amount of the purchase money mortgage. For example, let's say you agreed to buy the house for $115,000 and you obtained a mortgage from the bank for $75,000 and you paid $25,000 of your own money to the seller. That only totals $100,000. To make up the difference, the seller agreed to accept $15,000 in a **second** mortgage behind your bank's **first** mortgage position. That $15,000 is called a *purchase money mortgage* or *seller financing*. A real estate deal structured in a manner, such as the one in this example, can be said to have "creative financing." This means that the type of financing arrangements in the deal are different (creative) from a conventional or typical real estate transaction in the area. Creative financing deals are used when you hear the term "no money down" real estate. A "no money down" deal means that the buyer didn't have to make a down payment with cash since the seller agreed to accept the full "down payment" in the form of a second mortgage on the subject property that is being sold.

From an appraisal standpoint **you have to be careful** when you find out that a comparable sale has had a purchase money mortgage or creative financing involved in the deal. The reason for this is that the recorded sales price of the property may <u>not</u> indicate the **value** for the property if it had been an all cash equivalent sale. A seller can normally get a higher sales price for his/her property by offering buyers better terms, such as a purchase money mortgage agreement.

As we have seen by the ITAO table examples, the reason the seller can get a higher sales price is that often the seller will offer the buyer a lower interest rate for the purchase money mortgage than the buyer could obtain from a conventional mortgage lender. Also, if a buyer doesn't have a sufficient income to qualify for a large enough mortgage to pay the asking price of the house, the seller can offer a purchase money mortgage to help the buyer. This is known as giving the buyer "good terms" on the sale. When a buyer gets good terms then they're more willing to pay a higher price for the property. As a result, the sales price for a deal with good terms or creative financing can be inflated over what a typical buyer would have paid for that same house under a conventional mortgage loan and terms.

**Insured** or **Guaranteed Mortgages** help to protect the lender in the event of a foreclosure. However, the lender generally is not fully insured for their loan. Some Federal Housing Authority (FHA) and Veterans Administration (VA) loans are 95% guaranteed for the mortgage lender. This means that if the lender gives the buyer the loan on a property that meets the FHA or VA loan qualifications, then that loan will be insured for 95% of its value. For example, let's say the buyer stopped making the monthly loan payments. Well, if the bank foreclosed and didn't receive all of its money, then the FHA or VA would pay the lender up to 95% of the loan amount due to the insurance guarantee.

**Open End Mortgages** allow the borrower to add to the loan principal balance by borrowing more money without have to reapply for a new loan. These loans are commonly used for the construction of buildings. The builder gets additional funds in stages as the work progresses to complete the construction of the building. This gives the lender some type of security by not giving one large sum of money up front. The builder gets the funds when needed to complete the different stages of the construction process.

**Participation Mortgages** refer to more than one lender loaning money on the deal. For example, it's when several different banks put in a portion of the total loan funds for the transaction. This provides the lenders with some additional security and lowers the risk of the loan. If the loan is for many millions of dollars, then it would be a severe loss to just one lender if they had to foreclose on the loan. However, if many different banks are involved in lending the money, then the losses are spread out. Since spreading out the losses reduces the risk, the income also reduces because the different banks involved in the transaction have to share the profits of the loan.

Many insurance companies do this when they write very large insurance policies. If there was a claim against a multi-million dollar policy, then the losses are spread out over the different insurance companies that took part in writing the policy. They have to share the income from the yearly premiums but the tradeoff is that they don't have to pay all of the losses alone.

Individual and corporate investors do this all the time on large investments. They spread the risk by bringing partners in on a deal. Each partner will invest millions of dollars to get a share of the profits, while assuming their share of the risks. It covers them for the "downside" in case the deal goes bad financially.

**ARM** refers to **Adjustable Rate Mortgages**. These mortgages have an interest rate that is adjusted at specified intervals. The adjustments are based upon a certain index that must be available for the public to monitor. Some of the indexes they are linked to are the Prime lending rate, Treasury bills, etc. With these loans your monthly loan payment will change with each adjustment made. Often an ARM will have an adjustment cap and a lifetime cap. This means that the loan payment adjustment can only go up or down a certain percentage for each specified period and over the life of the loan.

> *You have to be very careful if you ever get an adjustable rate mortgage. Statistics that show that as many as 25% of adjustable rate mortgage loans are improperly calculated.*

You have to be "on your toes" if you ever get an adjustable rate mortgage. **There have been statistics that show as many as 25% of the adjustable rate mortgage loans are improperly calculated by the lenders!** When this happens, the borrower ends up paying the bank more money than the bank is owed. There are companies that provide a service that will properly calculate what your ARM loan payments and remaining loan balance should be. The fee for this service is usually inexpensive. If you have any doubts about an ARM loan, and you should due to the record of poor monitoring by the banks, then hire these services to make sure you're not overpaying on your loan.

**GPM** refers to **Graduated Payment Mortgages**. *(Some people jokingly call these "jip-um" mortgages)*. With these mortgages the payments are lower than the actual amortized loan payment would normally be. For example, let's say you have a 20 year amortized loan and the normal loan payment for that loan would be $1,000 a month. With a GPM the loan payment might only be $750 per month. However, the additional $250 that is needed to fully amortize the loan over the 20 year term is added to the outstanding loan principal balance. **This results in negative amortization and the principal balance of the loan <u>increases</u> instead of decreasing over time.** This growth continues until the loan payments are adjusted high enough to start to amortize the loan principal balance. In the early years of a graduated mortgage the loan payments made are not sufficient to cover the loan interest expense, nor for any loan principal payments. This loan interest payment shortfall is added to the loan balance amount. The purpose of this type of loan is that it enables the borrower to take out a loan with lower monthly payments in the early years. This will help someone get approved for a higher mortgage loan than they would if the loan had a normal amortization.

**Blanket Mortgage** is a mortgage covering at least two pieces of real estate as security for the same mortgage. A Blanket Mortgage can save a lot of time for someone who has multiple properties or vacant lots. It allows the borrower to use two or more properties for the security for one mortgage loan. The borrower will not have to take out separate mortgages for each property used as the collateral/security for the loan. For instance, let's say you bought a very large vacant lot and subdivided it into six smaller lots to build a house on each lot. Instead of having to get a separate mortgage for all six lots, which would be very time consuming and expensive with the closing costs and points, you could group all of the loans into one mortgage. This is more efficient and easier to manage.

**Package Mortgage** is a mortgage that covers the *Realty* plus the *Personalty*. The Personalty is also called *Chattels*. A *Package Mortgage* includes more than the real estate since it uses both real and personal property to secure a loan. For example, a condominium that is sold with the appliances included in the mortgage could be called a package mortgage.

> *You have to be careful though with assumable loans. Sometimes the original borrower is still held accountable for the repayment on the loan after someone else assumes it from him.*

An **Assumable Loan** is an outstanding loan balance that can be "assumed" or taken over by someone else other than the person who originally borrowed the money. For example, let's say you took out an assumable mortgage loan on your house. If you decided to sell your house down the road, then the buyer could assume your remaining loan balance. The buyer will just continue making the monthly loan payments right where you left them off when you sold the house. Generally all the buyer will have to do is pay a small "assumption" fee to the bank and fill out a new loan application. The buyer may not have to be approved and go through an entire loan process like you did when you first borrowed the money. **You have to be careful though with assumable loans. Sometimes the original borrower is still held accountable for the repayment on the loan after someone else assumes it from him.** If this were the case and the person you sold your house to stopped making payments on the loan, then the bank could come after you for the remaining funds owed to them. That's something that you certainly don't want to happen!

**Conventional Loan** is a loan from a bank that's not insured, like an FHA or VA loan, and it has market interest rates. The *Veterans Administration* (VA), the *Federal Housing Administration* (FHA), the *Federal National Mortgage Association* (FNMA) also known as "Fannie Mae," the *Government National Mortgage Association* (GNMA) also known as "Ginnie Mae," and the *Federal Home Loan Mortgage Corporation* (FHLMC) also known as "Freddie Mac," are all organizations that function on their own in the *Secondary Mortgage Market*. The purpose of the secondary market is that these organizations buy the mortgage loans from banks. They then package a group of loans together and sell them off to investors in the bond market as *Mortgage Backed Securities*. The benefit for the banks is that they get to replenish their funds after they sell off some loans in their portfolios. This is why banks have many of the current requirements for appraisals, termite inspections, etc. They need this documentation in order to meet the requirements to sell their loans on the secondary market. See section The VIP's - HUD, FHA, FNMA, GNMA, and FHLMC page 195.

A **Land Contract** is a document representing an installment sale. A *Land Contract* is also called an *Installment Sales Contract*. This refers to a sale of a property that does not pass the title to the buyer until all payments are made and the full purchase price is paid. For example, let's say you were selling your house and the buyer wanted to "assume" your existing mortgage loan. If your loan was <u>not</u> an assumable loan, then your lender would make you pay off the loan at the closing before you could pass clear title to the buyer. However, you could sell your property on a land contract and not tell the bank about it. The way it would work would be the buyer would take possession of the house but he wouldn't receive the deed or title until your mortgage loan was paid off and you had received the full purchase price for the house. You can agree to almost anything for the terms of any payments.

**However, it must be noted that a land contract is usually against the rules and agreements of any existing mortgages on a property and it should not be used to sell or buy a property.** The current mortgage holders usually have signed mortgage note saying that they will be paid off in full when the property is sold. Even though the deed or title does not pass to the new buyer at the new closing on the property, it's still considered a "sale". If the existing mortgage holders ever found out about such an agreement, then they can call the mortgage due and payable immediately! If you didn't have the funds to pay them in full, they could begin a foreclosure proceeding.

Another drawback to a land contract is that the buyer of the property may have no way of knowing if the current deed or title holder puts a new mortgage on the property. The buyer also will not know if any liens are recorded against the property *after* the original closing and *before* the deed or title is eventually passed to the new buyer. Basically, it's a very risky way of trying to buy or sell a house and I wouldn't recommend you get involved with a transaction like that.

**Negative Amortization** refers to the type of loan payment schedule where the monthly loan payments do not fully amortize the loan. As a result, the loan principal does not get reduced with each payment. The interest is reduced with the payments as the principal balance increases. With a negative amortization loan, your monthly payment on a mortgage, such as an ARM (Adjustable Rate Mortgage) or a GPM (Graduated Payment Mortgage), is not enough to cover the loan interest expense and principal payment. This loan payment shortage is added to your remaining loan balance. For example, this situation arises when the adjustable rate mortgage has a payment cap but the interest rate on the mortgage has increased. A benefit of negative amortization is that your payment doesn't have to increase just because the interest rate on your ARM increased. An ARM loan payment cap doesn't mean that the lender can't pass along an interest rate increase. Eventually, with a negative amortization loan the loan payment will eventually adjust to a level to allow the loan to amortize over its remaining life. The increase in the monthly loan payment needed to repay the larger loan over a shorter time span can be substantial. If rates have increased too high, then refinancing the loan may not be a viable option.

**Loan Principal** is the remaining balance or amount of the outstanding loan that is left to pay off. This does not include the interest amount on the loan.

**Loan Interest** is the remaining balance or amount of the outstanding interest left to pay off. This does not include the principal amount on the loan. When you pay loan interest you are basically paying "rent" for the use of borrowed money.

# Different Types Of Appraisal Accounts

Here's a summary of some of the services a professional real estate appraiser can provide depending upon their qualifications. See section Purpose Of A Real Estate Appraisal page 18 for more details:

◊ Residential and Commercial valuation estimates
◊ Estate planning and estate settlements
◊ Tax assessment review and advice
◊ Advice in eminent domain and condemnation property transactions
◊ Dispute resolution - including divorce, estate settlements, property partition suits, foreclosures, and zoning issues
◊ Feasibility studies
◊ Expert witness testimony
◊ Market rent and trend studies
◊ Cost/benefit or investment analysis, for example, what will be the financial return of remodeling a house, condo, or commercial property
◊ Land utilization studies
◊ Supply and demand studies

1. *Loan Origination Appraisals* - This type of appraisal account will be busier during good economic conditions and increasing sales of homes. During a good economy there will be higher employment percentages and more opportunity to make money. This leads to many people buying a nicer home or moving to a nicer area, which in turn leads to many new mortgage loan applications at the banks that will require appraisals.

2. *Refinance Loan Appraisals* - This type of appraisal account will generally be busier during times of lower interest rates for mortgage loans. During lower interest rate times many homeowners will refinance their existing mortgage. They can take advantage of the lower interest rates to reduce their current monthly mortgage payments. This leads to many refinance mortgage loan applications at the banks that will require appraisals.

> *Therefore, someone will be hired to do the job. Everyone will be much better off if the lender hires an "A to Z Appraiser" who does top quality work.*

3. *Foreclosure Appraisals* - This type of appraisal account will generally be busier during bad economic conditions and recessions. During a bad economy there will be higher unemployment which leads to more people falling behind with paying their bills and their mortgage loan payments. This in turn leads to bank foreclosure proceedings. New appraisals are needed after the properties are taken back by the lenders. It's a tragedy when someone loses their home due to foreclosure. However, as I've said earlier, you're not taking advantage of anyone or being unethical by appraising properties that are the result of a distressed sale or a foreclosure. All of these properties have to be appraised. Therefore, someone is going to be hired to do the job. Everyone will be much better off if the lender hires an **"A to Z Appraiser"** who does top quality work. Why make the situation worse by hiring another appraiser who is only concerned with the fee he earns and not the quality of his appraisal.

I've done a lot of foreclosure appraisals for lenders. After the bank takes the property back, they have it reappraised to decide what price to list it at for a quick sale. They do this to sell the property quickly and get as much of their money back as possible. By doing foreclosure appraisals, I've seen some very interesting properties and situations. I'm referring to aspects other than the sad fact that someone has lost their home due to a distressed situation. You might want to consider getting an account to do some foreclosure appraisals because it's great experience and you may find it to be very interesting work.

I've seen everything from very low valued Condos and Co-Ops, multi-million dollar single family houses, a State Supreme Court Judge's house, and even funeral homes that have been foreclosed on that I had to appraise. Some houses are in great condition after a foreclosure. I have seen cases of people that have put a lot of money into a house and then some bad luck hit them. They ended up losing their jobs or another unfortunate circumstance happened to them. Since they couldn't make the loan payments, the bank took the house back. I've also seen some houses that were *totally* destroyed after a foreclosure. I've seen cases of people who would destroy a house out of anger and revenge due to the bank foreclosing on them. I've also seen some dishonest builders and investors scam the banks out of millions of dollars. What they did was borrow the money and then just walk away from the house and kept the funds from the loan without even making one loan payment to the bank or mortgage lender.

4. *Tax Appraisals* - This type of appraisal account will generally be busier during times when the property taxes are raised. Many homeowners will dispute an increase in their property taxes, or the current amount of their taxes. They may feel that their property has been "over assessed" and that their

property taxes should be reduced. To dispute your property taxes, you need to have an appraisal done to estimate the market value of your property. Also, when someone dies and leaves real estate to their heirs, an estate tax has to be paid and appraisals are needed for that.

5. *Commercial Appraisals* - This type of appraisal account will generally be busier in a good economy when businesses are doing well. A commercial real estate appraisal refers to the appraisal of a building and/or site that deals with a non-residential property. This would generally be any building larger than a legal four family dwelling or a site that is commercially zoned by town hall. Commercial appraising is very involved and takes a lot more training, experience and classes than just doing residential appraisals. If you ever have the opportunity to work with a commercial appraiser you'll see what I mean. The fees charged for commercial appraisals are **much** higher than those charged for residential appraisals. However, along with the higher fees there is a much higher liability that's assumed by the appraiser if a mistake is made in the report. As with anything else in life: *The greater the rewards, the higher the risk and sacrifice to obtain those rewards.*

6. *Relocation Appraisals* - This type of appraisal account will generally be busier during times when the economy is doing well. During good economic times, companies are hiring and expanding their businesses. As a result, they have to transfer new and existing employees to different locations. Relocation firms always need real estate appraisals during the process of employees being transferred to a new location by their employers.

7. *Insurance Appraisals* - This type of appraisal account will generally be busier during a strong economy and real estate market. Insurance companies sometimes hire appraisers to do appraisal reports on properties before they give an insurance policy. This will enable the insurance company to know the correct value to insure the property for in case of fire or damage.

## Miscellaneous Notes

I remember Dr. Scribner responding to a question in our appraisal class about whether or not the appraiser should know the sales price of the subject property. Let's say the sales price is $91,000 and your appraisal is coming in at $90,000. Then you can make the value $91,000 because no one can measure value that accurately and why create problems with the deal for a minor difference from the sales price. This is one reason why you should know the sales price, as long as you're <u>not</u> biased by knowing it. Also, by knowing the sales price you can get some indication of the type of property and sales comparables you'll be evaluating ahead of time.

*This is one reason you should know the sales price as long as you're not biased by knowing it.*
*Also, by knowing the sales price you can get some indication of the type of property and sales comparables you'll be evaluating ahead of time.*

*Contract Rent* is the rent that's being paid according to the lease. Leases should have a *condemnation clause* in them. This will help protect the landlord in case the building gets condemned at a time when the tenant has below market rent. If this happened, the tenant could take the landlord to court to be compensated for the difference between what the market rent is for the area and what their contract rent is in the lease. If this happened a judge can award the tenant money since there's no condemnation clause in their lease. As the landlord, you certainly don't want that to happen!

*Urban Space* is space in a building in an urban area. For example, space in an office building in a built-up and populated city. *Floor Area Ratio*, (FAR) - how many feet of building can you put on a lot. *Loss Ratio* - the square feet of a building that is lost rental due to hallways, common areas, utility rooms, etc. Sometimes entire floors are called "mechanical floors" because they hold the operating systems for part of the building. These all reduce the total rentable square feet in the building. The lower the Loss Ratio is, then the higher the efficiency of the building. The efficiency percentage is based upon the size of the building that you're dealing with. For example, a 15% loss ratio could be considered low and a 25% loss ratio could be considered high.

# Finishing The Appraisal Report

## The Reconciliation Process

Before starting to write up your appraisal report you should sit down with all of your notes, photographs and maps and review your data. This will give you some sense of direction before you jump into the report and end up leaving important items out. When you write an appraisal report use wording that is in a business like and professional manner. Remember the person reading your report will be someone trying to use the appraisal to help them in a business and investment decision.

You also need to review section HUD and FHA Guidelines page 220 and section Sample State Real Estate Appraiser Guidelines page 297 for more details and rules about appraisal standards and how to fill out the standard appraisal report forms.

You have to reconcile the entire appraisal report as you write it up. While you're filling out the additional pages of the appraisal form, keep checking the other pages to make sure that you're being **consistent** with what you write. You can always go back and change things while you're writing up the report, so take your time and be thorough. There will be times when you're writing up the report and you realize that you need to obtain some more information. You may need this information to make sure your conclusions are accurate and consistent. When this happens, stop writing the report until you go out and get the necessary data. You're much better off taking your time and delaying the report than just rushing it to meet a deadline. Remember the saying, "haste makes waste."

> *You check for the accuracy and logic of your information to see that it makes sense and it's not way off base.*
> *You don't want any conflicting statements and/or measurements because then your entire appraisal report becomes questionable.*

Since every phase of the appraisal report is being reconciled, you're constantly reviewing your data to come up with a **supportive estimate of value.** You check for the accuracy and logic of your information to see that it makes sense and it's not way off base. You don't want any conflicting statements and/or measurements because then your entire appraisal report becomes questionable. Just remember to <u>be consistent</u> in all of your reports and on the front **and** back of the appraisal form reports!!! *(I think I've told you that enough times now, so I know you're never gonna forget it, right?)* There are items that are found in several areas on the form,

such as, square footage, room count, garages, condition, location evaluations, etc. Be careful and make sure that you list them consistently or else your entire appraisal report will be in question. Also, be careful not to show two different viewpoints, such as, showing indications that the real estate market is **increasing** in one section of the report, and then **decreasing** in another section of the same appraisal.

One of my instructors told our class that he was involved in a court case that had to deal with inconsistencies in an appraisal report for a commercial property. He said that the appraiser showed two conflicting viewpoints for the direction of the real estate market at the time of valuation for this property. The lender had to foreclose on this property. After the foreclosure, the lender found out that the market value was worth much less than they were led to believe by the appraisal report. The lender filed a lawsuit against the appraiser. They sued based on the assumption that they wouldn't have lent the money in the first place if the appraisal report was accurate. The lender believed that the report failed to accurately estimate the market conditions and value "as of" the date of the appraisal. In some areas of the appraisal report there was data showing a **declining** market and in other areas there was data showing an **increasing** market. These types of inconsistencies put the credibility of your entire appraisal report in question.

> *All factors in your field notes and report must be considered to come up with a supportive estimate of value.*

Just use your **common sense** and think about your reconciliation analysis. Make sure that your estimates and comments in the report make sense. Don't let a calculator make your decisions for you!! You're the one with the mind that has the ability to think and reason, not the calculator or computer. The calculator and computer are only used to assist you in your appraisal report. You have to reconcile the **entire** appraisal report and not just one section, such as the grid area on the form for the sales comparison approach. All factors in your field notes and report must be considered to come up with a **supportive estimate of value.**

Nothing is cut into stone in performing good, quality and thorough real estate appraisals. Appraisal techniques taught in classrooms are guidelines and recommendations, <u>not</u> the final say. You're the one who has seen the subject property and the sales comparables firsthand with your own eyes. *(At least you better have or I'm comin' to get ya!).* You're the one who has obtained the field notes and pertinent data. Therefore, you're the expert and the professional who has firsthand knowledge and experience with the property you're appraising. Use your own judgment on all appraisals to CYA *(Cover Your Assets)*. Now that doesn't mean that you shouldn't take advice from someone else in your area who has more knowledge than you do. Especially, if there's a review appraiser who is looking over your reports and signing their name to them. **Just remember that you put your *John Hancock* on the bottom line of every appraisal report. Therefore, it's your neck that's on the line if you screw up or cut corners.** Cover Your Assets and do good, quality work on all of your reports so you don't have problems later.

The reconciliation process considers all three approaches to value but you don't have to use all three as long as you have a valid reason. Let's say you decided not to use the Cost Approach since the building is too old or for some other reason. Well, you still have *considered* the Cost Approach in your report even though you didn't use it.

## *Signing-Off On The Appraisal Report*

When you sign-off on an appraisal report you don't want to create a lot of problems for yourself later. Problems can arise later if the client finds out that your data is inaccurate or your market value estimate is way off base. So make sure you know what you're doing and that you have sufficient information about the subject property, the comparable sales and the local market. **Don't** include any data that's PFA, which stands for *Plucked From the Air*. Meaning, don't make up information just to fill out sections of the report. As I said before, if you need to obtain more data, then take the time to go and get it before finishing the appraisal report.

> *Don't include any data that's PFA, which stands for Plucked From the Air. Meaning don't make up information just to fill out sections of the report.*

**It's *very important* that you understand the fact that when you sign an appraisal report, you will be held accountable for everything in it.** Also, when you sign-off on a report as the review appraiser, then you're just as liable for the accuracy of the data in that appraisal report as the appraiser himself. So don't just flip through a report and sign-off as the review appraiser. Make sure the data you're reviewing is accurate and that the appraiser that has viewed the property is competent and thorough.

Anyone can file a complaint against you for any of your appraisal reports if it's found to have serious inaccuracies and problems in it. It doesn't have to be your client who has to be the one to file a complaint against you. If someone off the street was given a copy of your report by a client they can create problems for you if you do poor quality work. You don't want one of your reports coming back to haunt you down

the road. The State Certification Committee in your State can bring you up in front of a review board. This will happen if you're guilty of doing poor appraisal reports that have serious inaccuracies and inconsistencies in them.

I had an experience with an *MAI* designated appraiser who was signing-off on appraisal reports as the reviewer and **he wasn't even reading the reports!!!** An MAI is a very high designation for an appraiser to get. I had gotten very busy at one point and I had to subcontract out some of my work. This was because my office couldn't handle all of the work we had and I didn't have the time to hire and train any new appraisers. The appraisal office that I had hired to do some of my appraisals ended up doing some of the worst appraisal reports I have ever seen. These appraisals were so bad that they weren't even worth the paper they were written on! There were so many inconsistencies and problems in these reports that it was amazing to me how anyone could sign-off on them. As a result, I had to throw away all of those reports. *(Of course I told them I wasn't paying their bill).* I called their office and told them that I was considering filing a complaint against them with the Appraisal Institute and the State Certification Board. Coincidentally, they never sent me another bill for their work and I never heard from them again.

What apparently had happened was that this MAI and his appraisal office were *only* concerned with pumping out as many reports per day as possible. They couldn't care less about the quality of the appraisals. All they wanted to know was how much money they could make each day. So learn a lesson from this experience like I did. If you ever get very busy and have to subcontract out some appraisal work or hire new appraisers quickly, you better make sure that they do quality work. You'll be in just as much trouble as them if you send in bad reports to anyone!

If you do poor quality work like that you're going to get sued and you'll end up losing your license, your certification, and your designation. There's no doubt about it. You might get away with doing garbage work for a short time, but eventually you're going to pay for it. If you lose your State license and/or certification than no one will accept your appraisals and you'll be out of work! If this happens then no one is going to hire you with a black mark on your record. You can't find work when you don't have the required State and Federal approvals to be an appraiser.

I'll tell you another bedtime war story from my own experience in the appraisal business. This should definitely give you a good reason to verify all information yourself and not to rely on someone else's word about it. I was doing a foreclosure appraisal for a bank that had to take a property back from a borrower because they stopped making their mortgage payments. In this particular case I found out later that there was a very dishonest Realtor involved in the transaction. *(You'll encounter plenty of them during your career!)* I had finished my on-site inspection of the property and I was leaving to obtain my sales comparables and other field data. This Realtor told me that she had some good comps for me to use back at her office. I said, *"Fine, I'll take a look at them."* There's nothing wrong with having someone assist you on an appraisal report in obtaining your data. The more information you have, the better off you are. In fact you'll usually need someone at town hall, a real estate office or some other place to assist you on most of your reports. You just have to verify that the information they're giving you is accurate before you use it in your appraisal report.

Anyway, I went back to this Realtor's office and she gave me three sales comparables that she said were good comps to use. The only problem with these sales was that they were handwritten on a sheet of paper and weren't from a published data source that was widely accepted. This immediately raised a red flag in my mind about the validity of these sales comps and it should for you too if you ever encounter a situation like that. Coincidentally, the sales prices of these comps appeared abnormal for that area. So I asked her where she obtained this data and comps from and she said that they were all verified by her as recent sales.

I took the comps and went to another office in the area to try to confirm the validity of these sales. I couldn't find any published data source that had these sales listed. So I concluded that they were intentionally falsified by this dishonest Realtor to try to alter the final estimate of value for the subject property. The incentive for this Realtor was to *"move the deal along"* so she could get her commission on the sale. *(Realtors do this all the time!)* I went back to her office and questioned her more about these comps she had given me and suddenly she started fumbling for answers. She ended up taking the sheet of paper into the back room and then coming out later and telling me, *"Oh, maybe I was mistaken about these sales."* She then ripped up this paper with the false comps on it, obviously to destroy the incriminating evidence. *(That Realtor is basically a white-collar criminal and guilty of fraud)*. This Realtor clearly intended to mislead me to line her own pockets with a sales commission on the deal. I'll tell you more about dishonest Realtors and other third parties later.

I was so angry about the dishonesty of that Realtor that I wrote a letter filing a complaint to the real estate authorities about her. *(Who knows if it did any good)*. You shouldn't hesitate to file a complaint against anyone who is dishonest in this, or any other business. If I had trusted that Realtor by not verifying her information, I could have been in big trouble down the road. Someone reading the appraisal report could have discovered later that those sales comparables were totally false!!

You have to keep all of your field notes in your file for every appraisal. You do the same amount of work for every appraisal no matter what type of report you're doing, such as, a written report, an oral report, one page update, etc. The five different types of appraisal reports are: Oral Report, Letter of Opinion, Form Report, Narrative Report, Demonstration Appraisal Report. A Letter of Opinion is an appraisal. An Opinion of Value is **not** an appraisal.

I'll give you some advice that one of my instructors gave our class about doing a *demonstration appraisal report*. A demonstration appraisal report is a narrative appraisal report that is required for candidates trying to get an appraiser designation from certain organizations. The purpose of it is to test the knowledge and competence of an appraiser on all aspects of appraising residential real estate. It's an extremely thorough and comprehensive report that must to be done if you wish to obtain a designation.

Our instructor told us that you should follow the check list located in the pamphlet published by the appraisal organization you will get the designation from. By using this checklist, you won't forget to include anything in your demonstration report. You must be consistent throughout your report and you can't have any disparities with your statements, facts, adjustments, etc. He also said that you should use a two-family house for your demonstration report. Furthermore, you should find your vacant land and sales comparables **before** you choose the subject property that you'll use. Have someone who is a knowledgeable appraiser review your report before you send it into the appraisal organization for grading and evaluation.

When appraising a building based on the building plans and specifications you should get a copy of the plans to keep in your own files. This is because the plans are always changing so you need a copy to CYA, *(Cover Your Assets)*. You should disclose in the report that your estimate of value is based upon the plans that you have been shown. You should state that the estimate of market value does not take into account any changes that have taken place from the time you originally saw those plans.

> *When doing an appraisal, you have to mention any of the three S's in your report to CYA (Cover Your Assets). The three S's stand for: Structural, Safety and Sanitary problems or hazards in a building.*

When doing an appraisal, you *have to* mention any of the three S's in your report to CYA. The three S's stand for: **S**tructural, **S**afety and **S**anitary problems or hazards in a building or site.

There is something else that you have to be careful of to CYA. You should never say that only one or two of the sales comparables were used as the strongest representation for the value estimate in an appraisal report. The reason for this is that attorneys will try to "knockout" the strong basis for your value estimate in your defense against a lawsuit. Do not strongly emphasize that your value estimate is based upon just one or two sales comps in your report. If you do, then if an attorney can knockout those comps, you'll be left with no defense in the case. This is another reason why you should <u>always</u> get more than the minimum number of sales comparables or data to fill out the appraisal form. The more sales comparables and market data you have, the stronger your appraisal report is. With a strong appraisal there will be much less of a chance anyone could question your report later on

There's nothing wrong with making a true statement in your report if you provided some additional weight on a few of the sales comparables you included. You have every right to give some more emphasis on a few of the better sales comps in your report to estimate market value. You will always have some sales that are better comps than others in relation to the subject property. That's why the estimate of market value **is not** just an average of the adjusted sales prices for all of the comps you used. During your reconciliation process you have to decide which sales carry more weight and are a closer indication to the estimate of market value of the subject property. Then use an estimate of value for the subject property that's closer to the adjusted sales prices of *those* comps. Since they're a better representation of the subject property, you'll have a closer estimate of value.

# Uniform Standards of Professional Appraisal Practice

The Appraisal Foundation, through its Appraisal Standards Board, publishes the *Uniform Standards of Professional Appraisal Practice* (USPAP), which is the generally accepted set of performance standards for appraisers. It is these standards that are enforced by state governments and various professional appraisal organizations. Violation of the USPAP standards can lead to disciplinary action by government regulators and appraisal organizations. A copy of the USPAP can be obtained from The Appraisal Foundation web site store. See section Appraisal Related Web Sites page 406.

The USPAP was one of the State appraisal courses that I took when I was starting out in appraising. I will use my own notes from my class notebook, along with my own comments and experience, as a guideline but I won't duplicate the USPAP course information. I will only highlight the most basic items that I made notes on while taking the class. These were the points raised by the class instructor's and my own experiences that I felt were important to write down and study. You should read through the full version of the USPAP and also take the State appraisal courses taught by their own instructors to get the most benefit from their expertise and training.

> *Unfortunately, some people have no concept of morals even after they take these courses. Just don't be one of those people and you'll make plenty of money in this business and you'll sleep well at night.*

The whole idea behind this course is to teach students the ethical requirements and the accepted minimum standards to be responsible and honest real estate appraisers. Unfortunately, some people have no concept of morals even after they take these courses. Just don't be one of those people

and you'll make plenty of money in this business and you'll sleep well.

◊ The appraisal report must be portrayed in a meaningful manner that is understood by the client. You **cannot** let the entire report nor any one section of the appraisal report be used to mislead the client nor anyone else. It is also unethical to knowingly use, or allow an employee or third party to use a misleading appraisal report, even if you don't sign the report.

◊ You cannot report a predetermined market value nor any oral market value estimates before doing a full appraisal. You cannot give an estimate of market value unless you do *all* of the aspects of an actual appraisal report. You're liable for any discrepancies if you quote someone a value and you end up being wrong. You're supposed to be an expert and professional in your field. So if someone asks you, *"What's my house worth?"* Just tell them that you cannot give them a market value estimate without doing all of the research and field work of a full appraisal report.

> *You cannot slant the estimate of market value, nor any other aspect of the appraisal report, to favor the client.*

◊ You cannot slant the estimate of market value, nor any other aspect of the appraisal report, to favor the client. This is a very important aspect to remember. Don't try to "move any deals along" or "fudge the numbers" to benefit your clients or a mortgage lender. If the market value estimate is not a price the client wants to hear, then that's too bad. You can't alter the appraisal report just to keep someone happy.

◊ Regardless of the type of appraisal your doing or the fee charged for the services it **must** be done according to the Federal and State Appraisal Standards. You can't cut corners just because you're not getting paid a high fee for additional work needed.

◊ You cannot base your appraisal fee on the amount of the market value estimate or any other stipulated result. You cannot have any undisclosed fees for a report. Regardless of the fee you charge, the work is always the same. You have to base your fees on the time and knowledge required to do the assignment, not on the value estimate. You can quote your fee on a range rather than a set price so you can have room for any additional work that is needed.

◊ It's OK to give a client a range of the market value estimate *only* if the client requests it and understands it. For example, you can appraise a house to be worth $195,000 to $200,000 if the client understands this estimate. The client also must agree that you will use a range for the market value estimate.

◊ You cannot advertise to the public in a false, misleading or exaggerated manner. For example, you can't advertise that your an *MAI* appraiser unless you actually have been given that designation.

◊    You must act in a disinterested and impartial manner for the appraisal assignment and report. If you have **any** interest at all in the subject property, appraisal assignment and/or report other than your regular fee, then you must disclose everything to the client and state it in the report.

◊    You must disclose *everything* in your appraisal report that is an ethical or standards requirement.

---

*You cannot discuss the value estimate or any other information of the appraisal report with anyone other than the client. You must respect the confidential nature of the appraiser-client relationship.*

---

◊    You cannot discuss the value estimate or any other information of the appraisal report with anyone other than the client. This is another important point to keep in mind at all times. You *must* respect the confidential nature of the appraiser-client relationship. If you give out copies of an appraisal report to show a potential client the quality of your work, then you must *first* get the approval of the client the appraisal was for. An alternative is that you must "white out" the pertinent names and information, such as the property address, the client, the dates, and the estimate of value on that appraisal report.

◊    You must retain your written records of the appraisal, and any consulting work, for a minimum of five years after the appraisal assignment. This is needed in the event that you have to go back and re-evaluate an old appraisal assignment or someone has questions on it later on after reviewing the report.

◊    It is the responsibility of the appraiser, before accepting any assignment, to identify the appraisal problem and have the experience and knowledge required to competently complete the assignment. If not, then you must disclose your lack of knowledge and/or experience to the client before accepting the assignment. You must take the steps necessary to complete the assignment competently. For example, if you were hired to appraise a commercial property and you have no prior experience in commercial appraising, then you will have to get help from an experienced commercial appraiser for this assignment. Furthermore, you're required to tell the client about your lack of experience before you take the job.

◊    An appraiser's files are his primary data source. Other data is a secondary source.

◊    As you already know - **You have to be consistent in your appraisal reports!!**

# Articles by Kenneth J. Jones

This section has some real estate and appraisal articles written by Ken Jones, *CTA, SCGREA, and licensed real estate broker.* I've included these articles since they discuss some real life situations you'll encounter in real estate and the appraisal business. The topics are discussed in a way that goes far beyond a typical classroom or course textbook analysis of these issues. **The author shows why it's important to use common sense, logic, reason, _and morals_ in all of your real estate and appraisal decisions.** These articles are reprinted with permission from Ken Jones, www.globalvaluations.com.

## The Cost Approach: It DOES NOT Indicate Fee Simple Market Value!

One of the more hotly debated issues within the real property appraisal and banking industries, as well as within those tax assessing jurisdictions required to base real property assessments upon *Market Value*, is the topic of whether or not the Cost Approach is appropriate for use in appraisal assignments of existing building improvements, regardless of their age (including brand-new structures), when the purpose of the assignment is to estimate *Market Value*, as defined in the Uniform Standards of Professional Appraisal Practice (USPAP), of the Fee Simple estate.

On the one side, we have a majority of real estate appraisers who have been educated in the application of this methodology, either directly or indirectly, in accordance with the text and teachings of the Appraisal Institute which states, *"the result [of the Cost Approach] is an indication of the value of the fee simple interest in the property." (1).* On the other side, we have a broad diversity of real estate professionals, including builders, developers, professional cost-estimators, contractors, real estate brokers, as well as the overwhelming majority of the buying and selling population who fail to act in accordance with those teachings. These groups, both knowingly and unknowingly, conduct their business activities consistent with fundamental economic principles, and do not regard the results from the use/application of the Cost Approach as an indication of *Market Value*, contrary to those teachings.

This paper is intended to 1) provide the reader with an examination of the differences between the current academic teachings and factual market activities, and 2) provide the practicing appraiser factual economic and USPAP based support with which to educate their clients to the fact that the use of the Cost Approach within *Market Value* appraisals of the Fee Simple or a lesser/partial estate is inappropriate.

In order to grasp the inherent problems with the common belief that the results of the Cost Approach provides an indication of the *Market Value* of the Fee Simple property rights, one must first know and understand that there is a substantial difference between **real estate**, which is the tangible aspect of the land and whatever structures are intended to be permanently affixed thereto, if any, and **real property**, which are the intangible, man-made *rights* to the use of the real estate, typically referred to as the *Bundle of Rights*, which include the rights to own, use, occupy, rent, reversion, sell, give away, or to do none of these things. **It's absolutely essential** to understand the fact that, when an appraiser is given an assignment to estimate *Market Value* of the Fee Simple or a partial/lesser interest, the *"thing"* being valued is **not** the tangible **real estate**, but the intangible **real property rights** inherent to that specific parcel of real estate.

The next fact that must be recognized is that, when estimating either the **reproduction cost-new** (the estimated cost to create an exact duplicate of the subject improvements, including the exact building materials used in its construction as well as its exact design, including its functional deficiencies) OR the **replacement cost-new** (the estimated cost to create a new building of the same use [warehouse, office building, multi-family, single family, etc.] using the latest, most modern building materials and optimum functional design features), the result of such an estimate **is merely an accounting** of all of the expenses necessary to create a physical structure, hence its former name *The Summation Approach*. The result of this **accounting procedure** which *is* the Cost Approach, **does not mean**, nor should it be mistaken to mean, that the typical market participant will pay the amount of that cost estimate, or any amount relative to it in exchange for the rights to that parcel of real estate.

In order to believe that this **accounting procedure** indicates the *Market Value* of the Fee Simple property rights requires one to ignore a number of fundamental economic laws, including the 4 specific essential components which must exist simultaneously in order for anything to be considered to have value, being: 1) **Utility**; it must serve a useful purpose, 2) **Desirability**; it must be desired by those to whom it has a use, 3) **Scarcity**; its supply must be less than its relative demand, and 4) **Affordability;** it must be affordable to those to whom it has utility and desirability.

Further, to believe that the Cost Approach **accounting procedure** can provide an indication of the *Market Value* of the Fee Simple, or any partial interest in those property rights, is also to ignore the *Principle of Contribution* which states that an item only has value to the extent that it contributes to the value of the whole, OR by the amount that the value of the whole is diminished by the absence of that item.

Let us now consider the actions of typical market participants. It doesn't matter if we were to consider typical investor types involved in sophisticated income producing properties, or the typical first home buyer; when it comes to deciding the price to pay for the property rights associated with a specific parcel of real estate their *"appraisal"* methodology is virtually identical in that, **neither** considers the Cost Approach accounting methodology.

*Why not?* Primarily because, in their eyes **it's irrelevant!** The fact that **the building is already there** eliminates the need to know what it would cost to build new and depreciate it to present value. **The investor only cares about** the amount of return from a subject property as an investment compared to returns from competitive investments, AND **the home buyer only cares about** the purchase price of house *A* relative to the purchase price of house *B*, plus consideration of the *Contributing Value*, if any, from any differences between the two houses that they, the typical buyer, may consider to be of value and in such subjective dollar amount(s), as they, the typical buyer, may attribute to such differences as the differences are perceived to contribute to the overall utility and desirability of each house. **As for the typical seller,** they are solely concerned with obtaining the highest price possible relative to the sales prices obtained by sellers of what they perceive to be competitive properties.

POINT OF FACT: The very premise of the Cost Approach accounting methodology is totally foreign to the typical buyer and seller of real estate which is supported by the virtual absence of such activity being undertaken in the market by those typical buyers and sellers of existing building improvements.

POINT OF FACT: In addition to their apparent recognition of the irrelevance of indications from the Cost Approach accounting procedure, the typical buyer and seller of real property haven't the technical knowledge nor the practical experience required to undertake the construction of a building in a competent, cost-effective, timely manner, thus, cannot possibly be considered capable of undertaking the development of the Cost Approach.

**IT SHOULD BE OF SERIOUS CONCERN** to every appraiser and every user of an appraisal report to ensure that the person providing estimates of cost-new has sufficient technical knowledge and practical experience in the disciplines of building design, construction and cost-estimating to be considered in compliance with the *Competency Provision* of USPAP when the use of the Cost Approach is appropriate.

Adding to the absence of economic support, thus, further undermining the credibility in the belief that the Cost Approach accounting procedure can provide an indication of the *Market Value* of the **real property rights** associated with a specific parcel of **real estate** is the topic of the currently taught and accepted methods by which appraisers *"depreciate"* cost-new estimates in order to theoretically obtain an indication of the present *"value"* of the already existing building and site improvements.

Most appraisers have been taught that buildings *"depreciate"*, or lose *"value"* 1) by means of the aging process, 2) through changes in standards of functional utility, as well as 3) from *"externalities"*; negative influences from outside the boundaries of a property.

Above all, *"depreciation"* as it is currently taught and practiced, is just another accounting procedure, which reinforces the distinct difference between the Cost Approach methodology, which is conducted in isolation from *"Market Forces"*, and the Sales Comparison and Income Capitalization methodologies which are solely and wholly the direct result of market activity. This is supported by the fact that there would be no need to obtain indications of *"depreciation"* from the other 2 true *Market* approaches, such as using the capitalized rent loss from the income approach; just one of many examples.

An analysis of the practice of *"Physical Depreciation"* due to the aging process finds the cost-new estimate is most commonly *"depreciated"* by either the economic or actual age/life method, both of which are based upon an **accountant-like Straight-Line depreciation model** developed by dividing the age (actual or effective) of the improvement by the estimate of its remaining life (physical or economic). In addition to the **fact** that this *"depreciation"* estimate is **not** derived from *"Market"* evidence, is the major problem that it assumes that all things within the structure, as well as any and all site improvements, *"depreciate"* at the same, constant, average annual straight-line rate. **Example:** A building with an actual age of 15 years and an estimated remaining life expectancy of 45 years has depreciated, according to this model, by a total of 25%, implying an **average annual Straight-Line rate** of 1.67% annually. Since markets simple don't work this way, this **accountants methodology** cannot reasonably be considered *"Market"* based nor *"Market"* related, therefore, it cannot possibly reach a conclusion nor provide an indication of *"Market Value"*.

Another contributing problem in this **accountants method of depreciation**, are the typically unsupported statements of estimated actual life expectancies. It seems, according to virtually every real estate appraisal report I've ever read, there isn't a house structure in the USA that will last longer than 50-60 years, nor an industrial building that will last longer than 40-50 years, with similarly short actual life expectancies stated for all other types of building improvements.

I'm certain, as I'm sure you are, that there are vast numbers of buildings throughout the United States that exceed 80-100 years of age being put to all types of uses. In fact, there probably isn't a building structure being built today in accordance with minimal building codes that will not physically last for at least 100 years, assuming normal ongoing maintenance. And, while it may not continue to provide **Contributing Value** to the land/site for that long a time period, it's more likely than not that it will physically stand **at least** that long, again, assuming normal maintenance.

This brings us to the next major topic when discussing the applicability of the currently applied and accepted methods of *"depreciation"*, which is the concern that many appraisal reports fail to demonstrate a working understanding of the implications from the term *"remaining economic life"*, · which, if you're not an appraiser, is the estimated amount of time into the future that the existing improvement(s) will continue to provide **Contributing Value** to the **Market Value** of the vacant land/site.

This problem begs the obvious question, *"How can an appraiser reasonably support their prediction of the amount of years that a structure is going to continue to provide Contributing Value to the Market Value of the vacant land/site?"*. With the most reasonable answer being, *"It probably can't be done."*.

While one can argue the merits and/or demerits of various methods of measuring *"depreciation"*, logic dictates that even the consideration of *"depreciating"* cost-new estimates is, by its nature, dealing solely with the physical aspect of the real estate, totally outside of and apart from the parameters required of the appraisal of **Market Value** of property rights.

A reasonable test, or challenge to this premise is to ask, *"What evidence links physical aging/depreciation to lower 'Market Value'?"*, which might reasonably be analyzed as follows. Consider a common occurrence; a 100 year-old dwelling at an adequate level of maintenance which has currently been sold for $150,000 which, for the sake of this example, is typical **Market Value** in its market. Its actual cost-new in 1893 may reasonably have been $3,500 with the **Market Value** of its site having been $300 with an overall **Market Value** of $4,200. And, while changes in the economic forces of supply and demand have increased the ratio of the **Contributing Value** of the land to the overall **Market Value**, the original question remains, *"What evidence links physical aging/depreciation to lower 'Market Value'?"*, with the answer having to be, *"There is no such evidence."* Thus, it would appear reasonable to conclude that, neither the accepted methods for measuring physical *"depreciation"* nor for forecasting *remaining economic life*, have a relationship to market reality, thus, cannot result in an indication of **Market Value**.

Observation and experience provide the conclusion that most appraisers who develop a cost-new estimate of existing building improvements in **Market Value**, as well as appraisal assignments for other types of value, use data provided by national cost estimating services. When using such a service, appraisers typically develop the cost-new estimate using the data which provides an estimate of **replacement cost-new**; seemingly an unreasoned selection which leads one to believe that this selection results from a lack of understanding of its

definition and value implications as evidenced when, almost invariably, the appraiser applies a negative charge against the cost-new estimate of the **replacement** building citing, *"functional inadequacies contained within the existing subject building improvement."* which, by the very definition of *"replacement cost-new"*, cannot possibly be considered because the replacement building is built to current optimal functional standards. If, in fact, the building whose cost-new is being considered **has** functional inadequacies, the only appropriate methodology for estimating its cost-new would be to calculate **reproduction cost-new** which would literally reproduce an exact duplicate of the subject, including all of its functional inadequacies, which, **again**, **would not provide for consideration of a negative charge against cost-new for functional inadequacies because they are already considered in the cost-new estimate,** leaving us with the question, *"Should functional depreciation caused by such inherent things as floor plan layout, ceiling height, etc., even be considered as 'depreciable' items in a cost-new estimate?"*, to which the answer must reasonably be *"No. Because using the appropriate cost-new estimate eliminates that consideration."*

Another major concern is the notion that the cost-new estimate of an existing building improvement should have a negative charge taken against it for *"economic/external obsolescence"*, a fictitious premise since, as all appraisers are required to know, when estimating the value of the land/site *as if vacant*, an appraiser is responsible to consider all social, economic, governmental, and environmental influences upon the vacant land/site in order to determine both its value and its **highest and best use**. This includes all **external**, or **locational** factors. In this undertaking, the appraiser is required to contrast the **Market Value** of the land/site **as if it was vacant,** against the estimated **Market Value** of the property as it is currently improved. In estimating the **Market Value** of the theoretically vacant land/site by the most appropriate method, every such method must include consideration of the **Contributing Value** influence upon the subject land/site from **LOCATIONAL FACTORS**, including any and all negative **external** influences upon the subject's **location**.

Further, if there is a negative influence upon the subject parcel of land/site from a source outside of its boundaries that would be so substantial as to render its land value at zero (or below zero, so as to have to carry the remainder of the negative value impact onto the proposed [actually existing] building improvement), **at that point in the valuation process**, an appraiser **must** conclude that the **highest and best use** of the subject land/site, **as if vacant**, is for it to **remain vacant** until such time as the source of the negative influence is removed or its impact is sufficiently diminished to the point where there would be measurable market demand for the development of the land/site with improvements that would meet all 4 tests for highest and best use at that future point in time.

This leads to, perhaps, the most important question to be asked, *"Is the use of the Cost Approach in appraisal assignments for the purpose of estimating the 'Market Value' of the Fee Simple estate of existing building improvements, regardless of their age, in compliance with*

*USPAP Provisions and Standards?"* Upon examining USPAP, we find that The *Appraisal Foundations* Preamble to the Provisions & Standards states, *"It is essential that a professional appraiser arrive at and communicate his or her analyses, opinions, and advice in a manner that will be meaningful to the client and will not be misleading in the marketplace."* The **Conduct** portion of USPAP's *Ethics Provision* states, *"An appraiser must perform ethically and competently in accordance with these standards and not engage in conduct that is unlawful, unethical, or improper.".* The clarifying comment regarding this statement of proper conduct says, *"The development of an appraisal, review, or consulting service based upon a hypothetical condition is unethical . . .",* which begs the question, *"What can be more hypothetical than pretending that an existing building isn't there?".* However, a terribly more disturbing question is, *"What could possibly be more misleading, hypothetical, and further from the reality of the activities in the market than having the appraiser develop a so-called "valuation" methodology which is virtually NEVER used by typical market participants?"* And, to those who would ask, *"What about the Principle of Substitution?",* be reminded, while it states that, if there are 2 items of equal utility the item with the lowest price will gain the widest distribution, this basic economic principle is based upon the premise **that both items currently exist!**

Further, to put forth the concept that the *typical* buyer would *typically* build a substitute building if it was more economical is only *"supported"* by a number of unreasonable hypotheticals, including 1) ignoring consideration of the highest and best use of the vacant site, 2) ignoring the economic supply/demand issues in an over-supplied market, 3) the assumption of the availability of a substitute parcel of vacant land able to be purchased at the same price as the **Market Value** of the subject site, 4) the ability and willingness of the typical buyer to pay normal front-end expenses for site plan engineering, architectural services and environmental evaluations, **all before negotiating the purchase price of the land** which may prove undesirable subsequent to these preliminary studies, in addition to considering 5) whether or not this *typical* market participant has the expertise to successfully conduct such an undertaking, which is quite unlikely, evidenced by the virtual absence of such undertakings in the market.

Therefore, based upon the realities of fundamental economic principles, as well as the actions of the virtual entirety of typical market participants, I believe that: 1. The results of developing a cost-new estimate of a tangible physical structure cannot possibly provide an indication of the **Market Value** of intangible **real property rights**, and 2. To develop a methodology during an appraisal assignment which is virtually **never** used by typical market participants, and to include that **never used** methodology in reporting that appraisal, is a gross misrepresentation of actual market activities, therefore, is misleading to the user of the report, and should reasonably be considered a serious violation of the USPAP Ethics Provision and Standards Rule 1 and 2. *(1) The Appraisal of Real Estate, 10th Edition, Appraisal Institute, Chicago, Illinois, p 313*

# Real Estate: The Best Investment

**Real estate is the safest, most reliable and most financially advantageous investment one can make.** But, don't just take my word for it. Let's examine the cold, hard facts regarding income-producing real estate as an investment. And, let's contrast those facts against facts about other investments. I believe, that after you review all these facts, you'll agree with my opinion.

## FACT 1: REAL ESTATE IS WITHIN YOUR PERSONAL CONTROL.

**Let's compare an investment in real estate to owning stock.** Aside from the problems of being able to understand the complex vagaries of operating a major corporation, then being able to successfully predict its future earnings and profitability, the most dangerous aspect of owning stock is the lack of control you have over the company and the unpredictable change in the price of its stock. Face it. The people who have the greatest impact over the change in the value of a stock is that hand full of professional money managers, each of whom has total control over literally billions of dollars. And, when these professional money managers buy and sell stock, they buy thousands of shares in one company in a single trade. So, on any given day, if a money manager in New York hears a rumor at a cocktail party on Wednesday night that causes him/her to sell a stock on Thursday morning, that single action can, and usually does, drive down the price of that stock.

It happens every day, in a micro-second, and without warning. With a mere push of a computer button, poof! The value of your 100 shares of stock just went from the $16.00 a share you paid yesterday, to $5.50 a share, and you just lost $1,050. Without any visible or predictable cause, some guy you don't even know just wiped out 65% of the value of your investment in the blink of an eye. This also assumes there hasn't been any illegal insider trading or other illegal hanky panky with the accounting, such as Enron, Global Crossing and WorldCom, among others, both known and yet to be discovered.

Yes, while it's true that the value of real estate also tends to be influenced by things beyond the control of the individual property owner, such influences are usually related to financial conditions in the local and general economies. More importantly, these conditions are public knowledge, and are openly and simultaneously available to everyone. Further, these general economic changes also tend to occur over relatively long periods of time (months and even years), giving property owners ample time to make any desired adjustments to preserve the value of their investment.

Well, as we can see, as compared to investing in real estate, buying stock is a very high-risk proposition; not at all a reliable, predictable investment. In fact, buying stock is more like taking your money and going to a gambling casino where anything can happen, and it's all beyond your control.

## FACT 2: TENANTS PROVIDE PREDICTABLE, STEADY AND RELIABLE INCOME.

**Let's compare the cash-flow from real estate to that from stocks and bonds.** Even the highest quality publicly traded companies sometimes reduce, and even eliminate paying dividends (profits) to stockholders. While most people think this only happens in economic "hard times," the fact is, that a company can have financial problems at any time for reasons that have nothing to do with how good or bad the general economy is doing. The recent bankruptcies of such business giants as K-Mart, MCI/WorldCom and United Airlines are just a few of the numerous examples of how a company can run into financial problems in an otherwise good economy.

As for bonds, the present interest rate (yield) on the most recently issued 5-year US Treasury Note is 3.30%, if held the full 5 years to maturity. Likewise, the 10-year US Treasury Bond pays 4.05%, again, if held the full 10 years to maturity. In addition to suffering these meager rates of return, you'll also have to pay income tax on the earned interest, both federal and state (if applicable). So, if you're in the 28% federal income tax bracket, your net profit on the 5-year Note will be only 2.38%, and only 2.92% on the 10-year (before state income tax, if applicable).

Now, using a very simple example of income from investment real estate as a comparison, let's say you bought a 1-family house for investment at a purchase price of $100,000, with $10,000 (10%) down payment, and you're collecting $1,000 a month in rent with the tenant paying all utilities. Even after making your mortgage payment of $539.60 a month ($90,000 @ 6% for 30 years), and paying your property tax of about $85.00 per month, as well as paying your homeowner insurance at another $30.00 per month, you'll still have $345.40 to put into your pocket at the end of every month, or $4,144.80 a year. So, your annual return (interest rate, if you will) on your $10,000 of invested cash is a whopping 41.45% (before income taxes).

So, even after paying your federal income tax on the rental profit (using the same 28% tax bracket), you still have $2,984.40 spendable cash in your hands; that's equal to 29.84% annual net on your invested cash. And, that doesn't even consider 1) the increase in the value of your property, 2) the increase in your equity position as a result of your tenant pay down your mortgage, and 3) the benefit of reducing you income tax liability from a little thing the I.R.S. calls "depreciation," that I'll get to in a moment.

**Well, what about the change in the value of stocks and bonds compared to real estate?** On January 14, 2000, the Dow-Jones Industrial average (DJI) closed at its all-time high of $11,723.00. By March 11, 2003, just over 3 years later, it closed at $7,524.06, having lost over 35% of its value from its all-time high. As of this writing (October 15, 2004) the DJI closed at $9,933.38; it has never reached the $11,000 level to date.

As for the National Association of Securities Dealers Automated Quotations (NASDAQ), the losses there are even worse. Again, on March 11, 2003, the NASDAQ closed at $1,271.47, having lost about 75% of its value from its all-time high of $5,048.62 set exactly 3 short years earlier on March 10, 2000. As of this writing, the NASDAQ closed at $1,911.50, never having reached 50% of its all-time high value to date.

So, what about real estate? Well, the people who bought real estate virtually everywhere in the United States at the same time these stock indexes were setting their all-time highs in the year 2000, now have property that has increased in value by between 50-100%. Plus, they've also had cash flowing into their pockets every month, while their tenants have been paying down their mortgage debt. And, in most cases, these property owners have refinanced their mortgages with lower interest rate loans that have boosted their net cash-flow even more.

## FACT 3: LEVERAGING: THE BENEFIT OF USING OPM (OTHER PEOPLE'S MONEY)

In today's market, a buyer with an average credit history can buy a piece of investment real estate with as little as 5-10% invested cash down payment, and sometimes with less. The remaining 90-95% of the purchase money is borrowed (OPM). This is called "leveraging." As a practical matter, leveraging allows you to stretch your buying dollars, reduces your risk (because you have very little invested), and it exponentially increases the overall value of your wealth by creating the opportunity to buy more than one property at one time.

## FACT 4: TENANTS WILL PAY OFF THE MORTGAGE, PAY ALL THE EXPENSES, AND PROVIDE YOU WITH CASH EVERY MONTH, EVEN IN ECONOMIC DOWNTURNS.

While the property owner may write the check for the monthly mortgage payment, the tenants actually pay the mortgage (and most, if not all other expenses of the property) with their rent payments to the owner. Remember, people always need a place to live and conduct business, even in economic hard times. And, while most people will sacrifice extras, such as a new car and new clothes, they really can't sacrifice on having a place to live or to conduct their business. And, with the spectrum of government rental housing assistance programs, such as HUD Section 8, you can pretty much depend on collecting the rent to pay your debts (and, put money into your pocket) in both good times and bad.

## FACT 5: INVESTMENT PROPERTY OWNERS GET A MAJOR INCOME TAX ADVANTAGE FROM "DEPRECIATION."

The I.R.S. provides owners of investment real estate an accounting expense benefit called "depreciation" which lowers the taxable income from their investment real estate. Although there's a table in the I.R.S. rules that regulates the amount of annual and overall depreciation that can be taken (depending on the type of property), the most important thing you should know is that depreciation is only an accounting procedure, and has nothing to do with the actual value of the real estate.

## FACT 6: YOU CAN SELL YOUR INVESTMENT PROPERTY AND LEGALLY PAY NO CAPITAL GAINS INCOME TAX.

That's right! Internal Revenue Code §1031 sets forth the conditions under which owners of investment real estate can sell their property, take the profits from that sale and buy more investment real estate while not having to pay a single penny in capital gains income tax on the profit from the original sale. This type of transaction is commonly referred to as a "1031 Exchange." Again, there are a few rules that must be followed, but it's really a pretty simple transaction that can save you thousands of dollars in income taxes. Using the 1031 Exchange also provides you with the opportunity to buy more investment real estate with higher net cash flows, as well as buying property with a greater potential for future value growth. And, don't be fooled by a common misunderstanding of the term "exchange." When used in the context of the 1031 Exchange, you do not literally have to "exchange" your property with someone else for their property. In the 1031 Exchange, the word "exchange" simply means selling one type of investment property and replacing it with another investment property of the same type. It's also referred to as a "like kind" exchange.

Moreover, it doesn't matter if you own a piece of vacant land and want to buy and office building, or if you own a 2-family and want to buy and industrial building. It's all real estate, and it's all the same, or "like kind" property, which the underlying criterion required for getting the benefit of the 1031 Exchange. And, while there are other criteria required to use the 1031 Exchange, they're relatively simple to understand, and will save you thousands of dollars when you want to "trade-in" your existing investment property for another one.

Let me leave you with this simple truth: If, on January 1, 1974, you invested $5,000 in a stock fund that tracked the performance of the Dow-Jones Industrials, on October 15, 2004 your investment would be worth $58,068. That's a return of 11.61 times our original investment. (This analysis does not consider the benefits of reinvestment of dividends on stocks, nor does it consider the benefits of net cashflow from rent or the income tax benefits of depreciation and the use of the 1031 Exchange). But, if on that same January 1, 1974, you invested that same $5,000 in a piece of real estate worth $30,000, and if the value of that real estate only increased on an average of 5% per year, on October 15, 2004 that property would be worth $134,790. That's 26.96 times your original $5,000 investment, based solely on the increased value of the property.[1] Additionally, your mortgage would be paid in full (by the tenants) and you would have had cash in your pocket virtually every month during that 30+ year period. In simple terms, you would have made a profit of $129,790 on the real estate while only making a profit of $53,068 on the stock, or about 2½ times more profit from the real estate investment.[1]

Finally, when you compare all of the benefits of investing in real estate with those associated with any other type of investment, it seems clear there is no safer, more dependable and financially advantageous investment than real estate.

## How Many Valuation Approaches Are Enough?

As I roam around the United States, both literally, by giving seminars and undertaking appraisal and consulting assignments, and figuratively, mostly through my work in the area of appraisal review, I'm continually amazed at statements made by appraisers in their attempts to support/defend their use of multiple (usually all 3) so-called valuation approaches in appraisal assignments wherein Market Value, as defined in USPAP, is the purpose of the assignment.

When in such discussions, I'll always inquire as to why they used either 2 or all 3 so-called valuation approaches. I hope to hear the only answer that is ethically and economically supported, which is, "I researched the market and found that there was no clear cut indication for any 1 of these approaches over another, and also found that the typical market participant actually uses both/all of these approaches in formulating *their* valuation decision." However, instead of hearing such a sound reasoning, I find that appraisers almost invariably respond with the following statement, "Although, I developed all 3 approaches, I found that only the (blank) approach was applicable, and that's what I relied upon.". This statement always prompts me to ask, "Well, if only the (blank) approach was applicable, why did you develop and include the other approach(es) at all?". Their response is virtually universal: "That's the way the client wanted me to do it."

Well, for a variety of economically and ethically sound reasons, appraisers who continue to develop valuation approaches that are not relevant to the property being appraised are likely to find themselves being exposed to serious questions of competence and ethical propriety, both of which are likely to include some rather adverse legal and financial consequences. Let me begin by stating that there are 2 general underlying premises upon which this article is based:
1. The valuation assignments discussed in this article deal solely with requests for estimates of Market Value, as defined in USPAP, and
2. The valuation assignments discussed deal with real estate which is improved with existing buildings.
**NOTE:** The valuation of vacant land is specifically excluded from discussion in this article due to the varying and differing methods of land valuation from methods of valuation for existing building improvements.

Within these parameters, we should acknowledge certain facts about the role and responsibilities of an appraiser when engaged to undertake a Market Value appraisal assignment. I'm confident that we are all agreed that, under the Market Value scenario, the appraiser is being asked to provide the client with a conclusion of the estimated value, or a range of values that accurately represents that value or range which is the "most probable" value for which the subject would sell, within and adhering to all of the parameters in the USPAP definition of Market Value. In analyzing this scenario a bit more deeply, I believe that we would also be agreed with the reasonable conclusion that, in order for an appraiser to come to an accurate estimate which would represent what that typical buyer and seller would agree upon as being the value of a specific property, the appraiser must a) employ the same valuation technique(s), and b) develop it/them in the same way as would the typical buyer and seller of that specific property; the rationale being that, the use of any other technique(s) or, developing the appropriate technique(s), but in a manner different from the manner commonly used by the typical market participants, would likely result in a distortion of the final value estimate, thus, failing to provide the answer initially asked of the appraiser.

So, what approach should the appraiser use? In the process of coming to an answer to that question we should first follow the steps of the competent appraiser during the process of undertaking the appraisal assignment. In what should be the normal course of investigating a subjects market area, the most important set of facts to be obtained are 1) the perception(s) of the state of economic conditions at present and into the reasonably foreseeable future, 2) the present and anticipated influence(s) upon local real property values from that/those economic influence(s), and 3) the specific valuation method(s) most commonly developed and relied upon by the majority of local market participants in concluding the value that **they** feel is fair and reasonable for that specific property type in that market area. In order to ascertain this information, an appraiser must identify and personally interview as many active market participants (buyers, sellers, owners, tenants, managers, and brokers) as possible for the specific type of property being appraised; ideally, the appraiser will interview a majority of those market participants.

**It's important to note** that, to interview active participants from a different market area or to interview those who are active participants in the subjects market area for a different type of property than the subject, is likely to result in a distorted, inaccurate valuation conclusion for the subject property. To demonstrate the validity of this statement, let's make an analysis of a reasonably common occurrence; the appraisal of a warehouse/distribution building that, for the sake of this example, we'll say is a 5-year old 150,000 SF tilt-up masonry building having a 30 FT clear span, a flat roof, 10 floor-height tailgate doors, a 2,400 SF office area, is in good condition and is well located with good proximity to major highway transportation routes between 2 major northeast markets. Further, this market area, in which there are 20 buildings physically similar to the subject, grew at a rapid rate until about 2 years ago. It's still somewhat active, with the infrequent creation of new buildings, and with sales occurring at the rate of about 1 per year.

As we should, we will make a closer examination of the subject's market area by attempting to interview the owner and occupant of each building which discloses the fact that, of the

20 buildings, 14 are owner-occupied, 5 are tenant occupied and 1 is vacant, having been built on spec(ulation). During our interviews we find that, of the 14 owner-occupants, 9 bought buildings that were existing new buildings built on spec which were vacant and available. Of the remaining 5 owner-occupants, 3 bought existing buildings from former owner-occupants, 1 was a tenant in his building who bought it from the bank in possession of the title, and the last had his building built-to-suit by a local developer through the efforts of a broker. During our interviews we were told that each buyer based his purchase price on the sales prices that other buildings had sold for; a few owners commented that it was, "pretty much like buying a house.".

When we asked them if they ever considered how much rent they could get from the building, they all agreed that they hadn't given it a thought because they weren't in the business of buying real estate for the purpose of generating rental income, rather, they were only interested in the use of the building for the purpose of housing their specific enterprise. Trying all angles, we asked if they ever considered the cost of building a new building; buying the lot and hiring sub-contractors to construct the building. To a man, after having a good chuckle, each said that they didn't know the first thing about constructing a building, didn't have the time to "fool around" with such a venture, and wouldn't know if they were getting a better or worse deal. Although he did admit that he talked to a developer about constructing a new building, he followed quickly by stating that, since there would have been virtually no physical nor financial benefit, he decided to buy an existing building.

In the process of interviewing the 5 tenants in the 5 rented buildings, we found that there were 2 different corporate owners of these 5 buildings. During the interviews with these 2 corporate owners, we found that each were land developers and building contractors who had built their buildings for the sole purpose of holding them as an investment and obtaining rental income, having no intention of selling any building within the next 10-15 years. Our interview with these developers also disclosed that one of them was the owner of the currently vacant building. When questioned as to their intentions for that building, the owner stated that his original intention was to rent this building as he did the others he owns in this market area. He also stated that, since the building has been standing vacant for almost 2 years with little or no hope for obtaining a tenant, he's now changed his strategy and will be seeking to sell the building to an owner-occupant, a decision based upon his analysis of the current trend of sales in this market area as being the only way to successfully market that building. The owner also stated that he will be formulating his sale price based upon the sales prices of similar buildings that were recently sold in the immediate market area.

In conferring with the brokers who are known to be active in marketing this type of property in this market area, as well as interviewing the actual buyers, owners, and sellers of the same type of building as the subject, we've gained insight into the thinking of the local market participants and found that all provided valuable information as to the valuation methods they use to estimate the value of this type of property in this market area, leading us to reasonably conclude:

1. 70% of all buildings of this type are owner-occupied.

2. The Cost Approach is an irrelevant methodology.

3. There is virtually no current nor reasonably anticipated probability of obtaining tenants for buildings of this type in this area, thus, there is no relevancy to development of the Income Capitalization Approach.

4. The current state of the market activity for this type of building in this market area is now, and is anticipated to remain primarily directed toward owner-occupied buildings, dictating the use of the Sales Comparison Approach.

Therefore, now that we have obtained market direction to answer the question of what valuation method(s) should be used in coming to an estimate of the value that would reasonably represent the price that would probably be paid for the subject property, it seems clear that, to use any method other than the Sales Comparison Approach would not be representative of the actions of the typical market participants in this market area, therefore, would result in:

1. A value estimate that would not represent what the typical market participant would conclude to be the value of the subject, AND

2. A misleading conclusion, which is an unethical act according to USPAP Ethics Provision/Conduct, that would have occurred as the result of failures to comply with USPAP Standards Rule 1-1(a), (b) & (c), as well as failure to comply with USPAP Standards Rule 2-1(a).

Further, in addition to being irrelevant to develop any other approach(es), to do so would likely be both confusing as well as misleading to the reader(s) and/or user(s) of the report. And, while this lesson has shown us how, in real life, something that we might think of as being perceived as a harmless "traditional" work habit actually has substantive consequences beyond what we might realize. The following is a real-life example of how the "harmless", and all too common, misuse of a so-called valuation methodology actually had a significant negative impact upon one appraiser.

In a real-life litigation event, an appraiser, who made an appraisal of a detached 1-family dwelling for a lender in a sale transaction, was named a Defendant in a lawsuit by a buyer who claimed that the appraiser intentionally mislead him (the buyer) into thinking that the house was worth substantially more than its actual value which caused him to purchase the house at a time when he (the buyer) knew that he could be placing himself at financial risk due to a possible negative change in his income. However, the buyer claimed, that, based upon the appraiser's "misleading" appraisal report, specifically the appraiser's estimate of the value of the house as indicated by the Cost Approach, the buyer had been convinced that the purchase of the house was a safe undertaking since, based upon the appraiser's Cost Approach indication, the buyer was convinced he could sell the house for more than he was paying. The buyer claimed that he was damaged when it turned out that, within 1 year, he could **not** sell the house for the same amount paid, much less the higher amount indicated in the Cost Approach section of the appraiser's report. This ultimately resulted in foreclosure, causing the buyer the loss of his equity investment, damaging his credit, and causing him severe emotional harm.

During a pre-trial procedure, the appraiser's lawyer attempted to have the suit dismissed citing a lack of merit and pointing out to the Court that:

1. The appraiser knew that the Cost Approach was inappropriate for the property type in that market area,

2. Stated in the report that it was an inappropriate method for that type of property in that market area, and

3. Also stated in the report that he (the appraiser) did not rely upon the indication of the Cost Approach in reaching his value estimate which was solely based upon the indication of the Sales Comparison Approach.

In its response, the Court concluded that, the appraiser, knowing the use of the Cost Approach was inappropriate for this type of property in the market area, could find no reasonable explanation for its inclusion in the appraiser's report other than for the specific purpose of misleading the reader(s) and user(s) of the report into thinking that the value of the house may have been substantially higher than its actual value. The Court further justified its conclusion by saying that, if the appraiser did not intend to mislead the reader(s) and user(s) of the report, he would not have included such a misleading indication.

The lesson to be learned is, there are definite and serious consequences that may (and do) result from the actions and words of an expert, such as an appraiser. The message: **An appraiser must act in an honorable, responsible manner.** What appraisers are supposed to do is quantify, in monetary terms, human activity as it relates to their actions in real estate markets. It logically follows that, if an appraiser 1) fails to sufficiently investigate that market area, 2) fails to identify the market participants, and interview those market participants for the purpose of a) obtaining and understanding *their* perceptions of value and the influences upon it for a specific property type, as well as b) understanding the methods that *they* use to determine the value of a specific property type, **THE APPRAISER HAS FAILED** to live up to his/her **moral, ethical, and legal responsibilities.** Failure to emulate the activity of those humans who are the makers of the market activity in a given area for a specific type of property is incompetent.

## Who's The Expert, Anyway?

In seminar after seminar, and in virtually every discussion that I have with appraisers regarding their reasoning pertaining to something that they did which was inappropriate and/or inconsistent with sound appraisal practice, or something that they failed to do in accordance with sound appraisal practice, the universal excuse used in an attempt to exonerate themselves from their failure to live up to their ethical responsibilities is, "Well, the client wanted me to do it that way.". Which begs the naturally logical follow-up questions, which are, "Who's the expert, anyway? You or the client?", to which they most frequently respond with a blank stare as if I asked them to comment on Einstein's theory of relativity; they haven't got a clue.

Believe it or not, the appraiser is the person who is recognized as the expert in matters of real property valuation. Maybe that's why there is a requirement that an appraiser demonstrate competence through examination of their work product, as well as prove that they have successfully completed various levels of specialized professional education before even being qualified to sit for written examinations to achieve recognition by credible professional appraisal organizations as well as to achieve the appropriate level of state licensure.

Then, there's always the wise guy who says, "Well, *I'm* the client, and, since *I'm* paying for the work, *I* have the right to tell the appraiser how *I* want it done.", to which I usually reply with the following analysis of his statement: "So, Mr. Client. It's your position that the customer is always right. Correct? (Reply : Right.) Well, Mr. Client. To carry on the logic of *your* premise, you'd have to agree that I would be correct in assuming that, if a cash paying drug addict/patient walked into his doctor's office and asked the doctor to give him a prescription for morphine, which was not otherwise justified by the addict's physical condition other than the fact that he was an addict, using your logic, the doctor would be obligated to write an illegal prescription to that patient merely because the patient was a paying customer. Right?" (No Reply)

After the absurdity in the original statement is recognized, I usually hear a chorus of whimpering that goes something like this: "I know your right, BUT, *if I don't do it the way the client wants it done, somebody else will.* " To this morally bankrupt statement, I usually reply: "Well, if I don't sell drugs to that kid, somebody else will." OR "If I don't sell that kid a gun, somebody else will. Right?" *WRONG!* When you, the professional expert, are hired by a client, you are *REQUIRED* to perform your service by applying your expertise in providing the client **what they NEED**, *NOT* **what they WANT!** The attitude that, "If I don't do it somebody else will", is nothing less than the utterance of the morally weak who, by this statement, are demonstrating how low they will stoop to justify unjustifiable deeds in exchange for money; the common word for such an act is *"prostitution"*.

I imagine that if we were able to go back in time to Germany during the period between 1938-1945, we might probably hear these same words uttered by those "good" citizens who helped their government to round up Jews, knowing full well that they were being sent to certain death. Yet, those same "good" citizens, being too concerned for themselves, knowingly let those people suffer and die because they didn't have the moral fiber to stand up and say, *"NO! I WON'T DO THAT! IT'S WRONG!"*. Therefore, if *YOU* don't live up to *YOUR* moral and ethical responsibility to perform *YOUR* service by applying *YOUR* expertise in the way that *YOU* know to be proper, then *YOU ARE THE PROBLEM.*

## What's the Value of the Land?

The valuation of a parcel of vacant land is arguably one of the most challenging, complex assignments which can be undertaken; it can be likened to the artist standing before a blank canvas asking, *"What can I make of this vacant space?"*. There are numerous, seemingly countless possible categories of considerations which include 1) all of the possible and probable legal uses to which a parcel of land might reasonably be put, 2) the physical constraints of the tangible land such as its location, topography, shape, accessibility, mineral(s), ecological/environmental limitations, availability of utilities, as well as 3) the economic consideration of measuring market supply and demand factors for certain specific types of developmental potential, if any.

Let's remember that, for appraisals that are being made for the purpose of estimating Market Value (as defined in USPAP), **it is the duty of the appraiser** to estimate the reasonably probable price that a typical buyer would be most likely to pay, and that the typical seller could reasonably anticipate receiving as payment as of a specific date, with both parties being well informed or well advised as to all of the uses and limitations of the parcel of land in question, and that both would be acting in what each believes to be their own best interest without the influence of undue stimulus. What's so important about reminding ourselves of the USPAP Market Value definition is, that it serves to remind us that it's the appraiser's responsibility to arrive at that value estimate by means of the same valuation technique(s) employed by typical market participants, because, failing to do so may likely result in a considerably different final value estimate than would be reached by those typical market participants.

As a point of fact, while land valuation assignments tend to require the gathering of copious amounts of data and their analyses, which is no small task, all too often the tremendous effort expended in that process is wasted because of substantially inaccurate conclusions of value resulting from the application of an inappropriate valuation methodology; the valuation methodology almost exclusively used by appraisers in the valuation of all vacant land is the sales comparison approach, an over-simplistic methodology that often fails to account for underlying economic influences that tend to determine the price paid for land. Worse, is that it's also out of touch with the manner in which actual market participants arrive at the value of land which typically involves their consideration of the certain economic factors beyond mere supply & demand. A further complication caused by this problem is that the inaccurate valuation estimate then tends to carry over into inaccurate conclusions of highest and best use. However, before getting into the discussion of more appropriate land valuation concepts, we should first acknowledge a market reality, which is that, virtually all land transactions that meet the USPAP definition of Market Value tend to fall into 1 of the following 2 general categories:

1) Land which is bought with the intention of immediate development for a specific use, hereinafter being referred to as **productive land**, and

2) Land which is bought without the intention of immediate development for a specific use, rather, being bought with the intention of keeping it in its current vacant state for an indeterminate time until such time as the market would demand that it be developed for a currently undetermined use; perhaps to be considered a speculative purchase, hereinafter being referred to as **non-productive land**.

In order to enable us to understand the different techniques used to estimate the value of either productive or non-productive land, it will also be necessary to acknowledge the fundamental concepts of our general economic system which, including the real estate market, is embodied within the Classical Economic school of thought that recognizes that there are 4 components or agents, all of whose individual presence are essential to the production of anything; these 4 components/agents, commonly referred to as the *Agents in Production,* are Labor, Capital, Coordination (Management) and Land. Under this, our system of economics, we recognize that the value of the Land component/agent is residual, meaning that, when the total sales price for the item produced is received, the value of the Land component/agent is what is left over after paying for the costs of Labor, Capital and Coordination (Management); the residual value attributable to the contribution of the Land component/agent in the creation of the item produced is referred to as *Excess Productivity*.

This leads us to the realization that we should also have a working understanding of the economic principle of *Contribution, or Contributory Value,* which recognizes that, a component of a whole entity only has value to the extent that it contributes to the value of that whole OR by the amount which the value of the whole is diminished/reduced by the removal/absence of that component. In consideration of the productive and non- productive vacant land sales, the questions to be answered are:

1) **What valuation technique/concept is typically used by typical market participants when transacting productive land?**

2) **What valuation technique/concept is typically used by typical market participants when transacting non-productive land?**

3) **What are the underlying economic concepts of each?**

4) **How and why do they differ from each other?**

## NON-PRODUCTIVE LAND:
Of the 2 categories, the more easily addressed is the valuation technique and underlying economic concepts most commonly recognized by typical participants in the transaction of non-productive land. As we've established, non-productive land is not being bought for the purpose of immediate development, rather, to be held for an indeterminate time to be developed with improvements of an undetermined nature, thus, it could reasonably be said that non-productive land tends to be bought for speculation. Therefore,

1. Since typical market participants in this type of transaction tend not to consider any definable economic factors/influences, other than those of general supply and demand, in the process of negotiating and arriving at a price which concludes in the meeting of the minds, and

2. Since these typical market participants tend to solely rely upon the prices paid for other parcels of vacant land which fall within the same category of non-productive/speculative transactions, compensating/adjusting those sales prices for physical, financial, and legal differences between the transactions of the sold parcels and that of their subject parcel, there cannot practically, nor ethically be any other way in which to estimate the present value of non-productive land than to emulate the valuation methodology of the typical market participants whose described valuation methodology can be emulated through the application of the sales comparison valuation methodology.

## PRODUCTIVE LAND:
Having recognized that emulating the actions of typical market participants is both the role and responsibility of the appraiser, then, adherence to this ethic requires the appraiser to consider and explore the possibility that sales prices/values for both types of land transactions (productive and non-productive) might not be arrived at using the same valuation technique. The existence of this possibility, therefore, mandates that the appraiser explore and understand any and all other valuation techniques/concepts that might exist so that the appraiser can employ those methods in carrying out their ethically competent and legal responsibilities when undertaking the appraisal assignment of both productive and nonproductive land.

Having explored, analyzed and participated in transactions of both productive and non-productive lands, I've found it a general truth that typical market participants involved in productive land transactions consider land as a component part of a greater entity using the same concept as previously described in the classical observation of the *Agents in Production*. The following scenario duplicates a common daily occurrence of the practical application of this methodology:

From a current market analysis, a developer believes that there may be sufficient market demand to warrant further economic study into the possible construction of a 20,000 SF retail strip shopping center along a major traffic route. Based upon his research, the developer concludes that, at a market rent of $14/SF plus tenant paid Common Area Maintenance (CAM), tenant paid proportional property taxes over the base year, and tenant paid utilities, the proposed building will achieve a stabilized occupancy of 90% at completion of construction into the foreseeable future, and the developer estimates landlord operating expenses at $3.35/SF. Using the income capitalization valuation methodology, the developer estimates the value of this proposed strip center, when completed and in place with stabilized occupancy, will be $1,540,000. The developer estimates that all of the costs and expenses, including his entrepreneurial profit, to create this proposed building and attain stabilized occupancy will total $1,153,000, excluding the cost of the land. To determine the **maximum** amount that the developer can afford to pay for the land, being the amount of its productive contribution to the value of the whole entity, the following process is undertaken:

**Estimated Value of Completed Entity: $1,540,000.**
Less:
Hard & Soft Costs (Labor): ‹1,000,000›
Interest on Construction Mortgage (Capital): ‹53,000›
Entrepreneurial Profit (Coordination): ‹100,000›

**Land (Excess Productivity): $387,000.**

Assuming the proposed improvement and necessary site improvements require a 2 acre site, the developer will research the market for offerings of land in the immediate area which will support the needs of this proposed project. He'll soon know the asking/offering prices of sites suitable for his project and, depending upon those asking/offering prices may find a bargain among them, which frequently indicates an inadequately informed seller, upon which the developer will seize, or he may alternatively find that the asking prices are far above the economic capacity of his project, again, perhaps, indicating uninformed sellers, or the possibility of an infeasible project proposal, and will forego its creation.

**VALUE INFLUENCE FROM UNDERLYING ECONOMICS:**
The contributing value of a given parcel of vacant land is its Market Value when the improvements upon it create an overall entity that produces the highest possible value of the land. However, as seen in this example, the value of the land, which is totally dependent upon the income generated by the greater entity, is substantially influenced from the income which can vary widely depending upon such things as:
1. use,
2. quality of construction in terms of materials, design & finish of the improvement(s),
3. quality of tenancy,
4. general supply & demand conditions for the type of improvement proposed, as well as
5. general economic conditions that impact the businesses that would typically occupy the proposed improvement(s). Evidence in the market of the contributory value of land to the total value of the whole entity is all around us.

Take, for a common example, the substantially higher prices for land typically paid by major fast food chains as opposed to other potential users of the exact same site; it's not uncommon to see these major chains pay double or even triple the prices that would otherwise be considered reasonable by other potential users. If you've ever asked yourself, *"Why?"*, you now have the answer. These major fast food chains see the land for what it is, a necessary agent in the production and sale of its product. Since major fast food chain stores frequently generate income dollars many times more than other potential

users, frequently into the multi-million dollar range from a single location, the value of the land component is determined as the residual of all costs of doing business and reflected as a percentage of the potential gross income from the site based upon a predetermined formula; a text book example of the economic principle of contribution.

It should be evident that there is more than 1 way to estimate the Market Value of a parcel of vacant land. It should also be clearly evident that applying an inappropriate valuation methodology is likely to result in an inaccurate value estimate, as well as an incorrect conclusion of highest and best use, which results in the following ways:

1. **Applying the sales comparison methodology instead of measuring the value of the economic contribution of a parcel of land whose highest and best use is for its immediate development with improvements of the same use as those created on the sold sites, although with differing economic potential.**
eg: A 2 acre site was sold for $645,000 and subsequently developed with a 20,000 SF retail improvement which was functionally super-adequate for its market. Instead of generating the $15/SF absolutely net with a 90% stabilized occupancy rate, the forecast upon which the developer based his purchase price of the site, the building is actually generating only $14.50/SF with only partial tenant expense contributions netting $9.80/SF at 87% occupancy which appears stabilized. If we assume that the subject of our appraisal is the 2 acre parcel in our earlier example, and if we relied upon this and other recent sales of sites with no other apparent differences, all of which were put into immediate production (productive land), we would rapidly find ourselves in the common dilemma of trying to determine why their was such a variance in the overall and unit prices among these sales. Further, unless we had knowledge of all of the underlying economic factors upon which each sites sales price was determined prior to the purchase, and all of the actual subsequent economic performance of the subsequently created entities, we could have no idea of the reasonableness, and perhaps the competence of the developer, nor would we have a clue that the developer of our so-called *"comparable"* sale both over-built the improvements and under estimated the NOI resulting in his substantial over-payment of the site.

2. **Applying the sales comparison methodology instead of measuring the value of the economic contribution of a parcel of land whose highest and best use is for its immediate development with improvements of a different use as those created on the sold sites.**
The best example is the common error of comparing the sale of a parcel of productive land whose sale price/value was determined by a its contributing economic value to a whole entity which produces either a substantially greater or lesser value than that to be created upon the subject parcel.
eg 1: Comparing the sale of a 1 acre parcel of vacant land sold at $500,000 with no other value influencing difference than the fact that it was put into immediate production by a major fast food chain as a retail outlet, then viewing this sale as being *"comparable"* to your subject, which is a 1 acre parcel that's going to be developed with an single unit owner

occupied retail carpet outlet.

eg 2: Comparing the sale of a 1 acre parcel of land sold at $120,000 with no other value influencing difference than the fact that it was put into immediate production by a local entrepreneur for use as a used car lot, then viewing this sale as being *"comparable"* to your subject, which is a 1 acre parcel that's going to be developed with a multi-unit, 2-story structure housing 2 retails on the 1st floor and 2 professional offices on the 2nd floor. In these 2 examples we can see that the land is likely to have a very different contributing value to each of these 4 users, all of which represent the highest and best use of each site. In turn, the contributing value of the land is reflected in the sales price of each site being reflective of the value of the land component as an agent in the production of the overall income.

**3. Applying the sales comparison methodology using non-productive land *"comparable"* sales when the parcel being appraised has a highest and best use as productive land; a highest and best use for its immediate development with improvements.**
This error will undoubtedly result in a substantially lower value than would reasonably be arrived at by the typical market participant who would recognize the higher value of the subject parcel in its contribution to the productive use of the site. While it's relatively common to find this occurrence in the appraisal of vacant land, it's a very dangerous position in which an appraiser finds him/herself having arrived at a value estimate based upon inappropriate data and methodology that could substantially alter the benefit or liability position of their client. Such an occurrence calls into serious question the competence and, perhaps, the ethics of the appraiser who could reasonably be perceived as either being incompetent or an advocate for his/her client, neither of which is a lesser evil.

**4. Attempting to apply the principle of contributing value in the appraisal of a parcel of non-productive land whose highest and best use is for it to remain vacant for an indeterminate period of time until such an indeterminate time in the future when the market demonstrates sufficient demand for its development with improvements that would represent its future highest and best use that are currently unknown.**
This error will undoubtedly result in a substantially higher value than would reasonably be arrived at by the typical market participant who would recognize the lower value of the subject parcel based upon the lack of economic evidence necessary to support the development of the site as put forth by the appraiser. Unlike the example in number 3, it's relatively difficult to sustain this type of an occurrence in the appraisal of non-productive vacant land, since, in order to reasonably support a highest and best use conclusion that it be developed with improvements, it's absolutely essential for the appraiser to provide reasonable market evidence to demonstrate both the demand for that improved use, as well as the underlying economic feasibility which would support its creation.

Given the remote possibility that an appraiser would attempt to fabricate or substantially distort factual market evidence, it would be an even more dangerous position in which an appraiser would find him/herself than in the case of number 3; having arrived at a value estimate based upon either inappropriate or non-existent data, then using a methodology that could substantially alter the benefit or liability position of their client. Such an occurrence would necessarily call into serious question the ethics of the appraiser, although lack of competency should not be ruled out.

So, when someone asks, *"What's the value of the land?"*, you now know there's much more involved in coming to that answer than most people are generally aware. Remember, if you ask the 1st basic question that must be answered, *"Is this land productive or nonproductive?"*, you'll probably have little problem in determining the appropriate valuation methodology. From there, it's a matter of becoming educated on the valuation methodology and putting it into practice.

# *Don't Dictate My Fee*

**When a listing agent sets the amount of the commission to be paid to a buyer agent, is the listing agent acting legally and ethically?**

As we all know, listing agents have a fiduciary responsibility to their clients, the sellers of real property. They're hired to provide services to market, as well as to promote the best interests of those clients. And, for performing these services, they're entitled to charge their clients a fee; a fee that should be freely negotiated solely between the listing agent their client, the seller.

Likewise, buyer agents also have a fiduciary responsibility to *their* clients, the buyers of real property. And, like listing agents, buyer agents are hired to provide services to accomplish their clients goal of purchasing real property by 1) seeking out, previewing and showing qualifying property, 2) performing due diligence, 3) providing counseling and advice, 4) preparing and negotiating offers to purchase, 5) assisting to arrange financing, and so on. And, for their services, buyer agents are equally entitled to charge a fee which should also be freely negotiated between the buyers agent and their client, the buyer. In fact, anti price-fixing laws and regulations require that *all* fees be freely negotiated between an agent and a client.

It's also pretty much the law of the land that a buyer agent and a listing agent are two different entities. However, it seems that many agents fail to recognize the fact that buyer and listing agents each have clients whose interests are both different and competing in the same transaction. This disturbing truth is evident on each and every multiple listing sheet in every multiple listing service that I've ever seen. For example, there's a section on virtually every MLS form that states the amount of the buyer agent fee; a fee that the listing agent has usually unilaterally and arbitrarily decided should be paid to the buyer agent. This is a legally and ethically dangerous practice, aside from being ludicrous on its face. It's like saying that a plaintiff's attorney has the right to dictate the amount of the fee that the defendant's attorney can be paid to represent the defendant.

Interestingly enough, even the National Association of REALTORS® seems to be perpetuating the outdated concept of a "shared" commission which is addressed in their 2004 Code of Ethics and Standards of Practice, from which the following quote has been taken:
Standard of Practice 16-16: REALTORS®, acting as subagents or buyer/tenant representatives or brokers, shall not use the terms of an offer to purchase/lease to attempt to modify the listing broker's offer of compensation to subagents or buyer/tenant representatives or brokers nor make the submission of an executed offer to purchase/lease contingent on the listing broker's agreement to modify the offer of compensation. (Amended 1/04)

It's pretty alarming when you consider, that on the one side, we have 1) state and federal anti price-fixing laws, as well as 2) state government real estate licensing departments with rules and regulations that require buyer agents to freely negotiate their fee with the buyer, while on the other side we find 1) these laws, rules and regulations are being totally ignored throughout the United States on a daily basis, and 2) those who are ignoring the laws are doing so with the assistance of the National Association of REALTORS® that consciously has taken an opposing position to these laws, rules and regulations as recently as January 2004.

Even most state licensing regulations provide, that if a listing agent wishes to act as a dual agent (and obtains the appropriate permissions from both his seller client and a buyer), the listing agent can then negotiate and agree to a fee for selling the property as a dual agent. But, arguably, the only other agents that can be legally <u>bound</u> to accept the selling commission for selling that property are the other agents in the same company as the listing agent, as real estate licensing laws generally dictate that all agents in the same listing company are also the listing agent and/or dual agent.

Frankly, I can't imagine that it's legal (much less, ethical) for a listing agent from ABC Realty to set the amount of the fee to be charged by a buyer agent from XYZ Realty, because it clearly denies the buyer and the buyers agent their legal right to freely negotiate the amount of the buyer agents fee. And, as the practice of "splitting the listing agents fee" denies the legal right of a buyer to freely negotiate the buyer agents fee, it also has the practical effect of forcing the buyer agent into a sub-agency relationship with the listing agent, thereby stripping the buyer agent of their independence. If you disagree with this observation, then please answer this question: When "splitting" a single fee, and when the amount of the split is dictated by one agency to another agency, isn't the dictating agency the superior agency, while the one being dictated to is the subordinate agency? (Duh!)

Another problem in this mix is the common thought that the seller pays the real estate commission. Let's make an objective analysis of this concept:

1. In fact, the seller virtually never brings money to the closing table. Consequently, the seller can't possibly pay any expenses, including the brokerage fee, out of his/her own pocket. The truth is, **the <u>seller brings the deed</u>** to the closing, and **<u>the buyer brings the money.</u>**
2. **All of the sellers debts related to the sold property <u>are paid by the buyer</u> solely from the buyers funds <u>prior</u> to the seller transferring title to the buyer and <u>prior</u> to the seller receiving any money from the buyer.** Why is this done? Because virtually all title insurance policies **require** that all debts against the property be paid in full before the title insurance policy takes effect (except in the case where the buyer assumes the sellers debt).

So, unless, <u>before going to the closing,</u> the seller pays off all of the existing debt and other expenses that either are or can become liens against the property (such as a mortgage, past due property taxes, utility bills and the like), all of the money used to pay the debts against the property, **including the real estate brokerage commission for all agents,** comes from the buyer. The bottom line is, that in virtually every transaction in which a brokers fee is paid, the money used to pay that fee *must* come from the buyer, because the seller has no money until after transferring the deed to the buyer, which is literally the last act of the closing.

Another illustration in support of the fact that the buyer pays all costs and fees in a real estate transaction is evident in another commonly misunderstood situation when it's said, **"the seller is paying the buyers closing costs."**

**FACT: In almost every instance of this type, the price of the property is increased by the anticipated amount of the buyer's closing costs.** This price increase takes place at either the time of originally offering the property for sale (because it may be common practice for buyers to finance their closing costs in that local market), or it's done at the time of the purchase contract negotiation.

Regardless. The increased price of the property **is always paid by the buyer** since those "seller paid" closing fees are actually built into the buyers mortgage. In the end, the reality is that the seller doesn't pay either the brokerage commission or the buyer's closing costs. But, back to the matter at hand. As to the amount of the fee / commission charged by each agency position, there's no particular need for the buyer agent to know how much the listing agent is charging in a given transaction, as there's no need for a listing agent to know how much the buyer agent is charging. In fact, the only time that the amount of the fee charged by either agency position *might* reasonably be disclosed to the other is at the time of contract negotiation when both agents are attempting to understand and deal with the net proceeds desired by the seller. But, even then, it's not particularly *necessary* to disclose the privately negotiated fee.

There are also few questions that gnaw at me regarding the current practice of listing agents publishing to the world the amount of the fee being paid by the seller.
1. Isn't it the fiduciary responsibility to a client that an agent keep the terms of their agency employment contract a private

matter between the client and the agent?

2. Doesn't the term "fiduciary" also apply to the amount of the fee the client has privately negotiated with their agent? Both buyer and buyer-agent, as well as seller and listing-agent?

3. Isn't it detrimental to both the sellers and buyers negotiating position to disclose the amount of commission each has agreed to pay, since that disclosure could provide an indication of their relative level of desire, or perhaps, desperation to either sell or buy?

As I see it, there are three simple steps that can and should be immediately implemented to eliminate this legally and ethically questionable practice:

## 1. Listing agents must never impose a fee or commission upon buyer agents when taking a listing.

When taking a listing, the listing agent should always advise the seller that the fee being charged by the listing agent is only for services rendered to the seller in connection with marketing the sellers property, which generally includes pricing and marketing advice, the placing of a sign, creating and placing various forms of advertising, submission to multiple listing service(s), promoting the property to other agents, negotiating for the sellers position at the time a proposed purchase contract is presented by a buyer-agent, assisting with post-contract duties, etc. Additionally, it should become the listing agents responsibility at the time of listing to negotiate a selling commission, but only for his/her own agency to sell the property as a dual agent (when obtaining the sellers written permission to act as a dual agent). It's also important that the seller acknowledge, in writing, that this selling commission is only for the agents in the listing agency who might sell the property as a dual agent.

## 2. Listing agents must advise seller clients of buyer agent relationships and fee arrangements.

When taking a listing, a listing agent should explain to the seller that buyers may hire a buyer agent to represent them, and further explain that the buyer agent fee is negotiated freely between buyer and the buyer agent, not by the seller or the listing agent. Also at the time of listing, a listing agent should explain to the seller that all fees for both the listing agent and the buyer agent are typically paid from the proceeds of the purchase. The listing agent should also assure the seller, in writing, there is no obligation to sell the property unless they (the seller) are satisfied with the amount of the net proceeds, after the payment of all brokerage fees.

## 3. Listing and buyer agents should not disclose the amount of their fee to anyone, including to each other, without the expressed written consent of their respective clients.

As a practical matter, the net proceeds to the seller is an essential factor to be dealt with when negotiating of a bona fide offer to purchase. However, it's not essential that either the sellers or buyers agent disclose the amount / rate of their fee to each other. However, there may be circumstances where disclosure by both agency positions might better serve to bring the buyer and seller to a meeting of the minds, although this decision should be left to the two agency positions to deal with as circumstances dictate, but always subject to the approval of their respective clients and acting their clients best interests.

In closing, it seems clear that the practice of listing agents setting the fees of buyer agents is legally and ethically dangerous since it denies the basic right of buyers to obtain the benefit of professional assistance through competitive pricing. This practice also reeks of an implied agent / sub-agent relationship between the listing and buyer agents, with the buyer agent becoming an unwilling subordinate agent to the listing agent. When we combine these problems with the fact that the majority of published fee splits are nearly identical within most market areas, we have, at the least, the appearance of an illegal, collaborative price fixing scheme rather than fees that have resulted from a free and open market driven by healthy competition. I believe, that unless the current practice of listing agents dictating the fees that are paid to buyer agents is eliminated immediately, there's little doubt that sooner, rather than later, there will be serious and costly repercussions that will have a substantial negative impact upon all in the real estate brokerage industry. A "black eye" that the industry does not need, and can easily avoid.

# The VIP's - HUD, FHA, FNMA, GNMA, and FHLMC

## Background and History – "About Them"

This chapter will include the "About Us" and other information from the following web sites. Visit their web sites for more information. I've included this so that you have a basic idea of what each of these organizations does. They are all VIP's - *very important players,* in the real estate, mortgage loan, and appraisal businesses!! These are the people who determine the guidelines for filling out the standard real estate appraisal and mortgage loan forms. They also determine what updates or changes are made to the forms. This chapter will discuss the appraisal forms that you are most likely to use for residential appraisal reports and the additional guidelines you need to follow to fill them out correctly. You can visit www.nemmar.com to view copies of the standard appraisal forms that you will likely encounter for residential appraisal reports. These forms and the guidelines to filling them out are updated periodically. I have also included section HUD and FHA Guidelines page 220 and section Sample State Real Estate Appraiser Guidelines page 297 for you to use as a reference. You should learn these guidelines and rules for doing appraisals and for filling out the standard appraisal forms for your reports. The HUD/FHA and State appraisal procedures, requirements, and the amount of information listed in those sections will probably seem overwhelming to you at first. However, as you become an experienced appraiser it will be much easier to remember the standards and rules you need to follow to appraise real estate and fill out those form reports. **So don't try to memorize everything right away. Just take your time and learn each section at your own pace.** The procedures outlined in those sections can help you when you encounter all types of situations on your appraisals. Remember, the guidelines are the **minimum** standards to follow. You should also try to *exceed* the minimum standards so that your reports are top-notch and your clients keep sending you referral business due to the high quality of your appraisal work.

*I have also included the sections HUD and FHA Guidelines page 220 and Sample State Real Estate Appraiser Guidelines page 297 for you to use as a reference. You should learn these guidelines for doing appraisals and for filling out the standard appraisal forms for your reports. The HUD/FHA and State appraisal procedures, requirements and the amount of information listed in those sections will probably seem overwhelming to you at first. However, as you become an experienced appraiser it will be much easier to remember the standards and rules you need to appraise real estate and fill out those form reports. So don't try to memorize everything right away. Just take your time and learn each section at your own pace. The procedures outlined in those sections can help you when you encounter all types of situations on your appraisals.*

◊  **U.S. Department of Housing and Urban Development** (HUD) - www.hud.gov
  ▫  HUD's mission is to increase homeownership, support community development and increase access to affordable housing free from discrimination. To fulfill this mission, HUD will embrace high standards of ethics, management and accountability and forge new partnerships - particularly with faith-based and community organizations - that leverage resources and improve HUD's ability to be effective on the community level.

◊  **Federal Housing Administration** (FHA) - http://www.hud.gov/offices/hsg/fhahistory.cfm
  ▫  *What is the Federal Housing Administration?* The Federal Housing Administration, generally known as "FHA", provides mortgage insurance on loans made by FHA-approved lenders throughout the United States and its territories. FHA insures mortgages on single family and multifamily homes including manufactured homes and hospitals. It is the largest insurer of mortgages in the world, insuring nearly 33 million properties since 1934.
  ▫  *What is FHA Mortgage Insurance?* FHA mortgage insurance provides lenders with protection against losses as the result of homeowners defaulting on their mortgage loans. The lenders bear less risk because FHA will pay a claim to the lender in the event of a homeowner's default. Loans must meet certain requirements established by FHA to qualify for insurance.
  ▫  *Why does FHA Mortgage Insurance exist?* Unlike conventional loans that adhere to strict underwriting guidelines, FHA-insured loans require very little cash investment to close a loan. There is more flexibility in calculating household income and payment ratios. The cost of the mortgage insurance is passed along to the homeowner and typically is included in the

monthly payment. In most cases, the insurance cost to the homeowner will drop off after five years or when the remaining balance on the loan is 78 percent of the value of the property -whichever is longer.

- *How is FHA funded?* FHA is the only government agency that operates entirely from its self-generated income and costs the taxpayers nothing. The proceeds from the mortgage insurance paid by the homeowners are captured in an account that is used to operate the program entirely. FHA provides a huge economic stimulation to the country in the form of home and community development, which trickles down to local communities in the form of jobs, building suppliers, tax bases, schools, and other forms of revenue.

- *The History of FHA:* Congress created the Federal Housing Administration (FHA) in 1934. The FHA became a part of the Department of Housing and Urban Development's (HUD) Office of Housing in 1965. When the FHA was created, the housing industry was flat on its back: - Two million construction workers had lost their jobs. - Terms were difficult to meet for homebuyers seeking mortgages. - Mortgage loan terms were limited to 50 percent of the property's market value, with a repayment schedule spread over three to five years and ending with a balloon payment. - America was primarily a nation of renters. Only four in 10 households owned homes.

- During the 1940s, FHA programs helped finance military housing and homes for returning veterans and their families after the war. In the 1950s, 1960s and 1970s, the FHA helped to spark the production of millions of units of privately-owned apartments for elderly, handicapped and lower income Americans. When soaring inflation and energy costs threatened the survival of thousands of private apartment buildings in the 1970s, FHA's emergency financing kept cash-strapped properties afloat. The FHA moved in to steady falling home prices and made it possible for potential homebuyers to get the financing they needed when recession prompted private mortgage insurers to pull out of oil producing states in the 1980s.

- By 2001, the nation's homeownership rate had soared to an all time high of 68.1 percent as of the third quarter that year. The FHA and HUD have insured almost 30 million home mortgages and 38,000 multifamily project mortgages representing 4.1 million apartments, since 1934. In the more than 60 years since the FHA was created, much has changed and Americans are now the best housed people in the world. HUD has helped greatly with that success.

◊ **Federal National Mortgage Association** (Fannie Mae) or (FNMA) - www.fanniemae.com

- For most of us, a home is more than simple shelter or a good investment. A home of our own is a dream come true and symbolizes who we are. At Fannie Mae, the home symbolizes who we are, too. Our public mission, and our defining goal, is to help more families achieve the American Dream of homeownership.

- We do that by providing financial products and services that make it possible for low-, moderate-, and middle-income families to buy homes of their own. Since Fannie Mae began in 1968 we have helped more than 61 million families achieve the American Dream of homeownership.

- We are proud of what we have accomplished. More Americans own homes today than at any time in history. As the leader of the housing finance system, Fannie Mae is working to expand homeownership opportunities by creating products and technologies that help more people own homes. We believe that by doing so, we make a positive contribution to families, communities, and the nation

◊ **Government National Mortgage Association** (Ginnie Mae) or (GNMA) - www.ginniemae.gov

- *Who we are. What we do. Why it makes a difference?* At Ginnie Mae, we help make affordable housing a reality for millions of low- and moderate-income households across America by channeling global capital into the nation's housing markets. Specifically, the Ginnie Mae guaranty allows mortgage lenders to obtain a better price for their mortgage loans in the secondary market. The lenders can then use the proceeds to make new mortgage loans available.

- Ginnie Mae does not buy or sell loans or issue mortgage-backed securities (MBS). Therefore, Ginnie Mae's balance sheet doesn't use derivatives to hedge or carry long term debt. What Ginnie Mae does is guarantee investors the timely payment of principal and interest on MBS backed by federally insured or guaranteed loans — mainly loans insured by the Federal Housing Administration (FHA) or guaranteed by the Department of Veterans Affairs (VA). Other guarantors or issuers of loans eligible as collateral for Ginnie Mae MBS include the Department of Agriculture's Rural Housing Service (RHS) and the Department of Housing and Urban Development's Office of Public and Indian Housing (PIH).

- Ginnie Mae securities are the only MBS to carry the full faith and credit guaranty of the United States government, which means that even in difficult times an investment in Ginnie Mae MBS is one of the safest an investor can make.

- *What Are Mortgage-Backed Securities?* Mortgage-backed securities (MBS) are pools of mortgages used as collateral for the issuance of securities in the secondary market. MBS are commonly referred to as "pass-through" certificates because the principal and interest of the underlying loans is "passed through" to investors. The interest rate of the security is lower than the interest rate of the underlying loan to allow for payment of servicing and guaranty fees. Ginnie Mae MBS are fully modified pass-through securities guaranteed by the full faith and credit of the United States government. Regardless of whether the mortgage payment is made, investors in Ginnie Mae MBS will receive full and timely payment of principal as well as interest.

- Ginnie Mae MBS are created when eligible mortgage loans (those insured or guaranteed by FHA, the VA, RHS or PIH) are pooled by approved issuers and securitized. Ginnie Mae MBS investors receive a pro rata share of the resulting cash flows (again, net of servicing and guaranty fees).

- Ginnie Mae I MBS requires all mortgages in a pool to be the same type (e.g. single-family) and have a first payment date no more than 48 months before the issue date of the securities. Each mortgage must be, and must remain, insured or guaranteed by FHA, VA, RHS or PIH. In addition, the mortgage interest rates must all be the same and the mortgages must be issued by the same issuer. The minimum pool size is $1 million; payments on Ginnie Mae I MBS have a stated 14-day delay (payment is made on the 15th day of each month).

- Ginnie Mae II MBS allows multiple-issuer pools to be assembled, which in turn allows for larger and more geographically dispersed pools as well as the securitization of smaller portfolios. A wider range of coupons is permitted in a Ginnie Mae II MBS pool, and issuers are permitted to take greater servicing fees — ranging from 25 to 75 basis points. The minimum pool size is $250,000 for multi-lender pools and $1 million for single-lender pools. Ginnie Mae II MBS have an additional five-day payment delay because issuer payments are consolidated by a central paying agent (payment is made on the 20th day of each month).

- Real Estate Mortgage Investment Conduits (REMICs) direct principal and interest payments from underlying mortgage-backed securities to classes with different principal balances, interest rates, average lives, prepayment characteristics and final maturities. Unlike traditional pass-throughs, the principal and interest payments in REMICs are not passed through to investors pro rata; instead, they are divided into varying payment streams to create classes with different expected maturities, different levels of seniority or subordination or other differing characteristics. The assets underlying REMIC securities can be either other MBS or whole mortgage loans. REMICs allow issuers to create securities with short, intermediate and long-term maturities — flexibility that allows issuers to expand the MBS market to fit the needs of a variety of investors.

- Ginnie Mae Platinum Securities provide investors with greater operating efficiency, allowing holders of multiple MBS to combine them into a single platinum certificate. Ginnie Mae Platinum Securities can be used in structured finance transactions, repurchased transactions as well as general trading.

◊ **Federal Home Loan Mortgage Corporation** (Freddie Mac) or (FHLMC) - www.freddiemac.com

- Freddie Mac is a stockholder-owned corporation chartered by Congress in 1970 to keep money flowing to mortgage lenders in support of homeownership and rental housing. Freddie Mac purchases single-family and multifamily residential mortgages and mortgage-related securities, which it finances primarily by issuing mortgage pass through securities and debt instruments in the capital markets. By doing so, we ultimately help homeowners and renters get lower housing costs and better access to home financing.

- *Our Mission:* Since the Great Depression, federal support for housing has been an enduring national public policy objective. In the late 1960s the mortgage market was unpredictable, interest rates varied widely from city to city across the country, and mortgages loans were sometimes hard to get. Neither government nor private banking interests could address the nation's housing finance needs alone. A new solution was needed. Congress created Freddie Mac's charter in 1970, with a clear mission for us: stabilize the nation's mortgage markets and expand opportunities for homeownership and affordable rental housing. Freddie Mac's Congressional charter lays the foundation of our business and the ideals that power our mission. The charter forms the framework for our business lines, shapes the products we bring to market and drives the services we provide to the nation's housing and mortgage industry.

- *Our Business:* Over the past 33 years, we have accomplished a great deal. As a participant in the secondary market for mortgage loans, we purchase mortgages from lenders across the country and package them into securities that can be sold to investors around the world. That's how we ensure that there is a continuous flow of funds to mortgage lenders and provide low- to middle-income homeowners and renters with lower housing costs and better access to home financing. But not all the loans we purchase are packaged into securities; we retain some in our own portfolio. We get the funds to do this by selling bonds to investors throughout the world. By offering investors a way to invest in mortgages on homes within the United States, we increase our ability to purchase mortgages from lenders and maintain a continuous flow of mortgage loan funds that in turn provide families with even more affordable mortgage financing. America's housing finance system is the envy of the world today. The combination of a Congressional charter and private-market discipline has allowed us to bring increased efficiency, strength and affordability to the market in all economic conditions.

- *Our Contributions:* We take our mission very seriously at Freddie Mac, and we know the difference we have made. Over the last 33 years, we have: - helped increase the homeownership rate in America to record levels by purchasing more than 35 million mortgages, - lowered mortgage rates, which reduces homeowners' interest payments and apartment rents, - helped make home mortgage credit readily available and eliminated regional disparities, - helped expand the variety of mortgage loan products available, - used technology to help cut down the time and cost of getting a mortgage loan, - and attracted investors from here and abroad to support America's mortgage lending needs.

- Consumers' lives are better because we've helped them become homeowners and renters of affordable, quality housing. Thanks to our contributions, homeownership in America has reached 68% today, and we're continuously working to increase that number. The goal is simple: to open more doors for more people than ever before.

# FHA Appraisal Roster – Appraiser FAQ's

APPRAISER FHA Roster Frequently Asked Appraisal Questions For Appraisers

**1.    How can I become registered on the FHA Appraisal Roster?**

To become eligible to perform appraisals acceptable for underwriting FHA insured loans, you must possess a current license/certification with credentials based on the minimum licensing/certification criteria by the Appraiser Qualifications Board (AQB) of the Appraisal foundation for each state in which you desire to perform FHA appraisals and pass the national FHA Appraisal Exam. For more detailed information, please review ML 03-09 on the HUD/FHA web site . Please **note that applications received without passing exam results will be rejected.**

Registration procedures for appraisers who are not currently on the FHA Roster are as follows:

1.   Submit proof of a valid state appraiser's license or certification with credentials based on the minimum criteria issued by the AQB for each state in which you desire to perform FHA appraisals
2.   Pass the FHA Appraiser Exam and retain exam results
3.   Complete the Register Designation Application (Form HUD-92563) including references for line 18
4.   Not be listed on the General Services Administration's Suspension and Debarment List, HUD's Limited Denial of Participation (LDP) List, or HUD's Credit Alert Interactive Voice Response System (CAVIRS)
5.   Submit copy of license(s)/certification(s), exam results, and Register Designation Application with original signature to:

U.S. Department of Housing and Urban Development
Office of Single Family Housing
451 7th Street, SW, Suite 9278
Attn: Appraisal Branch
Washington, DC 20410

Fax Number: (202) 401-0416                    Telephone Number: (202) 708-2121

Note that all appraisers submitting application materials must send documents to HUD, and not their Homeownership Center.

**2.    How does an appraiser know that she/he is on the FHA Roster?**

Appraisers can check the FHA Roster at https://entp.hud.gov/idapp/html/apprlook.cfm for their status and to make sure their information is correct. Appraisers will not receive a registration confirmation if approved. However, a denial letter will be sent from HUD to appraisers that are not approved. Appraisers noticing incorrect information should fax the corrected information to the (202) 4010416.

**3.    What FHA Roster procedure should an appraiser follow if his/her license expires?**

The appraiser must provide HUD with proof of renewed license(s)/cerification(s). (See FHA Roster question 1 for address.) An expired license will cause the appraiser to be ineligible to perform FHA appraisals.

**4.   How do lenders and underwriters know whether an appraiser is eligible to perform FHA appraisals?**

HUD will continue to maintain the FHA Roster and will approve only those appraisers who have passed the exam and met the eligibility requirements for placement on the Appraiser Roster. Lenders can ascertain an appraiser's roster status through FHA Connection or ECHO.

## FHA APPRAISER EXAM

**1.   How should an appraiser prepare for the FHA Appraiser Exam?**

Reading the entire Handbook 4150.2, the Valuation Conditions (VC) Form and the Homebuyer Summary provide all information needed to prepare the appraiser for the FHA Appraiser Exam. In addition, 200 exam questions are available to study in preparation for taking the exam. Familiarity with Uniform Standards of Professional Appraiser Practice (USPAP) is assumed due to regular licensing requirements.

**2.    Is there a list of approved training course providers for the FHA Appraiser Exam?**

HUD does not approve or disapprove specific training courses. However, industry groups, professional societies and trade organizations are prepared to provide FHA Appraiser Exam training courses. Contact the local chapter of your professional organization, if you subscribe to one, or the national organizations of the Appraisal Sponsors. The American Society of Appraiser (ASA), Appraisal Institute (AI), National Association of Independent Fee Appraisers (NAIFA) and National Association of Master Appraisers (NAMA) are some of the industry groups offering FHA courses. All the groups have web-sites and the AI offers a course "on line"

**3.    Where do appraisers go to take the FHA Appraiser Exam?**
Prometric administers the test for HUD through multiple testing centers in each state. Appraisers can view testing center locations at http://www.2test.com/tcl/index.jsp. A complete list of locations can be obtained by calling Prometric at (800) 503-8991.

**4.    How do appraisers register to take the FHA Appraiser Exam?**
Prometric's policy states that appraisers can register with a credit card (American Express, MasterCard or Visa) to take the exam by calling Prometric at (800) 503-8991. Prometric also allows walk-ins based on space availability. The cost of the exam is $75. Once registered, appraisers must cancel their testing appointments by 12:00 noon two days prior to the scheduled testing time to receive a full refund.

**5.    I am a handicapped appraiser and will need special accommodations to take the FHA exam. What do I need to do?**
You will need to first contact Single Family Housing of HUD at (202) 708-2121. You will need to provide proof of handicap condition (e.g., doctor's letter), a description of the special accommodation needed for you to take the exam, and the test location. HUD will then review the request, and when approved, will provide you with a special telephone number at Prometric to schedule your exam.

**6.    What should appraisers bring with them to take the exam?**
Prometric *requires* appraisers to bring two positive forms of identification, one bearing a photograph, both bearing signatures, for exam admittance. Examples of acceptable form of identification include: current driver's license, valid passport, military ID card and state identification card. Social Security cards are *not* considered acceptable forms of ID; however, credit cards are acceptable form of secondary identification. Note that you will be required to submit your Social Security Number on the exam. Please make sure you list it accurately.

**7.    What should appraisers do if the Official Score Report contains incorrect information?**
The appraiser should copy the Official Score Report, circle the error(s) in RED, attach a note explaining that this is a correction (per the appraiser/applicant) and mail to:

U.S. Department of Housing and Urban Development
Office of Single Family Housing
451 7th Street, SW, Suite 9278
Attn: Appraisal Branch
Washington, DC 20410

**8.    How can an appraiser find out which components of the FHA Appraiser Exam showed his/her strengths and weaknesses?**
The appraiser can only find out if she/he passed or failed the exam. Scores are not provided.

**9.    How many times will an appraiser need to take the FHA Appraiser Exam to remain registered?**
At this time, appraisers need only to pass the exam only once. However, there is not a limit to the number of times an appraiser may take the exam before passing it. Please note that after two failures, candidates are required to wait one month before registering again for the exam.

**10. If an appraiser has questions concerning the FHA Appraiser Exam and/or registration process, what are his/her resources?**
Resources for exam and/or registration are listed in the table below.

| Information/Service | Resource |
|---|---|
| Test Center Locations | • Quick List*<br>• Prometric at (800) 503-8991 |
| FHA Appraiser Exam Registration | • Prometric at (800) 503-8991 |
| FHA Appraiser Exam Preparation | • Handbook 4150.2*<br>• VC Form*<br>• Homebuyer Summary<br>• 200 exam questions*<br>• FHA Appraiser Exam Fact Sheet* |
| FHA Registration | • Form HUD-92563*<br>• FHA Roster |
| **Homeownership Centers** | |
| • Philadelphia HOC (800) 440-8647 | • Atlanta HOC (888) 696-4687 |
| • Denver HOC (800) 543-9378 | • Santa Ana HOC (888) 827-5605 |

**P 44.   HUD-92563   Roster Appraiser Designation Application   Page 1 of 3**

---

## Application for Fee or Roster Personnel Designation

Check One

[ ] **U.S. Department of Housing and Urban Development (HUD)**

[ ] **Department of Veterans Affairs (VA)**

HUD OMB Approval No. 2502-0548 (exp. 06/30/2006)

VA OMB Approval No. 2900-0113

**Respondent Burden:** Public reporting burden for this collection of information is estimated to average 30 minutes per response, including the time for reviewing instructions, searching existing data sources, gathering and maintaining the data needed, and reviewing the collection of information. These agencies may not conduct or sponsor, and a respondent is not required to respond to this collection of information unless that collection displays a valid OMB Control Number.

**Privacy Act Statement:** The information you provide will enable the designated agency to determine whether you qualify for designation in the position for which you are applying. The information will not be disclosed outside the designated agency without your consent except to verify its accuracy and, when relevant to civil, criminal, or regulatory investigations and prosecutions, including the routine uses identified in VA system of records, 17 VA 26, Loan Guaranty Fee Personnel and Program Participant Records, published in the Federal Register. It will not be otherwise disclosed or released outside of the designated agency except as required and permitted by law. The Department of Housing and Urban Development (HUD) is authorized to collect this information by Title I, Section 1 of the National Housing Act (Pub. L. 479, 48 Stat. 1246, 12 U.S.C., 1701 et seq.). The Housing and Community Development Act of 1987, 42 U.S.C. 3543 authorizes HUD to collect the SSN. The Department of Veterans Affairs (VA) is authorized to collect this information by Chapter 37, Title 38 U.S.C.

**Penalty:** The provision of the SSN to the VA is voluntary; the provision of the SSN to HUD is mandatory. Failure to provide any of the requested information could affect the decision to approve your application since this decision will be made only on the basis of available information we currently have on record. This may result in a delay in the processing of your application.

**Instructions:** Please use typewriter or print clearly. Mail the completed form to the VA Regional Office or the U.S. Department of Housing and Urban Development, Office of Single Family Housing, 451 7th Street SW, Suite 9270, Washington, DC. 20410. HUD/FHA appraisers and inspectors may ascertain roster status from HUD's web site at: www.hud.gov. If this application is to be submitted to the VA, an executed VA Form 26-6684, Statement of Fee Appraisers or Compliance Inspectors must be attached.

**Appraisers:** This application is to be submitted to HUD **only after** the appraiser is State licensed or certified to appraise and has passed the HUD/FHA Appraisal Examination.

**Compliance Inspectors:** This application is to be submitted to HUD **only after** the inspector is licensed or certified to inspect repairs and construction, when such licensing or certification is required by the State or local jurisdiction where work will be performed. Upon availability, all inspector applicants must provide evidence of passing the HUD/FHA Inspector Examination.

HUD/FHA appraisers and inspectors may ascertain roster status from HUD's web site at www.hud.gov.

**Designation being applied for:** [ ] Appraiser Real Estate   [ ] Compliance Inspector

| 1. Name of Applicant (first-middle-last) | 2. Date of Birth (mm/dd/yyyy) | 3. Social Security Number | HUD required / **VA Voluntary** |
|---|---|---|---|

**HUD required / VA Voluntary**
3a. Sex  [ ] (1) Male  [ ] (2) Female

3b. Race
[ ] (1) White Non-Hispanic
[ ] (2) Black Non-Hispanic
[ ] (3) American Indian / Alaskan Native
[ ] (4) Asian / Pacific Islander
[ ] (5) Hispanic
[ ] (7) Hispanic Black
[ ] (8) Asian Indian American

4. Residence Address (number and street or rural route, city or P.O., county, State, zip code)

5. Telephone Number (include area code)

6. Business Address (Address where field reviews are to be sent)

7. Business Phone (include area code)

8. Present Occupation

9. Name and Address of Present Employer

10. Education — No. of Years
a. High School
b. College
c. Degree(s) Awarded (If applicable)

11. Special Education or Training, Vocational, Business, or Special courses (Enter course and school name and location)
For HUD/FHA Appraisal and Inspector Examination (Enter city, State, and date (mm/dd/yyyy) of Examination; attach a copy of the certification.)

12. Professional Organizations of which you are a member

13. Registration/License Information (Attach copy(ies) of appraisal license)

| Kind | Registration/License No. | State Where Issued | Expiration Date (mm/dd/yyyy) |
|---|---|---|---|

14a. Have you been previously approved by VA or HUD for a Fee Position?
[ ] Yes (If "Yes," complete Items 14b & 14c)
[ ] No

14b. Office Name & Address

14c. Dates of Fee Activity for VA or HUD
From: (mm/dd/yyyy)   To: (mm/dd/yyyy)

All previous editions are obsolete       Page 1 of 3       form **VA 26-6681**       form **HUD-92563** (04/2002)
ref Handbooks 4145.1 Rev-2, 4910.1, 4150.1 REV-1, 4905.1 REV-1, 4150.2 CHG-1, Permanent Foundations Guide for Manufactured Housing

**P 45.   HUD-92563   Roster Appraiser Designation Application   Page 2 of 3**

15. Geographic Area(s) of Practice (List your appraisal/inspection area(s), e.g., Albany, NY; Ft. Worth, TX; Cleveland, OH, etc.)

16. State Principal Assignments during at least the past 5 years  (attach additional sheet as necessary)

| Period (mm/dd/yyyy) | Number of Assignments | Names of Clients or Organizations |
|---|---|---|
| | | |

17. Employment History During Past 10 Years (attach additional sheet as necessary)

| Dates (mm/dd/yyyy) From   To | Occupation | Name of Employer | Address |
|---|---|---|---|
| | | | |

18. For **VA**, List and Submit at least 3 letters attesting to your qualifications.  **HUD** requires three reference contacts only.

| References | Occupation | Address |
|---|---|---|
| | | |

19. **To be completed by HUD applicants only:**  To avoid the possibility of any conflict of interest and to ensure compliance with HUD appraisal and/ or inspector roster standards, the following certifications are to be completed by personnel qualified to receive assignments from HUD or HUD approved lending institutions for HUD/FHA mortgage insurance applications. The term "interest" refers to direct interest as well as any "interest" held by relatives, business associates, or other controlled persons.

**Note:**  Any of the following items that have been struck out and initialed are exempted from this certificate and are to be explained truthfully in an attached letter.

(a)  I certify that I do not own more than 10% interest in any lender doing business with HUD in the local HUD office jurisdiction.

(b)  I certify that I do not actively engage in the management or operation of a lending institution doing business with HUD.

(c)  I certify that I will not accept any assignments for fee work in a transaction in which I have an interest.

(d)  I certify that I am not currently suspended, debarred, or in any way disqualified from participating in HUD programs.

(e)  **For appraisers**, I certify that I will comply with HUD Handbook 4150.2, "Valuation Analysis for Home Mortgage Insurance" (and any updates to the Handbook, including Mortgagee letters) and all other instructions and standards, in performing all appraisals on properties that will be security for HUD/FHA insured mortgages.

(f) **For Inspectors,** I certify that I have a minimum of three years experience in one or more construction-related fields and that such experience has equipped me with a thorough familiarity and understanding of residential construction techniques as related to new construction and repairs of a structural nature. I certify I will conduct my inspections in accordance with HUD/FHA requirements.   I further certify that if licensing or certification is required by the state or local jurisdiction(s) in which I will operate, I will maintain such licensing or certification in good standing with the applicable jurisdiction for the duration of my tenure on the FHA Inspector Roster.  I further certify that I have read and fully understand the inspection requirements, including any update to those requirements, including Mortgagee Letters, in performing all inspections on properties that will be security for HUD/FHA insured mortgages and contained in the following documents:

(i)   HUD Handbook 4905.1 REV-1 (Requirements for Existing Housing, One to Four Family Units);

(ii)   HUD Handbook 4910.1 (Minimum Property Standards for Housing);

(iii)   HUD Handbook 4145.1 REV-2 (Architectural Processing and Inspections for Home Mortgage Insurance);

(iv)   HUD Handbooks 4150.1 REV-1 (Valuation Analysis for Home Mortgage Insurance) and 4150.2 CHG-1 (Valuation Analysis for Home Mortgage Insurance for Single Family One to Four Unit Dwellings);

(v)   Permanent Foundations Guide for Manufactured Housing (formerly known as HUD Handbook 4930.3G, Permanent Foundations Guide for Manufactured Housing);

(vi)   All applicable local, state, or Council of American Building Officials (CABO) code(s) for the jurisdictions in which I will operate; and

(vii)   The HUD requirements at 24 CFR 200.926

(g)   HUD or its authorized agent(s) may inspect my work files at my place of business during normal business hours after providing me reasonable notice of such inspection.

| 20a. Number of assignments you will accept per week | 20b. or Hours you will work | 20c. Maximum No. of assignments you will accept at one time | |
|---|---|---|---|
| | | | |

# P 46.    HUD-92563    Roster Appraiser Designation Application    Page 3 of 3

I, the undersigned, understand and agree that:

(a)  The approval of this application does not constitute my appointment as an agent or employee of HUD/FHA or DVA/VA.

(b)  In performing fee work my status is that of an independent contractor.

(c)  My sole interest in all transactions shall be to perform fee assignments as required by HUD or VA standards and criteria.

(d)  An appraisal/inspection is a substantial and material element in the determination of the eligibility of an application for FHA mortgage insurance, and HUD/FHA will rely upon the accuracy and truthfulness of an appraisal/inspection completed by me in approving any insurance.

### Warnings

I hereby certify that to the best of my knowledge all the information stated herein, as well as any information provided in the accompaniment herewith, is true, accurate, and complete. I further certify that I have read the Warnings set forth below.

Any person who knowingly presents materially false, fictitious, or fraudulent statements in a matter within the jurisdiction of HUD is subject to penalties, sanctions, or other regulatory actions, including but not limited to:

(i)  Fines and imprisonment under 18 USC 287, 1001, 1010, 1012, which provides for fines of a maximum of $25,000 for individual and $500,000 for organizations of imprisonment for up to 5 years, or both; or

(ii)  civil penalties and damages under 31 USC 3729, of not less than $5000 and not more than $10,000, plus 3 times the amount of damages which the government sustains; and

(iii)  administrative sanctions, claims, and penalties by HUD pursuant to 24 CFR Part 24, 28, and 30.

21. Date Signed (mm/dd/yyyy)    22. Applicant's Signature (do not print)

**Reviewing Official** Complete the following items

23. This Application has been reviewed and I hereby recommend
☐ Designation  ☐ Disapproval

24. Date of Action (mm/dd/yyyy)

25. Signature of Reviewing Officer

This applicant is being recommended in the county(ies) appraisal areas and/or State shown below

26. County(ies)

27. State

# FHA Appraisal Exam – 200 Sample Questions

Sample Final Test Questions for FHA Appraisal Exam

1. Valuations Conditions (VC) Form - VC requirements limit required repairs to those items necessary to:

2. If unable to view inspection and improvement in its entirety, the appraiser must:

3. VC-1 asks if there are "Overhead high voltage transmission lines within engineering (designed) fall distance." For the purposes of VC-1, what is an acceptable distance from the base of the tower?

4. When a property lacks connection to a public water supply, the appraiser must condition the appraisal on connection to a public supply, assuming:

5. Which of the following is **NOT** a requirement under VC-6 (Private Road Access and Maintenance)?

6. If the floor support system shows evidence of damage the appraiser will:

7. To ensure against conditions that could cause the building to deteriorate, all of the following are true **EXCEPT:**

8. In order to examine the roof, the appraiser should at a minimum:

9. Based on Handbook 4150.2, if a dwelling's primary heat source is a wood-burning stove:

10. During the summer, examination of the heating system must include:

11. It is a requirement that there is an installed heat or cool-air source:

12. The appraiser must flush toilets and run faucets to:

13. The appraiser's observation of the plumbing system must include all of the following **EXCEPT:**

14. In observing the electrical system the appraiser must:

15. Which of the following statements is true regarding garage doors?

16. In checking for health and safety deficiencies, the appraiser must operate:

17. Because of potential lead paint hazards, if the house was built before 1978, the appraiser should:

18. What is the owner-occupancy standard in a condominium project?

19. What is the completion standard for a condominium project?

20. A HUD/FHA Section 203 (k) mortgage **CANNOT** be used to:

21. The minimum threshold for required repairs under the Section 203 (k) program is:

22. For HUD/FHA appraisals, a Section 203 (k) appraisal requires:

23. "Eligible improvements" on a Section 203 (k) loan would **NOT** include:

24. A Section 203 (k) Consultant does **NOT:**

25. Which property type is **NOT** eligible for Section 203 (k) financing:

26. The subject property for a HUD/FHA Section 203 (k) mortgage:

27. In addition to the Uniform Residential Appraisal Report (URAR), the following documents must be submitted with **EVERY** FHA appraisal:

28. Appraisers should **NOT** require repair items that:

29. Which of the following would **NOT** be considered a required repair item:

30. On a 10-year-old, two-living-unit property, HUD/FHA requires as a minimum the following approach to value:

31. Before performing an appraisal on a property involving new or proposed construction, the appraiser must have the following documents:

32. A fully completed Builder's Certification form:

33. What repair items are required on a streamline refinance?

34. The minimum floor area for a manufactured home is:

35. After what construction date is a manufactured home acceptable?

36. Which road surface is **NOT** acceptable for HUD/FHA purposes?

37. HUD's requirements for a private road include:

38. What type of septic system is **NOT** acceptable?

39. What is the minimum distance between the private well and the septic tank for new construction?

40. The cost approach should be used in which of the following circumstances:

41. The cost approach for the HUD appraisal must be completed for:

42. Excess land is:

43. The appraisal of a property with excess land should:

44. The appraiser can be removed from the FHA register for six months to one year for square footage calculation errors of more than what percentage:

45. HUD does not discriminate in the selection of the appraiser on the basis of:

46. Ways to avoid discrimination, or to not encourage discrimination by others, include all of the following, **EXCEPT:**

47. Appraisers must be aware of Fair Housing regulations because:

48. A lender may request a reconsideration of the appraised value when:

49. Who is authorized to send additional comparables to the appraiser in HUD's reconsideration of an appraisal?

50. A vapor barrier for a crawl space is required when:

51. HUD requires repair of:

52. An existing property **MUST** always be rejected when:

53. Functional obsolescence is more likely to be present when the subject property:

54. An interior floor plan drawing is required when:

55. An appraisal performed under HUD general acceptable criteria for existing dwellings are to be done:

56. Which of the following properties would not require a termite inspection

57. A defective roof with _____ layers of all old shingles must be removed before reroofing.

58. If observed deficiencies exist in the property the appraiser must note them on this:

59. Required repairs are limited to those necessary to preserve:

60. All homes built prior to 19____ may contain lead paint

61. The _____ has the primary responsibility to determine if general acceptability criteria have been met prior to a loan.

62. A site must be graded to provide positive, rapid drainage away from perimeter walls of the dwelling and prevent:

63. Which of the following is **NOT** a Health and Safety deficiency?

64. FHA requires a minimum living area for all types of homes, other than manufactured housing:

65. The Cost Approach is required on FHA appraisals:

66. HUD's "3-S" Rule means:

67. Which of the following, if any, properties are not eligible for the 203K program?

68. Which of the following, are eligible property improvements under the 203K program for the first $5000 in repairs?

69. A 203K mortgage may be originated on a mixed-use residential property, provided:

70. What is the maximum percentage of commercial use permitted for a two-story building under the 203k program?

71. The Income Approach is always required if the property:

72. Which of the following is important for the HUD reviewer to keep in mind?

73. An interior floor plan drawing is necessary.

74. What should the appraiser do if at the time of inspection if repairs are in process?

75. Based on HUD's Handbook 4150.2, the verification process of comparable sales includes:

76. Which of the following conditions is not a consideration?

77. A comparable sale sold for $ 108,000 with a FHA mortgage of $100,000. The seller verified that "they paid 3 points" to the lender. What is the "net sale price"?

78. The most similar income property comparable sale had a sale price of $110,000. It had rents of $500 for each unit. The $110,000 comparable is similar to the duplex style of the subject, but the subject's rents are slightly lower ($475 per month) because they are smaller units. What is the indicated value for the subject, using a GRM? (rounded)

79. When the appraiser completes the cost approach for proposed construction, a marketing expense ratio of ___% is required.

80. The valuation condition segment sheet includes all but one of the following:

81. HUD defines Gross Living Area as :

82. According to HUD 4150.2 which square foot method is the most applicable for estimating replacement cost new:

83. Which of the following complete and make the following statement correct: "All flat roofs require _____ ?"

84. Any departure from HUD requirements should:

85. Which is the preferred method for developing the cost new of the existing subject improvements?

86. The appraiser must certify that the appraised value is based on the following:

87. When an appraiser finds a property in a condominium project that was not approved he/she should:

88. New single family construction requires:

89. Three and four family new construction requires:

90. The building sketch must show:

91. FHA requires the land value:

92. Final reconciliation is:

93. An appraisal reporting violation which has a square footage error of more than 10%, as a first offense will result in:

94. Failing to accurately report defects that costs over $5,000 to repair will result in (as a repeated offense):

95. Failing to recognize property in a special flood hazard area could result in:

96. Security bars on bedroom windows are acceptable if:

97. In the Site section of the sales comparison grid section the appraiser must enter which of the following as a response:

98. In the condition section of the Sales Comparison Grid section, the appraiser should make an adjustment for:

99. Comparable sales used in the appraisal must not be older than:

100. Adjustments to comparable sales must be:

101. Generally, a single line item adjustment on the URAR should not exceed:

102. A dwelling located in proximity to an underground high-pressure gas line is:

103. If appraising a single family home as a HUD real estate owned (REO), the appraiser must:

104. The "effective date" of an appraisal is:

105. For the typical HUD real estate owned (REO) property, the preferred "approach" to value is the:

106. On a FHA streamline refinance, which would not be considered a required repair?

107. When appraising a manufactured house, the appraiser cannot find the Federal Manufactured Home Construct & Safety Standard labels (tags) because the manufactured house (mobile home) has been bricked on the exterior veneer. The appraiser must:

108. Upon completion of the exam, the appraiser is placed on the FHA register for:

109. The selection of the appraiser is made by the:

110. The fee paid for the appraisal is:

111. The fee for a real estate appraisal must **NOT** include:

112. Under HUD guidelines, the fee for an appraisal is based upon:

113. The appraiser is required to state the full market assessed value in the:

114. The subject property is located in an area that is subject to hazards, which can not be cured. The appraiser must:

115. Assuming the current assessment does not represent the full market assessed value, the appraiser must have the which of the following to estimate the full market assessed value:

116. During the site visit the appraiser finds a property located next to a highly traveled roadway. The traffic noise is considerable yet several homes have sold on this same street. Access and the traffic flow are generally considered safe. According to HUD's Handbook 4150.2 the appraiser must:

117. Typically high-voltage power transmission lines are characterized as;

118. This type of property is not permitted within the 100-year floodplain.

119. The following photographs are required for an appraisal.

120. The appraiser must consider easements in the appraisal by:

121. According to HUD handbook 4150.2, gross living area includes the following types of space:

122. According to HUD's Handbook 4150.2, the analysis of conformity to the neighborhood for appraisal purposes requires:

123. The remaining economic life must:

124. The appraiser is responsible to determine the municipal zoning codes in order to:

125. Signs of soil contamination include the following:

126. According to HUD's Handbook 4150.2, the water supply for each living unit must contain the following:

127. The location of a domestic well must be:

128. Defective conditions in a property are characterized as:

129. If the roof must be repaired and there are already too many layers of shingles:

130. According to HUD's Handbook 4150.2 , the minimum distance between single family detached homes is:

131. HUD permits security bars in the windows of bedrooms under the following conditions:

132. One unit of a two-unit property is currently leased through the valuation date, while the remaining unit, which is much smaller, is owner occupied. The property rights appraised are:

133. During the site visit the appraiser notes several items which need to be repaired. Correcting all of the deficient items would require a major rehabilitation and repair costs are too extensive to estimate. The appraiser should:

134. What criteria does HUD permits the use of comparable listing in the sales comparison approach?

135. The fee for a real estate appraisal must not include:

136. The fee for an appraisal is based upon:

137. The selection of comparable sales is based upon the verification of the conditions of sale. The most applicable sales are generally:

138. The proper order of adjustments is:

139. The Income Approach is **NOT** required for the following property type.

140. The Income approach used for HUD relies upon the Gross Rent Multiplier (GRM). Which component is **NOT** required to calculate this multiplier?

141. The final analytical step is to reconcile the different approaches to value. According to HUD's Handbook 4150.2, the reconciliation must:

142. The Comprehensive Valuation Package (CVP) consists of the following three parts:

143. The purpose of the Home Buyer Summary is to:

144. The appraisal file must include all of the following items, **EXCEPT:**

145. HUD will monitor appraiser's performance using:

146. According to HUD's Handbook 4150.2, appraisal performance measures will include:

147. According to FIRREA the threshold for requiring state-certified appraisers is $250,000. Therefore HUD requires all appraisals performed for FHA to

148. Under the competency rule, HUD will permit all FHA Register Appraisers to perform appraisals for manufactured homes under which one of the following conditions:

149. All appraisers on the FHA Register must have a current state appraisal license. HUD also requires all appraisers to:

150. The four tiers of sanctions are:

151. A residential development should be processed as a Planned Unit Development (PUD) if it has one of the following minimum characteristics.

152. The approved list of condominium projects are available from the:

153. The appraiser is required to state the exposure period on the appraisal. The exposure period is defined as:

154. The previous sales history for a residential property must be considered and disclosed in the appraisal for _____ prior to the valuation date.

155. In developing the cost approach for properties on tribal trust lands:

156. In developing an appraisal for a single family home located on tribal trust land, HUD permits the appraiser to:

157. According to HUD's Handbook 4150.2, the appraiser may increase the value of a new or existing home by _____ for solar energy systems, assuming a full conventional back-up system.

158. The appraisal file must include all of the following items, **EXCEPT:**

159. HUD will monitor appraisers performance using:

160. According to HUD's handbook 4150.2, performance measures used to measure appraisers will include:

161. The subject property has an assessment and taxes well above comparable properties in the local market. The appraiser is required to:

162. If there is no method to relate the assessment to a full assessed market value or there is not a current assessment for properties such as new construction, then the appraiser must enter _____ on the VC form.

163. A letter may be obtained from a state authority stating that an oil or gas well on the subject property has been safely and permanently abandoned. If such a letter is not provided, the dwelling must be located at least _____ from the abandoned well.

164. Evidence of sinkholes or subsidence can include the following:

165. Flood maps are available from FEMA and Special Flood Hazard Areas (SFHA) have the following designations.

166. During the site visit, the appraiser walks the property line and sees that a garage and fence from an adjacent property has been built extending on to the subject property. The appraiser must:

167. The appraiser is required to access the attic to visually examine for:

168. According to HUD's Handbook 4150.2, the requirements for mechanical systems include:

169. According to HUD's Handbook 4150.2, the requirements for mechanical systems include all of the following, **EXCEPT:**

170. Conventional heating systems are required to maintain at least _____ in areas containing plumbing systems.

171. According to HUD's Handbook 4150.2, utility service must have all of the following , **EXCEPT:**

172. According to HUD's Handbook 4150.2, the following classifications of properties must comply with CABO Model Energy Code concerning energy efficiency standards and insulation.

173. In the property address section the appraiser is required to list the:

174. In the neighborhood section of the URAR the appraiser is required to list the:

175. In the neighborhood section of the URAR the appraiser is required to list the:

176. The subject property has a private well, the appraiser is required to check "yes' for VC-4 (Sewer & Water Supply) and require a:

177. The subject property has a community sewer system, the appraiser must always check _____ for VC-4 (Sewer & Water Supply).

178. According the HUD's Handbook 4150.2, evidence of termite infestation includes all of the following, **EXCEPT:**

179. Evidence that a private road or drive is required for VC-6. Evidence can be one of the following:

180. During the site visit, the appraiser finds a negative physical condition that does not require repair or inspection. Therefore, the appraisal must be based upon the:

181. For each specific item marked "YES" for VC-2 through VC-11 indicates a:

182. The homebuyer must receive a copy of the Homebuyer Summary Form that the _____ prepares and the _____ submits to the buyer.

183. If a supervisory appraiser and the appraisal trainee both prepare an appraisal report:

184. If an appraiser is sanctioned by HUD for an action that also violates USPAP, HUD will refer the administrative record to:

185. The FHA reviews appraiser performance and has four tiers of sanctions. Optional actions can include all of the following , **EXCEPT:**

186. The appraiser has a contractual responsibility to the:

187. The appraiser is required to identify the following intended users:

188. Basement apartments can be included in the gross livable area if the following requirements are met, **EXCEPT:**

189. The standard used to describe the extent of the appraisers inspection procedure for compliance with minimum property standards; is:

190. Section 223(E) is a mortgage insurance program specifically designed for:

191. HUD waives the following requirement for loans under the Section 223(E) mortgage insurance program:

192. The appraiser is required to state the current owner on the URAR. If the dwelling is not occupied by the current owner, the appraiser must provide the:

193. The borrower selects a HUD approved 203K Consultant to do all of the following, **EXCEPT:**

194. A conflict of interest can included one of the following situations:

195. The URAR prepared for HUD is considered a _____ report and a _____ analysis, under USPAP standards.

196. The levels of severity for all of the levels of violations listed in HUD's Handbook 4150.2 include the following, **EXCEPT:** .

197. Appraisal questions and comments can be directed to:

198. According to HUD's Handbook 4150.2, the special assessment is calculated:

199. New and proposed construction within Runway Clear Zone is:

200. According to HUD's Handbook 4150.2, the subject dwelling or related property improvement must be at least _____ feet from the outer boundary of the pipeline easement

# HUD/FHA – General Appraisal FAQ's

GENERAL Frequently Asked Appraisal Questions

## HOMEBUYER SUMMARY FORM

**1.   Is the Homebuyer Summary Form required for refinances?**
Yes, on refinances from conventional financing to FHA and on cash-out FHA to FHA refinances. The lender must ensure that the appraiser is fully informed on the type of appraisal that is being ordered. Appraisers may routinely wish to complete the Valuation condition (VC) Form and the Homebuyer Summary.

**2.        Is the Homebuyer Summary Form required for streamline refinances with appraisals?**
On streamline refinances with appraisals, all that is required is the VC form, not the Homebuyer Summary. Although FHA does not require repairs (except for lead based paint repairs) on streamline refinances with appraisals, the lender may require completion of repairs as a condition of the appraisal.

**3.        Is the Homebuyer Summary Form required for existing properties (over one year old)?**
Yes. The form is also required for existing properties less than one year old. The form is not required for proposed construction and properties under construction.

**4.        Should the Homebuyer Summary reflect only items needing repair, or should it also reflect certifications that may be required (termite inspections, well test, septic certifications, etc.)?**
The Homebuyer Summary should reflect ALL conditions noted on the VC Form; if none, the appraiser should so state.

**5.   If there are no repairs or conditions, is the Homebuyer Summary Form still required?**
Yes.


## VALUATIONS CONDITIONS (VC) FORM

**1.        Appraisers are concerned that a completed VC Form will be interpreted by some in the home purchase process as being equivalent to a Home Inspection. What measures are in place to ensure this will not happen? What role does the Lender play here?**
The VC Form is for use by lenders and will not typically be issued to the borrower(s). Purchasers are provided with the Homebuyer Summary, which specifically provides them with a summary of the observations of an appraiser who visited the property, plus reminds them that an appraisal is different from a home inspection. The Lender's role is to ensure that the borrower(s) understand the Homebuyer Summary and acknowledges receipt of the form. Also, Form HUD-92564-CN "For Your Protection: Get a Home Inspection" is presented to the buyer(s), and requires a signed acknowledgment, before or at the same time the contract is executed.

**2.        Is the VC Form required for existing properties (over one year old)?**
Yes. The VC form is also required for existing properties less than one year old. The form is not required for proposed construction or for properties under construction.

**3.        Is the VC Form required on a 203(k) case?**
The VC Form is not required on a 203(k) case. However, if the appraiser identifies repair conditions that were not noted in the Plan Review (Specifications of Repairs/Work Write-Up) for the 203(k) loan, the appraiser should notify the lender before proceeding any further with the appraisal.

**4.        Why is there a "no" response available in sections VC-2 through VC-13, but not in VC-1?**
"Yes" to any VC-1 item may make the property ineligible for FHA financing, as the condition cannot be remedied. "Yes" to VC-2 through VC-13 can usually be remedied.

**5.        What is the definition of "Readily Observable"?**
Observations made by the appraiser of conditions that are immediately discernable and noticeable during the typical site visit. The appraiser is not required to move furniture, equipment or cause damage to the property.

**6.        What is a representative sample?**
For multiple identical components such as windows and electrical outlets, one such component per room. For multiple identical exterior components, one such component on each side of the building.

**7.       Please explain the requirements for a termite inspection and are they also required for condominiums?**

If the structure is ground level, or if the structure is wood and touches the ground, a termite inspection is required. In those geographic areas, which are not susceptible to termite infestation, a termite inspection is not required. However, an appraiser must note any infestation, any damage resulting from previous infestation, repairs due to infestation, or repairs necessary due to infestation. For condominiums, termite inspections are required for the first floor units only. If the unit is located on the second floor or above, a termite inspection is not required.

**8.    Please address the eligibility of properties located within 300 feet of a gas station.**

The appraiser would note this on the VC Form, describe its impact on value or marketability on the URAR, and finish the appraisal. It would not necessarily render the property unacceptable. The DE Underwriter is required to provide a written disclosure to the borrower that the property is located within 300 feet of a gas station.

**9. Page 2-1-C of the Handbook states that, if a dwelling is less than 2 years old, the appraiser must indicate the year and month the home was completed. What is meant by the term "completed" and explain why this information is necessary.**

The purpose of this provision is for the application of the Cost Approach. The Handbook requirement will be reduced from two years to "thirteen months". "Completed" is defined as 100 percent complete.

**10.       Page 2-10 of the Handbook states that low voltage power lines may not pass over any structure on the property. What structure or structures are we discussing?**

"Structure" is limited to the primary living unit. Should the appraiser indicate that the lines pass over other structures they should keep in mind the safety of the occupants of the property. If the line(s) is/are considered unsafe, it should be noted on the VC Form to require correction of the condition to satisfy the safety issue.

**11.       If the appraiser is unable to take the required photographs to show the front, rear and sides of the improvements because of shrubbery, topography, etc., what should he/she do?**

The appraiser should make every attempt to take the required photographs. If not possible, the appraiser should so state on the appraisal report.

**12.       If the appraiser does not know the location of the private well or septic tank drain field, how can the distance between them be documented?**

If the appraiser is unable to make the determination, a condition requirement will be made on the VC Form. The DE Underwriter can clear the condition by obtaining satisfactory evidence from a qualified party that the distance requirements (between the two systems, and between the systems and property line) have been met.

**13. Section 3-6A-11 indicates that the crawl area space must be 18" – is this the distance from the bottom of the joists or from the sub-floor? Please clarify "Enter" for crawl space and attic areas.**

The Handbook will be clarified, as follows: "The minimum distance is 18 inches from the bottom of the joists". The appraiser will enter the crawl space (at a minimum entry of the head and shoulders) to observe conditions except: when access is obstructed, when entry could damage the property, or when dangerous and adverse situations are suspected. In any event, the crawl space and accessibility dictates the level of entry. However, the appraiser will visually examine the crawl space for inadequacies (see HUD HB 4150.2 Chapter 3-6 A-11 and Protocol for VC-8). The attic must be examined whether access is by pull-down stairway or scuttle. At a minimum head and shoulders entry. However, size and accessibility dictates the level of entry. The requirement to examine the crawl space and attic is not a new requirement nor has the requirement changed.

**14. When is a handrail necessary?**

A handrail is necessary usually when three or more risers are present. However, if a situation poses a safety issue for the occupants, a condition requirement should be made regardless of the number of risers.

**15. VC-11 references multiple broken windows. What if there is only one broken window?**

All broken windows should be repaired or replaced, as necessary.

## THE URAR AND OTHER ISSUES

**1.    Why can't appraisers use comparables over 12 months old, especially in rural areas where it is difficult to obtain comparables that are more recent?**

For FHA purposes, a sale over 12 months old is not acceptable as a comparable. The appraiser should go to a competing neighborhood; however, an older sale may be used as a fourth or fifth comparable sale to supplement the three comparables and to demonstrate market trends or marketability. For the three comparables, however, the search must be sufficient to capture comparables from the past 12 months.

**2.       On Page D-9, Room Grid, appraisers are instructed to enter the appropriate square footage for each designated room. Is this correct?**
No. The Handbook will be revised to reflect "enter the number of each type of room on each level. Show the appropriate area square footage for each designated level"

**3.       How are sales concessions to be addressed by the appraiser when completing the URAR?**
Sales concessions influence the price paid for real estate. It may be in the form of loan discount points, loan origination fees, settlement assistance, payment of condo/PUD fees, builder incentives or the inclusion of non-realty items in the transaction. As noted in Handbook 4150.2, Chapter 4 – The Valuation Process: sections 1-A, 6A-3, 6A-8, 6B, and under Sales or Financing Concession in the protocol section on Value Adjustments, appraisers are required to verify and analyze all sales on a cash-equivalent basis (interest rate buy downs, below market financing, owner financing, etc). As stated in the Appraisal of Real Estate, Eleventh Edition:

◊     In cash equivalency analysis, an appraiser investigates the sales price of comparable properties that appear to have been sold with non-market financing to determine whether adjustments to reflect typical market terms are warranted. First, sales with non-market financing are compared to other sales transacted with market financing to determine whether and adjustment for cash equivalency can be made. *Market evidence is always the best indicator of such an adjustment.* However, buyers rarely, if ever, rely on strict dollar for dollar cash equivalency adjustments.

The appraiser must verify all sales transactions for seller concessions and report those findings on the URAR. The amount of the negative adjustment to be made to each comparable with sales or financing concessions is equal to any increase in the purchase price of the comparable that the appraiser determines to be attributable to the concessions. It should be noted that the need to make negative adjustments and the amount of the adjustments to the comparables for sales and financing concessions are not based on how typical the concession might be for a segment of the market (large sales concessions can be relatively typical in a particular segment of the market and still result in sales prices that reflect more than the value of the real estate). The adjustment must reflect the difference between what the comparables actually sold for with the sales concessions and what they would have sold for without the concessions so that the dollar amount of the adjustments will approximate the reaction of the market to the concessions. In the case where the subject has a sales concession, and the comparable(s) did not, the appraiser does not add nor deduct for the subject's sales concessions (comparables are never adjusted upward or a sales concession).
The appraiser should be discussing the purchase agreement, including any sales concessions for the subject; on page two of the URAR in the section marked "analysis of any current agreement of sale".
Item 5 of the Definition of Market Value, (which is included with every residential appraisal) as shown above the Statement of Limiting Conditions and Appraiser's Certification states: "The price represents the normal consideration for the property sold unaffected by special or creative financing or sales concessions* granted by anyone associated with the sale."

◊     *Adjustments to the comparables must be made for special or creative financing or sales concessions. No adjustments are necessary for those costs which are normally paid by the sellers as a result of tradition or law in a market area; these costs are readily identifiable since the seller pays these costs in virtually all sales transactions. Special or creative financing adjustments can be made to the comparable property by comparisons to financing terms offered by a third party institutional lender that is not already involved in the property or transaction. Any adjustment should not be calculated on a mechanical dollar for dollar cost of financing or concessions but the dollar amount of any adjustment should approximate the market's reaction to the financing or concessions based on the appraiser's judgment. Verification of sales date and confirmation of seller concessions, if any, provides the lender client and FHA with a more thorough and accurate report on which to rely for mortgage lending and insurance decisions.

**4. What exhibits are required to be submitted with the appraisal in order to be in compliance with HUD's reporting requirements?**
An appraisal performed for HUD/FHA purposes requires that all sections of the Comprehensive Valuation Package (CVP) must be completed. The CVP constitutes the reporting instrument to HUD for FHA-insured mortgages. It consists of three parts. Part 1 is the fully completed URAR with the required attachments (addenda, maps, building sketch, photos, certifications, limiting conditions, etc.). Part 2 is the completed Valuation Condition Form (HUD-92564-VC), and Part 3 is the Notice to the Homebuyer report called the Homebuyer Summary (HUD-92564-HS). Appendix D of the Handbook 4150.2 explains the data requirements for the forms. The appraiser provides the lender/client with one original report plus one copy (containing original signature and photos).
Exceptions to these reporting requirements include new or proposed construction and some refinances. The Valuation Condition Form (Part 2) and the Homebuyer Summary Form (Part 3) are not required for proposed or under construction properties, however, both forms are required for existing homes that are less than one year old. The VC Form and the Homebuyer Summary are not required for the 230(k) appraisals, as the repairs should be addressed in the Plan Review/Specifications of Repairs. For Streamline refinances, the Homebuyer Summary is not required.

# HUD/FHA – Get A Home Inspection - FAQ's

<u>HUD/FHA - For Your Protection: Get a Home Inspection – FAQ's</u>

**1.    When is it mandatory to use the "For Your Protection: Get a Home Inspection" form?**
The form is mandatory for loans on dwellings that are more than 12 months old, excluding refinance transactions and Home Equity Conversions Mortgages.

**2.         When HUD is the seller (HUD Real Estate Owned [REO]), will the "For Your Protection" form be required?**
Yes.

**Homebuyer Summary:**

**1.         When is the use of the Homebuyer Summary mandatory?**
The Homebuyer Summary is mandatory for loans on all existing homes, except for 203(k) program loans and streamline financing.

**2.         Is the Homebuyer Summary required for existing properties (over one year old)?**
Yes. The form is also required for existing properties less than one year old. The form is not required for proposed construction and properties under construction.

**3.         Should the Homebuyer Summary reflect only items needing repair, or should it also reflect certifications that may be required (termite inspections, well tests, septic certifications, etc.)?**
The Homebuyer Summary should reflect ALL conditions noted on the VC sheet. If there are none, the appraiser should state this on the Homebuyer Summary.

**4.    If there are no repairs or conditions, is the Homebuyer Summary still required?**
Yes. If there are no repairs or conditions, the Homebuyer Summary should so state. **Valuation Conditions:**

**1.         When is the use of the Valuation Conditions Form mandatory?**
The Valuation Conditions (VC) Form is mandatory on all existing homes, except for 203(k) program loans and streamline refinancing without an appraisal.

**2.         We're concerned that a completed VC Form will be interpreted by some in the home purchase process as being equivalent to a Home Inspection. What measures are in place to ensure this will not happen? What role can the Lender play here?**
The VC Form is for use by lenders and will not typically be issued to the borrower(s). Purchasers are provided with the Homebuyer Summary which specifically provides them with a summary of the observations of an appraiser who visited the property, plus reminds them that an appraisal is different from a home inspection. The Lender's role is to ensure that the borrower(s) understand the Homebuyer Summary and acknowledges receipt of the form. Also, Form HUD-92564-CN "For Your Protection: Get a Home Inspection" is presented to the borrower(s) and signed on or before the contract is executed.

# *Valuation Analysis For Home Mortgage Insurance - FAQ's*

Valuation Analysis for Home Mortgage Insurance, Handbook 4150.2 - FAQ's:

**1.       Is the Valuation Conditions Form required for existing properties (over one year old)?**
Yes. The Valuation Conditions (VC) form is also required for existing properties less than one year old. The form is not required for proposed construction or for properties under construction.

**2.   Is the VC Form required in appraisals for refinancing?**
Yes.

**3.   Is a VC Form required for a 203(k) case?**
The VC Form is not required on a 203(k) case. However, if the appraiser identifies repair conditions that were not noted in the plan review for the 203(k) loan, the appraiser should notify the lender.

**4.       Why is there a "no" response available in sections VC-2 through VC-13, but not in VC-1?**
"Yes" to any VC-1 item may make the property ineligible for FHA financing as the condition cannot be remedied. "Yes" to VC-2 through VC-13 can usually be remedied.

**5.       Please define "Readily Observable".**
"Readily observable" is defined as observations made by the appraiser of conditions that are immediately discernable and noticeable during the typical site visit. The appraiser is not required to move furniture, equipment or cause damage to the property.

**6.       What is a representative sample?**
For multiple identical components such as windows and electrical outlets, a representative sample is one such component per room. For multiple identical exterior components, a representative sample is one such component on each side of the building.

**7.       Is the full assessed value required by Section A of the Addenda on Page D-34 of the Handbook to be "as repaired".**
No. This is the state's or local jurisdiction's full assessed value before applying any ratio or factor to arrive at property taxes. For most areas of the country this is an "as is" value.
The assessed market value is different from the assessment. The assessed market value is the assessor's opinion of market value used by the homeowner to determine if the taxes are reasonable. The assessment is often a fraction of the assessed market value used to calculate the taxes (assessment x tax rate = taxes). The assessment often does not relate to market value. The process to relate the assessment to the assessed market value is known as equalization. If there is no equalization method, the appraiser should indicate N/A as the assessed market value.

**8.       Please explain the requirement for a wood destroying insect inspection.**
A pest inspection is required for all structures except condominium units that are above ground level. The appraiser must note any infestation, any damage resulting from previous infestation, repairs resulting from infestation, or repairs necessary due to infestation. If the area in which the property is located is in a questionable probability area, that is, one that may or may not need a termite certificate, then the underwriter should contact the HOC for guidance. However, an appraiser must still check for signs of infestation even in those areas designated as not prone to infestation.

**9.       Regarding VC-9, does the flat roof inspection include porches?**
Yes, the requirement includes all roofs over all enclosed structures on the property. Flat roofs on condominium projects are covered by the condo's Home Owners Association. Nevertheless, the appraiser should always make comments on a project's overall condition.

**10.   If the roof cannot be observed because it is snow covered, what can the lender do to satisfy the condition?**
If it is unreasonable to expect the snow to clear within a reasonable amount of time, the appraiser may access the condition of the roof by observing the roof from the interior. The borrower must be informed that the roof was snow covered at the time of the appraisal to determine whether it is acceptable to the purchaser. The lender may also require additional requirements to satisfy this condition.

**11.       VC-1 indicates that properties located within 300 feet of a stationary storage tank containing more than 100 gallons of flammable or explosive material are ineligible. It is common to have oil, gas or propane tanks for residential heating purposes that are typically in excess of 100 gallons within 300 feet of property (especially with smaller lots) borders.**
HUD has increased the storage tank size to 1,000 gallons.

**12.   Please address the eligibility of properties located within 300 feet of a gas station.**
This would not necessarily render the property unacceptable. The Direct Endorsement (DE) Underwriter is required to provide a written disclosure to the borrower that the property is located within 300 feet of a gas station.

**13.      Please clarify VC-6 Private Road – "show evidence access is protected by a permanent recorded easement". Will the ALTA policy suffice?**
The title search should reveal recorded easements. However, it is the DE Underwriter's responsibility to determine if the title policy shows sufficient evidence of a permanent recorded easement.

**14.      Is there a requirement for smoke detectors?**
Although FHA strongly recommends them, smoke detectors are not a nationwide HUD requirement at this time. The 203(k) rehabilitation program requires that smoke detectors be installed adjacent to sleeping areas.

**15.      Page 2-1-C of the Handbook states that, if a dwelling is less than 2 years old, the appraiser must indicate the year and month the home was completed. Please define the term "completed" and explain why this information is necessary.**
The purpose of this provision is for the application of the Cost Approach. The Handbook requirement will be reduced from two years to *thirteen* months. "Complete" is defined as ready for occupancy with only minor finish items (e.g., touch-up painting, final grading and seeding) remaining.

**16.      Many properties will be eligible for FHA financing under the guideline for overhead high-voltage transmission lines because they are located within the fall distance of a radio or TV cable tower or satellite dish. Is there anything the lender can do to render these properties for insurance?**
The appraiser must indicate whether the dwelling or related property improvements is located within the easement serving a high-voltage transmission line, radio/TV transmission tower, cell phone tower, microwave relay dish or tower, or satellite dish (radio, TV cable, etc.). If the dwelling or related property improvements are located within such an easement, the DE Underwriter must obtain a letter from the owner or operator of the tower indicating that the dwelling and its related property improvements are not located within the tower's (engineered) fall distance.

**17.   Are appraisers competent to assess whether offensive noises and odors threaten the health and safety of the occupants of a property.**
Section 2-2K will be modified to reflect that the appraiser should review any nuisance and take it into consideration in the market analysis, making adjustments if appropriate. The appraiser should document the appraisal report, as necessary.

**18.      Regarding Section 3-1 of the Handbook, are black and white photographs acceptable?**
Yes, black and white laser printed copies of photographs, as well as photographs produced by digitized cameras which are of adequate size and clarity, are acceptable.

**19.      If the appraiser is unable to take the required photographs to show the front, rear and sides of the property because of shrubbery, topography, etc., what should he/she do?**
The appraiser should make every attempt to take the required photographs. If not possible, the appraiser should so state on the appraisal report.

**20.      Is it the appraiser's responsibility to determine the feasibility of connecting to public or community water and/or sewage systems?**
If the property has private water and/or sewage systems, the appraiser will annotate the VC Form (VC-4 as appropriate). It is the lender's responsibility to determine the feasibility/reasonableness of the connection cost. The appraiser should provide the lender with information about the location of public or community systems (e.g., the public water line is available directly in front of the subject property; or the public system is located approximately 100 feet from the property, but there are protected wetlands between the subject and the public system).

**21.      If the appraiser does not know the location of the private well or septic tank drainfield, how can the distance between them be documented?**
If the appraiser is unable to make the determination, a condition requirement will be made on the VC Form. The DE Underwriter can clear the condition by obtaining satisfactory evidence from a qualified party that the distance requirements (between the two systems, and between the systems and property line) have been met.

**22.      Handbook 4150.2 indicates that cisterns are not acceptable. Are there any exceptions to this?**
Yes. The HOCs have the authority to consider case-by-case waivers in areas where cisterns are typical. The lender contacts the HOC that has jurisdiction over the property for waiver procedures.

**23.      Handbook 4150.2 indicates that the crawl space must be 18 inches. Please clarify.**
The Handbook will be clarified, as follows: "A minimum distance of 18 inches from the ground to bottom of the joists is highly recommended but not mandated". The appraiser will enter the crawl space (at a minimum entry of the head and shoulders) to observe conditions except when access is obstructed, when entry could damage the property, or when dangerous and adverse situations are suspected.

In any event, the crawl space and accessibility dictates the level of entry. However, the appraiser will visually examine the crawl space for inadequacies (see HUD HB 4150.2 Chapter 3-6 A. 11 and Protocol for VC-8).

ATTIC: The attic must be examined whether access is by pull-down stairway or scuttle. At a minimum head and shoulders entry. However, size and accessibility dictates the level of entry. The requirement to examine the crawl space and attic is not a new requirement nor has the requirement changed.

## 24.    Are vapor barriers required in crawl spaces?

Typically no; however, if moisture problems are evident, a vapor barrier should be required.

## 25.  Handbook 4150.2 requires that the heating system must be able to maintain 50 degrees in all areas containing plumbing systems and that the system must be installed in accordance with the manufacturer's recommendations. How will the appraiser know this?

This requirement pertains only to dwellings that use wood-burning stoves or solar systems. If the appraiser is unable to make the necessary determinations, he/she should so state on the VC form by making a condition requirement. The lender may obtain a certification from a qualified firm that the system is properly installed to clear the condition requirement.

## 26. When is a handrail necessary?

Usually when there are three or more risers. However, if a situation poses a safety issue for the occupants, a condition requirement should be made regardless of the number of risers.

## 27.    Please clarify the requirements for lead-based paint repairs on condominium units.

The lead-based paint requirements relate only to the unit being appraised, not to the entire project. Section 3-6A-17 of the Handbook will be revised to reflect this correction. However, the appraiser should always comment on the overall condition of the condominium project.

## 28.  Regarding Section 3-6B-6, Bedroom Egress, what is "adequate' egress? Occupants of a bedroom must be able to get outside the home if there is a fire.

## 29.    In Section 4-5E, the construction ratings do not coincide with other agencies, such as Fanny Mae and Freddie Mac, or Marshall and Swift. Will this be changed in the future?

The reference to "fair" construction quality will be removed from the handbook in order to bring HUD's construction ratings in line with those of Fannie Mae, Freddie Mac and Marshall and Swift.

## 30.  Why can't appraisers use comparables over 12 months old, especially in rural areas where it is difficult to obtain comparables that are more recent?

A sale over 12 months old is not acceptable in the first there comparables. The appraiser should go to a competing neighborhood. An older sale may be used as a fourth or fifth comparable sale to supplement the three comparables, however, the search must be sufficient to capture comparables from the past 12 months.

## 31.   Can you explain how the appraiser is to handle financing concessions?

Sales concessions influence the price paid for real estate. It may be in the form of loan discount points, loan origination fees, settlement assistance, payment of condo/PUD fees, builder incentives or the inclusion of non-realty items in the transaction.

Appraisers are required to verify and analyze all sales on a cash-equivalent basis (interest rate buy downs, below market financing, owner financing, etc). As stated in the Appraisal of Real Estate, Eleventh Edition:

◊    In cash equivalency analysis, an appraiser investigates the sales price of comparable properties that appear to have been sold with non-market financing to determine whether adjustments to reflect typical market terms are warranted. First, sales with non-market financing are compared to other sales transacted with market financing to determine whether and adjustment for cash equivalency can be made. *Market evidence is always the best indicator of such an adjustment.* However, buyers rarely, if ever, rely on strict dollar for dollar cash equivalency adjustments.

The appraiser must verify all sales transactions for seller concessions and report those findings on the URAR. The amount of the negative adjustment to be made to each comparable with sales or financing concessions is equal to any increase in the purchase price of the comparable that the appraiser determines to be attributable to the concessions. It should be noted that the need to make negative adjustments and the amount of the adjustments to the comparables for sales and financing concessions are not based on how typical the concession might be for a segment of the market (large sales concessions can be relatively typical in a particular segment of the market and still result in sales prices that reflect more than the value of the real estate). The adjustment must reflect the difference between what the comparables actually sold for with the sales concessions and what they would have sold for without the concessions so that the dollar amount of the adjustments will approximate the reaction of the market to the concessions.

Comparables are never adjusted for the subject's sales concessions. If the subject has a sales concession, the appraiser should discuss the purchase agreement, including any sales concessions for the subject, on page two of the URAR in the section marked "analysis of any current agreement of sale".

Item 5 of the Definition of Market Value, (which is included with every residential appraisal) as shown above the Statement of Limiting

Conditions and Appraiser's Certification states: "The price represents the normal consideration for the property sold unaffected by special or creative financing or sales concessions* granted by anyone associated with the sale."

◊   *Adjustments to the comparables must be made for special or creative financing or sales concessions. No adjustments are necessary for those costs which are normally paid by the sellers as a result of tradition or law in a market area; these costs are readily identifiable since the seller pays these costs in virtually all sales transactions. Special or creative financing adjustments can be made to the comparable property by comparisons to financing terms offered by a third party institutional lender that is not already involved in the property or transaction. Any adjustment should not be calculated on a mechanical dollar for dollar cost of financing or concessions but the dollar amount of any adjustment should approximate the market's reaction to the financing or concessions based on the appraiser's judgment.

**32.     Section 8-1 on Manufacturing Homes requires inspection by a State Administrative agency when the appraiser observes changes to the original home. If the manufactured home has an addition, and there is no local agency to inspect such homes, are there alternatives to rejecting the property?**
The lender can obtain an engineer's report indicating that the structural changes or additions to the property were made in accordance with the HUD Manufactured Home Construction and Safety Standards, instead of rejecting the property.

**33.   On Page D-9, Room Grid, appraisers are instructed to enter the appropriate square footage for each designated room. Is this correct?**
No. The Handbook will be revised to reflect: "enter the *number of each type of room* on each level. Show the appropriate area square footage for each designated *level.*"

**34.   On Page D-29, VC-27, are you referring to fire retardant treated sheathing?**
Yes, this is a typographical error and will be corrected.

**35. Regarding VC-11, if an older garage door does not have the automatic reverse feature and/or does not stop when met with resistance, must the appraiser require that a new opener be installed?**
The appraiser must verify that the garage door does not drop with a heavy impact due to broken or missing components. If there is readily-observable evidence of a potential safety hazard, call for repair or replacement.

**36. VC-11 references multiple broken windows. What if there is only one window broken?**
Any broken window should be repaired or replace.

**37.   Page D-33, VC-13 indicates that the property does not meet completion standards if the completion rate is less than 2/3. What does this mean?**
This item will be removed from the Handbook and VC Form.

**38. In the Glossary of Terms, does the term "Dangerous or Adverse Situations" refer to the property being appraised or the performance of the appraiser?**
This definition refers to the property only. It is not intended to refer to the appraiser. The definition will be revised in the Handbook as follows:
◊   Situations that pose a threat of injury to the homeowner or occupant(s) and/or require the use of special protective clothing or safety equipment on the part of the homeowner or occupant(s).

**39.   Who performs the final inspection on properties "under construction" or "existing less than one year old"?**
If the property is under construction and not 100% complete, the appraiser will perform the appraisal, complete the URAR and all necessary exhibits, and require a final inspection. The final may be completed by a fee panel inspector or the HUD approved local jurisdiction or equivalent and Form HUD-92051, Compliance Inspection Report is required. If the property is 100% complete, the appraiser performs the appraisal and completes the URAR and all necessary exhibits. In this instance, the appraisal serves as the final inspection and Form HUD-92051, Compliance Inspection Report, is not required. For detailed guidance see HUD HB 4145.1 REV-2 Change 1, Paragraph 6-3, pages 6-16 and 6-17. However, in all cases, if the appraiser does not have the plans, specifications and construction documents as well as a completed builder's certification at the time the appraisal is to be performed, the appraiser may not complete the appraisal until this documentation is made available.

**40. The Handbook advises the appraiser to only talk to the DE Underwriter about an appraisal before it is completed. Also, no other person should talk to the appraiser. This seems to be a bit impractical. A lot of times the appraiser has small problems that would have nothing to do with the DE Underwriter. Does this mean that after a sponsored mortgage broker i.e. lender, orders an appraisal, we are not supposed to talk to the appraiser until it is received? A lot of times, an appraiser will call just to let us know a property isn't going to work, can't find a comparable, etc. Are we not to have that kind of relationship with the appraisers anymore?**

No one but the underwriter is to discuss the value with the appraiser until the appraisal is completed. The appraiser can discuss the physical characteristics or schedule an appointment with the seller or their representative. Consistent with the Financial Institution Reform and Recovery Act (FIRREA), the appraiser may not discuss the value with anyone else but the client. The client is the lender.

**41. Will there be revisions to Handbook 4150.2 coming out with changes already made?**
FHA will update the handbook as necessary.

**42.      Will appraisers be able to charge a higher fee for the increased reporting requirements?**
It is the Department's position that appraisal fees should not increase as a result of the recent changes. The appraisal process for HUD has remained largely unchanged. The new forms only require confirmation of pre-existing requirements already contained in the MPR.

**43.      Our appraisers are stating that the FHA appraisal cost for consumers will substantially increase because of the at least 1-2 hours more work and the requirement that appraisers inspect under the house and crawl in the attic for visual inspection. How do I address this statement?**
The reporting requirements have not changed. The appraiser has always been required to enter both the attic and crawl spaces to observe conditions.

# HUD and FHA Guidelines for
# Valuation Analysis for Single Family and
# One- to Four-Unit Dwellings

***Purpose of this Section:*** The following section contains appraisal guidelines for HUD and FHA appraisals. I've included this section to be used as a reference for you. These guidelines can help further clarify the appraisal topics discussed in this book. The text is written in a very formal and technical style of writing since it is used by HUD and FHA for their appraisal procedures. You don't need to try and memorize everything right away since it will seem overwhelming if you try to do that. Just take your time so you can learn at your own pace and refer back to this book as needed, like a reference manual.

*These guidelines can help further clarify the appraisal topics discussed in this book. The text is written in a very formal and technical style of writing since it is used by HUD and FHA for their appraisal procedures. You don't need to try and memorize everything right away since it will seem overwhelming if you try to do that. Just take your time so you can learn at your own pace and refer back to this book as needed, like a reference manual.*

These are the purposes of the HUD Updated Handbook 4150.2, July 1999 Valuation Analysis for Single Family and One- to Four-Unit Dwellings information:

◊ Provide guidance for appraisers on how to appraise existing, proposed and new construction of one- to four-family homes for which mortgages are to be insured by FHA.

◊ Introduce appraisers to the environment of greater accountability associated with recent HUD reforms.

**TABLE OF CONTENTS**

**FORMS AND REPORTS REFERENCED IN HANDBOOK 4150.2**
◊   HUD-92005: Description of Materials
◊   HUD-92541: Builder's Certification
◊   HUD-92544: Builder's Warranty
◊   HUD-92563: Roster Appraiser Designation Application (to be updated)
◊   HUD-92802: Application and Request for Manufactured Home Lot and/or Site Preparation
◊   Homebuyer Summary and Valuation Conditions Form
◊   Marshall and Swift Form 1007
◊   Freddie Mac 704 Form: Second Property Value Analysis and Report
◊   R.S. Means & Company Repair and Modeling Cost Data Book or the Home-Tech Remodeling and Renovation Cost Estimator
◊   Use of Materials Bulletin No. 100, Subject: HUD Building Product Standards & Certification Program for Solar Water
Heating Systems-August 15,1993
◊   Marshall & Swift Cost Handbook - New & Proposed Construction

◊   Marshall & Swift Guide to Construction Costs
◊   Form FW 68: Land Appraisal Report
◊   Uniform Standards of Professional Appraisal
◊   Permanent Foundation Guide for Manufactured Housing
◊   CABO Model Energy Code, 1992 Ed., Residential Buildings


## FOREWORD

**_PURPOSES OF HANDBOOK:_** These are the purposes of this Handbook:
◊   Provide guidance for appraisers on how to appraise existing, proposed and new construction of one- to four-family homes for which mortgages are to be insured by FHA.
◊   Introduce appraisers to the environment of greater accountability associated with recent HUD reforms.

**_HOME BUYER PROTECTION PLAN:_** On June 1, 1998, HUD launched the *Home Buyer Protection Plan.* The Plan reforms the appraisal process to ensure that home buyers seeking FHA-insured mortgages receive accurate and complete appraisals of the homes they seek to purchase. If homebuyers do not receive adequate appraisals, they may have to make extensive repairs to make their homes habitable. As a result of the additional financial burden, they may default on their FHA-insured mortgages.

**_THE NEW HUD VALUATION CONDITIONS FORM:_** As part of the *Home Buyer Protection Plan,* HUD has revised the Valuation Conditions (VC) Form. This new form:
◊   Requires submission of valuation condition information for all appraisals.
◊   Transforms the former VC form into a series of "yes-or-no questions" based on readily observable physical conditions of the subject property.
◊   Summarizes the information on the physical condition of the property for the Homebuyer.

**_THE PERFORMANCE MEASUREMENT FRAMEWORK:_** Another significant change reflected in this Handbook is the introduction of performance measures for appraisers. The performance measurement framework is designed to achieve improvements in the performance and professionalism of appraisers on the FHA Register. HUD will measure appraiser performance in the following five performance categories:
◊   Appraisal process
◊   Appraisal reporting
◊   Valuation conditions
◊   Maintaining state licensure
◊   Responsiveness to field review

As part of this new framework, HUD will develop statistical indicators to identify poor appraisals and appraisers, and will inform appraisers of its enforcement efforts.

**_ENFORCEMENT AND SANCTIONS:_** In addition to providing clear sanctions, HUD has enhanced enforcement efforts by creating an Enforcement Center. The Enforcement Center will provide administrative support for the management of the sanction process.

**_RESOURCES:_** Questions and comments can be sent electronically to REAC's Internet website at reacone@hud.gov. The Help Desk will be available be g on May 5,1999 Monday through Friday from 7:30 a.m. to 8:00 p.m. EST for questions. The telephone number is (888) 245-4860.

# 1    SELECTION OF APPRAISER

## 1-0    INTRODUCTION

The success of the FHA insurance program and HUD's ability to protect its financial interest begins with selecting qualified and knowledgeable appraisers.  This chapter presents the minimum requirements that appraisers must meet to be placed on the FHA Register.

## 1-1    FHA REGISTER

The FHA Register lists appraisers who are eligible to perform FHA single-family appraisals.  To conduct an appraisal for FHA insurance endorsement, the appraiser must be on the FHA Register.

◊    Appraiser achieves necessary credentials
◊    Appraiser applies to HUD
◊    HUD reviews application
◊    Appraiser placed on FHA Register

### A.    APPRAISER CREDENTIALS

To be eligible for placement on the FHA Register, all appraisers must be state-licensed or state-certified and must not be listed on any of these:

◊    GSA's Suspension and Debarment List (the government-wide list of parties excluded from federal procurement or non-procurement programs).
◊    HUD's Limited Denial of Participation List.
◊    HUD's Credit Alert Interactive Voice Response System (CAIVRS)

To be eligible to perform appraisals for FHA, the appraiser must also pass a HUD//FHA test on appraisal methods and reporting, which focuses on applied knowledge of the new Handbook 4150.2. A uniform national examination will be available June 1, 1999.  The examination contains fifty questions in a multiple-choice format.  The test will be administered by a national provider and the cost paid by the appraiser.  Appraisers currently on the FHA Register will be grandfathered until January 30, 2000.

### B.    REGISTER APPLICATION PROCESS

The application process is the first screening of the appraiser's qualifications to perform HUD/FHA appraisals.  To apply, appraisers must submit the following to FHA:

◊    Updated form HUD-92563 "Register Appraiser Designation Application".
◊    A copy of a current valid appraisal license and/or certification verification that the appraiser has passed the FHA Examination.

HUD will review this information to determine the appraiser's eligibility for the FHA Register.

### C.    APPLICANT REVIEW

To verify that the appraiser is eligible to perform HUD/FHA appraisals, REAC performs a detailed review of the appraiser's professional qualifications and checks for any negative information.  The review does the following:

◊    Verifies that the appraiser is state-licensed or state-certified under the Appraisal Qualifications Board (AQB) criteria.
◊    Verifies that the appraiser has passed the FHA Appraisals Methods and Procedures test.
◊    Pre-screens the appraiser's social security number in the HUD/FHA Credit Alert Interactive Voice Response System (CAIVRS).
◊    Reviews HUD records to ensure that the appraiser has no pending suspensions, disqualifications or debarments.
◊    Verifies with the appraiser's signature that there are no actions or pending judgments against the appraiser for waste, fraud, abuse or breach of professional ethics or standards.
◊    Reviews the previous period's performance, if applicable.

### D.    DESIGNATION TO THE FHA REGISTER

When the review of the application is complete, the appraiser is designated to the FHA Register.  New appraisers recently added to the FHA Register may be monitored and reviewed more frequently to ensure that their performance is consistent with HUD/ FHA guidelines and to monitor training needs. Because the initial application to the FHA Register will occur after the appraiser has become state-licensed or state-certified, the first term will coincide with the remaining period of state licensing for the home state.  After this initial period, the FHA Register period will be consistent with the home state license period. Each period, every appraiser must re-apply to the FHA Register, concurrent with the appraiser's application for state licensing and/or re-certification.  HUD reviews the appraiser's performance and compliance with new testing requirements and verifies that the appraiser is state-certified or state-licensed. For more information on the review process, see Chapter 6 of this Handbook.

## 1-2  LENDER SELECTION OF THE APPRAISER
&#9674;   Lender selects appraiser
&#9674;   Lender assigns appraiser
&#9674;   Lender transmits case #, if available
&#9674;   Appraiser performs appraisal
&#9674;   Lender reviews appraisal

When the lender selects an appraiser from the FHA Register, the FHA Connection processes a case number for the lender. The lender may assign the appraiser before receiving the case number, but the case may not be submitted for endorsement without the case number. The case number must be placed on all copies of the URAR as well as the VC form and summary. The mortgagee will give the appraiser:

&#9674;   The property address
&#9674;   Type of construction
&#9674;   Number of units
&#9674;   Other information necessary for the assignment

If the property is a condominium or a Planned Unit Development (PUD), the lender will verify that it is HUD-approved before ordering a case number or having an appraisal performed. The lender will give the appraiser the project name and ID number and all available property information. If it is proposed construction for a PUD or Condominium, it must be FHA-approved before ordering a case number. The name of the Condominium or PUD must be given.

### A.  NON-DISCRIMINATION POLICY
The Department's regulations on choosing appraisers state that there shall be no discrimination on the basis of race, color, religion, national origin, sex, age or disability. HUD expects lenders to comply with anti-discrimination requirements and affirmatively select female and minority appraisers for a fair share of appraisals commensurate with their representation on the FHA Register. HUD will monitor lenders' choice of appraisers by their sex and race.

### B. CONTRACTUAL RESPONSIBILITY OF APPRAISERS
The appraiser is hired by the lender, and therefore has a contractual responsibility to the lender. However, the appraiser provides services for HUD programs, and therefore, has an obligation to perform these services commensurate with the standards and requirements of HUD. This dual responsibility of the appraiser is recognized in the review and reporting requirements of HUD. The lender and the appraiser must meet their respective obligations as prescribed by HUD/FHA. Therefore, the intended user of the appraisal report is also HUD. These contractual obligations to the lender and HUD/FHA are in addition to the appraiser's legal obligations to his or her credentialing state.

### C.  COMMUNICATION WITH APPRAISERS
HUD/FHA mortgage insurance is initiated when a lender selects an appraiser from the FHA Register. Once the appraiser agrees to perform the appraisal, the appraiser is in a contractual relationship with the lender. The appraiser will send the completed appraisal directly to the lender. HUD advises the appraiser to discuss the appraisal only with the underwriter. No other individual should contact the appraiser before the appraisal has been completed. Real estate brokers and agents should consider the lender their sole source of information on the appraisal and all matters related to the appraisal.

### D.  APPRAISAL FEES
The appraiser and the lender will negotiate the price and due date. HUD does not establish fees or due dates. The fee is paid for market value estimate based on guidelines consistent with HUD policy and procedure established in this Handbook. The fee is not based on a requested minimum valuation, a specific valuation or the approval of a loan. Lenders may charge the borrower only what is customary and reasonable in the area to obtain an appraisal. Appraisal management firms may charge the mortgagor a fee for the appraisal that may encompass fees for services performed by the firm as well as fees for the appraisal itself. However, the total of these fees is limited to the customary and reasonable fee for an appraisal in the market area where the appraisal is performed. Such arrangements must comply with all aspects of the Real Estate Settlement Procedures Act (RESPA) and its implementing regulations, including restrictions against:

&#9674;   Kickbacks and referral fees
&#9674;   Charges for settlement services that were not actually performed
&#9674;   Payments in affiliated business arrangements other than return on ownership

## 2   SITE ANALYSIS

### 2-0 INTRODUCTION

This Chapter addresses the site requirements for FHA-insured mortgages. Before the valuation process can begin, subject properties must meet specific site requirements. The appraisal process is the lender's tool for determining if a property meets the minimum requirements and eligibility standards for a FHA-insured mortgage. In addition, these standards provide a context for the appraiser in performing the physical inspection of the property.

### 2-1 SITE REQUIREMENTS

The purpose of site analysis is to identify the various site characteristics that affect the marketability and the value of the subject property. Site analysis requires the following:
◊   Determining the desirability and utility of the site
◊   Determining the degree and extent to which the site, because of external influences, shares in the market for comparable and competitive sites in the community
◊   Forecasting the likely changes at the site because of justifiable future trends
◊   Appraising the current situation and knowledge of the various trends that could affect the valuation of the real property

The principal of change is fundamental to appraising real estate and to properly analyzing a site. Value is created and modified by economic, social and governmental changes that occur outside the property. Evaluate the direction of these trends and determine their effect, if any, on the current value of the subject property.

#### A.   NEIGHBORHOOD DEFINITION
The appraiser must clearly define the boundaries - north, south, east and west - of the subject neighborhood. By defining the neighborhood, the appraiser can extract pertinent information on which to base valuation conclusions.

#### B.   COMPETITIVE SITES
Sites are competitive when they are improved with, or appropriate for, residential properties that are similar in accommodations and sales price or rental range for similar residents or prospective occupants. Compare features of the subject site with the same features of competitive sites within the community. An acceptable site must be related to the needs of the prospective occupants and to the alternatives available to them in other competitive locations.

#### C.   DEFINITIONS - CONSTRUCTION STATUS
**Proposed -** No concrete or permanent material has been placed. Digging of footing and placement of re-bar is not considered permanent.
**Under Construction -** From the first placement of concrete (permanent material) to 100% completion. Finalized and ready to occupy.
**Existing -** 100% complete and has occupancy permit.
**Existing less than one year -** Appraisal performed less than one year since receipt of final occupancy permit issued. For model homes, age begins with issuing of permit to use as a model.
For any home less than 2 years old, list month and year completed in the age box on the URAR.

#### D.   ECONOMIC TRENDS
The appraiser must give consideration to, and include in the value analysis, the economic trends of a neighborhood and the general area, including:
◊   Price and wage levels (the purchasing power of community occupants)
◊   Employment characteristics
◊   The current supply and demand for residential dwellings, including projects under construction
◊   Taxation levels
◊   Building costs
◊   Population changes
◊   Activity of real estate sales market and mortgage interest rates

#### E.   LAND USE RESTRICTIONS
Site analysis determines the effects of actual and potential neighborhood land use on the subject site. The following factors form patterns for present and future land uses:

#### 1.   Zoning
The appraiser should consider the effect on the value of appropriate and well-drawn zoning ordinances. Land-use controls that receive public approval and are strictly enforced protect residential sites from adverse influences that diminish the desirability of sites. This must be noted on the URAR, and its effect must be quantified in the valuation analysis.

## 2.   Protective Easement/Covenants

Properly drawn protective covenants have proven more effective than zoning regulations in providing protection from adverse environmental influences.  When combined with proper zoning ordinances, these covenants provide the maximum legal protection to ensure that a developed residential area will maintain desirable characteristics or that a proposed or partially built-up neighborhood will develop in a desirable manner.  Protective easements and covenants should be superior to any mortgage and should be binding to all parties and all persons claiming under them.  These must be noted on the URAR and its effect must be quantified in the Valuation Analysis.

## 3.   Inharmonious Land Uses

The appraiser must identify all inharmonious land uses in a neighborhood that affect value.  Clearly define the current and long-term effect that inharmonious uses will have on the market value and the economic life of the subject property.  If inharmonious land use represents a serious detriment to either the health or safety of the occupants or to the economic security of the property, clearly note safety of the occupants or to the economic security of the property, clearly note this on the VC and URAR.  Recommend that the property be rejected by the Lender.

## 4.   Natural Physical Features

The appraiser must consider favorable and underlying topography and site features, including pleasing views, wood lots, broad vistas and climatic advantages.  Streets that are laid out with proper regard to drainage, land contours and traffic flow show good design and increase the desirability of the neighborhood.  This must be noted on the URAR and its effect must be quantified in the valuation analysis.

## 5.   Attractiveness of Neighborhood Buildings

The overall appeal of a neighborhood is strengthened if the buildings in a neighborhood harmonize with each other and their physical surroundings.  A pleasing variety that results in harmoniously blended properties is desirable but not mandatory.  The age of the structure is not in itself an important consideration; however, the maintenance of the structure over time has an important impact.  Consider the amount of rehabilitation that has taken place or is taking place in a neighborhood.  This must be noted on the URAR and its effect must be quantified in the valuation analysis.

## 6.   Neighborhood Character

Mobility and economic growth can alter neighborhood patterns.  Shopping, recreation, places of worship, schools and places of employment should be easily accessible.  This must be noted on the URAR and its effect must be quantified in the valuation analysis.

## 7.   Character of Neighborhood Structures

The appraiser must carefully analyze the age, quality, obsolescence and appropriateness of typical properties in a neighborhood.  Take into account the attitude of the user group as well as the alternative choices available to the specific market under consideration.  This must be noted on the URAR and its effect must be quantified in the valuation analysis.

## F.   COMMUNITY SERVICES

Community services include commercial, civic and social centers.  For a neighborhood to remain stable and retain a high degree of desirability, it should be adequately served by elementary and secondary schools, neighborhood shopping centers, churches, playgrounds, parks, community halls, libraries, hospitals and theaters.  A lack of services in the community should be noted and quantified in the valuation analysis.  The appraiser must note a change in these services and quantify the effect on value.

## G.   TRANSPORTATION

Ready access to places of employment, shopping, civic centers, social centers and adjacent neighborhoods is a requisite of neighborhood stability.  The appraiser must take into consideration the transportation requirements of the typical family and quantify the effect on value.

## H.   UTILITIES AND SERVICES

The appraiser must consider these utilities and neighborhood services: police and fire protection, telephone services, electricity, natural gas, garbage disposal, street lighting, water supply, sewage disposal, drainage, street improvements and maintenance.  Public services and utilities can affect value and must be quantified.  A lack of these services should be noted and quantified in the valuation analysis.

## I.   NEIGHBORHOOD CHANGE CONSIDERATIONS

As time passes, desirability changes residential areas in any location.  Therefore, give special consideration to the following:
   ◊   Infiltration of commercial, industrial or nonconforming use
   ◊   Positive and negative effect on value of gentrification

◊    Changes in the mobility of people (employment shifts)
◊    Weakly enforced zoning regulation or covenants

## J.  MARKETABILITY

The demand for home ownership in a neighborhood is directly related to the marketability of the homes in the neighborhood or in competitive neighborhoods.  Home ownership rates, vacancies and the marketing time of dwellings in a neighborhood help the appraiser determine the strength of market demand and the extent of supply.

## K.  SMALL COMMUNITY MARKET PREFERENCES

A small town may have its own set of standards in architectural design, livability, style of mechanical equipment, lot size, placement of structures, nature of street improvements and in all features of the physical property and environment.  Judge each in light of local standards and preferences.

## L.  OUTLYING SITES AND ISOLATED SITES

The segment of the market interested in purchasing homes in these sites compares the advantages and disadvantages of other outlying or isolated locations.

## M.  STUDY OF FUTURE UTILITY

The study of future utility is typically covered in the appraiser's Highest and Best Use Analysis and includes:
◊    Selecting possible uses
◊    Rejecting uses that are obviously lower or higher than the most probable use
◊    Analyzing differing motives of those buyers

The study of the future uses and utility of a particular property will lead the appraiser to the property's Highest and Best Use.

## N.  CONSIDERATION OF GENERAL TAXES AND SPECIAL ASSESSMENTS

When estimating value, account for general taxes and special assessments:
◊    General real estate taxes related to specific sites are a recurring periodic expense in the ownership of taxable real property and must be accounted for in the value estimate.
◊    Special assessments of various types are frequently an additional expense of ownership and must similarly be accounted for in the value estimate.

Determine the relative effect of the real estate tax and/or special assessment's burden on the desirability of the site.  Enter this information on the URAR.

### 1.  Assessment

The real estate tax liability is computed by multiplying the assessed value by the tax/millage rate, which is typically expressed in dollars per hundred or dollars per thousand of assessed value.  In the addendum to the VC, state the assessment, real estate tax liability and tax year.  State the assessed market value of the subject property in the addenda.
>    If there is no method to relate the assessment to market value, such as new construction where reasonable assessment may not exist, mark the assessed market value response as "N/ A".

### 2.  Special Assessment

A special assessment can be calculated in two ways:
◊    The same way as real estate taxes, or
◊    On a pro-rated basis

Determine how the special assessment is calculated and report the special assessment liability on the URAR.
>    If the property does not have special assessment, mark the URAR "N/A".
*For example:* An organization that services a community creates an annual operating budget.  Each property becomes liable for its percentage of that budget based on the percentage of front feet their property has compared to the total amount of front feet as a special assessment in this community.

## 2-2 SPECIAL NEIGHBORHOOD HAZARDS AND NUISANCES

Physical conditions in some neighborhoods are hazardous to the personal health and safety of residents and may endanger physical improvements.  These conditions include unusual topography, subsidence, flood zones, unstable soils, traffic hazards and various types of grossly offensive nuisances. When reporting the appraisal, consider site hazards and nuisances.
>    If site hazards exist and cannot be corrected but do not meet the level of unacceptability, the appraisal must be based upon the current state.
>    If the hazard and/or nuisance endangers the health and safety of the occupants or the marketability of the property, mark "YES" in VC-1 and return the unfinished appraisal to the lender.

The lender, who is ultimately responsible for rejecting the site, relies on the appraiser's site analysis to make this determination.  Guidelines for determining site acceptability follow.  The appraiser is required to note only those *readily observable* conditions.

## A.  UNACCEPTABLE SITES

FHA guidelines require that a site be rejected if the property being appraised is subject to hazards, environmental contaminants, noxious odors, offensive sights or excessive noises *to the point of endangering the physical improvements or affecting the livability of the property, its marketability or the health and safety of its occupants.* Rejection may also be appropriate if the future economic life of the property is shortened by obvious and compelling pressure to a higher use, making a long-term mortgage impractical. These considerations for rejection apply on a case-by-case basis, taking into account the needs and desires of the purchaser. For example, a site should not be considered unacceptable simply because it abuts a commercial use; some commercial uses may not appeal to a specific market segment while other commercial uses may. If the-condition is clearly a health and safety violation, reject the appraisal and return it to the lender. If there is any doubt as to the severity, report the condition and submit the completed report. The lender must clear the condition and may require an inspection or reject the property. For those conditions that cannot be repaired, such as site factors, the appraised value is based upon the existing conditions.

## B.  TOPOGRAPHY

There are special hazards caused by unique topography. For example, denuded slopes, soil erosion and landslides often adversely affect the marketability of hillside areas. When evaluating the site, consider earth and mud slides from adjoining properties, falling rocks and avalanches. These occurrences are associated with steep grades and must be considered in the site analysis.

## C.  SUBSIDENCE

Danger of subsidence is a special hazard that may be encountered under a variety of circumstances:

◊   Where buildings are constructed on uncontrolled fill or unsuitable soil containing foreign matter such as organic material
◊   Where the subsoil is unstable and subject to slippage or expansion

In mining areas, consider the depth or extent of mining operations and the site of operating or abandoned shafts or tunnels to determine if the danger is imminent, probable or negligible.

The appraiser must note any readily observable conditions, which indicate potential problems. Signs include fissure or cracks in the terrain, damaged foundations, sinkholes or settlement problems.

If there is a danger of subsidence, the specific site will be deemed ineligible unless complete and satisfactory evidence can be secured to establish that the probability of any threat is negligible.

>   If there is evidence of subsidence, the property is ineligible. Mark the "YES" column in VC-1 under subsidence.

## D.    OPERATING AND ABANDONED OIL OR GAS WELLS

Operating and abandoned oil and gas wells pose potential hazards to housing, including potential fire, explosion, spray and other pollution.

### 1.   Existing Construction

No existing dwelling may be located closer than 300 feet from an active or planned drilling site. Note that this applies to the site boundary, not to the actual well site.

### 2.   New or Proposed Construction

If an operating well is located in a single-family subdivision, no new or proposed construction may be built within 75 feet of the operating well unless mitigation measures are taken. This measure is designed to:

◊   Avoid nuisance during maintenance
◊   Diminish noise levels caused by pumping
◊   Reduce the likelihood of contamination by potential spills

The appraiser must examine the site for the existence of or any readily observable evidence of a well.

### 3.   Abandoned Well

A letter may be obtained from the responsible authority in the state government stating that the subject well was safely and permanently abandoned.

◊   When such a letter is provided, a dwelling may be located no closer than 10 feet from the abandoned well.
◊   When a letter is not provided, the dwelling must be located at least 300 feet from the abandoned well.

The lender is responsible for obtaining the letter; the appraiser must note the location of the well and verify the existence of the letter.

### 4.   Special Case - Proposed, Existing or Abandoned Wells

Hydrogen sulfide gas emitted from petroleum product wells is toxic and extremely hazardous. Minimum clearance from sour gas wells may be established only after a petroleum engineer has assessed the risk and state authorities have concurred on clearance recommendations for petroleum industry regulation and for public health and safety.

> If there is readily observable evidence that the conditions exist, mark the "YES" column in VC-1 under operating and abandoned wells.
> If an inspection by a qualified person verifies that the condition exists and is acceptable based on the standards defined above, account for the presence of wells in the valuation of the property.

## E.  SLUSH PITS

A slush pit is a basin in which drilling "mud" is mixed and circulated during drilling to lubricate and cool the drill bit and to flush away rock cuttings. Drilling mud normally contains large quantities of bentonite - a very expansive soil material. This results in a site with the potential for great soil volume change and, therefore, damage to structures. To be eligible for FHA mortgage insurance, all unstable and toxic materials must be removed and the pit must be filled with compacted selected materials.

> If a property is proposed near an active or abandoned well, call for a survey to locate the pits and their impact on the subject property.
> If there is any readily observable evidence of slush pits, mark the "YES" column in VC-1.

## F.   HEAVY TRAFFIC

Close proximity to heavily traveled roadways can have a negative effect on the marketability and value of sites because of excess noise and danger. Properties backing to freeways or other thoroughfares that are heavily screened or where traffic is well below grade and at a sufficient distance from the property may not affect value. For detailed noise acceptance levels, reference 24 CFR 51.103.

> If there is significant noise or unsafe traffic conditions that endanger the occupants or affect the marketability of the property, mark "YES" in VC-1.

Typically, traffic hazards cannot be corrected. Therefore, the appraiser must quantify the effect on value if the property is marketable. This adjustment should be supported by comparable transactions. This condition could be the reason that a lender ultimately rejects the property. Do not reject existing properties only because of heavy traffic if there is evidence of acceptance within the market and if use of the dwelling is expected to continue.

## G.  AIRPORT NOISE AND HAZARDS

Sites near, an airport may be subjected to the noise and hazards of low-flying aircraft. Appraisers must identify affected properties, review airport contour maps and condition the appraisal accordingly. Do not reject existing properties only because of airport influences if there is evidence of acceptance within the market and if use of the dwelling is expected to continue. HUD's position is that because the properties are in use and are expected to be in use into the near future, their marketability should be the strongest indicator of their acceptability. Marketability should account for the following:

◊   Plans for future expansion of airport facilities
◊   Prospective increases in the number of planes or flights using the field or specific runways
◊   The timing and frequency of the volume of flights
◊   Any other factors that may increase the annoyance of having the airport nearby excessive noise

If changes are likely, the appraiser must anticipate any adverse effect that these changes are likely to have on the marketability of the property. The appraiser should judge each situation on its merits. Compare the effect of aircraft activity on the desirability of a particular site with other sites that are:

◊   Improved with similar structures
◊   Considered competitive with those located in the subject neighborhood

## H.   SPECIAL AIRPORT HAZARDS

HUD requires that the buyer of a property located in a Runway Clear Zone/Clear Zone is advised that the property is located in such a zone and of the implications associated with that site. This includes the possibility that the airport operator could acquire the property in the future.

## 1.  New and Proposed Construction

New and proposed construction within Runway Clear Zones (also known as Runway Protection Zones) at civil airports or within Clear Zones at military airfields are ineligible for home mortgage insurance. Properties located in Accident Potential Zone I at military airfields may be eligible for FHA insurance provided that the property is compatible with Department of Defense guidelines. For more information, see 24 CFR 51.303(b). If new or proposed construction lies within these zones, mark "YES" in VC-1.

## 2.  Existing Construction

Existing dwellings more than one year old are eligible for FHA mortgage insurance if the prospective purchaser acknowledges awareness that the property is located in a Runway Clear Zone/Clear Zone. The lender will furnish this disclosure form to the buyer. For a sample of the buyer's acknowledgment certification, see HUD Handbook 4150.1, REV-1, Chapters 4-26 (a) and (b).

> Note whether the property is in a Clear Zone and condition the appraisal on the buyer's acknowledgment.

## I.  PROXIMITY TO HIGH PRESSURE GAS

A dwelling or related property improvement near high-pressure gas, liquid petroleum pipelines or other volatile and explosive products - both above ground and subsurface must be located outside of the outer boundary of the pipeline easement.

> If the property is less than ten feet away, mark "YES" in VC-1.

## J.  OVERHEAD HIGH-VOLTAGE TRANSMISSION LINES

No dwelling or related property improvement may be located within the engineering (designed) fall distance of any pole, tower or support structure of a high-voltage transmission line, radio/TV transmission tower, microwave relay dish or tower or satellite dish (radio, TV cable, etc.).  For field analysis, the appraiser may use tower height as the fall distance. For the purpose of this Handbook, a High-Voltage Electric Transmission Line is a power line that carries high voltage between a generating plant and a substation.  These lines are usually 60 Kilovolts (kV) and greater, and are considered hazardous.  Lines with capacity of 12-60 kV and above are considered high voltage for the purpose of this Handbook.  High voltage lines do not include local distribution and service lines. Low voltage power lines are distribution lines that commonly supply power to housing developments and similar facilities.  These lines are usually 12 kV or less and are considered to be a minimum hazard.  These lines may not pass directly over any structure, including pools, on the property being insured by HUD.

> If the property is within the unacceptable distance, mark "YES" in VC-1.

## K.  SMOKE, FUMES, OFFENSIVE NOISES AND ODORS

Excessive smoke, fog, chemical fumes, noxious odors, stagnant ponds or marshes, poor surface drainage and excessive dampness are hazardous to the health of neighborhood occupants and adversely affect the market value of the subject property.

> If these conditions threaten the health and safety of the occupants or the marketability of the property, mark "YES" in VC-1.  If, however, the extent of the hazard is not dangerous, account for its effect in the valuation of the property.
> Include other factors that may affect valuation such as offensive odors and unsightly neighborhood features such as stables or kennels.

## L.  FLOOD HAZARD AREAS

### Designation of Special Flood Hazard Areas

The Federal Emergency Management Agency (FEMA) determines Special Flood Hazard Areas nationwide, (SFHA).  FEMA issues Flood Hazard Boundary Maps to designate these areas in a community.  A special flood hazard may be designated as Zone A, AO, AH, Al-30, AE, A99, VO or Vl-30, VE or V.

◊  Only those properties within zones 'A' and 'V' require flood insurance.

◊  Zones 'B' or 'C' do not require flood insurance because FEMA designates only zones 'A' and 'V as "Special Flood Hazard Areas."

An appraisal report with a positive indication in a Special Flood Hazard Area (SFHA) activates a commitment requirement for flood insurance coverage.  The appraiser must quantify the effect on value, if any, for properties within a designated flood map. A lender shall reject a property in any of these circumstances:

◊  If the property is subject to frequently recurring flooding

◊  If there is any potential hazard to life or safety

◊  If escape to higher ground would not be feasible during severe flooding conditions

FEMA Maps:  For copies of FEMA's Flood Hazard Boundary Maps and Flood Insurance Rate Maps, contact:
Federal Emergency Management Agency (FEMA)
FEMA Map Service Center
P.O. Box 1038
Jessup, MD 20794-1038
Phone: 1-800-358-9616    Fax: 1-800-358-9620

### Eligibility of Properties for FHA Insurance

The lender is responsible for determining the eligibility of properties in Flood Zones, and relies on the appraiser's notation on the URAR.

### 1.  New and Proposed Construction

If any part of the property improvements essential to the property value and subject to flood damage are located within the 100-year floodplain, then the entire property, improved and otherwise, is ineligible for FHA mortgage insurance unless a Letter of Map Amendment (LOMA) or a Letter of Map Revision (LOMR) is submitted with the case for endorsement. Proposed construction where improvements are located, or to be located, within a designated Special Flood Hazard Area (SFHA) is ineligible for FHA insurance.  This is true regardless of whether the property is covered or will be covered by flood insurance unless the lender can furnish evidence of a LOMA, a LOMR or evidence that the property is not in a SFHA. For existing properties located in a SFHA, make the appropriate notation in the URAR.

> If the proposed improvements are located in a SFHA and there is no LOMA or LOMR mark "YES" in VC-1 and return the unfinished appraisal to the lender until these documents are retrieved.

### 2. Existing Construction

Market attitude and acceptance determine the eligibility of existing properties located in a designated SFHA. Flood insurance is required for properties accepted for mortgage insurance in a FEMA-designated SFHA.

### 3. Condominium

The Homeowners Association is responsible for maintaining flood insurance on the project as a whole, not each individual unit. The appraiser must verify the location of a condominium in the floodplain and make the correct notation in the URAR.

## M. STATIONARY STORAGE TANKS

Stationary Storage tanks containing flammable or explosive material pose potential hazards to housing, including hazards from fire and explosions.

> If the property is within 300 feet of a stationary, storage tank containing more than 1000 gallons of flammable or explosive material, the site is ineligible. Mark "YES" in VC-1 and return the unfinished appraisal to the lender.

# 3    PROPERTY ANALYSIS

## 3-0 INTRODUCTION

The FHA guidelines for property analysis include specific requirements to which appraisers must adhere for the appraisal to reflect an accurate valuation that win:

◊ Denote any deficiencies in the subject property
◊ Protect HUD's interest in that property

The property analysis includes General Acceptability Criteria for conducting the appraisal to address FHA minimum property requirements.

## 3-1 APPRAISAL REQUIREMENTS

◊ The appraiser must make a complete visual inspection of the subject property - interior and exterior - and complete the VC form.
◊ The appraiser must take photographs that show the sides, front and rear of the subject property and all improvements on the subject property with any contributory value. A photograph of the street frontage is also required.
◊ The appraiser is required to submit a single photograph of each comparable sale transaction in the addenda to the appraisal report.
◊ The map of proposed construction must clearly show proposed roadways.
◊ The appraiser must provide a copy of a local street map that shows the location of the property and each comparable sale.
◊ If the subject property is proposed construction and the improvement has not started, the appraiser should take a photograph that shows the grade of the vacant lot.

## 3-2 ANALYSIS OF SITE

For both proposed and existing construction, the appraiser must determine the present highest and best use for the site, disregarding improvements that may exist or are proposed for the site. This conclusion serves as the basis of comparison for estimating the market price of the land and discloses the extent to which the existing or proposed building improvements are appropriate or inappropriate for the site. This also forms the basis for selecting comparable land sales. The appraiser must analyze the site to:

◊ Establish the basis for comparing the market estimates of sites in the estimate of replacement cost of the property
◊ Determine suitability for the existing or proposed use

Carefully consider the topography, suitability of soil, off-site improvements, easements, restrictions or encroachments.

### A. TOPOGRAPHY

Proper topography and site grading can be important elements in preventing wet basements, damp crawl spaces, erosion of soils, and overflowing sewage disposal systems. To ensure proper protection, the appraiser must analyze the relationship of street grades, floor elevations, and lot grades. If the foundation or its bearing soils may be affected by seepage or frost, the dwelling is unacceptable unless the surface and subsurface water is diverted from the structures to ensure positive drainage away from the foundation.

### B. SUITABILITY OF SOIL

Consider the readily observable soil and subsoil conditions of the site including the type and permeability of the soil, the location of the water table, surface drainage conditions, compaction, rock formations and other physical features that affect the value of the site or its suitability for development.  Also observe the effects of the adverse features of the adjoining land.

## C.  OFF-SITE IMPROVEMENTS
Consider the off-site improvements adjoining the subject property, including street surface, curbs, sidewalks, curb cuts, driveways, aprons, etc., that are not contained within the legal boundaries of the site but enhance the market acceptance and the use and livability of the property.  Also consider these situations:
　　◊　Compare the subject property with the immediate neighborhood to determine the dominant off-site improvements required by the market.  Note any necessary off-site improvements that are not in existence or are proposed for the subject property and adjust for them in the market value.
　　◊　Any proposals for installing off-site improvements and levying assessments by the local governing body in the near future may affect value.  These proposals will necessitate a commitment condition that requires the installation of improvements and the payment of the assessment before or immediately after insurance endorsement.

## D.  EASEMENTS, RESTRICTIONS OR ENCROACHMENTS
Consider all easements, restrictions or encroachments and their impact on the market value of the subject property and list them on the appraisal.  These factors are often discovered during the survey and title report once the appraisal has begun.  Perform limited due diligence to verify the existence of these types of significant limiting factors.  Also record these items in the URAR which were considered in the value estimate.

## E.  ENCROACHMENTS
As a general rule, an encroachment will cause a property to be ineligible for FHA mortgage insurance.  However, there are exceptions to this rule and further information can be found by calling the lender.  The appraiser should identify any of these conditions:
　　◊　Encroachment of a dwelling, garage, another physical structure or other improvement onto an adjacent property, right-of-way or utility easement
　　◊　Encroachment of a dwelling, garage, another physical structure or improvements on the subject property
　　◊　Encroachment of a dwelling, garage or another physical structure into the setback requirement
An encroachment may be acceptable if the adjoining landowner or the local governing authority provides a perpetual encroachment easement that is filed in the County Clerk and Recorder's Office.  The Direct Endorsement under-writer will handle this issue under the General Waiver guidelines.

## 3-3 ANALYSIS OF PHYSICAL IMPROVEMENTS
Analysis of the physical improvements results in conclusions as to the desirability, utility and appropriateness of the physical improvements as factors in determining mortgage risk and the ultimate estimate of value.

## A.  GROSS LIVING AREA
Gross Living Area is the total area of finished, above-grade residential space.  It is calculated by measuring the outside perimeter of the structure and includes only finished, habitable, above-grade living space.  Finished basements and unfinished attic areas are not included in total gross living area.  The appraiser must match the measurement techniques used for the subject to the comparable sales.  It is important to apply this measurement technique and report the building dimensions consistently because failure to do so can impair the quality of the appraisal report.

## B.  BASEMENT BEDROOMS, BASEMENT APARTMENTS
As a rule basement space does not count as habitable space.  If the bedroom does not have proper light and ventilation, the room can not be included in the gross living area.  The following requirements apply to the valuation of below-grade rooms:
　　◊　The windowsill may not be higher than 44 inches from the floor.
　　◊　The windowsill must have a net clear opening (width x height) of at least 24 inches by 36 inches.
　　◊　The window should be at ground level; however, compensating factors may allow less.
In all cases, use reasonable care and judgment.  If these standards are not substantially met, the basement area cannot be counted as habitable space.

## C.  DESIGN
Design is the cohesive element that blends the structural, functional and decorative elements of a property into a whole.  With good design, the property's parts will be in harmony (each part with all the other parts).  The whole property, in turn, will be in harmony with its immediate site and environment. Because good design is recognized and desired, the economic life of properties and neighborhoods will be extended and prices will typically exceed those for properties offering the same number of rooms and area but lacking good design.  This competitive advantage usually continues through the entire economic life of the property. The appraiser must recognize this demonstrable price differential and reflect it in the comparative adjustments of market data and the final finding of value.

## D. CONFORMITY OF PROPERTY TO NEIGHBORHOOD

A residential property with good physical characteristics may not necessarily be good security for a mortgage loan, even if it is situated in a good location. The property may be entirely appropriate at another location, but not in its actual location. The property may be displeasing when viewed in relation to its surroundings, and it may not conform in other respects to the most marketable use in the particular neighborhood. When determining the effect of property-neighborhood relationships to marketability, consider elements other than similarity of physical characteristics.

**Analysis of the Elements of Conformity.** Analysis of Conformity requires consideration of Suitability of Use-Type, Appropriateness of Functional Characteristics, Harmony of Design and Relation of Expense of Ownership to Family Income Levels.

◊  *Suitability of Use-Type.* The term Use-Type refers to the use for which a dwelling is designed - single-family, two-family, etc. In most neighborhoods only one use-type is suitable. In some neighborhoods, however, because of their heterogeneous development, several use-types may be found suitable.

◊  *Appropriateness of Functional Characteristics.* Functional Characteristics refer to the living facilities provided in a residential property. They relate to site use and to arrangement, number and size of rooms. Usually well-defined neighborhood market preferences are observable.

Nonconformity may exist because of the placement of the house on the site. Carefully consider any deviation from the accustomed or accepted placement to determine whether it adversely affects desirability. If a site is substantially smaller than the size typical in the neighborhood, marketability may be limited. The shape or topography of a particular lot may make it less desirable than those typical of the area. The number, arrangement and size of rooms frequently conform to definite preferences in given neighborhoods. In some localities where one-story dwellings dominate, a two-story dwelling may meet considerable market resistance.

◊  *Harmony of Design.* Conformity of the exterior design of a structure with other structures in the immediate neighborhood is not important unless it contrasts inharmoniously with them. There may be considerable variety in the exterior design of dwellings in a neighborhood and yet each may present a pleasing appearance when viewed in relation to its surroundings. On the other hand, a dwelling may be without any architectural faults and yet clash so violently with the design of neighboring properties that marketability may be seriously limited.

◊  *Relation of Ownership Expense to Family Incomes.* Families usually select homes in neighborhoods where typical occupants have financial means similar to their own. A home that is too costly for these families to purchase or maintain will have limited marketability.

## 3-4  REMAINING ECONOMIC LIFE OF BUILDING IMPROVEMENTS

Because a building is subject to physical deterioration and obsolescence, its period of usefulness is limited. As a building deteriorates or becomes obsolete, its ability to serve useful purposes decreases and eventually ends. This may occur gradually or rapidly.

### A.  ECONOMIC LIFE VS.  PHYSICAL LIFE

◊  The *total physical life* of a building is the period from the time of completion until it is no longer fit or safe for use or when maintaining the building in a safe, usable manner is no longer practicable.

◊  The *total economic life* of a building is the period of time from its completion until it can no longer produce services or net returns over and above a return on the land value.

Economic life can never be longer than the physical life, but may be and frequently is shorter. A structure that is sound and in good physical condition with many years of physical life remaining may have reached the end of its economic life - if its remaining years of physical usefulness will not be profitable.

### B.  ESTIMATION OF REMAINING ECONOMIC LIFE

In predicting the remaining economic life of a building, consider these factors:

◊  The economic background of the community or region and the need for accommodations of the type represented

◊  The relationship between the property and the immediate environment the architectural design, style and utility from a functional point of view and the likelihood of obsolescence attributable to new inventions, new materials and changes in tastes

◊  The trends and rate of change of characteristics of the neighborhood and their effect on land values

◊  Workmanship, durability of construction and the rate with which natural forces cause physical deterioration

◊  The physical condition and probable cost of maintenance and repair, the maintenance policy of owners and occupants and the use or abuse to which structures are subjected

### C.  END OF USEFUL LIFE OF BUILDING IMPROVEMENTS

The useful life of a building has come to an end:

◊     When the building can no longer produce annual income or services sufficient to offset maintenance expense, insurance and taxes to produce returns on the value of the land

AND

◊     When rehabilitation is not feasible

The improvements on the lot at the time have no more value than the amount obtainable from a purchaser who will buy them and remove them from the site.

## 3-5  CODE ENFORCEMENT FOR EXISTING PROPERTIES

Local municipalities design local housing code standards; therefore, enforcement of such housing standards rests with the local authority.  HUD does not have the authority or the responsibility for enforcing local housing codes except for mortgages on properties to be insured under Section 221(d)(2)-a program with mortgage limits at $36,000.  Loans insured under Section 221(d)(2) of the National Housing Act require code enforcement.  The appraiser should contact the lender for further instructions if the mortgage is to be insured under Section 221(d)(2).

## 3-6  GENERAL ACCEPTABILITY CRITERIA FOR FHA-INSURED MORTGAGES

These criteria define standards for existing properties to be eligible for FHA mortgage insurance.  Underwriters bear primary responsibility for determining eligibility; however, the appraiser is the on-site representative for the lender and provides preliminary verification that these standards have been met.  Many of the requirements are technical and beyond the expertise of the appraiser.  They are presented here for reference, and the appraiser's responsibility is noted by category.  These criteria form the basis for identifying the deficiencies of the property that the appraiser must note in the VC form and that must be addressed by the lender before closing.  When examination of existing construction reveals noncompliance with the General Acceptability Criteria, an appropriate specific condition to correct the deficiency is required if correction is feasible.  If correction is not feasible and compliance can be effected only by major repairs or alterations, the lender will reject the property.  The appraiser is only required to note conditions that are readily observable.

**As-Repaired Appraisal.**  The appraiser prepares the valuation "as-repaired" subject to the conditions noted on the VC form.  Those items not listed on the VC will form the basis of comparison to comparable properties for physical conditions.  *Required repairs are limited to those repairs necessary to preserve the continued marketability of the property and to protect the health and safety of the occupants.*

**Deferred Maintenance.**  Any operable or useful element that will have reached the end of its useful life within two years should be replaced.  With respect to such deferred maintenance items, exercise good judgment in requiring repair.

**Replacement Because of Age.**  If an element is functioning well, do not recommend replacement simply because of its age.
>    If the septic system shows evidence of failure because of age, recommend a specific inspection.

**Valuation Conditions.**  The Valuation Conditions Form and its protocol help the appraiser evaluate the standards required by the General Acceptability Criteria.  The criteria are described below.  The appraiser must ascertain if the condition called for exists and mark yes if it does.
>    If the observed deficiencies exist, mark "YES" in the appropriate location on the Valuation Conditions Form, condition the appraisal on the requirement for repair or further inspection and prepare the appraisal "as-repaired" subject to the satisfaction of the condition.

The following guidelines are HUD's General Acceptability Criteria for existing properties.  They provide general guidance for determining the property's eligibility for FHA mortgage insurance.  For instructions on filling out the VC form, see the protocol in Appendix D.

### A.  GENERAL ACCEPTABILITY CRITERIA

These minimum requirements for existing housing apply to existing buildings and to the sites on which they are located.  The buildings may be:

◊     Detached
◊     Semidetached
◊     Multiplex
◊     Row houses
◊     Individual condominium units

These requirements also cover the immediate site environment for the dwelling, including streets, other services and facilities associated with the site.

### 1.  Subject Property

The subject property must be adequately identified as a single, marketable real estate entity.  However, a primary plot with a secondary plot for an appurtenant garage or for another use contributing to the marketability of the property will be acceptable if the two plots are contiguous and comprise a readily marketable real estate entity.

## 2.   Hazards
The property must be free of all known hazards and adverse conditions that:
◊   May affect the health and safety of the occupants
◊   May affect the structural soundness of the improvements
◊   May impair the customary use and enjoyment of the property

These hazards include toxic chemicals, radioactive materials, other pollution, hazardous activities, potential damage from soil or other differential ground movements, ground water, inadequate surface drainage, flood, erosion, excessive noise and other hazards on or off site.

>   If the property meets the acceptability guidelines in the VC protocol (Appendix D), quantify the deficiency's impact in the property valuation.
>   If the property does not meet the acceptability guidelines, note the appropriate hazard in VC-1 and explain.

In the appraisal of new and proposed construction, special conditions may exist or arise during construction that were unforeseen and necessitate precautionary or hazard mitigation measures.  HUD will require corrective work to mitigate potential adverse effects from the special conditions as necessary.  Special conditions include:
◊   Rock formations
◊   Unstable soils or slopes
◊   High ground water levels
◊   Springs
◊   Other conditions that may have a negative effect on the property value

The builder must ensure proper design, construction and satisfactory performance when any of these issues are present. For specific instructions about noting this information in the VC form, see VC-1 in the protocol (Appendix D).

## 3.   Soil Contamination
a.   Septic and Sewage
If a septic system is part of the subject property, the appraiser must determine whether the area is free of conditions that adversely affect the operation of the system.  Consider the following:
◊   The type of system
◊   Topography
◊   Depth to ground water
◊   Soil permeability
◊   The type of soil to a depth several feet below the surface

If in doubt about the operation of sewage disposal systems in the neighborhood, mark "YES" in VC-2, condition the appraisal on further inspection and prepare the appraisal "as-repaired" subject to satisfaction of the condition. The lender will contact the local health authority or a professional to determine the viability of the system.

b.   Other Soil Contaminants
The following conditions may indicate unacceptable levels of soil contamination: pools of liquid, pits, ponds, lagoons, stressed vegetation, stained soils or pavement, drums or odors.
>   If there is evidence of hazardous substances in the soil, require further inspection.  Mark "YES" in VC-2, condition the appraisal on further inspection and prepare the appraisal "as-repaired" subject to the satisfaction of condition.

c.   Underground Storage Tanks
During the site inspection, the appraiser must walk the property and search for readily observable evidence of underground storage tanks.  Evidence would include fill pipes, pumps, ventilation caps, etc.
>   If there is evidence of underground storage tanks, require further analysis.  Mark "YES" in VC-2, condition the appraisal on that requirement and prepare the appraisal "as-repaired" subject to the satisfaction of the condition.

## 4.   Drainage
The site must be graded to provide positive drainage away from the perimeter walls of the dwelling and to prevent standing water on the site.  Signs of inadequate draining include standing water proximate to the structure and no mitigation measures such as gutters or downspouts. For specific instructions about noting this information in the VC form, see VC-3 in the protocol (Appendix D).
>   If drainage is inadequate and needs improvement, mark "YES" in VC-3, make a repair requirement, condition the appraisal on that requirement and prepare the appraisal "as-repaired" subject to the satisfaction of the condition.

## 5.   Water Supply And Sewage Systems
Each living unit must contain the following:
◊   Domestic hot water

◊   A continuing and sufficient supply of potable water under adequate pressure and of appropriate quality for all household uses

◊   Sanitary facilities and a safe method of sewage disposal

Connection must be made to a public water/sewer system or a community water/sewer system, if connection costs to the public or community system are reasonable (3% or less of the estimated value of the property). If connection costs exceed 3%, the existing on-site systems will be acceptable provided they are functioning properly and meet the requirements of the local health department.

>    If the correction is feasible, require connection. Mark "YES" in VC-4, condition the appraisal on the requirement and prepare the appraisal "as repaired" subject to the satisfaction of the condition.

a.   Individual Water Supply and Sewage Disposal Systems

If water and sewer systems are not connected to public systems, the water well and/or septic system must meet the requirements of the local health authority with jurisdiction. If the local authority does not have specific requirements, the maximum contaminant levels established by the Environmental Protection Agency (EPA) will apply. If the authority is unable to perform the water quality analysis in a timely manner, a private commercial testing laboratory or a licensed sanitary engineer acceptable to the authority may take and test water samples.

◊   Each living unit must be provided with a sewage disposal system that is adequate to dispose of all domestic wastes and does not create a nuisance or in any way endanger the public health.

◊   Individual pit privies are permitted where such facilities are customary and are the only feasible means of waste disposal and, if they are installed in accordance with the recommendations of the local Department of Health.

>    If there is a well or septic system on the property, mark "YES" in VC4, condition the appraisal on further inspection by the lender and prepare the appraisal "as-repaired" subject to satisfaction of the condition.

A domestic well must be a minimum of 50 feet from a septic tank, 100 feet from the septic tank's drain field and a minimum of 10 feet from any property line.

>    Clearly show the location of private wells and septic systems on the site sketch and note the distance between the two.

b.   Unacceptable Conditions

The following water well conditions are unacceptable and must be noted in VC-4:

◊   Mechanical chlorinators

◊   Water flow that decreases noticeably when simultaneously running water in several plumbing fixtures (the well may not be able to provide a continuous, adequate supply of water)

◊   Properties served by dug wells unless a complete survey conducted by an engineer was delivered to the lender and subsequently given to the appraiser

◊   Properties served by springs, lakes, rivers or cisterns (3-6)

To be considered acceptable, the engineer's survey must include these items:

◊   A health report with no qualifications

◊   Indication that an inoperative well was cased, sealed and capped with concrete to a depth of at least 20 feet

◊   A pump test indicating a flow of at least 3-5 gallons per minute supply for an existing well, and 5 gallons per minute for a new well

◊   An acceptable septic report

◊   No indication of exposure to environmental contamination, mechanical chlorination or anything else that adversely affects health and safety

>    If these requirements for individual wells or septic tanks are not met, note them in VC-4 and prepare the appraisal "as-repaired" subject to further inspection.

The lender will require the engineer's follow-up report and will arrange for any required corrective measures.


## 6.   Wood Structural Components: Termites

Termites can cause serious problems in the wood structural components of a house and may go undetected for a long period of time. FHA requires maximum assurances that a home is free of any infestation. A pest inspection is always required for:

◊   Any structure that is ground level

◊   Any structure where the wood touches ground

Structures in a geographic area with no active termite infestation may not require a pest inspection. However, the appraiser must always note:

◊   Any infestation

◊   Any damage resulting from previous infestation

◊   Whether damage from infestation has been repaired or is in need of repair

Observe all areas of the property that have potential for termite infestation, including the bottoms of exterior doors and frames, and wood siding in contact with the ground and crawl spaces. Examine mud tunnels running from the ground up the side of the house for possible evidence of termite infestation.

>    If there is any evidence of termite infestation, require an inspection by a reputable licensed termite company. Mark

"YES" in VC-5, condition the appraisal on the requirement and prepare the appraisal "as-repaired" subject to the satisfaction of the condition.

For specific instructions on noting this information in the VC Form, see VC-5 in the protocol (Appendix D).

## 7.  Streets

Each property must be provided with safe and adequate pedestrian and vehicular access from a public or private street. Private streets must be protected by permanent recorded easements and have joint maintenance agreements or be owned and maintained by a HOA. All streets must provide all-weather access to all buildings for essential and emergency use, including access for deliveries, service, maintenance and fire equipment.  FHA defines *all-weather surface* as a road surface over which emergency vehicles can pass in all types of weather.  Streets must either be:

   ◊   Dedicated to public use and maintenance

 OR

   ◊   Retained as private streets protected by permanent recorded easements (when approved by HUD)

> If these requirements are not met, mark "YES" in VC-6 and prepare the appraisal "as-repaired" subject to the correction of this deficiency.

## 8.  Defective Conditions

A property with defective conditions is unacceptable until the defects or conditions have been remedied and the probability of further damage eliminated.  Defective conditions include:

   ◊   Defective construction
   ◊   Poor workmanship
   ◊   Evidence of continuing settlement
   ◊   Excessive dampness
   ◊   Leakage
   ◊   Decay
   ◊   Termites
   ◊   Other readily observable conditions that impair the safety, sanitation or structural soundness of the dwelling

The items outlined in VC-7: Structural Conditions, are meant to alert the appraiser and the lender to the possibility of defective conditions.  These items are readily identifiable characteristics that could indicate one of the defective conditions.

## 9.  Ventilation

Natural ventilation of structural space - such as attics and crawl spaces - must be provided to reduce the effect of excess heat and moisture that are conducive to decay and deterioration of the structure.  All attics must have ventilation to allow moisture and excessive heat to escape.  The appraiser must check the attic areas to determine whether the ventilation is adequate.

> If ventilation is not provided, make a condition for repair, mark "YES" in VC7 and prepare the appraisal 'as-repaired' subject to the satisfaction of the condition.

## 10.  Foundations

All foundations must be adequate to withstand all normal loads imposed.  Stone and brick foundations are acceptable if they are in good condition.  The appraiser must review the conditions in VC-8 for evidence of conditions that could indicate safety or structural deficiencies that may require repair.

> If the foundation is deficient, mark "YES" in VC-8 and prepare the appraisal "as-repaired" subject to the repair of the deficiencies.

## 11.  Crawl Space

To ensure against conditions that could cause the property to deteriorate and seriously affect the marketability of the property, it is required that:

   ◊   There must be adequate access to the crawl space; the appraiser must be able to access the crawl space for inspection. Access is defined as ability to visually examine all areas the crawl space. Specifically, the minimum distance is 18 inches.
   ◊   The floor joists must be sufficiently above ground level to provide access for maintaining and repairing ductwork and plumbing.
   ◊   The crawl space must be clear of all debris and trash and must be properly vented.
   ◊   The crawl space must not be excessively damp and must not have any water ponding.

> If these requirements are not met, mark 'YES" in VC-8 and prepare the appraisal "as-repaired" subject to repair of the deficiency.

## 12.  Roof

The covering must prevent moisture from entering and must provide reasonable future utility, durability and economy of maintenance.  When re-roofing is needed for a defective roof that has three layers of shingles, all old shingles must be removed before re-roofing. The details of the process are provided in the protocol. The appraiser must observe the roof to determine whether the deficiencies present a health and safety hazard or do not allow for reasonable future utility. The appraiser is only required to note readily observable conditions.

> If the roof is deficient, mark "YES" in VC-9 and prepare the appraisal "as repaired" subject to the repair of the deficiency. Flat roofs typically have shorter life spans and therefore require inspection.

> If there is a flat roof mark "YES" in VC-9 and prepare the appraisal "as repaired" subject to further inspection.

### 13. Mechanical Systems

These are the requirements for mechanical systems:

◊    Must be safe to operate

◊    Must be protected from destructive elements

◊    Must have reasonable future utility, durability and economy

◊    Must have adequate capacity and quality

The appraiser must observe the systems in VC-10 and determine if any of the conditions do not meet the above stated criteria.

> If the systems require repair, mark "YES' in VC-10, condition the appraisal on the repair or further inspection and prepare the appraisal "as-repaired" subject to the satisfaction of the condition.

> If systems could not be operated due to weather conditions, explain that in VC-10, condition the appraisal on assumed functionality, and make a note of this condition on the Homebuyer Summary - Part 3 of the Comprehensive Valuation Package.

### 14. Heating

Heating must be adequate for healthful and comfortable living conditions:

◊    Dwellings that use wood-burning stoves or solar systems as a primary heat source must have permanently installed conventional heating systems that can maintain a temperature of at least 50 degrees F. in areas containing plumbing systems. These systems must be installed in accordance with the manufacturer's recommendations.

◊    Properties with electric heating sources must have an acceptable electric service that meets the general requirements of the local municipal standards.

◊    All water heaters must have a non-adjustable temperature and pressure-relief valve. If the water heater is in the garage, it must comply with local building codes.

◊    All non-conventional heating systems - space heaters and others - must comply with local jurisdictional guidelines.

Solar energy systems are discussed in Appendix B.

### 15. Electricity

Electricity must be available for lighting and for equipment used in the living unit. Refer to the specific instructions in the protocol (Appendix D) for determining adequate electricity.

### 16. Other Health And Safety Deficiencies

The appraiser must note and make a repair requirement for any health or safety deficiencies as they relate to the subject property, including:

◊    Broken windows, doors or steps

◊    Inadequate or blocked doors

◊    Steps without a handrail

◊    Others

The appraiser must operate a representative number of windows, interior doors and all exterior and garage doors, as well as verify that the electric garage door operator will reverse or stop when met with resistance during closing. If conditions exist that require repair, mark "YES" in VC-11 and prepare the appraisal "as-repaired" subject to the satisfaction of the condition.

### 17. Lead-Based Paint And Other Hazards

If the home was built before 1978, the appraiser should note the condition and location of all defective paint in the home. Inspect all interior and exterior surfaces - wars, stairs, deck porch, railing, windows and doors - for defective paint (chipping, flaking or peeling). Exterior surfaces include those surfaces on fences, detached garages, storage sheds and other outbuildings and appurtenant structures.

> If there is evidence of defective paint surfaces, condition the appraisal on their repair, mark "YES" in VC-12 and prepare the appraisal "as-repaired" subject to the satisfaction of the condition.

For condominium units, the appraiser needs to inspect only the exterior surfaces and appurtenant structures of the unit being appraised and address the overall condition, maintenance and appearance of the condominium project.

> If the condominium project was built before 1978 and shows signs of excessive deferred maintenance or defective paint, mark "YES" in VC-13 and prepare the appraisal "as-repaired" subject to the satisfaction of the condition.

## B.   OTHER CRITERIA

There are other eligibility criteria that are not part of the VC form.  The lender bears primary responsibility for these; however, they are provided here so that the appraiser may reference them if questions arise during the property inspection.

### 1.   Party Or Lot Line Wall

There must be adequate space based upon market acceptability between buildings to permit maintenance of the exterior walls for detached homes.

### 2.   Service And Facilities

**Trespass.**  Each living unit must have the capacity to be maintained individually without trespassing on adjoining properties.

**Utilities.**  Utilities must be independent for each living unit except that common services - water, sewer, gas and electricity - may be provided for living units under a single mortgage or ownership.

- ◊   Each unit must have separate utility service shut-offs.
- ◊   Each unit must have individual meters.
- ◊   For living units under separate ownership, common utility services may be provided from the main service to the building line when protected by an easement or covenant and maintenance agreement acceptable to HUD.
- ◊   Individual utilities serving a unit must not pass over, under or through another unit, unless:
    - o   Provisions have been made for repairing and maintaining those utilities without trespassing on adjoining properties.

    OR

    - o   An easement of covenant is made for permanent right of access for maintenance and repair of utilities.
- ◊   If a single drain line in the building serves more than one unit, the building drain clean-outs must be accessible from the exterior.
- ◊   Other facilities must be independent for each living unit, except common services, such as laundry and storage space or heating, may be provided for two-to-four-living-unit buildings under a single mortgage.

**Dedication.**  Utilities must be located on easements that have been permanently dedicated to the local government or appropriate public utility body.  This information must be recorded on the deed record so that the utility services match the easement.

### 3.   Non-Residential Use Design Limitations

A qualified property must be predominantly residential in use and appearance.  Any nonresidential use of the property must be subordinate to its residential use, character and appearance.  A property, any portion of which is designed or used for nonresidential purposes, is eligible only if the type or extent of the nonresidential use does not impair and/or remove the property's residential character and appearance.

### 4.   Access Onto Property

Access to the living unit must be provided without passing through any other living unit.  Access to the rear yard must be provided without passing through any other living unit.  For a row-type dwelling, the access may be by an alley, easement or passage through the dwelling.

### 5.   Space Requirements

Each living unit must have the space necessary to ensure suitable living, sleeping, cooking and dining accommodations and sanitation facilities.

### 6.   Bedroom Egress

All bedrooms must have adequate egress to the exterior of the home.  If an enclosed patio (solid walls) covers the bedroom window, it is possible that the bedroom won't qualify as a habitable bedroom.  Security bars are acceptable if they comply with local fire codes.  Occupants of a bedroom must be able to get outside the home if there is a fire.

### 7.   Energy Efficiency

For new and proposed construction and properties less than one year old, all detached one- and two-family dwellings and one-family townhouses not more than three stories in height must comply with the CABO Model Energy Code, 1992 Edition, Residential Buildings, except for sections 101.3.1, 101.3.2, 104 and 105.  These sections remain:

- ◊   Section 101.3.2.2, Historic Buildings
- ◊   The Appendix

◊   HUD Intermediate MPS Supplement 4930.2 Solar Heating and Domestic Hot Water Systems, 1989 edition

Valuation procedures for solar energy systems can be found in Appendix B.3.

## C.  CONDITIONS NOT REQUIRING REPAIRS

Conditions that do not ordinarily require repair include any surface treatment, beautification or adornment not required for the preservation of the property. These are some examples:

◊   A wood floor's finish that has worn off to expose the bare wood must be sanded and refinished.  However, a wood floor that has darkened with age but has an acceptable finish does not need polishing or refinishing.

◊   Peeling interior paint and broken or seriously cracked plaster or sheetrock require repair and repainting, but paint that is adequate though not fresh does not need to be redone.

◊   Missing shrubbery or dead grass on an existing property does not need to be replaced.

◊   Cleaning or removing carpets is required only when they are so badly soiled that they affect the livability and/or marketability of the property.

◊   Installing paved driveways or aprons should not be required if there is an otherwise acceptable surface.

◊   Installing curbs, gutters or partial street paving is not required unless assessment for the same is imminent.

◊   Complete replacement of tile floors is not necessary if some tiles do not match, etc.

Avoid unnecessary requirements because they increase housing cost without adding any basic amenities to the property.

## D.  REPAIR CONDITIONS FOR NEW/PROPOSED CONSTRUCTION

The appraiser must develop the cost approach for new or proposed construction and the normal site development costs must be included in the lot value.  Where unusual cuts, fills, retaining walls, etc. are necessary to prepare the site for the proposed building improvements, estimate the amount by which the cost of the work exceeds the cost of preparing typical sites for similar structures from the Marshall and Swift Cost Handbook.  This estimate supplements the estimate of the replacement cost of building improvements.

◊   When estimating the market price of a site with unusual site characteristics that must be corrected, assume that the site is in the condition that will exist after the corrective work is completed.  Disregard the cost of the treatment, but use the value of the improved site in the estimate of the replacement cost of the property.

◊   Use the supplemental cost estimate to:
  o   Determine the extent to which the replacement cost of the property will exceed the cost of a substitute property produced by constructing identical  improvements on a typical site
  o   Indicate the extent to which value may be less than the replacement cost for that part in excess of the cost of preparing the typical site

◊   Do not include the cost of treating unusual site characteristics in the estimate of replacement cost of building improvements.  It is necessary to avoid including both the effect of site treatment and the cost of the work in the estimate of replacement cost of the property.

# 4    THE VALUATION PROCESS

## 4-0  INTRODUCTION

This Chapter addresses the development of the three approaches to value:
  ◊    Sales Comparison Approach
  ◊    Income Capitalization Approach
  ◊    Cost Approach

It also addresses their impact in arriving at a final value conclusion that reflects the conditions denoted on the Valuation Conditions (VC) Form.  These approaches form the foundation for developing a value and lead to the final reconciliation for an estimated market value. The VC form identifies key components of the property analysis and requires the appraiser to:
  ◊    Describe the results of the visual inspection
  ◊    Identify known conditions, if any
  ◊    Reconcile their findings with the approaches to value

This Chapter conforms to the current Uniform Standards of Professional Appraisal Practice (USPAP) and the requirements of the URAR.  In developing and coming to a conclusion about value, the appraiser must be aware of and comply with all state and federal laws and requirements.  Furthermore, strict compliance with USPAP is required for all FHA appraisals.

## 4-1  MARKET VALUE ESTIMATES

In accordance with HUD/FHA requirements, an appraiser must do the following:
  ◊    Define the type of value being considered for the property appraisal
  ◊    Ascertain the definition of market value appropriate for the appraisal
  ◊    Indicate whether the estimate is the most probable price that the property will sell for on the open market
>  Follow the standards of USPAP.  Key sections that are most applicable are provided below.

### A.  DEFINITION OF MARKET VALUE

The definition of market value that applies to HUD/FHA is cited from the Uniform Standards of Professional Appraisal Practice.  This is the definition of value which must be used for all appraisals performed for FHA-insured mortgages.

> *"The most probable price which a property should bring in a competitive and open market under all conditions requisite to a fair sale, the buyer and seller each acting prudently and knowledgeably, and assuming the price is not affected by undue stimulus."*

Implicit in this definition is the consummation of a sale as of a specified date and the passing of title from seller to buyer under conditions whereby:

1.   The buyer and seller are typically motivated.
2.   Both parties are well informed or well advised, and each is acting in what they consider their best interest.
3.   A reasonable time is allowed for exposure in the open market.
4.   Payment is made in terms of cash in United States Dollars or in terms of a financial arrangement comparable thereto.
5.   The price represents the normal consideration for the property sold unaffected by special or creative financing or sales concessions.

### B.      PROPERTY RIGHTS APPRAISED

Identifying property rights to be valued determines the criteria for selecting market data and for comparable transactions.  The following table is an example of property rights.

| Property Type | Occupancy | Property Rights Appraised |
|---|---|---|
| Single-family | Owner | Fee Simple |
| Two-to-Four family | One unit owner-occupied, other units rented | Leased Fee |
| All property types | Ground lease | Leasehold Estate |

The appraiser examines property rights to determine what rights, if any, the property owner has conveyed to others.  The conveyance of rights to others impacts the value of the property.  For example, a single-family owner-occupied property has fee simple property rights that are absolute and unencumbered - unlike a leasehold estate where property rights are specified to use and occupancy for a stated term.  The appraiser must determine to what extent, if any, the transfer of property rights impacts the property's value.

*Fee Simple* is defined as absolute ownership unencumbered by any other interest or estate.

*Lease Fee* is defined as an ownership interest held by a landlord with the right of use and occupancy conveyed by lease to others; usually consists of the right to receive rent and the right to repossession at the termination of lease.

*Leasehold Estate* is defined as the right to use and occupy real estate for a stated term and under certain conditions that have been conveyed by a lease.

## C.  PURPOSE
The purpose of an appraisal is the stated reason for performing an appraisal assignment.  The purpose is typically stated as the basis for an underwriting decision.  For HUD, the purpose is to determine market value for mortgage insurance purposes.

## D.  INTENDED USE OF APPRAISAL/FUNCTION
The intended use or function for all appraisals prepared for FHA is to support the underwriting requirements for an FHA-insured mortgage.

## E.  USE OF THE APPRAISAL
The use of the appraisal is to support FHA's decision to provide mortgage insurance on the real property that is the subject of the appraisal.  Therefore, intended users include the lender and HUD.

## F.  EFFECTIVE DATE OF VALUE
The effective date of value is either the date when the appraiser physically inspects the subject property or another date specifically defined by the lender.
> If another date is used as the effective date, indicate the alternative date and the date on which the subject property was physically inspected.

## G.  SCOPE
The appraiser must perform a complete appraisal as defined by USPAP, considering all of the applicable approaches to value and developing the appropriate approaches identified in this Handbook.  Departure is not allowed.

## H.  SPECIAL LIMITING CONDITIONS AND ASSUMPTIONS
The appraiser must adequately identify, report and quantify any extraordinary assumptions or limiting conditions that directly impact the valuation.  Examples include:
   ◊   A negative external influence (proximity to a municipal landfill, for example)
   ◊   Proposed road improvements
   ◊   A pending zone change

## 4-2  HUD/FHA REQUIREMENTS
HUD/FHA requirements for market value estimates are as follows:
   ◊   The appraiser must appraise the property to determine market value under the requirements detailed in Chapter 4-1 of this Handbook.
   ◊   The appraiser must evaluate the physical condition of the property and note it on the Valuation Conditions (VC) Form of the Comprehensive Valuation Package.  Note any necessary repairs.  If repairs are in process, disclose the extent or status of those repairs at the time of the appraisal.  Always base the value on the completion of repairs and include this as a special limiting condition when repairs are required and expected to be completed.
   ◊   The appraiser must evaluate whether the property is free of hazards, noxious odors, grossly offensive sights or excessive noises that may:
         o Endanger the physical improvements
         o Affect the livability of the property or its marketability
         o Affect the health and safety of its occupants
>  If any of these conditions exist, recommend correction of the problem or rejection of the property and explain.
For more information, see Chapter 2-2 of this Handbook.
   ◊   The appraiser must determine if the subject property possesses sufficient remaining economic life to warrant a long-term mortgage, assuming a reasonable level of continued maintenance.  If the property does not warrant a long-term mortgage it will be ineligible for FHA mortgage insurance.
   ◊   The appraiser must indicate if the property conforms to applicable Minimum HUD/VA Property Requirements detailed in Chapter 3.
>  If the property does not conform to the Minimum Property Requirements, note it in the VC section of the appraisal report and require correction of the deficiency or rejection of the property and explain.
>  If there are so many necessary repairs that an "as-repaired" value cannot be determined, or if correcting the deficiencies would require major rehabilitation/alterations, return the appraisal to the lender with a detailed explanation.

## 4-3  NEW AND PROPOSED CONSTRUCTION REQUIREMENTS
Before performing an appraisal for new or proposed construction, the appraiser must have the plans and specifications and a fully completed Builder's Certification.  The lender must provide this information to the appraiser prior to issuing the assignment.  Without these items, the property will not be acceptable for FHA insurance purposes.

### A.  NEW CONSTRUCTION
The appraiser must develop the cost approach for new construction less than one year old.  Appraise new construction in the same way that existing properties are valued under the specifications outlined in this chapter of the Handbook.  Also, consider using the Gross Rent Multiplier method when developing the income approach for three- or four-unit buildings.

### B.  PROPOSED CONSTRUCTION
Appraise proposed construction consistent with the methodology presented in this chapter.  USPAP requires that the appraiser be provided with written specifications of the proposed structure.  Specifically, the Lender must provide the appraiser with these documents:

- ◊   Builder's plans, specifications and construction documents
- ◊   Completed builder's certification (Form HUD-92541)
- ◊   Builder's Warranty (Form HUD-92544)
- ◊   The 10-year Warranty, when required (the Secretary has proposed a 1-year Home-Owner Warranty period)
- ◊   All reports and information available (i.e. sales agreement, title report, environmental assessments or studies and inspection reports)

>   If these documents are not provided, return the incomplete appraisal to the lender.  Check the box stating that the valuation is subject to completion and the value is contingent on the structure receiving a certificate of occupancy.

## 4-4 UNIQUE PROPERTY APPRAISALS
Appraisers are sometimes faced with unique properties: a log home, an extra small home, lower than normal ceiling heights, etc.  Eligibility of these properties depends on whether or not the property is structurally sound and readily marketable.  If a property meets these criteria, the appraiser estimates market value.  However, depending on the uniqueness of a property, the final determination to accept or reject the property is made by the lending institution's underwriter.  Excess land is another area in which to exercise caution.  Land is considered to be excess if it is:

- ◊   Larger than what is typical in the neighborhood

AND

- ◊   Capable of a separate use

- ◊   If there is excess land, describe it but do not value it.  In this instance, the appraisal is based upon a hypothetical condition.  A legal description of the portion being appraised is required.

## 4-5 COST APPROACH
The cost approach is an indication of value based on the premise that a buyer would not pay more for a property than the cost to construct a property of equal utility.  The cost approach is not necessarily the best indication of market value for many properties, but it is often applicable for new(er) or proposed construction and special use properties.  Such situations include the following for single family one- to four-unit dwellings:

| Property Age | Cost-Approach Requirement |
|---|---|
| Proposed Construction | Required |
| New Construction | Required |
| Existing, less than one year | Required |
| Existing, regardless of age | Market acceptability of cost as an indication of pricing and value |

Unless the cost approach is deemed reliable on the above table or considered applicable in the appraiser's judgment, developing this approach is not required for a HUD/FHA appraisal.  The reporting requirement of USPAP known as the departure rule does not apply because the appraiser must always use the cost approach to value when considered applicable.

### USPAP Requirements
Strict compliance with USPAP standards is required for all FHA appraisals.

### Reporting Requirements
>   If the cost approach was excluded, report it in the reconciliation and insert the rationale for its exclusion.

## A.  COST APPROACH METHODOLOGY

### 1.  Land Value Estimate
Standard Rule 1-3(b) of USPAP requires appraisers to "recognize that land is appraised as though vacant ... ". The appraiser estimates the value of the land because it is generally considered to be a permanent, non-depreciating asset. There are exceptions to this generally agreed upon premise, but the exceptions will rarely be a factor in FHA/HUD related appraisals.  Exceptions may include land with an erosion problem or a polluted property.

### 2.  Excess Land
Excess Land is defined as the area by which the plot exceeds the area of a readily marketable real estate entity.  This occurs when the subject lot is considerably larger than typical lots in the neighborhood and the excess is capable of separate use.  Generally, the defining characteristic is an excess portion that can be subdivided and marketed as an individual parcel.  However, in small communities and outlying areas, appraisers must use different criteria because the market may accept a wide variance in lot sizes.  This segment of the market may show wide differences in lot use.
>   If the plot contains excess land, delineate and appraise separately the readily marketable real estate entity and the existing or proposed improvements.  Describe the excess land but do not appraise it with the primary 1 - 4 family residential building that is subject to a mortgage.
The lender will require that the value of excess land be excluded from the maximum mortgage amount that will be calculated only on a reasonable amount of land and improvements.

### 3.  Sales Comparison Approach For Land Value
In areas with an active real estate market, the sales comparison approach is generally the primary method used.  This method allows for collecting, verifying and analyzing recent and similar land sales to be compared with the subject land.  Before a conclusion is reached, the comparable land sales **are** adjusted for differences between the sales and the subject property.

### 4.  Alsite
In areas with a significant lack of comparable sales to develop the sales comparison approach, use the Alsite method, which assumes a market-accepted ratio between land value and property value.  Although the value estimate from this method is inherently less accurate than that of the sales comparison approach, it is still an acceptable approach.
>   The appraiser must document, support and justify the chosen Alsite ratio.

### 5.  Extraction
Extraction is a method to deduct the depreciated contribution of the subject's improvement from the total sales price of the property.  The remainder represents an estimate of land value.  This approach is also inherently less accurate than the sales comparison approach.
>   The appraiser must document, support and justify the estimate of the depreciated contribution of the improvements.

## B.  IMPROVEMENT COST ESTIMATE
Replacement cost is the preferred method for developing the Cost New of the subject improvements.  Typically the appraiser uses the Replacement Cost New and quantifies all forms of depreciation, except obsolescence.  An alternative is the reproduction cost. HUD does not require a specific method. The replacement cost of property is estimated to enable the application of the substitution principle.  Estimates of the replacement/reproduction cost of property are not estimates of value, although they indicate the possibility that value, in an equivalent amount, may exist.  Value depends entirely upon usefulness, not on the cost.  Value tends to conform to cost, but this is not to imply that it is always equivalent to cost.

## C.  TYPICAL REPLACEMENT COST
The replacement cost estimate must reflect the costs typically found in an area - not necessarily the costs of a particular builder or owner.  This method is typically preferred to the reproduction cost.

## D.  UNUSUAL AND NON-TYPICAL COSTS
Some of the items or allowances in the cost estimate may not represent equivalent value in a particular case.  An owner might erect a house that would cost more than the houses that generally characterize the neighborhood, but the value of the home to the typical prospective owner in that neighborhood might be less than the replacement cost of the property.  The cost of construction also may be in excess of value at a given time.  Under some circumstances, a reduction in cost may be in prospect.  If construction costs decline, value may also decline if it was originally equal to cost.

## E.  RECOMMENDED METHODOLOGIES
Generally, the Marshall and Swift square foot method is the most applicable method for estimating the Replacement Cost New.  This is a simplified procedure and all appraisers must have the knowledge and skill to apply this methodology.  This method may not be used for custom-built homes or unique buildings that require the segregated cost method.  Typical

residential construction with which HUD is involved should be rated "fair," "average" or "good" quality. Mass produced, tract-built homes are rated either "fair" or "average," meeting only the minimum construction requirements of lending institutions, mortgage insurance agencies and building codes. Appraisers must review the basic description to determine the correct construction type. The appraiser will complete the cost approach for each proposed construction case based on the construction type and quality rating of the property as shown in the Marshall and Swift Cost Handbook.

> Reference on the form the pages and revision date where the figures were obtained (usually two pages).
> Include a marketing expense with the replacement cost of improvements and an applicable current multipliers.

## F.   REMAINING ECONOMIC LIFE

Remaining economic life is an estimate of the remaining time period in which the improvements continue to contribute value to the property (building and improvements). The appraiser must consider the effect, if any, of modifications or renovations on the improvements. This effect is typically expressed in years.

## 4-6 SALES COMPARISON APPROACH

This is often the most applicable approach in estimating the market value of a single-family one- to four-unit property. This approach relies on:

◊   The availability of sales data
◊   The volume of transactions
◊   The reliability of reporting the transaction data confirmed and developed under this approach

When developing a value indication by the sales comparison approach, always include the assumptions and data from the other approaches on the VC form.

### A.   DATA REQUIREMENTS

#### 1.   Sales Data vs.  Comparable Sale

Any transaction in the market is a sale, but not all sales are *comparable*. Consider the type of transaction and physical characteristics of any sale before considering the sale a *comparable*.

#### 2.   Selection of Comparable Sales for Analysis

Identify the relevant market based on the area in which the property competes and the forces/dynamics that affect the comparable sale properties. This is necessary in relating the sales to the subject. Consider the amount of time that has elapsed between the sale date and the effective date of the appraisal. Sales data should not exceed six months between the date of the appraisal and the sale date of the comparable, and must not exceed twelve months. An explanation is required for sales dates in excess of six months. Consider neighborhood and other external factors that influence property value, including real estate and non-real estate influences. For example, when most of the neighborhood's residents are employed by one major employer who is relocating out of the region, the neighborhood may experience a decline in values. The term "non-real estate influenced", however, must never include racial composition. Consider the quality and quantity of data available for the given assignment. A lack of quality data in a market may force reliance on data in a similar market not necessarily the subject's immediate market area. However, clearly explain and justify any sales from outside the subject's immediate market area

#### 3.   Excluded Sales Transactions

When using conventional sales data, the appraiser must be aware of the terms of the sale and adjust the conventional sales price to reflect any unusual terms. For example, there are sales that must be excluded; however, some transactions may be included but adjusted for factors such as below-market financing to provide a cash equivalent sales price.

#### 4.   Current Offerings and Listings Analysis

Using these types of sales are discouraged. However, under certain slow market conditions or in markets with rapidly increasing pricing, it may be acceptable to include properties offered for sale. Proceed with caution when analyzing and adjusting these offerings. Recognize the inherent negotiability in price between an offering and a consummated sale. Clearly label these comparables as offering, listing, under agreement, etc., but present them as additional comparable data only.

#### 5.   Sales in Escrow

If a bona fide transaction is imminent, sales in escrow are considered to be reliable indications of market pricing. Exercise care in identifying the planned date of closure for the sale and any extraneous circumstances that may impede the closing on the projected date.

#### 6.   Distressed Sales

Using distressed sales is strongly discouraged because of the special circumstances surrounding these transactions.

### 7.   Resite Sales

Using Resite sales from a corporate seller at a below market value is strongly discouraged when the purchaser is the Resite company because of the unusual circumstances surrounding these transactions. Both distressed and Resite sales are strongly discouraged because they fail to meet the test of "market value," particularly item No. 1: "The buyer and seller are typically motivated." However, these sales can exceed normal market transaction and affect market values.

### 8.   Confirmation of Sales and Transaction Information

The appraiser must verify all market and comparable information used in the appraisal process and is accountable for any information presented as "fact" used to develop the subject property's value estimate. Verification ensures that the information is accurate and meaningful and provides the appraiser with a firm understanding of market motivations and trends. The goal of the verification process is to ensure that only information that accurately reflects current market conditions and trends is presented and that meaningful conclusions can be reached from this information. During the verification process, it is necessary for the appraiser to gain an understanding of the motivations surrounding the sale in order to:

       ◊  Determine if the sale was arm's length and not distressed
       ◊  Understand current market conditions that influence value

Whenever possible, interview a party to the sale to determine the expectations and motivations for purchasing the property. Also, determine whether significant capital expenditures funded by the seller were made shortly after the transaction occurred. if so, determine whether the expenditure needs to be added back into the sale price to reflect the actual conditions surrounding the sale. The appraiser must verify sale information with the buyer, the seller or one of their representatives (broker, lender, lawyer, etc.). If the sale cannot be verified with someone who has first-hand knowledge of the transaction, use public records. However, the appraiser must clearly state how the sale was verified and to what extent. Do not use or rely heavily on any sale that was not verified with an involved party or one of their representatives because concessions have become more common in the market.

## B.   ADJUSTMENT PROCESS

Other factors that affect the use of comparable sales must be considered. Account for differences between the subject property and each comparable sale. The analysis of sales includes both quantitative and qualitative factors. *Remember that the comparable data is adjusted to the subject property.* Present these adjustments as dollar amount figures and justify and explain the rationale for all adjustments. This information must be contained in the appraiser file. The sequence of adjustments should follow this format:

       ◊  The sequence of adjustments are part of the URAR. All FHA appraisers should be familiar with the adjustment grid within the URAR. Adjustments are indicated as a dollar amount. If an adjustment is not necessary, the appraiser can either enter "equal" or $0 as the adjustment.
       ◊  An individual line item adjustment should not exceed +/- 10%. The total adjustments to the comparables should not exceed 15% net and 25% gross of the sales price. If adjustment exceeds a parameter, the appraiser must explain why as part of the appraisal report.

     Adjustments to the sales include:
     ◊  Property Rights Conveyed. Refer to the property right appraised section of this chapter. This adjustment is always the first adjustment made to all sales.
     ◊  Sales or Financing Concessions. Account for and adjust for any special sale or financing terms, including sales concessions, non-market financing terms, points, buy downs, closing terms and swaps/exchanges. The most common scenario involves the seller paying points in the form of settlement help to the buyer. To reflect the amount, adjust the sales price of the comparable sale downwards. Typically this amount will not exceed six percent of the sales price for typical transactions.
     ◊  Condition of Sale. Account for the conditions surrounding the sale, including foreclosure/ distressed sale, purchased by an adjoining owner, sold between family members, auctioned or any unusual factor that could be reflected in the price paid.
     ◊  Market Conditions. Account for changes that have occurred or are occurring from the date of sale of the comparable transaction to the date of appraisal, including appreciation, new development, availability of financing, loan terms, supply and demand.
     ◊  Property Adjustments. These are required if the difference between the sale and the subject is quantifiable and supported by the market.
         o  *Location* - Account for location considerations.
         o  *Physical Characteristics* - Account for physical differences between the comparables and the subject, including condition, view, design/ appeal and quality of construction. These are typically entered as individual categories.
         o  *Economic Characteristics* - Account for economic characteristics between the comparables and the subject, including occupancy, rent level, lease structure or terms.

◊    Non-realty items. Non-realty items, such as personal property, may be included in value. These items are deducted from or added to the total consideration to reflect the cash equivalent price paid for the real property only.

◊    Other adjustments. Include physical characteristics that can be based on a dollar amount. The quality and quantity of market data should guide the selection of the most applicable method.

### 1.  Support for Adjustments

Adjustments must be supported by the market. The appraiser must use caution in developing adjustments; not all differences between the sale properties and the subject property are recognized as price-influencing factors in the marketplace. Only those factors that are accepted as value-influencing factors warrant adjustments.

### 2.  Explanation of Adjustments

The appraiser must explain why an adjustment was made. If adjustments are made, the appraiser must explain the differences that support the adjustments made to each of the comparables as they relate to the subject property.

> Report the explanation on the URAR and maintain it in the work papers.

### 3.  Reconciliation of Adjusted Sale Prices

The appraiser must consider the strengths and weaknesses of each of the comparable sales and develop this data into an indication of value by the sales comparison approach.

> Report the final reconciled value indication by the sales comparison approach on the URAR.

## 4-7 INCOME APPROACH

When the motivations of the buyer and the marketability of the property are based on its income-producing potential, the income approach must be developed. This approach applies when the entire property or one or more of the units is leased, regardless of the rental amount and occupancy. The ability of the property to be attractive to a renter and/or investor supports the development of the income approach. Situations where the income approach applies are presented on the following chart.

| Property | Occupancy | Applicability Test |
|---|---|---|
| Single-family | Owner-occupied | Market indication of highest and best use as improved (either for rental or for owner-occupancy) |
| Single-family | Vacant | Market indication of highest and best use as improved (either for rental or for owner-occupancy) |
| Two-family | One unit is owner- occupied; the other is vacant. | Optional, depending on the availability and reliability of market data |
| Two-family | One unit is owner-occupied; the other is rented. | Required if the property is located in a neighborhood with other rental properties; otherwise, optional, depending on the availability and reliability of market data |
| Three-to-four Family | One unit is owner- occupied; other units are rented. | Required |
| One-to-four Family | Leasehold Estate | Required |
| One-to-four Family | Leased Fee Estate | Required |

### A.  DATA REQUIREMENTS

The appraiser must choose similar market rentals to compare to the subject property. Consider the transaction and physical characteristics of a rental before considering the rental as *comparable*.

### 1.  Confirmation Of Leases And Transaction Information

The appraiser must verify all comparable information used in the appraisal process. The appraiser is liable and accountable for any information presented as a "fact" in developing the value estimate. This ensures that the information is accurate and meaningful and provides the appraiser with an understanding of market motivations and trends. The goals of the verification process are to ensure:

◊    That only the information that accurately reflects current market conditions and trends is presented

◊    That meaningful conclusions can be reached from this information

If possible, interview the lessee or the lessor to determine their expectations and motivation for entering into the lease.

Verify lease information with the lessor/lessee or one of their representatives (broker, agent, lawyer, etc.). If this verification is not possible, clearly state how the lease was verified and to what extent. Do not rely heavily on any lease that was not verified with an involved party or one of their representatives.

### 2.  Adjustment Process

The appraiser must consider other factors that affect the use of comparable leases. The appraiser must account for differences between the subject property and the comparable leases to reconcile the actual lease income. This selection of comparable rentals is significant because the gross income multiplier should not be adjusted, only the comparable rental rate. These adjustments are typically presented as percentage or dollar amount figures. The appraiser must be able to justify and explain the rationale behind all adjustments. The sequence of adjustments should follow the same format as that presented in the sales comparison approach section; however, tailor the categories to the comparable rentals.

### 3.  The Income Projection

In developing the projected gross rent for the subject, the appraiser needs to review and analyze the leases in place on the effective date of the appraisal. Also, consider leases that will commence or terminate around the effective date of the appraisal and the impact, if any, on the property. The appraiser must take appropriate steps to ensure that the development of the income approach reflects the actual conditions at the subject property. If the subject is new, consider when the property income will stabilize. Include the justification for any assumption made - lease up time, for example. The income approach is typically based upon the "as stabilized" premises. Support this approach appropriately and clearly state the date when stabilized income will be achieved.

### B.  DEVELOPMENT OF RATES

The Gross Rent Multiplier (GRM) is the ratio between the sales price of a property and its gross rental income. This method is used to develop indications of a property value. The appraiser must consider the strengths and weaknesses of each comparable rental and develop an estimated multiplier that adequately reflects the income-generating ability of the subject property. This ratio is applied to the estimated income for the subject to conclude an indication of value by the income approach.

## 4-8 FINAL RECONCILIATION

The final analytical step in the valuation process is to reconcile value indicators. In this step, the appraiser must measure the strengths and weaknesses of each of the applicable approaches performed and develop this data into a single value estimate.

## 4-9 RECONSIDERATION OF APPRAISED VALUE

The underwriter may request reconsideration of the appraised value when new market data exists that may not have been reflected in the appraisal. The lender can select new comparables and request a reappraisal. This request from the lender must be in writing and maintained in the appraiser's work file. The appraiser must decide whether to use the new comparables and perform the reappraisal. If the comparables were available when the initial appraisal was performed, the lender may not offer pay for the reconsideration.

## 5    REPORTING THE APPRAISAL

### 5-0  INTRODUCTION

Accurate and thorough appraisal reporting is critical to the accuracy of underwriting for the mortgage insurance process.  The need for accuracy is greater for FHA-insured mortgages because buyers tend to have more limited income and lower equity in the properties.  This chapter presents the requirements for reporting complete and accurate appraisal information to HUD.  An appraisal performed for HUD/ FHA purposes requires that all sections of the Comprehensive Valuation Package (CVP) must be completed.  The CVP constitutes the reporting instrument to HUD for FHA-insured mortgages.

### 5-1  REPORTING THE APPRAISAL

When the appraisal is completed, submit the CVP and all required attachments - maps, photographs, sketches, etc. to the lender. Also, for new and proposed construction, submit the plans, specifications, construction documents and the completed builder's certification (Form HUD-92541).  Submit the original package and a complete copy to the lender.

The CVP is required for reporting the appraisal findings, analyses and conclusions about the observed conditions of the property. A complete HUD appraisal package includes three parts: the Uniform Residential Appraisal Report (URAR), the Valuation Conditions Form and the Homebuyer Summary.  These are described below.

### A.   PART 1: UNIFORM RESIDENTIAL APPRAISAL REPORT (URAR)

The URAR is the standard appraisal reporting form available through all lenders.  The following are required in reporting appraisal findings on the URAR:

◊    All information must be reported consistently with the HUD protocol in Appendix D of this Handbook.

◊    All findings must be reported consistent with Standard 2 of USPAP for a summary report.

◊    All boxes must be filled in and relevant factual data included, unless specifically noted.

◊    All calculations must be verified.

◊    Consistency between the sections must be verified.

#### 1.        Departure from HUD Requirements

HUD requirements are presented in this Handbook.  Any departure from these requirements must be explained in the URAR or as an attachment to the appraisal.  Present the reasoning, the result of such departure and any additional limitations to the use of the appraisal or the reported value as a result of this departure.  Departure from USPAP is not permitted for an appraisal submitted to HUD.

#### 2.        Certification

Within the URAR, the appraiser must certify that the reported value is an unbiased, independent valuation of the subject property.  This certification is consistent with that required by USPAP.  Of particular importance is the certification that the appraisal is not based on any of the following:

◊    A requested minimum value

◊    A specific value

◊    The approval of a loan as indicated

If the appraiser is subject to additional certifications in developing and reporting the appraisal, include them in the URAR report.  Such additional certifications may be the result of state certification requirements in certain jurisdictions or of relationships with professional appraisal and real estate organizations.

The assigned appraiser is required to sign the report making him/her fully and wholly accountable for the information presented on the URAR and in developing the appraisal findings.  If any party provided significant professional assistance, name this party on the certification and note the contribution.

#### 3.  Statement of Limiting Conditions

For each appraisal, the URAR includes the standard limiting conditions.  The appraiser must confirm these limiting conditions and strike any that do not apply. Also, if there are additional limiting conditions, clearly state them.  If the limiting conditions differ or are contrary to the limiting conditions stated on the URAR, fully disclose those limiting conditions and make them known in the value estimate.  Cite any value-influencing limiting conditions with the report of the estimate of market value. The repair conditions reported in the VC segment of the report constitute a limiting condition for the development of the appraisal because HUD appraisals estimate value "as-repaired." The reported estimate assumes that the noted deficiencies have been corrected.  It is, therefore, important that the appraiser certify to testing specific systems and examining all areas of the house to note the deficiencies.

## B.    PART 2: VALUATION CONDITIONS FORM

The Valuation Conditions (VC) Form specifically addresses physical conditions of the property- that may render the property uninhabitable or cause health and safety concerns.  Note the conditions observed during the walk-through on the VC form as of the date of appraisal.  A home inspection. is not required to complete the VC.  The VC form is divided into Site and Property Analysis as well as other property related information.

   ◊    VC-1 identifies the site hazards and nuisances that may render a location ineligible for FHA insurance.
   ◊    VC-2 through VC-11 identify the basic structural and mechanical components of the property and are the bases for determining if the property is habitable and eligible for FHA-insured financing.
   ◊    VC-12 and VC-13 provide further information on the property.
   ◊    The addenda include a provision for current market assessed value and a summary of estimated repair costs.

Each section must be completed entirely, based on the instructions in the protocol in Appendix D of this Handbook.  The appraiser must observe the property's components, test certain basic operations, view areas of the home that may include adverse conditions and report on readily observed adverse conditions.  In all instances, the observations are as of the effective date of value, as identified in the VC and appraisal segments.

   ◊    For each item in VC-1, a "YES" renders the property ineligible for FHA mortgage insurance.
   ◊    For each specific item in VC-2 through VC-11, "YES" indicates a limiting condition on the appraisal subject to the repair of the deficiency or further inspection.
   ◊    For each specific item in VC-2 through VC-11, "NO" indicates that the appraiser did not observe a deficient condition.

The appraiser may encounter a negative physical condition that does not require repair or inspection.  In this instance the appraisal is based upon the existing condition.  "NO" is not a substitute for a home inspection by a qualified professional home inspector, but merely indicates that the appraiser did not observe the condition during the property inspection for valuation purposes. For both "YES" and "NO" responses, exercise care and judgment in reporting the extent and the magnitude of the observed condition.  The mere presence of an item may not require an inspection or repair.  Likewise, depending on the condition observed, a minor observation may prove to be significant to the soundness of the property.  The property analysis relies heavily on the appraiser's judgment.  It is important to note all considerations as comments for each Valuation Condition. For detailed instruction regarding the Valuation Conditions Form, please see the protocol in Appendix D of this Handbook. Appraisals performed for HUD/FHA are not intended to protect the buyer: they protect HUD.  Many homebuyers mistakenly believe that a HUD appraisal and subsequent inspection is a guarantee that the property is free from defects when, in fact, the appraisal only establishes the value of the property for mortgage insurance purposes.  Buyers need to secure their own home inspection through the services of a qualified inspector and satisfy themselves about the condition of the property.  If available in a timely manner, home inspection reports should be sent to the appraiser; this affords the appraiser the opportunity to make valuation adjustments as needed.

## C.   PART 1: HOMEBUYER SUMMARY

This part summarizes required repairs from the appraiser's observation of the physical condition.  The Homebuyer Summary intends to protect the homebuyer by informing him/her of any material conditions that typically make the property ineligible for FHA mortgage insurance.

>    If any of the VC's are marked "YES" in the VC form, the appraiser must denote it in the appropriate box of the Homebuyer Summary and explain, in detail, the nature of the problem.

The summary also includes a notice to the homebuyer regarding the value of securing a home inspection, by a qualified inspector.

## 5-2  ACCESS TO FORMS

The Homebuyer Summary and Valuation Conditions Form are available electronically from the HUD Internet website: http://www.hudclips.org.

## 5-3  RECORD KEEPING

HUD reserves the right to request and review the appraiser's work files supporting an FHA-insured mortgage at any time and without prior notice.  Appraisers on the FHA Register must comply with the record-keeping and inspection requirements as a condition of performing appraisals for FHA-insured mortgages.

### A.   MINIMUM TERM FOR RECORD KEEPING

The appraiser is required to keep supporting documentation in addition to a copy of the CVP.  These files must be maintained for five years after the date of preparation or at least two years after final disposition of any judicial proceeding in which testimony was given, whichever expires last.  This is consistent with the Record Keeping Rule of USPAP.

### B.   DOCUMENTATION FILE REQUIREMENTS

Although there is no prescribed file for-mat or content, the appraiser's work files must include information to support all findings, observations and conclusions supporting the value estimate.  The files must indicate the rationale for adjustments and the market data analyzed in the development of the appraisal report.  The files must include documentation of the acceptance of the assignment and historical and factual information, such as photographs and maps.  A sample documentation file index is provided below.  This is not a comprehensive list of information.

## C.  SAMPLE DOCUMENTATION FILE

| Section | Supporting Data |
|---|---|
| Acceptance of assignment | File memorandum |
| | |
| **Property Description** | Legal description |
| | Photographs |
| | Floor plans |
| | Tax map and information |
| | Field notes from inspection |
| | Listing information |
| | Offer to purchase |
| | |
| **Neighborhood** | Notes from the field visit |
| | Photographs |
| | Demographic data |
| | |
| **Cost Approach** (if applicable) | Relevant Marshall Swift Valuation information |
| | Calculations performed |
| | Land Sales detail |
| | |
| **Sales Comparison Approach** | Sale details and photographs |
| | Transaction information |
| | Derivation of adjustments |
| | Interview notes |
| | |
| **Income approach** (if applicable) | Market rent comparable information |
| | Cap rate justification |
| | Historical financial statements |
| | |
| **VC Conditions Noted** | Photograph of condition |
| | Field notes |
| | Support for any assumed repairs |
| | Calculation of cost to repair a VC condition |
| | |

| Additional Information | Surveys |
|---|---|
| | Relevant market data |
| | Other sources of data |

## 6    APPRAISAL AND APPRAISER MONITORING

### 6-0  INTRODUCTION
The review process is a critical quality control and performance monitoring mechanism for HUD.  FHA will monitor appraisals and appraisers using statistical analysis and field reviews.  Through analysis of performance measures, FHA will identify candidates for field reviews.  By performing statistical analysis as well as field reviews, HUD maintains the capability to broadly track its portfolio and investigate it in greater depth.

### 6-1  MONITORING AND STATISTICAL ANALYSIS
The Real Estate Assessment Center (REAC) will conduct statistical analysis to track the performance of appraisers and properties and to identify problematic appraisals for review. If the review and subsequent analysis indicate behavior that is out of compliance with FHA guidelines, FHA may take enforcement action.  The performance categories below will guide the monitoring and enforcement efforts.

### 6-2  PERFORMANCE CATEGORIES
The following performance categories allow FHA to monitor each aspect of the appraiser's performance.  The table below lists examples of performance measures for each category.

| Performance Category | Performance Measure |
|---|---|
| Appraisal Process | Transaction quality |
| | Proof of analysis |
| | Relevance of data |
| | |
| Appraisal Reporting | Completeness |
| | Mathematical Accuracy |
| | |
| Valuation Conditions | Identified repairs |
| | |
| Maintenance of Professional | Maintenance of state licensure |
| | |
| Standards | Disciplinary actions |
| | |
| Field reviews | Supported findings |
| | Required record keeping |
| | Responsiveness to field review |

HUD expects a high level of professionalism, customer service, technical expertise and record keeping from appraisers.  The above measures demonstrate HUD's focus on:
    ◊   Complete, justifiable and accurate appraisals
    ◊   Qualified and competent appraisers
    ◊   Professionalism
    ◊   Accuracy

**6-3 APPRAISAL REVIEW PROCESS**

The oversight process includes statistical analysis of appraisals and field reviews. The reviews will be used to determine the reliability of the appraisal supporting FHA financing as well as the performance of the appraiser. To gauge an appraiser's performance, REAC will review a sample of appraisals performed for FHA over a specified time period and/or a specified number of appraisals performed.

# 7   REGULATORY ENVIRONMENT, ENFORCEMENT AND SANCTIONS

## 7-0 INTRODUCTION

This chapter describes the regulatory environment in which FHA single-family appraisals are performed and the enforcement and sanctions that are available to HUD and other government entities in that environment. Appraisers are subject to:

◊   Federal laws and regulations
◊   State licensing laws and regulations
◊   The requirements associated with any professional appraisal designations

This chapter enumerates these requirements and explains their connection to HUD's enforcement and sanctions processes.

## 7-1 REGULATORY ENVIRONMENT

### A.   FINANCIAL INSTITUTIONS REFORM, RECOVERY, ENFORCEMENT ACT OF 1989 ("FIRREA")

FIRREA instituted reform and regulation of real estate appraising through Title XI, the Real Estate Appraisal Reform Amendments. The amendments achieved the following:

◊   Established the Appraisal Foundation, comprising the Appraiser Qualifications Board (AQB) and the Appraisal Standards Board (ASB):
  ▪   The AQB determines the minimum education, examination and experience requirements for state-certified and state-licensed appraisers.
  ▪   The ASB promulgates the Uniformed Standards of Professional Appraisal Practice (USPAP).
◊   Required that only a state-certified or state-licensed appraiser may perform appraisals for federally related transactions
◊   Established that an appraiser trainee can sign an appraisal if a state-certified or state-licensed appraiser closely supervises the trainee, signs the appraisal report and inspects the property
◊   Established the definition of a "state-certified real estate appraiser" as someone who has satisfied the requirements in a state or territory whose criteria for certification meets the minimum criteria for certification by the Appraiser Qualification Board of the Appraisal Foundation
◊   Established the state agencies to license, certify and supervise appraisers

All appraisers performing services for FHA-insured mortgages must comply with USPAP in developing and reporting appraisals. Key aspects of USPAP include:

| Standard | Citation |
|---|---|
| Ethics Rule | Conduct management, confidentiality and recordkeeping |
| | |
| Competency Rule | Full responsibility of appraiser to have the knowledge and experience to complete the assignment competently or disclose any discrepancy before acceptance and take all necessary steps to correct |
| | |
| Departure Rule 1/ | Permits limited departures from acceptable portions of USPAP reducing the reliability of the valuation |
| | |
| Jurisdictional Exception | Individual portions of USPAP can be superseded by law or public policy |
| | |
| Standard 1 | In developing a real estate property appraisal, an appraiser must be aware of, understand and correctly employ the recognized methods and techniques that are necessary to produce a credible appraisal |

| | |
|---|---|
| Standard 2 | In reporting the results of a real estate property appraisal, an appraiser must communicate each analysis, opinion and conclusion in a manner that is not misleading |

In compliance with USPAP, unacceptable practices include:
◊ Estimating a specified (predetermined) value determined by the lender
◊ Fee splitting between lenders and appraisers
◊ Other practices that do not comply with HUD's standards

Also, USPAP contains statements on appraisal standards that have the full weight of USPAP. These statements were issued to clarify the existing standards. The ASB has also issued advisory opinions that currently do not establish new standards but offer advice on complex technical issues.

## B. FEDERAL FINANCIAL INSTITUTION REGULATORY AGENCIES

The Federal Financial Institution Regulatory Agencies issued a final rule on appraisals in June 1994. In general, the threshold for requiring state-certified appraisers to perform appraisals on federally related transactions was raised to Two Hundred Fifty Thousand Dollars ($250,000).

1/ FHA does not permit departure from USPAP. However, FHA requires an appraisal for all applications for single-family mortgage insurance, regardless of transactional value.

## C. FALSE, FICTITIOUS OR FRAUDULENT CLAIMS (18 U.S.C. *87, 1001) - CRIMINAL PENALTIES AND FINES

These statutes prescribe criminal penalties for any person who knowingly files a false claim on or against any department or agency of the United States Government.

## D. FALSE, FICTITIOUS OR FRAUDULENT CLAIMS ON HUD (18 U.S.C. 1010,    1012)- CRIMINAL PENALTIES AND FINES

These statutes prescribe criminal penalties for any person who knowingly files a false claim on or against HUD.

## E. FEDERAL FALSE CLAIMS ACT (31 U.S.C. 3729) - CIVIL FRAUD

The Federal False Claims Act defines the civil monetary damages imposed on any person who knowingly presents or files a false claim that was paid or approved by the United States Government.

## F. 24 CFR PART 28 - PROGRAM FRAUD CIVIL REMEDIES ACT (PFCRA)

These regulations define the administrative procedures for imposing civil penalties and assessments by HUD officials against any person who makes or submits false claims or false statements to Federal authorities or to their agents.

## G. 24 CFR PART 30 - CIVIL MONEY PENALTIES

These regulations define the money penalties that HUD may levy for submission of a false certification by another person - for example, an appraiser who makes a false certification at the bottom of the USPAP appraisal form about the truth/ correctness of the appraisal data.

## H. 24 CFR PART 24 - ADMINISTRATIVE SANCTIONS

These regulations define the administrative sanctions available to HUD officials for any person determined to have violated HUD regulations and policies.

## I. STATE LAWS AND PROFESSIONAL ORGANIZATIONS

The appraiser must adhere to all state and local laws relating to appraisal, licensing and certification requirements. Also, as a voluntary member of an appraiser's professional organization, the FHA appraiser should adhere to that organization's guidelines on appraiser conduct. However, HUD has no enforcement powers in private organizations.

### 1. State Certifications

Appraisers on the FHA Register must be licensed, certified-residential or certified-general appraisers. To perform appraisals for FHA, appraisers must maintain and be able to prove that they are so certified. While some states do not require an appraiser to be certified, they provide a licensing program so appraisers can meet federal guidelines. Appraisers must comply with the practices of their state unless the requirements of the state contradict those of the federal government; federal requirements preempt any and all state requirements. The appraiser must report to HUD any action or pending action that relates to appraisal reports prepared by the appraiser two years subsequent to the date on which the action was initiated. After disposition of any disciplinary action or adjudication of the action, the appraiser must provide HUD with the documentation and official findings within 14 days.

### 2. Professional Organizations

The appraiser may be a member or hold designations in professional organizations. Such involvement is encouraged, but not required. If the appraiser is a member, candidate or associate of any organization, the appraiser must report any adjudicated actions resulting in the suspension of the appraiser to HUD within 14 days of such action. On disposition of the-action or adjudication of the action, the appraiser must provide HUD with documentation and official findings. HUD reserves the right to suspend any appraiser found guilty of professional misconduct as adjudicated by the professional organization.

## 7-2 ENFORCEMENT

FHA intends to hold appraisers accountable for valuations that are inconsistent with USPAP or this Handbook. The Valuation Conditions Form must accurately reflect any site, structural or mechanical deficiencies. FHA recognizes that most appraisals are properly valued and do not indicate improper action. Accordingly, HUD emphasizes quality assurance, but will take enforcement action when necessary.

### A. STATE CERTIFICATION BOARDS

HUD will enforce actions against appraisers through existing state certification and licensing boards. HUD is required by law to refer appraisers to these boards if HUD considers the actions to be of such magnitude or frequency as to warrant such referral.

### B. PROFESSIONAL ORGANIZATIONS

HUD will cooperate with and refer cases to the enforcement arms of all applicable professional organizations.

## 7-3 APPLICABLE REMEDIES AND SANCTIONS

FHA will review appraiser and appraisal performance data. In making any determination, the following will be considered:

◊    The seriousness and extent of the non-compliant action
◊    The degree to which the appraiser is responsible for that action
◊    The frequency of the action(s)
◊    Any mitigating factors

HUD will impose sanctions on four tiers:

1. Notice of Appraisal Deficiencies and Remedial Education
2. Administrative Sanctions
3. Civil Sanctions
4. Criminal Sanctions

HUD expects that all appraisers performing appraisals for FHA are knowledgeable of HUD's policies and procedures. If, however, minor appraisal errors indicate lack of knowledge, HUD may require remedial education and training. For offenses arising from unethical behavior or for repeated offenses, HUD will apply more serious sanctions. All sanctions will be reported to the state regulatory agencies. The following sections generally define the actions taken under each tier. Generally, these penalties will be expunged after three years. A table providing examples of offenses and possible sanctions is included at the end of this chapter.

### A. NOTICE OF APPRAISAL DEFICIENCIES AND REMEDIAL EDUCATION

Education and training directives will be managed internally by HUD. If the evidence indicates that the appraisal deficiency is a matter of training, then the appraiser must undergo professional training. HUD will notify the appraiser and inform the appraiser of:

◊    The appraisal's deficiencies
◊    The findings that support the recommended training
◊    The recommended training
◊    The appraiser's right to refute the findings of the notice

The appraiser must appeal within 20 days from receipt of the notice if he or she disagrees with the findings. If the findings are adequately refuted, no action will be taken against the appraiser and the circumstances surrounding that particular incident will be noted in the appraiser's file. However, if the findings hold, the appraiser must comply with HUD's requirements for improved performance, including the type of training required and the time-frame for completion. This action will go on record in the appraiser's file.

### B. ADMINISTRATIVE SANCTIONS

Administrative sanctions will be managed internally by HUD and consist primarily of removal from the FHA Register for a specified time. Removal from the FHA Register can be imposed for noncompliance with FHA policies and requirements on appraisals. HUD will consider the seriousness of the appraiser's acts or omissions and any mitigating factors. HUD/FHA will notify the appraiser of the alleged violation and pending sanction in writing. If the appraiser believes that removal from the FHA Register is unwarranted, the appraiser must appeal in writing within 20 days and may arrange a meeting or conference call with FHA at a mutually acceptable time. If there is evidence and documentation of unacceptable performance, appraisers will be removed from the FHA Register at HUD/FHA's sole discretion. Upon any legally effected removal, HUD will notify the state licensing or certification agency in writing that such appraiser has been removed from the FHA Register. HUD will provide the state agency with:

◊   The state license or certification number of the appraiser
◊   The reason for removal
◊   Copy of the original appraisals
◊   Copy of the review report

In addition to removal from the FHA Register, administrative sanctions include sanctions under 24 CFR Part 24, Debarment, Suspension and Limited Denials of Participation (LDP) from HUD and government-wide programs.

## C.  CIVIL SANCTIONS

HUD will pursue civil sanctions by initiating an investigation of the alleged non-compliant action. A report containing the findings and conclusions of the investigation will be submitted to HUD's Office of the General Counsel or The Enforcement Center. If the Office of General Counsel or The Enforcement Center determines that the investigation report supports an action, the respective office will submit a written request to the Department of justice for approval to pursue civil sanctions. Civil sanctions are pursuant to Part 24 CFR 28-PFCRA and are described in Chapter 7-1.

## D.  CRIMINAL

If the non-compliant action is so egregious as to violate criminal law, HUD's Office of General Counsel or the Inspector General will refer the case to the Attorney General at the U.S. Department of Justice.

## E.   PERFORMANCE VIOLATIONS AND LEVEL OF SANCTION

The following chart outlines the type of sanction to be levied by the type of performance violation. For example, the appraiser may receive a Notice of Appraisal Deficiencies for a square footage error of less than 10% as a first offense. However, repeatedly making this mistake will result in removal from the FHA Register. If the violation is repeated so that it constitutes a pattern of misconduct, it may be considered gross negligence. The offense could also be considered gross negligence if the offense is so obvious that it could not have reasonably been the result of simple error. In this example, the sanction for gross negligence includes removal from the FHA Register and may include a Limited Denial of Participation or Debarment. Violations of intent include knowing and willful noncompliance with FHA/HUD requirements, as well as extensive or repeated intentional violations. In this example, the appraiser is guilty of intentional misconduct if he or she chooses to disregard the requirement. Sanctions at this level may include debarment and civil and/or criminal penalties. The Department may impose civil money penalties or other sanctions for minor violations if the Department determines that circumstances warrant.

### 7-4  PERFORMANCE AND SANCTION MATRIX

This is not an exhaustive list of violations. It is meant to highlight the ramifications for non-compliant performance. This does not preclude the Department from pursuing other remedies or related sanction(s); the Department reserves the right to take any such other actions and remedies in accordance with applicable law. Time frames are included for illustration and can vary depending on the degree of violation.

# 8    MANUFACTURED HOMES

## 8-0  DEFINITION

A Manufactured Home is a structure that is transportable in one or more sections.  In traveling mode, the home is eight feet or more in width and forty feet or more in length.  A Manufactured Home is designed and constructed to the Federal Manufactured Construction and Safety Standards and is so labeled.  When erected on site, the home is:

◊    At least 400 square feet
◊    Built and remains on a permanent chassis
◊    Designed to be used as a dwelling with a permanent foundation built to FHA criteria

The structure must be designed for occupancy as a principal residence by a single family.

## 8-1  PROPERTY STANDARDS FOR TITLE II MORTGAGE INSURANCE

The appraiser should be aware of the primary standards in this Handbook to prepare an appraisal for underwriting purposes.  These are the key standards:

◊    The site must be served by permanent water and sewer facilities approved by the local municipal authority, if available at the site.
◊    An all-weather roadway must serve the site.
◊    The entire property must be taxed as real estate.
◊    The towing hitch or running gear must have been removed.  The towing hitch or running gear must also have been removed for properties greater than one year.
◊    No part of the finished grade level under the home is below the 100-year flood level.
◊    Structural integrity must have been maintained during transportation and sufficient anchoring, support and stability must be evident.

All manufactured homes must have an affixed HUD seals(s) located on the outside of the home.  If the home is a multi-wide unit, each unit must have a seal.  These seals will be numbered sequentially.  If the tags are missing from the property, the appraiser must recommend rejection of the property and notify the lender.  In some states, a manufactured home may not be resold without a seal and homes without a HUD seal must be rejected.  In states where resale without a HUD seal is permissible, a manufacture's certification must be obtained verifying the date of the sale. The certification label/seal shall be located at the tall-light end of each transportable section of the manufactured home approximately one foot up from the floor and one foot in from the road side, or as near that location on a permanent part of the exterior of the manufactured home unit as practicable.  The roadside is the right side of the manufactured home when one views the manufactured home from the tow bar end of the manufactured home. (24 CFR 3280.11 (d))

◊    The home must be erected on a permanent foundation in compliance with the Permanent Foundation Guide for Manufactured Housing.  All proposed or newly constructed manufactured homes must meet the standards set forth in the Permanent Foundation Guide.  A licensed professional engineer's seal and signature (certification) is required to indicate compliance with the Foundation Guide.  The lender should furnish the appraiser with a design engineer's inspection of the foundation prior to the appraisal.
◊    Existing manufactured homes in place over one year are to be inspected by the appraiser for evidence of permanent concrete footings with tie-downs anchored to the footings.
◊    The appraiser must inspect the crawl space for the following: poured in place concrete footings placed below the frost line supporting the manufactured home carriage frame, tie-downs anchored to the footings, protection from the elements and enclosed with material imperious to rot and infestation and perimeter foundation-type construction with footings extended below the frost line.  The appraiser must require an engineering inspection if there is evidence of structural defects or other problems relating to the foundation or set-up of the home.
◊    The manufactured home must not have been constructed before June 15, 1976.  The unit must have been built to the manufactured housing construction safety standards as evidenced by having a small, red metallic label attached to it.  Any unit without this label is unacceptable.  If it has been removed, it cannot be reattached to make it acceptable for FHA insurance.
◊    New, never occupied homes that are transported directly from the manufacturer or directly from the dealership to the site are eligible for insurance.  For an existing manufactured home, evidence must be provided to verify that the home was assembled in accordance with the above paragraphs and has not been moved from its initial installation site.
◊    Additions or structural modifications may put the home at risk if changes were not performed in accordance with the HUD Manufactured Home Construction Safety and Standards.  If the appraiser observes changes to the original home, an inspection by the State Administrative agency, which inspects manufactured homes for compliance, must be required.  If there is no agency willing or able to inspect existing homes for compliance to the Manufactured Home Construction and Safety Standards, the manufactured home is unacceptable and should be rejected.

## 8-2 PROPERTY DESCRIPTION

Measurement is based on the overall length, including living areas and other projections that are at least seven feet in height. Length and width should not include bay windows, roof overhangs, drawbars, couplings or hitches. Each manufactured home must have a data plate with the name of the manufacturer and the construction date.

## 8-3 APPRAISER QUALIFICATIONS FOR MANUFACTURED HOMES CLASSIFIED AS PERSONAL PROPERTY

For all appraisals of manufactured homes classified as personal property, lenders must engage independent fee appraisers who have successfully completed a specialized course in manufactured home valuation based on the N.A.D.A. appraisal system. These independent fee appraisers must be knowledgeable in the business of manufactured home retail sales. Appraisal services may be obtained from an appraisal company if their appraisers meet these qualifications.

## 8-4 MANUFACTURED HOME LOT APPRAISALS

A manufactured home lot appraisal may be requested to estimate land value in determining the maximum loan proceeds allowable for a manufactured home lot loan or a combination loan (home and lot). A lot appraisal may also be requested to establish value for claim purposes on a foreclosed lot or manufactured home-and-lot combination. When appraising manufactured housing, appraisers should use normal single-family residential appraisal techniques (see Chapter 4 of this Handbook). Give special consideration to other manufactured homes as comparables in appraising manufactured homes. This will provide a comparable value indication from which to make justifiable conclusions. Therefore, make all efforts to obtain such comparables even though their distance from the subject may be greater than normally desirable.

If there are no manufactured housing sales within a reasonable distance from the subject property, use conventionally built homes. Make the appropriate and justifiable adjustments for size, site, construction materials, quality, etc. As a point of reference, sales data for manufactured homes can usually be found in local transaction records.

### A.  MANUFACTURED HOME LOT SITES

A manufactured home lot may consist of:

◊    An interest in a manufactured home condominium project (including an undivided interest in the common areas)

OR

◊    A share in a cooperative association that owns and operates a manufactured home park

The lot may be located within Native American Trust Lands if the borrower owns or leases the lot.

### B.  HOW TO PERFORM A MANUFACTURED HOME LOT APPRAISAL

In addition to the single-family residential appraisal techniques (see Chapter 4 of this Handbook), the appraiser must take the following steps when performing manufactured home lot appraisals:

◊    The appraiser must obtain Form HUD-92802, Application and Request for Manufactured Home Lot and/or Site Preparation and the FHA case number from the mortgagee.

◊    The appraiser must receive a copy of the design engineer's inspection of the foundation from the mortgagee.

◊    The appraiser must estimate the value of the lot by comparison with other lots offering similar amenities.

◊    When the appraisal is complete, the appraiser must send the original and one copy of the appraisal report, a photograph of the lot and one photograph of each comparable to the lender for review.

## 9    PLANNED UNIT DEVELOPMENTS AND CONDOMINIUMS

## 9-0 PLANNED UNIT DEVELOPMENT (PUD)

A PUD is defined as a mixed-use residential development of single-family dwellings in conjunction with rental, condominium, cooperative or town house properties. A residential development should be processed as a PUD if it has these minimum characteristics:

◊    A homeowner association that holds either title in fee or a lease of prescribed length on the common area

◊    Mandatory membership of all unit owners (or units) in the association

◊    The right of all unit owners to participate by vote in the operation of the association

◊    Lien supported assessment of the members to meet the association's budgeted operating costs (special assessments may be handled differently)

To be eligible for insurance endorsement, PUDs must be approved by HUD. The lender is responsible for obtaining a case number from HUD to ensure that the PUD is already approved. The appraiser should note whether there is a case number.

### A.  APPROACH TO VALUE

The approach to value for a PUD is the same as the approach to value for other types of developments (see Chapter 4 of this Handbook). Frequently, however, no valid comparisons are available that estimate market value. In these instances, appraisers should use the replacement cost estimate in valuation. Estimate the replacement cost of improvements, miscellaneous allowable costs and marketing expenses the same as any Section 203(b) case. If properties in similar developments in the area have been sold, then direct comparisons are possible and the Comparative Approach would be valid and should be used.

## B.  ESTIMATE OF MARKET PRICE

Estimating the market price of an equivalent site requires consideration of these factors not usually encountered in ordinary appraisals:

◊    Consider the size of individual sites when approaching the use of common areas and recreational facilities.

◊    If there are similar developments in the neighborhood, consider a comparison of common areas, including recreational amenities.

◊    If there are no similar developments, place more emphasis on the cost to produce a similar site with similar facilities and benefits.

◊    Distribute the pro rata supportable cost to maintain the common improvements, facilities and land owned by the homeowner's association to each site in the development (subdivision) and add it to the estimated value.

◊    To reflect additional amenities to the common areas, include an estimate on the Marshall and Swift Form 1007.  On line 32, cross out "landscaping cost" and enter additional amenities".

◊    Consider maintenance charges regarding cluster arrangements.  For example, note whether the advantages of cluster arrangements are negated by high maintenance charges.

◊    Before performing the assignment, check with the lender to ascertain that the project is on an approved list maintained by the Home Ownership Center (HOC).  Check the URAR item indicating that the property is within a PUD project.

## 9-1 CONDOMINIUMS

A condominium is a form of fee ownership or long-term leasehold of separate units or portions of multiunit buildings that provides for formal filing and recording of a divided interest in real property.  In contrast to a PUD, a joint share in ownership of the common area is part of the mortgaged property, and therefore, constitutes a measure of the security backing the mortgage loan.  FHA's interest is therefore more immediate and direct with respect to the common areas of condominiums than those of PUDS.  Before performing the assignment, the appraiser must check with the lender to ascertain that the project is on an approved list maintained by the HOC or by a DE underwriter who has performed a spot condominium approval.  The appraiser must check the URAR item indicating that the property is within a condominium project, and therefore, eligible for FHA endorsement.

## A.  DEFINITIONS

**Mortgage:**  a lien covering a fee interest or eligible leasehold interest in a one-family unit in a project, together with an undivided interest in the common areas and facilities serving the project.

**Family Unit:**  a one-family unit including the undivided interest in the common areas and facilities and such restricted common areas and facilities as may be designated.

**Common Areas and Facilities:**  areas that are for the use and enjoyment of the owners of family units located in the project, including the land, roof, main walls, elevators, staircases, lobbies, halls, parking spaces and community and commercial facilities.

**Restricted or Limited Common Areas and Facilities:**  areas and facilities restricted for use by a particular family unit or number of family units.

**Project:**  a structure or structures containing four or more units.

**Conversion:**  the creation of the condominium as of the date when all of the documents necessary to create a condominium regime have been recorded under state and/or local law.

**Tenant:**  the occupant named in the lease or rental agreement of a housing unit in a project on the date when:

◊    The condominium conversion documents are properly filed for the project, or

◊    On the date when the occupants are notified by management of intent to convert the project to a condominium, whichever is earlier.

**Bona fide Tenants' Organization:**  an association formed by the tenants to promote their interest in a particular project whose membership is open to each tenant and whose requirements apply equally to each tenant.

**Condominium Fee (Assessment):**  the apportionment of common expenses that are to be charged to a unit owner in a manner to be determined in the declaration or by-laws.  The charge may include costs for utilities on individual units and on common use buildings, security requirements, salaries for employees of the association and repairs to common facilities.

## B.  APPROACH TO VALUE

The approach to value for a single unit in a condominium project is similar to that for other home mortgage programs.  As in other home mortgage appraisals, value indications from the Sales Comparison and Income Capitalization Approaches are developed and considered (see Chapter 4 of this Handbook).  The cost approach can not be performed for a condominium unit.

### 1. Sales Comparison Approach

The appraiser should obtain sales data from any other units in the project and from other competitive condominium projects, including adjustments because of site factors, such as:

◊ Differences in views from the unit

◊ Proximity to recreation areas (swimming pools, clubhouses, tennis courts, etc.)

◊ Proximity to odors and the nuisance of incinerators proximity to garbage chutes or refuse areas proximity to noisy pumps or boiler rooms

Adjustments must also be made for the following:

◊ Differences in physical improvements within the dwelling that have been made by the owner-occupant

◊ Differences in preferences of purchasers between upper and lower floors and all other site factors

## APPENDIX A: VALUATION OF OTHER PROPERTIES

### A-1 REAL ESTATE OWNED (REO)

HUD's Real Estate Owned (REO) properties are a result of paying a claim to a lending institution and the lender transferring ownership of the property to HUD. Typically, REO properties were owned by the lender because the borrower defaulted on the mortgage. The appraiser must coordinate a specific time for a full site inspection of the property with the property manager. Generally, REO property is secured with the utilities turned off. However, the appraiser should attempt to have the utilities turned on to examine all building systems during the appraisal.

### A.  Appraiser Requirements

Requirements for appraisers who perform REO appraisals are the same as for appraisers of any other property. An appraiser of REO property must be state licensed and be a current member of the FHA Register.

### B. Appraisal Requirements - "As-Is" Value

REO properties are to be appraised "as-is". *The Dictionary of Real Estate Appraisal,* third edition, defines "as-is" market value as follows:

◊ "The value of specific ownership rights to an identified parcel of real estate as of the effective date of the appraisal; relates to that which physically exists and is legally permissible and excludes all assumptions concerning hypothetical market conditions or possible reasoning."

The "as-is" value is the market value for the property as it exists on the date of the appraisal. The appraisal shall consist of the Uniform Residential Appraisal Report (URAR) and the Valuation Conditions (VC) form. The appraiser shall indicate on the appraisal or an addendum to the appraisal if the property can be sold with FHA mortgage insurance (meets FHA minimum property requirements) either (1) in its as-is condition without repairs or (2) in its as-is condition with repairs costing $5,000 or less. If the property can be sold with FHA mortgage insurance by making $5,000 or less in repairs, the appraiser shall provide a list of the repairs and their estimated cost. If the property needs more than $5,000 in repairs to make it eligible for FHA mortgage insurance, the appraiser needs only to list the general areas of repairs and provide a statement that such repairs will exceed $5,000.

### C.  Effective Date of Value

The effective date of value is the date when the appraiser performs the site visit for the subject property. If another date is used as the effective date, the appraiser must specifically indicate:

◊ The alternative date

◊ The date when the subject property was physically inspected

### D.  Scope

The appraiser must perform the complete appraisal process, which includes considering all applicable approaches to value and developing appropriate approaches identified in this Handbook.

### E.  Purpose

The purpose of the REO appraisal is to help establish the sales price for the subject property. REO appraisals will estimate the "as-is" value of a foreclosed property owned by HUD.

### F.  Intended Use of Appraisal/Function

The intended use or function of a REO appraisal is to provide the 'as-is" value of foreclosed property for marketing and bidding purposes. Great reliance will be placed on the as-is value of the property for future sale. The as-is value supports FHA's sales price for the disposition of the property. The extent of repairs needed to the property will determine if it is offered for sale with FHA-insured financing or without insured financing. If the property meets minimum FHA property requirements without repairs, or meets FHA minimum property requirements with $5,000 or less of repairs, the property will be offered with FHA insured financing. If required repairs exceed $5,000, the property will be offered without Section 203(b) insured financing, but eligible for Section 203k insured financing.

## G.  Additional Requirements

The appraiser must value the subject property from the information gathered and arrive at an estimated market value of the subject property based on the requirements detailed in Chapter 4-Valuation Analysis-of this Handbook. Include all transaction data of the previous homeowner, date of that transaction and sale prices based on USPAP requirements. This provides a benchmark or frame of reference for the property and neighborhood market conditions. For properties where the interior cannot be inspected because of adverse occupants or other reasons, estimate the value based on an exterior inspection of the property. *Use the Freddie Mac 704 form, Second Mortgage Property Value Analysis Report, in conducting exterior estimates of value.* Prepare a narrative report on the outside condition and the apparent maintenance of the property in contrast to the neighborhood properties. Include the estimate of Value and include photographs of the exterior, as well. A building sketch is required, but a floor plan or room layout of the property is not required. The appraiser must consider and note the exposure period and estimate how long the property is expected to remain on the market. The exposure period differs from the marketing period. The exposure period estimates the length of time the property interest would have been offered on the market before the effective date of the appraisal. The concept of reasonable exposure encompasses not only adequate, sufficient and reasonable time but also adequate, sufficient and reasonable effect. The Valuation Analysis must be based upon a Reasonable Exposure Period. When appraising REO properties, the appraiser must adhere to all other valuation and appraisal requirements discussed in previous chapters.

## A-1.1   Approaches To Value

### A.  Cost Approach

Generally, the Cost Approach is not developed for REO properties. If the Cost Approach is justified, follow the specifications outlined in Chapter 4: Valuation Analysis. The appraiser is required to quantify repair costs in depreciation for an "as-is" value.

### B.  Sales Comparison Approach

Often, the Sales Comparison Approach is the most applicable approach to estimate the market value of a REO property. Appraisers must utilize sales comparables from other REO transactions from HUD, the Department of Veterans Affairs, Fannie Mae, Freddie Mac, or a conventional lender, as long as they include the following requirements:

   ◊   In the subject neighborhood or reasonable proximity
   ◊   Comparable property subject to reasonable adjustment
   ◊   Sold with a willing buyer and seller
   ◊   Exposed to the market for a reasonable period

If comparables such as these are not available, regular market comparables may then be used. Do not use distressed sales such as Sheriff Sales in the Sales Comparison Approach. These sales do not involve a willing seller nor are they exposed to the market under normal conditions. The resulting value indication derived from the use of such sales is not consistent with the definition of market value. Always use the sales comparison approach for one- and two- unit properties. This approach relies on:

   ◊   The availability of sales data
   ◊   The volume of transactions
   ◊   The mirroring of Sales Comparison Approach
   ◊   The market
   ◊   The ability to observe and report the most recent market trends

Data confirmed and developed under this approach has direct application to the other approaches used and should be considered therein. At least three comparable sales must be used with this approach. At all times, the appraiser must carry forth the assumptions and data from the other approaches and the VC form in developing a value estimate by the Sales Comparison Approach.

### C.  Income Approach

Generally, the Income Approach is not developed for one- or two-family REO properties. If the market indicates that the Income Approach is justified, follow the specifications outlined in Section 5: Valuation Analysis. For three- and four-unit properties, always use the income approach.

**A.1.2    Reporting Requirements**

An REO appraisal must be performed in accordance with the Uniform Standards of Professional Appraisal Practice (USPAP). Other reporting requirements are as follows:

◊   With each appraisal, the appraiser must provide a list of any buyer incentives that would enhance the marketability of the property to provide an incentive to buy the property un-repaired as opposed to repaired.

◊   For all property constructed before 1978, the appraiser must condition the appraisal on the completion of a lead-based paint test.

◊   For appraisals of vacant lots (land), complete Form FW 68, Land Appraisal Report, or an equivalent form.

**A-1.3    Reconciliation**

The final analytical step in the valuation process is to reconcile value indicators. In this step, the appraiser must measure the strengths and weaknesses of each applicable approach and develop this data into a single value estimate.

## A-2 APPRAISAL OF SINGLE FAMILY HOMES ON NATIVE AMERICAN LANDS

For purposes of this appraisal guidebook, if a lender specifically needs an appraisal under HUD/FHA's Section 248 program on Tribal Trust land or for HUD's Office of Native American Program (HUD/ONAP) Section 184 on Tribal Trust, allotted (which is also known as individual trust) and fee simple lands, these guidelines will apply. If the property is on allotted (or individual) trust or fee simple land located on Native American Reservations and it will be mortgaged under HUD/FHA's Section 203(b), the appraiser must use the basic appraisal methodology addressed in this handbook. Within designated Native American Reservations, treaties and tribal laws have created a variety of ownership patterns. Some parcels may be unrestricted fee simple, other parcels restricted tribal trust or allotted trust land. The appraiser must be familiar with the different restrictions and develop a reasonable value for the subject property. Following are the general designations.

### A.    FEE SIMPLE UNRESTRICTED

Fee simple unrestricted ownership is ownership real property which may be bought, sold and transferred between Native American or non-Native American purchasers without review by the Tribe or Bureau of Indian Affairs, (BIA). For the HUD/ FHA Section 203(b) program, appraisals must conform to all other standard HUD appraisal policies. For the HUD/ONAP Section 184 program, fee simple land on a reservation, the procedures utilized for tribal trust and allotted trust may be followed. Restricted Trust Land is land held by an individual Indian or Tribe which is subject to Federal restriction against alienation or encumbrance. Before any lien can be placed against restricted land, the transaction must be approved by the Bureau of Indian Affairs (BIA). All HUD loans must comply with this requirement and provide evidence in the HUD loan file. Lenders are encouraged to make contact with the appropriate BIA and Tribal realty officers early in the loan processing.

### B.    TRIBAL TRUST

Tribal trust lands are held in trust for the tribe by the United States government. Tribes may lease portions of the tribal trust land for the use of specific individuals, but ownership, through the Federal trust, remains with the tribe.

### C.    ALLOTTED (OR INDIVIDUAL) TRUST LAND

Land owned by individual tribal members but held in trust by the United States government. It is common for allotted trust lands to be owned by several individuals. If a prospective borrower proposes to use all or a portion of a fractionated property, all other owners must indicate acceptance of this arrangement by becoming parties to the mortgage or subdividing the subject parcel out to the individual for undivided ownership.

**A-2.1    PROPERTY RIGHTS APPRAISED**

### A.    TRIBAL TRUST LAND

HUD/FHA's Section 248 insures mortgages and HUD/ONAP's Section 184 guarantees mortgages on homes that are located on Native American Tribal Trust Land. For these properties, leased ownership of the underlying land remains with the tribe and will be subject to a long-term 50 year ground lease (or a 25 year lease with a 25 year renewable term). Determining the value for the leasehold estate is the purpose of the appraisal and the subsequent use is to provide supporting documentation for a HUD insured or guaranteed mortgage. Mortgages on tribal trust sites must include an acceptable lease signed by the mortgagor and Tribal authority and approved by the BIA.

### B.    ALLOTTED (OR INDIVIDUAL) TRUST LAND

Mortgages on allotted (or individual) trust sites do not involve a lease, but a specific mortgage rider is required. All HUD loans must have a Deed of Trust Rider attached approving the mortgage pursuant to 25 USC 483 (a) and approved by the BIA. HUD/ONAP's Section 184 guarantees mortgages on allotted trust land. Allotted trust land is held in trust by the federal government for individual Native Americans. The land is owned by the individual and value is given for the land. When appraising allotted trust land for Section 184, appraisers may follow the method given for Tribal Trust Land. HUD/FHA insures mortgages on homes that are located on allotted trust land under Section 203(b). The appraiser can use this data for background information, but must use the typical appraisal practices for FHA Section 203 addressed in Chapters 3 and 4 of this handbook. The appraiser must perform the complete appraisal process according to current USPAP and HUD/FHA standards. This includes consideration of all applicable approaches to value and complete development of all applicable approaches, as identified herein.

## A-2.2   APPROACHES TO VALUE

The appraiser must be familiar with the different restrictions and develop the appropriate value for the subject property. The supply of comparable sales and rental transactions vary by site and by tribes. Until sufficient sales exist on a reservation or within the specific Native American area to provide a reasonable sales comparison approach for determining the value of tribal trust leaseholds or allotted land sales, the appraiser must rely on other value indicators. The appraisal process must be documented more thoroughly than a typical market appraisal. USPAP Standards #1 and # 2 are effective to allow the appraiser to "correctly employ those recognized methods and techniques that are necessary to produce a credible appraisal." And "in reporting the results of a real property appraisal an appraiser must communicate each analysis, opinion and conclusion in a manner that is not misleading." An appraisal on trust land may rely more on the cost approach, or data developed from other tribes. HUD will accept the report if the appraiser has documented the search, information developed and conclusions clearly for the intended users to understand.

### A.   Cost Approach

The cost approach is often the primary indication of value based on the unique nature of the reservation setting. In conjunction with the completion of this approach on tribal trust sites, the value of the site as vacant does not apply. On the cost approach addenda to the URAR the value of the site is zero or a small leasehold value. if the land lease is at market and there was no upfront payment the lease-fee value is equivalent to the leasehold value, which is zero. This is the typical scenario and no value exists for the underlying land. The appraiser should enter the statement "subject is on Tribal Trust Land with annual rent not capitalized" in comments. If a market exists and the land was purchased, the value is estimated via traditional methods.

#### 1.   New Construction

Due to the flexibility allowed by law, HUD permits the inclusion of development costs for new construction, which can exceed market value, to be used in both Section 248 and Section 184. Following are instructions specific to new construction on tribal lands. The basic appraisal methodology is addressed in Chapter 4 of this handbook. In addition to including the cost of water, septic, and any other on-site costs in the cost approach, for lands within the reservation, the appraiser may provide an allowance for off-site development costs. The lesser of actual pro-rated costs or up to 10% of the cost of the construction of the subject house may be added for off-site infrastructure associated with development of the subject lot. This policy applies principally to new construction where such charges are assessed by tribally approved entities such as housing entities or housing authorities, or agreements with other federal or local government bodies for providing power, utilities, sewer/water and/or road construction. The costs to bring utilities; including public water, sewer, electricity, and telephone represent significant development costs. The traditional tract development of residential homes may not be a part of the local culture. Therefore, the utility costs to hook-up to any form of a public system in a more rural area can exceed local standards.

In remote areas, the construction costs in the Marshall & Swift guide or related cost manuals may have to be adjusted for transportation, labor or other costs not included in the basic estimate. Architect fees are not typically reflected in the base building costs. Due to special circumstances the normal Alsite for this fee may not automatically reflect the above actual cost. The appraiser must provide a supporting explanation in the adjustments to the construction costs.

#### 2.   Existing Construction

Where market sales are limited, HUD requires the cost approach to be completed on all tribal trust appraisals, including a credible estimate of depreciation.

### B.   Sales Comparison Approach

Native American communities are developing economies at varying rates and degrees. It is important for the lender and HUD to understand the economic factors which affect value. Therefore the appraiser must communicate the local tribal housing market. The sales comparison approach will generally be completed, and in remote areas may involve sales up to 18 months old. Where no credible comparables are available, a narrative justification that discusses the market, and provides any sales, rental or vacancy information pertinent to the subject will be acceptable to support value developed from the cost approach. In addition to the typical data sources the appraiser may obtain sales information from the local tribal or Bureau of Indian Affairs (BIA) realty office. Sales from other reservations within the region may be considered. Each situation will have unique factors and the appraiser should explain deviations from the sales comparison approach instructions outlined in Chapter 4 of this Handbook. The order of selection preferences for sales would depend on the type of land being appraised.
  ◊   Tribal Trust Leasehold sales (market sales between tribal members)
  ◊   Sales of allotted land trust between tribal members

◊   Fee Simple within the Reservation (residual value of the improvements by adjusting out the land contribution)
◊   Fee Simple proximate to the Reservation

For comparable sales that include land value, an adjustment is required to back-out the raw land value. This adjustment is required when comparing a fee simple comparable sale to a Native American trust sale transaction. Enter adjustments on the form under "Other" and label as "Raw Land Value," which is determined separately for each of the comparable sales.

### C.   Income Approach
The income approach is generally not developed with regard to Native American Trust Land. If the property includes a rental unit(s), the appraiser must provide an estimate of monthly rent for each unit and note whether or not the rent is limited to the tribal sub-market. If the appraiser determines that this approach is justified, the appraiser should complete the income approach according to the specifications outlined in Chapter 4 of this Handbook.

### A-2.3   Reconciliation of Value
The appraiser must determine the market value for the restricted trust properties from the limited data available. Value determination on trust land is an exception to typical HUD/FHA instructions; value is not limited to the lower of cost or market. Where market information is limited, greater weight may be given to the replacement cost approach. Document the decision process and the value.

### A-2.4   HUD/FHA REQUIREMENTS
On loans involving restricted trust land, with either Section 184 or Section 248, HUD waives the requirement of a strict interpretation of market value and will accept loans based on the above market cost approach. All other HUD health, safety, access, and property condition issues must conform to FHA requirements. The appraiser must indicate if the property is in need of, or in the process of receiving any repairs. Make appropriate requirements for repairs-to-be-completed and appraise the property "as repaired." The appraiser must indicate if the property conforms to the applicable Minimum Property Requirements of this Handbook. If it does not, the appraiser must recommend correction of the deficiency or rejection of the loan and explain. Tribally owned and maintained streets and utilities are considered publicly owned. Appraisers must require easements and a maintenance agreement for non-public, common ownership situations. HUD accepts tribal enforcement of building codes and inspections to the extent they are standard and enforced. At the point tribal support is not available, review and certification that the work complies with an appropriate national standard must be contracted out to a licensed or certified specialist. Example, a tribe issues building permits, but has no provisions for inspections. The lender/borrower must contract with a lender approved qualified specialist such as an engineer, architect or inspector. Inspection/approval by the Indian Health Service is acceptable for individual or community water and sewer systems. The remaining economic life must be estimated and reported but does not limit the mortgage. The subject property must possess sufficient remaining physical life to warrant a long-term mortgage. The mortgage term may not exceed the remaining physical life of the property.

#### A.   HUD/FHA Section 248 and HUD/ONAP Section 184 Requirements
For both Section 248 and Section 184 programs, the property must be free of hazards, noxious odors, grossly offensive sights or excessive noises which might endanger the physical improvements, affect the livability of the property, its marketability, or the health and safety of its occupants. If any of these conditions exist, the appraiser must recommend correction of the problem or rejection of the loan and explain. For both programs, the appraiser will make appropriate requirements to correct any observed or potential environmental problems. Many reservations have not been mapped for the 100-year flood plain. If the appraiser observes a possible flood plain problem, they are to require flood insurance on existing properties. The Underwriter may waive the flood insurance requirement if the borrower or the tribe provides an elevation certificate from a licensed engineer that the property is not at risk from flooding. Note that the lowest floor (including basement) for new construction must be at or above the 100-year flood elevation.

#### B.   REPORTING REQUIREMENTS
The appraiser must report if an approach was not developed and insert the rationale for exclusion of the approach. The appraiser must attach an addendum complete with the assumptions supporting the indication of value by the cost approach. The cost approach is reconciled to the other values, if any, on the URAR. The appraiser will indicate any work requirements or VC pursuant to outstanding instructions. The DE underwriter/lender must assure acceptable completion of any work requirements pursuant to existing instructions.

### A-2.5   INSTRUCTIONS FOR ASSISTED APPRAISAL PROCESSING IN APPRAISAL HIGH COST AREAS
To accommodate the special conditions associated with remote sites on Native American lands, the following assisted appraisal process is allowed. The assigned appraisers may network with local personnel where the high cost of real estate appraisals is a concern for underwriting single family mortgages in Native American communities. To minimize this problem, FHA and ONAP will allow the use of trained local personnel to perform the inspection, provide current analysis of the local market, and draft the appraisal report. The report must be forwarded to the assigned appraiser who win review the report, provide additional

documentation, sign the URAR and forward the report to the lender. Using the Assisted Appraisal Process is restricted to remote areas where licensed appraisers are not readily available. It may be used when the cost of transportation and/or time increases the cost of the appraisal to twice the cost of typical appraisals in the local urban areas. The process must be monitored and acceptable to the DE underwriter/lender. The assigned appraiser may use local subcontractors who:

◊    Have general real estate skills (construction, lending, sales, management) acceptable to the appraiser (such as Housing Authority staff, Tribal Designated Housing Entities (TDHE) staff or BIA realty personnel, local real estate professionals).

◊    Must comply with the Conflict of Interest limitations (have no personal or financial interest with the buyers or sellers of the property).

◊    An appraiser who signs a real property appraisal report prepared by another, even under the label of "review appraiser" must accept full responsibility for the contents of the report, USPAP Standard 2-5.

◊    The assigned appraiser is responsible for the entire appraisal and signs the URAR. The individual assisting in the report must document the extent of help provided and certify no conflict of interest exists in the certification.

◊    The assigned appraiser must be familiar with the Competency Rule in the USPAP. This includes key issues such as the unique property rights conveyed, the local market involved and market conditions. It is assumed the remote area markets will change slowly. If conditions have changed, an updated analysis is required. The assigned appraiser assumes all responsibility that the appraisal meets all HUD/FHA and ONAP program requirements.


## APPENDIX B: SPECIAL PROGRAMS
### B-1 203(K) REHABILITATION HOME MORTGAGE INSURANCE

The Section 203(k) program is HUD's primary program for rehabilitating and repairing single-family properties. A Section 203(k) mortgage provides financing for the acquisition and rehabilitation construction of a property. The mortgage is funded by a HUD-approved lender and insured by HUD/FHA. A Section 203(k) mortgage may be used to perform the following:

◊    Purchase a property and repair/renovate it.
◊    Purchase a dwelling on another site, move it onto a new foundation and repair/ renovate it.
◊    Refinance existing indebtedness and repair/ renovate a property.
◊    Repair/renovate a presently owned property.

The following table summarizes which properties are eligible under Section 203(k).

| Type of Property | Eligibility |
|---|---|
| Condominiums | Yes 2/ |
| Mobile homes | Yes |
| Cooperatives | No |
| Non-residential being converted to single family (1-4 unit) | Yes |
| Single family (over 1 year old) | Yes |

A 203(k) mortgage may be originated on a "mixed use" residential property provided that:

◊    The percentage floor area used for commercial purposes follows these standards:
   o   One story building          25%
   o   Two story building          49%
   o   Three story building        33%

◊    The commercial use will not affect the health and safety of the occupants of the residential property

◊    The rehabilitation funds will only be used for the residential functions of the dwelling and areas used to access the residential part of the property.


2/    Condominiums are eligible only if they meet the following requirements:

◊    FHA/VA approved
◊    Maximum loan does not exceed 100%
◊    Improvements are only within the unit walls
◊    Condominium is complete with no ongoing or anticipated addition of any units or common areas
◊    Unit owners have had control of the common area for at least one year
◊    The condominium association has proof of hazard, liability and flood insurance coverage
◊    Unit is owned fee simple
◊    There are no restrictive covenants or provisions restricting conveyance of the unit

◊   A minimum of 90% of the units in the project have been sold
◊   51 % or greater of the units in the project are owner occupied
◊   No single entity owns more than 10% of the units in a project with more than 30 units.
◊   No single entity owns more than 20% of the units in a project with less than 30 units.

## A.   ELIGIBLE IMPROVEMENTS
(B-1)   A minimum of $5,000 must be used in part for renovation and/or repair of an existing property.  Minor or cosmetic repairs or new fixtures alone, such as stoves and refrigerators, are not acceptable.  The repair or renovation may include:
   ◊   Making structural alterations such as repair or replacement of structural damage, additions to structure and finished attics and/or basements
   ◊   Eliminating health and safety hazards that would violate HUD's Minimum Property Standards
   ◊   Installing wells and/or septic systems and reconditioning plumbing
   ◊   Making changes for improved functions and modernization
   ◊   Making changes for aesthetic appeal and eliminating obsolescence
   ◊   Repairing or adding roofing, gutters and downspouts
   ◊   Making energy conservation improvements
   ◊   Landscaping, grading, repairing patios and terraces that improve the property equal to the dollar amount spent on the improvements
   ◊   Creating accessibility for the handicapped

## B.   INELIGIBLE IMPROVEMENTS
Any luxury item and/or improvement that does not become a permanent part of the subject property is not eligible, including:
   ◊   Additions or alterations to support commercial use or to equip or refurbish space for commercial use
   ◊   Recreational or luxury improvements, such as swimming pools, hot tubs, whirlpool baths and saunas
   ◊   Barbecue pits, bath houses, tennis courts, satellite dishes or tree surgery

## C.   BORROWER, PLAN REVIEWER AND APPRAISER
The borrower must have the following items prepared before an application, review or appraisal can occur:
   ◊   An existing plan of the structure
   ◊   A proposed plan detailing where structural or planning changes are contemplated
   ◊   Inspection reports from a qualified engineer or inspection service denoting the presence of rodents, dry rot or termites and evaluating the adequacy of the existing structural, heating, plumbing, electrical and roofing systems
   ◊   Specifications of repairs
   ◊   For site improvements, a plot plan denoting the location of the structure, walkways, drives and other relevant details
   ◊   Description of materials (HUD Form 92005 or similar form)

**203k Consultant:** The borrower selects a HUD approved 203(k) Consultant to do the following:
   ◊   Visit the site
   ◊   Prepare work write-up that specifies a description and cost of each work item
   ◊   Review the architectural exhibits for compliance with HUD's Minimum Property Standards
   ◊   Inspect any of the property's health and safety items noted on the drawings
In comparing the cost estimates with others projects, the consultant can use R.S. Means & Company Repair and Remodeling Cost Data Book or The Home-Tech Remodeling and Renovation Cost Estimator.  When the consultant has reviewed the property and respective plans, an appraisal can be requested.  The lender will hire the same or another 203(k) Consultant to inspect the rehabilitation during construction and sign off on all draw requests.

**Appraiser.** The appraiser is required to perform an "as-repaired" appraisal and to report it on the URAR.  When performing an "as-repaired" appraisal, appraise the subject property at its expected market value when the proposed rehabilitation and/or improvements are complete. Also, a lender may request an "as-is" appraisal to be recorded on a separate URAR.  Under an "as-is" appraisal, the subject property is appraised in its present condition to establish the value before rehabilitation.  Repair requirements or VC conditions are not included in the "as is" valuation. The appraiser must visit the property, review the architectural exhibits showing the proposed work and review the proposal for standard valuation conditions that may have been overlooked.  If conditions exist that impact the safety and health of the occupants, discuss these items with the plan reviewer to correct them in the architectural exhibits.

**B-2 SECTION 255: HOME EQUITY CONVERSION MORTGAGES (*REVERSE MORTGAGES*)**

A Reverse Mortgage allows a borrower aged 62 and older to borrow against the equity in a property that has limited outstanding debt. A subject property under this program must be a one- to four-unit dwelling in which the mortgagor occupies one of the units. The appraiser must perform the appraisal with the same standards and forms expected in an FHA single-family appraisal. It may be a unit in an approved condominium or Planned Unit Development (PUD). Manufactured homes are eligible if the home complies with outstanding FHA guidance. The same deficiencies and repair items must be noted on the URAR forms. In certain instances, the borrower is not required to treat any defective paint surfaces after closing for properties built before 1978.

**B-3 SECTION 223(E)**

Section 223(e) is a mortgage insurance program for properties located in older, declining urban areas. The program allows for the acquisition, repair and/or renovation or construction of a residential property. Under this program, FHA waives the requirement that the subject property have a remaining economic life of at least five years if the property is in a reasonably viable location where there is a need for affordable housing.

**Appraisal:** The property must comply with HUD's Minimum Property Requirements of , and the appraisal must denote any deficiencies on the VC form. When conducting an appraisal on a subject property eligible for this program, the appraiser must determine the remaining economic life by examining the pattern of recent changes in the adjacent sites' land use strategies that would be incompatible with single-family use. If the remaining economic life is less than five years, prepare a plan of the subject property denoting the land use patterns surrounding it. The physical life of the property must be sufficient to permit a long-term mortgage. Under this program, the physical life of a property can be substituted for the economic life because of the special risk provisions that compensates for the economic factors that adversely affect the property.

**B-4 TITLE I PROPERTY IMPROVEMENT AND MANUFACTURED HOME LOAN  PROGRAM**

Title I is two-loan programs, one for property improvements and one for the purchase of manufactured homes and/or lots on which the manufactured homes are to be placed. No appraisal is needed for a property improvement loan; however, an appraisal of any real property involved in a manufactured home is required or for any existing home. This would be:

◊   A manufactured home lot loan
◊   The lot portion of a combination loan for the purchase of a lot and manufactured home
◊   A used manufactured home

If a loan defaults, the lender repossessing the manufactured home under the Uniform Commercial Code or through judicial processes must request an N.A.D.A. appraisal. Appraisals of repossessed manufactured homes should be made before removal by the lender.

**B-5 SOLAR ENERGY**

To encourage the use of solar energy in homes, HUD will insure a mortgage up to 20 percent above the maximum allowable insurable amount in a geographical area if such increase is necessary to account for the increased cost of the residence due to the installation of a solar energy system which may not exceed 20 percent of the value of the property. An eligible solar energy system is defined as any addition, alteration, or improvement to an existing or new structure which is designed to utilize wind or solar energy to reduce energy requirements obtained from other sources. Active, passive and photovoltaic solar energy systems are permitted in this program, provided they are accompanied by operational 100 percent back-up conventional systems. The solar energy system's contribution to value will be limited by its replacement cost or by its effect on the market price of the dwelling. In the event that market data is not available to indicate the additional amount which would be paid for a property containing a solar energy system, the amount of increase would be the lesser of the actual cost of the solar system installed in the subject house or 20 percent of the market value of the property. The difference in added value contributed by the solar system in comparison to the conventional system must represent a reasonable proportion of the total value of the property and may never exceed 20 percent of the market value of the property without a solar energy system.

**A.  Appraisal Procedure**

The appraiser shall reflect in value the local market acceptance of solar heating equipment. Solar collectors must be located where they will be free from natural or man made obstructions to the sun.

**1.  Solar Hot Water Systems**

Acceptability. When such systems are proposed to be installed, they must comply with the provisions of Use of Materials Bulletin Number 100, Subject: HUD Building Product Standards and Certification Program for Solar Water Heating Systems, issued August 15,1993. [Use of Materials Bulletin are available for public inspection during regular business hours in the Office of Consumer and Regulatory Affairs, Department of Housing and Urban Development, Room 9156,451 7'h Street S.W., Washington, DC 20410. They will soon be available on the HUD Web Page.] When such a system is already installed in an existing home, the appraiser may request an inspection by a qualified solar system inspector/contractor for recommendations as to acceptability in operations, maintenance and life expectancy.

**2.   Photovoltaic Systems** [In Preparation]

**3.   Limits to Value**
The solar heating or hot water system's contribution to value will be limited by its replacement cost and by its effect on the market price of the dwelling.  In estimating market value by comparing a subject property that has a solar heating system to a recently sold comparable property with a fossil fuel system only, increased the sale price of the comparable by the amount typically paid in the market for the solar heating system.

**4.   Temporary Procedure**
Lack of Market Data.  In the event that market data is not available to indicate the additional amount which would be paid for a property which does include solar heating or hot water system, then the amount of the increase shall be the difference in cost between all heating equipment, including solar installed in the subject house, less the cost of all heating equipment installed in the comparable property without a solar installation. However, in making this adjustment based on differences in cost, the appraiser shall consider the ratio between the value added by a solar heating system and the value of the property with a conventional heating system only, to ensure that the contribution of a solar heating system to the total value represents a reasonable proportion of the total value of the property.

**5.   Responsibility for Temporary Limit**
The HOC will consider the costs of acceptable solar energy systems for homes of several sizes, and will consider the market prices of typical homes of these several sizes (without solar energy systems) in order to set a limit on the amount which a solar energy system can add to the estimated value of the subject property.  This limit shall be expressed as a percentage of the market value of the subject property (before consideration of the solar energy system) and this limit shall not exceed 20 percent of the market value of the subject property (without a solar energy system).

## APPENDIX C:  VALUATION REFERENCES

## C-1 RULES OF ROUNDING

### A.   PRECISION IN ROUNDING

Precision in calculating value estimates is critical to obtaining consistent valuations.  Because the final estimate is a result of several calculations, the degree of precision used in the calculations could alter the final value.  Therefore, it is important to remain consistent throughout the calculations.  Also, consistency in rounding across appraisals is important for HUD to remain fair in determining insurance eligibility.  Each value that HUD considers must be the result of the same rounding process so that values are not altered.

### B.  RULES OF ROUNDING

Numbers are rounded to the least precise number used in calculations.  For example, $55,156 x 3.2=$176,499, is rounded to $180,000 because the least precise number contained two digits (3.2). The number, $176,499, was rounded by counting two places to the right of the beginning of the number.

Significant digits determine the precision of the numbers used in calculations.  Significant numbers determine precision because precision is the closeness of the measurement, not the degree of accuracy.  The following rules define significant numbers:

| Rules of Rounding | Examples |
|---|---|
| All nonzero digits are counted. | 345 has three significant digits. |
| Zeros that precede the first nonzero digit are not counted. | 002 has one significant digit and .0001 has one significant digit. |
| Zeros surrounded by nonzero digits are counted. | 30005 has five significant digits. |
| Zeros that follow the last nonzero digit are sometimes counted. | 32.0 contains three significant digits because the zero is holding a place and could only serve that function. However, 300 may have one or three significant digits.  Note that 300 has three significant digits because the decimal holds the precision to the decimal place. |
| All zeros at the end of a number are ignored when counting significant digits. | 139,000 has three significant digits counting from left to right and ignoring all trailing zeros.  Trailing zeros after a decimal are considered significant because it is assumed that a person placed the trailing zeros after a number to define the degree of precision. |

### C.   RULES OF ROUNDING EXAMPLE

The series of calculations used when deriving the adjusted base cost and value under the cost approach demonstrate where the rules of rounding would apply.

|  | Not applying rules | Rules of Rounding |
|---|---|---|
| Square footage single family home | 1,800 | 1,800 |
| Good quality Class D | $68.87 | 68.87 |
| No air conditioning | (2.02) | 2.02 |
|  | $66.85 | 66.85 |
| Height Adjustment for 10 ft. | 1.06 | 1.06 |
| Floor area/ shape multiplier | 0.982 | 0.982 |
|  | 1,041 | 1.04 |

| Adjusted Base Cost | 69.59 | 69.52 |
|---|---|---|
| | | |
| Current Cost Multiplier | <u>1.01</u> | <u>1.01</u> |
| | 70.28 | 70.22 |
| | | |
| Local Area Multiplier | <u>1.21</u> | <u>1.21</u> |
| | 85.04 | 84.966 |
| | | |
| | **$153,073** | **$153,000** |

## C-2 THE VALUATION PROCESS

| THE VALUATION PROCESS |
|---|
| Definition of Problem<br>Identification of Real Estate<br>Identification of Property Rights to be Values<br>Date of Value Estimate<br>Use of Appraisal<br>Definition of Value |

| **PRELIMINARY ANALYSIS, DATA SELECTION AND COLLECTION** | | |
|---|---|---|
| **General** | | **Specific** |
| Social | | (Subject and Comps) |
| Economic | | Sales |
| Governmental | | Cost |
| Environmental | | Income/Expense |
| | | Site Improvements |

| HIGHEST AND BEST USE ANALYSIS |
|---|
| Land as though Vacant<br>Property as Improved |

| LAND VALUE ESTIMATE |
|---|

| **Application of the Three Approaches** | | |
|---|---|---|
| Sales Comparison | Income Capitalization | Cost |

| RECONCILIATION OF VALUE<br>INDICATIONS AND FINAL VALUE ESTIMATE |
|---|

| REPORT OF DEFINED VALUE |
|---|

## APPENDIX D: COMPREHENSIVE VALUATION PACKAGE PROTOCOL

### D-1 RESIDENTIAL APPRAISAL REQUIREMENTS
This section provides specific instructions to complete the Uniform Residential Appraisal Report (URAR).

### Section 1 - Subject
This section provides the factual data to identify the property and the parties to the appraisal process. Information should be supplied by the client who engages the appraiser and other qualified parties, through public records and from local government records.

| Field | Protocol |
|---|---|
| File Number | Insert the FHA Case Number at the top right corner of the page. |
| Property Address | Provide the property street number and name, city, state and zip code for the property being appraised. |
| Legal Description | Enter the legal description of the property and its county. If the property address has not clearly been identified, enter a legal description. The four types of legal descriptions are: lot and block system, geo-detail survey, government survey system and metes and bounds system. Attach this information as an addendum if the space provided is insufficient. |
| Property Tax Information | Enter the assessor's parcel number, tax year, the total amount of real estate taxes, including all relevant taxes (school district tax, fire district tax, etc.) and special assessment information. For newly constructed properties that have not been assessed, mark "N/ A". Special assessments can include municipal bond debt for off-site improvements. The assessment can be expressed as a percentage of the assessor's opinion of market value. |
| Ownership Information | Enter the name of the current owner. The borrower may not be the current owner, except in the case of refinance transactions. Indicate who occupies the property: the owner, an occupant (if there is not an executed lease and owner does not live there), a tenant or if the property is vacant. Indicate if it is a HUD REO (real estate owned) property, in which case the property was foreclosed and HUD is the current owner. |
| Property Rights Appraised | Select the appropriate ownership rights for the subject property as of the date of appraisal. For HUD/VA mortgages, indicate the project type. Is it a Planned Unit Development or a Condominium? If there are monthly association dues to cover common property, enter this information in the HOA$/ Mo. space. If the subject is a form of condominium ownership and maintained by an association, report the monthly fees in this space. |
| Neighborhood or Project Name | A neighborhood is defined as a group of complementary uses. Use judgment in describing the boundaries. Provide the factual information for the location of the property. Include the name of the subdivision, if applicable, or the local neighborhood designation. If the subject property is in a planned development, provide the name of the development. Provide map reference and census tract information. For properties located in an area without tract numbers, enter "N/ A." The map reference is optional. Census tract numbers have ten digits. To reach the US Census Bureau, call 301-457-4608 Monday through Friday from 8:30 a.m. to 5:00 p.m. EST. |
| Transaction Data | Provide the agreed-on sales price, (accepted offer) date of sale, and all financial terms implicit in the offer and the pending sales contract. If unable to obtain this information, document all efforts to obtain it. If sales concessions are indicated, comment on any consequent effect on value. |
| Lender/ Client | Enter the name and address of the individual and firm who engaged the appraisal. Generally, it is assumed that the lender is also the client. If the client is not the same person as the lender, include the client's name. If the client is the owner, enter "Client is Owner". |
| Appraiser | Enter the name and address of the appraiser(s) signing the certification of appraisal. |

## Section 2 - Neighborhood

This section should reflect the area surrounding the subject property and all changes in the neighborhood. The appraiser must inspect the site characteristics and surrounding properties and make determinations that will be incorporated into the valuation of the subject property. In all instances, the appraiser must check the most appropriate box for each line and characteristic. Failure to note conditions that may adversely affect the value of the property is poor appraisal practice and may violate the Uniform Standards of Professional Appraisal Practice.

| Field | Protocol |
| --- | --- |
| Location | Enter the type of area surrounding the subject property. When both "urban" and "declining" are checked, consider making a recommendation that the mortgage encumbering the property be insured under Section 223(e). |
| Built-up | Enter the built-up percentage - the percentage of available land that has been improved. Land such as a state park would not be considered available. |
| Growth Rate | Enter the growth rate. If many lots are available, the growth rate may be rapid, stable or slow, but if the neighborhood is fully developed, select the "stable" box. |
| Property Values | Check off the box describing the current trend in property values in the community. Comparing houses that have been sold and resold in recent years is an effective way to determine the market trends. Appraisers who use this method, however, should make sure to factor in any adjustments made to the property between sales. |
| Demand/ Supply | Mark the appropriate demand /supply value. To determine the equilibrium status of supply and demand in the neighborhood, compare the number of houses sold to the number of houses listed for sale in a recent time period. The similarity or difference between the number of houses sold and listed, not the absolute numbers, should determine the demand/supply level. |
| Marketing Time | Mark the appropriate marketing time - the typical length of time a property similar to the subject property would have to stay on the market before being sold at a price near its market value. |
| Predominant Occupancy | Enter whether the neighborhood's predominant occupants are tenants or homeowners. The transient nature associated with tenants tends to decrease the property value of a given neighborhood. Also, check off the appropriate percentage to indicate the percentage of the properties in the neighborhood that are vacant. |
| Single Family Housing | Indicate the high and low neighborhood prices and ages, and what would be the predominant value and age. |
| Present Land Use | Estimate each type of land usage in the neighborhood. If there is no land in the neighborhood with one of the classifications, enter a "0" or a "-". If a portion of the land consists of parks or other unspecified classifications, enter * and enter the actual percentages on the first line of the 'Neighborhood Characteristics' section. |
| Land Use Change | Select whether the land use is not likely, likely or in the process of changing. If a change is imminent or likely, detail what the future use will be. Changes in land use refer to conversion from one developed parcel use to another developed use and not for the development of previously vacant land. Explain any impact on value resulting from likely or in-process land use changes. |
| Neighborhood Boundaries and Characteristics | Provide a description of neighborhood boundaries and characteristics. Details regarding bordering street names and both physical and economic characteristics typical of the neighborhood win provide substantial details and understanding regarding neighborhood composition. A site map indicating subject site and comparables will also shed light on the neighborhood. NOTE: Race and the racial composition of the neighborhood are not appraisal factors. |
| Factors that Affect Marketability | Discuss factors that would attract residents or cause them to reject the neighborhood. These are typical factors important to discuss: Proximity to employment and amenities, including travel distance and time to local employment sources and community amenities Employment Stability, in terms of variety of employment opportunities and industries Appeal to Market regarding the overall appeal of the neighborhood as compared to competitive neighborhoods in the same market Convenience to Shopping with respect to distance, time and required means of transportation Convenience to School in terms of the distance and time for travel to school |
| Market Conditions | Discuss market conditions in the subject neighborhood that may have an effect on appraisal value. |

## Section 3 - Planned Urban Development (PUD)

The appraiser must complete this section if the subject property is a part of a Planned Unit Development. Otherwise, strike the section. A PUD is a project that includes common property and improvements owned and maintained by an owners' association for the use and benefit of the individual units in the subdivision.

| Field | Protocol |
|---|---|
| Project Information | Select whether or not the developer/builder is in control of the Home Owners' Association (HOA). |
| Number of Units in Subject Project | Enter the approximate total number of units in the subject project and the number of units currently for sale. |
| Common Elements/ Recreation | Describe the common areas and recreational facilities of the PUD, including all areas accessible for use by PUD owners. |

## Section 4 - Site

This information provides the description of the land underlying the subject property. Insert factual information on each of the lines provided and report the conclusions as directed. Consider all aspects of the physical description and reconcile them in the estimate of market value.

| Field | Protocol |
|---|---|
| Dimensions | List all dimensions of the site. If the shape of the site is irregular, show the boundary dimensions (85'X 150'X 195'X 250') and attach a sketch or legal description of the site. |
| Site Area | Enter the site area in square feet or acres. |
| Corner Lot | Enter "YES" or "NO". |
| Zoning Classification | Enter the zoning type used by the local municipality and describe the majority of uses permitted. For example: "Residential-Single Family" or "Residential One to Four Units". IMPORTANT: Do not use abbreviations; they vary among different communities. |
| Zoning Compliance | Determine whether the current use is in compliance with the zoning ordinances. Check whether it is Legal, Legal Non-Conforming, Illegal or No Zoning. Use "Historic," if applicable. If there is a non-conforming use, enter "Non-Conforming" and state whether it is a legal use that has been approved by the local zoning authority. If the existing property does not comply with all of the current zoning regulations (use, lot size, improvement size, off street parking, etc.) but is accepted by the local zoning authority, enter "Legal Non-Conforming". If the use is not legal, the property is not eligible for HUD mortgage insurance. |
| Highest and Best Use | This entry represents the highest and best use of the site in relation to the neighborhood and current market conditions. If current use represents the highest and best use, check "present use". If it does not, check "other use" and provide a detailed explanation. |
| Utilities | Check either the "Public" box or explain under "Other." Public utilities mean governmentally supplied and regulated. Public does not include any community systems sponsored, owned or operated by the developer or a private company not subject to government regulation or financial assistance. For individual and/or community systems, check "Other". If the electricity is underground, please state this on the form. |
| Off-site Improvements | Briefly describe the off-site improvements under "Type" and check Public or Private. The appraiser must state the type of all off-site improvements - streets, curbs, gutters, sidewalks, alleys and streetlights - and indicate whether they are publicly or privately maintained. For example: "Street-Asphalt; Public." Public refers to an improvement dedicated to and accepted by a unit of government - not including Home Owner's Associations. |
| Topography | Enter whether the lot is level or sloped. If the lot is sloped, estimate the slope degree. |
| Size | Enter descriptions such as typical, small or large. Compare the size of the structure to the typical size of competitive properties in the neighborhood. Explain all deficiencies, significant inadequacies and potential super adequacies and consider them in the estimate of value. |

| | |
|---|---|
| Shape | Enter the site configuration: triangular, square, rectangular or irregular. This entry must be consistent with the dimensions provided on the Dimensions Field. |
| Drainage | Enter whether Adequate or Inadequate. If Inadequate, be sure to explain and make requirement for correction on the VC form. Explain all deficiencies that do not require repair and consider them in the estimate of value. |
| View | Briefly describe the view from the property. Identify a view with a significant positive or negative influence on the value. Include a photograph if feasible. |
| Landscaping | Enter whether adequate or inadequate, relative to neighborhood. Explain all inadequacies and super adequacies and consider them in the estimate of value. For new construction, include a description of any landscaping included in the sale price. |
| Driveway Surface | Enter surface type such as concrete, asphalt or gravel. An all-weather surface is required. If it does not exist, mark it as a repair requirement on the VC. Explain all deficiencies that do not require repair (extreme slope, etc.) and consider them in the estimate of value. |
| Apparent Easements | Describe any apparent easements. Consider easements affecting the functional utility of the property in the conclusions of both the highest and best use and market value. If an easement adversely affects the subject property, note the effect in the Adverse Conditions field. Consider surface, sub-surface and overhead easements. |
| FEMA Flood Hazard Area | FEMA (Federal Emergency Management Agency) is responsible for mapping flood hazard areas. If any of the improvements on the property are within a Special Flood Hazard Area, mark "YES". Otherwise, mark "NO". Attach a copy of the flood map panel for properties located within flood plains. |
| FEMA Zone | If the property is in a FEMA Flood Hazard Area, enter the FEMA Zone and map date. Only properties within Special Flood Hazard Areas, such as zones "A" and "V", require flood insurance. Zones "B" and "C" do not. |
| FEMA Map Number Comments | Enter the FEMA Map number and page number. If it is not shown on any map, enter "Not on FEMA Maps." Enter any comments related to the site. For example, discuss apparent adverse easements, encroachments, special assessments, slide areas, illegal or non-conforming zoning use, etc. Discuss the observations with direct relationship to value and consider them in the final estimate of value. |

## Section 5 - Description of Improvements

This section describes the subject improvements. Enter factual information on each of the lines provided and report the conclusions. Consider all aspects of the physical description and reconcile them in the estimate of market value.

| General Description | |
|---|---|
| **Field** | **Protocol** |
| Number of Units | Enter the number of units being valued. The URAR is designed for 1 to 4 units. Otherwise, use the multi-family form. |
| Number of Stories | Enter the number of stories *above grade,* including half stories. Do not include the basement. |
| Type (Detached/Attached) | Fill in the Type, "Det" (Detached), "Att" (Attached), "S/D" (Semi-Detached) or "R" (Row). |
| Design (Style) | Enter a brief description of the house design style using historical or contemporary fashion. For example: Cape Cod, bi-level, split level, split foyer, town house, etc. Do not use builder's model name. Avoid generic descriptions such as Traditional or Conventional. |
| Existing/ Proposed | Enter "E" (existing), "P" (proposed) or "UC" (under construction). A "P" or "UC" requires plans and specifications for the appraiser to review. If Rehabilitation, enter "REHAB" instead of "E" or "P". |
| Age (Years) | Enter the actual age, date of completion of the construction. Construction records may be helpful if available. If the property is less than two years old, include both the month and year completed. If it is over two years old, insert the completed year only. |
| Effective Age(Years) | Enter the effective age of the site. A range is acceptable. The effective age reflects the condition of the property relative to similar competitive properties. The effective age may be greater than, less than or equal to the actual age. Note any significant difference between the actual and effective ages and explain in the Comments section. |

## Exterior Description

The appraiser must address all visible deficiencies. Deferred maintenance and physical obsolescence must be considered in the valuation process.

| **Field** | **Protocol** |
|---|---|
| Foundation | Specify the type of material used for the foundation: poured concrete, concrete block, wood, etc. |
| Exterior Walls | Enter the type of construction material: aluminum, wood siding, brick veneer, porcelain, log, stucco, etc. If a combination of materials, show the predominant portion first. |
| Roof Surface | Enter material type used for roof surface: composition, wood, slate, tile, etc. |
| Gutters and Downspouts | Enter type: galvanized, aluminum, wood or plastic. If partial, state the site. |
| Window Type | Describe the type: double-hung, casement or siding. Also, identify the window frame material: wood, aluminum, steel, vinyl, etc. |
| Storm/Screens | State if there are storm screens or not. Enter "YES", "NO" or "PARTIAL". |
| Manufactured House | Enter manufactured home (MH) or modular (MOD), or answer "NO" if neither. A manufactured mobile home must have the seal that signifies compliance with the Federal Manufactured Home Construction and Safety Standards. |

## Foundation

The appraiser must   address all visible deficiencies and may require a recommendation for an inspection.  Consider deferred maintenance and physical obsolescence in the valuation process.  This statement links to the VC report, the valuation and the need for a full inspection.

| Field | Protocol |
|---|---|
| Slab | Enter "YES" or "NO".  Indicate its percentage of total foundation. |
| Crawl Space | Enter "YES" or "NO".  If partial, include percentage of floor area.  Indicate its percentage of total foundation. |
| Basement | Enter "Full", "Partial" or "None". Indicate its percentage of total foundation. |
| Sump Pump | Enter "YES" or "NO". |
| Dampness | Enter "YES" or "NO". If damp, make requirement for correction in the VC segment. |
| Settlement | Enter "YES" or "NO". Provide a detailed explanation and check for cracks. |
| Infestation | Enter "YES" or "NONE APPARENT". Look for evidence of any type of insects and related damage. If there is any, require insect infestation inspection in the VC segment. |

## Basement

The appraiser is required to inspect the basement.  Address all visible deficiencies which may require a recommendation for an inspection.  Consider deferred maintenance and physical obsolescence in the valuation process.  This statement links to the VC report, the valuation and the need for a full inspection.

| Field | Protocol |
|---|---|
| Area Sq. Feet | Enter square feet of basement area. |
| % Finished | Enter the percentage of basement square footage (figure above) that is finished. This is a percentage of total basement area that is finished, not a percentage of the ground floor area. |
| Ceiling | Enter material type: drywall, lath and plaster or Celotex ceiling panels. |
| Walls | Enter material type: drywall, wood panel or cinder block. |
| Floor | Enter floor type: asphalt, tile or concrete. Comment if any part is earth. |
| Outside Entry | Enter "YES" or "NO". If "YES", use blank line below to describe what type of entry exists. |

## Insulation

If access is available, the appraiser must inspect the following components and note the observations. Note all irregularities in the type or presence of insulation in the Comments section .

| Field | Protocol |
|---|---|
| Roof | Make every effort to determine if insulation is present and the type.  Enter R-factor or show depth and site.  If the type cannot be determined, enter "Unknown".  Do not guess. Comment whether the insulation is (G)ood, (A)verage, (F)air, (P)oor or (U)ndetermined. |
| Ceiling | Make every effort to determine the type.  Enter R-factor or show depth and site.  If the type cannot be determined, enter "Unknown".  Do not guess. Comment whether the insulation is (G)ood, (A)verage, (F)air, (P)oor or (U)ndetermined. |
| Walls | Make every effort to determine the type. Enter R-factor or show depth and site. If the type cannot be determined, enter "Unknown". Do not guess. Comment whether the insulation is (G)ood, (A)verage, (F)air, (P)oor or (U)ndetermined. |
| Floor | Make every effort to determine the type. Enter R-factor or show depth and site. If the type cannot be determined, enter "Unknown". Do not guess. Comment whether the insulation is (G)ood, (A)verage, (F)air, (P)oor or (U)ndetermined. |

| None | Check this line if there is no insulation anywhere in the house. |
| Unknown | Check this line if unable to determine the presence of insulation. |

## Room List   (General Information)

| Field | Protocol |
|---|---|
| Room Grid | Enter the appropriate square footage for each designated room area. |

Comments about room design and count should reflect local custom.  A dining area built as an L-shape off the kitchen may or may not be considered a room depending on the size.  To determine whether one or two rooms should be counted, hypothetically insert a wall to separate the two areas that have been built as one:

◊   If the residents can use the resulting two rooms with the same or more utility without increased inconvenience, count the room as two.

◊   If the hypothetical wall would result in a lack of utility and increased inconvenience, count the room as one.

◊   This represents a hypothetical condition that must be reported in accordance with USAP.

◊   The room count typically includes a living room (LR), dining room (DR), kitchen (KT), den (DN), recreation room (REC) and one or more bedrooms (BR).  Typically, the foyer, bath and laundry room are not counted as rooms.  A room is a livable area with a specific use.

The following definitions and terms may be useful as a guide:

◊   Basement:  generally, *completely below* the grade. (Do not count the basement in the finished gross living area at the grade level.  Insert the size of the basement - The information must be consistent with the description in the Basement section.)

◊   Foyer:  the entrance hall of a house

◊   Level 1: includes all finished living areas at grade level

◊   Level 2: includes all finished living areas above the first level

| Field | Protocol |
|---|---|
| Finished Area Above Grade Contains | To complete this section, enter the total number of each room type at each level. DO NOT enter the dimensions. Enter total number of rooms, bedrooms, baths and square feet of Gross Living Area (above grade). |

Attach a building sketch showing the Gross Living Area Above Grade, including all exterior dimensions of the house, patios, porches, garages, breezeways and other offsets.  State "covered" or "uncovered" to indicate a roof or no roof (such as over a patio).

## Interior Materials/Condition

Enter the types of Materials and the Condition of the Materials (Good, Average, Fair, and Poor).  Make every effort to describe accurately and explain "Fair" and "Poor" rating on Line 103.  The rating must relate to the habitability of the house given local standards.

| Field | Protocol |
|---|---|
| Floors | Enter floor type - tile, hardwood, carpet - and note the condition. |
| Walls | Enter type of walls - plaster, drywall, paneled - and note the condition. |
| Trim/Finish | Enter type of molding - wood, metal, vinyl - and note the condition. |
| Bath Floor | Enter floor type - ceramic tile, vinyl, carpet. and note the condition. |
| Bath Wainscot | Enter type that protects walls from moisture - ceramic tile, fiberglass, etc. - and note the condition. |
| Doors | Enter type - wood, metal, etc. - and note the condition. |

## Heating

| Field | Protocol |
|---|---|
| Type | Enter type of heating system: hot water, steam, forced warm air, gravity warm air or radiant. |
| Fuel | Enter type of fuel used: coal, gas, oil or electric. |
| Condition | Enter condition of system. For example, enter Good, Average, Fair or Poor. If Fair or Poor rating, describe in Comments section. |

## Cooling

| Field | Protocol |
|---|---|
| Central | Enter "YES" or "NO" to signify the status of central air-conditioning in the house. |
| Other | Describe any other permanent means of cooling in the house, except for central air conditioning: permanently affixed fans, zoned air-conditioning, etc. |
| Condition | Describe any adverse or irregular conditions of the cooling system in Comments section. |

## Kitchen Equipment

Make an entry [X] in the boxes to indicate that these items exist. An entry in a box means that the item was considered part of the real estate and is included in the value. If an item is personal property, put a "P" in the box and do not include it in the estimate of value. Treat nonfunctioning equipment as existing, but as deferred maintenance in the valuation process.

| Field | Protocol |
|---|---|
| Refrigerator | Enter "X" if this item exists. Enter "P" if personal property. |
| Range/Oven | Enter "X" if this item exists. Enter "P" if personal property. |
| Disposal | Enter "X" if this item exists. Enter "P" if personal property. |
| Dishwasher | Enter "X" if this item exists. Enter "P" if personal property. |
| Fan/Hood | Enter "X" if this item exists. Enter "P" if personal property. |
| Microwave | Enter "X" if this item exists. Enter "P" if personal property. |
| Washer/Dryer | Enter "X" if this item exists. Enter "P" if personal property. |

## Attic

Describe any additional space - an attic, room above the garage, etc. - in terms of how it can actually be used. The essential question is whether it can be included in the above-grade living area. State the means of access and if it is heated and finished. Enter "X" if any of these items exist.

| Field | Protocol |
|---|---|
| None | Enter "X" if none of the following items exist. |
| Stairs | Enter "X" if this item exists. |
| Drop Stair | Enter "X" if this item exists. |
| Scuttle | Enter "X" if this item exists. |
| Floor | Enter "X" if this item exists. |
| Heated | Enter "X" if this item exists. |
| Finished | Enter "X" if the attic is finished. |

**Amenities**

| Field | Protocol |
|---|---|
| Number Of Fireplaces | Enter "X" if this amenity exists and the Provide a specific number, if more than one . |
| Patio | Enter "X" if this amenity exists. |
| Deck | Enter "X" if this amenity exists. |
| Porch | Enter "X" if this amenity exists. |
| Fence | Enter "X" if this amenity exists. |
| Pool | Enter "X" if this amenity exists.  Specify whether in-ground or above-ground.  Above-ground pools are typically considered personal property and are not included in the value. |

**Car Storage**

| Field | Protocol |
|---|---|
| None | If the property does not have a garage, carport or driveway, check "NONE". |
| Garage | If there is a garage, designate whether it is "Attached", 'Detached" or "Built-in" and indicate on the corresponding line the number of cars that may be parked. If there is a carport, enter the number of cars on the corresponding line.  Also indicate whether it is attached to or detached from the home. If there is no garage or carport, but there is a driveway, state "YES" and enter the number of cars that can be reasonably parked in the driveway. |

**Comments**

The completion of this section is critical to the estimate of market value.  The appraiser must discuss all adverse conditions and observed physical and functional deficiencies noted above.  If necessary, attach additional discussion in the addendum.

| Field | Protocol |
|---|---|
| Additional Features | Enter any additional features such as a pool size, special energy-efficient items, special fireplace features, other features not shown above or any other comments. Please elaborate on any special or unusual aspects of items. |
| Condition of the Improvements | Describe any physical, functional or external depreciation noted at the property. Provide a conclusion as to the overall condition of the improvements that is supported by the previous descriptive sections. Discuss any deficiencies or notable observations on attached pages, if necessary. |
| Adverse Environmental Conditions | List any adverse environmental conditions, including hazardous wastes, toxic substances and others. If the property was built before 1978 and there is evidence of cracking, chipping, peeling or loose paint, make this statement on lead-based paint: "Property built before 1978, lead-based paint corrective measures are required." Also, check the appropriate lead-based paint requirement in the VC Form. |

## Section 6 - Approaches to Value

### Cost Approach
If the subject property is new construction or the cost approach is recognized in the market as a basis for pricing, the appraiser must complete the cost approach and attach the following conclusions:

- ◊ Land value
- ◊ Cost new
- ◊ Estimates of depreciation (curable and incurable)
- ◊ An estimate of value

Consider the value by the cost approach in the reconciliation of market value.

### Sales Comparison Analysis
In selecting comparables, use the bracketing method. Ideally, one of the comparables should be a little larger (200 sq. ft. to 300 sq. ft.); another a little smaller; and the third should be approximately the same size - generally within a hundred square feet of the subject. If this is not possible, the appraiser should explain why.

DO NOT SELECT COMPARABLES BY SALES PRICE. All adjustments must be extracted from the market. Do not make an adjustment unless it has a material effect on value. Explain the reason for making any adjustments for site, site/view or design/appeal. Avoid using three builder sales from the same subdivision, if possible.

In some areas of the country it is customary for the builder or seller to pay closing costs for the buyer and include them in the sales price of the property. In other areas, this may occur occasionally or not at all. In those rare market areas where closing costs are the responsibility of the seller and are always paid by the seller and included in the sales price, the appraiser must note this under "Special Limiting Conditions of the Appraisal" in the Reconciliation Block.

Do not use as market data sales that are not verified and adjusted to reflect the terms and conditions of sale. Always select the most similar comparables. Use older sales only if more recent ones are not available and be sure to explain in the "Comments" section why any comparable over six months old was used. The appraiser must always use sales within one year of the valuation date.

The value factors of Site, Site, View, Design/Appeal, Quality of Construction, Age, Condition and Functional Utility are all subjective factors that require subjective adjustments. Be careful that adjustments are reasonable and not excessive. If a property is overvalued, there is a high probability that the reason can be traced to an excessive adjustment somewhere in this section. Make adjustments only if the dissimilarity has a noticeable effect on the value. Small differences do not usually require adjustments. Always explain subjective adjustments.

### Transaction Data
The appraiser must verify the following information with one of the following sources:

- ◊ Buyer
- ◊ Seller
- ◊ Broker
- ◊ Other parties involved and fully knowledgeable about the sale
- ◊ Available public records

Enter factual data in each line. Before making adjusi3nents, the appraiser must be knowledgeable and must have inspected the sale property.

| Field | Protocol |
| --- | --- |
| Address | Enter the address that can be used to locate each property. Enter community, if needed, to identify property. For rural properties, list site by road name, nearest intersection and side road. |
| Proximity to Subject | Enter proximity of straight-line distance in miles; for example, "one tenth of a mile west of subject". If comparable distance from the subject is more than a generally accepted distance, be sure to explain why the sale is applicable in the "Comments" section. |
| Sales Price | Enter total amount paid by buyer, including extra cost. |
| Price/Gross Livable Area | Enter price per square foot for living area above grade. |
| Data and/or Verification Source(s) | Enter data and verification source name(s) or others: tax stamps, MLS, etc. This is the data source for the price and property information. Also show type of financing such as Conventional, FHA or VA. |

**Adjustments to Sales Price**

Adjustments are made to the prices of the sale properties for price-influencing dissimilarities between each sale and the subject property. Not all dissimilarities require adjustment because not all dissimilarities achieve price differentials in the market. All adjustments must be supported by the actions of the market.

| Value Adjustments | |
|---|---|
| **Field** | **Protocol** |
| Value | For each adjustment item, enter the description of the adjustment and Adjustments whether it is an upward or downward adjustment. |
| Sales or Financing Concessions | Enter adjustment for sales concessions, if needed. Be sure to explain in "Comments" section and use Addendum if appropriate. Analyze all sales on a cash equivalent basis. |
| Date of Sale/Time | State the date of sale and enter the adjustment for changes in market conditions. |
| Site | Enter "Good", "Average" or "Fair", when compared to the subject and using the same standard as the subject. An adjustment for site in the same neighborhood is seldom justified. |
| Leasehold/Fee Simple | State whether the property was sold as fee simple or as a Leasehold Estate. An adjustment is required if the estate differs from the rights appraised for the subject property, and the difference is recognized by the local market. |
| Site | Enter the size of the lot. Make adjustments only for measurable differences. Small differences in lot sizes do not usually call for an adjustment if the size is typical. If necessary, consider the possibility of excess or surplus land. |
| View | Make adjustments only if the view is superior or inferior to the subject. A quality rating of (G)ood, (F)air or (P)oor is given here. If the subject has a superior view and adjustments are made, a photograph would be helpful. |
| Design and Appeal | Enter the style according to a description used by local custom and show appeal as (G)ood, (F)air or (P)oor. Adjustments are necessary for differences between the sale and the subject property. |
| Quality of Construction | Enter "Good", "Average" or "Fair" and the construction type: aluminum siding, wood siding, brick, etc. If a combination, show the predominant material first, such as brick/frame if it is mostly brick. Adjustments may also be warranted for interior construction quality and should be explained and justified. |
| Age/Condition | Enter the age of the subject and each comparable sale. Enter the condition of the subject and comparable. The adjustment for condition is typically required . Consider an adjustment in either age or condition. There is the tendency to duplicate the required adjustment when applied in each category. Consider any assumed repairs to the structure and the roof when determining the need for adjustments to the sales. Consider the conditions reported on the VC Form in making any adjustments. |
| Above Grade Room Count | Enter room count, consistent with the description of improvements on the front of the URAR - Commonly, three adjustments may be entered: The first may be an adjustment for "expendable space", such as a bath. A deficiency in the number of baths should be adjusted first. The second is a separate adjustment for a difference in square feet. The third is an adjustment for room count. These can be individual or separate adjustments that have been combined. All should be extracted from the market. But room count and bath adjustments should be on one line and square foot adjustment for size on another line. Explain any property that has an adjustment in both square feet and room count. Break down combination adjustments in the "Comments" section. |
| Gross Living Area | Enter the total square footage of the above grade living areas. |
| Basement & Finished Rooms Below Grade | Enter the type of improvements in the basement: bedroom, recreation room, laundry, etc. Include other fully or partially below grade improvements found in the subject property or comparables. Make appropriate adjustments to reflect differences between the comparables and the subject property. Explain any special features. Show number of square feet of *finished* area. |

| | |
|---|---|
| Functional Utility | Enter "Equal", "Superior" or "Inferior" as a total of the items rated in the Improvement Analysis compared to the subject. Use the "Comments" section frequently and explain special features. The category of functional utility typically is the place to deduct for functional obsolescence observed in the subject, recorded on Page 1 and not found in the comparables. Extract dollar adjustments from the market. For example, a poor floor design that includes two bedrooms so that the entrance to one is gained by passing through the other typically requires a negative adjustment for functional obsolescence. In such a case, the second bedroom would not be counted as a bedroom. |
| Heating/Cooling | Enter an adjustment for differences in building systems or condition. |
| Energy Efficient Items | Enter an adjustment for any energy efficient items: storm windows and doors, solar installations, replacement windows, etc. |
| Garage/Carport | Enter an adjustment for car storage. Calculate adjustments in accordance with market acceptance of carport value versus garage and size (one car, two cars, etc.). |
| Porch, Patio, Deck, Fireplace(s), etc. | Enter an adjustment for these features. Base any adjustments on local market expectations. If a lump sum adjustment is offered for multiple amenities, break it down in the "Comment" section. |
| Fence, Pool, etc. | Enter appropriate adjustments. For example, a pool located in an area that expects pools might bring a dollar premium in comparison to a comparable without a pool. |
| Net Adjusted(Total) | Check either [+] or [-] box to indicate if the total net adjustments will increase or decrease the value and note by how much. If any adjustment is excessive, review the comparables to determine if the best ones were selected. If the total adjustments appear excessive in relation to the sale price; the appraiser should reexamine the comparability of that sale. Explain any adjustment that appears to be excessive. |
| Adjusted Sale Price of Comparable | Total all of the adjustments and add them to or subtract them from the sales price of each comparable. Generally, adjustments should not exceed 10% for line items, 15% for net adjustments and 25% for gross adjustments. |
| Comments on Sales Comparison | Please comment on the Sales Comparison section, including the subject property's compatibility to the neighborhood, specific characteristics of the sales that affect the adjustment process, etc. The analysis must be reported and the effect concluded. |
| Date, Price and Data for Prior Sales Within One Year of Appraisal | This is in accordance with USPAP standards, which requires the appraiser to consider and analyze any prior sales of the property being appraised and the comparables that occurred within one year of the date of appraisal. |
| Further Analysis | Provide an analysis of any current agreement of sale, option or listing of the subject property and analysis of any prior sales of subject and comparables within one year of the date of appraisal. |
| Indicated Value by Sales Comparison Approach | Upon the basis of the adjusted data, enter the indicated value of the subject. DO NOT arbitrarily select the adjusted sales price that is midway between the lowest and highest adjusted sales price. DO NOT average the comparable sale prices to arrive at an Indicated Value. The final estimate of market value must be supported by the actions of the market. |

## Income Approach

In a single-family residential property, the income approach is generally not recognized as a basis for buying by the market. The approach typically provides minimal applicability in the estimate of market value.

If a three- or four-unit building is being appraised, the appraiser has attached the valuation by the income approach to the addenda of this report. When used, show the gross rent from each of the comparables at the bottom of the form under "Final Reconciliation."

For example:

◊ Comp. #1 Gross Rent = $1,000 (GRM 110); Comp. #2 Gross Rent = $1,200 (GRM 108),... To determine the appropriate gross rent multiplier to use, follow the same procedure as in the market approach. Select a GRM based upon comparable rentals. Be sure to explain the information.

The appraiser must also analyze and report on current market conditions and trends that will affect projected income or the absorption period to the extent these conditions affect the value of the subject property. This information should be consistent with the neighborhood information on the front of the URAR.

| Field | Protocol |
|---|---|
| Indicated Value by Income Approach | Select and enter the indicated value by the income approach. |

## Section 7 - Reconciliation

The appraiser must consider all appropriate approaches and all information relevant to the subject property and the market conditions in the estimate of market value.

| Field | Protocol |
|---|---|
| Market Value "As Is" or "Subject to Completion per Plans" | Check the box marked "as is" or "subject to completion per plans and specifications". Use the "as is" value only if there are no repairs required or if the property is being rejected. If the property is being rejected, the appraiser must provide an "as is" value. The value "subject to completion per plans and specifications" must be consistent with the expected date of completion of the construction. State any assumptions that affect the premise of completion and the resulting value. |
| Market Value, "Subject to Repairs" | The value "subject to repairs, alterations, inspections or conditions listed" must reflect consistency between the development of the approaches to value and the final estimate of value. The appraisal is completed "as repaired". The appraiser must indicate the extent of repairs and also note this in the Valuation Condition Form of the appraisal. Only required repairs will be completed, and the market value must reflect the existing physical characteristics. Report any special circumstances or unique agreements and consider them in the reported value estimate. |
| Conditions of Appraisal | In addition to any comments that the appraiser wants to make, the appraiser should enter taxes and insurance expenses and condominium or PUD common expenses as appropriate. The appraiser must also enter any Limiting Conditions. |
| Final Reconciliation | This entry should contain the appraiser's reasoning for arriving at the final value. |
| Date of Value | Enter the date when the property was inspected. |
| Appraiser Signature | The appraiser who performed the appraisal must sign the form. |
| Appraiser Name | The appraiser who performed the appraisal must print his or her name. |
| Date Report Signed | Enter the date when the appraiser signed the report. |
| State Certification | Enter the appropriate and valid State Certification number. |
| State License | Enter the appropriate and valid State License number and state. |
| Supervisory Appraiser | The FHA Register appraiser must use this portion of the form for all required information and is always required to inspect the property. |

**Attachments**

The appraiser must do the following:

- ◊  State in the space provided in the Final Reconciliation section: "See attached appraiser's certification and Statement of Limiting Conditions."
- ◊  Attach a copy of these certifications and limiting conditions to all copies of the appraisal report, or the report is not valid for HUD use.
- ◊  Clearly and distinctly discuss any additional or different limiting conditions to those provided in this Handbook.
- ◊  Attach any valuation detail and support for estimates of value by the Cost and Income approaches.
- ◊  Provide attachments for any observations of the physical aspects of the property that lead to a recommendation for a physical inspection.

Attach the following to the URAR:

- ◊  The appraiser's certification
- ◊  The statement of limiting conditions that HUD has adopted
- ◊  The certification number or license number and expiration date

Then forward the complete appraisal package to the lender.

| **Field** | **Protocol** |
|---|---|
| Definition of Market Value | "The most probable price which a property should bring in a competitive and open market under all conditions requisite to a fair sale, the buyer and seller, each acting prudently, knowledgeably and assuming the price is not affected by undue stimulus." |

**Statement of Limiting Conditions and Appraiser's Certification - Contingent and Limiting Conditions**

The appraiser's certification that appears in the appraisal report is subject to the following conditions: If the appraisal is based on a condition different or contrary to the conditions listed below, full disclosure of the differing limiting condition must be inserted and made known in the value estimate. Any value-influencing limiting conditions must be cited with the reporting of the estimate of market value.

| **Field** | **Protocol** |
|---|---|
| Matters of a Legal Nature. | The appraiser will not be responsible for matters of a legal nature that affect either the property being appraised or the title to it. The appraiser assumes good and marketable title and responsible ownership. If applicable, the appraiser must specifically change this limiting condition and address the limitations in the reconciliation of market value. |
| Sketch of Improvements | A sketch showing the approximate dimensions of the improvements has been provided in the report. If a sketch is not provided, the appraiser must report the lack of information to develop the sketch. Additional visual aides, such as photographs and brochures, are recommended as attachments. |
| Special Flood Hazard Area | The appraiser has examined available flood maps and has noted whether the property is located in a Special Flood Hazard Area. A copy of the flood map is attached to the appraisal report for any properties in a floodplain. |
| Court Testimony | The appraiser is not required to give testimony or appear in court because he/she performed the appraisal unless specific arrangements have been made beforehand. |
| Adverse Conditions | The appraiser has noted in the report any adverse conditions he/she has found. In addition, the appraiser has no knowledge of hidden conditions that would decrease the value of the property. Any observation or knowledge of adverse conditions must be reported and made apparent to the reader of the appraisal report. |
| Highest and Best Use Value | The appraiser has estimated the value of the land in the cost approach at its highest and best use and the improvements at their contributory value. These separate valuations of the land and improvements must not be used in conjunction with any other appraisal and are invalid if they are so used. |
| True and Correct Sources | The information that the appraiser used in the report was all from sources that he/she considers true and correct. |

| Disclosure of Contents | The appraiser will disclose the contents within the appraisal only as provided for in the USPAP. |
| Subject to Completion of Repairs | The appraiser has based his/her appraisal report and valuation conclusion for an appraisal that is subject to satisfactory completion, repairs, or alterations on the assumption that completion of the improvements will be performed in a workmanlike manner. |
| Distribution of the Appraisal Report | The appraiser must provide his/her prior written consent before the lender/client may distribute the appraisal report to anyone other than those that are outlined in the URAR. |

**Appraiser's Certification**
The appraiser must sign and certify that the following statements are true in the development and reporting of market value in this appraisal report. The appraiser must attach additional certification, if applicable, to meet specific reporting requirements for professional organizations and state certification and licensing.

| Field | Protocol |
| --- | --- |
| Sales Comparison Analysis | The statement affirms the process in which the appraiser performed the Sales Comparison Analysis. After comparing properties to the subject, the appraiser certifies that he/she made financial adjustments based on the market to determine an appropriate price for the subject property. |
| Factors that Impact Value | The appraiser has considered all factors that impact value and has not knowingly withheld any significant information from the report. The appraiser has reported true and correct information for all factors. |
| Personal, Professional Analysis | AR stated information in the report is the personal, unbiased and professional analysis, opinions and conclusions of the appraiser. |
| Interest in the Property/ Discrimination Clause | The appraiser has no interest in the property and has not performed the appraisal in any way on the basis of the race, color, religion, sex, handicap, familial status or national origin of either the prospective owners or occupants of the subject property or those properties in the vicinity of the subject. |
| Present or Future Interest in the Property | The appraiser has no present or contemplated future interest in the subject property, and neither employment nor compensation is contingent on the appraised value of the property. |
| Predetermined Value | The appraiser was not required to report a predetermined value and was not encouraged to report a value that favors the cause of the client or any related party. |
| USPAP Conformity | The appraisal was conducted in conformity with the Uniform Standards of Professional Appraisal Practice. An estimate of reasonable time for exposure in the open market is a condition in the definition of market value and is consistent with the reported estimate of Exposure Period on the URAR. |
| Interior and Exterior Inspection | The appraiser has inspected both the interior and exterior of the subject property and the exterior of all comparable sales analyzed and has noted any apparent adverse conditions in the report. |
| Professional Assistance | If the appraiser had significant professional assistance in the performance of the appraisal or the preparation of the report, he/she must name the individuals providing significant professional assistance and disclose the tasks performed by these people. |
| Professional Assistance Appraiser Signature | The appraiser must note any individual providing significant professional assistance in the reconciliation. In regards to certification and agreement with the Appraiser's Certification, the appraiser who performed the appraisal must sign in this field. |
| Appraiser Name | The appraiser must print his/her name. |
| Date Signed | The date that the appraiser certifies and agrees to the Appraiser's Certification should be entered in this field. |
| State Certification Number | The appraiser must enter the appropriate and valid State Certification number. |

| State License Number | The appraiser must enter the appropriate and valid State License number (if applicable) |
|---|---|
| Expiration Date of Certification or License | Enter the date State Certification or License Number expires. |

## D-2 VALUATION CONDITION REQUIREMENTS

This section describes the specific conditions of the subject property that the appraiser must review and note in the Valuation Conditions Form of the Comprehensive Valuation Package. The physical condition of existing building improvements is examined at the time of appraisal to determine whether repairs, alterations or additions are necessary - essential to eliminate conditions threatening the continued physical security of the property. Required repairs will be limited to necessary requirements commonly referred to as the three S's Rule:

◊  Preserve the continued marketability of the property **(Saleability)**
◊  Protect the health and safety of the occupants **(Safety)**
◊  Protect the security of the property **(Security)**

These are typical conditions that require repairs or replacements:

◊  Termite damage
◊  Damaged, inoperative or inadequate plumbing, heating or electrical systems
◊  Broken or missing fixtures
◊  Rotten or worn-out counter tops
◊  Any structural failure in framing members
◊  Defective paint surfaces
◊  Masonry and foundation damage
◊  Drainage problems
◊  Damaged floors worn through to the finish
◊  Broken plaster or sheetrock

The appraiser must review each of the conditions specified below and note "YES" if any of the deficiencies exist and "NO" if they do not exist, except for VC-1. Unlike the other VC's, where a "YES" mark indicates a limiting condition on the appraisal, in VC-1, "YES" renders the property ineligible and the appraisal must be returned to the lender. Guidelines are set forth below to assist in the examination of the property. To perform this analysis, the appraiser must have full access to all areas listed.

If unable to visually evaluate the improvement in their entirety, return the appraisal to the lender until a complete visual inspection can be performed. The appraiser is not required to disturb insulation, move personal items, furniture, equipment, plant life, soil, snow, ice or debris that obstructs access or visibility.

An inspection done in accordance with the guidelines listed below is visual and is not technically exhaustive. These guidelines are applicable to buildings with four or less dwellings units and their garages or carports. This inspection does not offer warranties or guarantees of any kind.

## SITE CONSIDERATIONS

This section considers the evidence of hazards. Hazards, as defined below, endanger the health and safety of the occupants and/or marketability of the property.

## VC-1 Site Hazards And Nuisances

The appraiser must note and comment on all hazards and nuisances affecting the subject property. These hazards endanger the health and safety of the occupants and/or the marketability of the property, including subsidence/ sink holes, slush pits, heavy traffic areas, airport noise and hazards, proximity to high-pressure gas or petroleum lines, immediate proximity to overhead high-voltage transmission lines, smoke, fumes, offensive noises and odors. For detailed descriptions of these hazards, see Chapter 2-2, Special Neighborhood Hazards and Nuisances, in this Handbook. These hazards will render a property ineligible, and the appraisal should be returned to the lender.

| **Field** | **Protocol** |
|---|---|
| Subsidence/Sinkholes (Handbook Chapter 2-2 C) | If there is surface evidence of subsidence, the location is **ineligible.** Mark "YES" in the VC. |
| Operating oil or gas wells within 300 feet of existing construction (Handbook Chapter 2-2 D) | If the property is located closer than 300 feet from an active or planned drilling site, the location is **ineligible.** Mark "YES" in the VC. |
| Operating oil or gas wells within 75 feet of new construction (Handbook Chapter 2-2 D) | If the property is built within 75 feet of an operating well, the location is **ineligible.** Mark "YES" in the VC. |
| Abandoned oil or gas wells within 1 0 feet of new | If the property is located closer than 10 feet from an abandoned well, the |

| | |
|---|---|
| or existing construction without a letter from State agency (Handbook Chapter 2-2 D) | location is **ineligible.** Mark "YES" in the VC. |
| Slush Pits (Handbook Chapter 2-2 E) | If a property is proposed near an active or abandoned well, call for a survey to locate the pits and their impact on the subject property. If there is any readily observable evidence of a slush pit, the location is **ineligible.** Mark "YES" in the VC. |
| Excessive noise or hazard from heavy traffic area (Handbook Chapter 2-2 F) | If there is excessive noise or unsafe traffic conditions that endangers the occupants or affects the marketability of the property the location may be **ineligible.** Mark "YES" in the VC. |
| New and proposed construction in Runway Clear Zone (Handbook Chapter 2-2 I) | If the property is proposed construction or construction existing less than one year and located within a Runway Clear Zone, (Runway Protection Zone), for civil airports or a Clear Zone at military airfields, the location is **ineligible.** Mark "YES" in the VC. |
| High-pressure gas or petroleum lines within 10 feet of property (Handbook Chapter 2-2 I) | If the property is less than ten feet from the outer boundary of a pipeline easement, the location is **ineligible.** Mark "YES" in the VC. |
| Overhead high-voltage transmission lines within engineering (designed) fall distance (Handbook Chapter 2-2 J) | If the property is located in the fall zone (tower height) of high voltage transmission lines, the location is **ineligible.** Mark "YES" in the VC. |
| Excessive hazard from smoke, fumes, offensive noises or odors (Handbook Chapter 2-2 K) | If excessive smoke, fog, chemical fumes or noxious odors result in hazards to the occupants, the location is **ineligible.** Mark "YES" in the VC. |
| Stationary storage tanks containing more than 1000 gallons of flammable or explosive material (Handbook Chapter 2-2 M) | If the property is within 300 feet of a stationary, storage tank containing more than 1000 gallons of flammable or explosive material, the site is **ineligible.** Mark "YES" in the VC. |

## PROPERTY CONSIDERATIONS

Any deficiency noted as "YES" is a limiting condition in the appraisal. Each condition requires repair or further inspection. The appraisal is prepared "as-repaired" and the valuation is limited by those noted conditions. For the mortgage to be eligible for FHA insurance, these conditions must be satisfied before closing.

## VC-2    Soil Contamination

| Field | Protocol |
|---|---|
| On-site septic system shows readily observable evidence of system failure (Handbook Chapter 3-6 A.3) | Visually inspect the septic system and its surrounding area. If there are obvious or readily observable signs of system failure, require further inspection to ensure that the system is in proper working order. Mark "YES" in the VC, condition the appraisal on the inspection or repair and prepare the appraisal "as-repaired" subject to satisfaction of the condition. |
| Surface evidence of an Underground Storage Tank (UST) on site (Handbook Chapter 3-6 A.3) | If there is any readily observable evidence of underground storage tanks, make a requirement for further analysis. Mark "YES" in the VC, condition the appraisal on that requirement and prepare the appraisal "as-repaired" subject to the satisfaction of the condition. |
| Proximity to dumps, landfills, industrial sites or other sites that could contain hazardous materials (Handbook Chapter 3-6 A.3) | Note the proximity to dumps, landfills, industrial sites or other sites that could contain hazardous wastes. If there is readily observable evidence of hazardous substances in the soil, make a requirement for further analysis. Conditions that could indicate soil contamination include pools of liquid, pits, ponds, lagoons, stressed vegetation, stained soils or pavement, drums or odors. If any of these conditions exist, the appraiser should call for an environmental assessment. Mark "YES" in the VC, condition the appraisal on an environmental assessment and prepare the appraisal "as-repaired" subject to the satisfaction of the condition. |
| Presence of pools liquid, pits, ponds, of Lagoons, stressed vegetation, stained | If there is readily observable evidence of on-site contamination, make a requirement for further inspection. Mark "YES" in the VC, condition the appraisal on the inspection |

| soils or pavement, drums or odors (Handbook Chapter 3-6 A.3) | or repair and prepare the appraisal "as-repaired" subject to satisfaction of the condition. |

## VC-3    Grading and Drainage

| **Field** | **Protocol** |
| --- | --- |
| Grading does not provide positive drainage from structure (Handbook Chapter 3-6 A.4) | Examine the subject property to determine if there is proper grading and drainage. Proper drainage may include gutters and downspouts or appropriate grading or landscaping to divert the flow of water away from the foundation. If the grading does not provide positive drainage from the structure, make a repair requirement. Condition the appraisal on the requirement, mark "YES" in the VC and prepare the appraisal "as repaired" subject to satisfaction of the condition. |
| Standing water proximate to structure (Handbook Chapter 3-6 A.4) | Note any readily observable evidence of standing water near the property that indicates improper drainage. If the standing water is problematic, make a repair requirement, condition the appraisal on the requirement, mark "YES" in the VC and prepare the appraisal "as repaired" subject to this condition. |

## VC-4    Well, Individual Water Supply and Septic

| **Field** | **Protocol** |
| --- | --- |
| Property lacks connection to public water (Handbook Chapter 3-6 A.5) | Note the source of domestic water. If the property is already connected to a public system, mark "NO' in the VC form. If the property is equipped with a well, determine whether connection to a public system is feasible. If connection is feasible (3% or less of the estimated value of the property), hookup is MANDATORY. Condition the appraisal on connection to hookup, mark "YES" in the VC and prepare the appraisal "as-repaired" subject to the satisfaction of that condition. For wells, condition the appraisal on the water-testing requirement. |
| Property lacks connection to public/community sewer system (Handbook Chapter 3-6 A.5) | Note the sewage connection-public/community or septic. If property is already connected to a public system, mark "NO" in the VC form. Determine whether connection to a public system is feasible. If connection is feasible, hookup is MANDATORY. Condition the appraisal upon its hookup, mark "YES" in the VC and prepare the appraisal "as-repaired" subject to the satisfaction of the condition. If the property is served by dug wells, springs, lakes, cisterns or rivers, it is **ineligible.**  Mark "YES" in the VC and explain. |

## VC-5    Wood Destroying Insects

| Field | Protocol |
|-------|----------|
| Structure and accessory buildings are ground level and/or wood is touching ground (Handbook Chapter 3-6 A.6) | If yes, require a pest inspection, mark "YES" in VC-5, condition the appraisal on that requirement and prepare the appraisal "as-repaired" subject to the satisfaction of the condition. |
| The house and/or other structures within the legal boundaries of the property indicate evidence of active termite infestation (Handbook Chapter 3-6 A.6) | Examine the subject property for readily observable evidence of wood boring insect infestation and excessive dampness or large areas where the vegetation is dead. Indications that a licensed pest control professional should be required for an inspection of the subject property include mud tunnels running from the ground up the side of the house, swarms around wood structures and small piles of wings around windows. If the above conditions exist, make the requirement for a termite inspection from a licensed pest control contractor, condition the appraisal on the requirement, mark "YES" in the VC and prepare the appraisal "as-repaired" subject to the satisfaction of the condition. Do not require a pest inspection based solely on the age of a property. Inspections are necessary whenever there is evidence of decay, pest infestation, suspicious damage or when it is customary to the area or required by state law. |

## VC-6    Private Road Access and Maintenance

| Field | Protocol |
|-------|----------|
| Property inaccessible by foot or vehicle (Handbook Chapter 3-6 A-7) | All roads must have vehicular and pedestrian access. If the property is inaccessible by foot or by vehicle, mark "YES" in the VC, make a repair requirement and prepare the appraisal "as-repaired" subject to the satisfaction of the condition. |
| Property accessible only by private road or drive (Handbook Chapter 3-6 A-7) | In all cases where a private road exists, submit evidence that the road is protected by a permanent recorded easement (non-exclusive, non-revocable roadway, driveway easement without trespass from the property to a public street/road) and that there is an acceptable maintenance agreement recorded on the property or that is owned and maintained by a Home Owners Association (HOA). If there is no such easement, mark "YES" in the VC, condition the appraisal on attaining the easement and prepare the appraisal "as repaired" subject to the satisfaction of the condition. |
| Property is not provided with an all-weather surface (gravel is acceptable) (Handbook Chapter 3-6 A-7) | FHA defines all-weather surface as a road surface over which emergency vehicles can pass in all types of weather. If the property is not provided with an all-weather surface, condition the appraisal on its repair, mark "YES" in the VC and prepare the appraisal as-repaired" subject to satisfaction of the condition. |

## VC-7    Structural Conditions

This chapter addresses the structural components of the subject property and the effect that their condition may have on the habitability and enjoyment of the property (Chapter 3-6). An appraiser must examine the flooring, framing, walls, ceiling, attic and roofing for structural soundness. The appraiser will examine the following conditions:

| Field | Protocol |
|-------|----------|
| Floor Support Systems (Handbook Chapter 3-6 A.8) | Examine the flooring/joists for any signs of water leakage or damage, holes, large cracks in concrete slabs, leakage and readily observable evidence of rodent or termite infestation/damage, temporary supports or jacks or piers. If these conditions exist, condition the appraisal on their repair, mark "YES" in the VC and prepare the appraisal "as-repaired" subject to the satisfaction of the condition. |
| Framing/Walls/Ceiling (Handbook Chapter 3-6 A.8) | Examine all framing, walls and ceilings for soundness, significant cracks that are visible in the exposed portions of the walls and could effect structure, gaping holes and significant water damage. If these conditions exist, condition the appraisal on their repair, mark "YES" in the VC and prepare the appraisal "as-repaired" subject to the satisfaction of the condition. |
| Attic (Handbook Chapter 3-6 A-8) | Enter the attic and observe the interior roofing for insulation, deficient materials, leaks or readily observable evidence of significant water damage, structural problems, previous fire |

| | |
|---|---|
| | damage, RFT sheathing, exposed and frayed wiring and adequate ventilation by vent, fan or window. If any of these deficiencies exist, condition the appraisal on their repair, mark "YES" in the VC and prepare the appraisal "as-repaired" subject to the satisfaction of the condition. |

## VC-8 Foundation Basement

| Field | Protocol |
|---|---|
| Foundation/Basement (Handbook Chapter 3-6 A.10) | Examine the foundation/basement for inadequate access, dampness or readily observable evidence of significant water damage and readily observable cracks or erosion that effect structural soundness. The foundation/basement must have a vapor barrier. If these deficiencies exist, condition the appraisal on their repair, mark "YES" in the VC and prepare the appraisal "as-repaired" subject to the satisfaction of the condition. |
| Crawl Space (Handbook Chapter 3-6 A.11) | Examine the crawl space for inadequate access, distance from floor joists to ground, insulation, ventilation and any other structural problems. Access to the space should be clear. Enter the crawl space to observe conditions except when access is obstructed, when entry could damage the property or when dangerous and adverse situations are suspected. Access should be provided by the homeowner/seller. The space should be adequate for maintenance and repair, typically greater than 18 inches. The support beams should be intact and of structural soundness. The space must not have excessive dampness or ponding of water. In houses where moisture is present, the problem must be corrected by installing a sump pump, correcting the exterior drainage or by providing proper cross-ventilation. If any of these inadequacies exist, condition the appraisal on their repair, mark "YES" in the VC and prepare the appraisal 'as-repaired" subject to the satisfaction of the condition. |

## VC-9    Roofing

| Field | Protocol |
|---|---|
| Condition of Roofing (Handbook Chapter 3-6 A.12) | View the roof from ground level to determine if the integrity of the roof is sufficient. Observe roof coverings, roof drainage systems, flashing, skylights, chimneys and roof penetrations and readily observable evidence of leakage or abnormal condensation on building components. It is not necessary to observe attached accessories, including but not limited to solar systems, antennae and lightning arrestors. Note if the roof covers the entire home, if the roof has been repaired or patched substantially, if the material used on the roof was suitable for the subject property and any other visible signs of deterioration resulting in holes, puddles, leakage, clogged or inadequate drains or missing sections. If the subject property has a flat roof, note that an inspection is required, mark "YES" in the VC and prepare the appraisal "as-repaired" subject to the satisfaction of the condition. Note any warranties still in effect and if the remaining physical life is at least two years. If the roof will last less than two years, call for a new roof. If a roof is completely snow-covered, re-inspect it later when weather permits. Condition the appraisal on repair of any of the roof items, mark "YES" in the VC and prepare the appraisal "as-repaired" subject to the satisfaction of the condition. |

## VC-10   Mechanical Systems

An appraiser must examine all mechanical, plumbing and electrical systems in the subject property to ensure that they are in proper working order. This examination entails turning on the applicable systems and observing their performance.

| Field | Protocol |
|---|---|
| Inoperable systems due to weather conditions (Handbook Chapter 3-6 A.13) | Explain in VC-10 Condition the appraisal on repair and assumed functionality, mark "YES" in the VC and prepare the appraisal "as-repaired" subject to the satisfaction of the condition |
| Furnace/Heating System and Air Conditioning (central) (Handbook Chapter 3-6 A.14) | Turn on the furnace/heating/air conditioning system to observe whether the system performs appropriately and that no unusual noises are heard, no odors or smoke are emitted indicating a defective unit, etc. Note significant holes/deterioration on the unit Determine whether there is an installed heat or cool-air source in each room by using the system's normal operating controls. It is not necessary to observe the uniformity of heat or cool-air to various rooms. Unit shuts down prior to reaching desired temperature In most instances it will be possible to activate the air conditioner in the winter and the heater in the summer. However, do not operate the systems if doing so may damage equipment or when outside temperatures will not allow system to operate. Note any noncompliance with this condition and explain it in the VC form. Turn on the hot water to ensure that the hot water heater is operating appropriately. If these conditions exist, condition the appraisal on the repair of the condition, mark "YES" in the VC and prepare the appraisal "as-repaired" subject to satisfaction of the condition. |
| Electrical System (Handbook Chapter 3-6 A.13) | Examine the electrical box to ensure that there are circuit breakers with no visible frayed wiring or exposed wires in living areas and that there is adequate amperage for the appliances present in the property. If the appliances present at the time of the inspection do not appear to be reasonable (undersized), determine if there is adequate amperage to run "standard" appliances, as per municipal code. |
| Electrical System (Handbook Chapter 3-6 A.13) | Ensure that the electrical switches and outlets operate property. Operate a representative number of installed smoke detectors, lighting fixtures, switches and receptacles inside the house, garage and on exterior walls. Note presence of sparks or smoke from outlets. It is not required to insert any tool, probe or testing device inside the panels, to test or operate any over-current or to dismantle any electrical device or control. It is not required to observe telephone, security, cable TV, intercoms or other ancillary wiring. If any of the above deficiencies exist, condition the appraisal on their repair, mark "YES" in the VC and prepare the appraisal "as-repaired" subject to the satisfaction of the condition. |
| Plumbing System (Handbook Chapter 3-6 A.5) | Flush the toilets and turn on all faucets to determine that the plumbing system is intact, that it does not emit foul odors, that faucets function appropriately, that both cold and hot water run and that there is no readily observable evidence of leaks or structural damage under fixtures. Turn on several cold water faucets in the house to check water pressure and flow. Flushing a toilet at the same time will also reveal any weaknesses in water pressure. If the property has a septic system, inspect it for any signs of failure such as odor, rust or surface evidence of malfunction. If any of the above deficiencies exist, condition the appraisal on their repair, mark "YES" in the VC and prepare the appraisal "as-repaired" subject to the satisfaction of the condition. |

## VC-11  Other Health and Safety Deficiencies

This chapter addresses the interior components of the subject property and the effect that their condition may have on the habitability and enjoyment of the property. The appraiser is not required to observe storm windows, storm doors, screens, shutters, awnings and similar seasonal accessories, fencing, garage door remote control transmitters, wallpaper, carpeting, draperies, blinds, household appliances or recreational facilities.

| Field | Protocol |
|---|---|
| Other Health and Safety Deficiencies (Handbook Chapter 3-6 A.14) | Operate a representative number of windows, interior doors and all exterior and garage doors. Verify that the electric garage door opener will automatically reverse or stop when met with reasonable resistance during closing. Note and make a repair requirement for any health or safety deficiencies as they relate to the subject property, including broken windows/doors/steps, inadequate/blocked doors and steps without a handrail. If any of the conditions exist, condition the appraisal on their repair, mark "YES" in the VC and prepare the appraisal "as-repaired" subject to the satisfaction of the condition. |

## VC-12  Lead-Based Paint Hazard

| Field | Protocol |
|---|---|
| Lead-Based Paint (Handbook Chapter 3-6 A.15) | If the home was built before 1978, note the condition of all defective paint surfaces and their location in the home. Comment on the deterioration of painted surfaces of the subject property Inspect all interior and exterior surfaces, such as walls, stairs, deck porch, railing, windows or doors for defective (chipping, flaking or peeling) paint. (Exterior surfaces include surfaces on fences, detached garages, storage sheds and other outbuildings and appurtenant structures.) If there is evidence of defective paint surfaces, condition the appraisal on their repair, mark "YES" in the VC and prepare the appraisal "as-repaired" subject to the satisfaction of the condition. |

## VC-13  Condominiums and Planned Urban Developments (PUD)

If the subject property is located in a Planned Unit Development or condominium setting, it must be on FHA's approval list or accepted through reciprocity. The property should meet the owner-occupancy standards and completion standards defined below.

| Field | Protocol |
|---|---|
| This project is not on FHA's approval list | Verify that the approval number exists. The lender must supply the approval number on the appraisal. If the project is not approved, mark "YES" in the VC and condition the appraisal on this information. |
| The property does not meet owner-and occupancy standards | The project must be at least 51% owner-occupied. If owner-occupancy rates are less than 51%, mark "YES" in the VC condition the appraisal on this information. |
| This property does not meet completion standards | The project must be at least 2/3 complete. If completion rate is less than 2/3, mark "YES" in the VC and condition the appraisal on this information. |

**Radon.** Currently, HUD does not require radon testing of homes that are to be insured by this agency.

**Addenda**

| Field | Protocol |
|---|---|
| A. Assessed Market Value | Enter the assessed market value in the VC addenda. (It varies by municipality but is entered only when the value is represented as current.) The total of all taxes should be included. Excessive taxes can have a negative effect and must be reflected in the value. If there is no method to relate the assessment to market value, such as for new construction, mark the assessed market "N/ A". |
| B. Estimated Repair Costs | Quantify the costs associated with the repairs in the VC. These costs relate strictly to repair and not marketability. Use standard cost information, such as Marshall and Swift, in preparing the estimate. |

## D-3 HOMEBUYER SUMMARY

The Homebuyer Summary intends to protect the homebuyer by informing him/her of any material conditions that typically make the property ineligible for FHA mortgage insurance. If any of the VC's are marked "YES" in the VC form, the appraiser must denote it in the appropriate box of the Homebuyer Summary and explain, in detail, the nature of the problem. The lender is legally bound to address these problems before closing on the property.

| Field | Protocol |
| --- | --- |
| Site Hazards | Mark "Y" under problem if any of the sections in VC-1 are marked "yes". |
| Soil Contamination | Mark "Y" under problem if any of the sections in VC-2 are marked "yes". |
| Grading and Problems Drainage | Mark "Y" under problem if any of the sections in VC-3 are marked "yes". |
| Well, Individual Water Supply and Septic Problems | Mark "Y" under problem if any of the sections in VC-4 are marked "yes". |
| Wood Destroying Insects | Mark "Y" under problem if any of the sections in VC-5 are marked "yes". |
| Private Road Access and Maintenance Problems | Mark "Y" under problem if any of the sections in VC-6 are marked "yes". |
| Structural Deficiencies | Mark "Y" under problem if any of the sections in VC-7 are marked "yes". |
| Foundation Deficiencies | Mark "Y" under problem if any of the sections in VC-8 are marked "yes". |
| Roofing Deficiencies | Mark "Y" under problem if any of the sections in VC-9 are marked "yes". |
| Mechanical Systems Problems | Mark "Y" under problem if any of the sections in VC-10 are marked "yes". |
| General Health and Safety Deficiencies | Mark "Y" under problem if any of the sections in VC-11 are marked "yes". |
| Deteriorated Paint | Mark "Y" under problem if any of the sections in VC-12 are marked "yes". |

## Glossary of Terms

◊ **Component:** A readily accessible and observable construction element of a system, including a floor, wall, framing or roof construction that can be considered individually - but not individual pieces such as boards or nails.

◊ **Dangerous or Adverse Situations:** Situations that pose a threat of injury and/or require the use of special protective clothing or safety equipment.

◊ **Dismantle:** To take apart or remove any component, device or piece of equipment that is bolted, screwed or fastened by other means and that would not be taken apart by a homeowner for normal household maintenance.

◊ **Household Appliance:** Kitchen and laundry appliances, room air conditioners and similar appliances.

◊ **HVAC:** Heating, ventilation and air-conditioning system - one combined system or separate systems.

◊ **Normal Operating Controls:** Devices used by homeowner in the operation of a system, such as a thermostat, wall switch or safety switch.

◊ **Observe:** The act of making a visual examination.

◊ **Operate:** To cause systems or equipment to function.

◊ **Recreational Facilities:** Spas, saunas, steam baths, swimming pools, tennis courts, playground equipment and other exercise equipment, entertainment or athletic facilities.

◊ **Representative Number:** For multiple identical components such as windows and electrical outlets, one such component per room. For multiple identical exterior components, one such component on each side of the building.

◊ **Roof Drainage Systems:** Components used to carry water off a roof and away from a building such as gutters, downspouts, leaders, splash blocks.

◊ **System:** A combination of interacting or interdependent components, assembled to carry out one or more functions.

# Sample State Real Estate Appraiser Guidelines

**Purpose of this Section:** The following section contains appraisal guidelines for licensed appraisers in one State in the USA. I've included this section to be used as a reference for you regardless of which State you live or work in. These guidelines can help further clarify the appraisal topics discussed in this book. The text is written in a very formal and technical style of writing since it is used by the State Department of Real Estate for their appraiser licensing procedures. You don't need to try and memorize everything right away since it will seem overwhelming if you try to do that. Just take your time so you can learn at your own pace and refer back to this book as needed, like a reference manual.

> These guidelines can help further clarify the appraisal topics discussed in this book. The text is written in a very formal and technical style of writing since it is used by the State Department of Real Estate for their appraiser licensing procedures. You don't need to try and memorize everything right away since it will seem overwhelming if you try to do that. Just take your time so you can learn at your own pace and refer back to this book as needed, like a reference manual.

**State Department of Real Estate**
**Office of Real Estate Appraisers**
Background: In 1989, Congress passed the Financial Institutions Reform, Recovery and Enforcement Act (FIRREA), commonly known as the "Savings and Loan Bailout Bill." Title XI of FIRREA contains the *Real Estate Appraisal Reform Amendments* which require each state to establish a program to license and certify real estate appraisers who perform appraisals for federally related transactions. Title XI additionally requires states to adhere to real estate appraiser qualifications criteria set by the Appraiser Qualifications Board (AQB) of The Appraisal Foundation.

**Office of Real Estate Appraisers (OREA)**
In response to FIRREA, in 1990 the State Legislature enacted the Real Estate Appraisers' Licensing and Certification Law (Business and Professions Code Section 11300, et seq.) This law created the Office of Real Estate Appraisers (OREA), which was organized in early 1991. OREA regulates real estate appraisers by issuing licenses and investigating complaints of illegal or unethical activity by licensed appraisers.

*APPRAISAL AND VALUATION*
**THEORETICAL CONCEPTS OF VALUE AND DEFINITIONS**

**Definition of Appraisal**
To appraise means the act or process of developing an opinion of value; an opinion of value. (USPAP, 2000 ed., pg. 10) It may be said that value is the present worth of all rights to future benefits, arising out of property ownership, to typical users or investors. An appraisal report is usually a written statement of the appraiser's opinion of value of an adequately described parcel of property as of a specified date. It is a conclusion which results from the process of research and analysis of factual and relevant data.

Real estate appraising methods are being standardized by virtue of the experience and practice of qualified people in all parts of the country who encounter the same types of valuation problems, and who by various methods and processes succeed in solving them in an equitable manner. It is natural, however, that differences of opinion may exist as to the value of specific parcels of real estate and the means of estimating their value.

**Property rights are measurable.** Real estate as a tangible thing can be measured. It includes both land and improvements and exists independent of any desire for its possession. To distinguish between its physical aspects and rights in and to real property, the latter are called *property interests* in real estate.

These interests - ownership in fee simple and other lesser interests - have been discussed in preceding chapters.
Property rights in real estate are normally appraised at Market Value. There are many definitions of Market Value, but a good working definition is the most probable price the property would bring if freely offered on the open market with both a willing buyer and a willing seller.

Rights in real property are referred to as "Bundle of Rights," which infers: right to occupy and use; to sell in whole or in part; to bequeath (give away); and, to transfer by contract for a specific period of time (lease). It also implies the right not to take any of these actions.

These rights are limited by: the government's power of taxation; eminent domain; police power (for safety, health and general welfare of the public, such as zoning, building codes); and, right of property to escheat (revert) to the state in the event the owner dies and leaves no heirs.

The rights in a property must be known by the appraiser before making a proper valuation, and the appraiser must also be able to distinguish between personal and real property. Market value is the object of most appraisal assignments, and appraisals mainly are concerned with fee simple estate valuation as opposed to partial interest value.

The widespread need for appraisals is apparent. Everyone uses real estate in one way or another and must pay for its use, which involves a decision about value. Practical decisions concerning value must be based upon some kind of an appraisal or evaluation of real property collateral.

The term evaluation has a special meaning and use for institutional lenders since passage of the Federal Institutions Reform, Recovery, and Enforcement Act (FIRREA). In reality, it is an appraisal, an estimate of value.

Although an appraisal may be transmitted orally, it is usually a written statement of an estimate of value and is referred to as an *appraisal report*.

## TRADITIONAL APPROACHES TO VALUE
Basically, there are three approaches to property valuation used by appraisers. Each gives a separate indication of value, yet the approaches are all interrelated and all use market comparison techniques. All three approaches are considered in each complete assignment. However, all three are not always employed, depending upon the property type and the process and report type agreed to by the client and the appraiser.

The approaches to value are: Sales Comparison (or Market Data) Approach; Cost Approach; and Income Capitalization Approach.

## THE APPRAISER'S ROLE IN THE REAL ESTATE PROFESSION
The appraiser, by reason of professional training, experience, and ethics is responsible for furnishing clients with an objective third party opinion of value, arrived at without pressures or prejudices from the parties involved with the property, such as an owner or lender.

The appraiser has a heavy personal and professional responsibility to be correct and accurate in opinions of value. Otherwise, the appraiser's clients may easily suffer loss and the appraiser's professional reputation may also suffer.

There has been considerable controversy in recent years concerning the appraiser's potential for influencing declining neighborhoods and discrimination in housing. The main thrust of the controversy charges that appraisers have tended to view declining neighborhoods as reducing in value without regard for individual home upgrading and homogeneous neighborhoods as being more stable in value than mixed neighborhoods. It has been claimed that loan appraisals in these declining or mixed areas have been unduly pessimistic and conservative because of these purported appraiser attitudes. This supposed conservatism, it has been declared, leads to further decline because favorable loans are not made.

Appraisers respond that the professional appraiser will only consider the factors actually affecting value, and lenders' policies for granting loans are beyond the appraiser's control. Lenders reply that the appraiser's opinion of value is the main basis for the loan and prudent lending practices must be followed.

In the making of thousands of daily appraisal decisions, there is probably some truth on all sides.

A proper appraisal does not contribute to either problem mentioned above. An accurate appraisal, resulting from the competency of a skilled appraiser, will reflect only the forces affecting value.

◊    **True forces affecting value.** It is necessary that appraisers be exceptionally sensitive to their roles in accurately assessing the true forces affecting value. In accomplishing this, the appraiser cannot allow the general neighborhood composite of ethnic, religious, or minority populations or the general condition of neighborhood improvement to detract from a clear and objective evaluation of the property appraised on its own merits.

It is also the appraiser's responsibility to keep the appraisals timely in a changing market.

It is no longer prudent to rely solely on past sales of comparable property. The appraiser must use all pertinent data and appraisal methods to insure the appraised value is, in fact, the closest estimate of the price the property would bring if freely offered on the open market.

World events of the late 70's resulted in interest rate and property appreciation spirals to historic highs, dramatic decline in construction, creative financing approaches to generate sales, and extraordinary levels of foreclosure and bankruptcy. Such times required exceptional appraiser sensitivity to the true market forces.

Occasionally appraisers have contributed to individual property problems by failing to understand or recognize contrary market trends.

The professional appraisal associations have responded with increased emphasis on education in current appraisal and financial techniques. The dynamics of such a volatile market require the appraiser to keep abreast of new techniques and market forces. Recognizing this, State statutes enforced by the Office Of Real Estate Appraisers (OREA) require continuing education for licensed and certified appraisers. Those requirements are set forth in the OREA portion at the end of this chapter.

## APPRAISAL REPORT

An appraisal report sets forth the data, analysis and conclusions of the writer. When put in writing, it protects both appraiser and client. Reports vary in scope and length. The following information should be included and is more specifically outlined in Standards 1 and 2 of the USPAP:

◊   A **final value conclusion** is expressed in terms of dollars for the property which is being appraised.

◊   The **value conclusion** can be made for any date in the past, and, with some care, for any date in the future. The time of inspection of the physical improvements is generally taken as the date of value unless otherwise informed by either the property owner, owner's attorney, or a court of law. The date of the final writing and delivery of the report is the date of the appraisal, not to be confused with the date of value.

◊   **Adequate description of the property.** The street address, including city and state, as well as a complete legal description as set forth by the deed in the County Recorder's Office, should be shown, and the physical structures should be clearly described. The length of this description will depend upon the length and extent of the report.

◊   The **latitude of the reasonings** in determining the *value conclusion* will depend upon the type of report and the complexity of the appraisal problem.

◊   **Market data, and other factual data.** This includes information on the city and neighborhood which affects the *value conclusion;* information gathered on the site, improvements and the environment of the neighborhood which should be processed by means of one or more of the approaches to value; and, the preliminary estimate of value should be reconciled by means of logic and reasoning in order to arrive at one *value conclusion* for the property. Lengthy details are usually omitted in letter form reports, but appraiser retains the information as backup.

◊   **Signature and certification.** Appraisal reports must be signed by the writer and in most instances are preceded by a statement to the effect that the writer has no present or contemplated interest in the property. Requisites of an appraisal are set forth in the USPAP, which was adopted in 1989 by the major appraisal organizations.

## LAYMEN'S TERMS FOR APPRAISAL REPORTS (USPAP Terminology)

◊   **Letter form report.** This type of report is generally used when the client is familiar with the area, and supporting data are not necessary. It consists of a brief description of the property, the type of value sought, the purpose served by the appraisal, the date of value, the value conclusion and the signature of the appraiser. This is known as a Restricted Use Report and is governed by Section 2.2(c) of the USPAP. Specific language is required to put readers on notice that this report type is for a single user for his/her single purpose.

◊   **Short form report.** This type of report is normally used by lending institutions, such as banks, insurance companies, saving and loan associations, and governmental agencies. Generally, it consists of simple check sheets or spaces to be filled in by the appraiser. The report varies from two to eight pages in length and includes the pertinent data about the property, with photos, maps, plats and sketches. Today these types of reports are classified as Summary Reports and are governed by Section 2.2(b) of USPAP. This category of report can also be a narrative format, but the data presented will be generally in a summary format with more information than a restricted report.

◊   **Narrative report.** This type of report can be a complete document including all pertinent information about the area and the subject property as well as the reasons and computations for the *value conclusion.* It includes: maps, photographs, charts and plot plans. It is written for court cases and out-of-town clients who need all of the factual data. It gives the comprehensive reasoning of the *appraiser* as well as the *value conclusions.* These reports are classified as Self-Contained Reports. They are governed by Section 2.2(a) of USPAP.

*Any of these report types could be done on a form or in a narrative format. The contents and the depth of discussion, not the format, define the report type in USPAP terms.*

## PURPOSES AND USES OF APPRAISALS

The basic purpose of an appraisal is to estimate a particular value, i.e., market value, check for support of sales price, loan value, investment value, etc. Some of the uses for requiring the estimate of value are:

**Transfer of ownership of property.**
- ◊ An appraisal assists buyers and sellers in arriving at a fair and equitable sales price. An appraisal of physical property may also include an opinion of its age, remaining life, quality or authenticity.
- ◊ The listing agent needs an estimate of value of the property before accepting a listing from the owner. If the agent can show by means of an appraisal the appraised fair market value of the property, and obtain a listing at that figure, a sale more likely will result. The real estate practitioner should be prepared to demonstrate a knowledge of both comparative and economic values.
- ◊ Where a trade is involved, appraisals tend to assist in clarifying the opinions of value formed by both parties to the trade.
- ◊ Valuations are necessary for the distribution of estate properties among heirs.

**Financing and credit.**
- ◊ The lender has an appraisal made of the value of the property to be pledged as security for a mortgage loan.
- ◊ Measuring economic soundness of real estate projects involves feasibility studies in relation to financing and credit.

**Appraisal for taxation purposes.**
- ◊ Appraisals are needed by governmental bodies to establish the proper relationship between land and improvements for real estate taxes (ad valorem taxation).
- ◊ Properties subject to estate taxes must be evaluated for the purpose of levying federal and state taxes.
- ◊ Appraisals of income-producing properties are necessary to property owners for the basis of depreciation. Normally, only improvements can be depreciated, not the land. An allocation of the market value between land and improvements is a requisite for accounting and taxation purposes.

**Condemnation actions.**
- ◊ With the right of eminent domain being vested in governmental agencies, it is important that properties under condemnation be evaluated at market value to properly estimate purchase price, benefits, and damages to the property being affected.

**Insurance Purposes.**
- ◊ Appraisals are based principally upon the cost of replacement. This is important for the purpose of insuring properties for fire insurance.
- ◊ Appraisals are useful in setting claims arising from insurance contracts after a property has been destroyed.

**Miscellaneous reasons for appraisals.**
- ◊ Catastrophic damage. Establishing fair market value of property before and immediately after the damage.
- ◊ Fair rental value for negotiation of leases.
- ◊ Appraisals for inheritance and gift tax purposes.
- ◊ Fraud cases.
- ◊ Damage cases.
- ◊ Division-of-estate cases. A distribution of property under the terms of a will, in divorce proceedings, or between rival claimants, frequently requires that the value of the property involved be determined by appraisal.

## PRINCIPLES OF VALUATION

A knowledge of basic assumptions, postulates or premises that underlie appraisal methods is essential to an understanding of the purpose, methods and procedures of valuation. The following principles of value influences are the more important for a general understanding of the appraisal process.

- ◊ **Principle of conformity.** Holds that maximum value is realized when land uses are compatible and a reasonable degree of architectural harmony is present. Zoning ordinances help set conformity standards.

- ◊ **Principle of change.** Real property is in a constant state of flux and change, affecting individual properties, neighborhoods and cities. The appraiser follows trends and influences and is sensitive to changes in conditions that affect the value of real estate. Economic, environmental, government, and social forces affect all markets, especially real estate.

- ◊ **Principle of substitution.** This principle is the basis of the appraisal process. Simply stated, value will tend to be set by the cost of acquiring an equally desirable substitute. The value of a property to its owner cannot ordinarily exceed the value in the market to persons generally, when it can be substituted without undue expense or serious delay. In a free market, the buyer can be expected to pay no more, and a seller can expect to receive no less, than the price of an equivalent substitute.

     A property owner states that owner's house is worth $95,000. Buyers in the market can obtain a substitute property with the same features and utility for only $90,000. The seller's house, therefore, has a value of approximately $90,000, not $95,000.

◊     **Principle of supply and demand.** Holds that price varies directly, but not necessarily proportionately, with demand, and inversely, but not necessarily proportionately, with supply. Increasing supply or decreasing demand tends to reduce price in the market. The opposite is also true.

◊     **Principle of highest and best use.** The best use of a parcel of land, known as its highest, best and most profitable use, is that which will most likely produce the greatest net return to the land over a given period of time. This net return is realized in terms of money or other amenities.

The application of this principle is flexible. It reflects the appraiser's opinion of the best use for the property as of the date of his appraisal. At one period of time, the highest and best use of a parcel of land in a downtown business district might be for the development of an office building; at another time, a parking lot may be the highest and best use.

A single-family house on a commercial lot may not be the highest and best use for the site. A four-unit apartment on multiple zoned land suitable for 30 units is probably not the long-term highest and best use of the land.

It is also useful to understand that highest and best use may not be only economic or profit-making in character. Environmental, aesthetic, and historical considerations are increasingly important in governmental views of highest and best use.

The Appraisal Institute, at Page 244 of the 10th Edition of *The Appraisal of Real Estate,* offers this definition for highest and best use:
> "The reasonably probable and legal use of vacant land or an improved property, which is physically possible, appropriately supported, financially feasible, and that results in the highest value."

The first reference in the definition applies to vacant land while the second applies to improved properties. This indicates that there may be two highest and best uses, one with the site vacant and the other as improved. These must be reconciled into a final highest and best use determination for the property being appraised.

Determining highest and best use includes assessing potential buyers' motives, the existing use of the property, potential benefits of ownership, the market's behavior, community or environmental factors, and special conditions or situations which come to bear on appraisal conclusions of value.

◊     **Principle of progression.** The worth of a lesser-valued object tends to be enhanced by association with many similar objects of greater value (inadequacy or under-improvement).

◊     **Principle of regression.** The worth of a greater-valued object is reduced by association with many lesser-valued objects of the same type (super adequacy or over-improvement).

◊     **Principle of contribution.** A component part of a property is valued in proportion to its contribution to the value of the whole property or by how much that part's absence detracts from the value of the whole. Maximum values are achieved when the improvements on a site produce the highest (net) return, commensurate with the investment.

◊     **Principle of anticipation.** Value is created by anticipated future benefits to be derived from the property. In the Fair Market Value Analysis, appraisers estimate the present worth of future benefits. This is the basis for the income approach to value. Simply stated, the income approach is the analysis of the present worth of projected future net income and anticipated future resale value. Historical data are relevant because they aid in the interpretation of future benefits.

◊     **Principle of competition.** Competition is created where substantial profits are being made. If there is a profitable demand for residential construction, competition among builders will become very apparent. This could lead to an increase in supply in relation to the demand, resulting in lower selling prices and unprofitable competition, leading to renewed decline in supply.

◊     **Principle of balance.** Value is created and sustained when contrasting, opposing, or interacting elements are in equilibrium, or balance. Proper mix of varying land uses creates value. Imbalance is created by an *over-improvement* or an *under-improvement.* Balance is created by developing the site to its highest and best use.

◊     **Principle of four-stage life cycle.** In due course, all material things go through the process of wearing or wasting away and eventually disintegrating. All property is characterized by four distinct stages: *growth, stability, decline, and revitalization.*

Single properties, districts, neighborhoods, etc., tend generally to follow this pattern of growth and decline. It is also evident this process is frequently reversed as neighborhoods and individual properties in older residential areas are renewed and restored.

Revitalization and modernization in inner-city older neighborhoods may result from organized government programs or as a result of changing preferences of individual buyers. Most neighborhoods remain in the mature or stable stage for many years, with decline being hardly noticeable as renewal becomes essentially an ongoing process.

## BASIC VALUATION DEFINITIONS
### Value Designations
There are many different designations or definitions of value. They may be divided into the following two main classifications:

◊   **Utility value,** which is value directed toward a particular use. This frequently is termed *subjective* value and includes valuation of amenities which attach to a property or a determination of value for a specified purpose or for a specific person.

◊   **Market value,** which represents the amount in money (cash or the equivalent) for which a property can be sold or exchanged in prevailing market conditions at a given time or place as a result of market balancing. It may be based on a "willing buyer" and "willing seller" concept. This is frequently termed the *objective* value, since it is not subject to restrictions of a given project.

Appraisers carefully define the value being sought. Types of values are Liquidation Value, Insurable Value, Investment Value and, of course, Assessed Value (for taxation).

The real estate market sometimes places great importance on real estate financing terms. Market Value might be estimated for specific financing arrangements: seller carry-back, balloon payments, renegotiable mortgages or other "creative" financing techniques.

### Market Value Defined
In appraisal practice, the term Market Value is defined by agencies that regulate federal financial institutions in the U.S. That definition is the one found in USPAP and is given as:
"The most probable price which a property should bring in a competitive and open market under all conditions requisite to a fair sale, the buyer and seller each acting prudently and knowledgeably, and assuming the price is not affected by undue stimulus."

Implicit in this definition is the consummation of a sale as of a specified date and the passing of title from seller to buyer under conditions whereby:
◊   buyer and seller are motivated;
◊   buyer and seller are well informed or well advised and acting in what they consider their best interest;
◊   a reasonable time is allowed for exposure in the open market;
◊   payment is made in terms of cash in United States dollars or terms of financial arrangements comparable thereto; and
◊   the price represents the normal consideration for the property sold, unaffected by special or creative financing or sales concessions granted by anyone associated with the sale.
(Source: *Uniform Standards of Professional Appraisal Practice,* Appraisal Foundation, 2000 Edition, page 160.)

### Legal Definition
The legal definition of Fair Market Value under State law is found in the Code of Civil Procedure, Section 1263.320, as follows:
"The fair market value of the property is the highest price on the date of valuation that would be agreed to by a seller, being willing to sell but under no particular or urgent necessity for so doing, nor obliged to sell, and a buyer, being ready, willing, and able to buy but under no particular necessity for so doing, each dealing with the other with full knowledge of all the uses and purposes for which the property is reasonably adaptable and available."

### VALUE vs. PRICE
When reference is made to the value of a property, generally fair market value is meant. Market price is what one might get from the sale of the property in terms of money. Sometimes value and price are the same, most particularly when there is no compulsion to buy or sell. Under other circumstances, there might be a wide difference between the market value of a property and the actual sale price. The appraiser must be careful to consider normal buyers and sellers attitudes for the type of property appraised. The appraiser is estimating actual market value not theoretical value.

The immobility of real estate makes it unique. Theoretically, there are no two parcels exactly alike and therefore no means of making a total comparison between properties. Circumstances of one buyer and one seller affect the sale price of a specific property, whereas the actions of many buyers and sellers of similar type properties determine the going rate for the sale or exchange of property on the open market.

Among the various types of value that have been designated from time to time are book value, tax value, market value, cash value, capital value, speculative value, par value, true value, exchange value, reproduction value, physical value, replacement value, insurance value, investment value, rental value, face value, depreciated value, leasehold value, sound value, sales value and cost value.

The real estate broker should be concerned mostly with the concept of Fair Market Value, or simply market value, for this is the basis upon which most property is generally bought and sold.

## VALUE vs. COST
Value can be distinguished from "cost" as well as from "price," for neither is necessarily synonymous with value. The principal differences may be explained as follows:

◊    **Value** has to do with the combined factors of present and future anticipated enjoyment or profit. The value sought in the appraisal of property may be said to be the discounted present worth of all desirable things (benefits) which may accrue from a skillful use of it. A conclusion in regard to these things will clearly be a matter of opinion: an intelligent estimate based on a thorough analysis of all available influencing factors and on reasonable and more or less warranted assumptions.

◊    **Cost** represents a measure of past (or prospective) expenditures in money, labor, material or sacrifices of some nature in acquiring or producing the commodity. While cost may be, and frequently is, a factor upon which value is partially based, it need not be, as it does not control present and future value. An example of this fact is the value of an apartment property as compared with an oil well (assuming that the building and drilling costs were the same). The oil well may prove to be a big producer and of great value, or it may prove to be a dry hole and of no value. An apartment building might be costly to build but have little value because of its bad location and high vacancy factor.

◊    **Price** is what one pays for a commodity, regardless of pressure motives or intelligence of the seller or buyer. Usually it is considered to be the amount of money involved in a transaction. Whether we receive in value more or less than what we pay for will depend on the soundness of judgment in the analysis or appraisal of value. Under an efficient market structure, price will usually tend to equal value, varying only as buyers and sellers have unequal knowledge, negotiating skills, or economic strength. Some factors influencing market price (as distinguished from value) are favorable financing, distress sale, forced purchase, uninformed purchaser or seller, misrepresentation of facts by the seller and high pressure sales practices.

Appraisers carefully distinguish between market value, cost and price in refining their appraisal conclusions.

## Purposes and Characteristics of Value
The purpose of a valuation or an appraisal is usually indicated in the value concept employed, for example: market value, assessed value, condemnation value, liquidation value, cash value, mortgage loan value, fire insurance value, etc. The purpose of an appraisal frequently dictates the valuation method employed and influences the resulting estimate of value.

◊    **Intended use.** The intended use of the report has become distinct from the purpose of the appraisal. This relates to how the process has been separated from the writing of the report (Standard 1 vs. Standard 2 in USPAP). The purpose of the appraisal may be, for instance, to help in settling an estate. The intended use of the report may be to communicate the value findings to heirs only, or may include attorneys and/or taxing authorities. The purpose helps to define how the appraisal process will be laid out. The intended use will help to determine which report type is most appropriate for communicating the results of the process.

◊    **Four elements of value.** There are only four elements of value, all of which are essential. These are utility, scarcity, demand (together with financial ability to purchase), and transferability. None alone will create value.
◊    For example, a thing may be scarce but, if it has no utility, there is no demand for it. Other things, like air, may have utility and may be in great demand, but are so abundant as to have no commercial value. *Utility* is the capacity of a commodity to satisfy a need or desire. To have utility value, real estate should have the ability to provide shelter, income, amenities or whatever use is being sought. Functional utility is an important test for determining value. Likewise, the commodity must be transferable as to use or title to be marketable.

Generally speaking, a commodity will have commercial or marketable value in proportion to its utility and relative scarcity. Scarcity is the present or anticipated supply of a product in relation to the demand for it. Utility creates demand, but demand, to be effective, must be implemented by purchasing power. Otherwise, a person desiring a product cannot acquire it.

Fundamental to the concept of value is the "highest and best use" principle, discussed earlier in this chapter. Location is a most important factor in determining highest and best use. Any analysis to reach a decision as to the "highest and best use" must include consideration as to the future supply and demand for such use within the area and a possible oversupply or undersupply with attendant effect on market demand and value.

## FORCES INFLUENCING VALUE

The value of real estate is created, maintained, modified and destroyed by the interplay of the following four great forces:

◊    **Environmental and physical characteristics.** Examples of physical characteristics include: quality of conveniences; availability of schools, shopping, public transportation, churches; similarity of land used; and types of physical hazards. Environmental considerations include climate, soil and topography, barriers to future development (oceans, mountains, etc.), transportation systems, and access to other areas/regions.

◊    **Social ideals and standards.** Examples of social forces include: population growth and decline; age, marriage, birth, divorce and death rates; and attitudes toward education, recreation, and other instincts and yearnings of mankind.

◊    **Economic influences.** Examples of economic forces are: natural resources; industrial and commercial trends; employment trends; wage levels; availability of money and credit; interest rates; price levels; tax loads; regional and community present economic base; new development trends; and rental and price patterns.

◊    **Political or government regulations.** Examples of political forces include: building codes; zoning laws; public health measures; fire regulations; rent controls; environmental legislation controlling types of new development; fiscal policies; monetary policies; government guaranteed loans; government housing; and credit controls.

Each and every one of these many physical, social, economic and political factors affect cost, price, and value to some degree. The four forces interweave and each one is in a constant state of change.

## FACTORS INFLUENCING VALUE

◊    **Directional growth.** In any estimate of value, attention should be given to "the city directional growth" as well as to "Urban Renewal Plans." The city directional growth refers to the manner and direction in which the city tends to expand.

Properties in the direction of growth or renewal in different sections of the city tend to increase in value, especially if the growth or renewal is steady and rapid.

◊    **Location.** Location is an exceptionally important value factor because location influences demand for the property. Location must not be described too generally, and is an effective value factor only when it is specifically related to highest and best use. Brokers often claim, "The three most important characteristics for any property are location, location and location."

◊    **Utility.** Utility includes the capacity to produce. This important factor involves judgment as to the best use to which a given property may be put. Building restrictions and zoning ordinances affect utility.

◊    **Size.** The width and depth of a parcel of land will often determine the possibilities and character of its use.

◊    **Corner influence.** Corner sites sometimes have higher unit value than a site fronting on one street only. Disadvantages include loss of privacy, higher cost as off-site improvements cost more and lot maintenance is more expensive, and setbacks may require a smaller size house. Commercial properties benefit from corner sites because of easy access and added exposure.

◊    **Shape.** Parcels of land of irregular shape generally cannot be developed as advantageously as rectangular lots.

◊    **Thoroughfare conditions.** The width of streets, traffic congestion, and condition of pavement have an effect on the value of frontage properties and to a lesser degree on other properties in the neighborhood.

◊    **Exposure.** The south and west sides of business streets are usually preferred by merchants because pedestrians seek the shady side of the street on warm afternoons and merchandise displayed in the windows is not damaged by the sun. This traditional view in older commercial districts is somewhat offset by new architectural concepts (e.g., shopping malls), parking and convenience.

◊    **Character of business climate.** Larger cities develop residential, shopping, financial, wholesale, and industrial districts.

◊    **Plottage or assemblage.** An added increment of value when several parcels of land are combined under one ownership to produce greater utility than when the parcels are under separate ownership.

In highly urbanized multiple residential and commercial areas plottage, or assemblage, makes it possible to gain that higher utility. An example of this would be a density bonus for the combining of residential lots. This principle may also apply to light industrial areas.

◊     **Topography and character of soil.** The bearing qualities of the soil may affect construction costs. Extensive foundations are usually necessary in soft earth. The type and condition of the topsoil affect the growth of grass, plants, shrubs and trees. Value may also be influenced by land contour and grades, drainage and view points.

◊     **Obsolescence.** Caused by external or economic changes which decrease the functional utility of a property, or by physical deterioration of the property.
     Changes in types and methods of construction, style of architecture, or interior arrangements for specific purposes may render a particular building out of date. Changes in the uses of neighboring property may also contribute to the obsolescence of a building. Careful appraisal will include the potential for remodeling, refurbishing or other method to restore value.

◊     **Building restrictions and zones.** These sometimes operate to depress values and at other times to increase values.
◊     For example, there may be a vacant lot on a residential street which will sell for only $150 a front foot for single family residential use but would sell for $600 per front foot as an apartment site. Or a vacant lot in a zoned area may sell for more per front foot as a business site because of the supply of business sites being restricted by zoning.

## Additional Factors Important for Residential Property
When appraising residential property, it is customary to make a direct comparison between the property being appraised (subject property) and comparable properties in the area which have sold recently. This is the market data or "sales comparison approach" method based upon the economic principle of substitution (i.e., the value of a particular property will not generally exceed the cost to purchase a similar, or substitute property which is equally desirable and available).

◊     **Gross rent multiplier.** An appraiser may also use a technique known as Gross Rent Multiplier (GRM) by comparing actual rentals and sales prices of properties comparable to the subject to get another indication of value by multiplying the monthly rent by an appropriate GRM. If a comparable property rents for $700 a month and sells for $84,000, which is 120 times the gross monthly rental ($84,000 ÷ $700 = 120), the indicated GRM applicable to the subject property is 120.
     GRM applies only to *rental* income. When part of a property's income comes from *nonrental sources,* an appraiser will use a similar gross income multiplier (GIM).

◊     **Square foot method.** In making a preliminary estimate of the value of residential property, it is usual to evaluate the lot and the present value of the building. An estimate of the cost of replacing a building is usually made by the square foot method. The square foot method requires measuring the building and dividing it into rectangles. Multiplying the length by the width of each rectangle will produce the square footage of that segment. The total square footage of the residence is obtained by adding together the square footage of all rectangular segments. The sum obtained thereby is multiplied by an appropriate construction cost per square foot, depending upon the type of construction involved. The result is known as the replacement cost of the residence. Depreciation is then taken from the replacement cost to give the present value of the improvements. The present value added to the land value represents an indication of the value of the subject property. In analyzing depreciation, special attention should be paid to the condition of the building, the exterior finish and roof, the interior fixtures, plans and workmanship, interior decoration, plumbing, heating, and electric fixtures, etc. Particular attention should be given to the inspection of the foundation and the underpinnings of the house in connection with possible termite infestation and soil problems such as subsidence or expansion.

◊     **Multi-family dwellings.** Trends and standards for residential dwellings vary in the markets, especially for multi-family structures. Appraisers must consider: the layout; adequacy of size; conveniences; safety features and comfort; adaptability for intended use; and cost and ease of maintenance.

## Additional Factors Important for Commercial Property
Commercial property is real property acquired for investment. Commercial structures are of many types, sheltering such businesses as shopping centers, banks, service establishments, restaurants, parking lots, retail stores and office buildings. A downtown, regional, or community commercial district is usually clearly defined and located on major streets. Store rentals and business leases are generally based on square footage of rentable area. In many localities the tenant pays, in addition to rent, all property expenses/charges such as taxes, insurance, maintenance, and assessments. Such a lease is a "net" (or, in some communities, a "net, net, net") lease.

Front footage valuations are still applicable in many downtown areas or location. In appraising such property, care must be used to properly evaluate such things as floor plans, utility, relationship of site area to improvements, obsolescence, parking accommodations, ratios of net rentable areas to gross area. Efficiency, safety, structural and design features are also very important, as are energy standards and efficiencies.

## Additional Factors Important for Industrial Property
Industrial lands are usually valued in terms of gross buildable area, either by square foot or by acre (e.g., 30 cents a square foot; $13,000 an acre). One of the reasons for valuing industrial land in terms of area is that the parcel is generally all usable. Indeed,

optimum efficiency of site, buildings and equipment are vital to the successful operation of industrial properties.
Industrial buildings are generally constructed of concrete or steel, including prefabrications, or tilt-ups. Industrial parks (groups of industrial buildings having similar uses) have grown in importance. These require plenty of parking space, storage facilities, excellent operating layouts, management services, and even room to expand. These properties are frequently designed and equipped to meet needs of specific occupants.

◊    **Topography.** The topography of undeveloped land is of importance, and consideration should be given to the cost of grading, if required.

◊    **Subsoil.** The character of the subsoil is frequently overlooked, and yet may be vital. Quicksand, rock, or other detriments may make a certain site unsuitable for a given industry. Drainage may also be an important factor.

◊    **Plottage value.** There is an added increment of value known as plottage which is gained from combining land parcels in an urban area into a reasonably sized industrial site.

◊    **Tract layouts.** In the study and valuation of unimproved but potentially valuable industrial lands, it is often necessary to have the assistance of a competent engineer who is familiar with plant and tract layouts.

## Additional Factors Important for Agricultural or Farm Lands

Present trends show larger and fewer farms, fewer farm buildings per acre, and fewer family-style operations. The type of buildings an appraiser usually finds on agricultural lands include residences, machine sheds, poultry sheds, multifunctional barns, silos, and various animal shelters. According to some experts in the field, farm buildings contribute less than 20% of the total property value.

One important factor in estimating the value of agricultural land is the nature and longterm trend of costs and prices for the crop grown or intended to be grown. For example, if the property is to be used as a dairy farm the appraiser must consider: whether the soil is suitable for hay and grain; water supply for the cattle and crops; proximity to markets; climatic conditions; labor conditions; etc.

Farm land valuation is highly specialized and often requires the assistance of soil and crop experts and appraisal specialists to evaluate irrigation systems and other equipment and machinery.

## ECONOMIC TRENDS AFFECTING REAL ESTATE VALUE
### Regional, National and Global Economics

Property values increase, decrease, or remain stable based on the interaction of the four forces influencing value. Appraisers must examine and evaluate these forces.

Economic trends and forces at higher levels (regional, national and international) affect property values at the local level. The real estate appraiser must recognize that the general pattern of statistical analysis that guides in interpreting value influences on a national level should be used in the general analysis of state and regional forces which in turn influence local property values.

An appraiser should follow national and regional economic trends, changes in national income levels, international developments and government financing policies because the greater the severity and duration of any economic swing, the wider and deeper is its influence. Conditions to be observed include: gross national product; balance of payments to other countries; national income levels; employment; price level indexes; interest rates; fiscal and monetary policies; building starts; and credit availability.

## Factors Influencing City Growth and Development

An appraiser is constantly concerned with the conditions and prospects of the local economy because the value of local real estate is largely determined by the health of the community, as measured by household purchasing power, population changes, employment diversification and stability, wage and price levels, and area growth potential, including environmental conditions.

Cities are classified generally by the functions that stimulate and determine their potential and growth. These classifications are:
◊    **Commercial.** Primary source of revenue stems from commercial enterprises. These are usually farming cities, cities located at railroad terminals or on ocean ports.

◊    **Industrial.** Primary source of revenue is derived from manufacturing and processing of commodities.

◊    **Extractive industry.** Primary source of revenue comes from natural resources, e.g., mining, fishing and lumber.

◊    **Political.** Primary source of revenue is government employment.

◊   **Recreation and health.** Primary source of revenue comes from tourist trade, vacation and health resorts.

◊   **Education.** The anchor point of these cities is a college or university.

## Population Trends
Because of the direct relationship existing between the value of real property and population growth, the appraiser should be concerned with population trends and other demographic factors affecting local population, such as: opportunities for employment; quality of local government; civic and social conditions; demand for goods and services; transportation and living conditions; and, opportunities for education and personal improvement.

## Neighborhood Analysis
A neighborhood may be defined as a group of similar land uses which are similarly affected by the operation of the four forces influencing value: utility, scarcity, demand(desire) and effective purchasing power. A common definition for a neighborhood is a grouping together of individuals within the community for similar purposes and interests, whether the reasons be commercial, industrial, residential, cultural or civic. The life cycle of a neighborhood includes growth in desirability, peak desirability, stability for a time, then deterioration. The cycle then tends to turn again as the neighborhood becomes more desirable due to change in use or renewal.

Neighborhood analysis is important because the neighborhood is the setting for the property to be appraised and the property has value, to a large extent, as it contributes to or detracts from the neighborhood.
A neighborhood tends to be a somewhat self-contained community, frequently defined by physical boundaries such as hills, freeways, or major streets and usually with some sense of community. In urban areas, the neighborhood tends to become somewhat blurred due to modern transportation and area-wide cultural, educational, recreational, and commercial services. In analyzing the "neighborhood" of the parcel to be appraised, a good starting point is to ascertain the community identity and boundaries.

After defining, even in vague terms, this community identity, an appraiser will look to common services and features, such as local shopping, street patterns, zoning boundaries, and cultural, religious, educational and recreational services. In short, an appraiser searches the local area by observation and through government and public utility investigation to find the factors most affecting use and value patterns in the area.

Neighborhood analysis also tends to define the best search area for comparable market data. As the appraisal progresses, the appraiser may extend or contract this search area.

Some sources of neighborhood data:
   ◊   U.S. Census tract maps and data (local library or vendors).
   ◊   City and county population demographics (planning departments).
   ◊   City, county, and state street and highway systems (city, county and state road/engineering/highway departments).
   ◊   Local zoning and general planning, including community plans (planning departments).
   ◊   School locations, capacities, policies (local school districts).
   ◊   Public utility services: water, sewer, natural gas, electric power, telephone (local public utility companies and government agencies).
   ◊   City and county economic statistics (local chambers of commerce).
   ◊   Local tax information (county tax assessor).
   ◊   If pertinent, private wells and septic laws (local health departments); national forest/park laws (local forestry and park dept.), etc.

## SITE ANALYSIS AND VALUATION
Although the location of the neighborhood and city must be weighed in analysis and valuation of a particular site, the location of the site itself, in relation to the neighborhood, is a very important factor.

Since sites in a neighborhood are not usually uniform in size, shape and other physical and economic characteristics, some are superior to others. It is important that the site be analyzed separately and evaluated in conformity with the principle of highest and best use.

Other reasons to separate the land from the value of an entire property, along with important factors contributing to site value, are discussed on the following pages.

## Legal Data of Site Analysis

### Legal description.
◊   An appraiser must determine the legal property description as set forth by a deed or official record.
◊   The proper legal description to locates the property physically within the neighborhood.

### Taxes.
◊   A comparison is made between the subject and similar properties to ascertain if the property being appraised has been fairly assessed (assessed value, tax rate and tax total). This comparison of properties is not as useful since the adoption of Proposition 13.
◊   The extent of the tax burden will have a bearing upon the desirability of the property, particularly when taxes are out of proportion to income.

### Zoning and General Plan.
◊   Copies of the latest zoning ordinances and general plan should be studied to inform the appraiser as to the present usages to which the land may be developed. Sometimes the highest and best use of land is limited by zoning restrictions.
◊   Proposed or contemplated changes in the existing ordinances should be determined, since this could have a bearing upon the valuation of the property. However, zoning by itself does not create value unless there is a demand for the land so zoned.

### Restrictions and easements.
◊   Public and private restrictions and easements affecting the land must be discovered.
◊   The restrictions and the types of easements on the property have a direct bearing upon the use and value of the site being appraised.

### Determination of existence of other interests in property.
◊   Life estates.
◊   Leases.
◊   These partial interests divide property values among the parties involved. This does not mean a mathematical division, but rather a division of the bundle of rights.

## Physical Factors Involving the Site
The physical features of the site should be compared with typical lots in the neighborhood.
Lot values will generally tend to cluster around a"site value, "... the price generally accorded a single, usable, typically-sized parcel of land in the area. Lots larger or smaller will tend to increase or decrease when compared to this usual "site value." A good view will also tend to increase lot value. The effect of topography (drainage, low spots, rock, etc.) can frequently be measured by the cost to cure the problem to make the site usable.

### Shape of a lot.
◊   The utility of the lot is the governing factor in irregular or odd-shaped lots.
◊   The total area of the lot is not the most important factor. A 50' x 150' lot containing 7,500 square feet is more valuable than a 25' x 300' lot (also 7,500 sq. ft.) because of utility.
◊   Irregular-shaped lots are frequently valued in terms of total site value expressed in dollars rather than in terms of unit values of price per square foot or frontage foot.

### Topography and soil conditions.
◊   Topography and the type of soil can have an adverse effect upon the site value if it makes building costs higher.

### Corner influence.
◊   In today's market, it has generally been found that corner single-family lots are not valued appreciably more than inside lots.
◊   Corner lots provide better light and more convenient access.
◊   On the other hand, corner lots result in more traffic noise and trespassing and, if applicable, greater special assessments for streets and lighting.

### Relation of site to surroundings.
◊   The site must be studied in its relationship to streets, alleys, transportation, and stores.
◊   Does the home-site abut commercial or multi-residential uses?
◊   Is it a key lot looking upon other back yards?
◊   If a corner lot, does a bus line stop at the comer?

**Availability of public utilities.**

**Title encumbrances and encroachments.**

**Landscaping and underground utilities.**

## METHODS OF SITE VALUATION
### A. Sales or market data comparison.
1. Sales and listings (data) of vacant sites are obtained and compared with the property being valued.
2. The data should be of comparable properties, including the same zoning and in the same or similar neighborhood. Since people make value, the data gathered should be from areas where the purchasing power or income levels are the same as the subject property.
3. The sales prices should be investigated to determine whether the price paid was the result of a true open market transaction reflecting fair market value. Listings may also be considered.
4. Some sources of comparable market data are:
    a. Title insurance company records.
    b. Tax assessor's records.
    c. Recorder's office.
    d. Multiple listing files.
    e. Financial news.
    f. Appraiser's personal files.
5. The verified market transactions should be compared with the subject parcel as to:
    a. Time.
        (1) Determine if prices have gone up, down, or remained stable from the time of each sale to the date of value.
        (2) A percentage factor or a dollar amount may be applied to the comparable sales in order to arrive at an adjusted price due to the time factor.
    b. Location.
        (l) Determine if the location of each comparable property is superior, equal or inferior to that of the subject property.
        (2) A percentage factor or dollar amount may be applied to the data in order to adjust for the difference in location.
    c. Characteristics of the lots.
        (1) The size, depth, and topography of the other properties are compared with the property being valued.
        (2) A percentage factor or dollar amount is determined for these characteristics and applied to the comparable properties to adjust their prices towards the property being appraised.
    d. The adjusted prices of the comparable properties are then compared and analyzed in order to arrive at an estimate of value for the property under study.

**Example.** Using only 3 lot sales (the minimum) as a demonstration.

| Sale No. | Price | Date | Size (feet) | Square Feet |
|---|---|---|---|---|
| 1 | $5,000 | October, 1995 | 50 x 120 | 6,000 |
| 2 | $4,750 | March, 1996 | 40 x 130 | 5,200 |
| 3 | $5,500 | June, 1996 | 50 x 120 | 6,000 |
| Subject | | | 50 x 150 | 7,500 |

Through investigation, it was found that prices have been increasing approximately 1% a month during the past year. Sale No. 1 is believed to be located in an area inferior to the subject. This lot would sell for about $500 more if located in the subject's block. Sale No. 2 is located in an area believed to be about $250 better than the subject. Sale No. 3 is also in a superior location, by the same $250 adjustment. The shape and topography of Sales No. 1 and No. 2 are better than the subject by an amount estimated to be $500 and $100 respectively. Sale No. 3's topography and utility appear about the same as the subject.

**Adjustments.**

| Sale No. | Time | Location | Characteristics | Adjusted $ | Adj. $/sq. ft. |
|---|---|---|---|---|---|
| 1 | +$500 | +$500 | -$500 | $5,500 | $.92 |
| 2 | +$240 | -$250 | -$100 | $4,640 | $.89 |
| 3 | +$110 | -$250 | 0 | $5,360 | $.89 |

The average adjusted price per square foot of the comparable sales is $.90. Therefore, the subject property has an indicated value as follows:

7,500 square feet x $.90 per square foot = $6,750

In actual practice, the use of more sales data is advisable in order to arrive at a well-supported adjusted price per square foot.

e. If all pertinent factors are considered, the adjusted prices will probably be in a fairly close range. If there is still a wide discrepancy, the appraiser will:
   (l) re-analyze work to find undisclosed pertinent factors;
   (2) reexamine data as being true examples of fair market transactions;
   (3) re-compute adjustments to insure accuracy; and
   (4) finally, discard the data or explain the apparent contradictions.

## B. Abstraction.
1. The abstraction method is used to obtain land value where there are no vacant land sales.
   a. Sales of houses in the same neighborhood on lots with similar characteristics are obtained.
   b. An estimate of the cost new of the improvements is made.
   c. An amount is deducted from cost new for depreciation.
   d. The depreciated cost of the improvements is deducted from the selling price of the property.
   e. The difference represents an approximation of land value.
**Example:** Appraised lot size is 65' X 100' = 6,500 sq. ft. Sale property is 6,000 sq. ft. lot with a single family residence and sold for $83,000. The sale building has an estimated cost new of $61,000 and an accrued depreciation estimated at $20,000. Land value by abstraction:

Price of sale property ................................................................$83,000
Less depreciated value of improvements:
   Cost new................................................................................$61,000
   Less accrued depreciation .................................................$20,000
Depreciated value .......................................................................$41,000
Indicated land value ...................................................................$42,000

Divide by lot size ................................................................ ÷ 6000 sq. ft.
Indicated lot value/sq. ft................................................... $7.00/sq.ft.
Multiply by subject lot size:
   65' x 100' = 6,500 sq. ft...................................................x 6,500
**Indicated value of lot ...........................................................$45,500**

**C. Plot Plan.** For better appraisal reporting, a plot plan can be prepared, with lot dimensions and improvements drawn to scale. It should show walks, driveways and other lot improvements and roof plans of the various structures on the site. The plot, together with pictures of the site, neighboring street and lot improvements are vital for an effective site analysis.

## ARCHITECTURAL STYLES AND FUNCTIONAL UTILITY
It is essential for an appraiser to have a working knowledge of building design and construction. Good basic design of both interior and exterior has a decided effect on the marketability of real estate. There is no substitute for appropriate materials and proper proportions and scale. The appraiser should be aware of imitations and new plastic replacements.

To achieve maximum value, architectural style and design should be related to the site. A typical stable neighborhood should be improved with homes of approximately the same size, age and style. A house that has an architectural style extremely foreign to its surroundings tends to encounter difficulty when offered for sale.

Or a home meets resistance in the market because of its style, which places it within a definite age group. Thus, if a certain style of architecture has lost its appeal because public taste has changed, this trend will have an adverse effect on value. Both real estate brokers and appraisers must be familiar with home styles and know the effect on value of misplaced styles. The appraiser must also be alert to resurgence of older properties in public acceptance.

This section: contains brief descriptions of various architectural styles in single family homes; explains how to determine quality of construction; and defines functional utility and its effect on marketability.

### Architectural Styles

◊ **Colonial.** Cape Cod and Cape Ann styles are: generally quite small in size - minimum with good taste; symmetrical-windows balanced on both sides of front door; either one or one and one-half stories with little head room upstairs; fairly steep gable or gambrel roof covered with wood shingles; and exterior of wood siding.

◊ **New England Colonial.** A square or rectangular, box-like structure having: maximum usable space; symmetrical windows balanced on both sides of front door; either two or two and one-half stories; gable roof covered with wood shingles; exterior of wood generally painted white; and impressive front entrance usually with transom fan of glass above the door.

◊ **Dutch Colonial.** A moderate-sized home generally not more than 50 feet wide, with a symmetrical front having: an entrance at the center, balanced by the windows; low-sweeping gambrel roof; exterior generally of stone; and either one and one-half story with dormer windows or two and one-half stories with dormer windows.

◊ **Georgian and Southern Colonial.** These styles have elaborate front entrances with plain or fluted columns; are generally of brick or wood; have prominent gabled roofs, often hipped; are very symmetrical; require large plots of land; large scale, not suitable for a small house; and either two, two and one-half or three stories.

◊ **English Elizabethan.** This style has gothic refined lines with molded stone around windows and doors; generally of brick, stucco, or stone; steep pitched roof, covered with slate or shingle; usually leaded metal casement windows; and requires a large building site.

◊ **English Half-Timber.** This style has protruding timber faces with stucco between the faces; lower story of heavy masonry; steep pitched roof; generally two stories; and requires a large lot area.

◊ **Regency.** A generally symmetrical style with front entrance in center; exterior of brick or stone; shutters on each side of windows; low hipped roof; two stories in height; and octagonal window on second floor over front door.

◊ **French Provincial.** Usually a large house on a sizable plot, masonry exterior walls with very high roofs; large high windows with long shutters; and one and one-half or two and one-half stories.

◊ **French Normandy.** Generally has turrets at entry; walls of brick or stone; unsymmetrical; and steep pitched shingle roof.

◊ **True Spanish.** Enclosed patios; red mission tiled roof; wrought iron decorations; and stucco walls (usually white).

◊ **Small Spanish.** Stucco exterior; flat composition roof with mission tile trim in the front; suitable for small lots; no patio; and one story only.

◊ **Monterey Spanish.** Two stories; stucco (generally white); red mission tiled roof; second story balconies; and decorative iron railings.

◊ **Modern and Contemporary.** Generally one story; usually flat or low pitched roof; often on concrete slab; large amount of glass; and indoor/outdoor living.

◊ **Bungalow or Ranch House.** One story; stucco with wood trim; often on concrete slab; shingle or shake roof; low and rambling; generally attached garage; and indoor/outdoor living.

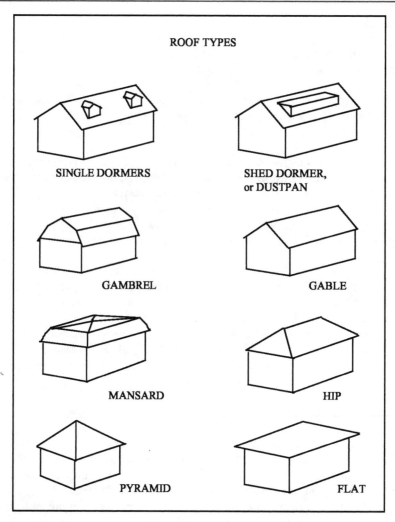

ROOF TYPES

SINGLE DORMERS

SHED DORMER, or DUSTPAN

GAMBREL

GABLE

MANSARD

HIP

PYRAMID

FLAT

## Building Quality

One of the most important reasons for inspecting a property is to determine its quality of construction and condition. The appraiser must be knowledgeable as to structural details of buildings. All exposed portions of a building should be closely inspected to ascertain the materials used, the present condition, and the type and quality of construction, which may be classified as follows:

A. **Low quality.**
    1. Competitive low cost house which does not exceed the minimum building codes.

B. **Fair quality.**
    1. Plain and inexpensive finishes on both interior and exterior.
    2. Cheap quality finish hardware, lighting fixtures, and heating.
    3. Generally erected in areas of low purchasing power.
    4. Typically, stucco exterior, concrete slab floor, composition roof.

C. **Average quality.**
    1. Meets VA and FHA standards.
    2. Usually purchased by persons of moderate income.
    3. Medium standard of construction with some low cost refinements.
    4. Usually of stucco exterior, hardwood flooring, composition roof or shingle.
    5. Finish hardware, lighting fixtures and heating of average quality.
    6. House found in large tract developments.

D. **Good quality.**
    1. Good architectural design, workmanship and materials.
    2. Stucco walls with wood and masonry trim, hardwood floors, shingle roofs.
    3. Usually has two bathrooms, forced air furnace or equal heating, good quality lighting fixtures and finish hardware.
    4. Usually has extra built-in equipment in kitchen.

E. **Very good quality.**
>    1. Generally, custom designed by architect.
>    2. Home contains many extra features.
>    3. Stucco walls with extensive wood or masonry trim, hardwood flooring, shake roofs.
>    4. Two or more bathrooms, forced air heating, very good quality finish hardware and lighting fixtures.
>    5. Custom fireplaces.

F. **Excellent quality.**
>    1. Custom designed by architect.
>    2. Extra features are of the highest quality and design.
>    3. Stucco walls with redwoods or cedars or other fine woods, stone trim, hardwood, marble and custom carpet floorings, clay tile, slate roofs, copper gutters and so on.
>    4. A bath with each bedroom, walk-in closets, zoned heating, special wood finishes such as teak, cherry, walnut, etc., designer lighting including recessed art lighting.
>    5. Custom fireplaces, custom libraries or bars, granite or marble counters in baths and kitchen, gourmet appliances.

## FUNCTIONAL UTILITY

Good architecture is concerned with room layout and functional utility as well as exterior style. A functional analysis of a property measures the conveniences and economy in the use of the property. The combined factors of usefulness and desirability have an effect on a property's marketability. The degree of its functional utility is important in any consideration of its marketability. Thus, marketability is the ultimate test of functional utility.

### Functional Utility Checklist
**A. Building.**
>    1. Living room.
>       a. Adequacy of floor and wall space for proper placement of furniture.
>       b. Circulation - should not have to pass through long living room to reach other parts of the house.
>       c. Fireplace should be away from the traffic flow.
>       d. Wall spaces - adequate for furniture arrangements.
>    2. Dining room or area.
>       a. Ease of access to kitchen.
>       b. Size of room or area governed by overall size of house. c. Best if room is nearly square.
>    3. Bedrooms.
>       a. Master bedroom should be of adequate size (minimum 10' x 12').
>       b. Other bedrooms (minimum 9' x 10') .
>       c. Cross ventilation should be provided.
>       d. Located away from family areas and kitchen for privacy.
>       e. Should not have to go through one bedroom to enter another.
>       f. Closet space should be adequate (minimum depth 2 feet; minimum area 6 square feet).
>       g. Proximate to full bath facilities.
>    4. Kitchen.
>       a. Workspace should be ample and efficient in plan.
>       b. Equipment should be centrally located to eliminate unnecessary foot travel.
>       c. Walls, ceilings and floors should be of easily maintained materials.
>       d. Adequate provision should be made for proper lighting and ventilation.
>       e. Kitchen should be conveniently located in relation to dining areas and family room.
>       f. Kitchen should have an exterior entrance.
>       g. Laundry facilities should be adjacent to kitchen.
>    5. Bathrooms.
>       a. Proper location with respect to other rooms.
>       b. If only one bathroom exists, it should be located off the central hall.
>       c. Bathroom should not open directly into kitchen or living room.
>       d. Adequate ventilation - exterior window or automatic exhaust fan is necessary.
>       e. Floors, walls, and ceilings easily cleaned and maintained.
>    6. Closets and storage.
>       a. At least one clothes closet per bedroom.
>       b. Adequate linen closet space.
>       c. Storage closets should be centrally located.
>       d. A storage area should be provided near the laundry equipment.
>       e. Exterior storage necessary if there is only a carport.

**B. Site.**
1. Construction should be related to the size of the building site.
2. The house should be so located on the land that it relates to the building site or "belongs."
3. Adequate front, rear and side yards are necessary for light and privacy. Yards may be clustered in planned unit developments.
4. A private service yard for drying clothes and storage of refuse should be convenient to the kitchen.
5. Entrance to the garage should be convenient and readily accessible.
6. Proper landscaping.
7. Recreational and garden facilities.
8. Adequate yard improvements.

**Guidelines for Considering Physical Characteristics of Real Property for FHA Insurance Purposes**
A. **Visual appeal of property.** How well will the property as a whole retain its market appeal?
1. Exterior design of structures.
a. Visual appeal based upon the probability of continuing market acceptance.
b. Certain architectural styles are short-lived in their acceptance and become obsolete.
2. Setting.
a. Measures the property's appeal in the market because of terrain, accessory buildings, walks, landscaping.
b. The dwelling and surroundings should present a pleasing and unified composition.
3. Interior design of dwelling.
a. The interior design should exhibit simplicity of treatment, harmony in proportions and refinement in design.
b. Interior permanent features should be up-to-date and of adequate construction.

B. **Livability of property.** The degree of usefulness, convenience and comfort which the property affords is determined by:
1. Site utilization.
a. Considers all aspects of the site and its arrangements as these affect the livability of the entire property.
b. The lot characteristics including size, shape, topography, orientation and natural advantages are considered.
2. Dwelling space utilization. Consideration is given to the size and efficient distribution of space within the structure.
3. Room characteristics. Consideration is given to the size and proportion of the rooms in relationship to the overall area of the dwelling. The following factors are considered:
a. Room orientation.
b. Circulation.
c. Privacy.
d. Closet and storage space.
e. Kitchen efficiency.
f. Service facilities.
g. Insulation.

C. **Natural light and ventilation.** The effect of natural light and natural ventilation on the desirability, livability and healthfulness is considered.
1. The proper amount or ratio of natural light to room area should be maintained.
2. Ventilation of all rooms is studied to measure its effect on desirability of the dwelling.
3. Cross ventilation desirable in all bedrooms.

D. **Structural quality.** The quality of structural design, materials, and workmanship is determined for the dwelling. The component elements to be considered are as follows:
1. Foundations.
2. Wall construction.
3. Partitions.
4. Floor construction.
5. Ceiling construction.
6. Roof construction.

E. **Resistance to elements and usage.** A determination is made as to the resistance of the dwelling to the effects of weather, decay, corrosion, fire, and deterioration. Consideration is given to three categories:
1. Lot improvements.
a. How is the soil protected from erosion?
b. Is the land properly graded so that the structure is not damaged by water?
c. The yard improvements such as walks and walls should be of adequate materials.

2. The building exterior. Analysis is made with reference to the resistance of the exterior of the building to the effects of the elements.

3. Building interior. Consideration is given to the resistance of interior surfaces and materials to determine wear and tear and deterioration.

F. **Suitability of mechanical equipment.** Measures the extent that the equipment contributes to the desirability and appeal of the dwelling through convenience, economy, and comfort. Consideration is given to:

1. Plumbing system.
2. Heating system.
3. Electric system.
4. Supplementary equipment.

## THE APPRAISAL PROCESS AND METHODS

Over time, well defined ground rules have been developed by professional appraisers to arrive at an estimate of value. This orderly, systematic procedure is known as the appraisal process. Not every step is used every time or necessarily in the same order. However, this comprehensive check list for the appraisal process should serve to give a better understanding of the importance of properly evaluating the various elements that influence market value and market price.

### Overview of the Appraisal Process

As governed by Standard 1 of USPAP, the orderly steps and considerations of the appraisal process are designed to answer two questions:

◊ What is highest and best use?

and

◊ What is this use worth?

To reach a legitimate conclusion:

A. Define the problem.
1. Identification of the property to be evaluated.
   a. Complete mailing address (including city and state).
   b Complete legal description (by lot, block and tract number, including county where recorded; by metes and bounds descriptions; or by the government survey system).
2. Description of use of property to be appraised.
   a. Vacant lot.
   b. Single-family residential.
   c. Multi-family residential.
   d. Special purpose (commercial, etc.)
3. Interests to be appraised.
   a. Which of the bundle of rights are to be evaluated? Rights affect value because they set the limits within which the property may be used.
   b. An appraisal estimates the value of the rights of ownership, not merely the physical land and its improvements.
   c. The extent of the research and the valuation opinion will vary depending upon which of the following rights are involved:
      (1) Fee Simple (complete ownership). (2) Easement across property. (3) Lessor's or lessee's interest. (4) Mineral Rights. (5) Miscellaneous interests.
4. Purpose and intended use of the valuation determine the types of information to be gathered and processed, such as:
   a. Fair value for sale of a home.
   b. Value for mortgage loan purposes.
   c. Value for insurance purposes.
   d. Value for condemnation proceedings.
   e. Miscellaneous purposes and functions.
5. Date of value is generally the date of the last inspection of the property, although it may be any time in the past. Prospective values may be rendered, such as for proposed developments where "future sales" are projected and discounted to present value.

B. Make a preliminary survey of neighborhood, site and data required for appraisal.
1. Make a preliminary estimate of the highest and best use of the subject property.
   a. Analysis of the site and improvements. Is it a proper improvement? Does the improvement meet the test? Take inventory of important site utilities and building construction features.
   b. Analysis of the neighborhood. What are the boundaries and what services are available?
2. The type of property determines the variety of specific data needed.

a. For a single-family home, emphasis will be placed on data concerning similar lots and improvements.

b. For a four-plex, emphasis will be placed on data concerning small multifamily units.

3. A definite plan facilitates the gathering of necessary data as indicated from the preliminary survey.

C. Collect other general and specific data. The value of a property is affected by demand and by purchasing power available. Data should be obtained on population trends, income levels, and employment opportunities. A number of sources should be investigated.

1. General data are obtained from government publications, newspapers and magazines.

2. Regional data (metropolitan area) are obtained from monthly bank summaries, regional planning commissions, and government agencies.

3. Community data (city) are obtained from the Chamber of Commerce, planning commission, city government, banks and savings and loan associations, and real estate boards.

4. Neighborhood data, obtained from personal inspection, real estate practitioners and builders active in the area, include:

   a. Age and appearance of the neighborhood.

   b. Hazards and adverse influences.

   c. Percentage build-out.

   d. Contemplated development.

   e. Proximity to schools, business, recreation, etc.

5. Obtain comparable market data, such as sales and listing prices, from:

   a. Assessor's records and county recorder's office.

   b. Title insurance and trust companies.

   c. Real estate boards and local real estate offices.

   d. Property owners in the neighborhood.

   e. Appraiser's/other appraisers' data bases.

6. Collect and analyze data regarding the subject property's improvements from:

   a. Assessor's office for age and other non-confidential information.

   b. City building department.

   c. Contractors in area.

   d. Personal inspection of improvements.

D. Analyze the data to conclude what is the highest and best use and the estimated worth of this use. As discussed later in this chapter, the following are the three approaches to value which will be used:

1. Sales Comparison Approach, formerly known as the Market Data Approach. Study of value as indicated by the prices of recent sales and reliable listings of properties similar to the appraised property.

2. Cost Approach. Study of value by adding the value of the land, if vacant, to the cost new, less accrued depreciation, of improvements

3. Income Approach. Study of value of the property as an income stream as it would be sold in the open market.

E. Make final estimate of defined value and write the report. The form and extent of the report will depend upon the purpose, type of property, and request of the client.

**The Departure Provision**

The Departure Provision sets forth the portions of the USPAP Standards that can be left out or departed from in the appraisal process. Care must always be given in departing from the full appraisal process, since the analysis not undertaken may have a material impact on the final value conclusion. In addition to Standard 1 and the Departure Provision, there is Statement 7 and Advisory Opinions 11, 12, 13 and 15 which provide additional valuable guidance in developing a proper appraisal process. These can all be found in the current edition of USPAP.

**METHODS OF APPRAISING PROPERTIES**

There are three approaches to consider in making a market value estimate. These approaches are:

◊   **Sales comparison approach.** Recent sales and listings of similar type properties in the area are analyzed to form an opinion of value.

◊   **Cost approach.** This approach considers the value of the land, assumed vacant, added to the depreciated cost new of the improvements. This is considered a substitute or alternative to buying an existing house.

◊   **Income approach.** The estimated potential net income of real property is capitalized into value by this approach.

Not only does each parcel of real estate differ in some respects from all other properties, but there are many different purposes for which an appraisal may be made. Each variation of purpose could result in a considerable, yet logical, variation of estimated value. For example the nature of the property, whether non-investment, investment or service; the purpose of the purchase, whether for use, investment or speculation; and the purpose of the appraisal, such as for sale, loan, taxation, insurance and the like, all constitute matters which will influence the proper methods of appraisal approach and the final result reached by the appraisal.

Consequently, the first step in any appraisal procedure is to have a clear understanding of the purposes for making the appraisal and the value to be sought. The adequacy and reliability of available data also are determining factors in the selection of the approaches to be employed. A lack of certain pertinent or up-to-date information may well eliminate an otherwise possible approach. When this is the case, it is not considered a departure from USPAP, since the approach was considered but not workable.

In other instances, proper procedures may only call for an appropriate discounting of conclusions drawn from such data. Thus, based on its adaptability to the specific problem, one method is subsequently the focus of the analysis and the other approach methods may not be employed. This is considered a limited appraisal and a departure from USPAP Standard 1.
In most appraisals, all three approach methods will ordinarily have something to contribute. Each approach method is used independently to reach an estimated value. Then, as a final step, by applying to each separate value a weight proportionate to its merits in that particular instance, conclusions are reached as to one appropriate value. This procedure is known as reconciliation.

## THE SALES COMPARISON APPROACH
This approach, formerly known as the market data comparison approach, is most generally adaptable for use by real estate brokers and salespersons. It lends itself well to the appraisal of land, residences and other types of improvements which exhibit a high degree of similarity, and for which a ready market exists. The principle of substitution is the basis of this approach. The buyer should not pay more for a property than the cost of acquiring a comparable substitute property. An analysis of market data is necessary in all three approaches to value.

The mechanics of the market comparison approach involve the use of sales and market data of all kinds in order to compare closely the property being appraised with other similar properties which have recently been sold or are offered for sale as to time of the sales, location of the sales and physical characteristics of the improvements. The sources used for determining value include actual sales prices, listings, offers, rents and leases, as well as an analysis of economic factors affecting marketability.

### Sources of Data
Sales or market data are obtained from many sources including:
◊ **Appraiser's own files.** Information gathered on previous assignments might provide information for the present appraisal.

◊ **Public records.** The county assessor's office keeps a record of all sales transactions recorded within the county. This information is kept confidential for the assessor's own use, but an owner can obtain needed information about owner's property from the assessor's office. The date of recording of any deed may be obtained from the recorder's office. The exact legal description as well as legal seller and buyer can be obtained from an inspection of the deed (or facsimile). The documentary transfer tax applies on all transfers of real property located in the county. Notice of payment is entered on the face of the deed or on a separate paper filed with the deed. Tax is computed at the rate of 55 cents for each $500 of consideration or fraction thereof. If a portion of the total price paid for the property is exempt because a lien or encumbrance remains on the property, this fact must be stated on the deed or on a separate paper filed with the deed.

◊ **Multiple listing offices, fellow appraisers or brokers.** Information on listings, offerings, and sales may frequently be obtained from real estate multiple listing facilities, real estate offices or by appraisers familiar with the area.

◊ **Legal property owner, sellers or buyers.** When viewing comparable sales and other pertinent data in an area, additional information is solicited by interviewing property owners living in the neighborhood. The appraiser should try to confirm the sales price and circumstances of the sale with buyer, seller and/or broker. If informed of the appraiser's purpose, parties will usually verify and explain the sale.

◊ **Classified ads and listings.** Ads are a source of information on properties currently being offered for sale. If possible, the appraiser's name should be on the mailing list of banks, savings and loan, and other institutions selling properties.
◊ Listing prices may often indicate the probable top market value of a specific property while bid prices may normally indicate the lowest probable value. Both are subject to variation based on motivation, but a reasonable number of properties falling into this category will provide a bracket within which a current fair value may be found. Offers are likely to approach market value more closely than are listings. However, an offer to purchase is not usually a matter of common knowledge.

### The Procedure
The procedure used in the sales comparison approach method is to systematically assemble data concerning comparable properties which are as "like-kind" to the subject as possible in regard to: neighborhood location; size (a comparable number of bedrooms and baths); age; architectural style; financing terms and general price range. The greater the number of good comparable data used,

the better the result, provided a proper analysis is made. The approach is based on the assumption that property is worth what it will sell for in the absence of undue stress, and if reasonable time is given to find a buyer. For this reason, the appraiser should look behind sales and transfers to ascertain what influences may have affected sales prices, particularly if only a few comparisons are available.

Proper comparisons between like properties are ideally based on an actual inspection. Inspections should determine: the condition of improvements at time of sale, not as of date of inspection; room arrangement and room count so that the utility of the data may be compared to the subject property; yard improvements and their influence upon the sales price; the sales price (from buyer, seller or broker), to determine if the sale was an arm's length or open market transaction; size and topography of the lot. For nearly comparable properties, negative (downward) adjustments should be imposed for the subject's poor repair, freakish design, existing nuisances, etc. Conversely, positive adjustments should be made for the subject's superior design, view, special features, better condition, higher quality of materials, landscaping, and the like.

Unless the sales being compared are of recent date, consideration must also be given to adjusting values in keeping with the economic trend of the district and the worth of the dollar. Financing terms receive value adjustment considerations, e.g., for favorable existing assumable financing, or perhaps seller-assisted financing.

**Units and elements of comparison.** The common units of comparison used by appraisers in the sales comparison approach are property components that can readily be used for comparison purposes: square footage; number of rooms; and number of units. Elements of comparison are characteristics in either the property or the transaction itself that cause prices to vary. These principal elements of comparison are financing terms, time (the market conditions at the time of the sale), sale conditions (no pressures/arm's length), location, physical characteristics, and income (if any) from the property.

Using the appropriate units and elements of comparison for the subject and each comparable, the appraiser assigns an estimated adjusted amount (dollar or percentage) for each difference found in the items of comparison (number of bathrooms, view, square footage, financing, forced sale). An adjusted price is thus established for each comparable property that should realistically reflect what the subject would sell for in the current market. The less comparable properties are then eliminated from consideration and greatest weight is given to the comparable sales most similar to the property being appraised. Through this judgment or reconciliation process, the appraiser arrives at the final estimate of value for the subject property.

**Advantages.** Some advantages of using the sales comparison approach are:
◊   It is the most easily understood method of valuation and in most common practice among real estate brokers and salespersons.
◊   It is particularly applicable for appraisal purposes involving the sale of single family residences and loan arrangements therewith. These make up the great bulk of real estate transactions.

**Disadvantages.** Some disadvantages of the comparison approach method are:
◊   Locating enough "nearly alike" properties which have recently sold or been listed.
◊   Adjusting amenities to make them comparable to the subject property. The greater the amount of adjustment or number of adjustments, the less reliable the comparable becomes.
◊   Older sales become less reliable in a changing market.
◊   Occasional difficulty confirming transaction details.
◊   Limitations in rapidly changing economic conditions and periods of high inflation and interest rates, when property appreciation rates may cause hazardous value conclusions.

### Application of the Procedure - Residential Sales
Like properties are always compared. The more current the data the better. The suggested order for making unit and element comparisons is in this sequence:
◊   finance terms
◊   time (market conditions)
◊   sale conditions
◊   location
◊   physical characteristics
◊   other (e.g., special considerations for income property)

### The steps.
◊   Research the market for bona fide "like-kind" recent market data. Select data. Verify.
◊   Select the appropriate units and elements of comparison. Adjust the sales price of each comparable (or eliminate it from consideration). The adjustment is always made to the comparable, not to the subject property.
◊   Each comparable will have its own value indication. Eliminate the less comparable properties. Set out comparison results

in chart or grid form. Using judgment and experience, reconcile or correlate the adjusted sales prices of the comparables and, by giving greatest weight to the sale that is most compatible to the subject property, assign an estimated value to the subject. Do not average the adjusted sales prices of the comparables. Reconciliation is a judgment process. It is not mechanical.

**Example.** Assume that the house to be appraised is a 2,400 square foot, 5-year old, single-family tract home located two blocks from the beach, with a fair view, stucco, 10 rooms, 4 bedrooms, 3 baths, 3 car garage. It is in good condition.

Prices have been increasing at 1% a month. The appraiser has selected from the neighborhood comparables which are equal in most of their financing and physical characteristics, except as shown on the rating chart. The value or sales price for the subject property is determined as shown on the chart below.

Adjust sales prices to indicate the appraised parcel value by subtracting the adjustment if the appraised parcel (subject) is inferior to the comparable and by adding the adjustment if the subject is superior to the comparable.

### SALES COMPARISON DATA APPRAISAL RATING GRID – SINGLE-FAMILY RESIDENCE TRACT HOME

| Elements/Units | Comparables | | | Subject |
|---|---|---|---|---|
| | Data 1 | Data 2 | Data 3 | |
| **Sales Price** | $164,000 | $176,000 | $178,000 | ? |
| **Adjustments** | | | | |
| Financing Terms… | Normal | Normal | Normal | Normal |
| Conditions of Sale … | Normal | Normal | Normal | Normal |
| Time (Sale Date) …. | June, 1995 | Nov., 1995 | April, 1996 | Aug., 1996 |
| Adjustment 1%/mo | +$22,960 | +$15,840 | +$7,120 | |
| Distance to Beach … | 1 Block | 3 Blocks | 4 Blocks | 2 Blocks |
| Adjustment | *(inferior) -$6,000 | *(superior) +$2,000 | *(superior) +$4,000 | |
| Garage | Equal | Equal | Equal | Equal |
| Age | Equal | Equal | Equal | Equal |
| Rooms | Equal | Equal | Equal | Equal |
| Bathrooms | Equal | Equal | Equal | Equal |
| View | None | Some | Fine | Fair |
| Adjustment | *(superior) +$4,000 | *(superior) +$1,000 | *(inferior) -$6,000 | |
| Square footage | 2,400 | 2,430 | 2,390 | 2,400 |
| Adjustment | 0 | 0 | 0 | |
| **Net Adjustments …** | $20,960 | $18,840 | $5,120 | |
| Adjusted Sale Price. | $184,960 | $194,840 | $183,120 | |
| **Indicated Value ….** | | | | **$185,000** |

* Inferior means the subject property is inferior to the comparable in this regard. Superior means the opposite. Subtract the adjustment if the subject property is inferior to the comparable property. Add the adjustment if the subject property is superior to the comparable property.

**Reconciliation:** Data 2 is close to the subject property in size, location, and view although not as good as the subject. Data 3 is the latest sale, but has the greatest difference in view and location. Data 1 is the oldest sale but is most useful for confirming the indication of value. Indicated value: $185,000.

## COST APPROACH

The Cost Approach views value as the combination of:
◊    the value of the land as if vacant; and
◊    the cost to reconstruct the appraised building as new on the date of value, less the accrued depreciation the building suffers in comparison with a new building.

The principle of substitution applies: i.e., value tends to be set by the price of an equivalent substitute. In the Cost Approach, the substitute is the cost of reconstructing the present building on a vacant site.

The total cost of the land as if vacant, plus the reconstruction cost new of the building with all direct and indirect expenses and profit, and before deduction of depreciation, will tend to set the upper limit of value. In this view, the cost new can be used as a benchmark for measuring the other approaches.

### The Procedure in Brief
◊    Estimate the value of the land as though vacant and available for development to its highest and best use.
◊    Estimate the replacement or reproduction cost of the existing improvements as of the appraisal date.
◊    Estimate the amount of accrued depreciation to the improvements from all causes (physical deterioration and/or functional or external obsolescence).
◊    Deduct the amount of the accrued depreciation from the replacement cost new to find the estimate of the depreciated value of the improvements.
◊    Add the estimated present depreciated value for the improvements to the value of the land. The result is an indication of the value for the subject property.

### Cost New Bases
The Cost Approach views the value of the building at its cost of reconstruction as new on date of value. There are three bases of reconstruction cost as new:
◊    Historic Cost indexed to Cost New;
◊    Reproduction Cost New; and
◊    Replacement Cost New.

Each basis has value to a cost-as-new study, but terms should not be confused.

**Historic cost indexed to cost new.** Historic Cost is the actual cost of the building when originally constructed, yesterday or fifty years ago. By use of price indices from building or engineering cost services, or from the original building contractor, Historic Cost can be "indexed" to Cost New on date of value. Indexed Historic Cost can be very useful if the building is fairly new and/or it is so unique that it is the only reliable value base. The advantage of Indexed Historic Cost is the accuracy of employing actual building costs. The disadvantage is that the older the costs are the less reliably they can be indexed. When considering Indexed Historic Costs, the appraiser should be certain that historic costs were normal costs at time of construction and that historic costs, as indexed, will accurately reflect Cost New on date of value.

**Reproduction cost new** is the cost, on date of value, of constructing a replica of the appraised building. This is a replica in actual design and materials. In this method, the cost-as-new estimate is made as if looking at plans of an exact duplicate of the present building. The advantage of Reproduction Cost New is the greater accuracy of duplicating the building in actual design and materials. The disadvantage is that advances in building construction and methods, materials and design make cost estimates of obsolete building construction very difficult and wildly distorted for materials no longer reasonably available or requiring large amounts of hand labor. Reproduction Cost New is most useful for study of refined methods of depreciation, unique construction, and occasional legal requirements for court testimony.

**Replacement cost new** views the building as if reconstructed with modern methods, design and materials that would most closely replace the use of the appraised building. For example, an older brick warehouse would be constructed today with concrete block or tilt-up cast slab construction. The advantage of Replacement Cost New is the ready availability of accurate current costs, and a better understanding by all parties of modern methods, design and materials. The disadvantage is the subjective decisions of proper current replacement materials and design for older construction. In actual practice, the Replacement Cost New is the most frequently used Cost Approach base.

### Steps in the Cost Approach
A. An estimate is made as to the land's current market value, assumed vacant and available for improvement to its highest and best use. Land value is usually based on a market approach utilizing comparable market data of similar sites in the area.

B. An estimate is made of the cost new of reconstructing the buildings and other improvements.
  1. The appraiser selects the proper cost new base:
    a. *Historic Cost* of appraised building indexed to cost new on date of value.
    b. *Reproduction Cost* of duplicating the replica of the appraised building using original materials and design on date of value.
    c. *Replacement Cost* of replacing the use and facility of the appraised building using modern materials, methods, and design on date of value.
  2. The appraiser completes property inspection, description, measurement, inventory, and plot plan of appraised building improvements and equipment, with notes regarding type, style, quality, and condition of building materials, workmanship and condition.
  3. The appraiser selects appropriate method of cost new estimating.
    a. The **Square-Foot Method** is the most common method used by appraisers on the West Coast to estimate the cost of construction. The property being appraised is compared with similar structures where costs are known, and which have been reduced to units per square foot of floor area. Standard type buildings whose costs are known are broken down to a cost per square foot of floor area. The building being appraised is compared with the most comparable standard building and its cost per square foot is used for the subject property. Adjustments must be made for size of building, and various exterior and interior features. Though adjustments cannot be made for many variables, this method, in most instances, is accurate enough for the real estate appraiser. The square-foot method can be used and applied faster than any other estimate.

    b. The **Cubic-Foot Method** is similar to the square-foot method, except the cubic contents of buildings are compared instead of the square footage of the floor area. This method is most popular in the Eastern United States. If used properly, it is more accurate than the square foot method, since the height as well as area of the building is taken into consideration. This method is most often used for industrial or warehouse buildings.

    c. The **Quantity Survey Method** involves a detailed estimate of all labor and materials for each component of the building. Items such as overhead, insurance, and contractor's profit must be added to direct costs. This is a very accurate but time-consuming method to arrive at costs. Because of the detail and time required, this method is seldom used, except by building contractors and professional cost estimators.

    d. The **Unit-in-Place Cost Method** entails calculation of the cost of units of the building as installed. The total costs of walls in place, heating units, roof, etc. are obtained on a square foot basis, including labor, overhead, and profit. This is a detailed, accurate method generally used for checking on new construction units. It is seldom used by appraisers because specialized knowledge is necessary to gather all elements of unit costs.

  4. The appraiser investigates cost sources and estimates cost-as-new of all buildings and improvements. Costs must be measured accurately. They are classified as direct (hard) costs and indirect (soft) costs. Indirect costs are usually associated with administration of the project while direct costs are expenditures for labor, equipment, materials, overhead and profit.
    a. Cost sources:
        (1) Costs of comparable buildings under construction.
        (2) Owners, builders, and/or contractors of comparable buildings.
        (3) The contractor of original building, if available.
        (4) Published cost services (usually handbooks providing current comprehensive cost data, by local areas and general construction types).
        (5) Professional cost estimators.
    b. The appraiser completes the cost estimate to include all:
        (1) Direct expenses of construction such as labor, materials and equipment and engineering for the building, site preparation, street and utility work, landscaping, etc.
        (2) Indirect expenses such as legal, title, appraisal and feasibility study fees, licenses, permits, *ad valorem* taxes during construction, demolition and removal costs, inspections, insurance during construction, financing charges, accounting, etc.
        (3) Developers' overhead, supervision, and profit; for planning, construction, and sale of the project to "turnkey" condition (that is, completely ready for a new purchaser/occupant) and selling costs.

C. The appraiser estimates the accrued depreciation and deducts from cost-as-new estimate. This amount must be deducted from the cost-as-new to determine the present value of the improvements. The difficulties of correctly estimating depreciation tend to increase with the age of the improvement. Experience and good judgment are among the necessary qualifications for making a realistic estimate of proper depreciation. There is no justification in assuming that improvements necessarily depreciate at a rate corresponding to their age.

D. The appraiser adds the land value to depreciated value of improvements for indicated value by Cost Approach.

## DEPRECIATION

In connection with the appraisal of real property, depreciation is defined as "loss in value from any cause." It is customarily measured by estimating the difference between the current replacement or reproduction cost new and the estimated value of the property as of the date the property was appraised.

Contrasting with depreciation is *appreciation* of value from inflation or special supply and demand forces relating to the specific property. Appreciation may reduce or offset entirely a normally anticipated decrease of value due to depreciation.

Depreciation includes all of the influences that reduce the value of a property below its cost new. The principal influences are often grouped under three general headings and subdivided as follows:

1. Physical deterioration resulting from:
    a. Wear and tear from use;
    b. Negligent care (sometimes termed "deferred maintenance");
    c. Damage by dry rot, termites, etc.; or
    d. Severe changes in temperature.
2. Functional obsolescence resulting from:
    a. Poor architectural design and style;
    b. Lack of modern facilities;
    c. Out-of-date equipment;
    d. Changes in styles of construction;
    e. Construction methods and materials obsolete by current standards; or
    f. Changes in utility demand such as desire for master bath or more garage space.
3. External obsolescence resulting from adverse environmental and economic influences outside the property itself, such as:
    a. Misplacement of improvement (not typical for neighborhood);
    b. Zoning and/or legislative restrictions;
    c. Detrimental influence of supply and demand; or
    d. Change of locational demand.

The first two categories of accrued depreciation are considered to be inherent within the property and may be curable or incurable. The third category is caused by factors external to the property and is almost always incurable.

### Appraisal and Income Tax Views - "Book" vs. Actual Depreciation

It is important to understand that "depreciation" is a word with two meanings: one for the appraiser and another for the owner concerned with tax position.

**Book depreciation.** Depreciation, for the owner's income tax position, is "book" depreciation, a mathematical calculation of steady depreciation from owner's original purchase price or cost basis. This "book" depreciation allows the owner to recover the cost of the investment over the "useful life" of the improvement. It accrues annually and is an income tax deduction. In this sense, the owner's accountant sees depreciation as a deduction from gross income.

Frequently, "book" depreciation results in negative gross income, at least on paper. The building seems to be losing value faster than the income replaces it. This gives the owner a "paper loss" that can be offset against other income. This "paper loss" or "tax shelter" is a motivating factor for purchase or exchange of many income properties.

"Book" depreciation is:
◊   an allowable deduction from cost for accounting or income tax purposes;
◊   determined by owner's policy and to meet IRS requirements; and
◊   deducted from owner's original (historic) cost.

"Book value" is the current value for accounting purposes of an asset expressed as original cost plus capital additions minus accumulated depreciation, based on the method used for the computation of depreciation over the useful life of the asset for income tax purposes. Depreciation is allowed on improvements only, not land.

The book value of the property may be ascertained at any given time by adding the depreciated value of the improvement to the allocated value of the land.

**Actual depreciation.** The "book" depreciation from owner's original cost is not the depreciation normally considered by the appraiser. The appraiser looks not to owner's original cost, but cost new on date of value. From this current cost new, the appraiser deducts the estimate of accrued "actual" (not book) depreciation. Depreciation (loss in value) is estimated only for improvements.

"Actual" depreciation used by appraisers is:
◊   loss in value;
◊   determined by market data, observed condition, etc.; and
◊   deducted from current reconstruction cost new.

Because accountants and appraisers select rates of depreciation for different purposes, accruals for book and actual depreciation vary considerably. While both estimators may use the same period as to the remaining economic life of the property and may also use the same method, additional considerations may affect the resultant rate. Whereas the accountant may be restricted because of accounting conventions, the appraiser is under no such restrictions.

The real estate agent who is determining values should understand the necessity for following proper appraisal procedures and should not rely on book values either to estimate accrued depreciation or for future depreciation accruals.

## METHODS OF CALCULATING ACCRUED DEPRECIATION

Accrued depreciation is depreciation which has already occurred up to the date of value. Remainder depreciation is depreciation which will occur in the future. Accrued depreciation may be classified either as curable or incurable. The measure between curable and incurable is economic feasibility. It is possible to physically restore or cure most depreciation such as by expensive restoration of old homes. However, in most circumstances, cure of deficiencies is measured by the economic gain (increased rents) compared with the cost of the cure. Three methods of estimating accrued depreciation are discussed next.

**Straight line or age-life method** is depreciation which occurs annually, proportional to the improvement's total estimated life.

For example, an improvement with an estimated total life of 50 years would be said to depreciate at an equal rate of 2 percent per year. (2 percent x 50 years equals 100 percent depreciation.)

The effective age of the building is generally used instead of the actual age. Effective age is the age of a similar and typical improvement of equal usefulness, condition and future life expectancy. For example, if a building is actually 25 years of age but is as well maintained and would sell for as much as adjoining 20-year-old properties, it would be said to have an effective age of 20 years.

The straight line method is: easy to calculate; used by the Internal Revenue Service; and easily understood by the lay person. However, in actuality, buildings do not depreciate in a straight line at a stated percentage each year, but will vary according to maintenance and demand for the type of structure.

The **cost-to-cure** or observed condition method (breakdown method) involves:
◊   Observing deficiencies within and without the structure and calculating their costs to cure. The cost to cure is the amount of accrued depreciation which has taken place.
◊   Computing an amount for physical deterioration or deferred maintenance for needed repairs and replacements.
◊   Determining and assigning a dollar value to functional obsolescence due to outmoded plumbing fixtures, lighting fixtures, kitchen equipment, etc.
◊   Measuring functional obsolescence which cannot economically be cured (e.g., poor room arrangements and outdated construction materials) and calculating the loss in rental value due to this condition.
◊   Calculating external obsolescence (i.e., caused by conditions outside the property) and determining the loss of rental value of the property as compared with a similar property in an economically stable neighborhood. The capitalized rental loss is distributed between the land and the building.

This is the most refined method of examining complex causes and cures of depreciation. However, it can be difficult to calculate minor or obscure depreciation accurately. Also, measurement by rental loss is sometimes difficult to substantiate.

A **combination** of the straight line and cost-to-cure methods may be used to:
◊   determine the normal depreciation as if the property is not suffering from undue depreciation; and,
◊   add any excess deterioration and obsolescence

For example: a house is 20 years old and has a remaining life estimated at 40 years for a total life of 60 years, thus depreciating at a rate of 1.67 percent a year. Effective age due to condition estimated at 15 years.

**Cost New ...** ............................................................................................$105,000
1.  Normal deterioration:
    1.67 percent x 15 years = 25 percent
    25 percent x $105,000 = ................................... ........................ $26,250
2.  Excessive physical deterioration:
    New roof, exterior painting ................................ ........................ $5,000
3.  Functional obsolescence, curable:
    Modernize bathroom ....................................... ........................ $3,900
4.  Functional obsolescence, incurable:
    Poor room arrangement results in rental loss of
         $40 per month when compared to normal house.
    Monthly gross multiplier 100.
    ...... $100 x $40 a month = ................................ ........................ $4,000
5.  External obsolescence:
    Estimated monthly rent of subject if located
         in ideal neighborhood (after curing physical and
    ...... and functional deficiencies) ................... ........................ $1,000
    Estimated rental loss due to external causes .... ........................    $50
    Yearly rental loss is 12 x $50 = $600
    Capitalization rate applicable to properties in ideal
         neighborhood (ratio of annual rent to value) = 10.5 percent
    Capitalized rental loss:
         $600 ÷ 10.5 percent = $5,700
    Ratio of land to building value:
         in ideal neighborhood, land 30 percent, building 70 percent.
    Economic obsolescence:
    70 percent x $5,700 .................................... ........................ $3,990

TOTAL ESTIMATED DEPRECIATION ...........................................................$43,140

**DEPRECIATED VALUE OF HOUSE** ...........................................................$61,860

**Reproduction or replacement cost method.** The subject property is improved with a duplex, two detached garages, a covered porch for each unit and common driveway and walk.

Measurements and current cost replacement figures for the improvements are as follows:
◊    Each unit of duplex is 25' x 35' @ $55.00 per sq. ft.
◊    Each detached garage is 21' x 25' @ $20.00 per sq. ft.
◊    Each covered porch is 6' x 10' @ $14.00 per sq. ft.
◊    Driveway is 20' x 100' @ $2.40 per sq. ft.
◊    Walk is 3' x 40' @ $2.40 per sq. ft.

The improvements are now 12 years old and it is determined that such improvements have a remaining economic life of 38 years. The current lot value, by comparison, is $45,000.00. Depreciation computations are based on the use of the straight line method.

**What is the replacement cost new and, using the cost approach method, what is the present value of this property?**
Each duplex unit (25' x 35' x $55.00) x 2 .......................................... $96,250.00
Each detached garage (21' x 25' x $20.00) x 2 ................................... 21,000.00
Each covered porch (6' x 10' x $14.00) x 2 ........................................ 1,680.00
Driveway (20' x 100' x $2.40) ............................................................ 4,800.00
Walk 3' x 40' x $2.40 ........................................................................... 288.00
Improvements – Total Replacement Cost New ................................... **124,018.00**

Depreciation:
    12 yrs. + 38 yrs. = 50 yrs. life of improvements when new
    100 ÷ 50 = 2 percent annual depreciation rate, or recapture rate.
    12 yrs. x 2 percent = 24 percent total depreciation to date.
    124,018 x 24 percent = Total depreciation in value to date.................. 29,764.00
    Total value of improvements less depreciation .................................. $94,254.00
    Plus lot value .......................................................................................... 45,000.00
    **Total Current Value by Replacement Cost Approach** ................. **$139,254.00**

**Market data method.** A comparative method is frequently used in residential appraisals where the property being appraised can be compared with market data of buildings of similar type and condition.

1. From the sales price of a comparable residential property, deduct an estimate of land value.
2. From the resulting total comparable improvement value, deduct the estimated contributory value of secondary improvements and landscaping.
3. The result is the value of the comparable main residence at its total depreciated value in place.
4. Divide this main residence value by the residence square footage. This yields depreciated unit value.
5. By multiplying the appraised building square footage by the unit value of the comparable residence, the total indicated depreciated value is found for the appraised residence.

| | |
|---|---|
| Sales price of comparable property | $180,000 |
| Less estimated land value | - 55,000 |
| Improvement Value | **125,000** |
| Less estimated value of secondary improvements and landscaping | - 23,000 |
| Value of comparable residence | 102,000 |
| Divide by area of comparable residence | ÷ 2,900 sq. ft. |
| Depreciated unit value of comparable residence | $35.17/sq.ft. |
| Multiply by size of appraised residence | x 2,850 sq. ft. |
| **Indicated depreciated value in place of appraised residence** | **$100,234** |

Advantage of the Market Data Method: This method is the most accurate measure of depreciation from the market. Disadvantage of the method: It is sometimes difficult to obtain truly comparable market data and occasionally difficult to accurately estimate land value and secondary improvement value for deductions for main residence value indication.

**Age-life method using effective age.** House has an actual physical age of 25 years with a remaining life of 25 years, thus depreciating at the rate of 2 percent a year. It is the opinion of the appraiser that the subject house is of the same condition and utility as similar houses that are only 20 years of age. Therefore, the house has been assigned an effective age of 20 years. The accrued depreciation would thus be 20 years times 2 percent or 40 percent.

| | |
|---|---|
| Calculated cost new | $120,000 |
| Accrued depreciation (40 percent x $120,000) | 48,000 |
| Depreciated value of improvement | 72,000 |
| Plus land value | 50,000 |
| **Indicated value by cost approach** | **$122,000** |

**Measuring physical deterioration.** A store building has a remaining useful life of 30 years and an effective age of 20 years. Present reproduction cost for the structure is $230,000. The roof is 75% deteriorated. A new roof will cost $10,000. The air conditioning and heating systems are 40% depreciated. Their installed cost new is $8,000. What is the total amount of physical deterioration?

The building, under the straight-line or age-life method, is 40% depreciated (100% ÷ 50 = 2% x 20 years effective age = 40%). This 40% depreciation to the building is to be applied to the amount of the building's reproduction cost less the depreciation already taken on the other components.

| | |
|---|---|
| Depreciation to roof (.75 x $10,000) | $7,500 |
| Depreciation to air conditioning and heater (.40 x $8,000) | $3200 |
| Depreciation to rest of building (.40 x $212,000) | $84,800 |
| **Total physical deterioration** | **$95,500** |

**Income approach - future depreciation.** Future depreciation is loss in value which has not yet occurred but will come in the future and is of significance in the capitalization of income method, which will be discussed next. In the income approach to valuation, depreciation is based on the remaining economic or useful life, during which time provision is made for the recapture of the value of improvements. It is the return "of" the investment, as differentiated from the return (interest and profits) "on" the invested capital. Under the income approach, this depreciation is usually measured by one of two methods: straight-line or sinking fund.

In straight-line depreciation, a definite sum is deducted from the income each year during the total estimated economic life of a building to replace the capital investment. If the appraiser estimates that a building will have a remaining life of 25 years, this method provides that 1/25 or 4 percent of the building's value be returned annually as a deduction from net income. The sinking fund method also includes a fixed annual depreciation deduction from income, but with yearly reserves from such funds deposited into a sinking fund which, with compound interest, will offset the depreciated value of the structure and be collectible at the end of the building's useful life. Accruals for future depreciation to replace the capital investment are in addition to and essentially different from both maintenance charges and reserves for periodic replacement of curable depreciation.

Should there be any estimated salvage value to the improvement at the end of its economic life, this amount need not be returned through the annual depreciation charge under either the straight-line or the sinking-fund method.

## INCOME (CAPITALIZATION) APPROACH

The income approach is concerned with the present worth of future benefits (the income stream) which may be derived from a property. This method is important in the valuation of income-producing property, although it can rarely be relied on as the only approach. An important consideration in this approach is the *net* income which a fully informed person using good management can expect to receive during the remaining useful life of the improvement. An alternative, using *gross* income and the Gross Rent Multiplier (GRM) is explained later in this chapter.

The process of calculating the present worth of a property on the basis of its capacity to continue to produce an income stream is called *capitalization*. The capitalization approach is based primarily on the appraisal concepts of comparison, substitution and anticipation.

### Appraiser's and Owner's Viewpoints

A real estate professional will understand that there are several differences in the owner's and appraiser's viewpoints on income property.

An owner purchases income property as an investment, based on personal desires and tax position. The owner frequently views the investment as equity in a financed property. "Equity" is the owner's down payment or the difference between the loan amount and the value or price of the property. The owner calculates the payments on the loan as an expense of owning the property, and deducts from income tax the interest paid on the loan and the "book" depreciation from the purchase price or cost basis. The owner can deduct only actual expenses, not reserves for future expenses, and can compute gross income only from income actually collected (or owed), not just projected. The owner looks for a profitable resale or exchange at a higher price or favorable tax position. In most cases, the appraiser will ignore these personal considerations.

The appraiser reconstructs expense and income into amounts the well-informed investor would anticipate, without specific regard for personal equity, spendable income, or tax consequences. Using methods outlined below, an appraiser analyzes an income property to ascertain its value to the market *generally, i.e.,* the Fair Market Value.

## CAPITALIZATION

Capitalization is the mathematical process of estimating the present value of income property based on the amount of anticipated annual net income it will produce. Capitalization converts the future income stream into an indication of present worth of property. There are several methods of capitalizing net income. Our discussion will deal with the *direct* method.

There are four types of capitalization (cap) rates used in the appraisal process:
◊    The *interest rate* is the rate of return *on* invested capital. It is the same as the yield rate or risk rate. It does not include any provision for the return *of* investment capital.
◊    The *recapture rate* is the rate at which invested funds are being returned to the owner.
◊    The *capitalization rate* is derived from the interest rate and the recapture rate.
◊    The *overall rate* is derived from the relationship between net income and value for the total property and theoretically provides in one rate for both return on, and recapture of, the capital investment. The overall cap rate is an income rate. *Any* interest in income producing property can be valued using this rate but appraisers apply it most commonly to fee simple estates.

Capitalization rates may be estimated by several methods:
◊    market or sales data;
◊    band of investment (uses a weighted average rate by combining a rate for mortgage loan money and a rate for investor's equity); or
◊    summation (has very limited use - involves building up a "safe" interest rate based on various risk/investment factors).

Of course, the market or sales data method involves an appraiser's systematic comparison of recent sales of similar properties. The appraiser analyzes each comparison property's sales price, rents, expenses, net income and cap rate, makes needed adjustments and selects an appropriate indicated overall cap rate for the property being appraised. This rate represents both the return *on* and the return *of* the investment. To ensure reliability of the selected rate, the appraiser uses judgment and experience to make certain the comparables and the subject property have similar age, physical, location, income, expense and risk characteristics.

**Capitalization rate formula.** The capitalization rate is a combination of the interest rate (return on the investment) and the recapture rate (return on the investment in improvements). If only the land produces income, the cap rate and interest rate are the same. However, when improvements contribute to the income production, a provision must be made for recapture of the value of the improvements before the end of their economic life. Land has no limited economic life; it will never wear out and thus will always be able to produce income. The building is a wasting asset and cannot be used indefinitely.

The most common method of providing for recapture of the investment in the improvements is the "straight line" method, with the building value recaptured in equal annual installments. The recapture rate is computed by dividing the remaining economic life of the improvements into 100%. Thus, the annual recapture rate for a building with an estimated remaining economic life of 40 years is 2.5% (100% ÷ 40). If the remaining economic life is 25 years, the recapture rate is 4%.

To find the indicated value of income property, divide the net annual income by the capitalization rate:

$$\text{Net Annual Income} \div \text{Capitalization Rate} = \text{Property Value}$$
or
$$I \div R = V$$

If any two factors in this formula are known, the third can be obtained.

$$I = R \times V$$
and
$$R = I \div V$$

## INCOME APPROACH PROCESS
The main steps to calculate value by capitalizing income are:
◊ Determine the net annual income;
◊ Select the appropriate cap rate by market comparisons; and Capitalize the income (divide the net annual income by the cap rate).

## Determining Net Annual Income
The procedures for determining net annual income are:
◊ Estimate potential gross income the property is capable of producing.
◊ Deduct from potential gross income an annual allowance for vacancy factor and rent collection loss. The remainder is called "effective" gross income or adjusted gross income.
◊ Deduct from adjusted gross income the estimated probable future annual expenses of operation (fixed expenses, variable expenses, reserves for replacements for building components or short-lived items) to obtain the net income of the investment property.

**Income and expenses.** The potential gross income used is the expected future income. In many cases, the immediate past or current income may be an indicator of future income. However, reliance solely upon past or current income is incorrect. The income to use is the one which the purchaser and seller anticipate over the remaining productive life of the improvement, as adjusted for foreseeable economic changes.

**Income estimates.** The gross income estimate for an income property is the potential or anticipated gross income from all sources (market rents, services, parking space fees and rentals, and coin-operated equipment, etc.). Gross income is estimated as of the date of the appraisal. Contract rent is the actual, or contracted, rent received from the property. Market rent is the rent the property should bring in the open market at the date of appraisal. Rents and vacancy factors and collection losses are based on current market rent data. The appraiser uses his/her judgment of the area in arriving at an allowance for vacancy and collection losses.

Rent data is obtained from the subject property's rent schedule and the appraiser's review of rents from similar recent sales in the area. Individual apartments or units of the comparables are compared with the subject property, using square footage, number of bedrooms, or similar items of comparison. It is assumed management for all properties is adequate. Cost of deferred maintenance or repairs is an adjustment item.

Market rent schedules and expenses are usually maintained on a monthly basis. Both must be converted to an annual basis.

**Expenses must be realistic.** The operating expenses (all expenditures necessary to produce income) are to be deducted from the effective gross income to find the net operating income expected from the property. The appraiser must use caution in extracting expense information from owner's operating statement as some items included on the operating statement, such as principal and interest payments on mortgages and depreciation allowance for income tax purposes, must be disregarded by the appraiser as not being allowable expense items.

These non-allowables may include entertainment expenses and other items of personal expense, and capital improvement expenditures. Since most operating statements are prepared by accountants for tax and accounting purposes, appraisers usually must reconstruct them to properly forecast annual expenses.

Expenses are generally classified as being one of the following:

◊ **Fixed expenses.** These are incurred annually with relatively little change from year to year. They are to be paid whether the property is fully occupied or not. These items include taxes, insurance, licenses and permits.

◊ **Variable expenses.** These expenses are incurred continually in order to maintain and give service to the property. They are variable depending upon the extent of occupancy and include items such as utilities, management fees, security, costs of administration, maintenance and repairs for structures, grounds and parking area maintenance, contracted services (e.g., rubbish removal) and payroll.

◊ **Reserves for replacements.** This is an annual allowance for replacing worn out equipment and building components, such as stoves, carpets, draperies, roof covering.

## Selecting the Cap Rate

The appraiser selects an appropriate overall capitalization rate ("present worth" factor) after market analysis of similar properties. This rate provides for return of invested capital plus a return on the investment).

The rate is dependent upon the return which investors will actually demand before they will be attracted by such an investment. The greater the risk of losing the investment, the higher will be the accompanying rate as determined in the market for such properties. By analyzing market prices, the rate can be approximated at any given time.

A variation of only 1 percent may make a substantial difference in the capitalized value of the income.

For example, based on an annual net income of $30,000, and a capitalization rate of 6 percent, the capitalized property valuation would be $500,000 (income ÷ rate). Capitalizing this same income at a rate of 7 percent would result in a value of only $428,500 (rounded).

## Capitalizing Net Annual Operating Income

The final step after having determined the net annual income and the capitalization rate is to capitalize the income. This may be merely the mathematical calculation of dividing the income by the rate if the income is considered to be in perpetuity. For example, the valuation of property which has an assumed perpetual annual net income of $30,000 and a capitalization rate of 5 percent is $600,000. The lower the rate, the greater the valuation, and the greater the assumed security of the investment. So called annuity tables are used in capitalizing incomes for fixed periods of varying duration.

As stated earlier, an important element in all capitalization rates is provision for a return of the investment on the improvements to the property during their remaining economic life. This may be called an amortization of such investments. It may be provided for by straight-line depreciation, which recovers a definite sum every year for the period of years estimated to be the economic life of the improvement, at the end of which time the cost of improvement will be accrued. It may also be provided for by other methods, such as establishing "sinking funds" or a declining balance depreciation. These are more technical procedures which are used by professional appraisers.

## INCOME APPROACH APPLIED

Using procedures just discussed, here are two examples for finding estimated value using the income approach.

1. How much should an investor pay for a 10 unit apartment house, 24 years old, estimated fair market rent per unit being $500 per month. Indicated vacancy factor is 7%. Acceptable cap rate is 8 percent. Fixed expenses are: taxes of $3,200 and insurance of $860. Operating expenses are: management - $3,960; utilities - $1200; waste removal - $600; reserves for replacement - $1,700.

Gross Scheduled Income (Annual) .................................................................$60,000
  (10 x $500 x 12 = $60,000)

Less Income Loss Due to Vacancy Factor ................................ ........................ $4,200
  (.07 x $60,000 = $4,200)

Effective Gross Income ........................................................ ........................ $55,800

Less Expenses
  Fixed
    Taxes ............................................................... $3,200

| | | |
|---|---:|---:|
| Insurance | 860 | |
| Total | | $4,060 |
| Operating | | |
| Management | 3,960 | |
| Utilities | 1,200 | |
| Waste Removal | 600 | |
| Total | | $5,760 |
| Reserves for Replacement | | |
| Roof | 800 | |
| Painting | 500 | |
| Carpeting | 400 | |
| Total | | 1,700 |

SUBTRACT TOTAL OF EXPENSES .............................................................. - 11,520
NET OPERATING INCOME (NOI) ................................................. .............. $44,280

Capitalization Rate Furnished By Owner is 8%.
Using formula $I \div R = V$
$44,280 \div .08 = $553,500
**Indicated Value (rounded)............................................. ................................ $555,000**

2. A small commercial building has rental income of $27,650 annually and suffers vacancy/collection losses of 5%. Expenses include: taxes $3,780; utilities $850; roof reserve $1,500; insurance $1,100; maintenance $2,000; repainting and fixture reserve $500; and management $2,000. The appraiser finds similar properties have cap rates ranging from 8.75% to 9.37%. Based on this market data the appraiser selects an indicated overall capitalization rate for the subject property of 9%. Using the Income Approach, what is the indicated value of the property?

| | | |
|---|---:|---:|
| Gross scheduled Income (Annual) | | $27,650 |
| Less Vacancy and Collection Loss (5%) | | 1,383 |
| Effective Gross Income | | 26,267 |
| Less Expenses | | |
| Fixed | | |
| Taxes | $3,780 | |
| Insurance | 1,100 | |
| Operating | | |
| Maintenance | 2,000 | |
| Utilities | 850 | |
| Management | 2,000 | |
| Reserve for Replacements | | |
| (Roof, Repainting and Fixtures) | 2,000 | |
| Subtract Total Expenses | | -11,730 |
| Net Operating Income (NOI) | | 14,537 |
| Indicated Overall Capitalization Rate 9% | | |
| $14,537 \div .09 = $161,522 | | |
| Indicated Total Value by Income Approach | | $161,522 |
| **Round Value to** | | **$161,500** |

## RESIDUAL TECHNIQUES
Suppose vacant land returns net income of $6000 a year and the applicable interest rate for this type of real property is 7 percent. Using the income method, the property has a value of $85,715 ($6,000 ÷ .07).

However, income from improved property is the result of the contribution of both land and buildings. The buildings have limited economic life and their value must be recaptured over their remaining economic life. Income attributable to land is deemed perpetual.

There are three methods to capitalize income from improved property. They are each a "residual technique" because capitalization is applied to the residual (leftover or unknown) net income attributable to the property as a whole, to the building, or to the land. The appropriate technique would be selected based on market data. The same net income figure applies in all three methods.

## Property Residual Technique
This is the simplest method of capitalizing the net income from improved property because the property is valued as a single unit

(used when the value of neither land nor improvements can be estimated independently). The property's total net income is capitalized directly at an overall rate developed from the market data, comparing similar income producing properties which are also similar in the way net income is estimated.

**Example.** The net income generated from real property is $32,000 annually and the overall cap rate selected from the market data approach is 9%. What is the value of the property?

- ◊    Income ÷ Rate = Value
- ◊    $32,000 ÷ .09 = Value
- ◊    Value = $355,556

## Building Residual Technique

If the value of the land is known and the value of the building is unknown, the property's value may be determined by the building residual technique. This technique allocates the net income of the property to both land and building. The procedure is:

1. Multiply the known land value by the applicable interest (i.e., return) rate on the land to determine the income attributable to land only.
2. Deduct income to the land from total net income to determine the balance ("residue") of the net income which represents the portion of the income attributable to/earned by the building
3. Capitalize the building's income at the overall cap rate (interest rate plus recapture rate) to derive the value of the building.
4. Add the capitalized value of the building to the land value to arrive at the value of the whole property.

**Example.** An appraiser estimates that a 60 unit apartment building has an estimated remaining economic life of 25 years. The annual net income of the property is forecast at $216,000. On the basis of several comparables, an appraiser estimates that the land value is $60,000 and the applicable rate of interest for this type of investment property is 8%. What is the indicated value of the property by the income approach?

| | |
|---|---|
| Annual net income of property | $216,000 |
| Less interest on $60,000 land value at 8% | 4,800 |
| Net income attributable to building | $211,200 |
|     Interest rate ................... 8% | |
|     Recapture rate ............... 4% | |
|     Cap rate ..................... 12% | |
| Indicated building value ($211,200 ÷ .12) | $1,760,000 |
| Land value (by comparison) | 60,000 |
| **Indicated property value** | **$1,820,000** |

## Land Residual Technique

If the building value is known and the land value is unknown and cannot be determined separately, the value of the property as a whole may be estimated by using the land residual technique. The land residual technique is similar to the building residual technique except that the appraiser must first find the income attributable to the improvements and the residue (balance) of the income is then attributable to the land. The procedure is:

1. Multiply the known improvement value by the applicable building capitalization rate (interest rate plus recapture rate) to determine the income attributable to the building only.
2. Deduct income to the building from the total net income to determine the residue (balance) of the net income attributable to/earned by the land.
3. Capitalize the land's income at the interest rate only (since it is not necessary to recapture the permanent land value) to derive the value of the land.
4. Add the capitalized value of the land to the building value to arrive at the value of the whole property by the land residual technique.

**Example.**  Same facts as the building residual technique example above.

| | |
|---|---|
| Annual net income of property | $216,000 |
| Less income attributable to building ($1,760,000 x .12) | 211,200 |
| Net income attributable to land | 4,800 |
| Indicated land value ($4,800 ÷ .08) | 60,000 |
| Building value | 1,760,000 |
| **Property value indicated by land residual technique** | **$1,820,000** |

## Finding the Overall Cap Rate - Example

A property sells for $250,000. Building value is $190,000. Remaining economic life is 25 years. Annual net income from building is $28,000. What is the interest rate for the building? What is the overall cap rate?

Recapture rate is 4% (100% ÷ 25).

| | |
|---|---|
| Building's net income ................................................................ | $28,000 |
| Recapture of building (.04 x $190,000) .......................................... | $7,600 |
| Net income after recapture ......................................................... | $20,400 |

Interest rate = $20,400 ÷ $190,000 = .1074 or 10.74%
The overall cap rate is the sum of the interest rate and recapture rate:
Interest Rate = 10.74%
Recapture Rate = 4%
Therefore, the Overall Cap Rate = 14.74%

## YIELD CAPITALIZATION ANALYSIS

Now preferred over the residual techniques discussed above, yield capitalization analysis is a method of converting economic benefits of ownership into present value by discounting each anticipated benefit at an appropriate yield rate, or by developing an overall capitalization rate that explicitly reflects the required yield rate and anticipated changes in income and/or value, if any. The *yield rate* is a rate of return on capital. This method simulates typical investor assumptions by using formulas that calculate the present value of future economic benefits based on specified rate of return requirements.

The future economic benefits that are typically considered in this analysis are periodic cash flows and reversion. The procedure used to convert these future economic benefits into present value is called *discounting*, and the required rate of return (or yield rate) is referred to as the *discount rate*. The discounting procedure is based on the assumption that the investor will receive an adequate rate of return *on* the investment, plus return *of* the capital invested. Unlike direct capitalization using market-extracted rates, the method and timing of the returns on and of capital are explicit in yield capitalization analysis. This valuation method can be used to value the fee simple interest in a property, or any property interest for which all future economic benefits can be estimated.

The most common form of yield capitalization analysis is called *discounted cash flow analysis*. In this valuation technique, each anticipated future economic benefit of ownership of the property or property interest being valued must be estimated. Next, each benefit is discounted to present value using a discount rate that reflects the risk associated with the characteristics of the investment. This rate cannot be extracted directly from sales (as can an overall capitalization rate), but must be based on market attitudes and expectations for rates of return for similar assets. Yield rates inherently include a safe, risk-free rate, along with premiums to compensate the investor for the added risk, illiquidity, and burden of management associated with the specific investment. The safe rate included in the yield rate includes an inflationary expectation for the anticipated term of the investment. The discounting process can be performed using formulas and factors obtained from financial tables, or by using financial calculators or personal computers.

The following discounted cash flow analysis example summarizes the application of yield capitalization analysis to a simple real estate problem. The property to be appraised is expected to produce a first-year net operating income of $100,000, which is expected to increase at 3 percent per year over a seven-year holding period. At the end of the holding period, it is anticipated that the property can be sold for $1,000,000 net of sales expenses. The appropriate yield rate for this investment is concluded to be 13 percent. The following table shows the anticipated cash flows, along with the present value factors and the calculated present value of each year's cash flow.

### Discounted Cash Flow Analysis

| | Year 1 | Year 2 | Year 3 | Year 4 | Year 5 | Year 6 | Year 7 |
|---|---|---|---|---|---|---|---|
| Net operating Income | $100,000 | $103,000 | $106.090 | $109,273 | $112,551 | $115,927 | $119,405 |
| Reversion | | | | | | | $1,000,000 |
| Total income | $100,000 | $103,000 | $106,090 | $109,273 | $112,551 | $115,927 | $1,119,405 |
| Present value factor | x 0.8850 | x 0.7831 | x 0.6931 | x 0.6133 | x 0.5428 | x 0.4803 | x 0.4521 |
| Present value | $88,500 | $80,659 | $73,531 | $67,017 | $61,093 | $55,680 | $53,983 |

TOTAL PRESENT VALUE: $902,339; rounded to $900,000.
(The present value factors in this analysis were calculated using a financial calculator, but could have been obtained from a set of financial tables.)

**GROSS RENT MULTIPLIER**
Value is the present worth of all rights to future benefits. The rights being obtained through the payment of rents are the use of the physical structure as well as the intangibles (amenities or satisfactions). Income properties such as large apartments and commercial stores are purchased for the income stream they produce, whereas single family homes are purchased for shelter plus the satisfaction (amenities of home ownership).

Standard capitalization techniques used for income producing properties do not measure intangibles such as pride of ownership and other amenities found in home ownership.

This indirect method of capitalization, the gross rental multiplier, will measure the market value of the combination of intangibles and tangibles found in single family and small income properties.

The gross rent multiplier is found by dividing the sales price of a house or other small income property by its monthly rent. For example: a $90,000 sales price divided by a monthly rent of $600 results in a gross rent multiplier of 150. If homes in the area were selling at prices equivalent to 150 times the monthly rental, then the 150 multiplier would apply to other comparable homes in the area.

**Method of Approach In Using the Gross Rent Multiplier**
1. Determine the fair or economic rent of the property being appraised by comparison with similar rental properties.
2. The gross rent multipliers of the sales one investigates are calculated by dividing the sales prices by the monthly rents.
3. The rent multipliers may then be tabulated showing how these properties varied from the subject property: i.e., better or poorer.
4. The gross rent multipliers are *not* averaged to arrive at one final multiplier. Rather,
   a. each property and its multiplier is compared to the subject property as to fair rent obtainable, location, size, condition, utility, and amenities; and
   b. after proper analysis, a judgment is made as to the appropriate gross rent multiplier.
5. The appraiser multiplies the selected gross rent multiplier by the fair rental of the subject property. The product is the value estimate.
6. Discounted Cash Flow Analysis (DCF) is a technique of income analysis which has grown to be a prominent method in recent years. It is defined as: "The procedure in which a discount rate is applied to a set of projected income streams and a reversion. The analyst specifies the quantity, variability, timing, and duration of the income streams as well as the quantity and timing of the reversion and discounts each to its present value at a specified yield rate. DCF analysis can be applied with any yield capitalization technique and may be performed on either a lease-by-lease or aggregate basis." *(Dictionary of Real Estate Appraisal,* 3rd edition, by the Appraisal Institute) For further study of this method, the reader is advised to seek additional education, as this is a rather technical process subject to misuse and abuse if not properly taught.

**SUMMARY**
It may be said that all three appraisal approaches to value (Cost, Sales Comparison, and Income Capitalization) should be considered and used when appropriate to the property type. The results are reconciled into one final estimate of value. As independent approaches, the sales comparison method is the most widely used. Investment property is frequently appraised by the income capitalization method, while the replacement cost method best lends itself to special purpose properties or newer properties.

The purpose of the appraisal will have a definite bearing in determining the method of valuation. For example, if the purpose is sale, purchase, exchange or condemnation, the value concept sought is current market value.

Reconciliation of the three indications of value derived through the market data, cost and income approaches leads to the final estimate of value or final value conclusion, which is the final step in the appraisal process. Reconciliation is a method of interpreting the data which have been gathered throughout the entire appraisal process into one final value conclusion. The primary facts which are analyzed and brought together are the estimates of value arrived at by reason of the three approaches to value.

Each approach to value results in only a preliminary estimate or an indicated value of the property. The indications resulting from each of the approaches give a range within which the final value conclusion lies. The result obtained by each of the methods of valuation will not be the same due to the many variables which are encountered, but they generally are within range of each other.

A thorough review of each of the approaches is made in order to narrow the range of preliminary answers. If the results from one particular approach appear to be at a great divergence from the other two, each phase of this approach should be reconsidered to account for the difference.

Greater weight, however, is generally given to one of the approaches over the other two, based on the quality of data in each. The final conclusion of value is not an average of the three approaches to value. After giving full consideration to each approach, the appraiser uses judgment and reasoning to arrive at one conclusion. The greatest confidence is placed in the approach which seems to produce the most reliable solution to the specific appraisal problem, realizing that it must be reasonable and capable of being supported convincingly.

The final value conclusion should not be reported in odd dollars and cents. If the final answer approximates $1,000, the answer could be rounded to the nearest $100; if $10,000, to the nearest $500; if $50,000, to the nearest $1,000 or more.

## APPRAISAL OF MANUFACTURED HOMES (MOBILEHOMES)
The appraisal of mobile homes attached to foundations on individual lots relies on the approaches outlined for other residential properties. The appraiser needs a technical understanding of mobile home construction for differences in cost studies. The market data approach works best in this appraisal effort.

Mobile home coaches in parks are on rental spaces or fee-owned spaces in a mobile home park subdivision. Again, the general principles of real property appraisal apply, except the appraiser needs the technical background in coach construction to best evaluate quality and features.

In many respects, the appraisal of a mobile home on a fee-owned space is similar to residential condominium appraisal. This includes consideration of homeowners association services and fees as well as CC&Rs covering operation of the park and space improvement requirements.

Mobile home appraisal is becoming another specialized opportunity in the appraisal profession. This is particularly true in the expanded market for mobile homes as low and moderate income housing.

## EVALUATING THE SINGLE FAMILY RESIDENCE AND SMALL SINGLE MULTI-FAMILY DWELLINGS
This section outlines basic premises which must be considered in making an appraisal of a single family residence and emphasizes some important factors to be weighed. It points out the differences that will be encountered between appraising new and used homes, and shows appraisal differences between a small multi-family dwelling and a single family home.

## NEW RESIDENCE
**Neighborhood analysis.**
A. Factors which make up the neighborhood must be determined and analyzed.
1. Type of occupants.
a. Income level.
b. Representative age groups and family sizes.
2. Type of improvement.
a. Is there a mixture of uses (e.g., single family, apartments, etc.)?
b. What is the age bracket of the improvements?
c. What is the price range of typical houses in the area?
3. Neighborhood trend.
a. Are there detrimental factors present which might tend to depress the market?
b. Is the trend away from single family houses to multi-family, commercial or industrial uses?
c. Is the neighborhood in a transitional stage from owner occupied homes to tenant occupancy?
d. Are there advantageous factors which indicate an increasing market demand or price level?
4. Changes in land use.
a. Zoning and restrictions.
b. Street and highway pattern.
c. Transportation.
d. Any encroachments?
e. Is utility increased? Decreased?
5. Community services.
a. Commercial.
b. Recreational.
c. Educational.
d. Cultural.
e. Governmental.

**Inspection of property.**
A. Relationship of the improvements to site.
1. The house, including outbuildings, should have a harmonious appearance on the site.

a. Is the house too large for the site?

b. Is the house properly oriented on the lot to take advantage of climatic conditions?

c. Over-built? Under-built?

B.   Exterior of house.

    1.   Determine the quality of construction. Inspect:

      a. Foundation.

      b. Walls.

      c. Roof.

    2. Determine the resistance to wear and tear and the action of the elements.

      a. Are there adequate gutters and drainspouts to take the water away from buildings?

      b. Are there satisfactory roof overhangs to protect the windows and walls?

    3.   Measure the exterior dimensions of the buildings in order to obtain their areas.

    4.   Examine and describe yard improvements for purposes of estimating their value.

C. Interior of house.

    1. Determine the quality of the building.

      a. Durability of building.

      b. Arrangement of floor plan and layout of space.

      c. Attractiveness of design.

      d. Grade and quality of materials used.

      e. Adequacy of heating, cooking, electrical, and plumbing equipment.

    2. Measure or take note of room sizes and placement of windows for adequate light and ventilation.

    3. Determine if the traffic pattern is functionally proper.

    4. Does the home have all the modern conveniences necessary for a new house in its price class?

**Verification through public records.**

A. Public records should be checked to verify the following about the property being appraised:

    1. Proper legal description.

    2. Correct street address.

    3. Size/dimensions of the lot.

    4. Location of the lot with respect to the nearest cross street.

    5. Any easements, restrictions or other reservations or interests affecting the property.

    6. The assessed value and taxes of the property.

    7. Any changes in zoning or street pattern.

B. Transfer of title of similar properties.

    1. Sales of single family vacant lots should be obtained and verified.

    2. Sales of improved single family residences within the same neighborhood should be recorded.

**Inspection of comparable sales.**

A. Vacant lots or improved similar properties should be inspected.

B. Similar or dissimilar features as compared to the subject property are recorded and the selling price, terms and reasons for sale or purchase must be verified by the seller or buyer.

**Application of approaches to value.**

A. Cost approach to value.

    1. From the information gathered in the inspection and the size, quality and cost classification, an estimate of cost is made of all improvements on the land.

    2. The land value is estimated from information gathered in the record search of vacant parcels.

    3. In the majority of instances, if the improvements are new and the highest and best use of the land, the estimate of value by means of the cost approach is equal to land value plus the new improvement costs.

B. Sales Comparison or market approach to value.

    1. The sales of similar type houses are compared to the subject as to time, location and physical characteristics.

    2. Necessary adjustment must be made between the sales and the subject.

    3. A preliminary estimate of value by means of the comparative approach is obtained.

C. Income approach to value.

    1. The economic rent of the subject is estimated by means of experience and comparison.

    2. Gross monthly multipliers of similar type properties are gathered and analyzed in order to arrive at one multiplier to apply to the subject.

    3. DCF may be applied for such properties as new condominium projects, subdivisions or any property with a variable type income over the holding period of the investment.

    4. A preliminary estimate of value by means of the income approach is obtained.

D. Reconciliation of the approaches.

1. Each approach is weighed and compared.
2. With a new property it will generally be found that the cost approach will carry the greatest weight in the correlation.
3. If the new subject property were located within a tract of similar type houses, market comparison would be given the most weight in the reconciliation.
4. After weighing all of the factors involved, one final value reconciliation for the property is set forth.

## OLDER RESIDENCE

**Neighborhood analysis.** In addition to the points covered under new residence, the following should be carefully considered when dealing with an older property in a built-up neighborhood:

A. Neighborhood trend.
    1. A check should be made to determine if proposed zoning changes are being considered by the local government.
    2. Contemplated changes might indicate that the best use of the subject is no longer thought to be for single family housing.

B. Inspection of property. In addition to the items covered under the new residence, consideration should be given to the following:
    1. A more careful inspection is made of the premises.
a. Note effects of dry rot and termites.
b. Look for deferred maintenance.
c. Inspect roof and attic for signs of water leaks.
d. Check foundation for settling.
    2. Room arrangement and functional utility.
a. An older home is more likely to have an out-of-date floor plan.
    b. The livability or utility is often obsolete as compared to a newly designed structure.
    3. Wiring and plumbing.
        a. Is the home under-wired for today's electrical appliances? Particular attention should be given to the kitchen.
        b. Are the plumbing lines being affected by encrustation? Will they have to be replaced shortly?
        c. Are the plumbing fixtures in the kitchen and bathrooms adequate and in good working condition?
    4. Heating plant and/or air conditioning unit.
a. Is unit(s) sufficient for size and quality of house?
    b. What would be entailed to install a new or more efficient unit? Would it be feasible?

C. Application of approaches. Each approach may be used in valuing an older property. The primary difference between valuing a new and old home is in the determination of depreciation as part of the cost approach.
    1. Consideration must be given to the inspection of the home in order to help the appraiser reach an opinion as to the effective age to be assigned.
    2. Physical curable deterioration must be calculated with care.
    3. Study must be made to determine if a functional item may be treated as curable or incurable.
    4. Items of economic depreciation will be more prevalent in an older neighborhood than a newer one.

## Definition of small multi-family dwelling.

A. In most instances, a small multi-family dwelling refers to a property which contains more than one but less than six living units. These units may be one of the following:
    1. Double bungalow or duplex.
    2. Triple bungalow or triplex.
    3. Small courts or numerous houses on a lot.
    4. Flats or small apartments.

## Reasons for purchasing residential properties.

A. There are three categories of residential properties.
    1. Single family homes.
    2. Small multi-family dwellings.
    3. Income producing multi-family dwellings.
B. Single family homes.
    1. Primary concern is given to amenities of home ownership.
    2. Cost of ownership is of secondary importance.
    3. Pride of location and architectural appeal is given consideration before purchasing.
C. Small multi-family dwellings are purchased for a combination of home ownership and income.
    1. Location, architectural attractiveness, and the amenities of ownership are given strong consideration by a purchaser.
    2. Income is of secondary importance.
    3. Typically, a buyer hopes to be able to reduce the cost of living by obtaining some rental income to decrease

expenses.

    4. The income received tends to offset real estate taxes, insurance, and maintenance costs.

    5. In some instances, rental income will also cover mortgage payments on the property.

    6. Usually, the owner of a small multi-family dwelling must do all management work.

D. Income producing multi-family dwelling.

    1. Large multi-family dwellings (above 10 to 15 units) are purchased primarily for the income stream to be produced.

    2. The net income or spendable income is the most important item considered by the buyer.

    3. Amenities of ownership have little influence in the buying decision.

E. Other reasons for purchase.

    1. Hedge against inflation.

    2. Means of forced saving.

    3. Chance for appreciation in value due to increasing demand in the area.

## Appraisal procedure.

A. Small multi-family units are appraised approximately the same as single family homes.

B. Cost factors, depreciation and estimates of land value are calculated in the same manner as with single family homes.

C. Small units cannot be considered as true income producing units. Therefore, in most instances, monthly gross multipliers are used instead of an income approach to value.

D. The market comparison approach differs to some extent from the comparative approach as used with homes.

    1. Less emphasis is placed on attempting to measure pride of ownership and amenities.

    2. The comparison approach can be refined to a greater degree.

        a. Comparisons may be made on a per unit basis.

        b. Comparison can be made on a per room basis.

    3. The appeal of the units from a renter's standpoint must be considered.

    4. The location factor as it relates to transportation and shopping may be given greater consideration than with a single family home.

## Amenities of multi-family dwellings.

A. Factors and amenities considered important by tenants of multi-family dwellings.

    1. Distance from employment centers.

    2. Public transportation.

    3. Distance to good shopping.

    4. Distance to parks and recreation.

    5. Distance from nuisances.

    6. Rent levels.

    7. Pride of ownership.

    8. Adequacy of off-street parking.

B. Factors considered important by the owner.

    1. Police and fire protection, rubbish collection.

    2. Vacancy rates in the area.

    3. Amount of taxes.

## TYPICAL OUTLINE FOR WRITING THE SINGLE FAMILY RESIDENCE NARRATIVE APPRAISAL REPORT

A. Title Page:

    1. "A market value appraisal of the single family residence known as (Address)."

    2. Name of client.

    3. The name and address of the appraiser

B. Table of Contents:

    1. Preface.

    2. Body of report.

    3. Addenda section.

C. Letter of Transmittal:

    1. Date.

    2. Name and address of addressee.

    3. Salutation.

    4. Authorization.

    5. Legal description or reference thereto.

    6. Purpose of appraisal, including type of value estimated.

    7. Date of evaluation.

    8. Reference to following report of pages, including exhibits as well as limiting conditions, factors considered and reasoning employed in arriving at the final conclusion of fair market value.

      9. Estimate of value (written and numbered).

      10. Certification of appraiser.

      11.Signature.

D.   Summary of Salient Facts and Conclusions:

      1.  Recap of pertinent information such as value estimate, date of value, purpose of appraisal, etc.

E.   Premise Section:

      1.  Statement of intended use of the appraisal report.

      2.  Statement of limiting conditions on which the appraisal is based, including full definition of value as estimated in report.

F.   Regional, City and Neighborhood Analysis:

      1.  Pertinent features.

      2.  Economic factors.

      3.  Significant trends.

G.   General Property Information:

      1. Record or legal owner.

      2. Legal description.

      3. Legal address.

      4. Location.

H.   Site Analysis:

      1.  Description of parcel:

         a. Size and shape.

         b. Topography and surface drainage.

         c. Soils including subsoil (foundational).

         d. Access.

         e. Landscaping, etc.

      2.  Street improvements and utilities.

      3.  Deed restrictions and zoning.

      4.  Assessed valuation and tax information.

      5.  Current use and adaptability.

      6.  Highest and best use.

I.   Improvement Analysis:

      1.  Basic description:

         a. Type and date of construction.

         b. Architectural form.

         c. Number of rooms.

      2.   Summary of square foot areas:

         a. Residence.

         b. Garage.

         c. Other structures, walks and drives.

      3.  Exterior description:

         a. Foundation and sub-structure.

         b. Exterior treatment.

         c. Roof design and cover.

         d. Porches.

      4.  Interior description:

         a. Room descriptions (space allotment; floor, walls and ceiling finish; built-ins and fixtures).

      5.   Mechanical Equipment:

         a. Heating and air conditioning.

         b. Electrical.

         c. Miscellaneous - garbage disposal, etc.

      6. Miscellaneous Improvements:

         a. Outbuildings.

         b. Patios and walks.

         c. Landscaping.

J. Analysis and Valuation:

      1. Statement of problem.

      2. Methods of appraisal.

      3. Investigation.

K. Estimate of Land Value:

      1. By market data approach.

2. By sales abstraction.
3. Economic approaches:
    a. As percentage of annual income classification.
    b. As percentage of total property value.
4. Reconciliation of various approaches.
5. Final estimate of land value.

L. The Cost Approach:
1. Reproduction cost estimate:
    a. Justification.
2. Estimate of accrued depreciation:
    a. Physical deterioration with justification: curable and incurable.
    b. Functional Obsolescence with justification: curable and incurable.
3. Economic obsolescence with justification.
4. Depreciated reproduction cost.
5. Addition of estimated land value.
6. Value indicated by cost approach.

M. The Market Data Approach:
1. Market data presentation including statement of source and verification: a. Summary of pertinent data (sales and listings).
2. Analysis of market data:
    a. Factors of adjustment.
3. Application of adjusted market data factors:
    a. Comparison by various common denominators: e.g., ratio of sales price to living area; ratio sales price to number of rooms.
    b. Direct property comparison.
4. Reconciliation of indications using reliability coefficients.
5. Value indicated by market data approach.

N.  The Income Approach:
1.   Seldom employed in analysis of single family residential property.
2.   Justified gross rent multiplier of neighborhood.
3.   Justified fair rental estimate for subject.
4.   Indicated value by income approach.

O.  Reconciliation and Discussion of Value Estimates:
1. State values estimated by three separate approaches.
2. Analysis:
    a. Major, but not exclusive, weight to approach that:
       ▫ Is most closely related to purpose of the appraisal;
       ▫ Is most appropriate for property classification concerned;
       ▫ Has greatest amount of supporting data;
       ▫ Most accurately reflects attitude of typical purchaser; and
       ▫ Is most sensitive to current trends.
3. State final value conclusions:
    a. Suggested arbitrary separation:
       ▫ Land; and
       ▫ Improvements.

P. Addenda Section:
1. Market data.
2. Market data map.
3. Plots, maps, pictures, charts, statistical and factual data pertinent to the value estimate and necessary as supporting evidence not included in body of report.

Q. Appraiser's Qualifications.

## CONCLUSION

In concluding this information on concepts, valuation and appraisal techniques, let us wave three warning flags. It is to be noted that there are subtle differences between *valuation* and *appraising*. The first is broader, tends to be economic in origin and emphasizes theory; the latter refers more to practice, methods and techniques. Next, anyone can make an appraisal, even a lay person, but the *worth* of an appraisal report is determined by the experience, knowledge, qualifications, and motives of the person behind it. Finally, let us not be deceived by any broad statement that appraising is an exact science. It is a science as is any of the other social sciences, but people and property cannot be appraised with the exactness and accuracy reached by the mathematical and physical sciences.

## ADDITIONAL PRACTICE PROBLEMS
The following are some additional practice problems with suggested solutions.

### Applying the Income (Capitalization) Approach
1. A 50 unit apartment building and lot are being appraised. The 30 two-bedroom units rent for $600 and the 20 one-bedroom units rent for $475 monthly, which rent is comparable to market rent in the area. Vacancy and collection losses are estimated to be 5% of potential gross income. The parking structure and laundry facility contribute an additional estimated $1,200 income per month. What is the property's (land and building) total estimated annual effective gross income?

**Solution.**

| | |
|---|---:|
| 30 x $600 = $18,000 x 12 = | $216,000 |
| 20 x $475 = $9,500 x 12 = | 114,000 |
| Apartment rental income | $330,000 |
| Plus other income: $1200 x 12 = | 14,400 |
| Potential Gross Annual Income | $344,400 |
| Less 5% vacancy/collection loss | -17,220 |
| Total annual effective gross income | $327,180 |

2.  The owner's operating statement shows the following annual expenses:

FIXED EXPENSES

| | | |
|---|---:|---:|
| Real Property Taxes | $7,200 | |
| Insurance | 2,200 | |
| License | 200 | |
| Capital Improvements | 22,000 | |
| Depreciation | 10,000 | |
| | | $41,600 |

OPERATING EXPENSES

| | | |
|---|---:|---:|
| Water | $9,000 | |
| Gas and Electricity | 6,000 | |
| Pool Service | 4,800 | |
| Gardening Maintenance | 1,200 | |
| Entertainment Expenses | 750 | |
| Building Maintenance | 10,000 | |
| Resident Manager Salary | 12,000 | |
| Refuse Service | 1,200 | |
| | | $44,950 |

RESERVES FOR REPLACEMENTS

| | | |
|---|---:|---:|
| Appliances, carpets, drapes | $6,000 | |
| Building components | 4,000 | |
| | | $10,000 |

**TOTAL EXPENSES** ............................................................ **$96,550**

After reconstructing owner's statement (determining proper allowable expense items), what is property's annual estimated net income?

**Solution.**

Deduct $32,000 (Capital Improvements and Depreciation) from fixed expenses and $750 (Entertainment Expense) from operating expense, as being improper deductions.

| | |
|---|---:|
| From problem #1, the effective annual gross income is | $327,180 |
| EXPENSES | |
| Fixed | $9,600 |
| Operating | 44,200 |
| Replacement Reserves | 10,000 |
| Total Expenses | - 63,800 |

**Estimated Annual Net Property Income** .................................. **$263,380**

3. The appraiser determined a proper capitalization rate for the above property is 9.5%. What is the estimated property value?
   **Solution.**
   $263,380 net income ÷ .095 cap rate = $2,772,421 estimated property value.

4. Suppose the net income of the property is only $189,000 and similar properties are valued at $1,929,000. What is the indicated overall cap rate?
   **Solution.**
   $189,000 (Income) ÷ $1,925,000 (Value) = 9.8% overall cap rate.

5. Given, based on comparative sales technique:

| | |
|---|---:|
| Sale price of an income property | $230,000 |
| Building value | $170,000 |
| Remaining estimated life of building | 40 years |
| Annual net income of property | $23,500 |

   What is the indicated interest rate for the property?
   **Solution.**
   (Improved properties have both an interest rate and a recapture rate included in the capitalization rate. The recapture rate applies only to the improvements, while the interest rate applies to both land and improvements.)

| | |
|---|---:|
| Estimated net income before recapture | $23,500 |
| Recapture for building: | |
| 100% ÷ 40 yrs. = 2.5% x $170,000 | $4,250 |
| Net income after building recapture | $19,250 |

   Interest Rate = $19,250 ÷ $230,000 = 8.3%

6A. Building Residual Technique Problem (Land value known; building value unknown.)
   Assume the following:

| | |
|---|---:|
| Annual net income from the whole property | $14,000 |
| Land value | $42,000 |
| Recapture rate for building (25 yrs remaining economic life) | 4% |
| Interest rate | 8% |

   What is (1) the building value and (2) the property value?
   **Solution.**

| | |
|---|---:|
| Net income of property | $14,000 |
| Income attributable to land: $42,000 x .08 = | $3,360 |
| Income attributable to building | $10,640 |

   Capitalization rate: 12% (8% + 4%)
   Formula: Present Value = Net income ÷ Capitalization Rate

| | |
|---|---:|
| Therefore, Indicated value of building = $10,640 ÷ .12 = | $88,667 |
| Plus land value | $42,000 |
| **Indicated property value by building residual technique** | **$130,667** |

$$\text{(\$130,700 rounded)}$$

6B. Land Residual Technique Problem (Building value known; land value unknown.) Assume the same figures as above in building residual technique problem, except building value is $88,700 and land value is unknown.
   What is (1) land value and (2) property value?
   **Solution.**

| | |
|---|---:|
| Net income | $14,000 |
| Less income attributable to improvements ($88,700 x .12) | -$10,644 |
| Income attributable to land | $3,356 |

| | | |
|---|---|---:|
| Indicated value of land = $3,356 ÷ .08 = $41,950 (rounded) | | $42,000 |
| Add improvement value | | $88,700 |
| **Indicated property value by land residual technique** | | **$130,700** |

7A. Assume that comparisons show comparable single-family houses in a neighborhood rent for about $380 per month and sell for an average of $45,600. What is the indicated gross rent multiplier for a subject property in this neighborhood?
   **Solution.**
        Formula: sales price ÷ gross monthly rent = gross rent multiplier
        Therefore, $45,600 ÷ $380 = 120
        The gross rent multiplier is 120

7B. Suppose that, when compared to other rentals, the above property lost $24 per month rental income due to poor kitchen location. What is the estimated depreciation attributable to incurable functional obsolescence?
   **Solution.**
        120 x $24 = $2,880

# FNMA and FHLMC Guidelines for
# Completing the URAR
# Manufactured Home Addendum

You can find this residential appraisal report form, along with a complete set of all residential appraisal forms, advice, updates and information on our web site at www.nemmar.com.

**_Purpose of this Section:_** This section provides Fannie Mae and Freddie Mac guidelines. These supplemental instructions provide directions to the appraiser for reporting the results of a complete appraisal on property that includes a Manufactured Home using:

> 1. The current Uniform Residential Appraisal Report (Freddie Mac Form 70 or Fannie Mae Form 1004) or Individual Condominium Unit Appraisal Report (Freddie Mac Form 465); and,
> 2. The Uniform Residential Appraisal Report Manufactured Home Addendum (Freddie Mac Form 70B 10-03) or the Manufactured Home Appraisal Report Addendum (Fannie Mae Form 1004C 6-03).

> The Uniform Residential Appraisal Report and the Addendum are referred to together in these Instructions as the "Appraisal Report".

1. Definition of Manufactured Home. A Manufactured Home is a one-unit dwelling built on a permanent chassis in accordance with the National Manufactured Construction and Safety Standards Act as promulgated by the Department of Housing and Urban Development (HUD) and affixed to a permanent foundation.

Other types of factory-built housing that are not subject to the National Manufactured Construction and Safety Standards Act, such as modular or panelized housing, are not considered Manufactured Homes.

2. Appraiser Qualifications. Manufactured Homes have marketability and valuation characteristics that are different from site-built homes; therefore, you must:

> ◊ Have adequate experience and must have previously completed real property appraisals of Manufactured Homes
> ◊ Have adequate education and/or training related to the appraisal of Manufactured Homes
> ◊ Understand the unique features that affect the quality of Manufactured Homes and the factory construction techniques for Manufactured Homes
> ◊ Understand the manufacturers' and federal, state and local requirements for the installation of Manufactured Homes
> ◊ Be knowledgeable concerning the local Manufactured Home market, and
> ◊ Have access to appropriate manufactured housing data sources to establish an opinion of value

You must not accept an assignment to appraise a Manufactured Home unless you have knowledge and experience in appraising this type of property in the subject market area. With you submittal of the Appraisal Report for a Manufactured Home, you are certifying that you meet the qualifications stated above.

3. Incomplete Information. If you appraise the Manufactured Home before it is delivered and permanently attached to the site, some of the information needed to complete the Form 70 or Form 465 and Form70B or Fannie Mae Form 1004C may not be available at the time you perform the appraisal. In that case, you may prepare the appraisal report subject to receipt and analysis of the previously unavailable information, and prepare a certificate of completion or appraisal addendum that includes your review and analysis of the previously unavailable information and certifies that the requirements and conditions of the appraisal have been satisfied. The certificate of completion or appraisal addendum must be prepared and signed by the appraiser and supervisory appraiser, if required on the Form 70 or Form 465 and Form 70B or Fannie Mae Form 1004C.

4. Neighborhood Description. You must describe the trends in the market conditions for Manufactured Homes in the subject area, including property values, supply and demand for Manufactured Homes, marketing time, price and age ranges and information regarding the terms of sale of competitive properties

5. Manufactured Home Identification. You must include the following information on the subject Manufactured Home:

> ◊ The number of sections comprising the Manufactured Home (single or multiple sections)
> ◊ For a new Manufactured Home, the retailer from whom the home was purchased

◊ The manufacturer's name
◊ Trade or model name
◊ Year of manufacture
◊ Serial number(s)/vehicle identification number(s) (VIN) for each section
◊ HUD label number(s) from either the HUD Data Plate or HUD certification label(s) for each section

The serial number(s) for the Manufactured Home is also known as the vehicle identification number(s)VIN. The serial number(s) is stamped on the frame front cross member of each section of the Manufactured Home or it can be found on the HUD Data Plate. The HUD label number(s) is the number that appears on the red metal HUD certification label(s) that is attached to the exterior of each section of the Manufactured Home or the HUD label number(s) that appears on the HUD Data Plate for each section of the Manufactured Home.

6. Site Information. You must provide detailed information on the site, including:

◊ Whether the site is on a public, community or private street and whether the street is properly maintained and with adequate access
◊ The size, configuration and topology of the site and the effect of site characteristics on the market acceptance, value and marketability of the property
◊ Confirmation that the wheels, axles, and towing hitches have been removed from the Manufactured Home
◊ Confirmation that the Manufactured Home is affixed to a permanent foundation system; if you cannot confirm this you must note that prominently on the Appraisal Report
◊ A description of the foundation type
◊ Confirmation that the Manufactured Home is permanently connected to a septic tank or sewage system and other utilities (e.g., water, electricity, etc.)
◊ Summary of comparable land sales and support for site value conclusion

7. Manufactured Home Quality. You must determine whether the Manufactured Home has total living space and individual room dimensions to be marketable and describe the overall condition of the subject Manufactured Home. You must rate the quality of construction of the subject Manufactured Home based on objective criteria such as the N.A.D.A. Manufactured Housing Appraisal Guide®, Marshall & Swift Residential Cost Handbook®, or other published cost service. You may consider characteristics such as the type of foundation, skirting, and roof pitch in determining the marketability and value of the Manufactured Home.

8. Determining Value of Manufactured Home. The appraised value of property including a Manufactured Home must be based only on the real property, including the site and the Manufactured Home. Non-realty items, such as insurance, warranties, or furniture must be excluded from the value conclusion.

9. Determining Value of Manufactured Home – Purchase Contract. For a purchase transaction, you must obtain from the lender:

◊ A complete copy of the executed contract for sale (Form 500, Manufactured Home Purchase Agreement, for a new Manufactured Home) of the Manufactured Home and land, or if the Manufactured Home and land are being purchased separately, a copy of the executed contract for each
◊ A copy of the manufacturer's invoice if a new Manufactured Home (e.g., not previously owned)

You must:

◊ Analyze the purchase contract and review the manufacturer's invoice, if applicable, and provide any comments in the Appraisal Report
◊ Match the serial number(s) from the HUD Data Plate or frame front cross member of each section of the Manufactured Home to the serial number(s) on the invoice so that you can accurately report the Manufactured Home information in the Appraisal Report

10. Determining Value of Manufactured Home – Comparable Sales Approach. The Appraisal Report must contain at least two comparable sales of Manufactured Homes of similar quality and similar configuration (i.e., single-wide comparable sales for a single-wide subject property and multi-wide comparable sales for a multi-wide subject property). You may use either site-built housing or a different type of factory built-housing as the third comparable sale if you explain the reason for selecting the comparable and make and support the appropriate adjustments in the Appraisal Report. More than three comparable sales are recommended if needed to develop an adequately supported opinion of value based on the sales comparison approach that is further supported by the cost approach to value.

If the Manufactured Home is in a controlled market (such as a new subdivision or project, a newly converted project or an area where the property seller owns a substantial number of units), at least one comparable sale must be outside the influence of the developer, builder or property seller. Re-sales from within the subject project or subdivision may be used to meet this requirement. When comparable sales from outside the subject project or subdivision are used, they must also be outside the influence of the subject property's developer, builder or property seller.

You may not create comparable sales by combining vacant land sales with the contract purchase price of the Manufactured Home. If you are unable to develop an appraisal based on at least two comparable sales of similar Manufactured Homes, you must note that prominently in the Appraisal Report.

11. Determining Value of Manufactured Home – Cost Approach. You must provide a detailed and supported cost approach to determining value. The sales comparison and cost approaches to value are complementary for the valuation of manufactured housing and should support the final value conclusion. The information must be sufficient to allow the lender to replicate the cost figures and calculations.

The Uniform Residential Appraisal Report Manufactured Home Addendum includes the minimum level of detail for the cost approach that should be provided. You must complete the Cost Approach section on the Freddie Mac Form 70B or Fannie Mae Form 1004C; you do not also need to complete the Cost Approach section on the Freddie Mac Form 70.

12. Determining Value of Manufactured Home – Other Sources. Traditional appraisal data sources may not provide sufficient quality Manufactured Home data for you to develop a supportable and well-documented appraisal. Although the MLS and public records information remain an important source of data, you should develop other sources such as Manufactured Home retailers and builders experienced in the installation of Manufactured Homes. You may also use the N.A.D.A. Manufactured Housing Appraisal Guide® and Marshall & Swift® Residential Cost Handbook to support your quality adjustments and value conclusions.

**Manufactured Home Appraisal Report Addendum (Form 1004C)**

Use of Form 1004C:
The appraiser uses this form to expand upon the information required in the Uniform Residential Appraisal Report (Form 1004) when reporting appraisals on manufactured homes. This addendum will be required as a standard exhibit to Form 1004 for all manufactured home mortgage applications taken on or after August 24, 2003.

The use of Form 1004C will help to ensure that the appraiser inspected, considered, and/or reported (as applicable) the necessary information for the property valuation and underwriting of a manufactured home. The supplemental information on this appraisal addendum will help the lender better understand the factors that may affect the value and marketability opinions and conclusions provided by the appraiser. This addendum also will require the appraiser to make supplemental certifications to address his or her knowledge and experience regarding the appraisal of manufactured homes.

Fannie Mae will continue to require market-based property valuations for manufactured homes demonstrated by a well-developed sales comparison approach to value. This means that the appraiser must develop and report in a concise format an adequately supported opinion of market value based on the sales comparison approach to value and further supported by the cost approach to value. The sales comparison and cost approaches to value are complementary for the valuation of manufactured housing and should support the final value conclusion.

This form must be printed on legal size paper using portrait format.

Instructions:
This form is completed in its entirety by the appraiser. The lender should retain the original of the completed form, and the appraiser should retain a copy.

# HUD Comprehensive Valuation Package -
# Forms 92564-VC and 92564-HS

You can find this residential appraisal report form, along with a complete set of all residential appraisal forms, advice, updates and information on our web site at www.nemmar.com.

On September 10, 1999 The *Department of Housing and Urban Development* (HUD) began requiring appraisers to complete the newly revised four page *Valuation Condition* (VC) checklist (form HUD-92564-VC). This form does not represent new requirements for FHA appraisals. The revised form incorporates FHA requirements existing prior to September 10, 1999 and clarifies items listed on the previous VC checklist.

Similar to the previous VC check sheet, FHA has emphasized that the appraiser complete the revised VC sheet by simply observing the condition of the property and its key components and systems. In this respect, nothing new is being required by either the forms or the governing Handbook. FHA is not requiring the appraiser to make a judgment about observed conditions which that appraiser does not feel qualified to make.

FHA appraisals are distinguished from conventional appraisals in that the property is appraised *"As Repaired"* rather than *"As Is"*. In order to make this distinction, the appraiser is required to have an intimate and up-to-date knowledge of the FHA Handbook 4150.2, *Valuation Analysis for Home Mortgage Insurance*. It is this knowledge that enables the appraiser to complete the VC form, and to reach an "as repaired" value. It is also this knowledge that appraisers eventually will be tested on by HUD in order to be listed on the *FHA Appraiser Roster*. Appraisers being added to the Roster since July 1, 1999 have successfully passed the examination. Appraisers already on the Roster before July 1 have until February 1, 2000 to pass the examination. Until this testing is completed, FHA will rely on an appraiser's previous certification to and understanding of the FHA requirements which they made when originally applying for Roster status. As a result, appraisers listed on the FHA Roster of Appraisers will be considered to be competent to perform an FHA appraisal including the VC and *Homebuyers Summary* forms without having passed the test until February 1, 2000.

FHA requires the homebuyer to sign two separate documents acknowledging the fact that an FHA appraisal is not a home inspection and that any conditions noted on the VC sheet are based on observations. The VC sheet is based on "readily observable conditions" rather than judgments by the appraiser. As stated in HUD's September 10, 1999 Mortgagee Letter 99-29, *"Appraisers who have passed state licensing exams and are familiar with the requirements of Uniform Standards of Professional Appraisal Practice (USPAP) will be able to review the instructions set forth in the Handbook and to accurately complete the Valuation Condition Sheet and Homebuyers Summary forms. The instructions are clear, concise, self-explanatory, and do not require an appraiser to perform work outside the scope of his or her expertise as defined by USPAP"*.

# Appraisal Form - URAR - FHLMC 70, FNMA 1004

You can find this residential appraisal report form, along with a complete set of all residential appraisal forms, advice, updates and information on our web site at www.nemmar.com.

Single Family Residential appraisal form. This is the most common appraisal report form and is a full appraisal analysis including all three of the approaches to market value.

**Uniform Residential Appraisal Report (Form 1004)**
Use of Form 1004:
The lender uses this form to obtain the appraiser's analysis and estimate of the value of single-family properties and PUD units that secure conventional first or second mortgages. This form may also be used for detached condominium units in projects that consist solely of detached dwellings and have no common area improvements (other than greenbelts, private streets, and parking areas), as long as the appraiser includes certain project information on the form (or in an addendum to it). It may also be used for two-family properties if each of the units is occupied as a principal residence by one of the co-borrowers or if the value of the second unit is relatively insignificant in relation to the total value of the property.

This form must be printed on legal size paper, using portrait format. When printing this form, you must use the "shrink to fit" option in the Adobe Acrobat print dialogue box.

Instructions:
This form is completed in its entirety by the appraiser. The lender should retain the original of the completed form, and the appraiser should retain a copy.

The Uniform Standards of Professional Appraisal Practice requires appraisers to identify their appraisal reports as a self-contained report, a summary report, or a restricted report by stating the applicable category at or near the beginning of the appraisal report form. The Appraisal Standards Board has expressed the opinion that Form 1004 is consistent with a summary appraisal report. Therefore, the appraiser should identify all appraisals reported on this form as summary appraisal reports.
The appraiser must provide his or her description and analysis of the neighborhood, site, and improvements. The appraiser must provide the lender with an adequately supported estimate of market value and a complete, accurate description of the property. The sales comparison analysis should include as comparables three other properties, and should provide specific sales or financing concession information for the comparables. In addition, the appraiser must attach the standard required exhibits listed in the Selling Guide--including the *Statement of Limiting Conditions and Appraiser's Certification* (Form 1004B)--to support each appraisal report.

PUD Units:
If the appraiser uses this form to document the appraisal for a PUD unit, he or she must complete the "Project Information for PUDs" section that immediately follows the "neighborhood" section of the form. Generally, there should be no need to attach an addendum to the form for appraisals of units in established PUD projects. However, it may still be necessary to use an addendum if the appraisal relates to units in a new PUD project for which the developer is still in control of the owners' association.

Detached Condominium Units:
If the appraiser uses this form to document the appraisal for a detached condominium unit in a project that consists solely of detached dwellings, he or she must provide the following project information on Form 1004 or in an addendum to it:
  ◊   If the project has been completed: number of phases _____ , number of units _____ , and number of units sold _____ ;
  ◊   If the project is incomplete: planned number of phases _____ , number of units _____ , and number of units sold _____ ;
  ◊   If the project is being developed in phases: total units in subject phase _____ , number of completed units _____ , number of sold units _____ , and number of rented units _____ ;
  ◊   A description of the common elements or recreational facilities;
  ◊   Owners' association fees per month for the subject unit: $ _____ ;
  ◊   The utilities that are included in the owners' association fees;
  ◊   A comment about whether the unit's owners' association fees are reasonable in comparison to those for units in other projects of similar quality and design; and
  ◊   A comment about whether the project appears to be well-maintained.

Two-Family Properties:
The appraiser may use Form 1004 to document the appraisal for a two-family property if the value of the second unit is relatively

insignificant in relation to the total value of the property. For example, if a two-family property consists of a legal basement rental unit and an owner-occupied main unit--and the property is located in a neighborhood in which rental basement units are commonly found--use of the Form 1004 is appropriate when the value of the basement unit is relatively insignificant. This is because the appraiser generally places more emphasis on the sales comparison analysis approach to value rather than on the income approach to value that typically is used for most rental properties.

The appraiser may also use Form 1004 if each unit of a two-family property is occupied as a principal residence by one of the co-borrowers.

# Appraisal Form - FHLMC 465, FNMA 1073

You can find this residential appraisal report form, along with a complete set of all residential appraisal forms, advice, updates and information on our web site at www.nemmar.com.

Condominium appraisal form. This is a full appraisal of a single condominium unit.

# Appraisal Form - FNMA 2055

You can find this residential appraisal report form, along with a complete set of all residential appraisal forms, advice, updates and information on our web site at www.nemmar.com.

Fannie Mae Interior Short Form appraisal report. This is not a full appraisal since it lacks the cost and income approaches to value and is based upon the market approach only.

# Appraisal Form - FHLMC 72, FNMA 1025

You can find this residential appraisal report form, along with a complete set of all residential appraisal forms, advice, updates and information on our web site at www.nemmar.com.

Small Residential Income Property Appraisal Report. This is a full appraisal report form used for two to four family building appraisals.

**Small Residential Income Property Appraisal Report (Form 1025)**
Use of Form 1025:
The lender uses this form to obtain the appraiser's analysis and estimate of value for either a conventional or a VA mortgage that is secured by a two- to four-family property.

This form must be printed on legal size paper, using portrait format. When printing this form, you must use the "shrink to fit" option in the Adobe Acrobat print dialogue box.

Instructions:
This form is completed in its entirety by the appraiser. The lender should retain the original of the completed form and the appraiser should retain the copy.

The Uniform Standards of Professional Appraisal Practice requires appraisers to identify their appraisal reports as a self-contained report, a summary report, or a restricted report by stating the applicable category at or near the beginning of the appraisal report form. The Appraisal Standards Board has expressed the opinion that the *Uniform Residential Appraisal Report* (Form 1004) is consistent with a summary appraisal report. Because Form 1025 is structured similarly to Form 1004 and requires an appraiser to provide essentially the same information as it relates to two-to four-family properties, an appraiser should also consider Form 1025 to be a summary appraisal report and should identify all appraisals reported on this form accordingly.

The appraiser should provide his or her description and analysis of the neighborhood, site, and improvements. The valuation should include both rental and sales comparables; however, the same properties do not have to be used as both a rental and a sales comparable. In addition, the appraiser must attach the standard required exhibits listed in the Selling Guide--including the *Statement of Limiting Conditions and Appraiser's Certification* (Form 1004B)--to support each appraisal report.

Units of Comparison:
If the comparable properties are not very similar to the subject property, the appraiser must reconcile the indicators of value--the value per unit, the value per room, the value per square foot of gross building area, and the value per the gross rent multiplier--to develop a valid unit comparison that can be used in the valuation process. The appraiser should indicate in his or her market data analysis (or in an addendum to the appraisal report form) the adjustments that were made, explain the reasons for each adjustment, and note which indicators were given the most weight.

Rent Forecasts:
The appraiser must comment on how well the rent comparables compare to the subject property. He or she should also note and explain any adjustments that were made to arrive at the gross monthly forecasted rent (unfurnished) for the subject property. When estimating stabilized or forecasted rents, the appraiser must base his or her estimate on the level of rents currently obtainable on the effective date of the appraisal, and must not use a projection of future rent values.

# *Appraisal Form - FHLMC 71A*

You can find this residential appraisal report form, along with a complete set of all residential appraisal forms, advice, updates and information on our web site at www.nemmar.com.

Freddie Mac Residential Income Property appraisal form.

# *Appraisal Form - FNMA 2075*

You can find this residential appraisal report form, along with a complete set of all residential appraisal forms, advice, updates and information on our web site at www.nemmar.com.

FNMA Desktop Underwriter Property Inspection report form. This is not an appraisal and does not provide an estimate of market value. This is a home consulting assignment as opposed to a home appraising assignment.

**Desktop Underwriter Property Inspection Report (Form 2075)**

Use of Form 2075:
Desktop Underwriter's enhanced risk assessment capability enables the use of the Desktop Underwriter® Property Inspection Report (Form 2075), which requires an exterior-only inspection of the subject property from the street by a state-licensed or state-certified appraiser without an estimate of market value for the property.

Form 2075 is not an appraisal report. When Desktop Underwriter recommends Form 2075, it has judged the reasonableness of the sales price as adequate collateral for the mortgage loan. Therefore, a property appraisal is not required for the specific transaction.

This form must be printed on legal size paper, using portrait format. When printing this form, you must use the "shrink to fit" option in the Adobe Acrobat print dialogue box.

Instructions:
When Desktop Underwriter recommends Form 2075, we will rely on the property valuation performed by the system's proprietary automated valuation model. Lenders are required to obtain an exterior-only property inspection of the subject property. No estimate of value is required. If the property inspection reveals adverse physical deficiencies or conditions, or the subject property does not conform to the neighborhood, the lender is required to upgrade to a complete interior and exterior appraisal reported on Form 2055.

The appraiser must attach any required exhibits to support each inspection report. The required exhibits for Form 2075 are a street map that shows the location of the subject property and a photograph that shows the front of the subject property.

# Appraisal Form - FHLMC 1000, FNMA 1007

You can find this residential appraisal report form, along with a complete set of all residential appraisal forms, advice, updates and information on our web site at www.nemmar.com.

Single Family Comparable Rent Schedule form. This form is usually required for non-owner occupied appraisal reports.

**Single-Family Comparable Rent Schedule (Form 1007)**
Use of Form 1007:
The lender uses this form to obtain the market rent for a conventional single-family investment property from the appraiser.

This form must be printed on letter size paper, using portrait format. When printing this form, you must use the "shrink to fit" option in the Adobe Acrobat print dialogue box.

Instructions:
The form is prepared by the appraiser as an attachment to the appraisal for a single-family investment property. The lender should retain the original of the form and the appraiser, the copy.

The form is designed to present the information needed to determine the market rent for a single-family property. It calls for information on the physical structure, location, and lease terms.

# Appraisal Form - FHLMC 998, FNMA 216

You can find this residential appraisal report form, along with a complete set of all residential appraisal forms, advice, updates and information on our web site at www.nemmar.com.

Operating Income Statement form. This form is used for One to Four-Family investment property and Four-Family Owner-Occupied property appraisal reports.

**Operating Income Statement (Form 216)**
Use of Form 216:
The lender should use this form to determine the amount of operating income that can be used in evaluating the applicant's credit on applications for conventional mortgages that are secured by one-family investment properties and all two- to four-family properties (including those in which the applicant occupies one of the units as a principal residence).

This form must be printed on legal size paper, using portrait format.

Instructions:
This form is prepared either by the loan applicant or the appraiser. If the applicant prepares the form, the appraiser must also include his or her comments about the reasonableness of the projected operating income of the property. The lender should retain the original of the completed form and the appraiser should retain the copy. The lender's underwriter uses the second page of the form to calculate monthly operating income and net cash flow for the property, and to explain any adjustments he or she made to the applicant's figures.

Rent Schedule:
The applicant (or appraiser) should complete this schedule by entering the current rents in effect, as well as market rents. Rental figures should be based on the rent for an "unfurnished" unit. The applicant should indicate which utility expenses he or she will provide as part of the rent and which must be paid separately by the tenants.

Income and Expense Projections:
The applicant (or appraiser) should complete all items that apply to the subject property, and should provide actual year-end

operating statements for the past two years.

If the applicant prepares the *Operating Income Statement* (Form 216), the lender should send the form and any previous actual operating and expense reports the applicant provides to the appraiser for review and comment. If the appraiser completes the form, the lender should make sure the appraiser has the operating statements; any expense statements related to mortgage insurance premiums, owners' association dues, leasehold payments, or subordinate financing payments; and any other pertinent information related to the property.

The lender's underwriter should carefully review the applicant's (or the appraiser's) projections (and, if the applicant prepared the form, the appraiser's comments concerning those projections). Based on the appraiser's comments, the lender should make any necessary final adjustments for inconsistencies or missing data.

Specific instructions for completing the projections for *effective gross income* follow. When the applicant will occupy one of the units of a two- to four-family property as a principal residence, income should not be calculated for the owner-occupied unit.
- ◊ **Annual Rental at 100% Occupancy**. Multiply the total monthly rental shown in the rent schedule by 12. If the lender disagrees with the applicant's figures, the reasons for the disagreement should be documented in writing.
- ◊ **Positive Adjustments**. Any additional income should be added to the rental income. The source of that income--such as parking, laundry, etc.--should also be shown.
- ◊ **Negative Adjustments**. The income should be reduced by the annual dollar amount of rent loss that can be expected as the result of anticipated vacancies or uncollectible rent from occupied units.

Specific instructions for completing the projections of *operating expenses* follow. Any operating expenses that relate to an owner-occupied unit in a two- to four-family property should not be included.
- ◊ **Heating, Cooking, Hot Water**. If any of these items are provided by the applicant as part of the rent for a unit, the projected cost and type of fuel used should be included. When the costs for heating relate to public areas only, an appropriate notation should be made.
- ◊ **Electricity**. This should include only those projected expenses that will be incurred by the applicant over and above any similar expense for heating, cooking, or hot water already taken into account. If the expense relates to the cost of electricity for public areas only, an appropriate notation should be made.
- ◊ **Water/Sewer**. These projected expenses should not be included when they are part of the real estate tax bill or when the units are serviced by an on-site private system.
- ◊ **Casual Labor**. This includes the costs for public area cleaning, snow removal, etc., even though the applicant may not elect to contract for such services.
- ◊ **Interior Paint/Decorating**. This includes the costs of contract labor and materials that are required to maintain the interiors of the living units.
- ◊ **General Repairs/Maintenance**. This includes the costs of contract labor and materials that are required to maintain the public corridors, stairways, roofs, mechanical systems, grounds, etc.
- ◊ **Management Expenses**. These are the customary expenses that a professional management company would charge to manage the property.
- ◊ **Supplies**. This includes the costs of items like light bulbs, janitorial supplies, etc.
- ◊ **Total Replacement Reserves**. This represents the total average yearly reserves that were computed in the "Replacement Reserve Schedule" portion of the form. Generally, all equipment that has a remaining life of more than one year--such as refrigerators, stoves, clothes washers/dryers, trash compactors, etc.--should be expensed on a replacement cost basis--even if actual reserves are not provided for in the operating statement or are not customary in the local market.

Operating Income Reconciliation:
The first formula in this section is used to determine the monthly operating income for a two- to four-family property when one unit is occupied by the applicant as his or her principal residence. The monthly operating income should be applied either as income or debt in accordance with the instructions on the form.

Both formulas must be used to determine the net cash flow for a single-family investment property or for a two- to four-family property that the applicant will not occupy. The net cash flow should be applied as either income or debt in accordance with the instructions on the form.

# Appraisal Form - HUD/FHA SA HOC GRM

You can find this residential appraisal report form, along with a complete set of all residential appraisal forms, advice, updates and information on our web site at www.nemmar.com.

HUD/FHA Three and Four-Unit Gross Rent Multiplier form. When using the URAR for three and four unit properties the appraiser is to complete the Gross Rent Multiplier calculations and analysis. If the FNMA 1025 - Small Residential Income Property Appraisal Report form is used, then completion of the GRM section on the form is acceptable. See section HUD/FHA Gross Rent Multiplier Form page 163 for an example of how this form filled out for an appraisal report.

# Appraisal Form - FHLMC 442

You can find this residential appraisal report form, along with a complete set of all residential appraisal forms, advice, updates and information on our web site at www.nemmar.com.

Freddie Mac Satisfactory Completion Certificate form.

# Appraisal Form - FHLMC 439, FNMA 1004B

You can find this residential appraisal report form, along with a complete set of all residential appraisal forms, advice, updates and information on our web site at www.nemmar.com.

Freddie Mac and Fannie Mae Statement of Limiting Conditions and Appraiser's Certification form.

**Statement of Limiting Conditions and Appraiser's Certification (Form 1004B)**
Use of Form 1004B:
Property appraisers use this form to evidence their understanding of Fannie Mae's definition of market value, to make certain required certifications, and to acknowledge contingent or limiting conditions to their appraisal reports.

This form must be printed on legal size paper, using portrait format.

Instructions:
The appraiser must execute a Form 1004B and submit it with each appraisal report he or she prepares.

The appraiser may not make any changes or deletions to this certification, although he or she may make additional certifications on a separate page or form. Acceptable additional certifications include those required by state law and those related to the appraiser's continuing education or membership in an appraisal organization. The appraiser may not add additional limiting conditions.

# Appraisal Form - ERC

You can find this residential appraisal report form, along with a complete set of all residential appraisal forms, advice, updates and information on our web site at www.nemmar.com.

Employee Relocation Council appraisal form. This is the form usually used for relocation appraisals. The appraisal can be for the transferring employee's current residence or the residential property he/she is purchasing in the new location.


# Appraisal Form - FNMA 1104

You can find this residential appraisal report form, along with a complete set of all residential appraisal forms, advice, updates and information on our web site at www.nemmar.com.

Freddie Mac Multi-Family Environmental Survey report form.


# Test Appraisal Form - FNMA 1004

You can find this residential appraisal report form, along with a complete set of all residential appraisal forms, advice, updates and information on our web site at www.nemmar.com.

Uniform Residential Appraisal Report (Test Form 1004)

Use of Test Form 1004:
The *Uniform Residential Appraisal Report* (Test Form 1004) is designed for one-unit property appraisals (including individual units in condominium and PUD projects) that are based on an interior and exterior property inspection. Test Form 1004 requires the appraiser to report whether the property has any physical deficiencies or conditions (such as needed repairs and deferred maintenance) and to determine if such conditions affect the livability or soundness or structural integrity of the property. In addition, the appraiser must report whether there are any adverse environmental conditions present in the improvements, on the site, or in the immediate vicinity of the property.

The sale history analysis section of the report form has been expanded. In addition, the report form requires the appraiser to identify the effective date of his or her data source(s), identify the current owner of record for the subject property as evidenced by public record data demonstrating the seller's ownership of the property for a purchase (or the borrower's ownership for a refinance transaction), provide information on any recent listing(s) for sale for the subject property, and indicate whether the listing(s) and prior sale(s) of the subject property and prior sale(s) of the comparable sales represent arm's length transactions.

All of our standard exhibits that are used to support an appraisal based on an interior and exterior property inspection are also required when using this test form.

# *Test Appraisal Form - FNMA 1004B*

You can find this residential appraisal report form, along with a complete set of all residential appraisal forms, advice, updates and information on our web site at www.nemmar.com.

Definitions, Statement of Limiting Conditions, and Appraiser's Certification (Test Form 1004B)

Use of Test Form 1004B:
The Definitions, Statement of Limiting Conditions, and Appraiser's Certification (Test Form 1004B) is designed to be used to report an appraisal of a one-unit property. The appraiser's certification was expanded to specifically address unacceptable appraisal practices and to address potential civil liability and/or criminal penalties for intentional or negligent misrepresentation(s).

# *Test Appraisal Form - FNMA 1004C*

You can find this residential appraisal report form, along with a complete set of all residential appraisal forms, advice, updates and information on our web site at www.nemmar.com.

Manufactured Home Appraisal Report (Test Form 1004C)

Use of Test Form 1004C:
The appraiser uses this form when reporting appraisals on manufactured homes. The use of Form 1004C will help to ensure that the appraiser inspected, considered, and/or reported (as applicable) the necessary information for the property valuation and underwriting of a manufactured home. The information specific to the appraisal of a manufactured home will help the lender better understand the factors that may affect the value and marketability opinions and conclusions provided by the appraiser.

Fannie Mae will continue to require market-based property valuations for manufactured homes demonstrated by a well-developed sales comparison approach to value. This means that the appraiser must develop and report in a concise format an adequately supported opinion of market value based on the sales comparison approach to value and further supported by the cost approach to value. The sales comparison and cost approaches to value are complementary for the valuation of manufactured housing and should support the final value conclusion.

This form must be printed on legal size paper using portrait format.

Instructions:
This form is completed in its entirety by the appraiser. The lender should retain the original of the completed form, and the appraiser should retain a copy.

# *Test Appraisal Form - FNMA 1004D*

You can find this residential appraisal report form, along with a complete set of all residential appraisal forms, advice, updates and information on our web site at www.nemmar.com.

Appraisal Update and/or Completion Report (Test Form 1004D)

Use of Test Form 1004D:
The lender uses this form for reporting an update of a prior appraisal and/or a certification of completion. The appraiser must identify the service(s) being reported by checking the appropriate box(s). This form must be printed on legal size paper, using portrait format.

Instructions:
This form is completed in its entirety by the appraiser. The lender should retain the original of the completed form and the appraiser should retain the copy.

Appraisal Update Report - An appraisal update is required when an appraisal will be more than four (4) months old on the date of the note and mortgage. When the original appraisal report will be more than 12 months old on the date of the note and mortgage, a new appraisal is required.

The appraiser must, at a minimum, review and concur with the prior appraisal, inspect the exterior of the subject property from the street, and review and analyze current market data in order to determine whether the property has declined in value since the effective date of the prior appraisal. The prior appraisal identified in the appraisal update is incorporated by reference in the Appraisal Update Report.

Certification of Completion - The certification of completion is used to confirm that the requirements or conditions established in the identified appraisal report have been met. The appraiser must certify that he or she reviewed the appraisal report and re-inspected the interior and exterior of the subject property.

The appraiser must determine if the improvements have been completed in accordance with the requirements and conditions stated in the original appraisal report. If they have not, the appraiser must describe the changes and explain the impact on the final value conclusion contained in the original appraisal report.

The appraiser must also identify when there are substantial changes from the subject data contained in the original appraisal report that do not adversely affect the analysis, opinions, or conclusions stated in the appraisal report.

The appraiser must attach any required exhibits to support each appraisal report.
- ◊ For an appraisal update and/or a certification of completion, the only required exhibits are descriptive photographs that show the front and rear of the subject property.

# Test Appraisal Form - FNMA 1025

You can find this residential appraisal report form, along with a complete set of all residential appraisal forms, advice, updates and information on our web site at www.nemmar.com.

Small Residential Income Property Appraisal Report (Test Form 1025)

Use of Test Form 1025:
The lender uses this form to obtain the appraiser's analysis and opinion of market value for transaction that is secured by a two- to four-family property.

This form must be printed on legal size paper, using portrait format. When printing this form, you must use the "shrink to fit" option in the Adobe Acrobat print dialogue box.

Instructions:
This form is completed in its entirety by the appraiser. The lender should retain the original of the completed form and the appraiser should retain the copy.

The report form provides a concise format to report the appraiser's analysis, opinions and conclusions. The appraiser is required to, at a minimum (1) perform an on-site inspection of the interior and exterior of the subject property, (2) inspect the neighborhood, (3) inspect each of the comparable sales from the street, (4) collect, confirm, and analyze data from reliable public and/or private sources, and (5) report his or her analysis, opinions, and conclusions in this appraisal report.
The valuation process includes current listing, rental and sales comparables; however, the same properties do not have to be used as both a rental and a sale comparable. In addition, the appraiser must attach the standard required exhibits listed in the Selling Guide--including the *Statement of Limiting Conditions and Appraiser's Certification* (Form 1004B)--to support each appraisal report.

Units of Comparison:
The appraiser must develop and analyze appropriate units of comparison including price per unit, price per room, price per bedroom, value per square foot of gross building area, and the value per the gross rent multiplier to arrive at a supportable opinion of market value. The appraiser should indicate in his or her market data analysis (or in an addendum to the appraisal report form) the adjustments that were made, explain the reasons for each adjustment, and note which indicators were given the most weight.

Rent Forecasts:
The appraiser must comment on how well the rent comparables compare to the subject property. He or she should also note and explain any adjustments that were made to arrive at the gross monthly forecasted rent (unfurnished) for the subject property. When estimating stabilized or forecasted rents, the appraiser must base his or her estimate on the level of rents currently obtainable on the effective date of the appraisal, and must not use a projection of future rent values.

# *Test Appraisal Form - FNMA 1073*

You can find this residential appraisal report form, along with a complete set of all residential appraisal forms, advice, updates and information on our web site at www.nemmar.com.

Individual Cooperative Interest Appraisal Report (Test Form 1073)

Use of Test Form 1073:
The Individual Cooperative Interest Appraisal Report (Test Form 1073) is designed for an appraisal of an individual cooperative unit based on an interior and exterior property inspection. When reporting the sales price for the subject cooperative interest and in the sales prices for the comparable sales, the pro rata share of the blanket mortgage(s) on the real estate is not to be included.

This form must be printed on legal size paper, using portrait format.

Instructions:
This form is completed in its entirety by the appraiser. The lender should retain the original of the completed form and the appraiser should retain the copy.

The sale history analysis section of the report form has been expanded. In addition, the report form requires the appraiser to identify the effective date of his or her data source(s), identify the current owner of record for the subject property as evidenced by public record data demonstrating the seller's ownership of the property for a purchase (or the borrower's ownership for a refinance transaction), provide information on any recent listing(s) for sale for the subject property, and indicate whether the listing(s) and prior sale(s) of the subject property and prior sale(s) of the comparable sales represent arm's length transactions.

New Projects:
For units in new (or recently converted) cooperative projects, the appraiser should select as comparables one closed or settled sale from the subject project (if one is available) and two closed or settled sales from outside the project. If closed or settled sales are not available in the subject project, the appraiser should use comparable sales from competing projects.

Established Projects:
For units in established cooperative projects (those that have resale activity), the appraiser should use as comparables two closed or settled sales from within the subject project (if available) and one closed or settled sale from a competing project.

All of our standard exhibits that are used to support an appraisal based on an interior and exterior property inspection are also required when using this test form.

# *Test Appraisal Form - FNMA 2055*

You can find this residential appraisal report form, along with a complete set of all residential appraisal forms, advice, updates and information on our web site at www.nemmar.com.

Exterior-Only Inspection Residential Appraisal Report (Test Form 2055)

Use of Test Form 2055:
The lender uses this form to document appraisals for one-family properties (including units in condominium or PUD projects) when Fannie Mae requires an appraisal based on an exterior-only inspection of the subject property. The revised format enables the appraiser to report his or her conclusions in a brief but comprehensive manner, which will be more efficient for reviewing and processing.

This form must be printed on legal size paper, using portrait format.

Instructions:
This form is completed in its entirety by the appraiser. The lender should retain the original of the completed form and the appraiser should retain the copy.

Test Form 2055 requires the appraiser to report in a clear and succinct yes/no format whether the property has any physical deficiencies or conditions (such as needed repairs and deferred maintenance) and to determine if such conditions affect the livability or soundness or structural integrity of the property. In addition, the appraiser must report whether there are any adverse environmental conditions present in the improvements, on the site, or in the immediate vicinity of the property.

The sale-history analysis section of the report form accommodates a three-year history for the subject property and the comparable sales as well as space for reporting the appraiser's analysis of the sale and listing history. The report form requires the appraiser to identify the effective date of his or her data source(s), identify the current owner of record for the subject property (as evidenced by public record data), provide information on any recent listing(s) for sale for the subject property, and indicate whether the listing(s) and prior sale(s) of the subject property and prior sale(s) of the comparable sales represent arm's length transactions.

# Health Concerns

## Asbestos Insulation

Asbestos has been used for insulation as far back in time as ancient Greece. Almost all older houses have had asbestos insulation on the heating pipes. A thin layer of asbestos can sometimes be found on old hot air ducts if there is a furnace. Old cast iron boilers had asbestos on the interior insulating walls as well. Believe it or not, asbestos used to be **required** to be installed in all new construction. That's why so many buildings have asbestos in them. It was considered a "miracle product" when it was widely used. *(Yeah, it performs miracles with your health!)* Many floors tiles and other products found in older homes have asbestos in them. Asbestos has great insulating and fireproofing qualities, the only problem is the public wasn't made aware of the health problems associated with it until it was too late. This is one area you have to be careful about. Asbestos really scares potential home buyers because of the health concerns with it.

> *Asbestos causes lung cancer when it comes loose from the pipes and the fibers get into the air.*
> *The asbestos fibers are like tiny daggers and when you breathe them in, they stick into your lungs.*

Asbestos causes lung cancer when it comes loose from the pipes and the fibers get into the air. The asbestos fibers are like tiny daggers and when you breathe them in, they stick into your lungs and stay there. The fibers cling to dust and can be stirred up off the floor when someone walks in a room where the fibers are located. There are about five different diseases related to exposure to asbestos. There are six different types of asbestos minerals.

I did an inspection for an attorney who handled a lawsuit filed by the relatives of residents from a town in Australia. This attorney told me that **every** resident from that town was killed due to the *Blue Asbestos* mine that most of them worked at. Supposedly Blue Asbestos is the most dangerous type of asbestos to be exposed to. Just by getting one fiber in your lungs can be fatal!!! Just one fiber will not only create scar tissue in that section of the lung, but it will spread to cover the entire lung over time. This attorney told me that all of the workers in the mine were killed due to breathing the Blue Asbestos at work. Their families were all killed because the mine workers would bring home the fibers in their clothes which would spread in their homes. Also, the rest of the people in this town were killed due to the Blue Asbestos fibers being blown around town by the wind.

An asbestos lab technician told me that Steve McQueen died of an asbestos related cancer. Supposedly Steve McQueen worked in the French Merchant Marine when he was younger and that's where he was overly exposed to asbestos. I'm not telling you these stories to try to scare you, I'm just letting you know about some potential health hazards you have to watch out for.

Asbestos pipe insulation usually has a white color and appears to have layers of ribbed cardboard in the middle sections. You'll probably see an off-white canvas covering over it. Old hot air heating ducts may have a very thin, white layer of asbestos around them. The only way to know for sure if any insulation is asbestos is to have a laboratory take a sample. You can charge an additional fee for this service if you'd like. I don't get involved in handling any asbestos myself and I don't recommend you do either.

Don't take any chances identifying asbestos in the house. Just tell the client when you see an asbestos type of insulation, and tell them the EPA recommendations. The Environmental Protection Agency has offices in every State that will provide anyone with free information and brochures. They provide information about Asbestos, Radon Gas, Oil Leaks, Lead in paint and water, and many other environmental and health concerns. Get the local number for your State office and obtain their brochures for more information. There are also classes you can take that are accredited by the EPA for more information about these items.

> *The EPA recommends that any asbestos insulation be professionally sealed or removed from the house by an EPA licensed asbestos contractor.*

The Environmental Protection Agency recommends that any asbestos insulation be *professionally* sealed or removed from the house by an EPA licensed asbestos contractor. This means, the homeowner, the plumber or any other repair person should not touch any asbestos in the house!! Often you'll see a residue from asbestos insulation on the heating pipes. Evidence of this is small white particles on sections of the pipes, usually around the joints. This indicates that a non-EPA licensed person removed the asbestos and it should immediately raise a red flag for you to notify the client.

Many times the homeowner will have a new boiler put in and some foolish contractor will just rip asbestos off the pipes not knowing what he's doing. Or worse, sometimes the contractor or the homeowner removes it intentionally just to get rid of it themselves. Big mistake on their part! When inspecting an older house you may not actually see the asbestos. If this were the case, you should assume that there was asbestos in the home at one time. It's better to be safe than sorry. Since asbestos was almost always used in older houses, it was probably unprofessionally removed and that's why you don't see it. I've found asbestos insulation on copper water supply pipes in houses that were built as late as 1960!!! When older houses have forced hot air heating systems, then there **really** is a problem if asbestos was used. I've found very thin layers of asbestos around forced hot air heating ducts and in the lining of furnaces. The furnace fan will circulate asbestos all over the house once it gets inside the air ducts. So not only will you have deadly fibers in the basement and behind the walls, you'll also have them in the livable rooms.

⚠️ Tell your client to have a laboratory take an air sample to learn what the asbestos fiber content is in the house. There's no way for you to determine this during an inspection. Don't take any chances with this stuff. Asbestos lawsuits are big bucks. I've only heard of one home inspector getting sued for asbestos. But I have heard of many contractors getting sued for hundreds of thousands of dollars for improperly removing asbestos.

Don't let the clients be fooled by any Realtors or other third parties telling them not to worry about the asbestos in the house. A common line that I hear Realtors and other third parties say to my clients on inspections is: *"This asbestos is just fine, the Environmental Protection Agency says all you have to do is to wrap it in tape or plastic."* That really bothers me when I hear that. What gives that third party the right to sugarcoat a decision that concerns someone else's health? You can bet that if that Realtor or third party was the person buying that house, they'd insist that the asbestos be removed. They'd also make sure it was removed by a licensed EPA contractor prior to closing! Yet it's OK for them to let someone else buy the house and leave the asbestos there.

I'll never forget the time that I started inspecting a house for a client before they had arrived at the site. I was in the lower level of the house with a dishonest Realtor to the transaction who was getting a commission on the sale. I mentioned that there was asbestos on the heating pipes and that some of it appeared to have been removed unprofessionally or had fallen off sections of the pipes. This Realtor got worried and asked me what type of health concern there was with breathing in asbestos fibers. I told her, *"The fibers are like tiny daggers that stick in your lungs and create scar tissue."* She just turned and practically ran for the stairway and said, *"I'm getting out of this basement now, I'll be waiting upstairs."*

When my client arrived, I told him about the asbestos. He then went upstairs and told this Realtor that he wanted it removed from the pipes prior to closing on the house. I could not believe it when I went back upstairs and the Realtor said to me, *"Why are you getting the client so scared about the asbestos?"* I felt like screaming at her! Just 15 minutes earlier this Realtor **ran** out of the basement because I told her about the asbestos on the pipes. Now suddenly she was worried because I might create problems with her deal by informing my client about the same health concern that she was so concerned about herself. I guess it's different when it's somebody else's lungs and not her own. Some people have an *amazing* ability to rationalize their actions. I'll talk more about this at the end of the book.

I tell my clients that they're better off having an EPA licensed contractor remove the asbestos from the house, as opposed to just having it wrapped professionally. The reason for this is that if the asbestos is left in the house and is only sealed, then when there's a pipe leak underneath the asbestos insulation, the covering will have to be removed. The asbestos will have to be exposed so that the pipe leak can be repaired. Once it's exposed, you have the problem all over again of fibers getting into the air of the house. Also, if the client has the asbestos removed from the house, as opposed to having it wrapped, then they don't have to worry about it bothering potential buyers when they sell the house.

When an Environmental Protection Agency licensed contractor removes asbestos, they seal the entire area where it's located. They work with completely sealed suits over their bodies. They then set up a vacuum to remove all of the dust from the area. When the asbestos is totally removed from the house, they take an air sample. The air sample is done to make sure the workers haven't left any fibers lying around that can be stirred up and breathed in later. Generally, any asbestos behind the walls is left alone. If there's no access to the asbestos and it can't be disturbed, there isn't that much of a health concern. Just let the EPA licensed asbestos contractor tell your client what to do. You only give recommendations from an appraiser's viewpoint.

# *Radon Gas*

While we're on the lovely topic of lung cancer, let's talk about radon. A radon lab technician told me the story about how radon was discovered. I thought you might find it interesting. There was a man who lived in Reading, Pennsylvania that worked for some type of nuclear laboratory. When he used to go to work, he would set off the radiation detectors at the lab. The radiation detectors are installed so that the nuclear lab can monitor their employees to see if they're being exposed to radiation inside the lab. The lab employees couldn't figure out why the detectors were setting off, so they tested his house for radiation. While studying the problem, they stumbled upon radon gas. *(Fortunately or unfortunately for mankind. I guess it's just another way to develop cancer. Like there aren't enough already!)*

Radon gas testing is a daily part of all real estate sales transactions. It's a great additional source of income and you should consider providing this service as well. Radon is a radiation gas that's released naturally by rocks and soil in the earth. The radiation gas is created by the natural breakdown or Uranium in the rocks and soil that leads to a by product called Radium. The radiation gas gradually seeps up from the ground and as long as it goes out into the open air it's not a problem. However, if the radon seeps through cracks in the foundation floor and walls it'll become trapped in the house and the levels will rise.

> *Some houses will be left vacant while they're being sold. The point is, that if a house has a high radon reading, don't let anyone tell the client that it's only because the house was sealed up.*

Some houses will be left vacant while they're being sold. Many people who think this will increase the radon level reading because no windows or doors are being opened. However, radon has a half life of only 3.825 days. Because of this fact, the maximum radon level that could build up would be just under a 4 day high level. After that point, some radon will decay and then be replenished by new radon gas entering the house. The point is, that if a house has a high radon reading, ***don't let anyone tell the client that it's only because the house was sealed up!*** Realtors like to use the excuse that a house was vacant and that's the only reason why it has a high radon reading. Don't let anyone make your client think that when he moves in, the radon level will be OK. If anyone says that, then tell that person to move into the house and call us in about 10 years after they have a chest X-ray.

As with asbestos and other environmental and health concerns, call your State Environmental Protection Agency office for their information, brochures and classes. The EPA considers radon to be the **number 2** leading cause of lung cancer behind smoking, so it's not something to take too lightly. Some experts feel that the EPA has over exaggerated the problem but I would let the client decide that for themselves. Don't try to make the decision for them.

The EPA uses a reading of 4 Pico Curies per liter to determine the maximum radon level in a house before mitigation is recommended. I'll give you some background so you have an idea of how Pico Curies are measured. The EPA office in my area says that one Pico Curie is the average indoor radon level and this is equal to getting about 100 chest X-rays per year. Now that may seem very high, but let me put it in the proper perspective. The EPA also informed me that the amount of radiation you receive from a normal chest X-ray, usually isn't as high as most people think. For example, with a reading of one Pico Curie per liter, the Environmental Protection Agency estimates that 3-13 people out of 1,000 will die of lung cancer. This is similar to a nonsmoker's risk of dying of lung cancer.

With a reading of 4 Pico Curies per liter, it's estimated that 13-50 people out of 1,000 will die of lung cancer. This is similar to five times the nonsmoker's risk of dying of lung cancer. However, you still may want to inform your client about this so that *they* can decide for themselves if the radon levels found are acceptable to them or not. Don't take it upon yourself to make the decision for your client.

*Mitigation* is the term used for the treatment to remove the radon problem by reducing the levels in the house. When a house is mitigated, the radon contractor will seal all open cracks in the lower level walls and floors that they can find. They then drill a hole in the foundation floor which looks like a sump pump pit. Instead of installing a sump pump in this pit, the contractor will install a fan with pipes leading to the outside of the house.

In some areas, the local codes require that these pipes discharge above the roof line. This will help prevent the radon from entering back into the house through an open window. The purpose of the mitigation is to vent all radon gas that builds up underneath the foundation, to the exterior of the house.

> *In some areas the radon levels tend to be higher than in other areas but all houses will get some radon gas reading!!! So don't let any Realtors, sellers, or other third parties talk your client out of getting an accurate radon test done.*

In some areas the radon levels tend to be higher than in other areas but all houses will get some radon gas reading!!! So don't let any Realtors, sellers, or other third parties talk your client out of getting an accurate radon test done. Sometimes they'll say to your client, *"Oh, you don't have to worry we don't have radon in this area."* HOGWASH!!!! All houses will have a radon reading, even if it's minor trace element readings of 0.5 Pico Curie per liter. This is because radon is everywhere according to the EPA. There is always an average of 0.4 Pico Curie per liter reading in the air of the atmosphere. EPA has found that the average indoor radon level is 1.5 Pico Curies per liter.

It's also important to inform your client that you might not have a high radon reading today but you might have a high reading a month from now. Or you might have a high reading and your neighbor might not and vice versa. The reason for this is that radon is a radiation gas that's unstable and it fluctuates. There are many factors that affect the radon level in a house, some of which include:

1    The time of the year and the climate.

2    The type of soil and rocky terrain in the area around and under the house.

3    The type of construction of the house.

4    And there are other reasons as well.

Because of these factors the Environmental Protection Agency recommends that you retest for radon every six months to make sure that the levels are acceptable. It's also another source of income to retest all of your client's homes every six months. *Believe it or not, radon can even be found in water!* That's another reason to have a laboratory analyze well water samples. You're not misleading people or trying to milk them for money. You're simply showing them the EPA recommendations for retesting times because of the unpredictability of radon.

According to the Environmental Protection Agency there currently is no evidence that there is a health problem with drinking water with radon in it. This is because radon becomes soluble (dissolves) in water. The colder the temperature of the water then the more radon will dissolve in it. The health concern of having radon in your water is that the gas is released into the air. The water releases the radon gas whenever you run the faucet or dishwasher, take a shower, flush a toilet, use the washing machine, etc. Anytime you aerate the water you will be releasing the radon gas into the house and this is when it becomes a health concern.

The current standards that the EPA uses for the acceptable levels of radon in the water are 10,000 to 1. Meaning that for each 10,000 Pico Curies per liter of radon gas that you have in your water, you will be releasing about one Pico Curie per liter into the air in the house. For example, let's say you have a radon water reading of 40,000 Pico Curies per liter. Then you will have 4 Pico Curies per liter escaping into the air of the house and this is the level at which EPA recommends mitigation. Currently there is no evidence of a correlation between a high radon reading in the air in relation to the radon reading in the water of a house. For example, let's say that you have a high radon reading in the air of your house. Well, this doesn't mean that you'll definitely have a high radon reading in the water of your house, and vice versa.

Air radon gas testing is usually done with a small, round metal canister that has charcoal inside. A canister is left in the house for about 3-5 days and then it's sealed and mailed back to the radon lab for analysis. Sometimes the seller or occupant of the house will ask you if there is a health risk of being in a house while a canister is there. Radon canisters don't emit anything hazardous. The charcoal inside the canisters merely absorbs the air in the room where they're placed so the lab can analyze them. Radon canisters do not present a health risk to the occupants of the house.

What makes a radon reading accurate is not the canister but the quality and sophistication of the lab's analyzing equipment. Don't just buy radon cans off the shelf of the local hardware store. The reason for this is that what makes a radon reading accurate **is not** the canister you use. The radon reading accuracy is determined by the sophistication of the lab's analyzing equipment. You could send the same canister to two different labs and get two different radon readings. That's another reason why you shouldn't let any third parties talk your client out of getting an accurate radon test done. Sometimes they'll say to your client: *"Oh, you don't have to test for radon, the seller already did that when they bought the house and he's willing to give you a copy of the test results for free!"* **(That sounds like the spider talking to the fly!)** How do you know how accurate the lab's equipment was that analyzed the seller's canister? How do you know the canister wasn't tampered with? Just because the seller had a low reading when he bought the house doesn't mean that there's a low reading in the house now. Remember, radon is always fluctuating.

> *As with radon canisters and well water samples, you want to make sure that you deal with a reputable laboratory for radon water analysis.*
> *The radon reading accuracy will depend on the sophistication of the lab's analyzing equipment.*

Water radon gas testing is usually done with a special water bottle. The water sample *must* be obtained without letting any aeration of the water which would release as much as 99% of the radon in the water sample. The testing bottle has to seal the faucet so that it traps all of the radon gas as the bottle is filled with the water. Special hoses are usually included with the testing bottles. As with radon canisters and well water samples, you want to make sure that you deal with a reputable laboratory for radon water analysis. The radon reading accuracy will depend on the sophistication of the lab's analyzing equipment. So check the lab out and make sure that they know what they're doing.

As an appraiser and home inspector I wonder sometimes what my exposure is to asbestos fibers and radon. But I guess there's risk in everything, even crossing the street, so I don't worry about it. If it bothers you, just talk to your physician or a local asbestos and radon lab for their advice.

## Health Concerns Photo Pages

P 47. In very old houses, you may find Rockwool or Vermiculite insulations. This off-white color insulation has a clumpy appearance. All older Rockwool and Vermiculite type of insulations should be tested for asbestos content. Any foam insulation should be tested for UFFI content. Contact your local EPA office for more information about these and other health and environmental hazards.

P 48. It is rare that you'll find asbestos insulation in good condition like this. This asbestos has not been disturbed and the metal brackets are still intact. As a result, there is less of a chance of asbestos fibers being breathed in by the occupants. However, it's always better to have all asbestos removed by a licensed EPA contractor. Call your local EPA for their advice about health hazards in a home.

P 49. This asbestos insulation on the heating pipes has been encapsulated. When an EPA licensed contractor encapsulates asbestos, they help reduce the health hazards of fibers getting in the air. However, as long as there is any asbestos in a house, there are going to be some fibers floating around. **Encapsulating this insulation does not totally eliminate the problem!**

P 51. *Here we are in asbestos heaven!* There are probably more asbestos fibers in this room than there are dust fibers. Almost always in older houses you'll find asbestos pipe insulation that is loose or has been removed unprofessionally. These conditions create very serious health hazards for the occupants of the house. Follow the EPA guidelines to resolve this.

P 50. Radon gas is considered by EPA to be the number two leading cause of lung cancer behind smoking. Radon is everywhere since it's created by a natural breakdown of rocks and soil. Stone foundation walls and dirt floors in the lower level increase radon gas levels. The large rock embedded in this basement will add radon into the air. A cement floor covering will help reduce this problem.

The insulation vapor barrier is installed upside down!

P 52. This photo and the one below show a radon mitigation system in the lower level of a house with the radon gas being vented outside above the roof.

Mitigation is the term used for the treatment to remove the radon problem by reducing the radon gas levels in the house. When a house is mitigated, the radon contractor will seal all open cracks in the lower level walls and floors that they can find. They then drill a hole in the foundation floor which looks like a sump pump pit. Instead of installing a sump pump in this pit, the contractor will install a fan with pipes leading to the outside of the house. In some areas, the local codes require that these pipes discharge above the roof line. This will help prevent the radon from entering back into the house through an open window. The purpose of the mitigation is to vent all radon gas that builds up underneath the foundation, to the exterior of the house.

P 53. While we're on the lovely topic of lung cancer, let's talk about radon. A radon lab technician told me the story about how radon was discovered. I thought you might find it interesting. There was a man who lived in Reading, Pennsylvania that worked for some type of nuclear laboratory. When he used to go to work, he would set off the radiation detectors at the lab. The radiation detectors are installed so that the nuclear lab can monitor their employees to see if they're being exposed to radiation inside the lab. The lab employees couldn't figure out why the detectors were setting off, so they tested his house for radiation. While studying the problem, they stumbled upon radon gas.
*(Fortunately or unfortunately for mankind. I guess it's just another way to develop cancer. Like there aren't enough already!)*

# What No One Else Tells You!!

## Reality Talk

I've included these last sections because I felt they're a very important part of giving you a complete picture of the real estate business in general. Some of these things you're going to have to experience for yourself to really see and understand what I mean. The school of hard knocks will always teach you the hard way, but you'll learn your lessons well! I won't include the icon keys for safety items and war stories in this section of the book. The reason I'm not including them is because this section is *filled* with war stories and safety issues and there would be icon keys for just about every paragraph! **Also, I'm not going to "pull any punches" in this section. I'm not going to paint some fairy tale, rosy picture or "sugarcoat" anything. I have written this section in a straight-forward, honest, direct, sincere – and sometimes <u>VERY BLUNT</u> manner!! I hope you are not shocked or offended by anything you read in this book. Everything I have written is the truth, the whole truth, and nothing but the truth.**

---

*Every single thing I mention in this book is from actual experiences that I have personally encountered or I have had friends in this business encounter them.*

*I've learned from my years in business and life that **money** is definitely a **truth serum** that **always** brings out the **<u>true</u>** character and integrity of a person and will reveal what they are really like deep down inside.*

---

After reading these sections you might say, *"This is just a bunch of negative and exaggerated examples of not trusting your fellow man."* Well, I've got news for you sweetheart, it may be negative and it may make you wonder about trusting your fellow man; but no matter what you call it, I call every bit of it **_Reality, Reality, Reality!!!!_** Every single thing I mention in this book is from actual experiences that I have personally encountered or I have had friends in this business encounter them. I only wish that I had a nickel for each time I've seen it happen. If I did, I wouldn't need to work anymore! You can go through life with blind faith and leave yourself wide open by trusting everyone. But just remember the old saying, *"A fool and his money are soon parted."* I have a lot of experience in all aspects of residential real estate. From this experience I could tell you war stories that would make your head spin. I've learned from my years in business and life that **money** is definitely a **truth serum** that **always** brings out the **<u>true</u>** character and integrity of a person and will reveal what they are really like deep down inside. If you want to see what

someone is *really* like deep down inside and if they're truly honest and have integrity, then look at the way they are when dealing with money. Don't focus on the front or image they portray in public because often that's not a good indicator. Instead look at their actions and how <u>honest</u> they are when dealing with money. *That's the true person deep down inside!* It's not how much money they have or don't have, because I know a lot more poor people who are far more honest and sincere than many of the wealthy people I've known. **Instead look at what the person does to get money and to keep money. Do they compromise their morals or cheat people for money? Are they shrewd and conniving when dealing with money? That's the key to the truth serum!** Money has a strange affect on many people. It becomes like an **addictive drug** that they can't enough of - regardless of how wealthy they become. The saying, *"show me a <u>rich man</u> and I'll show you a <u>crook</u>",* unfortunately is true in many cases.

## Third Parties To The Transaction

As I said in the beginning of the book, when I use the term "Third Parties", I'm talking about people involved in the transaction, not including you or your client. This could be any number of people. The list includes but isn't limited to: the seller, the Realtor or broker, the appraiser, the home inspector, the mortgage lender, the title company, the attorney, the builder or repair contractor, the mailman, the Tooth Fairy, Santa Claus, Easter Bunny the seller's dog or cat, and anyone else who may have an interest in the deal. Also, when I use descriptive adjectives and refer to *immoral, greedy, dishonest, incompetent, ignorant, etc.* Third Parties, it does <u>NOT</u> refer to **all** third party people, just those that match the particular adjective used. I also want to make it clear that throughout this book both males and females are being referred to whenever the pronouns *he* or *she* are used. Both males and females are also referred to when I give examples of war stories that I've encountered in the real estate business. When the pronouns "he" or "she" are used, they are interchangeable.

---

*Also, when I use descriptive adjectives and refer to "immoral, greedy, dishonest, incompetent, ignorant, etc." Third Parties, it does <u>NOT</u> refer to **all** third party people, just those that match the particular adjective used.*

---

"Third Parties" is a very broad term and I don't want any one person or group of people to think that they're being singled out when I use that term. I don't want anyone to think the term "third party" is directed at them personally. Realtors and other third parties are important people involved in the purchase and sale of real estate. They are a necessity and provide a vital service that helps the public to buy and sell property. The problem I have is that some Realtors and third parties can be very dishonest, greedy, incompetent, immoral, ignorant, or a combination of all of these undesirable qualities. To make matters even worse, they go a step further and think that they're *experts* in every aspect of real estate. These are the third party people that I'm referring to!! You need to understand that third parties, such as Realtors, **are not experts** in real estate. Realtors only need the equivalent of a few days of basic real estate classes to get a license. So don't think they know all the important aspects of investing in real estate. Even if a Realtor has many years of experience as a real estate agent and/or investor, they're not knowledgeable in **all** aspects of real estate. They cannot give you advice like a qualified real estate appraiser, home inspector, builder, real estate attorney, etc. can in each particular field of expertise.

---

**In case you didn't know, most of the time the Realtor works for the seller, not the buyer.**

---

In case you didn't know, most of the time the Realtor works for the **seller**, not the buyer. Sometimes the Realtor will represent the buyer as a "buyer's agent" but that's not very common. Some states require Realtors to sign an agreement with potential sellers and buyers clearly stating whom they're working for. One reason for this may be that some home buyers don't realize that the Realtor often represents the seller. This means that when you go into a real estate office looking to buy a house, the Realtor that shows you the properties listed for sale has a **fiduciary responsibility** to the **seller** of the house! Even though a buyer goes into the real estate office looking for houses, the Realtor still works for the seller. In this case the Realtor is responsible for looking out for the seller's best interest, and <u>not</u> the buyer's. Some buyers don't know this and mistakenly think that the Realtor is looking out for **their** best interest only. *(Some Realtors only look out for THEIR OWN best interests, regardless of whether they represent the seller or buyer! It's as though some Realtor's believe their fiduciary responsibility is only to fill their own pockets with sales commissions.)*

---

**An educated home buyer or seller is a dishonest Realtor's worst nightmare!!**

---

**An educated home buyer or seller is a dishonest Realtor's worst nightmare!!** I've seen plenty of greedy, ignorant, dishonest Realtors and third parties get angry because my clients wanted to take my advice and check everything out about the house they were planning to buy or sell. I think the last thing a greedy, dishonest, ignorant, immoral and/or incompetent third party person wants is an **educated home buyer or seller**. That's because an educated home buyer or seller is a careful, intelligent person who checks everything out before making a big investment. This can take a few days to check the town hall records, get repair

estimates, etc. If a home buyer or seller wants to verify items by checking the documentation themselves, getting repair estimates **prior** to closing, etc., these Realtors and third parties criticize them and say things like, *"Oh, this buyer or seller is just a worrier. They're making a big fuss over nothing. They should just close on the house and forget about it."* These third parties can cost a home buyer or seller tens of thousands of dollars. They do this by pressuring your client into **not** checking everything out **before** the closing. Far too many people are buying and selling their homes with their eyes closed. Hopefully, my educational materials will open your eyes *nice and wide* when you decide to buy or sell your house!

Sometimes the seller of the house, the Realtor, or some other third party will tell you something, such as the air-conditioning system, works just fine. However you find that you can't operate the system by its normal controls. If the seller, Realtor, or other third party get very defensive about the situation and insist that the system works properly, just tell them to go ahead and turn it on so you can evaluate the air-conditioning. Don't get in an argument with them just say, *"Great, **you** turn it on and I'll be more than happy to evaluate the A/C for my client."* This way you dump it back in their lap and leave it up to them to turn on the system.

Now remember, I said this in the beginning of the book and I'll say it again. You're a guest in someone else's house! So don't be rude or get into an argument with anyone at the subject property. You have to always be diplomatic and professional in this or any other business to be successful. You also have to respect the seller's property. Don't go into someone's house and start taking the place apart by poking holes I the walls and moving furniture all around. You have to treat their home and personal belongings as you want someone to treat your home and personal belongings during an inspection. Some seller's get very upset and worried during an appraisal and/or a home inspection because it can make or break a real estate deal. So remember to always be polite and courteous during an appraisal.

Now don't get me wrong when I tell you this by thinking you have to be a marshmallow during the appraisal. As an **"A to Z Appraiser"** you still have to do a very thorough inspection. This means that you have to evaluate all visible and accessible areas in the house and on the property. Don't be afraid to probe the visible wood beams on the inside and outside of the house. When you probe the wood beams and exterior trim work you're going to leave marks and some minor cosmetic damage. This can't be helped and it's a necessary part of properly evaluating the structural members for rot and wood destroying insect infestation. However, because probing will leave visible marks in wood, you don't want to go around damaging the interior finished floor moldings, doors and window sills. Just use your common sense when deciding what wood areas are finished coverings that shouldn't be probed and what wood areas <u>have to</u> be probed during your inspection.

I once did an inspection and I was probing the moldings at the base of the garage door trim work. This is a very common area to find rot and wood destroying insect infestation because the wood is in close contact with the soil. The wood was so rotted at the base of the door trim work that the probe went right through it. A hole that was a few inches in diameter was left in the wood. This is going to happen to you when you probe rotted and damaged wood. There's nothing wrong with you leaving this wood damaged because if the wood is very solid, then it won't fall apart when you probe it. However, if the wood needs to be replaced then it will fall apart and leave some damage. Don't worry about leaving the wood with some cosmetic damage because it has to be replaced anyway due to the rot and/or wood destroying insect damage. All your doing is showing your client and all third parties that the wood needs replacing.

Anyway, after I probed this garage door molding, I told the client and the third parties that this section of wood needed to be replaced because it was all rotted out. About three days later I got a phone call from the Realtor. She said that the seller was going to have their attorney contact me because the seller felt that *"I seriously hurt the market value of their property."* It was such a ridiculous comment that even the Realtor said the seller was crazy to make that claim. I was never contacted by the seller's attorney because the seller must have realized that they had no basis for a complaint against me. They realized that the wood was rotted out and the probing damage was done during an inspection that they allowed me to do at their home.

## *Verify Everything With The Documentation*

Often the seller or the Realtor will tell you or your client that something, such as the roof or heating system, was just recently replaced. Another example is that they will tell you that the asbestos was removed by a licensed EPA contractor. **That's fine, then just tell the client to get copies of all of the receipts and documentation for the work performed. Recommend that the client call the contractors personally.** This will enable them to talk with the contractors to find out important information. The client should ask the contractors if there was anything about the work they did at the subject property that would be helpful or important for the client to know. Sometimes the contractor will inform your client that the seller wanted to save some money on the job. This could be due to the fact that the house was on the market for sale. As a result, the seller may have told the contractor to cut corners and not do the proper repair work. This is done to cover up a problem so potential buyers won't see any inadequate repair work.

You also need to check with the local building department to make sure that this information is accurate and if any permits and final approvals were required. **Almost *always* permits and approvals are required so don't take it for granted that everything was filed and taken care of. Often you'll have the seller, the Realtor, or another third party tell you or your client that all the building permits and** approvals have been obtained for some work done at the site. Or else many times third party people will say that building permits and approvals were not needed for some work done at the site. That's fine, then just tell the client to obtain all receipts and documentation for the work done. Also, you and the client need to check with the local building department to make sure that this information is accurate and that all permits and *final* approvals were obtained if they were required for the work done.

> *Whenever you make ANY changes to a house or site from the time of the original construction, you have to file the necessary permits and obtain all final approvals from the local municipality.*

**Whenever you make ANY changes to a house or a site from the time of the original construction, you have to file the necessary permits and obtain all final approvals from the local municipality.** *(Contrary to popular belief, this is an accurate statement and I'm the only guy I know of that tells his client's the facts about checking the records at town hall. Realtors don't want your client checking town hall records because then he may know too much and be an educated buyer.)* This pertains to ***all repairs*** done at the house and site, such as: replacing the heating or air-conditioning systems; upgrading the electrical system; replacing the roof shingles; finishing a basement or attic; putting an addition on a house; adding a deck or a swimming pool; installing or updating a bathroom or kitchen; and anything else other than minor maintenance like painting. The reason you have to obtain permits and approvals for this repair work is that the local building department inspectors have to check the work out. They have to make sure the work is done properly and safely.

Local building inspectors are needed to ensure that all construction and repair work at least meets the minimum building codes in that town. By meeting the building code standards, it will help protect the occupants of the house from unsafe conditions. For example, let's say an electrician installs new branch wires and outlets in a remodeled bath or kitchen. How do you know the wires and outlets are properly installed? The answer is - you don't!! Once the walls are sealed up there's no way for the house occupants to see any loose or exposed wires. Unsafe electrical conditions could lead to a fire or someone getting electrocuted. This is why the local building inspector has to sign-off on repair work in stages. In most areas, the inspector will view the contractor's work before it's sealed up with a finished covering, such as sheetrock, flooring, etc. Then the building inspector will give the OK to seal up the work. A final inspection is conducted when the repair job is completed. It's similar to new house construction. The building inspector goes out to view the work in different stages during the construction process. Each inspection must receive an approval before further construction can continue. This process allows the inspector to sign-off on work that will be covered up when completed.

There is a second reason why the local municipality wants you to file for permits and approvals for all repair work. When you put an addition on a house, add a deck, a pool, or upgrade the house, you're then increasing the property's market value. As a result, the tax assessor may want to raise your property taxes because now the house is worth more money.

# The Sad Truth

I was doing an appraisal once, and a woman at town hall told me a few tragic war stories. They emphasize the importance of obtaining all permits and final approvals for repair work. She said that there had been two recent occasions with insurance agents that came by her office. These agents were checking the records on two houses in that town. One insurance company was involved in a lawsuit filed by a contractor against a homeowner. This contractor was doing some repair work in the attic area of a house. There had been work done a few years earlier by another contractor in this attic area. Well, the second contractor was working and **he fell through the ceiling!** This contractor sued the homeowner for millions of dollars. The basis of the lawsuit was that the prior repairs did not have a permit and final approval from the town building inspector for the work done.

The other insurance agent that came into this woman's office at town hall was also handling a lawsuit for millions of dollars. She told me that a child was swimming in someone's pool along with the homeowner's children. Unfortunately, something shot out of the pool water filter device and hit this boy in the eye. **The boy is now blind in one eye!** His family sued the homeowner because they didn't have a *final* plumbing inspection approval for the pool equipment which included the pool water filter.

An attorney gave one of my clients another very good reason why it's imperative to get all final permits and approvals. He said that someone could get hurt on your property due to repairs or upgrading that wasn't done properly or safely. If this happens and you don't have permits and approvals for the work, you could be sued. We've already seen this in the stories I just mentioned. **However, to make matters even worse, your insurance company may try to refuse paying the claim if you lose in court. The insurance company may tell you that it's your negligence for not making sure that all valid permits and approvals had been obtained!** You certainly don't want to get stuck in a position like that. Especially, when someone gets injured.

# Check Town Hall... Or Else

Years ago the records at local municipalities were all kept on paper and in file cabinets so it was a lot more work to find what you needed. Now everything is in computer databases which greatly simplifies checking the records on a property. **Don't** just take it for granted that the permits and approvals have been obtained for any work performed. Many people will add to the original construction or make repairs without filing for permits. They might do the work themselves or else they hire a contractor who doesn't know what he's doing, or else he's too lazy, and he won't file any permits for the work. Recommend to the client that he/she verify this information and you must check it out as well. If it's true and all permits and approvals have been obtained, then great, everyone's happy. But if it's not true, then you don't want to get stuck holding the bag for the problems that will come up later.

> *Don't take it for granted that the permits have been obtained for any work performed. Many people will add to the original construction or make repairs without filing for permits.*

**Don't let any Realtors, sellers, or other third parties talk you or your client out of verifying this information!** Almost always a seller or Realtor will say:
*"Oh, yes they have all the permits for that work,"* or *"Oh, you don't need to file a permit for that in this area,"* or *"Yes, we do have a C of O,"* or *"The asbestos was removed by a licensed EPA contractor."*

> *Don't let any Realtors or other third parties talk you or your client out of verifying this information at town hall.*

**Verify everything they say by looking at the written documentation with your own two eyes and tell the client to do the same!!!!** If the third party's information is wrong, then you and your client will end up paying the price for it. Just because someone has a Certificate of Occupancy it doesn't mean that the building department has approved all of the work done at the site. A *C of O* is issued when the house is built and it's generally only used to state the legal occupancy of the house. That's why it's called a *Certificate of Occupancy*. Even if a C of O is required for any repairs done at the site, this **does not** mean that the contractor or the homeowner had the C of O updated to include the repairs that were done. **If town hall isn't notified that the work is being done, then the C of O doesn't magically get updated on its own!**

> *Even if a C of O is required for any repairs done at the site, this **does not** mean that the contractor or the homeowner had the C of O updated to include the repairs that were done. **If town hall isn't notified the work is being done, then the C of O doesn't magically get updated on its own!***

In some areas, a new C of O is not issued when repairs or upgrading is done at the subject property. These areas will just require that the homeowner obtain permits and approvals from the town building and zoning departments. So don't make the client think that because there's a C of O, there are no violations or no missing permits and approvals.

# You Have The Right To...

**You must go down to town hall personally to check _ALL_ records pertaining to the subject property!** This will enable you to verify all information in the real estate listing and any other data sources. You and the client can also confirm any other information that has been represented about the house. **If you or the client send a third party to town hall to check the records, and they miss something, it's the client's neck and money that's on the line!** So go and check the records yourself. Because if it's your mistake for not verifying certain information, then the client may want you to reimburse them for any expenses they incur.

Your client has a **right** to know everything about the subject property. Often a Realtor, or other third party to the transaction will say, _"Oh, you don't need to check the town hall records. The attorney, appraiser and the title company all take care of that for you."_ DON'T BELIEVE THAT FOR A MINUTE!!!! If you or your client leave the town hall records check to someone else, then you'll both probably learn the hard way that important items are often missed. I went through this experience myself when my brother and I were selling one of our rental properties. The buyer was getting a FHA mortgage loan. With these loans, the lender requires a more extensive search into the property records than the search done for a conventional mortgage loan. This search turned up a list of building violations and missing permits that were from a **prior owner** of the property. Even though the violations were not caused by my brother and I, we still were held responsible for them. **The reason for this is that the building department doesn't care who owns the house. All they care about, is that the property is safe and everything adheres to the local building codes.**

After these problems surfaced, my attorney contacted the title company that we had paid for the title insurance policy and the title records search. Our title company said that there is a clause in just about all title policies dealing with this type of situation. The clause states that the title company **is not responsible** for any building, zoning or other violations. A title company is only concerned with the _ownership interest_ in the subject property. Ownership interest is what is stated in the deed for the property. This has _absolutely nothing_ to do with building permits, zoning, taxes, and many other aspects at town hall. As a result, we spent thousands of dollars and delayed the closing for months, in order to resolve these old violations created by a prior owner. This experience should put an end to any third parties trying to convince your clients that the attorney, appraiser, and title company check town hall thoroughly. That is, unless the appraiser is an **_"A to Z Appraiser."_**

I've done foreclosure appraisals for banks, where the banks had the houses re-appraised after they took back the titles through foreclosure proceedings. During my appraisals, I turned up problems in the deeds that weren't identified when the banks originally loaned the mortgage money. So now the banks had to spend the time and money to correct mistakes created by the prior owners of these properties. This situation could happen to you and your clients if you don't follow my advice.

Here's some history trivia I found on several web sites about property titles and legal ownership of real estate:
_**Did you know that Abraham Lincoln's family lost their homes several times because of "cloudy" title?**_
On June 12, 1806, Thomas Lincoln married Nancy Hanks. (Little is known about Abe Lincoln's mother except that she came from a very poor Virginia family. She was completely illiterate and signed her name with an X.) After their marriage the Lincolns moved from a farm on Mill Creek in Hardin County, Kentucky, to nearby Elizabethtown. There Thomas Lincoln earned his living as a carpenter and handyman. In 1807 a daughter, Sarah, was born. In December 1808 the Lincolns moved to a 141-hectare (348-acre) farm on the south fork of Nolin Creek near what is now Hodgenville, Kentucky. On February 12, 1809, in a log cabin that Thomas Lincoln had built, a son, Abraham, was born. Later the Lincolns had a second son who died in infancy. When Abraham Lincoln was two, the family moved to another farm on nearby Knob Creek. Life was lonely and hard. There was little time for play. Most of the day was spent hunting, farming, fishing, and doing chores. Land titles in Kentucky were confusing and often subject to dispute. Thomas Lincoln **lost his title** to the Mill Creek farm, and his claims to **both** the Nolin Creek and Knob Creek tracts were challenged in court. In 1816, therefore, the Lincolns decided to move to Indiana, where the land was surveyed and sold by the federal government. In the winter of 1816 the Lincolns took their meager possessions, ferried across the Ohio River, and settled near Pigeon Creek, close to what is now Gentryville, Indiana.

Even **Daniel Boone**, the first pioneer of Kentucky wilderness, lost every inch of his once vast landholdings because he had _"the wrong kind of title papers."_ It was the anxiety and outright losses of the Lincolns and other hardworking Americans that gave rise to today's title insurance industry. The first land title insurance company was founded in Philadelphia in 1876. Just a few years later in 1889, the firm that was to become _First American Title Insurance Company_ was established to protect buyers against the hidden hazards of real estate ownership: forgeries; faulty surveys; hidden liens; conveyances by a minor or mentally incompetent person; the false representation of a married person as being single; and many other title defects. Even the most complete search of records may not reveal all the defects in a real estate title.

# Is The Listing Accurate?

Let me give you another newsflash so I make this point very clear about checking all records at the town hall. Many people think the information in a real estate listing is always accurate. THAT'S NONSENSE!!!! If you read the bottom of all real estate listings and other data sources, you'll see a statement such as, *"Data Is Believed Accurate But Not Warranted."* Do you know what that means? Well, I'll tell you anyway. It's a caveat which means that if the information in the real estate listing or data source is wrong, then you cannot hold the listing Realtor or data company accountable for the error. In most areas, Realtors are not required to check the records at town hall to verify the information that the seller tells them to fill out a real estate listing. On a daily basis I see cases where a real estate listing states: the subject property has a 200 amp electrical system, when it only had 100 amps; or the house was connected to the city sewer system, when it actually had a septic system; or the size of the lot was one acre, when it was less than one acre; or the square footage and age of the house was incorrect on the real estate listing, etc.

> *Let me give you another newsflash to make it clear about checking all records at the town hall. Many people think that the information in a real estate listing is always accurate. THAT'S NONSENSE!!!!*

So, remember to tell your clients **not to rely on the information found in real estate listings!** If there is a *"know-it-all"* Realtor at the site they're probably going to tell your client that you're wrong. The Realtor will say that their real estate listing is 100% accurate. **If any Realtors dispute the advice you give to your clients, then just tell that Realtor or other third party to put their money where their mouth is!** Let me explain this since it's a great way to silence an immoral, greedy, or ignorant Realtor or other third party: If any Realtors dispute the advice you give to your clients, **then just tell them to write a signed statement that they want to guarantee to your client that if the Realtor or other third party are wrong, then THEY will pay the bill – not your client!** Just about every time I get a Realtor who earns a commission on the sale disputing what I say, I prove them wrong. Once you respond confidently and firmly (but not rudely) to know-it-all Realtors, it usually shuts them up for the rest of the inspection or appraisal. I can't even count the number of times that I've had a know-it-all Realtor tell my clients and I, *"My real estate listing is 100% correct, I checked it myself."* Before the inspection or appraisal is over, I always seem to find something in the listing that's inaccurate. When this happens, these Realtors never seem to admit that they were wrong. Someone needs to inform ignorant Realtors that maybe they don't know as much about real estate as they think they do. We'll talk more about this later.

> *If any Realtors dispute the advice you give to your clients, then just tell that Realtor or other third party to put their money where their mouth is! Just tell them to write a signed statement that they want to guarantee to your client that if the Realtor or other third party are wrong, then THEY will pay the bill – not your client!*

Realtors *(some of them)* and other data source employees don't intentionally put inaccurate information into a listing sheet. They generally rely on the seller to provide the information, or else the Realtor may think that they know what they're doing. The seller or the Realtor may unintentionally make a mistake. So it's not that they're trying to hide the truth from potential buyers. It's just that someone can make a mistake with the data. That's why all records need to be checked at town hall. This will help prevent incorrect information from going unnoticed.

At town hall the records will show: the amount of taxes on the house, the square footage and age of the house, the acreage of the site, if there are any building violations, if there are any easements or encroachments, if there are problems with the title and deed of the property, and a lot more. All of this information is very valuable to you and the client. Most people don't even realize how much information is open for the public to view at their local town hall records department. If you're thorough in your trip to town hall and you end up finding something out that's important, then you'll look like a hero. Your client will thank you for finding the important information.

## A Catch 22 Position

In just about any house you go into, you can find some upgrading or repairs that have been done which require permits and approvals. You'll also find that there are missing permits and approvals for some of this work in almost *every* house you go into! It's very common because there are very few homeowners who know that permits and final approvals are needed for all repair work done in a house. Many contractors don't bother with the permits, unless the homeowner insists on seeing them upon completion of the job. When you or your client find missing permits, just tell the client it's a common problem. Don't make the client think this is the *only* house without all valid permits and approvals. Just tell them to find out what is required to obtain the final approvals from the town for the work done.

> *You'll also find that there are missing permits and approvals for some of this work in almost every house you go into! It's very common because there are very few homeowners who know that permits and final approvals are needed for all work done.*

Sometimes your clients will ask you, *"What will happen if I do go to town hall to check about valid permits and approvals for the finished basement or attic, the addition, deck, pool, extra apartment, etc. and they aren't on file in the building department."* Well, if you or your client tell the building inspector that you checked for the permits and approvals and you can't find them, then you might raise a red flag in his mind. This could lead to the building inspector going to the subject property. The building inspector could file a building code violation against the property for the work done. A violation could be issued because there are no permits on file. Usually the only way to get building violations removed is to have the work pass the local building code standards. What will happen is the building inspector will tell the homeowner that if the work doesn't meet the local building code standards, then they must hire a licensed contractor to make the necessary repairs. Repairs will be needed to bring the work up to meet the minimum standards before a valid permit and approval can be obtained and the violation will be removed.

**You can run into serious problems in certain situations when permits and approvals need to be obtained <u>after</u> the work has already been done.** One case is when the repair work was not permitted by the building or zoning codes. For example, the local codes may not allow the homeowner to finish a basement or attic to use as livable space, build a small addition or garage, etc. When this occurs, the only option is to remove all of the work done. The building inspector can't approve something that is against the law of the town! I've had clients that took my advice and checked town hall prior to closing. They found garages that were built too close to the neighbors' property line; pools that were not allowed on the site; additions and enclosed porches that had to be dismantled; finished basements and attics that were against the zoning and fire codes, etc. None of these problem conditions could be approved without getting zoning variances and changes made to the building and fire codes. In order to sell these houses, the sellers had to dismantle all the repair work done to the house and site. That can turn into a nightmare and take a lot of time, money and aggravation to accomplish.

A more common problem when permits need to be obtained after the work has already been done occurs **when the work is not accessible to view.** For example, if there has been some electrical wiring, plumbing or foundation repairs. Usually this type of work will be sealed up after the repairs are completed. The building inspector can't sign-off on something that he can't see! As a result, the only way to get the permits and final approvals will be to open up the walls, floors, ceilings, etc so the inspector can view the repairs. I've had this situation come up on many occasions when I notified my clients about missing permits. This also can turn into a nightmare.

**So it can be a *Catch 22* for the client.** If they don't raise a red flag at the building department, then the missing permits might not create a problem for the closing when the client **purchases** the property. However, if your client doesn't clear up this matter prior to buying the house, then it might come up when he goes to **renovate, refinance or sell** the house down the road. Then your client will be stuck wasting his own time and money fixing a problem that someone else had created! I wouldn't take the chance if I were buying the house. From your standpoint as the appraiser, you're **required** to mention the building code violations that you know about in your written report. It's true that only an inspector from the local town hall can do a building code inspection. However, you still need to inquire about any known violations. You also must take any violations into consideration when estimating market value because it will have a negative affect on the purchase price offered by a typical buyer. So whether the client clears up the problem isn't your concern. However, you must mention it in your report to CYA.

# *People Who Have No Right To Remain Silent*

Sometimes you'll find that the seller, the Realtor, or another third party won't want to answer any preinspection questions. Or a dishonest Realtor will tell the seller not to be home for the appraisal appointment so they don't get involved in the appraisal process. They just say something like, *"I've been selling real estate for 10 years now and I've never seen it done this way before by asking the owner all these questions."* **They are talking out of ignorance!** The reason they've never seen it done this way is that they've never seen a good, thorough and knowledgeable real estate appraiser before!!!

> *The Realtors may say, "I've been selling real estate for 10 years now and I've never seen it done this way before by asking the owner all these questions." They are talking out of ignorance!*

Also, some people rationalize their actions to a point where it just blows my mind. They are intentionally dishonest and lie to you by **not** saying anything and by **not** being home to answer your questions. I have done many inspections and appraisals where I encountered Realtors, sellers, and other third parties who **intentionally** tried to hide something from my client and any other potential buyers. Once I was checking the lower level of a house that was located on the side of a hill. In one corner there were some plywood boards leaning up against the foundation wall. I moved the boards to see what was behind them and I found **serious structural cracks in the foundation wall.** I was really angry about the seller's attempt to hide this. The house was located on a hill and with a serious structural crack like that, it could have cost someone their life!! What <u>didn't</u> surprise me is that I later learned the listing Realtor <u>knew</u> about the structural crack but, *as usual,* <u>didn't</u> tell any potential buyers about it. If you're in this business long enough, *(and sometimes that only needs to be about a year),* you'll get used to seeing how some Realtors will do *anything* to earn a sales commission.

Sellers and Realtors often don't tell home buyers about known problems with a house. They just keep quiet and hope the buyer's home inspector or appraiser don't detect the problems. They think it's a game of "hide and seek". **Hide** the known problems and it's the home inspector and/or appraiser's job to **seek** out and find them. *Wrong – it doesn't work like that!* That's not a nice game of hide and seek like your kids play. That's called **FRAUD** and you can go to jail for it!! I'll give you a few more examples that I've experienced. One was a client I had that was buying a house with an old, forced hot air heating system. A thin layer of asbestos insulation was on the air ducts and in the lining of the furnace. **This creates a serious health hazard because the asbestos fibers are blown throughout the entire house.** The dishonest Realtor **never mentioned a word** to my clients about this asbestos problem. As soon as I saw the asbestos during the inspection, I told the client about this health hazard. Suddenly the Realtor jumps into the conversation and says, *"The owner already has found a contractor to remove the*

*asbestos from the air ducts so the client doesn't need to worry about it."* When I asked the Realtor if the owner was going to have the asbestos in the livable rooms removed, she said, *"there was no need to do that."* **It's so typical that the Realtor would say there's no need to do that. After all, the dishonest Realtor isn't going to be living in that house and breathing those asbestos fibers!**

I did an inspection once and found <u>severe</u> rot and powder post beetle damage to the main girder beam and floor joists of a house. My awl went right through the main girder and floor joists while I was probing the beams in the crawl space. This beam, along with many of the floor joists, had to be replaced. Replacing a main girder beam is not easy since the house has to be lifted up with jacks to replace the beam. Moreover, on the exterior of the house I found most of the siding had buckled and had to be replaced. This siding damage was from water problems due to the lack of a roof overhang (soffit, fascia and eaves) on the house which was a design by some architect who thought it would be "unique" and "set the house apart". *(Yeah, this "unique" design certainly "set the house apart". It was the only house around with all the siding destroyed from water drainage off the roof!).* My client had to spend a lot of time and money on the home inspection and in getting repair estimates. **Afterwards, my client found out that the seller and the Realtor had <u>known</u> about these problems *BEFORE* the home inspection.** This immoral stunt is done all the time by dishonest Realtors and sellers. Another buyer had backed out of a prior offer on this house because these problems were detected by their home inspector. Had the dishonest Realtor and seller told my client the TRUTH, and not tried to hide the truth from him/her, then my client, along with all other potential buyers, could have gotten repair estimates from contractors *first*, and then decided if they wanted to continue with the deal. At that point, my client could have hired me to inspect the house and find any additional problem conditions that were not disclosed up-front to him/her and other potential buyers by the Realtor and seller. *(I think once I saw in a dictionary this definition listed for the <u>TRUTH</u> - Something dishonest Realtors have a very, very difficult time dealing with, so they avoid it like the plague!)*

I have done many inspections where I would find personal items intentionally placed by a third party to cover termite and water damage. Luckily I detected these problems so my clients didn't get hit with any surprises after they moved into the houses. However, since the third party never told me or my client about these problems and left it up to us to find them on our own with their little game of "hide and seek", then what is that called? **Dishonest, Immoral, and Fraud!!** Plain and simple.

Let's say the appraiser and the client didn't happen to notice a problem condition that a third party to the deal knew existed but never told them about. How can that third party morally justify their actions by not mentioning the problem condition to the appraiser and/or the client? You can call it a *business negotiating decision by the third party;* you can call it a *mistake that is the fault of the buyer's appraiser and/or home inspector;* you can blame the *buyer for not hiring a more thorough appraiser and/or home inspector;* or you can call it *good or bad luck*. But no matter what you call it, and I don't care how you rationalize it, it **has to** be called one thing - *DISHONEST!* The third party person simply is not telling someone something they know that person should and would want to know about. Let alone the fact that they are **legally required to disclose** all known defects - unless they want to commit **fraud!** Whatever happened to the golden rule in today's world? *"Do onto others as you would want others to do onto you."* People should ask themselves: *If I were buying this house, would I want the seller to tell me about this problem?*

I'm using this example to make you realize there are dishonest and ignorant people out there that rationalize their unethical actions, which you probable already know. However, often people get too emotionally involved in the decision to buy or sell their home and this clouds their judgment. When that happens, they are more susceptible to being scammed or cheated by "smooth talking" salespeople and third parties in the deal. Often the same person who refuses to answer your questions, or doesn't tell you about a problem they know you should be informed about, is the same guy that brags how he goes to church every Sunday because he's such a good, ethical person in society.  BALONEY!! They can't hide behind that excuse.

There is something that you might consider when you're dealing with a dishonest person like that. You might want to inform them that if something comes up after your client buys the house that they knew about, then your client can sue the seller, the Realtor, and other third parties. **That's because you *cannot* intentionally hide a problem from anyone, whether you're the buyer or the seller.** Just about all houses are sold in *"As Is"* condition. This doesn't mean that the seller has a *license to steal,* nor does it mean that the seller can commit *fraud.* A lot of people believe that an "As Is" sale means that the Realtors and sellers don't have to tell anyone about known problem conditions at the property. That's totally false! The old theory of "buyer beware" is no longer valid. When a house is sold in "As Is" condition, it means that the seller is *required* **to disclose all known defects** to the buyer and the buyer agrees to accept the house with those known problems. The seller doesn't have to be a home inspector, however, they do have to inform you about the problems they know about and they cannot hide them from you.

Realtors and some other third parties have a *fiduciary responsibility* to lay all the cards out on the table for the client, whether it is the buyer or the seller. **They are required to disclose to the buyer and the seller any problem conditions that they know about.** Since they're professionals in the real estate business, they are held to a higher standard than the public. As a result, they can be found liable for something they knew about, **or that they should have known about,** if they did not inform the buyer or seller about the problem condition.

## Talk To The Neighbors

You can find out an awful lot about a house and the area it's located in by talking to the neighbors who live next to the subject property. I try to do this whenever I have the opportunity and I always encourage my clients to talk to the neighbors themselves. The people who live near the subject property usually have been there for at least a few years. They can tell you the good and bad points of the area. The best part about their responses to your questions is that they have no incentive to lie to you or your client! They're not involved financially in the sale of the subject property, and as a result, you'll get an unbiased second opinion for free!

> *You can find out an awful lot about a house and the area it's located in just by talking to the neighbors who live next to the subject property.*

Obviously, if the neighbor is a relative or close friend of the seller then their responses may be biased to help "move the deal along." But that's why you and your client should talk to several neighbors in the area and not just one of them. Don't feel like you're being rude or imposing on the neighbors either. You'll be amazed at how people like to talk to someone who's truly interested in listening to what they have to say. It gives people a feeling of importance and makes them feel like they're doing someone else a big favor. Especially, if the person they're helping will be a future next door neighbor.

Some questions that you and your client's can ask the neighbors are:

1   Do you ever have any water problems in your house? *(This is a **great** question to ask. If the subject property gets water from a high groundwater table, then most of the houses in the area may have the same problem unless they're located on higher ground.)*

2   Does the local municipality raise property and/or school taxes often?

3   Is it a quiet area or are there any noise problems?

4   How are the schools and public transportation?

5   *(If the house is located on a Private street)*, What are the rights and responsibilities of the homeowners to use and maintain the street?  What are the fees for the street maintenance, paving, snow plowing etc.?

6   Is there anything about the area that you would find helpful to know if you were buying this house?

*So you don't believe me that talking to the neighbors is helpful?*  Well, I'll tell you another war story and then maybe you'll change your mind. I tell all my clients to speak to the neighbors before they buy a house. This will enable them to find out anything interesting about water problems, noise problems, etc. One client of mine was buying a house with a septic system on the site. He took my advice and asked a few of the neighbors about water problems and septic problems in the area. Well, he was awfully surprised to find out that the area had a high groundwater table. **This not only created water problems in their basements during heavy rains, but it also forced them all to have their septic systems replaced!!** New septic tanks were needed due to the excessive water in the ground over the years. This client ended up having *a lot* more to calculate into his purchase price after finding out this information. He certainly was grateful to me for giving him that advice. So learn a lesson from this and recommend that **all** of your clients talk to the neighbors. They might end up finding out something very helpful and you'll end up looking like a hero for it.

# Be Totally Objective - Part 1

**Don't tell the client to buy or not to buy the house for any reason!!!!** This is one point that really bothers Realtors and I have to side with them on this one. Your job as an appraiser is to tell the client the estimated market value of the house *only!!* I'll repeat my statement again so you get it straight. Don't tell the client to buy or not to buy the house for any reason!

> *The condition of the house does not make it a good deal or a bad deal. Price is the ONLY factor on whether it's a good deal or not!*

If the house is in poor condition just include the repair estimates and the negative affect on the market value in your appraisal report. The condition of a house does not make it a good deal or a bad deal. **Price is the *ONLY* factor on whether it's a good deal or not!** Here's why:

◊ I've seen people buy houses in great condition but they were paying too high a purchase price for the house. Therefore it's a bad deal because they were paying much more than the market value price of the house.

◊ At the same time, I've seen people buy houses that are in terrible condition that need a lot of work. However, they were getting a great deal because they were buying the house well below market value. If you added up all the repairs and upgrading costs, and then added it to the purchase price, they could sell the house for much more than they paid for it after renovations.

The point is that you have no right telling the client whether or not to buy the house. You're hired to only estimate the market value - and that's what your training and expertise are focused on. As a result, **it's none of your business** if your client decides to buy a house that you don't like or that you wouldn't buy for any reason. After you notify the client of the market value of the property, it's totally up to the client how much, if anything, they want to pay for the property. After you

explain the valuation analysis in your appraisal report, it's none of your business even if they want to pay too much for the property. Perhaps there's an amenity value for them and that's why the client doesn't mind paying a high price?

You may not like the house for several different reasons: perhaps it's too old for your tastes; or it's a Cape Cod style and you only like Colonial style homes; or you feel that there's too much renovation work needed on and in the house; or it's not in a good area of town that you would want to live in, etc. The point I'm making is that all of these are your own *subjective* judgments and opinions! You have to be totally *objective* when you're appraising a house. Even though you might not want to buy that house or condo, maybe your client has different tastes and likes than you do. Also, maybe the client can't afford to buy a house in great condition or in a good section of town.

I've inspected houses that when I would write down the style of the house, such as Ranch, Cape Cod, Colonial, Tudor, etc. that I would be tempted to write down *"hideous"* because the house was so dreadful looking. However, I'm not paid to tell the client whether I would live in the house. So I keep my subjective comments and opinions to myself.

# Be Totally Objective - Part 2

**Don't ever tell any lender to give a loan or not to give a loan on a property!!!!** This situation may come up if you do appraisal and/or inspection work for a bank. A mortgage lender may ask you if they should make a loan, or you may throw in your two cents on your own. I'll repeat it again so you don't forget it. Don't ever tell any lender to give a loan or not to give a loan on a property!

Every once in a while I hear an appraiser or inspector saying that they recommended that the lender approve or not approve someone's mortgage loan. That blows my mind when they do that! Your job as an appraiser is to **only** interpret the market data that you have obtained as it relates to the subject property. You don't include your own **subjective** opinions or biases.

As an appraiser, you know **nothing** about the potential borrower's income, personal debts, past credit history, possible court judgments and lawsuits against them, total monthly living expenses, job stability, etc. Only the borrower and the lender know that type of information. So I don't care how nice the house you're appraising is; or how bad the condition of the house is; or what type of area it's located in; or whatever else you find out about it during your field work. And I don't care if it's the nicest house you've ever seen or the worst house you've ever seen. If you tell the lender to make the loan just because the house is selling for a great price and it's in excellent condition, **then you better be willing to put your money where your mouth is!** Because what happens if that guy borrows the money and then the house is destroyed due to a lack of maintenance and then he stops making his loan payments on the mortgage. *(I've seen this happen many, many times with foreclosure appraisals and inspections I've done for banks).* The bank is going to get stuck holding the bag for the loan. The bank will end up losing money on the foreclosure sale, even though you told them what a great loan they'd be making!

It's the same scenario if you stick your nose somewhere it shouldn't be by telling the lender <u>not</u> to make the loan. I don't care if it's the worst house you've ever seen or if it's in the worst section of town and you would <u>*never*</u> buy it. How do you know that the guy buying that house isn't some multimillionaire? What if he's going to renovate that house and donate it to a poor family or to a local charity? If the lender listened to you, then he wouldn't make the loan. *(Oh yes, I forgot you have a crystal ball to read the future. You can see that this loan will go sour for the lender!)*

> *You can put all of the objective comments you want in the appraisal report. But just keep your subjective opinions and your nose out of the lender's and the borrower's business.*

**Don't take any of this personally. It's not meant to insult you.** It's just meant to open your eyes to some of the realities of the real estate business. The point I'm trying to make is that you must estimate market value based upon the data you obtain and everything that affects the value of the subject property. You can put all of the **objective** comments you want in the appraisal report. But just keep your **subjective** opinions and your nose out of the lender's and the borrower's business. You're not hired to be a nosy "busy body." There are already <u>far too many</u> busy body, know-it-all Realtors and other third parties in the real estate business. You're hired to estimate market value ONLY! There are many times that I see people talk out of ignorance by thinking that they're a know-it-all. And I'm not being a hypocrite myself because I certainly don't think I have all of the answers.

## *Negotiating Realities To Assist Your Client*

Another point that I agree with Realtors on is the fact that **it's none of your business if the client does or does not want to negotiate with the seller after your appraisal!** You have <u>no</u> right sticking your nose into anything other than the appraisal itself. If the client asks you to help him out further with some negotiations, then you can provide this service if you would like. It's up to you. But let the client ask for your help, don't volunteer it.

Sometimes your client will ask you for your advice. They may want to know if any repairs or differences between the purchase price and the value estimate of your appraisal report should be negotiated with, or paid for by the seller. Tell them that it all depends on the flexibility of the seller. Some people

are negotiable and some aren't. However, if he asks the seller, there are only two answers he can get, and one of those is great!

It's similar to finding termite damage in a house. In many states the seller of the house is **required** by law to pay for the removal of any termites found on the property. However, the seller doesn't have to sell you the house if he doesn't want to. He can just say, *"Fine I'll pay for the termite treatment but I'm going to raise the sales price by the same amount".* The point is, just tell the client that whether or not something is negotiable will always depend on the flexibility of the seller.

> *The seller is more likely to hire the guy who's the cheapest to save himself a few bucks. After all, he's selling the house and he's not going to have to live with any poor quality repairs in the home.*

However, there is a **very important** concept that you want to tell your client about negotiating repairs or other factors that come up during your appraisal. Most of the time, if the seller is flexible, the seller will agree to have the repairs done at his own expense. You want to inform your client that if the seller has the repairs fixed at his expense, then he's probably going to get several estimates. Which contractor do you think the seller is going to hire: The guy who does high quality work at a high price or **the guy who does low quality work at a low price?** I'd say the seller is more likely to hire the guy who's the cheapest to save himself a few bucks. After all, he's selling the house and he's not going to have to live with any poor quality repairs in the home. I think your client might agree with that conclusion as well. So you should inform your client about this possibility.

Also, if the seller hires the contractor and pays him with his own check, then **that contractor is responsible to the seller and not to your client.** Therefore, if the contractor does poor quality work and your client buys the house and finds problems with the repair work done, then your client has no legal recourse. That contractor was *hired and paid* by the <u>*seller*</u> of the house and not by your client. Therefore, that contractor is generally only liable to the seller for his work. What are your client's chances of getting the seller to come back from his new home to your area to file a complaint and demand compensation against that contractor for poor quality work?  ZERO!!!!  Now, I'm not an attorney so you have to check this and all other legal aspects I'm telling you about with your own legal counsel. But the point I'm making is pretty clear. Just inform the client of these ideas and let the client decide what action they want to take. You'll find that this type of information is very helpful to your clients and you'll look like a hero when you open their eyes to it.

When hiring repair contractors you need to notify your client about some basic concepts. In most areas, contractors must be licensed and insured to do any repair work. The local town hall could verify this information. Insurance coverage should be for the general contractor plus any subcontractors they hire to assist them. For large construction jobs, the client should see if the contractor is bonded. *Bonding* means that the contractor can insure the quality of their work and that the job will be completed on time. A bonded contractor will have to place a bond before they start the job for it to be valid. For small construction jobs, bonding may be too much to ask from a contractor.

The client should check with the local Better Business Bureau and other organizations to determine if the contractor is reputable. The contractor should provide references of former clients they have done work for. This can help the client to find out about the contractors track record. However, if the contractor does provide your client with names, he's going to make sure he doesn't give them phone numbers of unhappy customers! This is where the client's own judgment will come into play in deciding if a contractor is reputable.

All aspects of agreements with contractors should be clearly stated in the written price estimate. **The client should have a time limit and a price cap on the repair work. This will prevent the contractor from "dragging their feet" to complete the job. A price cap will prevent cost overruns and excess fees added after the work has begun.** A statement should be put in the estimate that the contractor will provide the homeowner with all permits and final approvals from town hall. Any warranties for the repair work should be in writing. If the seller has hired contractors to make repairs, the client needs to speak with them about warranties. The client should find out how long the warranties are in effect and if they are transferable to the new owners.

There's another aspect that you need to inform your client about regarding negotiating with the seller. That is there will be times when some Realtors or other third parties will tell your client, *"Oh, there's no way the seller is going to reduce his price. He's already giving the house away and he has two backup offers waiting if you don't buy the house now."* HORSE MANURE!!!! I've heard that line used 100,000 times, not only while doing home inspections and appraisals, but also when buying my own rental properties. I've seen my own offers accepted by sellers that some know-it-all Realtor told me would never be accepted. I've also seen many clients get offers accepted when a Realtor or other third party told them the seller would never accept it.

So don't let yourself or your client be intimidated by anyone. It's your client's money and future, **he/she** has to be the one to decide how much he/she wants to pay for a house. Don't you or any third party make the decision for them. Any Realtors involved in the transaction have a *fiduciary responsibility* to the buyer or the seller. This means that they are **required to present any and all purchase offers from all potential buyers to the seller that they know about.** No matter how low or ridiculous the offer might seem, it still has to be presented to the seller. It doesn't matter if someone offers the seller less than 1/2 the asking price. They have to present the offer to give the seller the opportunity to accept it or reject it.

# Don't Let Your Client Be Pressured

**Tell the client not to be pressured or rushed into *any* decisions by the imaginary backup offers on the subject property.** Some Realtors, sellers, or other third parties want your client to believe that imaginary backup offers really exist. Also, tell your client not to become too emotionally involved in any deal. They should look at the property as though it were a typical business decision. They should put their personal emotions aside because they're spending a fortune on this financial investment. You have to make the client realize that they're not buying a **_CAR_** they're buying a **_HOUSE!!_** There's a big difference between the two. One is a normal expense everyone has to incur occasionally. The other is the biggest financial decision most people will ever make.

> *They should put their personal emotions aside because they're spending a fortune on this financial investment. You have to make the client realize that they're not buying a CAR, they're buying a HOUSE!!*

Harry Helmsley, who was clearly a brilliant real estate investor, was quoted as saying, *"The minute you fall in love with a building you're in trouble."* Meaning, that **if you get too emotionally attached to a property, you forget to look at it like a business decision. When this happens, you often end up paying too much for the property.** You have to be objective all the time and be able to make the hard decisions and walk away from a deal at any time.

Since I do home inspections, appraisals, and have owned rental properties myself, I see this happen to potential home buyers all the time. Many people get too emotional about buying a house and they only look at the cosmetic appeal of the house or the location it's in. You have to take a step back and look at the purchase as though it was strictly a business decision. **Too often people get convinced that if they don't make a high-priced offer on the house right away, then another buyer will come along and steal it right from under them.** Sure, there's a potential that if the house really is a good deal then someone else will come along and buy it sooner than you will. But this happens a lot less often than most people believe, or are led to believe by some Realtors involved in the transaction.

Often a Realtor or seller will rush a potential home buyer into making an offer and/or signing contracts on a home sooner than they should. They tend to put the "fear of God" into the home buyer. They tell the buyer, *"You have to make a high offer and sign the contracts right away. If you don't, someone else will buy it because there's a backup purchase offer on this house."* There are a million ways that a real estate deal can be killed. Many of those so-called "backup offers" are either imaginary or will fall through. Some reasons real estate deals fall through are: the seller and buyer don't agree on a final price and terms; the buyer or seller gets *"cold feet,"*; problems come up during the home inspection and/or appraisal; the mortgage loan is denied; etc. I have personally seen an awful lot of real estate deals fall through due to any number of reasons.

I had an excellent real estate attorney, named Walter Kehm, that handled all of my legal work when I first started buying rental properties. He used to say that *"Real estate deals are like a trolley car, if you let one go there will be another one coming by in 20 minutes."* I have found this statement to be very true from my own experiences in the real estate business. Not only in my own investments, but in the home inspection and appraisal experience I have had with my clients as well.

Many times I've had clients who decided not to purchase a home because of the problems that were found during the home inspection and/or appraisal. The seller's of these houses would not renegotiate with the buyer, and as a result, the deal never went through. In every one of these cases, the client continued to look at other houses which were for sale. Within a few months, these clients eventually found a nicer home at a better price than the deal they walked away from. They had benefited by waiting to find the best deal that they could, rather than rushing to purchase the first *decent* house they could find. So learn a lesson from this and don't let yourself or any of your clients be rushed into buying a house. A home is the biggest investment most people will make, so it's prudent that they take their time and think it through completely.

Also, some sellers and third parties will just wait until they find a buyer that hires an appraiser and/or home inspector that isn't as good, honest and thorough as you are. When this happens then that buyer will be going into the deal with their eyes **closed**. You want your client to go into the deal with their eyes **open**. Just because someone else might come along and pay too much for the house, doesn't mean that your client should beat them to it and over pay for the property.

You have to assist your client in their investment decision. That's what you're being paid for. You want your client to know all of the good and bad points about the subject property. **Sometimes the truth hurts and people don't want to hear bad things about a house that they've fallen in love with. But that's too bad because what you're telling them is REALITY!!** So let them know that your job is to open their eyes to aspects about buying a house that most other buyers don't have a clue exist. If someone else goes into the deal with their eyes closed and pays too much for the property, then all I can say is that they should have hired an ***"A to Z Appraiser and/or Home Inspector,"*** like your client did!

Now at the same time, if your client is still willing to pay the same price for the house even after you open their eyes, then fine. It's *none of your business* what the client does after you inform them about potential costs and problems with the subject property. You've done your professional and ethical responsibility by informing them ahead of time; and that's all you're required to do. **It's their money and their future,** so keep your nose out of it from that point on.

# Lay All The Cards On The Table

An important concept that I want you to clearly understand, is that **your job is to lay all the cards out on the table for your clients. Don't leave any skeletons hidden in the closet.** Tell them about all the different aspects and realities of their investment, both good and bad, of what we've discussed, plus any that you learn from your own experiences. If all the cards are laid out, then the client can make an intelligent and educated decision about their real estate purchase or mortgage loan. <u>Don't</u> make any decisions for the client. It's **their** money and **their** future, so let **them** decide. Your job is to just give the client the facts and your <u>objective</u> opinions, both good and bad. *(I've said that so many times by now I'm turning blue in the face. I just want to make sure you don't forget it.)*

> *If all the cards are laid out, then the client can make an intelligent and educated decision about their real estate purchase. Don't make any decisions for the client. It's their money and their future, so let them decide.*

If you're not sure about telling your client something, then just ask yourself: *"Is this something that can affect the market value of the subject property?"* and *"If I were the person buying this house or condo, would I want someone to inform me about this or not."* and *"Would I feel this is something that I would want to know about?"*

If you, or any third parties, try to make the decisions for the client, then you're not helping them out. It's similar to a person going to a doctor for a routine physical. If the doctor finds a problem condition from the test results, he should tell the patient what he found and the possible treatments. The doctor should then let the patient choose what action or treatment to take. Now the doctor is the professional and an expert in this field of medicine. Therefore, he should provide the patient with some objective advice and alternatives. With the doctor's advice and alternatives, the patient can then make an intelligent and educated decision on their own.

However, what would happen if the doctor decided, on his own, to not tell the patient about the problem condition? Let's say the doctor just rationalized in his own mind that the patient didn't need to know about the problem condition. Perhaps the doctor felt that the condition might go away on its own over time. Maybe the doctor would think that if he told the patient, he would only worry the patient unnecessarily. Does that doctor have a right to make a decision like that with someone else's life? Or should that doctor lay all of the cards out on the table for the patient to decide? You tell me. I think the doctor should let the patient decide. When a doctor doesn't inform a patient properly about their health condition, it brings to mind the old saying, *"Doctors bury their mistakes."* Unfortunately, I've seen first hand experiences where some doctors buried their mistakes. A doctor shouldn't filter out anything the client should know. And neither should an appraiser, a home seller, a Realtor, an attorney, a home inspector, nor anyone else. Unfortunately, many times people do filter out information that someone has a **right** to know about.

Tony Fasanella was one of my instructors for the State appraisal course called *"The Standards of Professional Practice."* Tony constantly stated to our class that the key to honest, ethical and professional conduct was **disclosure, disclosure, disclosure** of all aspects in an appraisal report. This meant that you don't hide anything from the client, nor do anything that will give someone a false impression or lead them to a wrong conclusion. That includes what you say verbally and what you put in the written report.

I feel bad about creating headaches for the seller or Realtor when I detect problem conditions during an inspection or appraisal. I like to help people, not make their life more difficult *(unless they're dishonest)*. But it's not my fault when I find problems with a house during an inspection or appraisal. The way I look at it is that I didn't **create** the problems - I only **identified** the problems which my client has a right to know about. So don't feel guilty about creating headaches for anyone if you're telling the **truth**. Your job is not to kill real estate deals, it's to identify all the negative and positive aspects of a house. Even though you don't create the negative aspects, the sellers and Realtors still get angry at you. They look at you like you're an idiot merely because they're ignorant to the facts.

# *Safety Concerns*

Remember that when you're doing an appraisal you **have to** mention any of the three S's in every appraisal report. You also have to mention anything that affects the value of the subject property. The three S's stand for: $\underline{S}$tructural, $\underline{S}$afety and $\underline{S}$anitary problems or hazards in a building. Safety hazard items such as tripping hazards in the steps, walks and patios; loose and missing handrails; improper deck construction and guardrails; leaning retaining walls; loose electrical grounding cables, etc., may seem like minor items to repair. However, these are things that can cause someone to get seriously hurt if they're not repaired immediately and properly.

◊ An uneven section in a walkway might not seem like much, but what happens if the person that trips, falls and hits their head?

◊ A leaning retaining wall will crush a child if it collapses on top of them.

◊ A missing or loose handrail could cause someone to fall down the steps.

> *If you make a mistake and forget to include a negative aspect that affects market value, you could end up costing the client some money. However, if you miss a safety hazard, you could end up costing someone their LIFE!*

If you think I'm overreacting then this next story should wake you up. I heard this story from a home inspection conference. A home inspector was sued because he neglected to check the deck on a house and it had very bad termite infestation. The woman who bought the house went out on the deck one day and it collapsed and left her paralyzed from the neck down. This is certainly a **horrible tragedy** for everyone involved in that incident. But the point I want to make very clear is <u>**do not take chances with safety items!!**</u> If you make a mistake and forget to include something in your appraisal report that negatively affects market value, you could end up costing the client some **money** by buying a house or granting a loan for more than they should have. However, if you miss a safety hazard, you could end up costing someone their <u>***LIFE!***</u> Don't wait for accidents to happen. Just remember the saying - *"An ounce of prevention is worth a pound of cure!"*

> *Don't let any Realtors influence your decisions because you want them to refer some more of their clients to you. If you just "move the deal along" to satisfy a Realtor, you're going to get sued eventually. There's no doubt about it.*

Now I don't want you to think that you have to walk around the house with a microscope to detect every possible tripping hazard. Just do good, thorough appraisals and **<u>be honest</u>**. Don't let any dishonest Realtors to the transaction influence your decisions because you want them to refer some more of their clients to you. If you just *move the deal along* to satisfy a Realtor who may have recommended you for the appraisal, then you're going to get sued eventually. There's no doubt about it. And if that's how you're doing your appraisals, then you *<u>DESERVE</u>* to get sued!!

Believe me, there are enough appraisers out there that either don't know what they're doing or are just plain dishonest and greedy. They're out to make as much money as possible without caring who gets hurt by it. Tony Fasanella and Dr. David Scribner were excellent instructors for the appraisal courses I had to take for the State Certification requirements. I remember Tony talking about dishonest appraisers. He said that people like that *"have no business being in this business."* I agree with him completely, and I hope you do too.

# Don't Over Exaggerate Problems Or Repairs

Now at the same time, don't be like some appraisers and over exaggerate everything as being bad just to Cover Your Assets. This is another aspect that bothers Realtors and I agree with them on this point as well. If you're a doomsday appraiser then you're not doing the client any good because you're over exaggerating things and your market value estimates will be way off base by being too conservative. Don't unnecessarily make the client think that the house is a dump and about to collapse on top of you when it really isn't so bad, or that the house isn't worth $10.

> *All houses will have some problems because no house is perfect. So you want to be reasonable in your conclusions and evaluations to the client*

**All houses will have some problems because <u>no</u> house is perfect. So you want to be reasonable in your conclusions and evaluations to the client.** If the house needs a new roof, don't make the client think that *no one* would ever consider buying this house because they will have to sleep with an umbrella over their bed the whole time they live there! Just tell him to get an estimate for a new roof. Plain and simple. You're going to see many houses that have older roofs that will need replacing. Don't make the client think that this is the **only** house around that needs a new roof. A roof can be an expensive item to repair. However, if he puts a new roof on the house, he'll increase the property's market value. He also won't have to worry about any roof leaks for 20 years. Replacing roofs, heating systems, appliances, etc. is all part of normal house maintenance. Some items are more expensive than others, and some items last longer than others. Whether your client buys this house, or the house next door, he's going to have to do the same basic maintenance to either one over time. The only difference may be how soon he has to do the repairs and maintenance. Just tell him to get estimates on the items that need it, so he knows what his repair costs will be *before the closing*.

You're also going to see many houses that have negative aspects that affect their market value. Whether it is a locational problem, functional problem, physical depreciation, environmental problem, etc. Despite the extent of the problems, all houses will have **some** market value. If the house is located in a low income section of town, don't make the client think that *no one* would ever consider buying this house because of its location! Just make sufficient adjustments for the property location and any other negative aspects in your report. This way you can accurately estimate the market value. Don't make a big deal over something that merely needs a price adjustment in the report. Just be honest and reasonable in your evaluations, plain and simple.

There's risk in everything in life, even crossing the street. What you and your client need to do is eliminate as much risk as possible in their purchase or loan on the subject property. You can never eliminate <u>all</u> of the risk, but you just want to narrow it down as much as possible. Having a good, thorough home inspection and appraisal done; checking the records at town hall; getting estimates for items that you determine need to be repaired; having certain things further evaluated; etc. all help to reduce the risk for you and your client. The more that is checked out then the more the risk is reduced. It's that basic. It's like buying an insurance policy for you and your client. So if you don't get lazy and cut corners, then at least if something does go wrong, then you won't look back and kick yourself for missing something you should have checked out further.

**You also have to make sure that you're knowledgeable enough so that you can give the client enough information to help him in his real estate investment. You can't just tell the guy to get a whole host of contractors to come in and evaluate the different aspects of the house further because you're not sure about *anything*.** I've seen this done by some home inspectors and believe me, you're going to have an unhappy client if you do this to someone. I once was doing a foreclosure appraisal for a bank and they sent me a copy of the home inspection report for this house. The bank had paid a very high price for the inspection. This bank didn't know that I did home inspections. They ended up hiring a home inspector that was recommended by a dishonest Realtor who wanted to *move the deal along* to get a commission. *(How unusual for a Realtor to do that!?)*. There were other factors that came up during my appraisal process which indicated further that this Realtor was dishonest. I told the banker that I couldn't believe it when I read this inspection report and found out the price the bank paid for it. This inspector wrote a four or five page report that told the bank <u>absolutely nothing about the house!</u> This inspection report basically told the lender that since the inspector wasn't sure about *anything*, the bank needed to hire many different contractors to evaluate: the heating system, the well water system, the septic system, the electrical system, the structural beams, the swimming pool, the roof, etc. Do you believe that? I'm amazed that the bank even paid this incompetent crook that calls himself a home inspector! They should've told him to "whistle Dixie" for his inspection fee and then replace the greedy Realtor for recommending this incompetent knucklehead that called himself a "home inspector".

There's nothing wrong with recommending to your client that they get estimates for repairs that are needed. Or if there are items that you think a licensed contractor should evaluate further. However, don't charge somebody a fee if you can't evaluate *anything* about the subject property!

# Is It Possible To Build A... ?

There is something else that you need to be aware of. There will be times when your client will ask you if it's possible to make some changes or additions to the house or site. Virtually anything can be done from a construction standpoint. However, what your client needs to find out is:

1   What the costs will be for the work.

2   If the zoning and building department regulations will allow the work to be done.

For example, I often have clients ask me, *"Can we put an addition on the house?"*, or *"I'd like to build a dormer and finish the attic space to make another bedroom. Is that possible?"*, or *"Since there's a steep slope in the backyard, will we be able to build a large deck."*

When you get asked questions like that, just tell the client to check with the zoning and building departments. The client needs to find out if these departments will allow the work to be done. If the zoning and building department employees say *"yes,"* then tell the client to get estimates from licensed contractors for the work they want done. There's nothing complex about it.

**Don't over exaggerate your answer by responding with,** *"Well, if you want to put an addition on the house, then you might as well forget about buying this place. That will just be a lot of work and aggravation for nothing. Just go find yourself a larger house to buy."*

**At the same time don't under estimate your answer by telling them (like some Realtors would),** *"Of course you can put a dormer in the attic area Mr. Client. The zoning and building departments are really flexible around here. They always bend the rules to help out homeowners. My friend Joe is a carpenter and he can do all of the work needed for next to nothing."*

# Report Writing

We've pretty much covered just about every aspect of the real estate appraisal business, and the appraisal process itself. Now we'll talk about writing up the appraisal report after leaving the job site. Don't hand the client a checklist style appraisal report at the site. You have to think about what you're going to write in your report, before you mail it out to your client. In my opinion, any appraiser that gives a brief checklist style report to their clients, gives a black eye to the whole profession. Appraisers who give their clients a brief, meaningless checklist report should be embarrassed!

An **"A to Z Appraiser"** provides a written appraisal report that's informative and useful to their clients. Your written report has to have narrative comments to assist the client and explain everything in an easy to understand fashion. That's why the checklist style reports are such a joke. Checklist style reports don't tell the client anything about the house! A narrative report will educate the client about the subject property in a manner that is easy for an average person to understand. Also, remember not to use construction jargon terms or have comments that only a professional in the industry will be able to understand. When writing your reports you have to think about what you want to say and think about the person who will be reading it.

I'll use an analogy from high school that you probably can relate to. Do you remember when you were in school and you were given a homework assignment to do a written report? Well, you didn't give the teacher your report at the end of the class did you? You had to go home and think about what you were going to write so that it would be a quality homework assignment. *(Or at least you should have).* If you shouldn't cut corners for a written report for school, then you shouldn't cut corners for a written report for an appraisal client.

A very important point to remember is this: ***What you put in the written report is what you will be held accountable for!!!!*** This simply means, that I don't care how many times you told the client over the phone that the railroad tracks in the guy's back yard have a negative impact on market value. If you don't put it in the written report, then you have **no defense** when you get an angry client calling you up 10 months later about not being able to sleep because the trains pass by his house every night at 3:00 in the morning and toot their horns! You won't even remember the house, let alone the locational problems of it 10 months earlier.

**In appraisal reports, you're required to disclose everything that you know which has an affect on the market value of the subject property.** Everything must be disclosed in a way that can't be misinterpreted or twisted around. You should always have a notepad at the job site and you should be taking field notes throughout the appraisal. Don't make the mistake of leaving anything to memory. You'll find out the hard way that when you get back to your office to write the report up, you'll have forgotten a lot. Moreover, you won't remember some of the details clearly. This is even more true when you start to get really busy and you sometimes have to do two appraisal inspections in one day. You'll have a hard time remembering if a problem condition was in the first or second house you inspected that day. That is, unless you have very detailed notes from the job site.

Organize your notes and your appraisal so that you don't forget to include anything in the written report. Make sure you take your time at the job site and in writing the report so you don't leave anything out. **When you take field notes and write your report make sure to include anything the client mentioned that concerned them or that they had questions about.** When the client is concerned about a particular aspect of the house or condo, then it's an indication that this is an item they'll **expect** to see in the report. The client will also become angry if they buy the house and discover that you improperly evaluated the item. For example, let's say the client asks a few questions about any possible easements in the front yard. Well, you better make sure you evaluate the deed and all other pertinent documents at town hall to try to figure out if there's an easement. On top of that, make sure your conclusions are put in the written report. If you don't, the client may buy the house and discover you missed this item during your appraisal and didn't mention it in your report. When this happens, then at the very least, you'll have a dissatisfied client who won't recommend you.

I'm not trying to scare you. I'm just telling you the facts. Cover Your Assets in all of your written reports. You basically try to CYA on all appraisals due to the possibility of unreasonable clients. While taking the appraisal courses one of my instructors told me about a very good commercial appraiser who was threatened with a lawsuit by an unreasonable client. Apparently there were many loan foreclosures on properties taken back by this particular mortgage lender. The lender was threatening to sue many of the appraisers they had hired for the original market value estimates. This lender was claiming that these appraisers over estimated the market value at the time of the original appraisal reports. Many of these appraisers gave in to that type of threat. They just had their E & O insurance carrier payoff the lender to get rid of the matter rather than spend a lot of money on legal fees defending themselves. This particular appraiser knew he was right and simply told the lender that he was going to fight them in court. This appraiser also didn't want a "black mark" on his record for something that he didn't do wrong.

I take my hat off to that appraiser for having the guts and determination to stand up for what he knew was right. Coincidentally, the lender dropped the lawsuit because they had no case against the appraiser. Do you believe that! Some people *(like that client)* have no concept of logic and they can be so unreasonable. An unreasonable client, such as the one in this case, will rationalize their actions by saying to themselves: *"Well, let's sue everybody in sight and see who breaks under the pressure and pays us a few bucks for nothing."*

If something isn't visible or accessible and/or can't be accurately evaluated, then tell the client that, and tell them to have it checked out further if any doubts exist. If you haven't

been able to evaluate some aspect of the appraisal report to the point where you feel comfortable in telling them it's a thorough and complete report, then tell the client that. Ask the client for more time to check things out further before you complete your report.

**Be very careful about giving cost estimates for repairs. You might end up paying the difference between what you quoted the client and what they ended up paying for the work.** Tell the client to call a contractor and get estimates on their own. Otherwise, make sure you know what the costs will be and leave some margin for error. Be very careful about recommending any contractors. If you do, make sure they're very honest. If the client uses anyone that you recommend and the client ends up in court with that person, then your client might become angry with you. They could become angry with you for referring the contractor who didn't do a good job.

Don't let the war stories scare you, just be aware it can happen to anyone. It's just part of normal, everyday business problems to deal with in any business. You get paid more because a lot of knowledge is required to be a skilled appraiser. As a result, there's more liability. Look at the liability doctors have to assume in their profession. That's why they get paid so much.

> *Any areas of the house that are inaccessible due to furniture, personal belongings, finished areas, etc. should be stated in your report.*
> *This way the client will have a written record that you don't have a magic wand, X-ray vision, or a crystal ball.*

**Any areas of the house that are inaccessible or not visible due to furniture, personal belongings, finished areas, etc. should be stated in your written report.** This doesn't mean that you have to take out a ruler and write the exact location of every piece of furniture, carpeting, wall covering, picture, etc. Just use your common sense and mention anything that's hidden but would normally be accessible and visible during a typical appraisal assignment. For example, some of the inaccessible areas that should be mentioned would include:  a finished basement or attic, a garage that's filled with storage items, a locked room, etc. Also, anything you couldn't evaluate properly during your field work should be stated in your report. **This way the client will have a written record that you don't have a magic wand, X-ray vision, or a crystal ball** *(which some people might be surprised to find out).*

If you think it sounds strange to state in the written report that you can't see behind finished and inaccessible areas, then I'll tell you another bedtime war story so you understand why. I once did an inspection and there was a section of the ceiling on the top floor of the house that had some brown water stains. The water stain wasn't that large and it didn't appear to be recent. You'll find this condition often in attics where there will be old water stains from roof leaks that have since been repaired. I told the client at the inspection site and in the written report that there probably was some damage to the areas behind the sheetrock ceilings. I explained that I can't detect this damage because it's not visible. When the client applied for his mortgage loan, the bank appraiser went through the house and mentioned the water stains on the ceiling in the appraisal report as well.

About three weeks after the date I did the inspection, I got a phone call from this client. He said that he needed a letter from me stating that the roof was in good condition and that it wasn't leaking. He said that the bank read what the appraiser had put in his report about the water stains. As a result, they required this letter for a final approval to lend him the mortgage money to buy the house. I told the client that I can't give him a letter stating that the roof is definitely not leaking and that everything is in good condition. He kept pushing the point of how he needed a letter because he felt that anything would help to satisfy his lender. I told him that I would not make any statements that could be misinterpreted. Furthermore, I said that the only thing I could write would be what I had stated in the written inspection report and that was: *"the water stains did not appear to be recent and appeared to have been from a prior roof leak but there could be damage behind the finished areas."* This statement turned out to be exactly what had happened. The seller of the house had a roof leak in that area before having the house last reroofed. After the new roof was installed, the water leak stopped. The only problem was that the seller was too cheap to pay to have the damage to the roof rafters repaired. There was no attic for me to view this damage due to the design of the house!

Well, about a month later I got a phone call from this client. He told me that after he closed on the house, he had a contractor open that section of the ceiling. Beneath the ceiling covering they found extensive water damage to the roof rafters. The client was unhappy because he felt that I didn't tell him *"strongly"* enough that there could be damage behind the sheetrock ceiling. Do you believe that!!! What more do I have to do? I told him at the site and I put a statement in the written report! I guess he felt I should have beat him over the head with the idea to make him understand it more clearly. In reality, this client **himself** was the main cause of his problem! This client, like many people who buy homes in an emotionally excited state, made the mistake of not taking a step back and looking at the deal like a typical business decision. He was overly eager and excited about buying a house because the real estate market values were appreciating very quickly during those years. He knew buying a home would make him money, like a business investment, but he was **too emotionally excited** to take the time to check everything out and get repair estimates *BEFORE* the closing! This happens when people let their emotions get too involved in their home search. So learn a lesson from this and don't leave anything to the imagination. When you start to book a lot of appraisals you'll have a hard enough time remembering a house you appraised one month ago; let alone if you have to remember details about it a year later.

# The Report Is Totally Confidential

There is an important point to remember about the contents of the **entire** written report, as well as any other aspects you learn about during the appraisal process. **That is the report and any other aspects of the appraisal are the property of the person who commissioned the appraisal and paid the fee, which is your client.** Your client is the one who owns the contents of that report once he has received it and paid you for your services. **Therefore, the contents of the report is <u>confidential</u> information for the client only!!!** When I say that your client "owns" the contents of the report, it doesn't mean that they own the copyrights to the report text. It means that the information and data in the report is the property of the client for their use in evaluating the subject property.

> *Many times a Realtor or seller will ask you for a copy of the appraisal report or about other aspects that you evaluated. <u>Don't give it to them without the client's consent!!!</u>*

Many times a Realtor or seller to the transaction will ask you for a copy of the appraisal report or ask you about some of the other aspects that you evaluated during your appraisal. <u>**Don't give the report nor any information about the report to them without the client's consent!!!**</u> That's a very important point that I will repeat to make sure you don't forget it: Don't give the report nor any information about the report to them without the client's consent!!! It's none of their business to see what's in the written report unless the client wants them to see it. The client may want to negotiate with the seller on some items you noted during your appraisal and report. If the report gets into anyone else's hands, then it can diminish the client's negotiating position. It's similar to playing poker. You wouldn't show your hand to other players of the game, would you?

If you send a copy of the written report to a Realtor or seller, then you can weaken your client's position. Your client's position is weakened because the third party will know what's in the report. You should also make your client aware of this when you book the job over the phone and at the job site. Tell your client about the poker game analogy so that you dump it back into their lap. This way the **client** makes the decision as to who gets any additional copies of the written report.

**I recommend to my clients' that they <u>don't</u> give a copy of the written report to anyone but their own attorney.** I've hardly ever seen a copy of the written appraisal report benefit my client when it was given to a Realtor, seller, or any other third parties. The reason for this is simple. Let's say the seller doesn't agree with me when I tell my client about a problem condition at the house. **The seller is <u>not</u> going to change his mind just because he sees that I wrote the statement on paper.** On top of that, I've often seen copies of the report *hurt* my clients' position when it was given to a third party. Let's say you told the client that the roof is very old but it's not leaking at this time. The Realtors and sellers will use this statement **against** the client. They'll say, *"As long as the roof isn't leaking, the seller isn't obligated to replace it."* This totally disregards the fact that the roof will leak and need replacing in the near future.

**Tell your client there's a better approach to negotiate rather than giving the seller a copy of your report. A written estimate from a licensed contractor can be much more helpful and convincing.** Your client gets two benefits from this. *First*, the client can show the seller and Realtor a second opinion in writing that confirms what you're telling them. *Second*, the client will have a repair estimate **prior** to closing. This way they'll know what the costs will be whether they do the work now or later.

There's another reason why you don't want to send a copy of the written report to any dishonest Realtors. The reason is that the written reports have a **very nasty** habit of floating around when they're not in your client's hands. You don't want your report ending up in someone else's hands, especially not another appraisal company. If you're an **"A to Z Appraiser"** then you have to worry about your competitors trying to steal your ideas and information that they find in your written reports.

I actually had a local Realtor threaten me once with legal action about this topic. Along with my home inspection and appraisal reports I send out a letter to the client. This Realtor threatened me because this letter states some benefits and reasons why the client shouldn't give out copies of the written report to anyone else. This Realtor not only threatened me with legal action, but even went a step further. The Realtor told all of the other people in that real estate office to tell their client's not to use me on their home inspections. *(Fine, don't recommend me to your clients because I'm not interested in referrals from dishonest Realtors who only refer inspectors that "move the deal along" to benefit a greedy, immoral, and ignorant Realtor! My concern and fiduciary responsibility is to MY CLIENTS, not to any Realtors or other third parties.)* This Realtor was getting a commission on the sale and represented the seller in the transaction, as is almost always the case. **Realtors who represent the seller know that they have no legal right to see the written report nor any of the test results,** such as radon and water tests. That's okay. I get enough work from satisfied clients so I don't need any work from any greedy or dishonest Realtors. As an **"A to Z Appraiser,"** you won't either.

## Appraisal Referral Realities

**You will find that the vast majority of Realtors and some other third parties won't recommend you for appraisals if you're too honest and too thorough.** They won't recommend you because you may kill their deals by finding problems with the house or condo. If that happens, then they'll end up losing their commission, their fee, or their profit on the sale. People like that will only refer customers to you with strings attached. **If you don't** *move the deal along* **by not telling the client about any problems in the house, then they get angry and won't recommend you again.** Don't bother with these types of people. It'll be very hard to avoid them in business, so just try to ignore them. You can get more than enough business from honest people. You don't want to *"sell your soul"* just to make money, so who cares if they don't recommend you.

---

*You will find the vast majority of Realtors won't recommend you for appraisals if you're too honest and too thorough.*

---

Honest Realtors and third party people will recommend a good, thorough appraiser. They know that a good appraiser will satisfy the client that the estimated market value of the house or condo has been thoroughly evaluated. Unfortunately, you may find that the honest third party people who will recommend you if you're good, can be **extremely** outnumbered in some areas. And I'm not talking about your clients, because they'll *always* recommend you if you're good. You just want to do business with the honest third party people so you can sleep with a clear conscience at night.

The only way you're going to make big money on a steady basis in this business is to have satisfied **clients** who refer customers to you. If you have steady referrals from former clients, then you won't even have to advertise and your phone will ring off the hook for appraisal jobs. That's when you know you have a rock solid business that's going to make you a lot of money for a long, long time. And you want to be in this for the long term. The people that make the most money in this business, are the ones who have the most satisfied clients. Even in a recession, they still make money, because houses are still sold when the economy is bad. The only difference is that houses sell for less money, but they still need to be appraised.

---

*There's a big difference between referrals from satisfied clients who you've done appraisals for, and referrals from Realtors who send customers to you just because you "move the deal along."*

---

There's a **big** difference between referrals from **satisfied clients** who you've done appraisals for, and referrals from **Realtors** and third parties who send customers to you just because you "move the deal along." If you just *move the deal along* and don't do a thorough and professional appraisal, then the client is going to know that after the appraisal is over. They might not say anything to you, but they just won't recommend you to their friends or business associates. I've seen it before in some other appraisal companies. They get all of their business from dishonest Realtors because they don't tell the client about anything wrong with the house, nor give an accurate estimate of the market value, and they just *move the deal along.* These appraisers end up being **owned** by **dishonest Realtors** and other third parties because the third parties have control over their income. I don't know about you, but I don't like anybody having leverage over me.

> *They get all of their business from dishonest Realtors because they don't tell the client about anything wrong with the house, and they just "move the deal along." These appraisers end up being owned by the dishonest Realtors.*

**Let me explain how you will be "owned" by the dishonest Realtors if you get most of your business from** *their* **referrals because you** *move their deals along.* With these types of referrals from dishonest Realtors and third parties, you can't tell the client about anything **important** being wrong with the house. The only thing they want you to tell the client is if some **minor** repairs are needed – but nothing else! Also, you have to "fudge the numbers" by slanting the market value estimate in your appraisal report so the deal closes and the Realtor gets their commission. If you do tell your client about important or costly repairs that are needed with the property, and it creates *any* problems or kills the deal, then the Realtor gets angry and **will** **never** **recommend you to their clients again!!** Regardless of the fact that you were being **honest** with the client, they still won't recommend you anymore.

**Dishonest Realtors and third parties don't want you to say** *anything* **that will throw a monkey wrench into their deal!** It doesn't matter how many other deals you *moved along* for the dishonest Realtor or other third party person. If you create problems with, or kill, just *one* of their deals; then that's it, you're cut off and they tell their clients not to hire you for appraisals anymore! And if the dishonest Realtors cut you off after you've been catering to them and *kissing their ass* for a long time just to get referral business from them, **then you're** *really in trouble!* You're in trouble because you don't have satisfied clients to refer you for future appraisals. Then your phone stops ringing and your appraisal income goes down to nothing. The reason you won't have satisfied clients recommending their friends to hire you for their appraisal needs, is because the clients will know after they hired you that you were "in bed" with the dishonest Realtor and you were just *moving the deal along* to satisfy the **Realtor** and *NOT* your **client**!! People aren't stupid. Your clients might not notice *during* your appraisal that you're compromising your morals and "hanging them out to dry" just to keep the Realtor that recommended you happy. However, your clients will notice they've been scammed *after* your appraisal and/or the deal closes. Especially when the problems that you should have told the client about start "coming out of the woodwork".

*You don't believe me?* I've heard quite a few war stories about appraisers who can't find any new business due to the poor quality of their work in the past. I've even seen it happen firsthand with a local home inspection company in my area. This home inspection company was run by an older man that just *moved deals along* for the Realtors. When the older inspector retired and a new inspector came in and started doing good, honest and thorough inspections, **the phone stopped ringing!** All of the dishonest Realtors and third parties stopped using the new inspector because he didn't cater to them and *move the deals along* like the older inspector had. The phone didn't ring from client referrals either. This is because none of the former clients would recommend anyone to this inspection company. They wouldn't recommend anyone because they knew the work was of such a poor quality from the older inspector. This created a terrible reflection on the company name, even after the older inspector retired. To make matters even worse, the only phone calls that did come in were from **unhappy** former clients of the old inspector. These people called to *complain* about the inspection services he did. They didn't call to refer more inspection business to them.

**There's another drawback to getting all of your referrals from dishonest third parties.** What happens is, the client buys the house or makes the loan and then finds out after the fact, that there are some problems. The client decides that the appraiser should've noticed these problems during the appraisal and told the client about them. Or possibly the market value estimate was way off base. So what does the client do? He gets angry because he knows the appraiser wasn't thorough or professional, and he sicks his attorney on the appraiser and files a lawsuit. Real estate appraisers like that end up being sued out of business.

> *So you see, the only way to make it in this, or any other business, is to do good, honest and professional work. If you "sell your soul" then your income and your reputation are going to pay dearly for it.*

So you see, the only way to make it in this, or any other business, is to do good, honest and professional work. If you *"sell your soul"* then your income and your reputation are going to pay dearly for it. And you won't even sleep well at night. I've found that some people have an **amazing ability to rationalize their actions,** no matter how bad they are. So let the dishonest Realtors and other third parties sell their souls. Just don't ever compromise your own integrity. Too many people compromise their integrity for money. I think that money is like a truth serum. It brings out the true character of a person, deep down inside, whether they're good or bad. There's an awful lot of *"white collar crime"* that goes unnoticed and unpunished because people rationalize their actions. They deliberately hide problems from the clients. Then they kid themselves thinking that there's nothing wrong with burying things underneath a blanket of deception.

I've had many Realtors and sellers complain because my home inspections take three or four hours. They also complain because of the amount of research and time I spend on my appraisals. They don't want you to be too thorough or to spend too much time in the house, or on writing the report. My clients never complain because I spend three or four hours inspecting a house they're planning to buy. *So why do Realtors* and sellers complain about it? They seem to forget, that my fiduciary responsibility is to my **client** and not to any **Realtors or third parties**. However, if **they** were buying the house, well then, it would be a **totally different story**. I'll talk more about hypocrites later.

I'm certainly not being a hypocrite myself or talking out of ignorance. I let my track record and integrity speak for itself: Less than *one percent* of my clients have ever called me up to say that they were unhappy with my services. I've even **turned away** business by being honest with people. There are many dishonest Realtors whose business I have turned away. I told these Realtors that I didn't want their referrals for clients. The reason for this is that I knew they would complain if I did a thorough home inspection or appraisal. Other examples are, I've done appraisals and inspections on houses that were taken back in foreclosures, or the houses were part of estate sales after someone had died. These houses had all of the utilities turned off at the time I arrived to do the inspection. You can't do a proper appraisal and/or home inspection on a house without any utilities turned on! The reason for this is that you won't be able to test any of the operating systems. I would be up-front and honest with my clients. I'd tell them that rather than go ahead with the inspection, they'd be better off waiting until the utilities were turned on. If they delay the inspection, I wouldn't have to charge them a fee for a limited home inspection. Sometimes these deals would fall through because another buyer would come along **before** the utilities were turned on, or some other reason. Therefore, as a result of being up-front and honest, I would lose money. However, I'd rather lose the money, then do the inspection and not feel good about it. I hope that's the way you run your business also.

**If you go into this business, then you're going to come across many dishonest Realtors and other third parties who will try to get you to** *"move their deals along."* I'm letting you know ahead of time that's it's going to happen, so don't say I didn't warn you about this. Often what dishonest Realtors will do is try to *butter you up* when you first show up at the subject property. Sometimes they'll even call you up before you go out to the site and try to butter you up. What they say to you is, *"Oh, can I have one of your business cards. Our office is always looking for new appraisers to recommend to our clients."* **They lie to you by saying this to make you think that they're going to refer their future clients to you for appraisal or home inspection work.** However, it's the same old con game that they're playing. If you don't *"move their deal along,"* then your business cards will end up in their garbage can as soon as the Realtors get back to their office. *(I have an awful lot of business cards and brochures that have ended up in dishonest Realtor's garbage cans. My cards ended up in their garbage because I was too honest and thorough with my clients* **Remember, an educated home buyer or seller is a dishonest Realtor's worst nightmare!!!)**

So remember, don't let any Realtors or other third parties butter you up on an appraisal. Be on your guard when they ask you for your business card so they can *supposedly* refer other clients to you. **Translated into English, what they're really saying to you is,** *"Don't tell the buyer that anything's wrong*

with the house and we'll give you some referral business. This way the both of us can cheat and deceive people and line our pockets with dirty money."

You'll also come across another offshoot for this type of Realtor and third party dishonesty if you go into this business. **Dishonest Realtors will sometimes say to you,** *"It's not **what** you say to the client, it's **how** you say it that matters."* **Translated into English, what they really mean by saying this to you is,** *"Don't tell the buyer that something, such as the heating system is old and can die at anytime. Just tell them that it's working properly now because that's all they need to know. Don't mention anything to them about getting estimates to replace it."*

**They want you to "sugarcoat" everything so it all sounds fine and dandy in greedy Realtor fairytale land.** Basically, dishonest and greedy Realtors ONLY want you to mention if some **minor** maintenance and repairs are needed on the property – and that's it!

## Some Good Reasons For Federal Regulations

In my opinion, there is an *urgent* need for Federal legislation. The legislation should prevent anyone who will benefit by the sale of a property from recommending a home inspector or an appraiser to a client. The reason I say this is that, **it is a total conflict of interest if they recommend an inspector or appraiser!!!** I can't believe that laws have not been passed which prevent this conflict of interest. If someone will gain a profit or a commission on the sale of a property, then don't you think that there's an obvious problem if they recommend a home inspector or an appraiser? The problem is due to the temptation of the Realtor or third party to make sure the deal goes through, at any cost, so they can get paid. Furthermore, most of the time, Realtors and third parties who get a commission on the sale work for the seller!! This means that their fiduciary and legal responsibility is to get the best deal possible for the ***seller***, not the ***buyer***. Therefore, how can these third party people say that they're looking out for the buyer's best interest, by recommending a thorough and unbiased home inspector or appraiser? Again, it's a total conflict of interest if they recommend a home inspector or an appraiser!

> *Legislation should prevent anyone who benefits by the sale of a property from recommending a home inspection or appraiser. I say this because, it's a total conflict of interest if they recommend an inspector or appraiser!!!*

Believe me, I'm no rocket scientist and I can see as clear as day that there's a problem here that needs to be fixed. I also think that there is an *urgent* need for another type of Federal legislation. This legislation should require all Realtors and third parties involved in a real estate transaction, who receive a commission on the sale, to make certain recommendations to the seller and the buyer. However, the recommendations *should not* be a conflict of interest.

◊ The recommendation they should be required to make to the **seller** is: *"The seller should hire an **independent** real estate appraiser that they select on their own, without any involvement or encouragement of the Realtors or any other third parties. An appraisal is recommended to give the seller an unbiased estimate of market value for the subject property. This appraisal should be done **before** the seller lists the property for sale."*

◊ The recommendation they should be required to make to the **buyer** is: *"The buyer should hire an **independent** real estate home inspector that they select on their own, without any involvement or encouragement of the Realtors or any other third parties. An inspection is recommended to give the buyer a thorough and professional home inspection of the subject property. This home inspection should be done **before** the buyer signs any contracts to purchase the subject property."*

If these ideas were enforced by Federal legislation, then it would greatly help everyone in the country with the biggest investment of their lives. This type of legislation would also improve the integrity of the real estate business *tremendously*. Now don't get me wrong here. If an attorney wants to recommend a home inspector or an appraiser to a client they're representing, then that's fine. In a case like this, the attorney is only looking out for **their client's interests**. The attorney will get paid a fee, regardless of whether the deal goes through or not. Therefore, they don't have a conflict of interest and a financial commission incentive to *move the deal along* by recommending an incompetent home inspector or appraiser - **like a dishonest, greedy Realtor or other third party does.** I hope you see the difference between these two situations.

In the front of the book I list the benefits of having an appraisal done by an independent, honest and thorough real estate appraiser. (See section Benefits Of Knowledge Of Appraisals page 20). I think they're all valid reasons that are based on a foundation of solid facts. These facts reinforce my opinions about the need for Federal legislation. I've seen many examples of sellers who have been deceived by dishonest Realtors and other third parties. **This deception could have been prevented, if the seller had been educated about the benefits of getting an unbiased appraiser to estimate the market value of their property.** The way dishonest Realtors and third parties cheat sellers' is by deceiving them as to the true market value of their property.

I had a client that hired me to do an appraisal of their house before they listed it for sale. The woman who owned the house was a very nice, easy-going person. She told me that she and her husband purchased the house just three years earlier for about $500,000. There was a Realtor who was involved in the transaction. At the time they purchased the property, this Realtor told the couple: *"You're getting a **rock bottom** price, and you're **stealing** this house for $100,000 **below** market value."* The woman who was my client told me, that she and

her husband asked this same Realtor to list their house for sale, three years later. Well, this Realtor told them: *"The market has gone way down because of the recession. You're going to have to sell the house for $100,000 **less** than what you paid for it, three years earlier."*

Luckily, my client and her husband didn't believe that the real estate market had dropped that drastically in only three years. The reason a greedy, dishonest Realtor may want to list a house for sale at a very low price is that the house will sell very quickly and that listing Realtor can make a fast commission on the sale. Also, if the **listing** Realtor has home buyers looking for houses in that area, then he/she may even be able to also be the **selling** Realtor on the deal by calling one of her home buyer clients and telling them about this *"great low-priced house that's just come on the market and hasn't even been listed yet in the MLS!!"* **If the listing Realtor is also the selling Realtor, then he/she will get twice the commission percentage on the sale! That's a greedy, dishonest Realtor's incentive to low-ball a seller with their listing price.** I did an extremely thorough appraisal, using six sales comparables that had sold within the past six months. These sales comps were all located within <u>two blocks</u> of the subject property. My appraisal market value estimate was just about the same price the client had paid for the house. There was a recession that caused prices to drop in the area. However, at the time my clients were going to sell the property, the market had rebounded so they wouldn't have to take a loss. This is a perfect example of how the public gets cheated by dishonest and/or incompetent Realtors who call themselves *"real estate professionals."*

This appraisal client made a statement to me about Realtors that I have found to be very true. She said that *"Realtors talk out of both sides of their mouth."* During all of my experience in this business **I've found that some Realtors will say *anything* to sell a house. It's similar to a prostitute - they "screw" people for money!!**

> *I've seen ENDLESS examples of buyers who have been deceived by dishonest Realtors and other third parties to the transaction.*

I've seen ***ENDLESS*** examples of buyers who have been deceived by dishonest Realtors and third parties. I'd be one of the richest people around if I had a nickel for each time I've seen this happen. All of this deception could have been prevented, if the buyer had been educated about the benefits of getting an **unbiased** home inspector to evaluate the condition of the subject property. The way dishonest Realtors and other third parties cheat buyers is by deceiving them as to the true condition of the house they're purchasing. For example, let's say a buyer wants to have an inspection done on a house they're thinking about buying. They will ask a Realtor or other third party that's involved in the deal to recommend a home inspector to them. **A dishonest Realtor or other third party will give the buyer three names of home inspectors that won't say anything bad about the subject property. This way the deal won't be delayed or renegotiated due to problem conditions found during the inspection.** After the

REA From A to Z

buyer closes on the house and moves-in, they find out about all the repairs that are needed and all of the problems with the house. The buyer then realizes that these are the things that the home inspector should have told them about. But by that time, it's too late. It's already a done deal.

---

*The reason a dishonest Realtor or other third party gives the buyer a list of three names is another con game. All three of the inspectors on that list are incompetent crooks with no integrity or morals!*

---

**The reason a dishonest Realtor or other third party gives the buyer a list of three names is another con game. All three of the home inspectors on that list are incompetent crooks with no integrity or morals that are "in bed" with the Realtor and they "screw" the clients for money – like prostitutes!** The dishonest Realtor or other third party has those inspectors in their back pocket. They're partners in crime. They're cheating the public by "moving deals along" and people don't realize they've been scammed until it's too late. The buyer can call the Realtor or third party to complain about the incompetent home inspector they recommended. However, the Realtor or third party gets off the hook by saying, *"Well, Mr. Buyer, I'm very sorry you found problems with the house that didn't come out during the inspection. However, I gave you three names to call. You should have hired inspector #2 on the list instead of inspector #3."* If you don't believe all of this, then just ask other home inspectors that are very thorough and knowledgeable. See what they tell you.

**One way you will certainly be able to know if you are a very honest, thorough and knowledgeable appraiser is based upon what greedy, dishonest Realtors think of you.** For example, when potential clients call me for price quotes, I tell them that they want to hire the appraiser that's **HATED BY THE REALTORS!!!!** I explain that the last thing the client should do is use an appraiser (or home inspector) recommended by the Realtor due to the <u>conflict of interest concerns</u>. You know that you're an **excellent** appraiser or inspector when the dishonest and greedy Realtors *HATE YOUR GUTS!!!* They hate my guts but that's OK with me because I don't want nor need business from criminals anyway! It's fine when the **honest** Realtors that I know recommend me to their clients. But I still make it **very clear** to the client on the phone when they are booking the job, that I represent the <u>client</u> and will tell them all known problems I find at the house and site, **regardless** of whether or not it kills the deal and costs the Realtor who recommended me to lose their commission. It's always a pleasure to meet and work with an **honest** Realtor that can accept terms like that – terms that are for my client's best interests only!

## You Get What You Pay For

I don't mean to scare you by talking about dishonesty and lawsuits. But this is how the whole idea of Federal and State regulations and licensing came about for real estate appraisers. During the 1980's real estate prices were rising through the roof, *(pardon the pun)*. The banks and savings and loans kept lending mortgage money on over-priced real estate transactions. A reason for this may be that they figured they couldn't lose money. If the buyer didn't make the mortgage payments then the lender could foreclose. If that happened, then the property would be worth more than the bank had lent and they would make a profit anyway.

Well, that's not how it turned out. Everybody ended up losing in a big way. When the recession hit the economy in 1989 an awful lot of banks lost billions of dollars due to real estate loans that had gone sour. The Savings and Loan bailout was estimated to cost over 250 billion dollars. Banks could foreclose on the properties but they couldn't resell them to get their funds back. Everybody loses in that type of situation including the homeowner, bank, the economy, the local town, etc.

The whole reason the *Resolution Trust Corporation* (RTC) was created was to take over insolvent banks. After taking over these banks, the RTC would try to sell the bank assets to investors to recoup some of the losses. The *Federal Deposit Insurance Corporation*, FDIC, and the *Federal Savings and Loan Insurance Corporation*, FSLIC, had to pay the depositors in the insolvent banks. Customers that had bank accounts were paid the insurance amount for their deposited money. Any funds that the RTC could not recoup with the sale of assets from insolvent banks were left to the American taxpayer to pay.

To try to prevent this whole mess from ever happening again, the Federal Government made some new rules. The government had to regulate some occupational group involved in the real estate industry. Since the banks and savings and loans were already regulated, they looked at real estate appraisers. In 1989 Congress passed the *Financial Institutions Reform, Recovery and Enforcement Act* of 1989 (FIRREA), more commonly known as the *Savings and Loan Bailout Bill*. Title XI of FIRREA set up a real estate appraiser regulatory system involving the Federal government, the States and *The Appraisal Foundation*. *The Appraisal Subcommittee* (ASC) of the *Federal Financial Institutions Examination Council* has the authority to ensure that the States and the Foundation meet the requirements that the States use certifying appraisers and the standards of professional practice to which appraisers are held by the States (the *Uniform Standards of Professional Appraisal Practice* - USPAP).

Many bankers felt that they would not have made many real estate loans which ended up being foreclosed on if the appraisers had been more cautious during the 1980's real estate boom. The bankers felt that the appraisers erred because they kept arriving at inflated estimates of market value in their reports. On the other hand, many appraisers felt that many bankers and mortgage brokers had unfairly pressured them in the 1980's. The pressure on the appraisers was to arrive at high estimates of market value in their reports. The high estimates were necessary in some reports so that the lender or broker could grant the mortgage loan and earn a profit or a commission fee. Before the Federal requirements, just about anyone could call themselves a real estate appraiser. The only way to differentiate between appraisers and to measure their competence was to ask if they were designated by one of the large appraisal organizations that existed.

The current regulations may not be enough to eliminate the potential for future problems. Problems such as those encountered with bad real estate loans in the 1980's may happen again. I think a very important aspect that's being overlooked will all of the licensing requirements is the standard amount that mortgage lenders pay appraisers. **Real estate appraisers are highly underpaid for the amount of work needed to do a thorough and high quality appraisal report.** If you're a thorough appraiser, you can earn a six figure income in this business. However, I still think there are far too many lenders that are *only* concerned with how inexpensively they can have a licensed appraiser do their property valuation reports. **They're so penny wise and dollar foolish it's amazing!** If you pay an appraiser more money than the lowest fee possible, then you can insist that he provide you with higher quality appraisal reports. If the appraiser is getting paid a reasonable fee for the work involved to do a thorough report, then he's going to spend much more time on the assignment. The appraiser will make a bigger effort to do the best work that he can.

I met an appraiser once who owned a business that did work for insurance companies. His appraisal firm did replacement value appraisals on homes. These are needed for insurance companies prior to writing some homeowner's policies. This appraiser was telling me about how insurance companies don't want to spend *any* money on these appraisals. He would get calls from insurance companies all over the country looking for someone to handle their appraisal work. When he told them his fee, their response was always, *"That's more money than we're paying now for these appraisals. You have to lower your prices."* After hearing this, the appraiser would ask the insurers why they called him if they already had an appraisal company handling their work. The insurers response would be, *"We're not happy with the quality of the work we're getting from the appraiser."* The appraiser would answer, *"That's why I charge more!"* **It's a simple concept that some people don't seem to understand. If you want top quality work, then you have to pay more for it.**

According to the Federal and State Appraisal Standards, an appraiser has to do the same amount of work for all of their reports, **no matter what they're being paid.** You can't cut corners because you're not getting paid enough on a particular assignment. If you take shortcuts, you're going to make mistakes and you'll end up regretting it. Unfortunately, many people forget this. That's why you have lazy and unqualified appraisers who are only concerned with mailing out as many reports as possible to clients. These appraisers don't have any concern about the quality of the work in their reports. The

reason for this lack of concern is that these appraisers feel that they're not getting paid enough to spend sufficient time on each report. I think some lenders might want to refresh their memories about this old saying: *"You get what you pay for!"*

By doing so many foreclosure appraisals, I can tell you that I've seen the results of this problem firsthand on many occasions. I've seen what a nightmare it becomes for a mortgage lender to have to foreclose on a property. I've seen lenders lose a ton of money in foreclosures. One of the aspects that play a big part in those loans being granted in the first place is the appraisal report. Some of these lenders would never have granted the loan if they had hired a more thorough, competent appraiser to estimate the market value of the property. *"Oh yes, but I forgot, those lenders are very intelligent businessmen. After all, they saved an extra $100 or $150 by hiring the cheapest appraiser in town. They didn't need to hire a competent, honest and knowledgeable appraiser and pay the extra amount by billing the loan applicant for the additional appraisal fee."* All those lenders had to do was to charge the mortgage loan applicant $100 to $150 more for the appraisal reports. If they had, then they could have saved themselves tens of thousands of dollars in losses for many of the loans that had gone sour! And I'm not talking about the lender paying the higher fee to get a good, competent appraisal done. The appraisal fee for mortgage loan applications is passed on to the potential borrower when they hand in their loan application. It makes me sick to my stomach to think that the American taxpayer paid for the whole failure of the banking industry due to foreclosures and a recession in the 1980's and early 1990's.

Surprisingly, in 2003 some major mortgage lenders began using *electronic appraisals* which are touted as a fast-growing "alternative" to traditional, full-cost appraisals. See Electronic Appraisals section page 93 for more information on why using electronic appraisals is a **HUGE mistake** for banks and mortgage lenders. "Intelligent" decisions like that may come back to haunt these lenders later with foreclosure loans and enormous financial losses – as it did in the late 1980's

Here's another example of "intelligent" mortgage lenders that focus on the **minor** costs and disregard the **major** costs: In 2004 real estate appraisers were complaining that one of their **biggest** problems was intimidation and pressure on them to "*hit the number*" desired by mortgage loan officers and others involved in real estate deals to *move the deal along*. Appraisers had been complaining for years that they are frequently pressured to value homes at the price needed to make the sale or refinancing loan go through. Appraisers who don't cooperate with loan officers say they are either: **1)** Blackballed those lenders and third parties, **2)** Receive no further appraisal assignments from those lenders, or **3)** Are not paid their fees for the appraisal report. *This is a very serious issue,* **especially if the appraiser is faced with being blackballed and losing that lender as a client. The long-term financial loss in income to that appraiser and appraisal firm can be huge!** Over 6,000 appraisers had signed an industry-wide petition demanding an end to this type of pressure from mortgage lenders.

Legislation that includes the specific federal ban sought by appraisers was introduced in the House of Representatives by Rep. Jan Schakowsky (D-Ill.). The bill, known as the *Save Our Homes Act* (H.R. 2531), is primarily aimed at curbing "**predatory lending**" practices. The language of the bill would amend the Federal *Truth in Lending Act* to prohibit a creditor or mortgage broker from *"influencing the independent judgment of an appraiser with respect to the value of real estate that is to be covered by a conforming home loan or is being offered as security according to an application for a conforming home loan."* The Schakowsky bill language would allow appraisers to report and document illegal pressure from lenders and mortgage brokers to federal authorities. Any infraction of this bill would constitute a violation of the *Truth in Lending Act*, subjecting the violator to a Federal lawsuit and fines of $10,000 per violation. Regulations implementing the ban would have to be drafted by the Federal Reserve. The language in the bill would appear to cover a wide range of situations, including loan officers "shopping" a contract by faxing competing appraisers the price "needed" for the deal. Appraisers that were unable to "pre-comp" the subject property *(provide a preliminary valuation hitting the number)* **never get the appraisal assignment!**

Appraisers feel that even more serious than this are forms of pressure where appraisers who already have an assignment are asked to "fudge the numbers" and bump up the value estimate of their appraisal report by the $10,000, $50,000, or more needed to close the sale or refinancing deal. Inflated appraisals are dangerous for banks and other financial institutions, and they **force appraisers to violate their own professional and ethical standards** <u>to earn their income.</u>

# Handling Client Complaints

No matter how good you are, you're going to get a few complaints from clients because you can't satisfy everyone all the time. It's the same problem in every other business. So you might as well get ready to deal with it now. The bright side is that the better you are, the fewer complaints you'll get. It's that simple. If you don't like headaches or aggravation, then just do good, thorough appraisals and you'll minimize the complaints as much as possible. As I've said earlier, I've only had less than one percent of my clients call me complain about my services. Of these complaints, I was only wrong one time where it was my fault for missing something that I should have seen. I had just started out in the home inspection business and I under-estimated the age of a roof for a client. This roof was in <u>excellent</u> condition so I told the client it was younger than it actually was. However, my client was informed about my mistake **before** he signed the contracts to buy the house. As a result, he didn't have any financial loss or problems due to my error. Moreover, I paid the client a refund on his inspection fee since I felt bad that I had made a mistake and didn't properly determine the correct age of the roof. If you have a track record like that, then you'll be doing just fine. You will be able to consider the quality of your work superior to the competition.

> *No matter how good you are, you're going to get a few complaints from clients because you can't satisfy everyone all the time. It's the same problem in every other business.*

When you get a complaint from a client after they have purchased the house you had appraised, it may be due to the fact that they didn't read the written appraisal report **prior to** the closing. Believe it or not, many people get so excited and emotional about buying a house that they tend to overlook very important factors. This is why you **have to** send your clients a thorough, professional, and narrative appraisal report. The written report should include explanations and comments describing the details about the subject property in the report. Don't be like a lot of other appraisers out there and send your clients a brief checklist report that doesn't tell them anything. If you send your clients a brief checklist report you'll end up regretting it eventually.

Some people will just assume that if they attended the on-site inspection, then they know enough about the house and they won't bother reading a long, narrative appraisal report. They also will just assume that they don't need to bother with getting estimates for any problem conditions prior to closing on the house. They'll just wait until after they move-in and worry about getting estimates later. This is a <u>**BIG mistake**</u> on the client's part because you know the old saying, *"When you **assume**, you make an **Ass** out of **U** and **Me**."*

I've had this exact situation happen with one of my home inspection client's. This client had purchased a house and **didn't follow my professional recommendations. I had told this client, verbally and in the written inspection report, to have the siding checked out by a licensed contractor <u>before</u>**

**closing on the house.** There were many damaged and missing shingles on the house. These shingles were located in areas too high to reach with a ladder, unless you were a house painter with an exceptionally long ladder – which home inspectors are not required to use. I also told this client that when I asked the seller the preinspection questions, the seller said that the house had been treated for carpenter ant damage a few years ago. **I told the client to speak to the exterminator who had done the carpenter ant treatment; get all documentation for the work; and find out the extent of the damage and the treatment. Furthermore, I told this client to hire their own exterminator to evaluate this information and treat the house again.**

This client had decided they didn't need to worry about following any of my recommendations until *after* they moved into the house. Well, wouldn't you know it, I got a phone call from them a few months after they moved into the house. **They told me that the reason the shingles were falling off the house was because of the carpenter ant damage.** I asked the client how they found out about the cause of this problem. He said that they hired a contractor, <u>*AFTER*</u> they bought the house, to evaluate the damaged shingles and the prior owner's carpenter ant treatment.

If this client had listened to me at the inspection site and read the written inspection report, they would have eliminated all these problems **before** they bought the house! However, the client either did <u>not</u> listen to me clearly at the inspection site and did <u>not</u> read the written report; or the client did listen to me and did read the report but they just decided, on their own, <u>not</u> to follow my professional recommendations. Therefore, in a case such as this, the **client cannot blame anyone but themselves** for being negligent and foolish.

> *This is a perfect example of why you have to stress to your clients, and put a statement in the written reports, recommending that they get repair estimates and eliminate any questions, concerns or problems -*
> *BEFORE BUYING THE HOUSE!!!!*

This is a perfect example of why you have to stress to your clients, and put a statement in the written reports, recommending that they get repair estimates and eliminate any questions, concerns or problems - *<u>BEFORE BUYING THE HOUSE!!!!</u>* Just tell the client not to get too emotional or excited about their purchase and not to *assume* anything. If they check everything out before they buy the house, then it becomes the *seller's* responsibility to remedy any problems. However, if the client doesn't check everything out before they buy the house, then it becomes the *buyer's* responsibility to remedy any problems.

If you're a thorough real estate appraiser, then sometimes when you get a complaint from a client, it's because they have been deceived by a dishonest and/or ignorant contractor. All of your written reports should have a statement that warns your clients about this problem, before it's too late. What happens is this: The client closes on the house and then moves-in to their new home. While they're living there or during some remodeling work, they find items that need to be repaired that weren't identified in the appraisal report. Since you're a thorough *"A to Z Appraiser"* the reason these items weren't identified during the on-site inspection, is because they weren't visible or accessible during the inspection. This happens all the time with termites and water problems. The client will open up a floor, wall or ceiling during remodeling work. When it's all open, they find damage from termites or water leaks. **Obviously, the appraiser can't identify a problem if it's not visible!!** *(Well, at least you would think that it's obvious to people).* Unfortunately, there are some people who don't realize you can't see behind floors, walls and ceilings. These people always think they hired *Clark Kent*, alias *Superman*, to do their appraisal!

What happens next, is the client will then unknowingly call up a dishonest and/or ignorant contractor. They will ask the contractor to come to the house and give them an estimate for the repairs needed. The contractor goes to the house and looks at the damage. He sees dollar signs in his eyes and immediately turns to your client and says, *"You mean your appraiser or home inspector didn't see this? Your appraiser or inspector should have seen this damage and told you about it. You should sue that appraiser or inspector to get reimbursed for the repairs I have to do."* Then to put the icing on the cake, this moron that calls himself a contractor, hands your client a ridiculous estimate for the repairs. The estimate is usually so high, that it's from the planet Mars!

> *What a dishonest contractor tries to do is distract your client's attention by pointing the finger at the appraiser for not seeing the damage.*

What a dishonest contractor tries to do is distract your client's attention by pointing the finger at the appraiser or home inspector for not seeing the damage. While your client is angry and furious with you, they don't even think about getting a second repair estimate to verify what this contractor is telling them. A dishonest contractor tries to look like the *Knight in Shining Armor* that rides in on his white horse to save your client from the evil real estate appraiser or inspector. Because of this, your client thinks the contractor knows what he's talking about and that the appraiser or home inspector is wrong. **Actually, it's the other way around!**

The contractor knows *nothing* about what is involved with an on-site appraisal inspection. The contractor also wasn't even at the house at the time of your inspection. Moreover, the contractor has <u>no</u> idea if the damage was visible or accessible at the time of the inspection. Sometimes, the contractor even has <u>no</u> idea if the damage **even existed** at the time of the inspection. Therefore, how can this ignorant contractor say that you should have seen the damage and notified your client about it?

> *When a dishonest or uneducated contractor scares a client, they do it to steal their money. When an "A to Z Appraiser" scares a client, they do it to save them money.*

All a contractor like that will succeed in doing is raise your client's blood pressure due to the client's anger. After that, they will then rip-off your client, unless someone else opens the client's eyes to the truth. When a dishonest or uneducated contractor scares a client, they do it to **steal** their money. When an *"A to Z Appraiser"* scares a client, they do it to **save** them money. What I mean by this is a contractor, such as the one I've described, will steal your client's money by deceiving them into paying a grossly overcharged repair bill. They get the client all emotionally pumped up with anger, and while the client's attention is distracted, they lower the boom on them with a gigantic repair bill. On the other hand, an *"A to Z Appraiser"* will save your client money by opening their eyes to the true risks and realities of buying a house. You may get the client scared by telling them about the potential pitfalls and hazards of a huge investment like a home. It's to the client's advantage to know all of the problems and risks in purchasing or selling a home if they don't check all of the records at town hall; the potential for damage and termites behind walls, floors, and ceilings; the health concerns of radon and asbestos; the risks of not pumping and internally inspecting a septic system; etc.

You might be saying to yourself, *"OK, now this author has really gone over the deep end. He's talking about the emotional state of real estate appraisal clients."* Well, let me give you a few war stories that show you the reality of this situation. These are two of the clients that consist of the less than one percent that have ever called me to complain about my services. I think you'll see why I feel that I was right in both cases and the home inspection clients were misled by lying contractors.

A client of mine had moved into a house that I had inspected for her. She called to say that she had replaced the water heater and the oil burner for the boiler. She told me the price she paid for the repairs and I immediately knew that she had been cheated by a dishonest contractor. I asked her why the contractor said the repairs were needed and if she had gotten any other estimates, before hiring this guy. The contractor told her that the oil burner and the water heater were unrepairable and both had to be replaced. She then said that she didn't get any other estimates for the repairs and this contractor was the only person who evaluated the damage. I then told the client to check the written inspection report and let me know what it said about these two items. The water heater was only three years old and was operating fine at the time of the inspection. The oil burner was also operating properly at the time of the inspection. Both items were covered under a warranty and service contract with the manufacturer and oil delivery company. My client ended up realizing that these items didn't need to be replaced at all. On top of that, this immoral contractor charged her more than **twice** what she should have paid, even if they did need to be replaced! Since this guy was such a crooked contractor, I am positive that these items may only have needed a minor repair or tune-up in the first place. However, the client was told that it was my fault by the contractor. She didn't find out the truth until it was too late and the money was spent on the repairs.

*(This next story is a real beauty).* Another client of mine called me after they moved into their new home. They had a contractor come in to give them a price quote to remove the old carpets and install new carpeting. This contractor found some damage **underneath** the existing carpet in a corner and one other small area. The hardwood floor underneath had buckled in two places. The contractor had only lifted the **one corner of the carpet** and he told the client, *"Didn't your home inspector see this damage underneath the carpet? This entire hardwood floor and carpet are going to cost you $5,000 to replace. Your home inspector should have seen this."* Not surprisingly, my client was angry about not being told of this damage before closing on the house. Fortunately, the client called me up before he let this blockhead, that calls himself a floor contractor, replace the hardwood floor. When I saw the damage in person, I could not believe anyone would have told my client that I was negligent. My client and I, both confirmed that the corner where the damage was found had been buried in boxes, toys and furniture at the time of the inspection. We also both confirmed, that the other damaged area was covered with a large couch at the time of the inspection. Impressions from the furniture were still visible in the carpets surrounding the damaged areas. **Therefore, it became very clear to both of us that the seller *intentionally* made sure we didn't see the damage at the time of the inspection.**

I was angry that the seller was such a crook and that he would stoop so low and hide damage on purpose. However, what really annoyed me, was the ignorance of the floor contractor! When I finally looked at the damaged area underneath the corner of the carpet, I realized that the contractor had no right to accuse me of being negligent. **The damaged area could be easily repaired by replacing a few of the buckled boards.** It didn't even matter if the wood matched exactly or not. The client had told the contractor they wanted to cover the floor with a new carpet anyway. Luckily the client had taken my advice and called a second contractor to give them an estimate. While I was there, the second floor contractor came by the house. **His price quote was a $500 repair job, not a $5,000 repair!**

You should have a statement in all of the written reports that you send out to warn your clients about this type of situation. Let them know that some contractors will try to blame the appraiser and/or the home inspector. These contractors will then grossly overcharge the client for repairs that may never have been needed in the first place. Tell your clients to call you **before** they have any repairs done which they believe you should have identified during the on-site inspection. If they call you **before** the repairs are done, both you and they will have a chance to clear up the situation before it's too late.

You also want to warn your clients if you find out that the seller or any third parties have intentionally lied about some aspect of the subject property. I've had this happen on a few occasions and it should immediately raise a red flag in your mind about the property and that person's integrity. **If you catch someone lying about some aspect of the property, then there probably will be other hidden problems.** There could be damaged areas or something that's not visible which can create a problem after your client moves-in. If this happens to you, then make sure that you and your client verify as much information as possible, before they sign contracts.

There's a very important point that you need to remember. If you get an angry phone call from a client who complains that you missed something during your inspection: **Don't jump down their throat and tell them they're crazy!** You have to stay calm and be very reasonable and diplomatic when you deal with an angry or hostile person. Don't make the mistake of telling the client that he's insane if he thinks you should have seen damage that was hidden at the time of the inspection. By yelling back at the client, all you will succeed in doing is getting him even more furious at you. Just calmly tell the client that you want to come by the house to see the problem in person. This is for your benefit as well as the client's benefit. By seeing the damage in person, it will enable you to help solve the problem before they make any unnecessary or overpriced repairs.

Your client can get angry and all pumped up because they're looking at a very large repair bill. Moreover, the contractor is blaming *you* for not seeing the problem. As a result, the client is told by the contractor that *you* should pay for the repair. An angry client is concentrating on what repairs you *didn't* tell them about, before they bought the property. You have to make them realize how much you *did* tell them about, before they bought the property. As an **"A to Z Appraiser"**: your on-site inspection lasted up to several hours; you used more than the minimum three sales comparables; you checked all records at town hall; you warned them about radon; you told them to get estimates and further evaluations for some items; you sent them a narrative and informative written report; etc. Would they have gotten that much information if they hired another appraiser in the area? How much risk did you help them eliminate? How much money did you save them? How much more thorough and professional was your appraisal, as compared to the competition? Would any homeowner, including them, allow an appraiser to come into their house and rip up the carpets, move the furniture, and open up the walls, floors and ceilings?

As long as you're logical and reasonable, the client will understand that you didn't cheat them. Your client will be complaining because **they're ignorant**, not because **you're negligent**. There's a big difference between the two. The client is ignorant because they don't know the Standards in the industry for performing an appraisal. When they're annoyed, they might not stop, take a step back, and think about the situation in a logical fashion. The client might not realize that an appraiser can't pull up carpets, or move furniture, or open up walls, floors and ceilings. You have to look at the situation from their perspective. The client is looking at a big repair bill and they think it's your fault. Once you explain the limits of an on-site inspection and ask the client questions, *(like the ones mentioned above)*, your client will understand that you haven't been negligent. After that your client will gradually calm down and recognize that you're the best appraiser in the area that they could have hired. Therefore, if you didn't see the damage, or if it wasn't visible, then no other appraiser would have identified the problem either.

> *A client of this limited mentality cannot comprehend that an appraiser doesn't travel on a magic carpet with a wand, emerald slippers, and Aladdin's lamp.*

Now, let's say that after you calmly explain all of this logic and reason, your client is still angry with you for missing something that you **clearly had no way of identifying.** If this is the situation, then I hate to have to clue you in. But you're dealing with a **basket case!** You have to tell this type of client that they need to call *Clark Kent "Superman"* for their next real estate appraisal. This is the type of person that I've been warning you about to CYA in all of your written reports. A client of this limited mentality cannot comprehend that an appraiser doesn't travel on a *magic carpet* with a *wand*, *emerald slippers*, and *Aladdin's lamp*. So bite your tongue, say your prayers, and try not to lose your patience with a person like that.

## Know-It-All People

There will be times when you'll get a hostile seller, Realtor, or other third party to a transaction who will become very defensive by saying the market value of the house is higher than what your appraisal comes in at for a pre-purchase appraisal; and lower than your market value estimate for a pre-listing for sale appraisal. **You'll find that these types of people are all experts in everything, yet they have no facts or knowledge to back up their statements.** Just don't be intimidated by anyone - not even the client. If you're knowledgeable enough, you'll have plenty of confidence. So don't let anyone *"ruffle your feathers"* while doing your appraisal reports.

> *You'll find that these types of people are all experts in everything, yet they have no facts or knowledge to back up their statements.*

Once you learn this material well enough and you get 10 or so appraisals under your belt you'll start to get a lot more confidence. That's why you shouldn't let any know-it-all Realtors or other third party people try to contradict you on any of your appraisals. When I say *know-it-all* people, I'm talking about people involved in the transaction, other than your client.

You don't want to be arrogant or rude with your attitude. There will be times that you'll *think* you're right but you might find out later that you're *wrong*. You don't want to end up putting your foot in your mouth later. So just be confident, knowledgeable and honest. Don't imitate them by being a know-it-all yourself because two wrongs don't make a right. If that person is honest and sensible, they will realize that you are much more knowledgeable than they are. For example, lets say you're looking for good, comparable sales for the subject property that have sold within the last six months. Many times some Realtors and other third parties to the transaction will give you some comps to assist you in your report. After reviewing these comparables, you may feel that they aren't good enough to use in order to properly estimate market value for the subject property. You will want to look for some better comps yourself, or at least you have to try to find better sales to use in your report. **You can't just take someone else's word that the comparables they give you are the *only* sales to use. After all, it's your neck that's on the line when you sign-off on that appraisal report!!** This isn't uncommon and it happens all the time. Since the person giving you the sales comparables is not a State Certified Appraiser, then they don't know what you have to look for to properly evaluate the comparables you use in an appraisal report.

If this were the case, and you had a know-it-all person involved in the deal, they might say to you, *"Well, I've been in the real estate business for 10 years now. I know this area like the back of my hand and these are the ONLY good comps you can use for that house."* Just tell that person that if they want to **guarantee to your client** that these are the best comparable sales to use and if the market value estimate is inaccurate due to the sales comparables that they're giving you, then go ahead and put it in writing for my client. But don't expect me, the appraiser, to get stuck holding the bag in eight months after this guy buys the house or grants the loan and then finds out the estimate of market value was way off base! That type of comeback will usually put an end to any know-it-all's comments. **Basically you're telling that person that if they know so much more about appraising than you do, then they should be willing to put their *money* where their *mouth* is. A know-it-all's reaction will be totally different when it's *their* neck and money that's on the line, as opposed to yours or your clients!**

It's amazing to me when I come across ignorant Realtors and other third parties who have taken a few basic classes related to some of the different aspects of real estate and - *Abracadabra* - they're instant experts in every aspect of real estate!! *(Or at least they think they are.)* They become **legends in their own minds**. They think that after they take a few real estate related classes and tests *(that just about anyone with a pulse can pass),* and a few years of experience as a real estate agent, they instantly have more knowledge than: every home inspector, every real estate appraiser, every real estate investor, every real estate attorney, every home buyer and every seller. I don't know how they do it. They must be giving out some magical pills or secret potion at these classes!

You may also come across sellers that get hostile. Sellers can get hostile when you try to tell your client about some problem conditions and items that need to be repaired at the subject property. Don't let them ruffle your feathers. My first real estate attorney used to say that there are two things that you can't tell a man: <u>One is:</u> That his property is overpriced; <u>The other is:</u> ...*(Well, I've decided that it wouldn't be appropriate for me to repeat the other item in this book. So I won't tell you. I'll just leave you in suspense.)*

# *Certified, Licensed Or Just A Dreamer?*

As an appraiser you'll come across Realtors and third party people who will say to you, *"Oh, I'm a certified real estate appraiser too. I don't work for an appraisal office, but I've done many appraisals for my clients."* They usually make a comment like that when they think they have better comps or information than you do to estimate market value of the subject property. I've found a problem with these people saying this to me. **The problem is that I've <u>never seen one of them</u> that have an actual Certification or License number issued to them by the State they work in. That can only lead to one conclusion. <u>They're not State certified or licensed real estate appraisers!!!!</u> Period.**

Some people have an amazing ability to kid themselves and rationalize things. If you're a State Certified or Licensed real estate appraiser, then you would have a State license number and documentation to prove it. This would verify that you have taken all the required classes; you have all the required fee-paid real estate appraisal experience; and you have passed all the required State appraisal examinations. There's no *if, ands* or *buts* about it! So the next time some Realtor or third party tells you that they know what they're talking about and you don't because they're an "appraiser," ask them the following questions:

1. Did you take the equivalent of the State appraisal **Course 1** and did you successfully pass the course examination?

2. Did you take the equivalent of the State appraisal **Course 2** and did you successfully pass the course examination?

3. Did you take the equivalent of the State appraisal **Course Standards of Professional Practice Part A and Part B** and did you successfully pass both course examinations?

4. Have you done at least **250 Fee-Paid Real Estate Appraisals** that have all of the requirements necessary to be considered as actual appraisal reports?

5. Did you pay the required application fees and did you take the State Certification real estate appraisal examination and did you successfully pass the exam?

6. Do you have a State Certification or License number issued to you?

After they get finished answering *"No"* to all of the above questions, ask them a few more. This way they might realize that they don't know more than you do about appraising. Ask them questions like:

7. What's the proper appraisal definition of market value?

8. How do you estimate the Physical Depreciation using the Age/Life Method?

9. What's the difference between Physical, Functional and External Depreciation?

10. When is the Cost Approach effective and should it be used to estimate the market value of single family houses?

11. What are the standard three approaches to estimate market value?

12. What price per square foot do you use to accurately reflect this market when you're adjusting for the different gross living area sizes between the subject property and the comparable properties?

Now don't be arrogant or rude about it, or be a wise guy yourself, just politely make them realize that **you're** the knowledgeable and professional real estate appraiser. It's fine if any Realtors or other third party people offer you some advice and try to assist you on your appraisal. There's nothing wrong with that, and often it'll help you out a lot. Just don't let anyone push you around or get an attitude with you. You don't want anyone to have an attitude like they've got all the answers and you're out to lunch or on cloud 9.

Most States have a minimum experience requirement of 250 Fee-Paid appraisals. These appraisals must have all the requirements necessary to be considered actual appraisal reports for State and Federal Certification experience. What this means is that you have to do at least 250 *actual appraisal reports.* These consist of appraisals that a client has hired you to do for them. Furthermore, the client has to have paid you **specifically** for doing the appraisal report. To elaborate further, it's when you're commissioned by a client to do an appraisal report only, and not in combination with, another real estate related service. The purpose of their payment to you is just for the appraisal and you're not being paid for some other real estate related service that you provide the client. Also, the appraisal *must have all the requirements* of a full appraisal report. Meaning that you must at least have all of the information, addendums, adjustments, math calculations, the three approaches to value, etc. that are found on the standard appraisal forms.

Realtors do what is called a *Comparative Market Analysis,* (CMA). Many Realtors improperly think that they

actually do appraisals, like a licensed and qualified appraiser, when they do a CMA. They think that an appraisal consists of taking a few recent sales in their area and then writing a brief description of what they believe someone's house is worth based on these comps. **Chicken feed!!! That's a CMA. That is not an appraisal report and you might want to clue them in on this.** Also, tax assessors for the city have to reassess houses occasionally for tax increases. What the assessor will do is simply make across the board increases based upon rising prices and tax rates. They don't even have to go out and look at the property in many cases! They just punch in some new tax rates into a computer and it updates all the property tax files. These **are not** appraisals either.

As I said in the beginning of the book, the reason for the Federal and State certification and licensing process is that they basically want you to take some classes and work under someone else's guidance. It is recommended that you do this until you get some experience under your belt. This has many benefits to it and it will really help you out in your beginning stages. You won't spend a lot of time *"spinning your wheels"* trying to learn the business.

## *Tell Your Client To Ignore The Hypocrites*

I'm bothered by dishonest and/or ignorant Realtors and other third party people who inaccurately tell your client that everything is just fine and dandy about the house they're interested in buying. They may tell your client that nothing needs to be repaired when in reality there are repairs needed. They may also tell your client the market value is what *they* estimate and not the price the appraiser has arrived at. I'm bothered by this because they're such **hypocrites!** *(Of course these Realtors and third party people know better than you as to what's good for your client. You're just very well trained and experienced in doing appraisals, but somehow they know more than you do.)* Do you think they would make the same comments and statements if **THEY** were buying the house or making the loan and not your client? *NOT A CHANCE!!!* That's what makes them such hypocrites. I'll give you some imaginary examples that will make you laugh but you'll have to agree that they do get the point across.

*Do you think they would make the same comments and statements if they were buying the house and not your client? NOT A CHANCE!!!*

What if **they** were your client at the inspection and you said to them, *"According to the owner, the septic system hasn't been pumped clean in two years. The septic system is underground and can't be seen. The typical buyer in this area would hire a septic contractor to pump the system and do an internal inspection just to make sure it's OK. Therefore, my recommendation is that you have it checked out further to be sure everything's all right."*

Could you picture that third party person, *(if they were your client)*, turning to you and saying, *"Oh, well I don't need to get the septic pumped and internally inspected. This loan application will be approved anyway because there's no way the borrower will default on the loan. After all the septic only has to be pumped every 2-3 years so there's still another year before any maintenance is needed on the system."*

What if you said to them, *"I tried to turn on the air-conditioning system by using the normal thermostat control on the wall. It won't turn on so you should have the system checked out by a licensed A/C contractor to determine what repairs are needed."*

Could you picture that third party person responding to that by saying, *"You're wrong Mr. Appraiser, I don't need to get a contractor to check out the A/C system. The seller and the Realtor both told me that it works fine. They just can't seem to turn it on now. It must be a loose wire inside the thermostat. My husband can fix that himself after we move in."*

How about if you told them, *"You have a lead water main line in the house. You have to get an estimate to have a new water main line installed. Lead is a very serious health concern for adults and especially for children."*

Of course they'd answer this by saying, *"You're totally over exaggerating. My friend lives right down the block and he has four children. They have been living with a lead water main in their house for 14 years and not one person in his family has been sick a day in their life."*

Let's say you found asbestos and you informed them, *"There is some asbestos on the visible heating pipes in the lower level. The Environmental Protection Agency recommends that you have it professionally removed by an EPA licensed contractor for safety. It will not only be a health benefit but it will also help when you go to sell the house down the road to have the asbestos professionally removed."*

Of course they would answer this by saying, *"Oh no, I only have to wrap some duct tape around the asbestos. I don't need to hire EPA licensed contractors. That whole asbestos thing is just an over reaction by some alarmist people in the asbestos removal business who are trying to make money by scaring people."*

What if you found termite damaged wood and you said to them, *"There is some termite damage in the base of the garage door. I didn't see the termites crawling inside the wood but then again, it's very, very rare to actually see them in the damaged areas. It's highly recommended that you have the house treated by a licensed Pest Control Operator because the termites could be in nonvisible areas of the house."*

Upon hearing this, their response would be, *"As long as there are no active termites crawling around in the visible areas of the house or in the damaged wood, then I have no need to be concerned with getting the house treated by a PCO. My friend Ralph told me the only time a treatment is necessary is when you actually see the termites. Ralph knows what he's talking about; he teaches math at the university."*

---

> He said, *"They wheel the Bible out when it's good for them and then they wheel it back in when it's not good for them."*

Now these examples may seem a little bit carried away and they do have some humor in them. There is a point that I'm trying to make with these examples. **That is there's no way any third party who contradicts you on an appraisal would have the same reaction and comments if they were the ones buying the house or granting the loan money, as opposed to your client.** I had a teacher in one of my religion classes in high school who used a great example that fits this type of situation perfectly. He was talking about how some people hide behind the Bible with their actions and use it only when it's **convenient** and when it benefits them. He said, *"They wheel the Bible out when it's good for them and then they wheel it back in when it's not good for them."* People who do that are kidding themselves and are hypocrites by their actions.

It's no different with a third party that contradicts the facts during an appraisal. They're simply being **hypocrites** when they contradict you. **They're hypocrites and contradicting you because it benefits *THEIR* wallet and not your *client's!*** All you're trying to do is tell your client the facts and realities about buying a house or securing a mortgage loan with the property. It doesn't matter if they're buying this house, or the house down the block. **You just want your client to go into the deal with his/her eyes open.**

Don't over exaggerate things but at the same time don't let some ignorant, greedy or immoral seller, Realtor, or other third party try to sugar coat anything either. **And if you ever have a real problem with a seller, a Realtor, or another third party contradicting what you say to your client just ask them,** *"What if the tables were turned and YOU were buying this house and my client told YOU not to worry about the asbestos,* (or whatever else you're discussing). *Would YOU take his word for it and not listen to the appraiser that YOU hired who is the expert in his field?"* **Don't be surprised if they swallow their tongue or fumble for words to answer a question like that.**

# *Straight Talk*

Not all people who dispute or contradict what you tell the client will be dishonest. They may just be ignorant about the topic their discussing. This will happen all the time throughout your life. Some people think they've got all the answers to everything! But what's funny about it, is that these kinds of people never have anything to prove that they know what they're talking about. There's an old saying that describes the difference between a Wise Man and a Fool: *"A Wise Man* **Knows** *He Doesn't Know Everything, But A Fool* **Thinks** *He Does."* So be a Wise Man in everything you do. Don't be a Wise Guy or a Fool in life.

> *There's an old saying that describes the difference between a Wise Man and a Fool: "A Wise Man Knows He Doesn't Know Everything, But A Fool Thinks He Does."*

When I bought my first real estate book and audio tape series I heard all of the negative comments, criticism and laughter from everyone! These negative comments and criticism came from family, friends and anyone else I mentioned the books and audio tapes to. I practically had to *hypnotize* my brother to buy that first house with me, because the critics were starting to worry him too. You'll probably hear some of the same negative comments and criticism from buying **this** book as well! Everyone gave me 10,000 reasons why I would fail with the real estate tapes and *"lose it all."* They all said it was a *"get rich quick scheme"* that was just a pipe dream. Not one person ever stopped to even think of just **one** reason why it would work!! I had enough guts, confidence and foresight to go ahead and listen to those tapes and read those books anyway, despite all the criticism around me. Thank God I did, because I proved to myself that I was right all along. Things did work out well, as I had anticipated.

That experience, and many others as well, have taught me a very good lesson that I'll never forget. **I've learned that you have to follow your own gut feelings and instincts with all of your decisions in life.** Often when you do something that's out of the norm of some people's standards, they criticize you for it. I think it's because some people have no foresight or ambition. You just have to ignore people like that, let their narrow minded and negative thinking limit **them** and not you. You have to dare to be your own person and to be different if you feel strongly about something. Now don't get the wrong impression by this. I don't want you to think that you shouldn't listen to anyone in life and think that you've got all the answers yourself. **I'll listen to advice from anyone, but whether I follow that advice is my decision to make. I won't just take someone else's advice with blind faith, because free advice is often only worth what you paid for it.** What I'll do is take advice from anyone and then use my own gut feeling and judgment from my experiences to make a final decision. This way, if I find out later that the decision I made was a mistake, then I can't **blame** anyone else but myself for it. However, if I find out later the decision I made was correct, then I don't **owe** anyone else but myself for it.

I'll give you some actual examples from history that I read about. These examples are from a *Dale Carnegie* book with a chapter titled: *"Remember That No One Ever Kicks A Dead Dog."* That phrase refers to the fact that when you're kicked or criticized it's often done because it gives the kicker a feeling of importance. It often means that you're accomplishing something that's worthy of attention. Many people get satisfaction out of denouncing those who are better educated or more successful.

A former president of Yale University, Timothy Dwight, apparently took huge delight in denouncing a man who was running for President of the United States. This president of Yale warned that if this man were elected President of the United States, *"We may see our wives and daughters the victims of legal prostitution, soberly dishonored, speciously polluted; the outcasts of delicacy and virtue, the loathing of God and man."* Sounds almost like a denunciation of Adolph Hitler, doesn't it? But it wasn't. It was a denunciation of Thomas Jefferson, the author of the Declaration of Independence and the patron saint of democracy. Pretty incredible that someone, who was well educated at Yale, could have made a statement like that about Thomas Jefferson.

What American do you suppose was denounced as a *"hypocrite,"* *"an impostor,"* and as *"little better than a murderer?"* A newspaper cartoon depicted him on a guillotine with the big knife ready to cut off his head. Crowds jeered and hissed at him as he rode through the streets. Who was he? George Washington. Do you believe that! I think it's absolutely amazing how some people say things out of sheer ignorance without knowing the truth or the facts. We're all guilty of doing it at one time or another. Just remember those two stories from history so you don't do it too often.

So, the next time someone criticizes you or disputes something you're saying, don't get angry and argue back. Just look at where it's coming from and ask yourself:

◊ Is this person more successful than I am?

◊ Does this person have any background or experience in the topic they're disputing?

◊ Does this person really know what they're talking about, or do they just think they know what they're talking about?

If the person has nothing to prove that they know what they're talking about, then just ignore them because they're talking out of ignorance. You don't want to get aggravated over someone or something trivial.

# *Motivational Talk*

I hope you're beginning to see the inner workings of the different aspects of Real Estate from a point of view that the vast majority of the public doesn't have a clue exists. **These are the realities of the real estate business.** I could tell you the truth or I could paint a perfect picture that you'd rather hear about instead, but then I'd be lying to you. I don't mean to be negative. I just want to open your eyes to some important information. You might want to inform your clients about some of this information when they call you for price quotes. You'll find that they appreciate it and will thank you because they didn't know or realize the realities of the real estate business discussed in this book.

*Every business has aspects about it that the public is unaware of. This makes the uninformed public susceptible to being taken advantage of, due to their lack of awareness.*

If you find some of these things hard to believe, then don't take my word for it. Talk to other home inspectors and appraisers in your area that are honest and do good, quality work. See if they confirm or dispute what I'm telling you. It's no different from any other business. Every business has aspects about it that the public is unaware of. This makes the uninformed public susceptible to being taken advantage of, due to their lack of awareness. Now, I'm not trying to be a doomsayer by any means. I **strongly** believe that anyone, from any background can achieve anything they want in life. But I do have an awful lot of battle wounds and scars from trusting people too much. My battle wounds aren't all from my experiences in the appraisal and home inspection business, but are also from past experiences in my personal and business life. After learning my lessons, I got up every day and licked my wounds and kept moving forward. By the time I got into the appraisal and home inspection business I wizened up a lot.

It's OK to lose a few **battles**. You just want to make every effort you can to win the **war** - *and don't take any prisoners along the way!* Like the saying goes, you have to *Go For It* with everything you do! Don't sit around and **let** things happen, you have to go out and **make** things happen in your life. I started with nothing and made it on my own and I'm certainly no rocket scientist. Therefore, I firmly believe that anyone, no matter who you are or where you come from, can become successful. Some people have more obstacles and hurdles to overcome than others do because of the circumstances in their lives. But everyone can be successful if they have enough ambition, desire, and motivation. You can provide a real benefit to society in just about anything that you set your mind to doing. The only key is that you have to be willing to work very hard. You also have to make all of the sacrifices necessary to attain the level and success that you're looking for. If you live an honest life and leave this world a little better off then when you got here, then you can consider yourself a success.

I remember when my brother and I bought our first rental property. There was a perfect example of how anyone could become successful, despite their current situation or where they came from. The woman who sold us the house had two sons. One son had worked hard to move out of the low income area he was born in. This son then went on to medical school and became a successful dentist. He later married another dentist and was living a nice lifestyle with his wife and children. The other son, who grew up in the same house, was a total failure in life. This second son was living in his mother's house and was receiving money from welfare and other public assistance programs. He was too lazy to work and his mother actually had to **evict** him from her house to sell it! This son refused to move when his mother told him she was selling the house. Because of this, we had to wait an extra four months to buy the house until the seller could evict her own son. So here were two people, from the exact same home, where one became successful and happy and the other was a failure and miserable in life. It's all up to you. Your own ambition will make the difference. I had a friend that used to say, *"You live by the consequences of your own actions."*

*I read a quotation from Teddy Roosevelt that said "It's hard to fail, but it's worse never to have tried."*

I read a quotation from Teddy Roosevelt that said *"It's hard to fail, but it's worse never to have tried."* Albert Einstein, the most profound thinker of his time, confessed that he was wrong **99%** of the time. I read that Thomas Edison tried over a **thousand** different ways before he got a light bulb to work. *Can you imagine the difference it would've made in history if those people just gave up on their efforts?* Here's another example of someone who was clearly one of the greatest leaders in history and how much he struggled and had to overcome in his life. In 1831 this man **failed** in business. In 1832 he was **defeated** in running for State Legislator. In 1833 he **failed** again in another business. In 1835 his fiancée **died**. In 1836 he had a **nervous breakdown**. In 1843 he ran for Congress and was **defeated**. In 1848 he tried again to run for Congress and was **defeated**. In 1855 he tried running for the Senate and he **lost**. In 1856 he ran for Vice President and he **lost**. In 1859 he ran for the Senate again and he was **defeated**. In 1860 this man, **Abraham Lincoln**, was elected the 16th President of the United States of America.

You're going to make mistakes in your personal and business life, no matter how careful and honest you try to be. It's just a part of life that everyone experiences so don't let it get you down. Try to look at it in a different way by saying *"You don't make mistakes, you just learn lessons."* What you want to try to do is have more successes than failures. **Mistakes and failures aren't bad, they just give you more experience to make better decisions in the future.** Don't be like a cat that sits on a hot stove. It'll never sit on a *hot* stove again, but it'll never sit on a *cold* stove either. I met someone once that told me that *"Nothing is Bad, Everything Has A Purpose."* That's a very true statement. Look back at the majority of the mistakes you've made, and all the bad things that have happened to you over the years. At the time they happened, they seemed much worse then they do now. Often those mistakes or bad experiences led to something better or more profitable for you in the long run. **They say that things** that happen to us aren't bad. It's the way that we react to them, that makes them seem bad.

Take care of the important things in your personal and business life and the little things will take care of themselves. Don't spend all of your time worrying about minor problems. People spend 90% of their time harping on a problem and only 10% of their time trying to find a solution to the problem. Don't step over **dollars** to pick up **pennies** either. People spend most of their time worrying about saving pennies and cutting costs and only a small portion of their time concentrating on *increasing their income* with new opportunities.

> *You may wonder whether the hard work and sacrifices will be worth it. If you do, just remember this old saying, "You don't pay a price for success, you pay a price for failure"*

As I said in the beginning of the book, this isn't a *"get rich quick scheme."* It takes a lot of time, sacrifice and hard work to make a lot of money in any business. If it was easy to become rich, then everybody would be doing it! When you do become successful, you'll look back at all the hard work and sacrifices that you made and it will seem like a small price to have paid. It's like taking an exam in school. While you're studying for the exam it seems like such hard work. But when the test is over and you do well, then you look back on the studying you had to do and it doesn't seem so bad after all. You may wonder if the hard work and sacrifices will be worth it. If you do, then just remember these sayings, *"You don't pay a price for success, you pay a price for failure"* and *"Every dog has his day."*

## Conclusion

I hope you feel we've covered every aspect of the real estate appraisal business from A to Z. I hope now you realize what I meant when I said in the beginning of the book that I wasn't going to paint some fairy tale, rosy picture. Also, that I was going to tell it like it is without holding anything back. You might have found some of this information to be very surprising to learn. I certainly did when I started out in this business. I hope I've given you enough information so that you don't make the same mistakes that I did.

I can't think of anything we've missed. However, as I've said earlier, you have to keep feeding your mind with the new technologies and aspects of this business that are coming into the market. Don't get lazy now. Remember to keep feeding your mind with new information and training. The more knowledge you have, the more money you'll make. If you're knowledgeable and honest, then you'll really make some big money.

I want to take the time now to commend you on getting this far through the book. I've heard statistics that have shown that **less than 10%** of the people who purchase self-improvement books and audio CDs, ever even read the books and/or listen to the CDs one complete time. To me that's an amazing statistic. People spend their hard earned money on something, and then they get lazy or distracted and they don't follow through with it. They purchase books and CDs and read 1/2 of the book or listen to 1/2 of the CD, and then they put them on a shelf to collect dust.

I take my hat off to you. You have the ambition, willpower and the foresight to make an attempt at improving your own life, as well as the life of others. By getting this far in this book, you've shown that you're part of the minority within the majority. And that's a unique group of people who really want to have a positive impact on their own lives and the lives of the people around them. Abraham Lincoln said that *"A man who follows a crowd will never be followed by a crowd."* So be a leader in everything you do.

> *As I said in the beginning of this book: Please send me an email and let me know what you think of this book and any recommendations you might have for improvements or new products. I accept positive and negative comments since both help me to improve the next version of my products. I am always looking to improve my products and services and I greatly appreciate customer feedback and suggestions.*

As I said in the beginning of this book: Please send me an email and let me know what you think of this book and any recommendations you might have for improvements or new products. I accept positive and negative comments since both help me to improve the next version of my products. I am always looking to improve my products and services and I greatly appreciate customer feedback and suggestions.

*I invite you to view our web site at www.nemmar.com to see the other real estate products we offer that will save you thousands of dollars when you buy, sell, or renovate a home. You can sign up online to receive our __free__ real estate newsletter with articles and product updates that will definitely help you profit in real estate.*

I invite you to view our web site at www.nemmar.com to see the other real estate products we offer that will save you thousands of dollars when you buy, sell, or renovate a home. You can sign up online to receive our **free** real estate newsletter with articles and product updates that will definitely help you profit in real estate.

Thank you very much for the trust and confidence that you placed in me by purchasing this book. Due to your referrals our business keeps growing, and so will yours. Good luck, and I sincerely wish you the best in all your endeavors. I hope that someday I get a chance to meet you.

I'll tell you one last story before I go. I will never forget the time that I was following up with some of my clients to see how they were doing in the homes they purchased that I had inspected and/or appraised for them. One client bought a condo that I had inspected for him. His name was Dan Rones. When I called to find out how Dan was doing, his father answered the phone since he was now living in the condo. What his father told me on the phone left me absolutely stunned and I will never forget that conversation. Dan was 33 years old and just about to start law school when he had a brain aneurysm in his sleep and died. Due to the severe shock of losing his son, his father had a stroke the week after the funeral and became paralyzed in both legs and one arm.

In business and life we often get so caught up and in a way "trapped" in trying to earn a living and take care of the problems and tasks that confront us on a daily basis. It's often hard to take a step back and "smell the roses" that are all around us. *(I know I have a hard time doing it)*. The sad and tragic story of Dan Rones and his father brings to mind the old saying, *"I cried the blues*

*'cause I had **no shoes**. Until upon the street I saw a man that had **no feet**!"*

I heard another saying that's interesting - and true, *"If you look over your right shoulder, you'll always see someone **that you wish you were.** But if you look over your left shoulder, you'll thank God **you're who you are.**"*

Life is short and precious. If you truly live an honest and moral life and leave this world a little better off then when you got here, then you can consider yourself a success. Success is *not* measured by how big your **wallet** is. Success is measured by how big your **heart** is. I will now leave you with a famous *Gaelic Blessing:*

**May the road rise to meet you,**
**May the wind be always at your back,**
**May the sun shine warm upon your face,**
**And the rains fall soft upon your fields,**
**And until we meet again,**
**May God hold you in the palm of His Hand.**

The Author

P 54. Top: Is this what they meant when they said:
*"A man's home is his castle"*

Bottom: That's me, the author, doing a home inspection
and appraisal for a client - *in 3 feet of snow!*

## More Nemmar Products

### Energy Saving Home Improvements From A to Z ™

*Don't let your dream house be a money pit in disguise!* Our **5-star rated** book that teaches you how to **save** thousands of dollars **and** help the environment by making minor improvements to your home. You'll learn how to **lower your utility bills by 50%**, live more comfortably, and help the environment. Includes many photographs with detailed descriptions.

### Home Inspection Business From A to Z ™

*The REAL FACTS the other books don't tell you!* Our **number one** selling home inspection book. This is **definitely** the best home inspection book on the market and has been called the "Bible" of the inspection industry. *Every* aspect of home inspections is covered with precise steps to follow. Includes many photographs with detailed descriptions.

### Real Estate Appraisal From A to Z ™

*The REAL FACTS the other books don't tell you!* Our **number one** selling appraisal book. This is **definitely** the best real estate appraisal book on the market. *Every* aspect of real estate appraising is covered with precise steps to follow. Includes sample professional appraisal reports and many photographs with detailed descriptions.

### Real Estate From A to Z ™

*Don't let your dream house be a nightmare in disguise!* You'll learn information the professionals use to inspect, appraise, invest, and renovate real estate. This book covers every aspect of Real Estate from A to Z and contains abbreviated versions of our three **5-star rated** books: *Home Inspection Business, Real Estate Appraisal, and Energy Saving Home Improvement From A to Z.*

### DVD's - Home Inspection From A to Z ™

Our **5 star rated** DVD's have two hours of video plus you get the 80 page *HIB **DVD** Companion Guidebook!*
**OPERATING SYSTEMS** DVD topics including: heating systems, air-conditioning, water heaters, plumbing, well water system, septic system, electrical system, gas service, and auxiliary systems. Health Concerns topics including: asbestos insulation, radon gas, and water testing.
**INTERIOR and EXTERIOR** DVD topics including: roof, chimneys, siding, eaves, gutters, drainage and grading, windows, walkways, entrances and porches, driveways, walls and fences, patios and terraces, decks, swimming pools, exterior structures, wood destroying insects, garage, kitchen, bathrooms, floors and stairs, walls and ceilings, windows and doors, fireplaces, attics, ventilation, insulation, basement/lower level, and water penetration.

### Home Buyer's Survival Kit ™

***Don't buy, sell, or renovate your home without this!*** Includes: Four of our **top selling** books – *Real Estate Home Inspection Checklist From A to Z, Energy Saving Home Improvements From A to Z, Home Inspection Business From A to Z,* and *Real Estate Appraisal From A to Z.* Plus, you get both of our *Home Inspection From A to Z* – **DVD's.** As an added bonus you also get the 80 page *HIB **DVD** Companion Guidebook.*

### Narrative Report Generator *and* On-Site Checklist

*The report generator and checklist the others don't have!* CD-Rom with the *best* Narrative Report Generator and On-Site Checklist on the market! These will enable you to *easily* do 30 page narrative, professional home inspection reports to send to your clients. These will assist you at the inspection site to be sure that you properly evaluate the subject property. Designed to walk you through the entire inspection process with very detailed instructions on how to properly evaluate the condition and status of **all** aspects of a home in a fool-proof, step-by-step system and create professional, narrative reports.

### Appraiser and Home Inspector "A to Z Coach" School Training ™

**Personal One-to-One Training** with an "A to Z Coach" where you are the only student! Your training is personalized to meet your specific requirements and needs. Your questions are answered to make sure you learn everything you need to know about real estate - from Asbestos to Zoning. No crowded classrooms filled with students - unlike other real estate training schools. You'll learn how to become a highly paid Real Estate Appraiser or Home Inspector from top experts with many years of experience in the business!

**Telephone and Email Training** with an "A to Z Coach" via telephone and email. Our training school meets and exceeds the standards of all the leading home inspection and appraisal organizations. Regardless of where you live, you can enroll as a student in Nemmar Real Estate Training's "A to Z Coach" School.

**Just some of our books, CD's, DVD's and much more!**

**Email info@nemmar.com for prices.**

**Visit us at www.nemmar.com**

**Everything You Need To Know About Real Estate
From Asbestos to Zoning** ™

*Real Estate Home Inspection Checklist From A to Z* ™

*Energy Saving Home Improvements From A to Z* ™

*Home Inspection Business From A to Z* ™

*Real Estate Appraisal From A to Z* ™

*Real Estate From A to Z* ™

**Nemmar Real Estate Training**

**info@nemmar.com**

**www.nemmar.com**

# Appraisal Related Web Sites, State Real Estate Appraiser Boards, Real Estate Terminology Glossary, & Index

# *Appraisal Related Web Sites*

Here are some web sites related to real estate appraisals and appraisers that you may find helpful. The descriptions for each listing below are from their web sites and not necessarily our endorsement. Evaluate each site on your own to determine the quality and value of the information, products, or services they provide.

◊   **Appraisal Foundation** - www.appraisalfoundation.org - The Appraisal Foundation, a not-for-profit educational organization dedicated to the advancement of professional valuation, was established by the appraisal profession in the United States in 1987.

◊   **Appraisal Subcommittee** - www.asc.gov - The ASC's mission is to ensure that real estate appraisers, who perform appraisals in real estate transactions that could expose the United States government to financial loss, are sufficiently trained and tested to assure competency and independent judgment according to uniform high professional standards and ethics.

◊   **Association of Appraiser Regulatory Officials** - www.aaro.net - The mission of the Association of Appraiser Regulatory Officials shall be to improve the administration and enforcement of real estate appraisal laws in member jurisdictions.

◊   **Foundation of Real Estate Appraisers** - www.frea.com - The Foundation of Real Estate Appraisers (FREA) was founded in 1991 to fill a gap in the market for appraiser continuing education. At the time, obtaining education was expensive and difficult. It involved earning a designation that required thousands of dollars in classes from an association, and years of subservient service to someone who was already designated. Today, with over 8,000 members, FREA is the largest professional organization for appraisers and home inspectors in the country. FREA provides E&O insurance, education and other benefits to its members.

◊   **Appraisal Institute** - www.appraisalinstitute.org - The Appraisal Institute is an international membership association of professional real estate appraisers, with more than 18,000 members and 99 chapters throughout the United States, Canada and abroad. Its mission is to support and advance its members as the choice for real estate solutions and uphold professional credentials, standards of professional practice and ethics consistent with the public good.

◊   **National Association of Independent Fee Appraisers** - www.naifa.com - NAIFA is all about being in a professional family of appraisers from its candidate members up through the ranks to our national officers. From this website you can find out who we are and how to contact our national staff and NAIFA Officials, both elected and appointed. NAIFA's Officials and National's staff members are committed to serving our membership in a professional and courteous manner.

◊   **American Society of Appraisers** - www.appraisers.org - The American Society of Appraisers is an organization of appraisal professionals and others interested in the appraisal profession. International in structure, it is self-supporting and independent. The oldest and only major appraisal organization representing all of the disciplines of appraisal specialists, the society originated in 1936 and incorporated in 1952.

◊   **American Society of Farm Managers and Rural Appraisers** - www.asfmra.org - The mission of the American Society of Farm Managers and Rural Appraisers is to represent professionals in financial analysis, valuation, and management of agricultural and rural resources.

◊   **U.S. Department of Housing and Urban Development (HUD)** - www.hud.gov - HUD's mission is to increase homeownership, support community development and increase access to affordable housing free from discrimination. To fulfill this mission, HUD will embrace high standards of ethics, management and accountability and forge new partnerships - particularly with faith-based and community organizations - that leverage resources and improve HUD's ability to be effective on the community level.

◊   **Federal Housing Administration (FHA)** - http://www.hud.gov/offices/hsg/fhahistory.cfm - What is the Federal Housing Administration? The Federal Housing Administration, generally known as "FHA", provides mortgage insurance on loans made by FHA-approved lenders throughout the United States and its territories. FHA insures mortgages on single family and multifamily homes including manufactured homes and hospitals. It is the largest insurer of mortgages in the world, insuring nearly 33 million properties since its inception in 1934.

◊   **Federal National Mortgage Association (Fannie Mae) or (FNMA)** - www.fanniemae.com - For most of us, a home is more than simple shelter or a good investment. A home of our own is a dream come true and symbolizes who we are. At Fannie Mae, the home symbolizes who we are, too. Our public mission, and our defining goal, is to help more families achieve the American Dream of homeownership. We do that by providing financial products and services that make it possible for low-, moderate-, and middle-income families to buy homes of their own. Since Fannie Mae began in 1968 we have helped more than 61 million families achieve the American Dream of homeownership.

◊ **Government National Mortgage Association (Ginnie Mae) or (GNMA)** - www.ginniemae.gov - Who we are. What we do. Why it makes a difference? At Ginnie Mae, we help make affordable housing a reality for millions of low- and moderate-income households across America by channeling global capital into the nation's housing markets. Specifically, the Ginnie Mae guaranty allows mortgage lenders to obtain a better price for their mortgage loans in the secondary market. The lenders can then use the proceeds to make new mortgage loans available.

◊ **Federal Home Loan Mortgage Corporation (Freddie Mac) or (FHLMC)** - www.freddiemac.com - Freddie Mac is a stockholder-owned corporation chartered by Congress in 1970 to keep money flowing to mortgage lenders in support of homeownership and rental housing. Freddie Mac purchases single-family and multifamily residential mortgages and mortgage-related securities, which it finances primarily by issuing mortgage pass through securities and debt instruments in the capital markets. By doing so, we ultimately help homeowners and renters get lower housing costs and better access to home financing.

## *DATA SOURCES*

◊ **CoStar Group** - www.costar.com - Today, savvy commercial real estate professionals exchange, share and access information like never before. They recognize the advantages of using new information technologies. And tens of thousands of them rely on the CoStar Group for electronic commercial real estate information.

◊ **CourthouseDirect.com** - www.courthousedirect.com - CourthouseDirect.com is committed to providing fast, accurate and affordable courthouse documents and research by using the potential of the Internet to cut cost and save time associated with obtaining public records and thereby eliminating inefficiencies and revolutionizing the delivery of courthouse information nationwide.

◊ **Market Data Center** - www.marketdatacenter.com - The Redlink - a friendly, state of the art, online data retrieval system. It provides complete records on single family and condominium properties, including up to 35 years of historical data. Data includes sales recordings, tax information and property characteristics for all metro Atlanta counties. The data is collected directly from the county courthouse and assessor offices and is available online 24 hours a day. It requires MDC customized software. The RedBook - a printed compilation of current real estate appraisal report data collected from a variety of sources. MapMerge - Easy access to county tax assessor records, plat maps, county ownership digests and up-to-date sales records. Our software is the only system that allows you to merge the data you need to customize your reports and maps. Through cross referencing and incorporation of multiple criteria you also have the flexibility you need to most effectively manage your data.

## *FLOOD HAZARD INFORMATION SOURCES*

◊ **FloodSource** - www.floodsource.com - Many companies could benefit from having access to current flood hazard information. From this idea, FloodSource™ emerged to provide reliable, affordable flood hazard data - quickly and easily. As a result, FloodSource™ is now a leading provider of flood hazard information to the surveyor, appraiser, real estate, insurance, and flood determination industries.

◊ **InterFlood** - www.interflood.com - InterFlood is from a la mode, a provider of appraisal technology in North America. We provide mortgage transaction software and e-commerce tools, and flood hazard information.

◊ **Ordinance.com** - www.ordinance.com - Developed in conjunction with site plan design professionals, the ordinance.com website is a direct result of the frustration that you have experienced in working with paper copies of zoning and planning ordinances. The site is designed to be used by professionals submitting site plan and subdivision review documents on behalf of their clients. Also, provides tax map and flood map info.

◊ **Flood Insights** - www.floodinsights.com - Getting a flood zone determination by typing an address online. Enter the address and Flood Insights returns the Flood Zone, Community Number, Map Panel, Panel Date, Census Tract, and all other pertinent information. Plus, it returns a map suitable for your appraisal reports.

# State Real Estate Appraiser Boards

Here is the contact information for the State real estate appraiser boards. Some of this information may be outdated over time due to address and employee changes at the board offices. You can contact the appraisal office in your State to get more information on appraisal licensing exams, requirements, updated regulations and rules for real estate appraisers, etc.

◊   ALABAMA
Alabama Real Estate Appraiser Board
P.O. Box 304355
Montgomery, AL 36130-4355
PHONE: 334-242-8747
FAX: 334-242-8749
http://www.reab.state.al.us/

◊   ALASKA
Board of Certified Real Estate Appraisers
333 Willoughby Avenue
P.O. Box 110806
Juneau, AK 99811-0806
PHONE: 907-465-2542
FAX: 907-465-2974
http://www.dced.state.ak.us/occ/papr.htm

◊   ARIZONA
Arizona Board of Appraisal
1400 W. Washington, Suite 360
Phoenix, AZ 85007
PHONE: 602-542-1539
FAX: 602-542-1598
http://www.appraisal.state.az.us/

◊   ARKANSAS
Arkansas Appraiser Licensing & Certification Board
2725 Cantrell Road, Suite 202
Little Rock, AR 72202
PHONE: 501-296-1843
FAX: 501-296-1844
http://www.state.ar.us/alcb/

◊   CALIFORNIA
Office of Real Estate Appraisers
1102 Q Street, Suite 4100
Sacramento, CA 95814
PHONE: 916-440-7878
FAX: 916-440-7406
http://www.orea.ca.gov/

◊   COLORADO

State of Colorado Board of Real Estate Appraisers
1900 Grant Street, Suite 600
Denver, CO 80203
PHONE: 303-894-2166
FAX: 303-894-2683
http://www.dora.state.co.us/Real-Estate/appraisr/appraisr.htm

◊   CONNECTICUT
Department of Consumer Protection
Real Estate Appraisal Division
State Office Building, Room G-8A
165 Capitol Avenue Hartford, CT 06106
PHONE: 860-566-1568
FAX: 860-566-7630
http://www.state.ct.us/dcp/

◊   DELAWARE
Delaware Council on Real Estate Appraisers
861 Silver Lake Blvd.
Dover, DE 19904
PHONE: 302-744-4500
FAX: 302-739-2711
http://www.state.de.us/research/profreg/realesapp.htm

◊   DISTRICT OF COLUMBIA DCRA/OPLA
941 N. Capitol Street, NE, Rm. 7200
Washington, DC 20002
PHONE: 202-442-4320
FAX: 202-442-4528
http://dc.gov/agencies/detail.asp?id=24

◊   FLORIDA
Florida Department of Business and Professional Regulation
1940 N. Monroe Street
Tallahassee, FL 32399-0750
PHONE: 407-317-7013
FAX: 407-317-7281
http://www.state.fl.us/dbpr/re/index.shtml

◊   GEORGIA
Georgia Real Estate Appraiser Board
International Tower
229 Peachtree Street, NE, Suite 1000
Atlanta, GA 30303-1605
PHONE: 404-656-3916
FAX: 404-656-6650
http://www.georgia.gov/

◊   HAWAII
Hawaii Real Estate Appraiser Program
P.O. Box 3469
Honolulu, HI 96801
PHONE: 808-586-2704
FAX: 808-586-2689
http://www.ehawaiigov.org/serv/pvl

◊   IDAHO
Idaho Real Estate Appraiser Board
Bureau of Occupational Licenses
Owyhee Plaza
1109 Main Street, Suite 220
Boise, ID 83702-5642
PHONE: 208-334-3233
FAX: 208-334-3945
http://www2.state.id.us/ibol/rea.htm

◊   ILLINOIS
Illinois Real Estate Appraisal Administration
500 E. Monroe Street, Suite 500
Springfield, IL 62701-1509
PHONE: 312-793-7254
FAX: 217-782-2549
http://www.obre.state.il.us/

◊   INDIANA
Indiana Professional Licensing Agency
302 W. Washington, Room EO12
Indianapolis, IN 46204-2700
PHONE: 317-234-3009
FAX: 317-232-2312
http://www.in.gov/pla/

◊   IOWA
Iowa Real Estate Appraiser Examining Board
1920 S.E. Hulsizer Avenue
Ankeny, IA 50021-3941
PHONE: 515-281-7468
FAX: 515-281-7411
http://www.state.ia.us/government/com/prof/home.html

◊   KANSAS
Kansas Real Estate Commission
1100 SW Wannamaker Road, Suite 104
Topeka, KS 66604
PHONE: 785-271-3373
FAX: 785-271-3370
http://www.ink.org/public/kreab/

◊   KENTUCKY
Kentucky Real Estate Appraisers Board
2480 Fortune Drive, Suite 120
Lexington, KY 40509
PHONE: 859-543-8943
FAX: 859-543-0028
http://www.kyappraisersboard.com

◊   LOUISIANA
Louisiana Real Estate Commission
5222 Summa Court
P.O. Box 14785 (70898-4785)
Baton Rouge, LA 70809
PHONE: 225-765-0191
FAX: 225-765-0637
http://www.lreasbc.state.la.us/

◊   MAINE
Maine Board of Real Estate Appraisers
35 State House Station
122 Northern Avenue
Augusta, ME 04333
PHONE: 207-624-8603
FAX: 207-624-8637
http://www.state.me.us/pfr/led/appraisers/index.htm

◊   MARYLAND
Maryland Deptartment of Licensing & Regulation
Real Estate Appraisers Commission
500 N. Calvert Street, Suite 302
Baltimore, MD 21202
PHONE: 410-230-6165
FAX: 410-333-6314
http://www.dllr.state.md.us/

◊   MASSACHUSETTS
Commonwealth of Massachusetts
Division of Registration
239 Causeway Street, Suite 500
Boston, MA 02114-2130
PHONE: 617-727-3055
FAX: 617-727-2669
http://www.state.ma.us/reg/home.htm

◊   MICHIGAN
Department of Consumer & Industry Service
Bureau of Occupational & Professional Regulation
P.O. Box 30018
Lansing, MI 48909
PHONE: 517-241-9236
FAX: 517-373-1044
http://www.cis.state.mi.us/bcs/appr/

◊   MINNESOTA
Minnesota Department of Commerce
85-7th Place East, Suite 60
St. Paul, MN 55101
PHONE: 612-296-6319
FAX: 612-296-4328
http://www.commerce.state.mn.us/index.htm

◊   MISSISSIPPI
Mississippi Real Estate Commission
2506 Lakeland Drive, Suite 300
PO Box 12685
Jackson, MS 39236-2685
PHONE: 601-932-9191
FAX: 601-932-2990
http://www.mrec.state.ms.us/

◊   MISSOURI
Missouri Real Estate Appraisers Commission
3605 Missouri Blvd.
Jefferson City, MO 65102
PHONE: 573-751-0038
FAX: 573-526-2831
http://www.pr.mo.gov/appraisers.asp/

◊   MONTANA
Board of Real Estate Appraisers
301 S. Park Avenue, Suite 400
P.O. Box 200513
Helena, MT 59620-0513
PHONE: 406-841-2381
FAX: 406-841-2313
http://discoveringmontana.com/dli/bsd/license/licensing_board
s.htm

◊   NEBRASKA
Nebraska Real Estate Appraiser Board
301 Centennial Mall South
State Office Bldg., 5th Fl.
Lincoln, NE 68509-4963
PHONE: 402-471-9015
FAX: 402-471-9017
http://www.appraiser.ne.gov

◊   NEVADA
State of Nevada, Real Estate Division
788 Fairview Drive, Suite 200
Carson City, NV 89710-5453
PHONE: 775-687-4280
FAX: 702-687-4868
http://www.red.state.nv.us/

◊   NEW HAMPSHIRE
New Hampshire Real Estate Appraiser Board
State House Annex, Room 426
25 Capitol Street
Concord, NH 03301-6312
PHONE: 603-271-6186
FAX: 603-271-6513
http://webster.state.nh.us/nhreab/

◊   NEW JERSEY
Board of Real Estate Appraisers
Division of Consumer Affairs
124 Halsey Street
P.O. Box 45032
Newark, NJ 07101
PHONE: 973-504-6480
FAX: 973-648-3536
http://www.state.nj.us/lps/ca/nonmed.htm

◊   NEW MEXICO
New Mexico Real Estate Appraisers Board
2055 S. Pacecho, Bldg. 300
P.O. Box 25101
Santa Fe, NM 87504
PHONE: 505-476-7100
FAX: 505-476-7094
http://www.rld.state.nm.us/

◊   NEW YORK
Department of State
Division of Licensing Services
84 Holland Avenue
Albany, NY 12208-3490
PHONE: 518-473-2728
FAX: 518-473-2730
http://www.dos.state.ny.us/lcns/appraise.htm

◊　NORTH CAROLINA
North Carolina Appraisal Board
P.O. Box 20500
Raleigh, NC 27619-0500
PHONE: 919-420-7920
FAX: 919-420-7925
http://www.ncappraisalboard.org/

◊　NORTH DAKOTA
North Dakota Appraisal Board
P.O. Box 1336
Bismarck, ND 58502-1336
PHONE: 701-222-1051
FAX: 701-222-8083
http://discovernd.com/

◊　OHIO
Ohio Division of Real Estate
615 Superior Avenue, N.W., Room 525
Cleveland, OH 44113
PHONE: 216-787-3100
FAX: 216-787-4449
http://www.com.state.oh.us/ODOC/real/

◊　OKLAHOMA
Oklahoma Real Estate Appraiser Board
2401 NW 23rd St, Ste 28
Oklahoma City, OK 73107
Mailing Address:
P.O. Box 53408
Oklahoma City, OK 73152-3408
PHONE: 405-521-6636
FAX: 405-522-3642
http://www.oid.state.ok.us/

◊　OREGON
Appraiser Certification and Licensure Board
Department of Consumer & Business Services
1860 Hawthorne Avenue, NE
Suite 200
Salem, OR 97303
PHONE: 503-485-2555
FAX: 503-485-2559
http://www.cbs.state.or.us/

◊　PENNSYLVANIA
Pennsylvania State Board of Certified Real Estate Appraisers
2601 North Third Street
Harrisburg, PA 17110
PHONE: 717-783-4866
FAX: 717-787-7769
http://www.dos.state.pa.us/

◊　RHODE ISLAND
Department Of Business Reg. Licensing
Division of Commerce
Licensing & Regulation Real Estate Appraisal Section
233 Richmond Street, Suite 230
Providence, RI 02903
PHONE: 401-222-2255
FAX: 401-222-6098
http://www.dbr.state.ri.us/real_estate.html

◊　SOUTH CAROLINA
South Carolina Real Estate Appraisal Board
P.O. Box 11847
Columbia, SC 29211-1847
PHONE: 803-896-4455
FAX: 803-896-4402
http://www.llr.state.sc.us/pol.asp

◊　SOUTH DAKOTA
South Dakota Department of Revenue and Regulation
445 East Capitol Avenue
Pierre, SD 57501-3185
PHONE: 605-773-3178
FAX: 605-773-3018
http://www.state.sd.us/state/executive/dcr/dcr.html

◊　TENNESSEE
Tennessee Real Estate Appraiser Commission
500 James Robertson Parkway
Suite 620
Nashville, TN 37243
PHONE: 615-741-1831
FAX: 615-741-6470
http://www.state.tn.us/commerce/boards/treac/index.html

◊　TEXAS
Texas Appraiser Licensing & Certification Board
P.O. Box 12188
Austin, TX 78711-2188
PHONE: 512-465-3900
FAX: 512-465-3910
http://www.talcb.state.tx.us

◊   UTAH
Utah Division of Real Estate
Department of Commerce
Box 146711
Salt Lake City, UT 84145
PHONE: 801-530-6711
FAX: 801-530-6756
http://www.commerce.utah.gov/dre/index.html

◊   VERMONT
Secretary of States Office
Vermont Board of Real Estate Appraisers
P.O. Box 109 State Street
Montpelier, VT 05609-1106
PHONE: 802-828-3228
FAX: 802-828-2484
http://vtprofessionals.org/opr1/appraisers/

◊   VIRGINIA
Department of Professional & Occupational Regulation
3600 West Broad Street, 5th Floor
Richmond, VA 23230-4817
PHONE: 804-367-2039
FAX: 804-367-2475
http://www.state.va.us/dpor/apr_main.htm

◊   WASHINGTON
Business & Professions Division
P.O. Box 9015
Olympia, WA 98507-9015
PHONE: 360-753-1062
FAX: 360-586-0998
http://www.wa.gov/dol/bpd/appfront.htm

◊   WEST VIRGINIA
Licensing and Certification Board
2110 Kanawha Blvd., East, Suite 101
Charleston, WV 25311
PHONE: 304-558-3919
FAX: 304-558-3983
http://www.state.wv.us./appraise/

◊   WISCONSIN
Wisconsin Dept. of Regulation & Licensing
Business & Design Professions
P.O. Box 8935
Madison, WI 53708-8935
PHONE: 608-261-2392
FAX: 608-267-3816
http://drl.wi.gov/index.htm

◊   WYOMING
Certified Real Estate Appraiser Board
First Bank Building
2020 Carey Avenue, Suite 100
Cheyenne, WY 82002-0180
PHONE: 307-777-7141
FAX: 307-777-3796
http://realestate.state.wy.us/

## Appraiser Boards outside the USA:

◊   AMERICAN SAMOA
American Samoa Government
Pago Pago, 96799
American Samoa
PHONE: 684-633-4116
FAX: 684-633-0000

◊   GUAM
Government of Guam
Dept. of Revenue & Taxation
Bldg 13-1, 2nd Fl. Mariner Ave, Tiyan
P.O. Box 23607
Barrigada, GU 96913
PHONE: 671-475-1844
FAX: 671-472-2643

◊   MARIANA ISLANDS
Board of Professional Licensing
Commonwealth of Northern Mariana Islands
P.O. Box 502078
Saipan, MP 96950
PHONE: 670-234-5897
FAX: 670-234-6040

◊   PUERTO RICO
Government of Puerto Rico
Department of State
Puerto Rico Board of Examiners
Hortencia #240, Round Hills
Trujillo Alto, PR 00976
PHONE: 809-722-2122
FAX: 809-721-8399

◊   VIRGIN ISLANDS
Dept. of Licensing and Consumer Affairs
Government of Virgin Island
No. 1 Sub Base, Room 205
St. Thomas, VI 00802
PHONE: 809-773-2226
FAX: 809-778-8250

# *Real Estate Terminology Glossary*

**A.L.T.A Title Policy:** (American Land Title Association) A type of title insurance policy issued by title insurance companies which expands the risks normally insured against under the standard type policy. It is a lender's policy, but available to any one willing to pay for the extra coverage.

**Abandonment:** To release a claim, as a Declaration of Abandonment when a property has been homesteaded.

**Abatement of Nuisance:** Extinction or termination of a nuisance.

**Abstract:** A brief summary.

**Abstract of Judgment:** A condensation of the essential provisions of a court judgment.

**Abstract of Title:** A summary or digest of the conveyances, transfers, and any other facts relied upon as evidence of title, together with any other elements of record which may impair the title.

**Abstraction:** A method of valuing land. The indicated value of the improvement is deducted from the sale price.

**Acceleration Clause:** Clause in trust deed or mortgage giving lender the right to call all sums owing him to be immediately due and payable upon the happening of certain event.

**Acceptance:** When the seller or agent's principal agrees to the terms of the agreement of sale and approves the negotiation on the part of the agent and acknowledges receipt of the deposit in subscribing to the agreement of sale, that act is termed an acceptance.

**Access Right:** The right of an owner to have ingress and egress to and from his property.

**Accession:** Acquire title by having property added to your property.

**Accretion:** An addition to land from natural causes. Example: From the gradual action of the ocean or river waters.

**Accrued:** Accumulated up to this point in time. Accrued interest, accrued depreciation.

**Accrued Depreciation:** The difference between the cost of replacement new as of the date of the appraisal and the present appraised value.

**Acknowledgment:** A formal declaration before a duly authorized officer by a person who has executed an instrument that such execution is his act and deed.

**Acquisition:** The act or process by which a person procures property.

**Acre:** A measure of land equaling 4,840 square yards, or 43,560 square feet, or a tract about 208.71 feet square.

**Actual Notice:** Knowledge of the existence of a thing or fact.

**Administrator:** A person appointed by the probate court to administer the estate of a person deceased.

**Adjusted Book Value:** Cost of acquisition minus depreciation (if allowed) plus capital improvements. Used when figuring profit for income tax.

**Adjusted selling price:** Selling price minus expenses of sale. Used when figuring profit for income tax.

**Ad Valorem:** According to valuation.

**Adverse Possession:** The open and notorious possession and occupancy under an evident claim or right, in denial or opposition to the title of another claimant.

**Affiant:** A person who makes a sworn or affirmed statement.

**Affidavit:** A statement or declaration reduced to writing, sworn to or affirmed before some officer who has authority to administer an oath or affirmation.

**Affirm:** To confirm, to aver, to ratify, to verify.

**Affirmation:** A solemn Declaration made by a person who objects to taking an oath.

**A.F.L.B.:** Accredited Farm and Land Broker.

**Agency:** The relationship between principal and agent which arises out of the contract, either expressed or implied, written or oral, wherein the agent is employed by the principal to do certain acts dealing with a third party.

**Agreement for Purchase and Sale:** A land contract.

**Agreement of Sale:** A written agreement or contract between seller and purchaser in which they reach a meeting of minds on the terms and conditions of the sale.

**Agreement to Convey:** A land Contract.

**Alienation:** The transferring of property to another, the transfer of property and possession of lands, or other things, from one person to another.

**Alienation Clause:** Clause in a loan document providing for full payment if the property is sold.

**Aluuvion; (Alluvium):** Soil deposited by accretion. Increase of earth on shore or bank of a river.

**Amenities:** Satisfaction of enjoyable living to be derived from a home; conditions of agreeable living or a beneficial influence arising from the location or improvements.

**Amortization:** The liquidation of a financial obligation on an installment basis; also, recovery, over a period, of cost or value.

**Amortized Loan:** A loan that is completely paid off, interest and principal, by a series of regular payments that are equal or nearly equal. Also called a level payments loan.

**Anticipation, Principle of:** Affirms that value is created by anticipated benefits to be derived in the future.

**Appraisal:** An opinion of value of property.

**Appraiser:** One qualified by education, training and experience who is hired to estimate the value of real and personal property based on experience, judgment, facts, and use of formal appraisal processes.

**Appurtenance:** Something annexed to another thing, which may be transferred incident to it. That which belongs to other things, as a barn, dwelling, garage, or orchard is incident to the land to which it is attached.

**Assemblage:** Putting together two or more parcels to increase the total value.

**Assessed Value:** A value placed upon property by a public officer or board, as a basis for taxation.

**Assessment**: The valuation of property for the purpose of levying a tax or the amount of the tax levied.

**Assessor**: The official who has the responsibility of determining assessed values.

**Assets**: Everything of value, both real and personal property, owned by a business.

**Assignment**: A transfer or making over to another of the whole of any property, real or personal, in possession or in action, or of any estate or right therein.

**Assignor**: One who assigns or transfers property.

**Assigns; Assignees**: Those to whom property shall have been transferred.

**Assumption Agreement**: An undertaking or adoption of a debt or obligation primarily resting upon another person.

**Assumption Fee:** A lender's charge for changing over and processing new records for a new owner who is assuming an existing loan.

**Assumption of Mortgage:** The taking of title to property by a grantee, wherein he assumes liability for payment of an existing note secured by a mortgage or deed of trust against the property, becoming a co-guarantor for the payment of a mortgage or deed of trust note.

**Attachment:** Seizure of property by court order, usually done to have it available in event a judgment is obtained in a pending suit.

**Attest:** To affirm to be true or genuine; an official act establishing authenticity.

**Attorney-In-Fact**: One who is authorized to perform acts for another under a power of attorney; power of attorney may be limited to specific act or acts, or be general.

**Avulsion:** The sudden tearing away or removal of land by action of water flowing over or through it.

**Bailment:** The delivery of goods or money to another in trust.

**Balloon Payment:** Where the final installment payment on a note is greater than the preceding installment payments and it pays the note in full, such final installment is termed a balloon payment.

**Band of Investment:** A method of computing the capitalization rate by considering the return demanded by the holders of various loans, and the owner.

**Base and Meridian:** Imaginary lines used by surveyors to find and describe the location of private or public lands.

**Bearing Wall or Partition**: A wall or partition supporting any vertical load in addition to its own weight.

**Bench Mark:** A location indicated in a durable market by surveyors.

**Beneficiary:** 1.) One entitled to the benefit of a trust; 2.) One who receives profit from an estate, the title which is vested in a trustee; 3.) The lender on the security of a note and deed of trust.

**Bequeath:** To give or hand down personal property by will; to leave by will.

**Bequest:** That personal property which is given by the terms of a will.

**Betterment:** An improvement upon property which increases the property value and is considered as a capital asset, as distinguished from repairs or replacements where the original character or cost is unchanged.

**Bilateral Contract:** A contract in which both parties agree to perform certain acts.

**Bill of Sale:** A written instrument given to pass title of personal property from vendor to vendee.

**Binder:** A notation of coverage on an insurance policy, issued by an agent, and given to the insured prior to issuing of the policy.

**Blanket Encumbrance:** An encumbrance that covers more than one parcel of property.

**Blanket Mortgage:** A single mortgage that covers more than one piece of real estate.

**Blighted Area:** A declining area in which real property values are seriously affected by destructive economic forces, such as encroaching inharmonious property usages, infiltration of lower social and economic classes of in habitants, and/or rapidly depreciating buildings.

**Board Foot:** A unit of measurement of lumber,, one foot wide, one foot long, one inch thick; 144 cubic inches.

**Bona Fide:** In good faith; without fraud.

**Book Depreciation:** The depreciation shown on the accounting books of the owner. Used for income tax calculation.

**Book Value:** Value of the property as shown on the accounting books of the owner.

**Boot**: Profit gained in exchange of properties on which income tax is not deferred. May be anything of value, including mortgage relief.

**Bounds:** Boundaries in a metes and bounds description.

**Breach:** The breaking of a law, or failure of duty, either by omission or commission.

**B.T.U.:** British Thermal Unit. The quantity of heat required to raise the temperature of one pound of water one degree Fahrenheit.

**Building Line:** A line, set by law, a certain distance from the street line in front of which an owner cannot build on his lot. (Setback)

**Building Residual:** A method of appraising. The value of land is subtracted from the value of the property leaving the value of the building.

**Bulk Sale:** The sale of merchandise in bulk rather than in the ordinary course of business.

**Bundle of Rights:** Beneficial interests or rights.

**Bylaws:** The rules of an organization such as a homeowners association.

**C.C. & R.s:** Covenants, Conditions and Restrictions affecting the use of a property.

**Capacity:** Having legal competence to sign binding contracts.

**Capital:** Assets of a permanent nature used in the production of an income, such as: land, buildings, machinery, equipment, etc.

**Capital Gain:** Profit from the sale of property.

**Capital Loss.** Loss from the sale of property.

**Capitalization:** In appraising, determining value of property by considering net income and percentage or reasonable return on investment.

**Capitalization Rate; Cap Rate:** Calculated by dividing the net operating income by the offering price of the property. The lower the rate, the higher the selling price…and the higher the rate, the lower the selling price. Selling Price = Net Operating Income/Cap Rate Example: If the net operating income of a apartment building is $100,000 and the Cap Rate is 10%, the selling price would be $1,000,000. ($100,000/10%). Lowering the Cap Rate to 8% increases the selling price to $1,250,000 ($100,000/8%). Raising it to 12% reduces the selling price to $833,333 ($100,000/12%). It answers the question, "How much am I willing to pay for this cash flow?"

**Cash Flow:** Cash left at the end of a period of time (usually a year) from the operation of income property or a business. Do not subtract depreciation when computing cash flow.

**Caveat Emptor:** "Let the buyer beware". The buyer must research purchase and buy at her own risk.

**Certificate of Reasonable Value (CRV);** The Veterans Administration appraisal commitment of property value.

**Certificate of Title**: A certification of the ownership of land. The first step to obtaining title insurance.

**C.C.I.M.:** Certified Commercial Investment Member.

**Chain of Title:** A history of conveyances and encumbrances affecting the title from the time the original patent was granted, or as far back as records are available.

**Change, Principle of:** Holds that it is the future, not the past, which is of prime importance in estimating value.

**Chattel:** Personal property.

**Chattel Mortgage:** A personal property mortgage - Security Agreement.

**Chattels Real:** An estate related to real estate, such as a lease on real property.

**Chattels**: Goods or every species of property movable or immovable that are not real property.

**Chose in Action:** A personal right recoverable by a court suit.

**Closing Statement:** The final accounting of a sale given by escrow to the buyer and seller.

**Cloud On The Title:** Any conditions revealed by a title search that affect the title to property; usually relatively unimportant items that can be removed with a quitclaim deed or court action.

**Code:** A group of laws.

**Collateral:** The property subject to the security interest.

**Collateral Security:** A separate obligation attached to contract to guarantee its performance; the transfer of property or of other contracts, or valuables, to insure the performance of a principal agreement.

**Collusion:** An agreement between two or more persons to defraud another of his rights by the forms of law, or to obtain an object forbidden by law.

**Color Of Title:** That which appears to be good title, but which is not title in fact.

**Commercial Paper:** Bills of exchange used in commercial trade.

**Commercial Acre:** A term applied to the remainder of an acre of newly subdivided land after the area devoted to streets, sidewalks and curbs has been deducted from the acre.

**Commingling:** Mixing client's money or property with the agent's.

**Commitment:** A Pledge, or a promise, or firm agreement.

**Common Law:** The body of law that grew from customs and practices developed and used in England "since the memory of man runneth not to the contrary."

**Community:** A part of a metropolitan area that has a number of neighborhoods that have tendency toward common interests and problems.

**Community Apartment Project:** A subdivision where the buyer receives a deed to the whole property and the right to use an apartment. Each owner is a tenant in common.

**Community Property:** Property accumulated through joint efforts of husband and wife.

**Compaction:** Whenever extra soil is added to a lot to fill in low places or to raise the level of the lot, the added soil is often too loose and soft to sustain the weight of the buildings. Therefore, it is necessary to compact the added soil so that it will carry the weight without the danger of their tilting, settling or cracking.

**Comparable Sales:** Property sales that have similar characteristics as the subject property and are used for analysis in the appraisal process.

**Comparison Approach:** Appraising by comparing recent sales prices of similar properties.

**Compound Interest:** Interest paid on original principal and also on the accrued and unpaid interest that has accumulated.

**Condemnation:** The act of taking private property for public use by a political subdivision; declaration that a structure is unfit for use.

**Condition:** Provision that the transfer of property depends upon another uncertain event.

**Condition Precedent:** A condition that must be fulfilled before title can be transferred.

**Condition Subsequent:** A condition that provides that if the owner fails to do something his title may be defeated and he may lose the property.

**Conditional Commitment:** A commitment of a definite loan amount for some future unknown purchaser of satisfactory credit standing.

**Conditional Sale Contract:** A contract for the sale of property stating that delivery is to be made to the buyer, title to remain vested in the seller until the conditions of the contract have been fulfilled.

**Condominium:** Individual fee ownership of units in a multi-family structure, combined with joint ownership of common areas of the structure and the land.

**Confirmation of Sale:** A court approval of the sale of property by an executor, administrator, guardian or conservator.

**Consideration**: Anything of value given to induce entering into a contract; it may be money, personal services, or even love and affection.

**Construction Loans**: Loans made for the construction of homes or buildings disbursed to the builder during construction and after periodic inspections.

**Constructive Eviction**: A disturbance of a tenant's possession by the landlord.

**Contiguous:** Touching at any point. Contiguous lots.

**Contingent**: Dependent upon an uncertain future event.

**Contour:** The surface configuration of land.

**Contract:** An agreement to do or not to do a certain thing.

**Contribution, Principle of:** Appraising principle used when considering proposed improvements.

**Conventional Loan:** A loan made without government backing.

**Conversion:** Change from one character or use to another.

**Conveyance:** Transfer of the title of land from one to another. Denotes an instrument that carries from person to another an interest in land.

**Corner Influence:** The added value of a corner lot.

**Correlation:** To bring the indicated values developed by the three approaches used in the appraisal process into mutual relationship with each other.

**Cost Approach:** An analysis in which a value estimate of a property is derived by estimating the replacement cost of the improvements, deducting there from the estimated accrued depreciation, then adding the market value of the land.

**Covenant:** Agreements written into deeds and other instruments promising performance or nonperformance of certain acts or stipulating certain uses or non-uses of the property.

**C.P.M.:** Certified Property Manager.

**C.R.E**: Counselor of Real Estate – Member of the American Society of R.E. Counselors.

**Cul-De-Sac:** Street open at one end only.

**Curable Depreciation:** Items of physical and functional obsolescence, which are customarily repaired or replaced by a prudent property owner.

**Curtesy:** The right, which a husband has in a wife's estate at her death.

**Damages:** The indemnity recoverable by a person who has sustained an injury, either in his person, property, or relative rights, through the act or default of another.

**Dealer Property:** Property held for sale to customers. Profit is considered ordinary income for income tax.

**Debtor:** The party who "owns" the property that is subject to the security interest. Sometimes known as the mortgagor or pledgor, etc.

**Deciduous Trees:** Lose leaves in autumn and winter.

**Declaration of Abandonment**: Document recorded to terminate a homestead.

**Declaration of Homestead**: Document recorded to establish a homestead to protect the owner against judgment liens.

**Declaration of Restrictions:** Recorded list of restrictions imposed on a subdivision by a subdivider.

**Declining Balance Depreciation:** Method of computing depreciation for income tax purposes.

**Deed:** Written instrument that, when properly executed and delivered, conveys title.

**Deed of Trust:** Document by which naked, legal title is transferred to a trustee as security for a loan.

**Default:** Failure to fulfill a duty or promise or to discharge an obligation; omission or failure to perform any act.

**Defeasance Clause:** The clause in a mortgage that gives the mortgagor the right to redeem his property upon the payment of his obligations to the mortgagee.

**Deferred Maintenance**: Existing buy unfulfilled requirements for repairs and rehabilitation.

**Deficiency Judgment:** A judgment given when the security pledge for a loan does not satisfy the debt upon its default.

**Demand:** Desire for property. One of four elements that create value.

**Demise:** Transfer to another of an estate for years, for life, or at will.

**Deposit Receipt**: Document used when accepting earnest money to bind an offer. Basic contract between buyer and seller.

**Depreciation:** Loss of value in real property brought about by age, physical deterioration or functional or economic obsolescence. Broadly, a loss in value from any cause.

**Descent:** Acquiring property by inheritance when the deceased dies intestate.

**Desist and Refrain Order:** An order directing a person to desist and refrain from committing an act in violation of the law.

**Devise:** A gift of real property by will.

**Devisee:** one who receive real property by will.

**Devisor:** One who leaves real property by will.

**Directional Growth:** Direction toward which the residential section of a city is destined or determined to grow.

**Discount:** An amount deducted from the face amount of a loan.

**Discount Points:** Prepaid interest demanded by lender when loan is negotiated. A premium paid for the privilege of borrowing at the stated interest rate.

**Documentary Transfer Tax:** Tax collected when a deed is recorded. Stamps are affixed to the deed.

**Dominant Tenement:** The land that is benefited by an easement appurtenant.

**Dower:** The right that a wife has in her husband's estate at his death.

**Earnest Money:** Deposit accompanying an offer.

**Easement:** Created by grant or agreement for a specific purpose, an easement is the right, privilege or interest that one party has in the land of another.

**Economic Life:** The period over which a property will yield a return on the investment, over and above the economic or ground rent due to land.

**Economic Obsolescence:** A loss in value due to factors outside the subject property, but adversely affecting the value of the property.

**Economic Rent:** The reasonable rental expectancy if the property were available for renting at the time of it valuation.

**Effective age of Improvement:** The number of years of age that is indicated by the condition of the structure.

**Effective Gross income:** The maximum rent from income property minus vacancies.

**Effective Interest Rate:** Percentage of interest that is actually being paid by the borrower for the use of the money.

**Egress:** Means of leaving/exiting the property.

**Emblements:** Growing annual crops. The right of a tenant farmer to harvest his crop after his lease expires.

**Eminent Domain:** The right of government to acquire property for necessary public use by condemnation; the owner must be fairly compensated.

**Encroachment:** Trespass: the building of a structure or construction of any improvements partly or wholly on the property of another.

**Encumbrance:** Anything that affects or limits the fee simple title to property, such as mortgages, easements or restrictions of any kind. Liens are special encumbrances that make the property security for the payment of a debt or obligation, such as mortgages and taxes.

**Endorsement:** The signature of the payee on the back of a negotiable instrument.

**Equitable Title:** The title held by a vendee under a land contract.

**Equity:** The interest or value that an owner has in real estate over and above any liens.

**Equity Redemption:** The right to redeem property during the foreclosure period.

**Erosion.** The wearing away of land by the action of water, wind or glacial ice.

**Escalation:** The right reserved by the lender to increase the amount of the payments and/or interest upon the happening of a certain event.

**Escheat:** The reverting of property to the state when heirs capable of inheriting are lacking.

**Escrow:** The deposit of instruments and funds with instructions to a third neutral party to carry out the provisions of an agreement or contract.

**Estate:** As applied to real estate, the term signifies the quantity of interest, share, right and equity, of which riches or fortune may consist, in real property.

**Estate at Sufferance:** Estate of a tenant after his right to possess the property has ended.

**Estate for Life:** A freehold estate, not of inheritance, but which is held by the tenant for his own life or the life or lives of one or more other persons.

**Estate for Years:** An interest in lands by virtue of a contract for the possession of them for a definite and limited period of time. A lease may be said to be an estate for years.

**Estate in Fee:** A fee estate. The greatest degree of ownership of real property.

**Estate of will:** The occupation of lands and tenements by a tenant for an indefinite period, terminable by one or both parties.

**Estimated Remaining Life:** Period of time (years) it take for the improvements to become valueless.

**Estoppel:** Doctrine that bars one from asserting rights that are inconsistent with a previous position or representation.

**El Al:** And others.

**Et Ux:** And wife.

**Eviction:** Putting out a tenant when his right to possess the property has ended.

**Exception:** Withholding part of a property when it is conveyed.

**Exclusive Agency Listing:** Written instrument giving one agent the right to sell property for a specified time, but reserving the right of the owner to sell the property himself without the payment of a commission.

**Exclusive Right to Sell Listing:** Written agreement between owner and agent giving agent the right to collect a commission if the property is sold by anyone during the term of his agreement.

**Exculpatory Clause:** A clause that releases the landlord from liability due to injuries.

**Execute:** To complete, to make, to perform, to do, to follow out; to execute a contract is to perform the contract to follow out to the end, to complete.

**Executed Contract:** Where both parties have completely performed.

**Executor:** Person named in a will to carry out its provisions as to the disposition of the estate of a person deceased.

**Extended Coverage:** A broad form title insurance policy that protects the owner against additional risks.

**Federal Housing Administration:** Federal agency that insures lenders making F.H.A. loans.

**Federal Notional Mortgage Association:** "Fanny Mae". A secondary money market that buys and sells existing loans to stabilize the money market.

**Fee:** An estate of inheritance in real property.

**Fee Simple:** In modern estates, the terms "fee" and "fee simple" are substantially synonymous.

**Fee Simple Absolute:** Fee simple ownership with no qualifications or limitations.

**Fee Simple Defeasible:** Fee simple ownership with a condition that, if broken, could result in loss of title to the property.

**Fiduciary:** A person in a position of trust and confidence, as between principal and broker.

**Financing Statement:** The instrument that is filed in a loan on personal property in order to give public notice of the security interest and thereby protect the interest of the secured parties in the collateral.

**Finder's Fee:** Fee paid to a person for information.

**Fixtures:** Items attached to the land or improvements, that usually cannot be removed without agreement, and, therefore, they become real property; plumbing fixtures, items built into the property, etc.

**Foreclosure:** Procedure whereby property pledged as security for a debt is sold to pay the debt in event of default in payments or terms.

**Forfeiture:** Loss of money or anything of value due to failure to perform.

**Freehold Estate:** A fee simple or life estate.

**Frontage:** Land bordering a street.

**Front Foot:** Property measurement for sale or valuation purposes; the property measured by the front foot on its street line – each front foot extending the depth of the lot.

**Functional Obsolescence:** A loss of value due to adverse factors from within the structure that affect the utility of the structure.

**Future Benefits:** The anticipated benefits the present owner will receive from his property in the future.

**General Lien:** A lien that affects all property of a person.

**General Partnership:** Partnership where all partners can participate in management and liability.

**Gift Deed:** A deed for which the consideration is love and affection and where there is no material consideration.

**Graduated Lease:** Lease that provides for a varying rental rate.

**Grant:** Technical term made use of in deeds of conveyances of lands to impart a transfer.

**Grant Deed:** Deed conveying the title. It has two implied warranties.

**Grantee:** The purchaser; a person to whom a grant is made.

**Granting Clause:** The action clause of a grant deed.

**Grantor:** Seller of property; one who signs a deed.

**G.R.I.:** Graduate, Realtors Institute.

**Gross Income:** Total income before any expenses are deducted

**Gross Rent Multiplier:** A figure, which, times the gross income of a property, produces an estimate of value of the property.

**Ground Lease:** An Agreement for the use of the land only, sometimes secured by improvements placed on the land by the user.

**Ground Rent:** Earnings of improved property credited to earnings of the ground itself after allowance is made for earnings of improvements, often termed economic rent.

**Guarantee of Title:** Opinion of title condition backed by a fund to compensate in case of negligence. A forerunner of title insurance.

**Hard Money Loan:** the borrower receives actual cash and not just credit.

**Hereditaments:** Anything capable of being inherited.

**Highest & Best Use:** Appraisal phrase meaning that use which, at the time of an appraisal, is most likely to produce the greatest net return to the land and/or buildings over a given period of time.

**Holder in Due Course:** One who has taken a note, check or bill of exchange in due course: 1. Before it was overdue; 2. In good faith and for value; 3. Without knowledge that is has been previously dishonored and without notice of any defect at the time it was negotiated to him.

**Holographic Will:** Will entirely handwritten and signed by the testator.

**Homestead:** Home upon which the owner or owners have recorded a Declaration of Homestead, protects home against judgments up to specified amounts.

**Hypothecate:** To give a thing as security without the necessity of giving up possession of it.

**Implied:** Presumed or inferred rather than expressed.

**Impounds:** A trust –type account established by lenders for the accumulation of funds to meet taxes, FHA mortgage insurance premiums, and/or future insurance policy premiums required to protect the lenders security. Impounds are usually collected with the monthly mortgage payments.

**Improvements:** Things built on land that becomes a part of the real property.

**Income Approach:** One of the three methods in the appraisal process; an analysis in which the estimated income from the subject residence is used as a basis for estimating value.

**Income property:** Property that produces rent.

**Increment:** An increase. Most frequently used to refer to the increase of value of land that accompanies population growth and increasing wealth in the community. The term unearned increment is used in this connection since values Are supposed to have increased without effort on the part of the owner.

**Ingress:** Means of entering property.

**Inherit:** To acquire property by will or succession.

**Injunction:** A writ or order issued under the seal of a court to restrain one or more parties to a suit or proceeding from doing an act that is deemed to be inequitable or unjust in regard to the rights of some other party or parties in the suit or proceeding.

**Installment Note:** Note that provides that payments of a certain sum or amount be paid on the dates specified in the instrument.

**Installment Sales Contract:** A land contract.

**Instrument:** Written legal document created to effect the rights of the parties.

**Intangible Value:** An asset that is not physical. Goodwill, patent rights, etc.

**Interest Rate:** The percentage of a sum of money charged for its use.

**Intestate:** A person who dies having made no will.

**Intestate Succession:** Inheriting property when the deceased had no will or a defective will.

**Inventory:** A list of the stock and fixtures of a business.

**Inverse Condemnation:** When the government damages property and the owner sues the government for damages.

**Involuntary Conveyance:** Transfer of title without the owner's permission.

**Involuntary Lien:** A lien imposed against property without consent of an owner: taxes, special assessments, federal income tax liens, etc.

**Irrevocable:** Incapable of being recalled or revoked: unchangeable.

**Irrigation Districts:** Quasi-political districts created under special laws to provide for water services to property owners in the district: an operation governed to a great extent by law.

**Joint And Several Note:** A note signed by two or more persons in which they are liable jointly and individually for the full amount of the loan.

**Joint Note:** Note signed by two or more persons who each have liability for payment of part of the loan.

**Joint Tenancy:** Joint ownership by two or more persons with right of survivorship: all joint tenants own equal interest and have equal rights in the property.

**Joint Venture:** A syndicate formed for a single purpose.

**Judgment:** The final determination of a court of competent jurisdiction of a matter presented to it: money judgments provide for the payment of claims presented to the court, or are awarded as damages, etc.

**Junior Lien:** Lien that does not have first priority.

**Junior Trust Deed:** Trust deed that does not have first priority.

**Jurisdiction:** The authority by which judicial officers take cognizance of and decide causes: the power to hear and determine a cause: the right and power that a judicial officer has to enter upon the inquiry.

**Key Lot:** Lot that has adjoining on its side the rear of another lot.

**Laches:** Delay or negligence in asserting one's legal rights.

**Land Contract:** A contract ordinarily used in connection with the sale of a property in cases where the seller does not wish to convey title until all or a certain part of the purchase price is paid by the buyer, often used when property is sold on small down payment.

**Land Residual:** A method of appraising. The value of the building is subtracted from the value of the property, leaving the value of the land.

**Land Sales Contract:** A land contract.

**Lateral Support:** The support that the soil of an adjoining owner gives to his neighbor's land.

**Lawful Object:** Legal purpose. One of the four essential elements of a contract.

**Lease:** Contract between the owner and tenant, setting forth conditions upon which tenant may occupy and use the property and the term of the occupancy.

**Leasehold;** the interest of one who leases property. A less than freehold estate.

**Legacy:** A gift of personal property by will.

**Legal Description:** A description recognized by law: a description by which property can be definitely located by reference to government surveys or approved recorded maps.

**Legatee:** Person to whom personal property is given by will.

**Less-Than-Freehold Estate:** The interest of one who leases property. The right of exclusive possession. A leasehold.

**Lessee:** One who contracts to rent property under a lease contract.

**Lessor:** An owner who enters into a lease with a tenant

**Leverage:** Making money with borrowed money.

**Liabilities.** The debts owed by a business.

**License:** Personal, revocable, non-assignable permission to do some act on the land of another.

**Lien:** A form of encumbrance that usually makes property security for the payment of a debt or discharge of an obligation: examples – judgments, taxes, mortgages, deed of trust, etc.

**Life Estate:** Estate limited in duration to the life or lives of one or more designated persons.

**Limited Partnership:** Partnership composed of some partners whose contribution and liability are limited.

**Liquid Assets:** Assets readily convertible to cash.

**Liquidate:** Selling property to secure cash.

**Liquidate Damages Clause**: A clause in a contract specifying the damages in the event of a breach of contract.

**Lis Pendens:** Suit pending, usually recorded so as to give constructive notice of pending litigation.

**Listing:** Employment contract between principal and agent authorizing the agent to perform services for the principal involving the latter's property.

**Loan Broker:** Person who negotiates the loans.

**Loan Closing:** When all conditions have been met, the loan officer authorizes the recording of the trust deed or mortgage and disbursal of funds.

**Loan Commitment:** Lender's contractual commitment to a loan based upon the appraisal and underwriting.

**Loan-To-Value Ratio:** The amount of the loan expressed as a percentage of the appraised value.

**M.A.I.:** Member of the Appraisal Institute.

**Margin of Security:** The difference between the amount of the mortgage loan and the appraised value of the property.

**Marginal Land**: Land that barely pays the cost of working or using.

**Market Data Approach:** One of the three methods in the appraisal process. A means of comparing similar type residential properties, that have recently sold, to the subject property.

**Market Price:** The price paid, regardless of pressures, motives or intelligence.

**Master Plan:** General plan for the future development of a community.

**Material Fact:** Fact is material if it is one that the agent should realize would be likely to affect the judgment of the principal in giving his consent to the agent to enter into the particular transaction on the specified terms.

**Mechanic's Lien:** A lien placed on property by laborers and material suppliers who have contributed to a work of improvement.

**Megalopolis:** Large geographical area composed of a group of adjacent cities.

**Menace:** A threat to commit duress.

**Meridians:** Imaginary north-south lines that intersect base lines to form a starting point for the measurement of land.

**Metes & Bounds:** Term used in describing the boundary lines of land, setting forth all the boundary lines together with their terminal points and angle.

**Mile:** 5,280 lineal feet.

**Minors:** All persons under the age of majority, usually 18.

**Misplaced Improvements:** Improvements on land that do not conform to the most profitable use of the site.

**Monument:** A fixed object and point established by surveyors to establish land locations.

**Moratorium:** the temporary suspension, usually by statute, of the enforcement of liability for debt.

**Mortgage:** An instrument recognized by law by which property is hypothecated to secure the payment of a debt or obligation: procedure for foreclosure, in event of default, is established by statue.

**Mortgage Guaranty Insurance:** Insurance against financial loss available to mortgage lenders from a private company.

**Mortgagee:** One to whom a mortgagor gives a mortgage to secure a loan or performance of an obligation: a lender.

**Mortgagor:** One who gives a mortgage on his property to secure a loan or assure performance of an obligation: a borrower.

**Multiple Listing:** A listing, usually an exclusive right to sell, taken by a member of an organization composed of real estate brokers, with the provision that all members will have the opportunity to find an interested client: a cooperative listing.

**Mutual Consent: Agreement.** Usually evidenced by an offer and an acceptance. One of four essential elements of a contract.

**Mutual Water Company**: A water company organized by or for water users in a given district with the object of securing an ample water supply at a reasonable rate. Stock is issued to users.

**N.A.R.:** National Association of Realtors.

**Naked Legal Title:** The right to sell the property if the trustor defaults. This right is given by the trustor to the trustee in a trust deed.

**Narrative Appraisal:** Summary of all factual materials, techniques and appraisal methods used by the appraiser in setting forth his value conclusions.

**Negotiable:** Capable of being negotiated: assignable or transferable in the ordinary course of business.

**Net Income:** Gross income of income property minus the vacancies and allowable expenses equals the net income.

**Net Listing:** A listing that provides that the agent may retain as compensation for his services all sums received over and above a net price to the owner.

**Net Worth:** The assets of a business or individual minus the liabilities equals the net worth.

**Notarize**: To witness a signature on a document and to place a notary public's seal on that document.

**Notary Public:** An official of the state who witnesses an acknowledgment by a person who has signed a document.

**Note:** A signed written instrument acknowledging a debt and promising payment.

**Notice of Completion:** Document that is recorded when an improvement is completed on a property.

**Notice of Default:** A Document that is recorded and delivered to the borrower when a default has occurred under a deed of trust.

**Notice Of Intent To Sell In Bulk:** A document that is recorded and published when merchandise is sold in bulk rather than in the ordinary course of business.

**Notice Of Non-esponsibility:** A notice provided by law designed to relieve a property owner from responsibility for the cost of work done on the property or materials furnished therefore: notice must be verified, recorded and posted.

**Notice To Quit:** Notice to a tenant to vacate rented property.

**Novation:** The substitution of a new obligation for an existing one with the intent to extinguish the original contract. A new contract that takes the place of an existing one.

**Non-cupative Will**: An oral statement made in anticipation of immediate and pending death.

**Obsolescence:** Loss in value due to reduced desirability and usefulness of a structure because its design and construction become obsolete: loss because of becoming old fashioned and note in keeping with modern needs, with consequent loss of income.

**Offset Statement:** Statement by owner of property of lien against property, setting forth the present status of liens against said property.

**Open-End Mortgage:** Mortgage containing a clause that permits the mortgagor to borrow additional money after the loan has been reduced, without rewriting the mortgage.

**Open Listing:** An authorization given by a property owner to a real estate agent wherein said agent is given the nonexclusive right to secure a purchase: open listings may be given to any number of agents.

**Option:** A right given for a consideration to purchase or lease a property upon specified terms within a specified time.

**Optionee:** Receiver of an option. Usually a potential buyer.

**Optionor**: Giver of an option. Usually a potential seller.

**Or More Clause**: A clause in a loan document allowing the borrower to pay additional sums at any time.

**Oral Contract:** A verbal agreement that is not reduced to writing.

**Ordinance:** City or county law.

**Orientation:** Placing a house on its lost with regard to its exposure to the sun, winds, privacy from the street and protection from outside noises.

**Over Improvement:** An improvement that is not the highest and best use for the site on which it is placed, by reason of excess size or cost.

**Ownership:** The right to the use of the property to the exclusion of others.

**Package Mortgage:** A loan where the security is both real and personal property.

**Par Value**: Market value, nominal value.

**Parole:** Oral. Verbal.

**Partial Release Clause:** A clause in a blanket mortgage or trust deed allowing for reconveyance of title of part of the property when part of the loan is paid off.

**Partnership:** A contract of two or more persons to unite their property, labor or skill, or some of them, in prosecution of some joint or lawful business, and to share the profits in certain proportions.

**Participation:** In addition to interest on mortgage loans on income properties, a small percentage of gross income is required, sometimes predicated on certain conditions being fulfilled, such as minimum occupancy or a percentage of net income.

**Party Wall:** A wall erected on the line between two adjoining properties, which are under different ownership, for the use of both properties.

**Patent:** Instrument used to convey title to government land.

**Percentage Lease:** Lease on property, the rental for which is determined by amount of business done by the lessee. Usually a percentage of gross receipts from the business with provision for a minimum rental.

**Periodic Tenancy:** Leasehold estate continuing from period to period until the landlord or the tenant gives notice.

**Personal Property:** Any property that is not real property.

**Plaintiff:** The party who brings a court suit.

**Planned Development Project:** A type of subdivision similar to a standard subdivision except there is an area owned in common by all owners of the subdivision.

**Plat:** A map or plan of parcels of land.

**Pledge:** The depositing of personal property by a debtor with a creditor as security for a debt or engagement.

**Plottage Increment:** The appreciation in unit value created by joining similar ownerships into one large single ownership.

**Points:** Prepaid interest demanded by lender when loan is negotiated.

**Police Power:** The right of the state to enact laws and enforce them for the order, safety, health, morals and general welfare of the public.

**Power of Attorney:** An instrument authorizing a person to act as the agent of the person granting it.

**Power Of Sale:** Right given to the trustee to sell the property under a deed of trust if the borrower defaults. A mortgage can also contain the power of sale clause.

**Prepayment:** Provision can be made for the loan payments to be larger than those specified in the note. The controlling language is usually "$ _____ a month or more." If the payments state a definite amount then one must look to the prepayment privilege in the trust deed.

**Presumption:** A rule of law that courts and judges shall draw a particular inference from a particular fact, or from particular evidence, unless and until the truth of such inference is disproved.

**Prima Facie:** Presumptive on its face.

**Primary Mortgage Market:** Place where the loan is originated.

**Principal.** The employer of an agent.

**Priority:** The order in which liens are paid when property is sold to satisfy debts.

**Private Restriction:** A Limitation placed on the use of the property by the seller.

**Privity:** Mutual relationship to the same rights of property, contractual relationship.

**Probate:** A court hearing to dispose of the property of the deceased person.

**Procuring Cause:** That cause originating from series of events that, without break in continuity, results in the prime object of an agent's employments producing a final buyer. Profit and Loss Statement: Financial document showing the profit or loss of a business during a given period of time.

**Progression:** The worth of a lesser valued residence tends to be enhanced by association with many higher valued residences in the same area.

**Promissory Note:** Following a loan commitment from the lender, the borrower signs a note, promising to repay the loan under stipulated terms. The note establishes personal liability for its repayment.

**Property:** Anything of which there may be ownership.

**Proration:** To divide or prorate equally or proportionately to time of use.

**Purchase and Installment Sale back:** Involves purchase of the property upon completion of construction and immediate sale back on a long-term installment contract.

**Purchase and Leaseback:** Involves the purchase of property and immediate leaseback to the seller.

**Purchase-Money Mortgage or Trust Deed:** A trust deed or mortgage given as part or all of the purchase consideration for property.

**Quiet Enjoyment:** Right of an owner to the use of property without interference of possession.

**Quitclaim Deed:** A deed to relinquish any interest in property that the grantor may have.

**Quiet Title:** A court action brought to establish title, to remove a cloud on the title.

**Range:** A strip of land six mile wide determined by a government survey, running in a north-south direction.

**Real Estate Trust:** A special arrangement under federal and state law whereby investors may pool funds for investments in real estate and mortgages and yet escape corporation taxes.

**Real Property:** Property that consists of land, that which is affixed, and that which is appurtenant to it. General considered immovable.

**Recapture:** The rate of interest necessary to provide for the return of an investment. Not to be confused with interest rate, which is a rate of interest on an investment.

**Reconveyance:** The transfer of the title of land from one person to the immediate preceding owner. This particular instrument or transfer is commonly used when the performance or debt is satisfied under the terms of a deed of trust, when the trustee conveys the title he had held on condition back to the owner.

**Recording:** Filing for record in the office of the county recorder or other proper government official.

**Redemption:** Buying back one's property after a judicial sale.

**Rehabilitation:** The restoration of a property to satisfactory condition without drastically changing the plan, form or style of architecture.

**Release Clause:** This is a stipulation that, upon the payment of a specific sum of money to the holder of a trust deed or mortgage, the lien of the instrument as to a specific described lot or area shall be removed from the blanket lien on the whole area involved.

**Release Statement:** Document filed to release the encumbrance when personal property is used for security for a loan.

**Reliction:** Gaining title to land by the gradual receding of water.

**Remainder:** An estate that takes effect after the termination of the prior estate, such as a life estate.

**Replacement Cost:** The cost to replace the structure with one having utility equivalent to that being appraised, but constructed with modern material, and according to current standard, design and layout.

**Request For Notice Of Default:** Document that is recorded by the holder of a junior loan so he may be notified if buyer defaults on other loans.

**Rescission Of Contract:** The abrogation or annulling of contract; the revocation or repealing of contract by mutual consent by parties to the contract, or for cause by either party to the contract.

**Reservation:** A right retained by a grantor when conveying property.

**Restriction:** Term as used relating to real property means the owner is restricted or prohibited from doing certain things relating to the property, or using the property for certain purposes.

**Return on The Investment:** Interest paid on a loan. The profit received on investment in income property.

**Reversion:** The right to future possession or enjoyment by the person, or his heirs, creating the preceding estate.

**Reversionary Interest:** The interest that a person has in lands or other property, upon the termination of the preceding estate.

**Rider:** An Amendment to a contract.

**Right Of Survivorship:** Right to acquire the interest of a deceased joint owner; Distinguishing feature of a joint tenancy.

**Riparian Rights:** The right of a landowner to water on, under, or adjacent to hid land.

**Sales Contract:** A contract by which buyer and seller agree to terms of sale.

**Sale-Leaseback:** Where the owner of property wishes to sell the property and retain occupancy by leasing it from the buyer.

**Sandwich Lease:** Leasehold interest that lies between the primary lease and the operating lease.

**Satisfaction:** Discharge of mortgagee, trust deed or judgment lien from the records upon payment of the evidenced debt.

**Seasoned Loan:** Loan that has been in existence long enough to show a pattern of payments.

**Secondary Financing:** A loan secured by a junior mortgage/trust deed on real property.

**Secondary Mortgage Market:** Place where existing loans are bought and sold.

**Secured Party:** This is the party having the security interest. Thus the mortgage, the conditional seller, the pledgee, etc., all referred to as the secured party.

**Security Agreement:** Agreement between the secured party and the debtor that creates the security interest.

**Section:** Section of land is established by government survey and contains 640 Acres.

**Separate Property:** Property owned by a husband and wife that is not community property.

**Servient Tenement:** Property burdened by an easement.

**Setback Ordinance:** An ordinance prohibiting the erection of a building or structure between the curb and the setback line.

**Severalty Ownership:** Owned by one person only.

**Sheriff's Deed:** Deed given by court order in connection with sale of property to satisfy a judgment.

**Situs:** Location. Land.

**Social Obsolescence:** Economic obsolescence.

**Special Assessment:** Legal charge against real estate by a public authority to pay cost of public improvements, sidewalks, etc.

**Specific Performance:** An action to compel performance of an agreement.

**S.R.A.:** member of the Society of Real Estate Appraisers.

**Statute:** A law enacted by a legislative body.

**Statute Of Frauds:** State law that provides that certain contracts must be in writing in order to be enforceable buy law.

**Statute of Limitations:** A state law that prevents court action by an injured party in a contract if not taken within specific time limits.

**Straight Line Depreciation:** Definite sum set aside annually from income to pay cost of replacing improvements, without reference to interest it earns.

**Straight Note:** Promissory note where the principal is paid in a lump sum at the end of the term.

**Subject To Mortgage:** When a grantee takes a title to real property subject to an existing mortgage, he is not responsible to the holder of the promissory note for the payment of any portion of the amount due. The maker of the note is not released from his responsibility.

**Sublease:** A lease given by a lessee.

**Subordinate:** To make subject to, or junior to.

**Subordination Clause;** Clause in a junior or a second lien permitting retention of priority. A subordination clause may also be used in a first deed of trust permitting it to be subordinated to subsequent liens. Example: the liens of construction loans.

**Subpoena:** Process to cause a witness to appear and give testimony.

**Subrogation:** The substitution of another person in place of the creditor, to whose rights he succeeds in relation to the debt. Often used where one person agrees to stand surety for the performance of a contract by another person.

**Succession:** Acquiring property of a deceased person who died intestate.

**Surety:** One who guarantees the performance of another; guarantor.

**Survey:** The process by which a parcel of land is measured and its area is ascertained.

**Syndicate:** Group of investors who pool their money for a common investment.

**Take-Out Loan:** Loan arranged by the owner or builder-developer for a buyer. The construction loan made for construction of the improvements is usually paid from the proceeds of this loan.

**Tangible Personal Property:** Personal property having substance that can be delivered from one person to another.

**Tax-Free Exchange:** A "like kind" exchange of properties for the purpose of deferring income tax.

**Tax Sale:** Sale of property after a period of nonpayment of taxes.

**Tenancy At Sufferance:** An estate held by a tenant when his right to possess the property has expired.

**Tenancy At Will:** An estate for an indefinite period that may be terminated at the will of either the landlord or the tenant.

**Tenancy From Period-To-Period:** Leasehold estate continuing from period to period until the landlord or the tenant gives notice.

**Tenancy In Common:** Ownership by two or more persons who hold undivided interest, without right of survivorship; interests need not be equal.

**Tender:** An offer of performance. If it is unjustifiably refused, it places the other party to a contract in default.

**Tenement:** All rights in land that pass with a conveyance of the land.

**Time If Of The Essence:** One of the essential requirements to forming of a binding contract; contemplates a punctual performance.

**Title:** Evidence that owner of land is in lawful possession there of; and instrument evidencing such ownership.

**Title Insurance:** Insurance written by a title company to protect property owner against loss if title is imperfect.

**Title Vesting:** The way that title is held by the owner.

**Torrens Title:** A system of land registration operated by a state.

**Tort:** Wrongful act; wrong, injury; violation of a legal right.

**Township:** A territorial subdivision six miles long, six miles wide and containing 36 sections, each one mile square.

**Trespass:** An invasion of an owner's rights in property.

**Trust Deed:** Deed given by borrower to beneficiary to be held pending fulfillment of an obligation, which is ordinarily repayment of a loan.

**Trust Account:** A neutral bank account maintained by a broker for the deposit of money entrusted with him.

**Trustee:** One who holds property in trust for another to secure the performance of an obligation.

**Trustee's Deed:** A deed given by trustee when property is foreclosed and sold at a trustee's sale.

**Trustor:** One who deeds his property to a trustee to be held as security until he has performed his obligation to a lender under terms of a deed of trust.

**Underwriting:** The technical analysis by a lender to determine the borrower's ability to repay a contemplated loan.

**Undivided Interest:** The interest of a co-owner in real property. His interest cannot be separated without court action.

**Undue Influence:** Taking any fraudulent or unfair advantage of another's weakness of mind, or distress or necessity.

**Unilateral Contract:** An exchange of a promise for an act. Only one party is bound to perform. The giver of an option.

**Unlawful Detainer Action:** A court suit to evict a tenant.

**Use Tax:** A tax charged on goods purchased from out-of-state and used within a state, like a sales tax.

**Usury:** On a loan, claiming a rate of interest greater than that permitted by law.

**Valuation:** Estimated worth or price. The act of valuing by appraisal.

**Variable Interest Rate:** Interest rate in a loan that can be changed upon the happening of a certain event.

**Variance:** Rezoning of a single parcel.

**Vendee:** Purchaser; buyer.

**Vendor:** Seller.

**Verification:** Sworn statement before a duly qualified offer to correctness of contents of an instrument.

**Vested:** Bestowed upon someone: secured by someone, such as title to property.

**Void:** To have no force or effect: that which is unenforceable.

**Voidable:** That which is capable of being adjudged void, but is not void unless action is taken to make it so.

**Voluntary Lien:** Any lien placed on property with consent of, or as a result of, the voluntary act of the owner.

**Waive:** To relinquishing, or abandon; to forego a right to enforce or require anything.

**Waiver:** Relinquishing a right.

**Warehousing:** Using existing loans as security for another loan. Warehousing involves mortgage portfolios.

**Warranty Deed:** A deed used to convey real property that contains warranties of title and quiet possession, and the grantor, thus, agrees to defend the premises against the lawful claims of their persons.

**Waste:** The destruction, or material alteration of, or injury to premises by a tenant for life or years.

**Will:** A document that provides for the disposition of property upon a person's death.

**Wraparound Mortgage:** Involves the borrower entering into a second mortgage. This arrangement represents the means by which he can add to his development without refinancing the first mortgage at substantially higher current rates.

**Writ of Execution:** A court order used to sell property to satisfy a debt.

# Index

☺ As you can see the last word in this book is "**zoning**" in the index. Like I said, my books cover:

*Everything You Need To Know About Real Estate From <u>A</u>sbestos to <u>Z</u>oning!* ™